Blackstone's Statutes on

Public Law & Human Rights

33rd edition

edited by

John Stanton

Senior Lecturer in Law, The City Law School, City, University of London

OXFORD
UNIVERSITY PRESS

OXFORD
UNIVERSITY PRESS

Great Clarendon Street, Oxford, OX2 6DP,
United Kingdom

Oxford University Press is a department of the University of Oxford.
It furthers the University's objective of excellence in research, scholarship,
and education by publishing worldwide. Oxford is a registered trade mark of
Oxford University Press in the UK and in certain other countries

First published by Blackstone Press 1988

Thirtieth edition 2020
Thirty-first edition 2021
Thirty-second edition 2022
Thirty-third edition 2023

Published in the United States of America by Oxford University Press
198 Madison Avenue, New York, NY 10016, United States of America

British Library Cataloguing in Publication Data
Data available

ISBN 978–0–19–889040–9

Printed in the UK by
Bell & Bain, Ltd., Glasgow

Blackstone's Statutes
Unsurpassed in authority, reliability, and accuracy

The titles in the Blackstone's Statutes series are a collection of carefully reviewed and selected unannotated legislative material and official documents.

We make every effort to ensure titles in the series meet the needs of their target market. They are reviewed by lecturers to match university courses closely and are expertly edited to be manageable in size, whilst retaining their comprehensive coverage.

The editors only include material from legislation that will be valuable to students and lecturers and it is therefore abridged where necessary.

Conventions used in *Blackstone's Statutes on Public Law & Human Rights*
Omissions are indicated with asterisks *****
Repeals are indicated with ellipsis . . .
The material in this book is reproduced in its most up-to-date form, and all amendments are incorporated within square brackets. Supplementary notes and details of amending provisions are generally not included.

All statutes have been enacted but some very recent legislation may not yet be in force.

Contents

Part I	**Legislation of the UK Parliament, and other legislatures within the UK**	**1**

Alphabetical contents

Thematic contents

Editor's preface

The UK Constitution is uncodified. This means that it is not contained in one document such as we might find in many other countries in the world but is instead contained within a wide range of sources that have been introduced at various points throughout our long history. Though these sources include a range of legal, non-legal, written and unwritten instruments and rules, the most prominent sources are Acts of Parliament, or statutes. Not all Acts—nor all Acts included within this book—are what we might call 'constitutional statutes'. In the opinion of Laws LJ in *Thoburn v Sunderland City Council*,[1] 'a constitutional statute is one which (a) conditions the legal relationship between citizen and state in some general, overarching manner, or (b) enlarges or diminishes the scope of what we would now regard as fundamental constitutional rights'.[2] Whilst there are undoubtedly a number of statutes here included that easily fall within that category, more broadly, this book sets out a selection of statutory material pertaining to Public Law and Human Rights in the United Kingdom. In addition to these, various other constitutional sources are also included: the European Convention on Human Rights and the UK–EU Withdrawal Agreement to name just two.

It is both the privilege and the responsibility of the editor to select such material that they deem appropriate to the study of Public Law. 'Statute books' have typically served as an aid to the study of law—particularly as a tool of reference in examinations (where permitted by an institution's regulations)—and the contents of this book have very much been guided by those identifying materials relevant to the Public Law courses at their own institutions. It goes without saying, though, that not all sources will be useful to everyone. I hope, though, that some of it proves valuable.

The latest edition is up to date as of the end of March 2023. Over the last year, changes have been made to many existing aspects of the UK constitutional order. On this basis, the 33rd edition includes updates to the Public Order Act 1986, the Northern Ireland Act 1998 and the Tribunals, Courts and Enforcement Act 2007, whilst the Coronavirus Act 2020—prominent in recent editions—has largely been repealed and is omitted.

Part I, as before, sets out an array of legislation enacted by the UK Parliament and other legislatures across the UK. Part II is dedicated to instruments of EU law and the UK–EU Withdrawal Agreement. Though aspects of EU law—and EU relevant legislation—have ceased to be of legal relevance, their historic value justifies their inclusion here. The now repealed European Communities Act 1972 is included (in Part II) for that reason. Part III sets out certain other constitutional materials, including notable human rights instruments and the Ministerial Code. Part IV contains Codes, A, C and G of the PACE Codes. This book is for academics and students of law. Comments are therefore welcome as to how it might better complement your teaching and your courses. I welcome such input.

I am thankful to Luke Sarabia at Oxford University Press for his work on this collection. Any errors are my own.

John Stanton
London, April 2023

---

[1] [2003] QB 151.
[2] [2003] QB 151, [62].

New to this edition

The 33rd edition of *Blackstone's Statutes on Public Law & Human Rights* has been fully revised and updated with all relevant legislation through to the end of March 2023 including:

- Updates to the Public Order Act 1986
- Updates to the Northern Ireland Act 1998
- Updates to the Tribunals, Courts and Enforcement Act 2007

Part I

Legislation of the UK Parliament, and other legislatures within the UK

Magna Carta

(Statute 25 Edw. 1, 1297)

Territorial extent: England and Wales, Northern Ireland

The Great Charter of the Liberties of England, and of the Liberties of the Forest; confirmed by King Edward, in the Twenty-fifth Year of his Reign.

Edward by the grace of God King of England, Lord of Ireland, and Duke of Guyan, to all archbishops, bishops, &c. We have seen the Great Charter of the Lord Henry sometimes King of England, our father, of the liberties of England in these words:

Henry by the grace of God King of England, Lord of Ireland, Duke of Normandy and Guyan, and Earl of Anjou, to all archbishops, bishops, abbots, priors, earls, barons, sheriffs, provosts, officers, and to all bailiffs, and other our faithful subjects, which shall see this present charter, greeting: Know ye, that we, unto the honour of Almighty God, and for the salvation of the souls of our progenitors and successors Kings of England, to the advancement of holy church and amendment of our realm, of our meer and free will, have given and granted to all archbishops, bishops, abbots, priors, earls, barons, and to all freemen of this our realm, these liberties following, to be kept in our kingdom of England for ever.

Chapter 1   Confirmation of liberties
First, we have granted to God, and by this our present charter have confirmed, for us and our heirs for ever, that the church of England shall be free, and shall have all her whole rights and liberties inviolable. We have granted also, and given to all the freemen of our realm, for us and our heirs for ever, these liberties underwritten, to have and to hold to them and their heirs, of us and our heirs for ever.

Chapters 2–8   ...

Chapter 9   *****

Chapters 10–28   ...

Chapter 29   Imprisonment, etc contrary to law
No freeman shall be taken or imprisoned, or be disseised of his freehold, or liberties, or free customs, or be outlawed, or exiled, or any other wise destroyed; nor will we not pass upon him, nor condemn him, but by lawful judgment of his peers, or by the law of the land. We will sell to no man, we will not deny or defer to any man either justice or right.

Chapters 30–36   ...
*****

The Bill of Rights (1688)

(1 Will. & Mar. sess 2, c. 2)

An Act declaring the Rights and Liberties of the Subject and Setleing the Succession of the Crowne.

Territorial extent: England and Wales, Northern Ireland (for Scotland see the equivalent Act of the Scottish Parliament, the Claim of Right 1689)

Whereas the lords spirituall and temporall and comons assembled at Westminster lawfully fully and freely representing all estates of the people of this realme did upon the thirteenth day of February in the yeare of our Lord one thousand six hundred eighty eight present unto their Majesties then called and known by the names and stile of William and Mary Prince and Princesse of Orange being present in their proper persons a certaine declaration in writeing made by the said lords and comons in the words following viz

The heads of declaration of lords and commons, recited—Whereas the late King James the Second by the assistance of diverse evill councillors judges and ministers imployed by him did endeavour to subvert and extirpate the Protestant religion and the lawes and liberties of this kingdome.

Dispensing and suspending power—By assumeing and exerciseing a power of dispensing with and suspending of lawes and the execution of lawes without consent of Parlyament.

Committing prelates—By committing and prosecuting diverse worthy prelates for humbly petitioning to be excused from concurring to the said assumed power.

Ecclesiastical commission—By issueing and causeing to be executed a commission under the great seale for erecting a court called the court of commissioners for ecclesiasticall causes.

Levying money—By levying money for and to the use of the Crowne by pretence of prerogative for other time and in other manner then the same was granted by Parlyament.

Standing army—By raising and keeping a standing army within this kingdome in time of peace without consent of Parlyament and quartering soldiers contrary to law.

Disarming Protestants, etc—By causing severall good subjects being protestants to be disarmed at the same time when papists were both armed and imployed contrary to law.

Violating elections—By violating the freedome of election of members to serve in Parlyament.

Illegal prosecutions—By prosecutions in the Court of King's Bench for matters and causes cognizable onely in Parlyament and by diverse other arbitrary and illegall courses.

Juries—And whereas of late yeares partiall corrupt and unqualifyed persons have beene returned and served on juryes in tryalls and particularly diverse jurors in tryalls for high treason which were not freeholders.

Excessive bail—And excessive baile hath beene required of persons committed in criminall cases to elude the benefitt of the lawes made for the liberty of the subjects.

Fines—And excessive fines have beene imposed.

Punishments—And illegall and cruell punishments inflicted.

Grants of fines, etc, before conviction, etc—And severall grants and promises made of fines and forfeitures before any conviction or judgement against the persons upon whome the same were to be levyed.

All which are uterly and directly contrary to the knowne lawes and statutes and freedome of the realme.

And whereas the said late King James the Second haveing abdicated the government and the throne being thereby vacant his Highnesse the Prince of Orange (whome it hath pleased Almighty God to make the glorious instrument of delivering this kingdome from popery and arbitrary power) did (by the advice of the lords spirituall and temporall and diverse principall persons of the commons) cause letters to be written to the lords spirituall and temporall being protestants and other letters to the severall countyes cityes universities boroughs and cinque ports for the choosing of such persons to represent them as were of right to be sent to Parlyament to meete and sitt at Westminster upon the two and twentyeth day of January in this yeare one thousand six hundred eighty and eight in order to such an establishment as that their religion lawes and liberties might not againe be in danger of being subverted, upon which letters elections haveing beene accordingly made.

The subject's Rights—And thereupon the said lords spirituall and temporall and commons pursuant to their respective letters and elections being now assembled in a full and free representative of this nation takeing into their most serious consideration the best meanes for attaining the ends aforesaid doe in the first place (as their auncestors in like case have usually done) for the vindicating and asserting their auntient rights and liberties, declare

[1] Suspending power—That the pretended power of suspending of laws or the execution of laws by regall authority without consent of Parlyament is illegall.

Late dispensing power—That the pretended power of dispensing with laws or the execution of laws by regall authoritie as it hath beene assumed and exercised of late is illegall.

Ecclesiastical courts illegal—That the commission for erecting the late court of commissioners for ecclesiasticall causes and all other commissions and courts of like nature are illegal and pernicious.

Levying money—That levying money for or to the use of the Crowne by pretence of prerogative without grant of Parlyament for longer time or in other manner than the same is or shall be granted is illegal.

Right to petition—That it is the right of the subjects to petition the King and all commitments and prosecutions for such petitioning are illegal.

Standing army—That the raising or keeping a standing army within the kingdome in time of peace unlesse it be with consent of Parlyament is against law.

Subject's arms—That the subjects which are protestants may have arms for their defence suitable to their conditions and as allowed by law.

Freedom of election—That election of members of Parlyament ought to be free.

Freedom of speech—That the freedome of speech and debates or proceedings in Parlyament ought not to be impeached or questioned in any court or place out of Parlyament.

Excessive bail—That excessive baile ought not to be required nor excessive fines imposed nor cruell and unusuall punishments inflicted.

Juries—That jurors ought to be duly impannelled and returned . . .

Grants of forfeitures—That all grants and promises of fines and forfeitures of particular persons before conviction are illegal and void.

Frequent Parliaments—And that for redresse of all grievances and for the amending strengthening and preserving of the lawes Parlyaments ought to be held frequently.

The said right claimed, tender of the crown, regal power exercised, limitation of the crown, new oaths of allegiance, etc—And they doe claime demand and insist upon all and singular the premises as their undoubted rights and liberties and that noe declarations judgements doeings or proceedings to the prejudice of the people in any of the said premisses ought in any wise to be drawne hereafter into consequence or example. To which demand of their rights they are particularly encouraged by the declaration of his Highnesse the Prince of Orange as being the only meanes for obtaining a full redresse and remedy therein. Haveing therefore an intire confidence that his said Highnesse the Prince of Orange will perfect the deliverance soe farr advanced by him and will still preserve them from the violation of their rights which they have here asserted and from all other attempts upon their religion rights and liberties. The said lords spirituall and temporall and commons assembled at Westminster doe resolve that William and Mary Prince and Princesse of Orange be and be declared King and Queene of England France and Ireland and the dominions thereunto belonging to hold the crowne and royall dignity of the said kingdomes and dominions to them the said prince and princesse dureing their lives and the life of the survivour of them. And that the sole and full exercise of the regall power be onely in and executed by the said Prince of Orange in the names of the said prince and princesse dureing their joynt lives and after their deceases the said crowne and royall dignitie of the said kingdoms and dominions to be to the heires of the body of the said princesse and for default of such issue to the Princesse Anne of Denmarke and the heires of her body and for default of such issue to the heires of the body of the said Prince of Orange. And the lords spirituall and temporall and commons doe pray the said prince and princesse to accept the same accordingly. And that the oathes hereafter mentioned be taken by all persons of whome the oathes of allegiance and supremacy might be required by law instead of them and that the said oathes of allegiance and supremacy be abrogated.

I A B doe sincerely promise and sweare that I will be faithfull and beare true allegiance to their Majestyes King William and Queen Mary

Soe helpe me God

I A B doe sweare that I doe from my heart abhorr, detest and abjure as impious and hereticall this damnable doctrine and position that princes excommunicated or deprived by the Pope or any authority of the see of Rome may be deposed or murdered by their subjects or any other whatsoever. And I doe declare that noe forreigne prince person prelate, state or potentate hath or ought to have any jurisdiction power superiority preeminence or authoritie ecclesiasticall or spirituall within this realme.

Soe help me God*

Acceptance of the crown, the two Houses to sit, subjects' liberties to be allowed, and ministers hereafter to serve according to the same, William and Mary declared King and Queen, limitation of the crown, papists debarred the crown, every King, etc, shall make the declaration of 30 Car 2, if under 12 years old, to be done after attainment thereof, King's and Queen's assent. Upon which their said Majestyes did accept the crowne and royall dignitie of the kingdoms of England France and Ireland and the dominions thereunto belonging according to the resolution and desire of the said lords and commons contained in the said declaration. And thereupon their Majestyes were pleased that the said lords spirituall and temporall and commons being the two Houses of Parlyament should continue to sitt and with their Majesties royall concurrence make effectuall provision for the settlement of the religion lawes and liberties of this kingdome soe that the same for the future might not be in danger againe of being subverted, to which the said lords spirituall and temporall and commons did agree and proceede to act accordingly. Now in pursuance of the premises the said lords spirituall and temporall and commons in Parlyament assembled for the ratifying confirming and establishing the said declaration and the articles clauses matters and things therein contained by the force of a law made in due forme by authority of Parlyament doe pray that it may be declared and enacted that all and singular the rights and liberties asserted and claimed in the said declaration are the true auntient and indubitable rights and liberties of the people of this kingdome and soe shall be esteemed allowed adjudged deemed and taken to be and that all and every the particulars aforesaid shall be firmly and strictly holden and observed as they are expressed in the said declaration. And all officers and ministers whatsoever shall serve their Majestyes and their successors according to the same in all times to come. And the said lords spirituall and temporall and commons seriously considering how it hath pleased Almighty God in his marvellous providence and mercifull goodness to this nation to provide and preserve their said Majestyes royall persons most happily to raigne over us upon the throne of their auncestors for which they render unto him from the bottome of their hearts their humblest thanks and praises doe truely firmly assuredly and in the sincerity of their hearts thinke and doe hereby recognize acknowledge and declare that King James the Second haveing abdicated the government and their Majestyes having accepted the crowne and royall dignity as aforesaid their said Majestyes did become were are and of right ought to be by the lawes of the realme our soveraigne liege lord and lady King and Queene of England France and Ireland and the dominions thereunto belonging in and to whose princely persons the royall state crowne and dignity of the said realmes with all honours stiles titles regalities prerogatives powers jurisdictions and authorities to the same belonging and appertaining are most fully and rightfully and intirely invested and incorporated united and annexed. And for preventing all questions and divisions in this realme by reason of any pretended titles to the crowne and for preserveing a certainty in the succession thereof in and upon which the unity peace

---

* **Editor's Note:** For the modern version of this effectively obsolete oath, see the Schedule to the Accession Declaration Act 1910.

tranquillity and safety of this nation doth under God wholly consist and depend the said lords spirituall and temporall and commons doe beseech their Majestyes that it may be enacted established and declared that the crowne and regall government of the said kingdoms and dominions with all and singular the premisses thereunto belonging and appertaining shall bee and continue to their said Majestyes and the survivour of them dureing their lives and the life of the survivour of them and that the entire perfect and full exercise of the regall power and government be onely in and executed by his Majestie in the names of both their Majestyes dureing their joynt lives and after their deceases the said crowne and premisses shall be and remaine to the heires of the body of her Majestie and for default of such issue to her royall Highnesse the Princess Anne of Denmarke and the heires of her body and for default of such issue to the heires of the body of his said Majestie And thereunto the said lords spirituall and temporall and commons doe in the name of all the people aforesaid most humbly and faithfully submitt themselves their heires and posterities for ever and doe faithfully promise that they will stand to maintaine and defend their said Majesties and alsoe the limitation and succession of the crowne herein specified and contained to the utmost of their powers with their lives and estates against all persons whatsoever that shall attempt any thing to the contrary. And whereas it hath beene found by experience that it is inconsistent with the safety and welfaire of this protestant kingdome to be governed by a popish prince … the said lords spirtuall and temporall and commons doe further pray that it may be enacted that all and every person and persons that is are or shall be reconciled to or shall hold communion with the see or church of Rome or shall professe the popish religion … shall be excluded and be for ever uncapeable to inherit possesse or enjoy the crowne and government of this realme and Ireland and the dominions thereunto belonging or any part of the same or to have use or exercise any regall power authoritie or jurisdiction within the same And in all and every such case or cases the people of these realmes shall be and are hereby absolved of their allegiance and the said crowne and government shall from time to time descend to and be enjoyed by such person or persons being protestants as should have inherited and enjoyed the same in case the said person or persons soe reconciled holding communion or professing … as aforesaid were naturally dead And that every King and Queene of this realme who at any time hereafter shall come to and succeede in the imperiall crowne of this kingdome shall on the first day of the meeting of the first Parlyament next after his or her comeing to the crowne sitting in his or her throne in the House of Peeres in the presence of the lords and commons therein assembled or at his or her coronation before such person or persons who shall administer the coronation oath to him or her at the time of his or her takeing the said oath (which shall first happen) make subscribe and audibly repeate the declaration mentioned in the Statute made in the thirtyeth yeare of the raigne of King Charles the Second entituled An Act for the more effectuall preserveing the Kings person and government by disableing papists from sitting in either House of Parlyament But if it shall happen that such King or Queene upon his or her succession to the crowne of this realme shall be under the age of twelve yeares then every such King or Queene shall make subscribe and audibly repeate the said declaration at his or her coronation or the first day of the meeting of the first Parlyament as aforesaid which shall first happen after such King or Queene shall have attained the said age of twelve years. All which their Majestyes are contented and pleased shall be declared enacted and established by authoritie of this present Parliament and shall stand remaine and be the law of this realme for ever And the same are by their said Majesties by and with the advice and consent of the lords spirituall and temporall and commons in Parlyament assembled and by the authoritie of the same declared enacted and established accordingly

2   Non obstantes made void
… noe dispensation by non obstante of or to any statute or any part thereof shall be allowed but … the same shall be held void and of noe effect except a dispensation be allowed of in such statutes …

3   …

Crown and Parliament Recognition Act 1689

(2 Will. & Mar., c. 1)

An Act for Recognizing King William and Queene Mary and for avoiding all Questions touching the Acts made in the Parliament assembled at Westminster the thirteenth day of February one thousand six hundred eighty eight

Territorial extent: England and Wales, Northern Ireland (effectively extended to Scotland by the Union with Scotland Act 1706, below)

Wee your Majestyes most humble and loyall subjects the lords spirituall and temporall and commons in this present Parlyament assembled doe beseech your most excellent Majestyes that it may be published and declared in this High Court of Parlyament and enacted by authoritie of the same that we doe recognize and acknowledge your Majestyes were are and of right ought to be by the laws of this realme our soveraigne liege lord and lady King and Queene of England France and Ireland and the dominions thereunto belonging in and to whose princely persons the royall state crowne and dignity of the said realms with all honours stiles tiles regalities prerogatives powers jurisdictions and authorities to the same belonging and appertaining are most fully rightfully and intirely invested and incorporated united and annexed. And for the avoiding of all disputes and questions concerning the being and authority of the late Parliament assembled at Westminster the thirteenth day of February one thousand six hundred eighty eight wee doe most humbly beseech your Majestyes that it may be enacted and bee it enacted by the King and Queenes most excellent Majestyes by and with the advice and consent of the lords spirituall and temporall and commons in this present Parlyament assembled and by authoritie of the same that all and singular the Acts made and enacted in the said Parlyament were and are laws and statutes of this kingdome and as such ought to be reputed taken and obeyed by all the people of this kingdome.

The Act of Settlement (1700)

(12 & 13 Will. 3, c. 2)

An Act for the further Limitation of the Crown and better securing the Rights and Liberties of the Subject.

Territorial extent: England and Wales, Northern Ireland; effectively extended to Scotland by the Union with Scotland Act 1706

1   The Princess Sophia, Electress and Duchess dowager of Hanover, daughter of the late Queen of Bohemia, daughter of King James the First, to inherit after the King and the Princess Anne, in default of issue of the said princess and his Majesty, respectively; and the heirs of her body, being Protestants

Whereas in the first year of the reign of your Majesty and of our late most gracious soverign lady Queen Mary (of blessed memory) an Act of Parliament was made intituled (An Act for declaring the rights and liberties of the subject and for setling the succession of the crown) wherein it was (amongst other things) enacted established and declared that the crown and regall government of the kingdoms of England France and Ireland and the dominions thereunto belonging should be and continue to your Majestie and the said late Queen during the joynt lives of your Majesty and the said Queen and to the survivor and that after the decease of your Majesty and of the said Queen the said crown and regall government should be and remain to the heirs of the body of the said late Queen and for default of such issue to her royall Highness the Princess Ann of Denmark and the heirs of her body and for default of such issue to the heirs of the body of your Majesty And it was thereby further enacted that all and every person and persons that then were or afterwards should be reconciled to or shall hold communion with the see or church of Rome or should professe the popish

Union with Scotland Act 1706

(6 Anne, c. 11)

An Act for an Union of the Two Kingdoms of England and Scotland.

Territorial extent: England, Wales and Scotland (by the combined effect of this Act and the equivalent Act of the Parliament of Scotland (APS, XI, 406)); subsequently applied to Northern Ireland

Most Gracious Sovereign

Whereas articles of union were agreed on the twenty second day of July in the fifth year of your Majesties reign by the commissioners nominated on behalf of the kingdom of England under your Majesties great seal of England bearing date at Westminster the tenth day of April then last past in pursuance of an Act of Parliament made in England in the third year of your Majesties reign and the commissioners nominated on the behalf of the kingdom of Scotland under your Majesties great seal of Scotland bearing date the twenty-seventh day of February in the fourth year of your Majesties reign in pursuance of the fourth Act of the third session of the present Parliament of Scotland to treat of and concerning an union of the said kingdoms And whereas an Act hath passed in the Parliament of Scotland at Edinburgh the sixteenth day of January in the fifth year of your Majesties reign wherein 'tis mentioned that the estates of Parliament considering the said articles of union of the two kingdoms had agreed to and approved of the said articles of union with some additions and explanations and that your Majesty with advice and consent of the estates of Parliament for establishing the Protestant religion and Presbyterian Church government within the kingdom of Scotland had passed in the same session of Parliament an Act intituled Act for securing of the Protestant religion and Presbyterian Church government which by the tenor thereof was appointed to be inserted in any Act ratifying the treaty and expresly declared to be a fundamental and essential condition of the said treaty or union in all times coming the tenor of which articles as ratified and approved of with additions and explanations by the said Act of Parliament of Scotland follows.

Article I   The kingdoms united; ensigns armorial

That the two kingdoms of England and Scotland shall upon the first day of May which shall be in the year one thousand seven hundred and seven and for ever after be united into one kingdom by the name of Great Britain and that the ensigns armorial of the said United Kingdom be such as her Majesty shall appoint and the crosses of St. George and St. Andrew be conjoyned in such manner as Her Majesty shall think fit and used in all flags banners standards and ensigns both at sea and land.

Article II   Succession to the monarchy

That the succession to the monarchy of the United Kingdom of Great Britain and of the dominions thereto belonging after her most sacred Majesty and in default of issue of her Majesty be remain and continue to the most excellent Princess Sophia Electoress and Dutchess dowager of Hanover and the heirs of her body being protestants upon whom the crown of England is settled by an Act of Parliament made in England in the twelfth year of the reign of his late Majesty King William the Third intituled An Act for the further limitation of the crown and better securing the right and liberties of the subject And that all papists and persons marrying papists shall be excluded from and for ever incapable to inherit possess or enjoy the imperial crown of Great Britain and the dominions thereunto belonging or any part thereof and in every such case the crown and government shall from time to time descend to and be enjoyed by such person being a protestant as should have inherited and enjoyed the same in case such papist or person marrying a papist was naturally dead according to the provision for the descent of the crown of England made by another Act of Parliament in England in the first year of the reign of their late Majesties King William and Queen Mary intituled An Act declaring the rights and liberties of the subject and settling the succession of the crown.

Article III   Parliament

That the United Kingdom of Great Britain be represented by one and the same Parliament to be stiled the Parliament of Great Britain.

Article IIII   Trade and navigation and other rights

That all the subjects of the United Kingdom of Great Britain shall from and after the union have full freedom and intercourse of trade and navigation to and from any port or place within the said United Kingdom and the dominions and plantations thereunto belonging and that there be a communication of all other rights privileges and advantages which do or may belong to the subjects of either kingdom except where it is otherwise expressly agreed in these articles.

Article V   ...

Article VI   Regulations of trade, duties, etc

That all parts of the United Kingdom for ever from and after the union shall have the same allowances encouragements and drawbacks and be under the same prohibitions restrictions and regulations of trade and liable to the same customs and duties on import and export and that the allowances encouragements and drawbacks prohibitions restrictions and regulations of trade and the customs and duties on import and export settled in England when the union commences shall from and after the union take place throughout the whole United Kingdom...

Articles VII, XVI   *****

Articles VIII–XV, XVII   ...

Article XVIII   Laws concerning public rights; private rights

That the laws concerning regulation of trade customs and such excises to which Scotland is by virtue of this treaty to be liable be the same in Scotland from and after the union as in England and that all other laws in use within the kingdom of Scotland do after the union and notwithstanding thereof remain in the same force as before (except such as are contrary to or inconsistent with this treaty) but alterable by the Parliament of Great Britain with this difference betwixt the laws concerning publick right policy and civil government and those which concern private right that the laws which concern publick right policy and civil government may be made the same throughout the whole United Kingdom. But that no alteration be made in laws which concern private right except for evident utility of the subjects within Scotland.

Article XIX   Court of Session etc

That the Court of Session or Colledge of Justice do after the Union and notwithstanding thereof remain in all time coming within Scotland as it is now constituted by the Laws of that Kingdom and with the same authority and privileges as before the Union Subject nevertheless to such regulations for the better Administration of Justice as shall be made by the Parliament of Great Britain and that hereafter none shall be named by Her Majesty or Her Royal Successors to be ordinary Lords of Session but such who have served in the Colledge of Justice as Advocates or Principal Clerks of Session for the Space of Five years or as Writers to the Signet for the Space of ten years with this provision that no Writer to the Signet be capable to be admitted a Lord of the Session unless he undergo a private and publick Tryal on the Civil Law before the Faculty of Advocates and be found by them qualified for the said Office two years before he be named to be a Lord of the Session yet so as the Qualifications made or to be made for capacitating persons to be named ordinary Lords of Session may be altered by the Parliament of Great Britain And that the Court of Justiciary do also after the Union and notwithstanding thereof remain in all time coming within Scotland as it is now constituted by the Laws of that Kingdom and with the same authority and privileges as before the Union Subject nevertheless to such regulations as shall be made by the Parliament of Great Britain and without prejudice of other rights of Justiciary...And that the heretable rights of Admiralty and Vice Admiralties in Scotland be reserved to the respective proprietors as rights of property Subject nevertheless as to the manner of exercising such heretable rights to such regulations and alterations as shall be thought proper to be made by the Parliament of Great Britain And that all other Courts now in being within the Kingdom of Scotland do remain but Subject to alterations by the Parliament of Great Britain And that all inferior

Courts within the said limits do remain Subordinate as they are now to the supreme Courts of Justice within the same in all time coming And that no Causes in Scotland be cognoscible by the Courts of Chancery Queen's Bench Common Pleas or any other Court in Westminster Hall and that the said Courts or any other of the like nature after the Union shall have no Power to cognosce review or alter the Acts or Sentences of the Judicatures within Scotland or stop the Execution of the same . . .

Articles XX–XXIV *****

Article XXV   Laws inconsistent with the articles, void

That all laws and statutes in either kingdom so far as they are contrary to or inconsistent with the terms of these articles or any of them shall from and after the union cease and become void and shall be so declared to be by the respective Parliaments of the said kingdoms.

   As by the said articles of union ratified and approved by the said Act of Parliament of Scotland relation being thereunto had may appear.

*****

5   Cap 8 ante, and the said Act of Parliament of Scotland to be observed as fundamental conditions of the said union; and the said articles and Acts of Parliament to continue the union

And it is hereby further enacted by the authority aforesaid that the said Act passed in this present session of Parliament intituled An Act for securing the Church of England as by law established and all and every the matters and things therein contained and also the said Act of Parliament of Scotland intituled Act for securing the Protestant religion and Presbyterian Church government with the establishment in the said Act contained be and shall for ever be held and adjudged to be and observed as fundamental and essential conditions of the said union and shall in all times coming be taken to be and are hereby declared to be essential and fundamental parts of the said articles and union and the said articles of union so as aforesaid ratified approved and confirmed by Act of Parliament of Scotland and by this present Act and the said Act passed in this present session of Parliament intituled an Act for securing the Church of England as by law established and also the said Act passed in the Parliament of Scotland intituled Act for securing the Protestant religion and Presbyterian Church government are hereby enacted and ordained to be and continue in all times coming the complete and intire union of the two kingdoms of England and Scotland.

*****

Union with Ireland Act 1800

(39 & 40 Geo. 3, c. 67)

*An Act for the Union of Great Britain and Ireland**

Territorial extent: United Kingdom

Whereas in pursuance of his Majesty's most gracious recommendation to the two houses of Parliament in Great Britain and Ireland respectively, to consider of such measures as might best tend to strengthen and consolidate the connection between the two kingdoms, the two houses of the Parliament of Great Britain and the two houses of the Parliament of Ireland have severally agreed and resolved, that, in order to promote and secure the essential interests of Great Britain and Ireland, and to consolidate the strength, power and resources of the British empire, it will be advisable to concur in such measures as may best tend to unite the two kingdoms of Great Britain and Ireland into one kingdom, in such manner, and on such terms and conditions, as may be established by the Acts of the respective Parliaments of Great Britain and Ireland:

---

   * Editor's Note: Pursuant to art. 2 of the Irish Free State (Consequential Adaption of Enactments) Order 1923 (SI 1923/405), 'references . . . to "the United Kingdom" or "the United Kingdom of Great Britain and Ireland," or "Great Britain and Ireland" or "Great Britain or Ireland," or "the British Islands" or "Ireland" shall . . . be construed as exclusive of' the Republic of Ireland.

And whereas, in furtherance of the said resolution, both houses of the said two Parliaments respectively have likewise agreed upon certain articles for effectuating and establishing the said purposes, in the tenor following:

Article First

That it be the First Article of the Union of the kingdoms of Great Britain and Ireland, that the said kingdoms of Great Britain and Ireland shall, upon the first day of January which shall be in the year of our Lord one thousand eight hundred and one, and for ever after, be united into one kingdom, by the name of the United Kingdom of Great Britain and Ireland, and that the royal stile and titles appertaining to the imperial crown of the said United Kingdom and its dependencies, and also the ensigns, armorial flags and banners thereof, shall be such as his Majesty, by his royal proclamation under the great seal of the United Kingdom, shall be pleased to appoint.

Article Second

That it be the Second Article of Union, that the succession to the imperial crown of the said United Kingdom, and of the dominions thereunto belonging, shall continue limited and settled in the same manner as the succession to the imperial crown of the said kingdoms of Great Britain and Ireland now stands limited and settled, according to the existing laws and to the terms of union between England and Scotland.

Article Third

That it be the Third Article of Union, that the said United Kingdom be represented in one and the same Parliament, to be stiled the Parliament of the United Kingdom of Great Britain and Ireland.

Article Fourth

*****

That it shall be lawful for his Majesty, his heirs and successors, to create peers of that part of the United Kingdom called Ireland, and to make promotions in the peerage thereof, after the union; provided that no new creation of any such peers shall take place after the union, until three of the peerages of Ireland which shall have been existing at the time of the union shall have become extinct; and upon such extinction of three peerages that it shall be lawful for his Majesty, his heirs and successors, to create one peer of that part of the United Kingdom called Ireland; and in like manner so often as three peerages of that part of the United Kingdom called Ireland shall become extinct, it shall be lawful for his Majesty, his heirs and successors, to create one other peer of that said part of the United Kingdom; and if it shall happen that the peers of that part of the United Kingdom called Ireland shall, by extinction of peerages or otherwise, be reduced to the number of one hundred exclusive of all such peers of that part of the United Kingdom called Ireland as shall hold any peerage of Great Britain subsisting at the time of the union or of the United Kingdom created since the union, by which such peers shall be entitled to an hereditary seat in the House of Lords of the United Kingdom then and in that case it shall and may be lawful for his Majesty, his heirs and successors, to create one peer of that part of the United Kingdom called Ireland, as often as any one of such one hundred peerages shall fail by extinction, or as often as any one peer of that part of the United Kingdom called Ireland shall become entitled by descent or creation to an hereditary seat in the House of Lords of the United Kingdom; it being the true intent and meaning of this article, that at all times after the union it shall and may be lawful for his Majesty, his heirs and successors, to keep up the peerage of that part of the United Kingdom called Ireland to the number of one hundred, over and above the number of such of the said peers as shall be entitled by descent or creation to an hereditary seat in the House of Lords of the United Kingdom:

*****

... that the persons holding any temporal peerages of Ireland existing at the time of the union shall, from and after the union, have rank and precedency next and immediately after all the persons holding peerages of the like orders and degrees in Great Britain subsisting at the time of the union; and that all peerages of Ireland created after the union shall have rank and precedency with the peerages of the United Kingdom so created, according to the dates of their creations; and that all peerages both of Great Britain and Ireland now subsisting or hereafter to be created shall in all other respects from the date of the union be considered as peerages of the United Kingdom; and that the peers of Ireland shall, as peers of the United Kingdom, ... enjoy all privileges of peers as fully as the peers of Great Britain, the right and privilege of sitting in the House of Lords and the privileges depending thereon ... only excepted.

Article Fifth

*****

Article Sixth

That it be the Sixth Article of Union, that his Majesty's subjects of Great Britain and Ireland shall from and after the first day of January one thousand eight hundred and one be entitled to the same privileges and be on the same footing, as to encouragements and bounties on the like articles, being the growth, produce or manufacture of either country respectively, and generally in respect of trade and navigation in all ports and places in the United Kingdom and its dependencies; and that in all treaties made by his Majesty his heirs and successors, with any foreign power, his Majesty's subjects of Ireland shall have the same privileges and be on the same footing as his Majesty's subjects of Great Britain:

That from the first day of January one thousand eight hundred and one all prohibitions and bounties on the export of articles, the growth, produce or manufacture of either country, to the other shall cease and determine; and that the said articles shall thenceforth be exported from one country to the other without duty or bounty on such export;

That all articles, the growth, produce or manufacture of either country (not herein-after enumerated as subject to specific duties), shall from thenceforth be imported into each country from the other free from duty other than such countervailing duties ... as shall hereafter be imposed by the Parliament of the United Kingdom, in the manner herein-after provided; ...
...

That any articles of the growth, produce or manufacture of either country, which are or may be subject to internal duty or to duty on the materials of which they are composed, may be made subject, on their importation into each country respectively from the other, to such countervailing duty as shall appear to be just and reasonable in respect of such internal duty or duties on the materials; ... and that upon the export of the said articles from each country to the other respectively, a drawback shall be given equal in amount to the countervailing duty payable on such articles on the import thereof into the same country from the other; and that in like manner in future it shall be competent to the united Parliament to impose any new or additional countervailing duties, or to take off or diminish such existing countervailing duties as may appear, on like principles, to be just and reasonable in respect of any future or additional internal duty on any article of the growth, produce or manufacture of either country, or of any new or additional duty on any materials of which such article may be composed, or of any abatement of duty on the same; and that when any such new or additional countervailing duty shall be so imposed on the import of any article into either country from the other, a drawback, equal in amount to such countervailing duty, shall be given in like manner on the export of every such article respectively from the same country to the other:

That all articles, the growth, produce or manufacture of either country, when exported through the other, shall in all cases be exported subject to the same charges as if they had been exported directly from the country of which they were the growth, produce or manufacture:
...

Article Seventh

...

Article Eighth

That it be the Eighth Article of Union, that all laws in force at the time of the union, and all the courts of civil and ecclesiastical jurisdiction within the respective kingdoms, shall remain as now by law established within the same, subject only to such alterations and regulations from time to time as circumstances may appear to the Parliament of the United Kingdom to require; ... provided ... that all laws at present in force in either kingdom, which shall be contrary to any of the provisions which may be enacted by any Act for carrying these articles into effect, be from and after the union repealed.

*****

Official Secrets Act 1911

(1 & 2 Geo. 5, c. 28)

An Act to re-enact the Official Secrets Act 1889, with Amendments.

Territorial extent: United Kingdom. See also s. 10(1)

1   Penalties for spying

(1) If any person for any purpose prejudicial to the safety or interests of the State—

(a) approaches [inspects, passes over] or is in the neighbourhood of, or enters any prohibited place within the meaning of this Act; or

(b) makes any sketch, plan, model, or note which is calculated to be or might be or is intended to be directly or indirectly useful to an enemy; or

(c) obtains, [collects, records, or publishes,] or communicates to any other person [any secret official code word or pass word, or] any sketch, plan, model, article, or note, or other document or information which is calculated to be or might be or is intended to be directly or indirectly useful to an enemy;

he shall be guilty of felony...

(2) On a prosecution under this section, it shall not be necessary to show that the accused person was guilty of any particular act tending to show a purpose prejudicial to the safety or interests of the State, and, notwithstanding that no such act is proved against him, he may be convicted if, from the circumstances of the case, or his conduct, or his known character as proved, it appears that his purpose was a purpose prejudicial to the safety or interests of the State; and if any sketch, plan, model, article, note, document, or information relating to or used in any prohibited place within the meaning of this Act, or anything in such a place [or any secret official code word or pass word], is made, obtained, [collected, recorded, published], or communicated by any person other than a person acting under lawful authority, it shall be deemed to have been made, obtained, [collected, recorded, published] or communicated for a purpose prejudicial to the safety or interests of the State unless the contrary is proved.

2   ...

3   Definition of prohibited place

For the purposes of this Act, the expression 'prohibited place' means—

[(a) any work of defence, arsenal, naval or air force establishment or station, factory, dockyard, mine, minefield, camp, ship, or aircraft belonging to or occupied by or on behalf of His Majesty, or any telegraph, telephone, wireless or signal station, or office so belonging or occupied, and any place belonging to or occupied by or on behalf of His Majesty and used for the purpose of building, repairing, making, or storing any munitions of war, or any sketches, plans, models, or documents relating thereto, or for the purpose of getting any metals, oil, or minerals of use in time of war];

(b) any place not belonging to His Majesty where any [munitions of war], or any [sketches, models, plans] or documents relating thereto, are being made, repaired, [gotten] or stored under contract with, or with any person on behalf of, His Majesty, or otherwise on behalf of His Majesty; and

(c) any place belonging to [or used for the purposes of] His Majesty which is for the time being declared [by order of a Secretary of State] to be a prohibited place for the purposes of this section on the ground that information with respect thereto, or damage thereto, would be useful to an enemy; and

(d) any railway, road, way, or channel, or other means of communication by land or water (including any works or structures being part thereof or connected therewith), or any place used for gas, water, or electricity works or other works for purposes of a public character, or any place where any [munitions of war], or any [sketches, models, plans] or documents relating thereto, are being made, repaired, or stored otherwise than on behalf of His Majesty, which is for the time being declared [by order or a Secretary of

State] to be a prohibited place for the purposes of this section, on the ground that information with respect thereto, or the destruction or obstruction thereof, or interference therewith, would be useful to an enemy.

4–6   ...

7   *****

8   Restriction on prosecution
A prosecution for an offence under this Act shall not be instituted except by or with the consent of the Attorney-General:
...

9   Search warrants
(1)   If a justice of the peace is satisfied by information on oath that there is reasonable ground for suspecting that an offence under this Act has been or is about to be committed, he may grant a search warrant authorising any constable . . . to enter at any time any premises or place named in the warrant, if necessary, by force, and to search the premises or place and every person found therein, and to seize any sketch, plan, model, article, note, or document, or anything of a like nature or anything which is evidence of an offence under this Act having been or being about to be committed, which he may find on the premises or place or on any such person, and with regard to or in connexion with which he has reasonable ground for suspecting that an offence under this Act has been or is about to be committed.

(2)   Where it appears to a superintendent of police that the case is one of great emergency and that in the interests of the State immediate action is necessary, he may by a written order under his hand give to any constable the like authority as may be given by the warrant of a justice under the section.

10   Extent of Act and place of trial of offence
(1)   This Act shall apply to all acts which are offences under this Act when committed in any part of His Majesty's dominions, or when committed by British officers or subjects elsewhere.
*****

Parliament Act 1911

(1 & 2 Geo. 5, c. 13)

An Act to make provision with respect to the powers of the House of Lords in relation of the House of Commons, and to limit the duration of Parliament.

Territorial extent: United Kingdom

Preamble
Whereas it is expedient that provision should be made for regulating the relations between the two Houses of Parliament:

And whereas it is intended to substitute for the House of Lords as it at present exists a Second Chamber constituted on a popular instead of hereditary basis, but such substitution cannot be immediately brought into operation:

And whereas provision will require hereafter to be made by Parliament in a measure effecting such substitution for limiting and defining the powers of the new Second Chamber, but it is expedient to make such provision as in this Act appears for restricting the existing powers of the House of Lords:

1   Powers of House of Lords as to Money Bills
(1)   If a Money Bill, having been passed by the House of Commons, and sent up to the House of Lords at least one month before the end of the session, is not passed by the House of Lords without amendment within one month after it is so sent up to that House, the Bill shall, unless the House of Commons direct to the contrary, be presented to His Majesty and become an Act of Parliament on the Royal Assent being signified, notwithstanding that the House of Lords have not consented to the Bill.

(2) A Money Bill means a Public Bill which in the opinion of the Speaker of the House of Commons contains only provisions dealing with all or any of the following subjects, namely, the imposition, repeal, remission, alteration, or regulation of taxation; the imposition for the payment of debt or other financial purposes of charges on the Consolidated Fund, [the National Loans Fund] or on money provided by Parliament, or the variation or repeal of any such charges; supply; the appropriation, receipt, custody, issue or audit of accounts of public money; the raising or guarantee of any loan or the repayment thereof; or subordinate matters incidental to those subjects or any of them. In this subsection the expressions 'taxation', 'public money' and 'loan' respectively do not include any taxation, money, or loan raised by local authorities or bodies for local purposes.

(3) There shall be endorsed on every Money Bill when it is sent up to the House of Lords and when it is presented to His Majesty for assent the certificate of the Speaker of the House of Commons signed by him that it is a Money Bill. Before giving his certificate, the Speaker shall consult, if practicable, two members to be appointed from the Chairmen's Panel at the beginning of each Session by the Committee of Selection.

2   Restriction of the powers of the House of Lords as to Bills other than Money Bills

(1) If any Public Bill (other than a Money Bill or a Bill containing any provision to extend the maximum duration of Parliament beyond five years) is passed by the House of Commons [in two successive sessions] (whether of the same Parliament or not), and, having been sent up to the House of Lords at least one month before the end of the session, is rejected by the House of Lords in each of those sessions, that Bill shall, on its rejection [for the second time]* by the House of Lords, unless the House of Commons direct to the contrary, be presented to His Majesty and become an Act of Parliament on the Royal Assent being signified thereto, notwithstanding that the House of Lords have not consented to the Bill:

Provided that this provision shall not take effect unless [one year has elapsed] between the date of the second reading in the first of those sessions of the Bill in the House of Commons and the date on which it passes the House of Commons [in the second of those sessions].

(2) When a Bill is presented to His Majesty for assent in pursuance of the provisions of this section, there shall be endorsed on the Bill the certificate of the Speaker of the House of Commons signed by him that the provisions of this section have been duly complied with.

(3) A Bill shall be deemed to be rejected by the House of Lords if it is not passed by the House of Lords either without amendment or with such amendments only as may be agreed to by both Houses.

(4) A Bill shall be deemed to be the same Bill as a former Bill sent up to the House of Lords in the preceding session if, when it is sent up to the House of Lords, it is identical with the former Bill or contains only such alterations as are certified by the Speaker of the House of Commons to be necessary owing to the time which has elapsed since the date of the former Bill, or to represent any amendments which have been made by the House of Lords in the former Bill in the preceding session, and any amendments which are certified by the Speaker to have been made by the House of Lords [in the second session] and agreed to by the House of Commons shall be inserted in the Bill as presented for Royal Assent in pursuance of this section:

Provided that the House of Commons may, if they think fit, on the passage of such a Bill through the House [in the second session], suggest any further amendments without inserting the amendments in the Bill, and any such suggested amendments shall be considered by the House of Lords, and, if agreed to by that House, shall be treated as amendments made by the House of Lords and agreed to by the House of Commons; but the exercise of this power by the House of Commons shall not affect the operation of this section in the event of the Bill being rejected by the House of Lords.

3   Certificate of Speaker

Any certificate of the Speaker of the House of Commons given under this Act shall be conclusive for all purposes, and shall not be questioned in any court of law.

---

* **Editor's Note:** The words in square brackets in s. 2 were substituted by the Parliament Act 1949.

4   Enacting words

(1) In every Bill presented to His Majesty under the preceding provisions of this Act, the words of enactment shall be as follows, that is to say:-

'Be it enacted by the King's most Excellent Majesty, by and with the advice and consent of the Commons in this present Parliament assembled, in accordance with the provisions of [the Parliament Acts 1911 and 1949], and by authority of the same, as follows.'

(2) Any alteration of a Bill necessary to give effect to this section shall not be deemed to be an amendment of the Bill.

5   Provisional Order Bills excluded

In this Act the expression 'Public Bill' does not include any Bill for confirming a Provisional Order.

6   Saving for existing rights and privileges of the House of Commons

Nothing in this Act shall diminish or qualify the existing rights and privileges of the House of Commons.

7   ...

*****

Official Secrets Act 1920

(10 & 11 Geo. 5, c. 75)

An Act to amend the Official Secrets Act 1911.

Territorial extent: United Kingdom

1   Unauthorised use of uniforms; falsification of reports, forgery, personation, and false documents

(1) If any person for the purpose of gaining admission, or of assisting any other person to gain admission, to a prohibited place, within the meaning of the Official Secrets Act 1911 (hereinafter referred to as 'the principal Act'), or for any other purpose prejudicial to the safety or interests of the State within the meaning of the said Act—

    (a) uses or wears, without lawful authority, any naval, military, air-force, police, or other official uniform, or any uniform so nearly resembling the same as to be calculated to deceive, or falsely represents himself to be a person who is or has been entitled to use or wear any such uniform; or

    (b) orally, or in writing in any declaration or application, or in any document signed by him or on his behalf, knowingly makes or connives at the making of any false statement or any omission; or

    (c) ... tampers with any passport or any naval, military, air-force, police, or official pass, permit, certificate, licence, or other document of a similar character (hereinafter in this section referred to as an official document), ... or has in his possession any ... forged, altered, or irregular official document; or

    (d) personates, or falsely represents himself to be a person holding, or in the employment of a person holding office under His Majesty, or to be or not to be a person to whom an official document or secret official code word or pass word has been duly issued or communicated, or with intent to obtain an official document, secret official code word or pass word, whether for himself or any other person, knowingly makes any false statement; or

    (e) uses, or has in his possession or under his control, without the authority of the Government Department or the authority concerned, any die, seal, or stamp of or belonging to, or used, made or provided by any Government Department, or by any diplomatic, naval, military, or air force authority appointed by or acting under the authority of His Majesty, or any die, seal or stamp so nearly resembling any such die, seal or stamp as to be calculated to deceive, or counterfeits any such die, seal or stamp, or uses, or has in his possession, or under his control, any such counterfeited die, seal or stamp;

he shall be guilty of a misdemeanour.

(2) If any person—

(a) retains for any purpose prejudicial to the safety or interests of the State any official document, whether or not completed or issued for use, when he has no right to retain it, or when it is contrary to his duty to retain it, or fails to comply with any directions issued by any Government Department or any person authorised by such department with regard to the return or disposal thereof; or

(b) allows any other person to have possession of any official document issued for his use alone, or communicates any secret official code word or pass word so issued, or, without lawful authority or excuse, has in his possession any official document or secret official code word or pass word issued for the use of some person other than himself, or on obtaining possession of any official document by finding or otherwise, neglects or fails to restore it to the person or authority by whom or for whose use it was issued, or to a police constable; or

(c) without lawful authority or excuse, manufactures or sells, or has in his possession for sale any such die, seal or stamp as aforesaid;

he shall be guilty of a misdemeanour.

(3) In the case of any prosecution under this section involving the proof of a purpose prejudicial to the safety or interests of the State, subsection (2) of section one of the principal Act shall apply in like manner as it applies to prosecutions under that section.

2, 3 *****

4, 5 ...

6 Duty of giving information as to commission of offences

[(1) Where a chief officer of police is satisfied that there is reasonable ground for suspecting that an offence under section one of the principal Act has been committed and for believing that any person is able to furnish information as to the offence or suspected offence, he may apply to a Secretary of State for permission to exercise the powers conferred by this subsection and, if such permission is granted, he may authorise a superintendent of police, or any police officer not below the rank of inspector, to require the person believed to be able to furnish information to give any information in his power relating to the offence or suspected offence, and, if so required and on tender of his reasonable expenses, to attend at such reasonable time and place as may be specified by the superintendent or other officer; and if a person required in pursuance of such an authorisation to give information, or to attend as aforesaid, fails to comply with any such requirement or knowingly gives false information, he shall be guilty of a misdemeanour.

(2) Where a chief officer of police has reasonable grounds to believe that the case is one of great emergency and that in the interest of the State immediate action is necessary, he may exercise the powers conferred by the last foregoing subsection without applying for or being granted the permission of a Secretary of State, but if he does so shall forthwith report the circumstances to the Secretary of State.

(3) References in this section to a chief officer of police shall be construed as including references to any other officer of police expressly authorised by a chief officer of police to act on his behalf for the purposes of this section when by reason of illness, absence or other cause he is unable to do so.]
*****

The Statute of Westminster 1931

(22 & 23 Geo. 5, c. 4)

An Act to give effect to certain resolutions passed by Imperial Conferences held in the years 1926 and 1930.

Territorial extent: As indicated in the Act

Whereas the delegates of His Majesty's Governments in the United Kingdom, the Dominion of Canada, the Commonwealth of Australia, the Dominion of New Zealand, the Union of South Africa, the Irish Free State and Newfoundland, at Imperial Conferences holden at Westminster in the years of our Lord nineteen hundred and twenty-six and nineteen hundred and thirty did concur in making the declarations and resolutions set forth in the Reports of the said Conferences:

And whereas it is meet and proper to set out by way of preamble to this Act that, inasmuch as the Crown is the symbol of the free association of the members of the British Commonwealth of Nations, and as they are united by a common allegiance to the Crown, it would be in accord with the established constitutional position of all the members of the Commonwealth in relation to one another that any alteration in the law touching the Succession to the Throne or the Royal Style and Titles shall hereafter require the assent as well of the Parliaments of all the Dominions as of the Parliament of the United Kingdom:

And whereas it is in accord with the established constitutional position that no law hereafter made by the Parliament of the United Kingdom shall extend to any of the said Dominions as part of the law of that Dominion otherwise than at the request and with the consent of that Dominion:

And whereas it is necessary for the ratifying, confirming and establishing of certain of the said declarations and resolutions of the said Conferences that a law be made and enacted in due form by authority of the Parliament of the United Kingdom:

And whereas the Dominion of Canada, the Commonwealth of Australia, the Dominion of New Zealand, the Union of South Africa, the Irish Free State and Newfoundland have severally requested and consented to the submission of a measure to the Parliament of the United Kingdom for making such provision with regard to the matters aforesaid as is hereafter in this Act contained:

1 Meaning of 'Dominion' in this Act
In this Act the expression 'Dominion' means any of the following Dominions, that is to say, the Dominion of Canada, the Commonwealth of Australia, the Dominion of New Zealand, ... the Irish Free State and Newfoundland.

2 Validity of laws made by Parliament of a Dominion
(1) The Colonial Laws Validity Act 1865 shall not apply to any law made after the commencement of this Act by the Parliament of a Dominion.

(2) No law and no provision of any law made after the commencement of this Act by the Parliament of a Dominion shall be void or inoperative on the ground that it is repugnant to the law of England, or to the provisions of any existing or future Act of Parliament of the United Kingdom, or to any order, rule or regulation made under any such Act, and the powers of the Parliament of a Dominion shall include the power to repeal or amend any such Act, order, rule or regulation in so far as the same is part of the law of the Dominion.

3 Power of Parliament of Dominion to legislate extra-territorially
It is hereby declared and enacted that the Parliament of a Dominion has full power to make laws having extra-territorial operation.

4 Parliament of United Kingdom not to legislate for Dominion except by consent
No Act of Parliament of the United Kingdom passed after the commencement of this Act shall extend, or be deemed to extend, to a Dominion as part of the law of that Dominion unless it is expressly declared in that Act that that Dominion has requested, and consented to, the enactment thereof.*

*****

* **Editor's Note:** This section has been repealed in relation to Canada by the Canada Act 1982, s. 1, Sch. B and in relation to Australia by the Australia Act 1986, s. 12.

Public Order Act 1936

(1 Edw. 8 & 1 Geo. 6, c. 6)

An Act to prohibit the wearing of uniforms in connection with political objects and the maintenance by private persons of associations of military or similar character; and to make further provision for the preservation of public order on the occasion of public processions and meetings and in public places.

Territorial extent: England and Wales, Scotland (s. 8: Scotland only). The amendment to s. 2(5) substituting 'three months' for 'one month' does not apply to Scotland.

1 Prohibition of uniforms in connection with political objects

(1) Subject as hereinafter provided, any person who in any public place or at any public meeting wears uniform signifying his association with any political organisation or with the promotion of any political object shall be guilty of an offence:

Provided that, if the chief officer of police is satisfied that the wearing of any such uniform as aforesaid on any ceremonial, anniversary, or other special occasion will not be likely to involve risk of public disorder, he may, with the consent of a Secretary of State, by order permit the wearing of such uniform on that occasion either absolutely or subject to such conditions as may be specified in the order.

(2) Where any person is charged before any court with an offence under this section, no further proceedings in respect thereof shall be taken against him without the consent of the Attorney-General [except such as are authorised by [section 6 of the Prosecution of Offences Act 1979]] so, however, that if that person is remanded in custody he shall, after the expiration of a period of eight days from the date on which he was so remanded, be entitled to be [released on bail] without sureties unless within that period the Attorney-General has consented to such further proceedings as aforesaid.

2 Prohibition of quasi-military organisations

(1) If the members or adherents of any association of persons, whether incorporated or not, are—

(a) organised or trained or equipped for the purpose of enabling them to be employed in usurping the functions of the police or of the armed forces of the Crown; or

(b) organised and trained or organised and equipped either for the purpose of enabling them to be employed for the use or display of physical force in promoting any political object, or in such manner as to arouse reasonable apprehension that they are organised and either trained or equipped for that purpose;

then any person who takes part in the control or management of the association, or in so organising or training as aforesaid any members or adherents thereof, shall be guilty of an offence under this section:

Provided that in any proceedings against a person charged with the offence of taking part in the control or management of such an association as aforesaid it shall be a defence to that charge to prove that he neither consented to nor connived at the organisation, training, or equipment of members or adherents of the association in contravention of the provisions of this section.

(2) No prosecution shall be instituted under this section without the consent of the Attorney-General.

(3), (4) *****

(5) If a judge of the High Court is satisfied by information on oath that there is reasonable ground for suspecting that an offence under this section has been committed, and that evidence of the commission thereof is to be found at any premises or place specified in the information, he may, on an application made by an officer of police of a rank not lower than that of inspector, grant a search warrant authorising any such officer as aforesaid named in the warrant together with any other persons named in the warrant and any other officers of police to enter the premises or place at any time within [three months] from the date of the warrant, if necessary by force, and to search the premises or place and every person found therein, and to seize anything found on the premises

or place or on any such person which the officer has reasonable ground for suspecting to be evidence of the commission of such an offence as aforesaid:

Provided that no woman shall, in pursuance of a warrant issued under this subsection, be searched except by a woman.

(6) Nothing in this section shall be construed as prohibiting the employment of a reasonable number of persons as stewards to assist in the preservation of order at any public meeting held upon private premises, or the making of arrangements for that purpose or the instruction of the persons to be so employed in their lawful duties as such stewards, or their being furnished with badges or other distinguishing signs.

3–5A ...

6 *****

7 Enforcement

(1) Any person who commits an offence under section two of this Act shall be liable on summary conviction to imprisonment for a term not exceeding six months or to a fine not exceeding [the prescribed sum], or to both such imprisonment and fine, or, on conviction on indictment, to imprisonment for a term not exceeding two years or to a fine [of any amount] or to both such imprisonment and fine.

(2) Any person guilty of [any offence under this Act other than an offence under section 2...] shall be liable on summary conviction to imprisonment for a term not exceeding three months or to a fine not exceeding [level 4 on the standard scale], or to both such imprisonment and fine.

(3) ...

8 Application to Scotland

This Act shall apply to Scotland subject to the following modifications:—

(1) Subsection (2) of section one and subsection (2) of section two of this Act shall not apply.

(2) In subsection (3) of section two the Lord Advocate shall be substituted for the Attorney-General and the Court of Session shall be substituted for the High Court.

(3) Subsection (5) of section two shall have effect as if for any reference to a judge of the High Court there were substituted a reference to the Sheriff and any application for a search warrant under the said subsection shall be made by the procurator fiscal instead of such officer as is therein mentioned.

(4) The power conferred on the sheriff by subsection (5) of section two, as modified by the last foregoing paragraph, shall not be exercisable by an [honorary sheriff].

(5), (6) ...

9 Interpretation, etc

(1) In this Act the following expressions have the meanings hereby respectively assigned to them, that is to say:—

...

'Meeting' means a meeting held for the purpose of the discussion of matters of public interest or for the purpose of the expression of views on such matters;

'Private premises' means premises to which the public have access (whether on payment or otherwise) only by permission of the owner, occupier, or lessee of the premises;

'Public meeting' includes any meeting in a public place and any meeting which the public or any section thereof are permitted to attend, whether on payment or otherwise;

['Public place' includes any highway and any other premises or place to which at the material time the public have or are permitted to have access, whether on payment or otherwise;]

...

(2) ...

(3), (4) *****

*****

Statutory Instruments Act 1946

(9 & 10 Geo. 6, c. 36)

An Act to repeal the Rules Publication Act, 1893, and to make further provision as to the instruments by which statutory powers to make orders, rules, regulations and other subordinate legislation are exercised. [26th March 1946]

Territorial extent: United Kingdom

1 Definition of 'statutory instrument'

(1) Where by this Act or any Act passed after the commencement of this Act power to make, confirm or approve orders, rules, regulations or other subordinate legislation is conferred on His Majesty in Council or on any Minister of the Crown then, if the power is expressed—

(a) in the case of a power conferred on His Majesty, to be exercisable by Order in Council;

(b) in the case of a power conferred on a Minister of the Crown, to be exercisable by statutory instrument,

any document by which that power is exercised shall be known as a 'statutory instrument' and the provisions of this Act shall apply thereto accordingly.

[(1A) Where by any Act power to make, confirm or approve orders, rules, regulations or other subordinate legislation is conferred on the Welsh Ministers and the power is expressed to be exercisable by statutory instrument, any document by which that power is exercised shall be known as a 'statutory instrument' and the provisions of this Act shall apply to it accordingly.]

(2) Where by any Act passed before the commencement of this Act power to make statutory rules within the meaning of the Rules Publication Act, 1893, was conferred on any rule-making authority within the meaning of that Act, any document by which that power is exercised after the commencement of this Act shall, save as is otherwise provided by regulations made under this Act, be known as a 'statutory instrument' and the provisions of this Act shall apply thereto accordingly.

2 Numbering, printing, publication and citation

(1) Immediately after the making of any statutory instrument, it shall be sent to the King's printer of Acts of Parliament and numbered in accordance with regulations made under this Act, and except in such cases as may be provided by any Act passed after the commencement of this Act or prescribed by regulations made under this Act, copies thereof shall as soon as possible be printed and sold by [or under the authority of] the King's printer of Acts of Parliament.

(2) Any statutory instrument may, without prejudice to any other mode of citation, be cited by the number given to it in accordance with the provisions of this section, and the calendar year.

3 Supplementary provisions as to publication

(1) Regulations made for the purposes of this Act shall make provision for the publication by His Majesty's Stationery Office of lists showing the date upon which every statutory instrument printed and sold by [or under the authority of] the King's printer of Acts of Parliament was first issued by [or under the authority of] that office; and in any legal proceedings a copy of any list so published...shall be received in evidence as a true copy, and an entry therein shall be conclusive evidence of the date on which any statutory instrument was first issued by [or under the authority of] His Majesty's Stationery Office.

(2) In any proceedings against any person for an offence consisting of a contravention of any such statutory instrument, it shall be a defence to prove that the instrument had not been issued by [or under the authority of] His Majesty's Stationery Office at the date of the alleged contravention unless it is proved that at that date reasonable steps had been taken for the purpose of bringing the

purport of the instrument to the notice of the public, or of persons likely to be affected by it, or of the person charged.

(3) Save as therein otherwise expressly provided, nothing in this section shall affect any enactment or rule of law relating to the time at which any statutory instrument comes into operation.

4 Statutory instruments which are required to be laid before Parliament

(1) Where by this Act or any Act passed after the commencement of this Act any statutory instrument is required to be laid before Parliament after being made, a copy of the instrument shall be laid before each House of Parliament and, subject as hereinafter provided, shall be so laid before the instrument comes into operation:

Provided that if it is essential that any such instrument should come into operation before copies thereof can be so laid as aforesaid, the instrument may be made so as to come into operation before it has been so laid; and where any statutory instrument comes into operation before it is laid before Parliament, notification shall forthwith be sent to [the Speaker of the House of Commons and the Speaker of the House of Lords] drawing attention to the fact that copies of the instrument have yet to be laid before Parliament and explaining why such copies were not so laid before the instrument came into operation.

(2) Every copy of any such statutory instrument sold by [or under the authority of] the King's printer of Acts of Parliament shall bear on the face thereof—

  (a) a statement showing the date on which the statutory instrument came or will come into operation; and

  (b) either a statement showing the date on which copies thereof were laid before Parliament or a statement that such copies are to be laid before Parliament.

(3) *****

5 Statutory instruments which are subject to annulment by resolution of either House of Parliament

(1) Where by this Act or any Act passed after the commencement of this Act, it is provided that any statutory instrument shall be subject to annulment in pursuance of resolution of either House of Parliament, the instrument shall be laid before Parliament after being made and the provisions of the last foregoing section shall apply thereto accordingly, and if either House, within the period of forty days beginning with the day on which a copy thereof is laid before it, resolves that an Address be presented to His Majesty praying that the instrument be annulled, no further proceedings shall be taken thereunder after the date of the resolution, and His Majesty may by Order in Council revoke the instrument, so, however, that any such resolution and revocation shall be without prejudice to the validity of anything previously done under the instrument or to the making of a new statutory instrument.

(2) *****

6 Statutory instruments of which drafts are to be laid before Parliament

(1) Where by this Act or any Act passed after the commencement of this Act it is provided that a draft of any statutory instrument shall be laid before Parliament, but the Act does not prohibit the making of the instrument without the approval of Parliament, then, in the case of an Order in Council the draft shall not be submitted to His Majesty in Council, and in any other case the statutory instrument shall not be made, until after the expiration of a period of forty days beginning with the day on which a copy of the draft is laid before each House of Parliament, or, if such copies are laid on different days, with the later of the two days, and if within that period either House resolves that the draft be not submitted to His Majesty or that the statutory instrument be not made, as the case may be, no further proceedings shall be taken thereon, but without prejudice to the laying before Parliament of a new draft.

(2) *****

*****

7–11A   *****

[11B   Application in relation to retained direct EU legislation etc

(1) For the purposes of this Act, if any retained direct EU legislation confers a power, which is expressed to be exercisable by Order in Council or statutory instrument, to make, confirm or approve any orders, rules, regulations or other subordinate legislation, this Act applies in relation to any document by which that power is exercised as if the retained direct EU legislation were an Act passed after the commencement of this Act.

(2) For the purposes of this Act, if regulations under the European Union (Withdrawal) Act 2018 or the Direct Payments to Farmers (Legislative Continuity) Act 2020 confer a power, which is expressed to be exercisable by Order in Council or statutory instrument, to make, confirm or approve any orders, rules, regulations or other subordinate legislation, this Act applies in relation to any document by which that power is exercised as if the regulations conferring the power were an Act passed after the commencement of this Act.]
*****

Crown Proceedings Act 1947

(10 & 11 Geo. 6, c. 44)

An Act to amend the law relating to the civil liabilities and rights of the Crown and to civil proceedings by and against the Crown, to amend the law relating to the civil liabilities of persons other than the Crown in certain cases involving the affairs or property of the Crown, and for purposes connected with the matters aforesaid.   [31st July 1947]

Territorial extent: United Kingdom (ss. 2, 4, 11, 21, 40), England and Wales, Northern Ireland (ss. 1, 17)

PART I SUBSTANTIVE LAW

1   Right to sue the Crown
Where any person has a claim against the Crown after the commencement of this Act, and, if this Act had not been passed, the claim might have been enforced, subject to the grant of His Majesty's fiat, by petition of right, or might have been enforced by a proceeding provided by any statutory provision repealed by this Act, then, subject to the provisions of this Act, the claim may be enforced as of right, and without the fiat of His Majesty, by proceedings taken against the Crown for that purpose in accordance with the provisions of this Act.

2   Liability of the Crown in tort
(1) Subject to the provisions of this Act, the Crown shall be subject to all those liabilities in tort to which, if it were a private person of full age and capacity, it would be subject—

(a) in respect of torts committed by its servants or agents;

(b) in respect of any breach of those duties which a person owes to his servants or agents at common law by reason of being their employer; and

(c) in respect of any breach of the duties attaching at common law to the ownership, occupation, possession or control of property:

Provided that no proceedings shall lie against the Crown by virtue of paragraph (a) of this subsection in respect of any act or omission of a servant or agent of the Crown unless the act or omission would apart from the provisions of this Act have given rise to a cause of action in tort against that servant or agent or his estate.

(2) Where the Crown is bound by a statutory duty which is binding also upon persons other than the Crown and its officers, then, subject to the provisions of this Act, the Crown shall, in respect of a failure to comply with that duty, be subject to all those liabilities in tort (if any) to which it would be so subject if it were a private person of full age and capacity.

(3) Where any functions are conferred or imposed upon an officer of the Crown as such either by any rule of the common law or by statute, and that officer commits a tort while performing or purporting to perform those functions, the liabilities of the Crown in respect of the tort shall be such as they would have been if those functions had been conferred or imposed solely by virtue of instructions lawfully given by the Crown.

(4) *****

(5) No proceedings shall lie against the Crown by virtue of this section in respect of anything done or omitted to be done by any person while discharging or purporting to discharge any responsibilities of a judicial nature vested in him, or any responsibilities which he has in connection with the execution of judicial process.

(6) No proceedings shall lie against the Crown by virtue of this section in respect of any act, neglect or default of any officer of the Crown, unless that officer has been directly or indirectly appointed by the Crown and was at the material time paid in respect of his duties as an officer of the Crown wholly out of the Consolidated Fund of the United Kingdom, moneys provided by Parliament, [the Scottish Consolidated Fund] ..., or any other Fund certified by the Treasury for the purposes of this subsection or was at the material time holding an office in respect of which the Treasury certify that the holder thereof would normally be so paid.

3 *****

4 Application of law as to indemnity, contribution, joint and several tort-feasors, and contributory negligence

(1) Where the Crown is subject to any liability by virtue of this Part of this Act, the law relating to indemnity and contribution shall be enforceable by or against the Crown in respect of the liability to which it is so subject as if the Crown were a private person of full age and capacity.

(2) ...

(3) Without prejudice to the general effect of section one of this Act, the Law Reform (Contributory Negligence) Act 1945 (which amends the law relating to contributory negligence) shall bind the Crown.

5–10 ...

11 Saving in respect of acts done under prerogative and statutory powers

(1) Nothing in Part I of this Act shall extinguish or abridge any powers or authorities which, if this Act had not been passed, would have been exercisable by virtue of the prerogative of the Crown, or any powers or authorities conferred on the Crown by any statute, and, in particular, nothing in the said Part I shall extinguish or abridge any powers or authorities exercisable by the Crown, whether in time of peace or of war, for the purpose of the defence of the realm or of training, or maintaining the efficiency of, any of the armed forces of the Crown.

(2) Where in any proceedings under this Act it is material to determine whether anything was properly done or omitted to be done in the exercise of the prerogative of the Crown, ... a Secretary of State may, if satisfied that the act or omission was necessary for any such purpose as is mentioned in the last preceding subsection, issue a certificate to the effect that the act or omission was necessary for that purpose; and the certificate shall, in those proceedings, be conclusive as to the matter so certified.

12–16 *****

PART II JURISDICTION AND PROCEDURE

17 Parties to proceedings

(1) [The Minister for the Civil Service] shall publish a list specifying the several Government departments which are authorised departments for the purposes of this Act, and the name and

address for service of the person who is, or is acting for the purposes of this Act as, the solicitor for each such department, and may from time to time amend or vary the said list.

Any document purporting to be a copy of a list published under this section and purporting to be printed under the superintendence or the authority of His Majesty's Stationery Office shall in any legal proceedings be received as evidence for the purpose of establishing what departments are authorised departments for the purposes of this Act, and what person is, or is acting for the purposes of this Act as, the solicitor for any such department.

(2) Civil proceedings by the Crown may be instituted either by an authorised Government department in its own name, whether that department was or was not at the commencement of this Act authorised to sue, or by the Attorney General.

(3) Civil proceedings against the Crown shall be instituted against the appropriate authorised Government department, or, if none of the authorised Government departments is appropriate or the person instituting the proceedings has any reasonable doubt whether any and if so which of those departments is appropriate, against the Attorney General.

(4), (5) *****

18 *****

19 ...

20 *****

21 Nature of relief

(1) In any civil proceedings by or against the Crown the court shall, subject to the provisions of this Act, have power to make all such orders as it has power to make in proceedings between subjects, and otherwise to give such appropriate relief as the case may require:

Provided that:—

    (a) where in any proceedings against the Crown any such relief is sought as might in proceedings between subjects be granted by way of injunction or specific performance, the court shall not grant an injunction or make an order for specific performance, but may in lieu thereof make an order declaratory of the rights of the parties; and

    (b) in any proceedings against the Crown for the recovery of land or other property the court shall not make an order for the recovery of the land or the delivery of the property, but may in lieu thereof make an order declaring that the plaintiff is entitled as against the Crown to the land or property or to the possession thereof.

(2) The court shall not in any civil proceedings grant any injunction or make any order against an officer of the Crown if the effect of granting the injunction or making the order would be to give any relief against the Crown which could not have been obtained in proceedings against the Crown.

22–27 *****

PART IV MISCELLANEOUS AND SUPPLEMENTAL

28, 29, 31–33, 35, 37–38 *****

30, 34, 36, 39 ...

40 Savings

(1) Nothing in this Act shall apply to proceedings by or against, or authorise proceedings in tort to be brought against, His Majesty in His private capacity.

(2)–(5) *****

*****

Life Peerages Act 1958

(1958, c. 21)

An Act to make provision for the creation of life peerages carrying the right to sit and vote in the House of Lords.   [30th April 1958]

Territorial extent: United Kingdom

1   Power to create life peerages carrying right to sit in the House of Lords

(1) . . . Her Majesty shall have power by letters patent to confer on any person a peerage for life having the incidents specified in subsection (2) of this section.

(2) A peerage conferred under this section shall, during the life of the person on whom it is conferred, entitle him—

>   (a) to rank as a baron under such style as may be appointed by the letters patent; and

>   (b) subject to subsection (4) of this section, to receive writs of summons to attend the House of Lords and sit and vote therein accordingly,

and shall expire on his death.

(3) A life peerage may be conferred under this section on a woman.

(4) Nothing in this section shall enable any person to receive a writ of summons to attend the House of Lords, or to sit and vote in that House, at any time when disqualified therefor by law.

*****

Obscene Publications Act 1959

(7 & 8 Eliz. 2, c. 66)

An Act to amend the law relating to the publication of obscene matter; to provide for the protection of literature; and to strengthen the law concerning pornography.   [29th July 1959]

Territorial extent: England and Wales

1   Test of obscenity

(1) For the purposes of this Act an article shall be deemed to be obscene if its effect or (where the article comprises two or more distinct items) the effect of any one of its items is, if taken as a whole, such as to tend to deprave and corrupt persons who are likely, having regard to all relevant circumstances, to read, see or hear the matter contained or embodied in it.

(2) In this Act 'article' means any description of article containing or embodying matter to be read or looked at or both, any sound record, and any film or other record of a picture or pictures.

(3) For the purposes of this Act a person publishes an article who—

>   (a) distributes, circulates, sells, lets on hire, gives, or lends it, or who offers it for sale or for letting on hire; or

>   (b) in the case of an article containing or embodying matter to be looked at or a record, shows, plays or projects it [, or, where the matter is data stored electronically, transmits that data.]

. . .

[(4) For the purposes of this Act a person also publishes an article to the extent that any matter recorded on it is included by him in a programme included in a programme service.

(5) Where the inclusion of any matter in a programme so included would, if that matter were recorded matter, constitute the publication of an obscene article for the purposes of this Act by virtue of subsection (4) above, this Act shall have effect in relation to the inclusion of that matter in that programme as if it were recorded matter.

(6) In this section 'programme' and 'programme service' have the same meaning as in the Broadcasting Act 1990.]

2 Prohibition of publication of obscene matter

(1) Subject as hereinafter provided, any person who, whether for gain or not, publishes an obscene article [or who has an obscene article for publication for gain (whether gain to himself or gain to another)] shall be liable—

    (a) on summary conviction to a fine not exceeding [the prescribed sum] or to imprisonment for a term not exceeding six months;

    (b) on conviction on indictment to a fine or to imprisonment for a term not exceeding [five years] or both.

(2) ...

(3) A prosecution ... for an offence against this section shall not be commenced more than two years after the commission of the offence.

[(3A) Proceedings for an offence under this section shall not be instituted except by or with the consent of the Director of Public Prosecutions in any case where the article in question is a moving picture film of a width of not less than sixteen millimetres and the relevant publication or the only other publication which followed or could reasonably have been expected to follow from the relevant publication took place or (as the case may be) was to take place in the course of [an exhibition of a film]; and in this subsection 'the relevant publication' means—

    (a) in the case any proceedings under this section for publishing an obscene article, the publication in respect of which the defendant would be charged if the proceedings were brought; and

    (b) in the case of any proceedings under this section for having an obscene article for publication for gain, the publication which, if the proceedings were brought, the defendant would be alleged to have had in contemplation.]

(4) A person publishing an article shall not be proceeded against for an offence at common law consisting of the publication of any matter contained or embodied in the article where it is of the essence of the offence that the matter is obscene.

[(4A) Without prejudice to subsection (4) above, a person shall not be proceeded against for an offence at common law—

    (a) in respect of [an exhibition of a film] or anything said or done in the course of [an exhibition of a film], where it is of the essence of the common law offence that the exhibition or, as the case may be, what was said or done was obscene, indecent, offensive, disgusting or injurious to morality; or

    (b) in respect of an agreement to give [an exhibition of a film] or to cause anything to be said or done in the course of such an exhibition where the common law offence consists of conspiring to corrupt public morals or to do any act contrary to public morals or decency.]

(5) A person shall not be convicted of an offence against this section if he proves that he had not examined the article in respect of which he is charged and had no reasonable cause to suspect that it was such that his publication of it would make him liable to be convicted of an offence against this section.

(6) In any proceedings against a person under this section the question whether an article is obscene shall be determined without regard to any publication by another person unless it could reasonably have been expected that the publication by the other person would follow from publication by the person charged.

(7) In this section ['exhibition of a film'] has the [meaning given in paragraph 15 of Schedule 1 to the Licensing Act 2003].

3 *****

4 Defence of public good

(1) [Subject to subsection (1A) of this section] a person shall not be convicted of an offence against section two of this Act, and an order for forfeiture shall not be made under the foregoing section, if it is proved that publication of the article in question is justified as being for the public good on the ground that it is in the interests of science, literature, art or learning, or of other objects of general concern.

[(1A) Subsection (1) of this section shall not apply where the article in question is a moving picture film or soundtrack, but—

(a) a person shall not be convicted of an offence against section 2 of this Act in relation to any such film or soundtrack, and

(b) an order for forfeiture of any such film or soundtrack shall not be made under section 3 of this Act,

if it is proved that publication of the film or soundtrack is justified as being for the public good on the ground that it is in the interests of drama, opera, ballet or any other art, or of literature or learning.]

(2) It is hereby declared that the opinion of experts as to the literary, artistic, scientific or other merits of an article may be admitted in any proceedings under this Act either to establish or to negative the said ground.

[(3) In this section 'moving picture soundtrack' means any sound record designed for playing with a moving picture film, whether incorporated with the film or not.]

*****

Criminal Law Act 1967

(1967, c. 58)

An Act to amend the law of England and Wales by abolishing the division of crimes into felonies and misdemeanours and to amend and simplify the law in respect of matters arising from or related to that division or the abolition of it; to do away (within or without England and Wales) with certain obsolete crimes together with the torts of maintenance and champerty; and for purposes connected therewith.   [21st July 1967]

Territorial extent: England and Wales

PART I FELONY AND MISDEMEANOUR

1 *****

2 ...

3 Use of force in making arrest, etc

(1) A person may use such force as is reasonable in the circumstances in the prevention of crime, or in effecting or assisting in the lawful arrest of offenders or suspected offenders or of persons unlawfully at large.

(2) Subsection (1) above shall replace the rules of the common law on the question when force used for a purpose mentioned in the subsection is justified by that purpose.

*****

Parliamentary Commissioner Act 1967

(1967, c. 13)

An Act to make provision for the appointment and functions of a Parliamentary Commissioner for the investigation of administrative action taken on behalf of the Crown, and for purposes connected therewith.   [22nd March 1967]

Territorial extent: United Kingdom

The Parliamentary Commissioner for Administration

1 Appointment and tenure of office

(1) For the purpose of conducting investigations in accordance with the following provisions of this Act there shall be appointed a Commissioner, to be known as the Parliamentary Commissioner for Administration.

(2) Her Majesty may by Letters Patent from time to time appoint a person to be the Commissioner....

[(2A) A person appointed to be the Commissioner shall hold office until the end of the period for which he is appointed.

(2B) That period must be not more than seven years.

(2C) Subsection (2A) is subject to subsections (3) and (3A).]

[(3) A person appointed to be the Commissioner may be—

(a) relieved of office by Her Majesty at his own request, or

(b) removed from office by Her Majesty, on the ground of misbehaviour, in consequence of Addresses from both Houses of Parliament.]

[(3A) Her Majesty may declare the office of Commissioner to have been vacated if satisfied that the person appointed to be the Commissioner is incapable for medical reasons—

(a) of performing duties of his office; and

(b) of requesting to be relieved of it.]

[(3B) A person appointed to be the Commissioner is not eligible for re-appointment.]

(4), (5) …

2   *****

3   Administrative provisions

(1) The Commissioner may appoint such officers as he may determine with the approval of the Treasury as to numbers and conditions of service.

[(1A) The Commissioner may appoint and pay a mediator or other appropriate person to assist him in the conduct of an investigation under this Act.]

(2), (2A), (3) *****

3A   *****

[4   Departments etc subject to investigation

(1) Subject to the provisions of this section and to the notes contained in Schedule 2 to this Act, this Act applies to the government departments, corporations and unincorporated bodies listed in that Schedule; and references in this Act to an authority to which this Act applies are references to any such corporation or body.

(2) Her Majesty may by Order in Council amend Schedule 2 to this Act by the alteration of any entry or note, the removal of any entry or note or the insertion of any additional entry or note.

(3) An Order in Council may only insert an entry if—

(a) it relates—

(i) to a government department; or

(ii) to a corporation or body whose functions are exercised on behalf of the Crown; or

(b) it relates to a corporation or body—

(i)   which is established by virtue of Her Majesty's prerogative or by an Act of Parliament or an Order in Council or order made under an Act of Parliament or which is established in any other way by a Minister of the Crown in his capacity as a Minister or by a government department;

(ii) at least half of whose revenues derive directly from money provided by Parliament, a levy authorised by an enactment, a fee or charge of any other description so authorised or more than one of those sources; and

(iii) which is wholly or partly constituted by appointment made by Her Majesty or a Minister of the Crown or government department.

[(3A) No entry shall be made if the result of making it would be that the Parliamentary Commissioner could investigate action which can be investigated by the Public Services Ombudsman for Wales under [the Public Services Ombudsman (Wales) Act 2019].]

[(3B) No entry shall be made in respect of—

(a) the Scottish Administration or any part of it;

(b) any Scottish public authority with mixed functions or no reserved functions within the meaning of the Scotland Act 1998; or

(c) the Scottish Parliamentary Corporate Body.]

(4) No entry shall be made in respect of a corporation or body whose sole activity is, or whose main activities are, included among the activities specified in subsection (5) below.

(5) The activities mentioned in subsection (4) above are—

(a) the provision of education, or the provision of training otherwise than under the Industrial Training Act 1982;

(b) the development of curricula, the conduct of examinations or the validation of educational courses;

(c) the control of entry to any profession or the regulation of the conduct of members of any profession;

(d) the investigation of complaints by members of the public regarding the actions of any person or body, or the supervision or review of such investigations or of steps taken following them.

(6) No entry shall be made in respect of a corporation or body operating in an exclusively or predominantly commercial manner or a corporation carrying on under national ownership an industry or undertaking or part of an industry or undertaking.

(7) Any statutory instrument made by virtue of this section shall be subject to annulment in pursuance of a resolution of either House of Parliament.]

(8) *****

5 Matters subject to investigation

(1) Subject to the provisions of this section, the Commissioner may investigate any action taken by or on behalf of a government department or other authority to which this Act applies, being action taken in the exercise of administrative functions of that department or authority, in any case where—

(a) a written complaint is duly made to a member of the House of Commons by a member of the public who claims to have sustained injustice in consequence of maladministration in connection with the action so taken; and

(b) the complaint is referred to the Commissioner, with the consent of the person who made it, by a member of that House with a request to conduct an investigation thereon.

(1A)–(1C) *****

(2) Except as hereinafter provided, the Commissioner shall not conduct an investigation under this Act in respect of any of the following matters, that is to say—

(a) any action in respect of which the person aggrieved has or had a right of appeal, reference or review to or before a tribunal constituted by or under any enactment or by virtue of Her Majesty's prerogative;

(b) any action in respect of which the person aggrieved has or had a remedy by way of proceedings in any court of law:

Provided that the Commissioner may conduct an investigation notwithstanding that the person aggrieved has or had such a right or remedy if satisfied that in the particular circumstances it is not reasonable to expect him to resort or have resorted to it.

(2A) *****

(3) Without prejudice to subsection (2) of this section, the Commissioner shall not conduct [an investigation under subsection (1) of this section] in respect of any such action or matter as is described in Schedule 3 to this Act.

(4) Her Majesty may by Order in Council amend the said Schedule 3 so as to exclude from the provisions of that Schedule such actions or matters as may be described in the Order; and any statutory instrument made by virtue of this subsection shall be subject to annulment in pursuance of a resolution of either House of Parliament.

(4A)–(4C) *****

(5) In determining whether to initiate, continue or discontinue an investigation under this Act, the Commissioner shall, subject to the foregoing provisions of this section, act in accordance with his own discretion; and any question whether a complaint is duly made under this Act shall be determined by the Commissioner.

(5A)–(9A) *****

6 Provisions relating to complaints

(1) A complaint under this Act may be made by any individual, or by any body of persons whether incorporated or not, not being—

    (a)   a local authority or other authority or body constituted for purposes of the public service or of local government or for the purposes of carrying on under national ownership any industry or undertaking or part of an industry or undertaking;

    [(b) any other authority or body within subsection (1A) below.

(1A) An authority or body is within this subsection if—

    (a) its members are appointed by—

        (i)   Her Majesty;

        (ii) any Minister of the Crown;

        (iii) any government department;

        (iv) the Scottish Ministers;

        (v)   the First Minister; or

        (vi) the Lord Advocate, or

    (b) its revenues consist wholly or mainly of—

        (i)   money provided by Parliament; or

        (ii) sums payable out of the Scottish Consolidated Fund (directly or indirectly).]

(2) Where the person by whom a complaint might have been made under the foregoing provisions of this Act has died or is for any reason unable to act for himself, the complaint may be made by his personal representative or by a member of his family or other individual suitable to represent him; but except as aforesaid a complaint shall not be entertained under this Act unless made by the person aggrieved himself.

(3) A complaint shall not be entertained under this Act unless it is made to a member of the House of Commons not later than twelve months from the day on which the person aggrieved first had notice of the matters alleged in the complaint; but the Commissioner may conduct an investigation pursuant to a complaint not made within that period if he considers that there are special circumstances which make it proper to do so.

(4) [Except as provided in subsection (5) below] a complaint shall not be entertained under this Act unless the person aggrieved is resident in the United Kingdom (or, if he is dead, was so resident at the time of his death) or the complaint relates to action taken in relation to him while he was present in the United Kingdom or on an installation in a designated area within the meaning of the Continental Shelf Act 1964 or on a ship registered in the United Kingdom or an aircraft so registered, or in relation to rights or obligations which accrued or arose in the United Kingdom or on such an installation, ship or aircraft.

(5) *****

7 Procedure in respect of investigations

(1) Where the Commissioner proposes to conduct an investigation pursuant to a complaint under [section 5(1) of] this Act, he shall afford to the principal officer of the department or authority concerned, and to any person who is alleged in the complaint to have taken or authorised the action complained of, an opportunity to comment on any allegations contained in the complaint.

(1A) *****

(2) Every [investigation under this Act] shall be conducted in private, but except as aforesaid the procedure for conducting an investigation shall be such as the Commissioner considers appropriate in the circumstances of the case; and without prejudice to the generality of the foregoing provision the Commissioner may obtain information from such persons and in such manner, and make such inquiries, as he thinks fit, and may determine whether any person may be represented, by counsel or solicitor or otherwise, in the investigation.

(3), (4) *****

8 Evidence

(1) For the purposes of an investigation under [section 5(1) of] this Act the Commissioner may require any Minister, officer or member of the department or authority concerned or any other

person who in his opinion is able to furnish information or produce documents relevant to the investigation to furnish any such information or produce any such document.

(1A) *****

(2) For the purposes of any [investigation under this Act] the Commissioner shall have the same powers as the Court in respect of the attendance and examination of witnesses (including the administration of oaths or affirmations and the examination of witnesses abroad) and in respect of the production of documents.

(3) No obligation to maintain secrecy or other restriction upon the disclosure of information obtained by or furnished to persons in Her Majesty's service, whether imposed by any enactment or by any rule of law, shall apply to the disclosure of information for the purposes of an investigation under this Act; and the Crown shall not be entitled in relation to any such investigation to any such privilege in respect of the production of documents or the giving of evidence as is allowed by law in legal proceedings.

(4) No person shall be required or authorised by virtue of this Act to furnish any information or answer any question relating to proceedings of the Cabinet or of any committee of the Cabinet or to produce so much of any document as relates to such proceedings; and for the purposes of this subsection a certificate issued by the Secretary of the Cabinet with the approval of the Prime Minister and certifying that any information, question, document or part of a document so relates shall be conclusive.

(5) *****

9 Obstruction and contempt

(1) If any person without lawful excuse obstructs the Commissioner or any officer of the Commissioner in the performance of his functions under this Act, or is guilty of any act or omission in relation to any investigation under this Act which, if that investigation were a proceeding in the Court, would constitute contempt of court, the Commissioner may certify the offence to the Court.

(2) Where an offence is certified under this section, the Court may inquire into the matter and, after hearing any witnesses who may be produced against or on behalf of the person charged with the offence, and after hearing any statement that may be offered in defence, deal with him in any manner in which the court could deal with him if he had committed the like offence in relation to the Court.

(3) *****

10 Reports by Commissioner

(1) In any case where the Commissioner conducts an investigation under this Act or decides not to conduct such an investigation, he shall send to the member of the House of Commons by whom the request for investigation was made (or if he is no longer a member of that House, to such member of that House as the Commissioner thinks appropriate) a report of the results of the investigation or, as the case may be, a statement of his reasons for not conducting an investigation.

(2) In any case where the Commissioner conducts an investigation under [section 5(1) of] this Act, he shall also send a report of the results of the investigation to the principal officer of the department or authority concerned and to any other person who is alleged in the relevant complaint to have taken or authorised the action complained of.

(2A) *****

(3) If, after conducting an investigation under [section 5(1) of] this Act, it appears to the Commissioner that injustice has been caused to the person aggrieved in consequence of maladministration and that the injustice has not been, or will not be, remedied, he may, if he thinks fit, lay before each House of Parliament a special report upon the case.

(3A), (3B) *****

(4) The Commissioner shall annually lay before each House of Parliament a general report on the performance of his functions under this Act and may from time to time lay before each House of Parliament such other reports with respect to those functions as he thinks fit.

(5) For the purposes of the law of defamation, any such publication as is hereinafter mentioned shall be absolutely privileged, that is to say—

  (a) the publication of any matter by the Commissioner in making a report to either House of Parliament for the purposes of this Act;

(b) the publication of any matter by a member of the House of Commons in communicating with the Commissioner or his officers for those purposes or by the Commissioner or his officers in communicating with such a member for those purposes;

(c) the publication by such a member to the person by whom a complaint was made under this Act of a report or statement sent to the member in respect of the complaint in pursuance of section (1) of this section;

(d) the publication by the Commissioner to such a person as is mentioned in subsection (2) [or (2A)] of this section of a report to that person in pursuance of that subsection.

11, 11A, 11AA, 11ZAA, 11B, 11C *****

Supplemental

12   Interpretation

(1), (2) *****

(3) It is hereby declared that nothing in this Act authorises or requires the Commissioner to question the merits of a decision taken without maladministration by a government department or other authority in the exercise of a discretion vested in that department or authority.

13, 14 *****

*****

Section 5   # SCHEDULE 3

MATTERS NOT SUBJECT TO INVESTIGATION

1. Action taken in matters certified by a Secretary of State or other Minister of the Crown to affect relations or dealings between the Government of the United Kingdom and any other Government or any international organisation of States or Governments.

2. [(1) Action taken, in any country or territory outside the United Kingdom, by or on behalf of any officer representing or acting under the authority of Her Majesty in respect of the United Kingdom, or any other officer of the Government of the United Kingdom other than,

(a) action which is taken by an officer (not being an honorary consular officer) in the exercise of a consular function on behalf of the Government of the United Kingdom;

(b) action which is taken by an officer within a control zone or a supplementary control zone; or

(c) action which is taken by a British sea-fishery officer.]

(2) *****

3. Action taken in connection with the administration of the government of any country or territory outside the United Kingdom which forms part of Her Majesty's dominions or in which Her Majesty has jurisdiction.

[4. Action taken by the Secretary of State under the Extradition Act 2003.]

5. Action taken by or with the authority of the Secretary of State for the purposes of investigating crime or of protecting the security of the State, including action so taken with respect to passports.

6. The commencement or conduct of civil or criminal proceedings before any court of law in the United Kingdom, of [service law proceedings (as defined by section 324(5) of the Armed Forces Act 2006) (anywhere)], or of proceedings before any international court or tribunal.

[6A. Action taken by any person appointed by the Lord Chancellor as a member of the administrative staff of any court or tribunal, so far as that action is taken at the direction, or on the authority (whether express or implied) of any person acting in a judicial capacity or as a member of the tribunal.]

[6B. (1) Action taken by any member of the administrative staff of a relevant tribunal so far as that action is taken at the direction, or on the authority (whether express or implied), of any person acting in his capacity as a member of the tribunal.

(2) In this paragraph, 'relevant tribunal' has the meaning given by section 5(8) of this Act.]

[6C. ...]

7. Any exercise of the prerogative of mercy or of the power of a Secretary of State to make a reference in respect of any person to ... the High Court of Justiciary or the [Court Martial Appeal Court.]

8. [(1)] Action taken on behalf of ... the Secretary of State by [a local authority, [NHS England], [an integrated care board]] ... [or] [a Special Health Authority] ...

[(2) For the purposes of this paragraph, action taken by [a local authority, [NHS England], [an integrated care board] or] ... Special Health Authority ... in the exercise of functions of the Secretary of State shall be regarded as action taken on his behalf.]

9. Action taken in matters relating to contractual or other commercial transactions, whether within the United Kingdom or elsewhere, being transactions of a government department or authority to which this Act applies or of any such authority or body as is mentioned in paragraph (a) or (b) of subsection (1) of section 6 of this Act and not being transactions for or relating to—

(a) the acquisition of land compulsorily or in circumstances in which it could be acquired compulsorily;

(b) the disposal as surplus of land acquired compulsorily or in such circumstances as aforesaid.

10. [(1)] Action taken in respect of appointments or removals, pay, discipline, superannuation or other personnel matters, in relation to—

(a) service in any of the armed forces of the Crown, including reserve and auxiliary and cadet forces;

(b) service in any office or employment under the Crown or under any authority [(to which this Act applies)]; or

(c) service in any office or employment, or under any contract for services, in respect of which power to take action, or to determine or approve the action to be taken, in such matters is vested in Her Majesty, any Minister of the Crown or any such authority as aforesaid.

[(1A) Sub-paragraph (1)(a) shall not apply to any action (not otherwise excluded from investigation by this Schedule) which is taken by the Secretary of State in connection with the provision of any allowance, grant, supplement or benefit under—

(a) the Naval, Military and Air Forces etc (Disablement and Death) Service Pensions Order 2006 (SI 2006/606); or

(b) the Armed Forces and Reserve Forces (Compensation Scheme) Order 2011 (SI 2011/517).]

[(2) Sub-paragraph (1)(c) above shall not apply to any action (not otherwise excluded from investigation by this Schedule) which is taken by the Secretary of State in connection with—

(a) the provision of information relating to the terms and conditions of any employment covered by an agreement entered into by him under section 12(1) of the Overseas Development and Cooperation Act 1980 [or pursuant to the exercise of his powers under Part 1 of the International Development Act 2002] or

(b) the provision of any allowance, grant or supplement or any benefit (other than those relating to superannuation) arising from the designation of any person in accordance with such an agreement.]

[(3) Sub-paragraph (1)(c) does not apply to any action (not otherwise excluded from investigation by this Schedule) which is taken by the Treasury in connection with—

(a) the provision of information relating to the terms and conditions of any employment covered by an agreement entered into by the Treasury pursuant to the exercise of the Treasury's powers under Part 1 of the International Development Act 2002, or

(b) the provision of any allowance, grant or supplement or any benefit (other than those relating to superannuation) arising from such an agreement.]

11. The grant of honours, awards or privileges within the gift of the Crown, including the grant of Royal Charters.

[12. (1) Action not otherwise within this Schedule which is taken in the course of administrative functions exercised at the direction, or on the authority (whether express or implied), of a judge of any court established under the law of England and Wales or Northern Ireland.

(2) In this paragraph 'judge' includes—

(a) a person appointed under section 89 of, and Part 2 or 3 of Schedule 2 to, the Supreme Court Act 1981, and

(b) a Master or District Judge appointed under section 70 of, and Schedule 3 to, the Judicature (Northern Ireland) Act 1978.]

*****

Immigration Act 1971*

(1971, c. 77)

An Act to amend and replace the present immigration laws, to make certain related changes in the citizenship law and enable help to be given to those wishing to return abroad, and for purposes connected therewith.   [28th October 1971]

Territorial extent: United Kingdom

1–3 *****

[3ZA   Irish citizens]

[(1)   An Irish citizen does not require leave to enter or remain in the United Kingdom, unless subsection (2), (3) or (4) applies to that citizen.

(2)   This subsection applies to an Irish citizen if the Irish citizen is subject to a deportation order made under section 5(1).

(3)   This subsection applies to an Irish citizen if—

(a) the Secretary of State has issued directions for the Irish citizen not to be given entry to the United Kingdom on the ground that the Irish citizen's exclusion is conducive to the public good,

(b) the Secretary of State has given the Irish citizen notice of the directions, and

(c) the directions have not been withdrawn.

(4)   This subsection applies to an Irish citizen if the Irish citizen is an excluded person for the purposes of section 8B (persons excluded under certain instruments).

(5)   Where subsection (2), (3) or (4) applies to an Irish citizen, section 1(3) does not permit the Irish citizen to enter the United Kingdom without leave on arriving in the United Kingdom on a local journey from any place in the common travel area.]

*****

Local Government Act 1972

(1972, c. 70)

An Act to make provision with respect to local government and the functions of local authorities in England and Wales; to amend Part II of the Transport Act 1968; to confer rights of appeal in respect of decisions relating to licences under the Home Counties (Music and Dancing) Licensing Act 1926; to make further provision with respect to magistrates' courts committees; to abolish certain inferior courts of record; and for connected purposes.   [26th October 1972]

Territorial extent: England and Wales

*****

---

* **Editor's Note:** The section here set out is that added by the Immigration and Social Security Co-ordination (EU Withdrawal) Act 2020.

PART VII MISCELLANEOUS POWERS OF LOCAL AUTHORITIES

111   Subsidiary powers of local authorities

(1) Without prejudice to any powers exercisable apart from this section but subject to the provisions of this Act and any other enactment passed before or after this Act, a local authority shall have power to do anything (whether or not involving the expenditure, borrowing or lending of money or the acquisition or disposal of any property or rights) which is calculated to facilitate, or is conducive or incidental to, the discharge of any of their functions.

(2) For the purposes of this section, transacting the business of a parish or community meeting or any other parish or community business shall be treated as a function of the parish or community council.

(3) A local authority shall not by virtue of this section raise money, whether by means of rates, precepts or borrowing, or lend money except in accordance with the enactments relating to those matters respectively.

(4) In this section 'local authority' includes the Common Council.

112   Appointment of staff

(1) Without prejudice to section 111 above but subject to the provisions of this Act, a local authority shall appoint such officers as they think necessary for the proper discharge by the authority of such of their or another authority's functions as fall to be discharged by them and the carrying out of any obligations incurred by them in connection with an agreement made by them in pursuance of section 113 below.

(2) An officer appointed under subsection (1) above shall hold office on such reasonable terms and conditions, including conditions as to remuneration, as the authority appointing him think fit.

[(2A) A local authority's power to appoint officers on such reasonable terms and conditions as the authority thinks fit is subject to section 41 of the Localism Act 2011 (requirement for determinations relating to terms and conditions of chief officers to comply with pay policy statement) [and in relation to a local authority in Wales, section 143A of the Local Government (Wales) Measure 2011 (functions of the Independent Remuneration Panel in relation to [remuneration] of [chief executives]).]]

(3) Subject to subsection (4) below, any enactment or instrument made under an enactment which requires or empowers all local authorities or local authorities of any description or committees of local authorities to appoint a specified officer shall, to the extent that it makes any such provision, cease to have effect.

The reference in this section to committees of local authorities does not include a reference to any committee of which some members are required to be appointed by a body or person other than a local authority.

(4)–(6) *****
*****

PART XI GENERAL PROVISIONS AS TO LOCAL AUTHORITIES

Legal proceedings

222   Power of local authorities to prosecute or defend legal proceedings

(1) Where a local authority consider it expedient for the promotion or protection of the interests of the inhabitants of their area—

   (a) they may prosecute or defend or appear in any legal proceedings and, in the case of civil proceedings, may institute them in their own name, and

   (b) they may, in their own name, make representations in the interests of the inhabitants at any public inquiry held by or on behalf of any Minister or public body under any enactment.

(2) In this section 'local authority' includes the Common Council[, a corporate joint committee] [and a fire and rescue authority created by an order under section 4A of the Fire and Rescue Services Act 2004] [and the London Fire Commissioner].

*****

Byelaws

235 Power of councils to make byelaws for good rule and government and suppression of nuisances

(1) The council of a district [...] and the council of a London borough may make byelaws for the good rule and government of the whole or any part of the district [principal area] or borough, as the case may be, and for the prevention and suppression of nuisances therein.

(2) The confirming authority in relation to byelaws made under this section shall be the Secretary of State.

[(2A) Subsection (2) does not apply to byelaws of a class prescribed by regulations under section 236A(1).]

(3) Byelaws shall not be made under this section for any purpose as respects any area if provision for that purpose as respects that area is made by, or is or may be made under, any other enactment.

*****

Local Government Act 1974

(1974, c. 7)

An Act to make further provision, in relation to England and Wales, with respect to the payment of grants to local authorities, rating and valuation, borrowing and lending by local authorities and the classification of highways; to extend the powers of the Countryside Commission to give financial assistance; to provide for the establishment of Commissions for the investigation of administrative action taken by or on behalf of local and other authorities; to restrict certain grants under the Transport Act 1968; to provide for the removal or relaxation of certain statutory controls affecting local government activities; to make provision in relation to the collection of sums by local authorities on behalf of water authorities; to amend section 259(3) of the Local Government Act 1972 and to make certain minor amendments of or consequential on that Act; and for connected purposes. [8th February 1974]

Territorial extent: England and Wales

*****

PART III LOCAL GOVERNMENT ADMINISTRATION

23 The Commissions for Local Administration

(1) For the purpose of conducting investigations in accordance with this Part [and Part 3A] of this Act, there shall be—

    (a) a body of commissioners to be known as the Commission for Local Administration in England, ...

    (b) ...

[but [the Commission] may include persons appointed to act as advisers, not exceeding the number appointed to conduct investigations.]

(2) The Parliamentary Commissioner shall be a member of [the Commission].

[(2A) ...]

(3) In the following provisions of this Part of this Act the expression 'Local Commissioner' means a person, other than the Parliamentary Commissioner, [...] [or an advisory member] who is a member of [the Commission].

[(3A) ...]

(4) Appointments to the office of ... Commissioner shall be made by Her Majesty on the recommendation of the Secretary of State...

[(4A) Subject to subsections (5) to (6), a Commissioner shall hold and vacate office in accordance with the terms of his appointment.]

[(5) A Commissioner's appointment may be a full-time or part-time appointment and, with the Commissioner's consent, the terms of the appointment may be varied as to whether it is full-time or part-time.

(5A) A Commissioner must be appointed for a period of not more than 7 years.

(5B) A Commissioner shall, subject to subsection (6), hold office until the end of the period for which he is appointed.]

(6) A ... Commissioner may be relieved of office by Her Majesty at his own request or may be removed from office by Her Majesty on grounds of incapacity or misbehaviour ...

[(6A) A person appointed to be a Commissioner is not eligible for re-appointment.]

(7) The Secretary of State shall designate two of the Local Commissioners for England as chairman and vice-chairman respectively of the Commission for Local Administration in England ...

(8) ...

(8A)–(13) *****

23A *****

24 ...

[24A   Power to investigate]

[(1) Under this Part of this Act, a Local Commissioner may investigate a matter—

    (a) which relates to action taken by or on behalf of an authority to which this Part of this Act applies,

    (b) which is subject to investigation under this Part of this Act by virtue of section 26, and

    (c) in relation to which subsection (2), (3) or (5) is satisfied.

(2) This subsection is satisfied if, in relation to the matter, a complaint which satisfies sections 26A and 26B has been made to a Local Commissioner.

(3) This subsection is satisfied if, in relation to the matter—

    (a) a complaint which satisfies sections 26A and 26B has been made to a member of an authority to which this Part of this Act applies, and

    (b) the complaint has been referred, or is treated as having been referred, to a Local Commissioner under section 26C.

(4) Any question whether subsection (2) or (3) is satisfied in relation to a matter shall be determined by a Local Commissioner.

(5) This subsection is satisfied if—

    (a) the matter has come to the attention of a Local Commissioner, and

    (b) section 26D applies to the matter.

(6) In determining whether to initiate, continue or discontinue an investigation, a Local Commissioner shall, subject to the provisions of this section and sections 26 to 26D, act in accordance with his own discretion.

(7) Without prejudice to the discretion conferred by subsection (6), a Local Commissioner may in particular decide—

    (a) not to investigate a matter, or

    (b) to discontinue an investigation of a matter,

if he is satisfied with action which the authority concerned have taken or propose to take.]

25   Authorities subject to investigation

(1) This Part of this Act applies to [the following authorities]—

    (a)   any local authority,

    [(aaa) the Greater London Authority,]

    [(aa)   ...],

    [(ab)   a National Park Authority [for a National Park in England],]

    (b)   any joint board the constituent authorities of which are all local authorities,

    [(ba)   ...

    (bb)   any development corporation established for the purposes of a new town,

(bbb) ...]
(bc)   ...
(bd)   any urban development corporation established by an order under section 135 of the Local
       Government, Planning and Land Act 1980 [for an urban development area in England],]
[(be) any housing action trust established under Part III of the Housing Act 1988 [for a
       designated area in England]],
[(bf) the [Homes and Communities] Agency,]
[(bg) [a fire and rescue authority [in England] constituted by a scheme under section 2 of the
       Fire and Rescue Services Act 2004 or a scheme to which section 4 of that Act applies;]
[(c)   any joint authority established by Part IV of the Local Government Act 1985;]
[(cza) the London Fire and Emergency Planning Authority;]
[(ca) any police and crime commissioner;]
[(caa) any Mayor's Office for Policing and Crime;]
(cb)   ...
[(cc) Transport for London...]
[(cd) ...]
[(ce) any economic prosperity board established under section 88 of the Local Democracy,
       Economic Development and Construction Act 2009;
(cf)   any combined authority established under section 103 of that Act;]
[(d)   in relation to the flood defence functions of the Environment Agency, within the
       meaning of the Water Resources Act 1991, the Environment Agency and [any Regional
       Flood and Coastal Committee]] [; and
(e)   The London Transport Users' Committee.]

(2) Her Majesty may by Order in Council provide that this Part of this Act shall also apply, subject to any modifications or exceptions specified in the Order, to any authority specified in the Order, being an authority which is established by or under an Act of Parliament, and which has power to levy a rate, or to issue a precept.

(3)–(8) *****

26   Matters subject to investigation

[(1) For the purpose of section 24A(1)(b), in relation to an authority to which this Part of this Act applies, the following matters are subject to investigation by a Local Commissioner under this Part of this Act—

(a)   alleged or apparent maladministration in connection with the exercise of the author-
      ity's administrative functions;
(b)   an alleged or apparent failure in a service which it was the authority's function to
      provide;
(c)   an alleged or apparent failure to provide such a service.
[(d) an alleged or apparent failure in a service provided by the authority in the exercise of
      public health functions of the Secretary of State (within the meaning of the National
      Health Service Act 2006) in pursuance of arrangements made under section 7A, 65Z5
      or 75 of the National Health Service Act 2006;
(e)   an alleged or apparent failure to provide a service in pursuance of such arrangements].

(1A) Subsection (1) is subject to the following provisions of this section.]

(2)–(4) ...

[(5) Before proceeding to investigate [a matter], a Local Commissioner shall satisfy himself that—

[(a) [the matter has] been brought, by or on behalf of [the person affected] to the notice of
      the authority to which [it relates] and that that authority has been afforded a reasonable
      opportunity [to investigate the matter and to respond]; or
(b)   in the particular circumstances, it is not reasonable to expect [the matter to be] brought
      to the notice of that authority or for that authority to be afforded a reasonable oppor-
      tunity [to investigate the matter and to respond].]

(6) A Local Commissioner shall not conduct an investigation under this Part of this Act in respect of any of the following matters, that is to say,—

    (a) any action in respect of which the [person affected] has or had a right of appeal, reference or review to or before a tribunal constituted by or under any enactment;

    (b) any action in respect of which the [person affected] has or had a right of appeal to a Minister of the Crown [. . .]; or

    (c) any action in respect of which the [person affected] has or had a remedy by way of proceedings in any court of law:

Provided that a Local Commissioner may conduct an investigation notwithstanding the existence of such a right or remedy if satisfied that in the particular circumstances it is not reasonable to expect the [person affected] to resort or have resorted to it.

[(6A) A Local Commissioner shall not conduct an investigation under this Part of this Act in respect of [any action taken by or on behalf of an authority in the exercise] of any of the authority's functions otherwise than in relation to England.]

(7)–(13) *****

[26A Who can complain

(1) Under this Part of this Act, a complaint about a matter may only be made—

    (a) by a member of the public who claims to have sustained injustice in consequence of the matter,

    (b) by a person authorised in writing by such a member of the public to act on his behalf, or

    (c) in accordance with subsection (2).

(2) Where a member of the public by whom a complaint about a matter might have been made under this Part of this Act has died or is otherwise unable to authorise a person to act on his behalf, the complaint may be made—

    (a) by his personal representative (if any), or

    (b) by a person who appears to a Local Commissioner to be suitable to represent him.

26B Procedure for making complaints

(1) Subject to subsection (3), a complaint about a matter under this Part of this Act must be made—

    (a) in writing, and

    (b) before the end of the permitted period.

(2) In subsection (1)(b), 'the permitted period' means the period of 12 months beginning with—

    (a) the day on which the person affected first had notice of the matter, or

    (b) if the person affected has died without having notice of the matter—

        (i) the day on which the personal representatives of the person affected first had notice of the matter, or

        (ii) if earlier, the day on which the complainant first had notice of the matter.

(3) A Local Commissioner may disapply either or both of the requirements in subsection (1)(a) and (b) in relation to a particular complaint.

26C Referral of complaints by authorities

(1) This section applies where a complaint about a matter is made to a member of an authority to which this Part of this Act applies.

(2) If the complainant consents, the complaint may be referred to a Local Commissioner by—

    (a) the member of the authority to whom the complaint was made,

    (b) any other member of that authority, or

    (c) a member of any other authority to which this Part of this Act applies which is alleged in the complaint to have taken or authorised the action complained of.

(3) Subject to subsection (4), a referral under this section must be made in writing.

(4) A Local Commissioner may disapply the requirement in subsection (3) in relation to a particular referral.

(5)–(8) *****

26D   Matters coming to attention of Local Commissioner

(1) This section applies to a matter which has come to the attention of a Local Commissioner if—

(a) the matter came to his attention during the course of an investigation under this Part [or Part 3A] of this Act,

(b) (subject to subsection (3)) the matter came to his attention—

(i)   before the person affected or his personal representatives had notice of the matter, or

(ii) in any other case, before the end of the permitted period, and

(c) it appears to the Local Commissioner that a member of the public has, or may have, suffered injustice in consequence of the matter.

(2) In subsection (1)(b)(ii), 'the permitted period' means the period of 12 months beginning with—

(a) the day on which the person affected first had notice of the matter, or

(b) if the person affected has died without having notice of the matter, the day on which the personal representatives of the person affected first had notice of the matter.

(3) A Local Commissioner may disapply the requirement in subsection (1)(b) in relation to a particular matter.]

27   [Members of the public]

(1) [In this Part of this Act, 'member of the public' means an individual or a body of persons, whether incorporated or not, other than—]

(a) a local authority or other authority or body constituted for purposes of the public service or of local government, [(including [the Welsh Ministers, the National Assembly for Wales Commission or the] the National Assembly for Wales)], or for the purposes of carrying on under national ownership any industry or undertaking or part of an industry or undertaking;

(b) any other authority or body whose members are appointed by Her Majesty or any Minister of the Crown or government department [or by the [Welsh Ministers]], or whose revenues consist wholly or mainly of moneys provided by Parliament [or the [Welsh Ministers]].

(2) …

28   Procedure in respect of investigations

(1) Where a Local Commissioner proposes to [investigate a matter under this Part of this Act], he shall afford to the authority concerned, and to any person who is alleged in the complaint [(if any), or who otherwise appears to the Local Commissioner,] to have taken or authorised [the action which would be the subject of the investigation], an opportunity to comment on [the matter].

(2) Every [investigation under this Part of the Act] shall be conducted in private, but except as aforesaid the procedure for conducting an investigation shall be such as the Local Commissioner considers appropriate in the circumstances of the case; and without prejudice to the generality of the preceding provision

(a) the Local Commissioner may, as well as adopting different procedure for different cases, adopt different procedure for cases of different descriptions; and]

(b) the Local Commissioner may obtain information from such persons and in such manner, and make such inquiries as he thinks fit, and may determine whether any person may be represented (by counsel or solicitor or otherwise) in the investigation.

(3) *****

(4) The conduct of an investigation under this Part of this Act shall not affect any action taken by the authority concerned [or any other person], or any power or duty of [the authority concerned or any other person] to take further action with respect to any matters subject to the investigation.

[(5) The differential procedure authorised by subsection (2)(a) includes (in particular) procedure for cases of a particular description that is expected to be faster than that for at least some other cases.]

29 Investigations: further provisions

(1) For the purposes of an investigation under this Part of this Act a Local Commissioner may require any member or officer of the authority concerned, or any other person who in his opinion is able to furnish information or produce documents relevant to the investigation, to furnish any such information or produce any such documents.

(2) For the purposes of any such investigation a Local Commissioner shall have the same powers as the High Court in respect of the attendance and examination of witnesses, and in respect of the production of documents.

(3)–(10) *****

30 Reports on investigations

[(1) If a Local Commissioner completes an investigation of a matter, [under this Part of this Act], he shall prepare a report of the results of the investigation and send a copy to each of the persons concerned (subject to subsection (1B)).

(1A) A Local Commissioner may include in a report on a matter under subsection (1) any recommendations that he could include in a further report on the matter by virtue of section 31(2A) to (2BA).

(1B) If, after the investigation of a matter is completed, the Local Commissioner decides—

    (a) that he is satisfied with action which the authority concerned have taken or propose to take, and

    (b) that it is not appropriate to prepare and send a copy of a report under subsection (1),

he may instead prepare a statement of his reasons for the decision and send a copy to each of the persons concerned.

(1C) If a Local Commissioner decides—

    (a) not to investigate a matter, or

    (b) to discontinue an investigation of a matter,

he shall prepare a statement of his reasons for the decision and send a copy to each of the persons concerned.

(1D) For the purposes of subsections (1) to (1C), the persons concerned are—

    (a) the complainant (if any),

    (b) any person who referred the matter under section 26C(2),

    (c) the authority concerned, and

    (d) any other authority or person who is alleged in the complaint, or who otherwise appears to the Local Commissioner, to have taken or authorised the action which is or would be the subject of the investigation.]

(2), (2AA), (2AB) *****

(2A) ...

[(2B) Subsections (3) to (8) apply in the case of a report under subsection (1).]

(3) Apart from identifying the authority or authorities concerned the report shall not...—

    (a) mention the name of any person, or

    (b) contain any particulars which, in the opinion of the Local Commissioner, are likely to identify any person and can be omitted without impairing the effectiveness of the report,

unless, after taking into account the public interest as well as [the interests of the complainant (if any) and of other persons], the Local Commissioner considers it necessary to mention the name of that person or to include in the report any such particulars.

[(3AA) Nothing in subsection (3) above prevents a report—

    (a) mentioning the name of, or

    (b) containing particulars likely to identify,

the Mayor of London or any member of the London Assembly.]

(3A) ...

(4) Subject to the provisions of subsection (7) below, the authority concerned shall for a period of three weeks make copies of the report available for inspection by the public without charge at all reasonable hours at one or more of their offices; and any person shall be entitled to take copies of, or extracts from, the report when so made available.

[(4A) Subject to subsection (7) below, the authority concerned shall supply a copy of the report to any person on request if he pays such charge as the authority may reasonably require.]

(5) Not later than [two weeks] after the report is received by the authority concerned, the proper officer of the authority shall give public notice, by advertisement in the newspapers and such other ways as appear to him appropriate, that [copies of the report will be available as provided by subsections (4) and (4A)] above, and shall specify the date, being a date [not more than one week after the public notice is first given] from which the period of three weeks will begin.

(6) *****

(7) The Local Commissioner may, if he thinks fit after taking into account the public interest as well as [the interests of the complainant (if any) and of other persons], direct that a report specified in the direction shall not be subject to the provisions of subsections (4) [, (4A) and (5) above.]

(8) *****

31 Reports on investigations: further provisions

[(1) This section applies where a Local Commissioner reports that there has been—
  (a) maladministration in connection with the exercise of the authority's administrative functions,
  (b) a failure in a service which it was the function of an authority to provide, or
  (c) a failure to provide such a service.]

(2) The report shall be laid before the authority concerned and it shall be the duty of that authority to consider the report and, within the period of three months beginning with the date on which they received the report, or such longer period as the Local Commissioner may agree in writing, to notify the Local Commissioner of the action which the authority have taken or propose to take.

[(2A) If the Local Commissioner—
  (a) does not receive the notification required by subsection (2) above within the period allowed by or under that subsection, or
  (b) is not satisfied with the action which the authority concerned have taken or propose to take, or
  (c) does not within a period of three months beginning with the end of the period so allowed, or such longer period as the Local Commissioner may agree in writing, receive confirmation from the authority concerned that they have taken action, as proposed, to the satisfaction of the Local Commissioner,

he shall make a further report setting out those facts and making recommendations.

[(2B) Where the report relates to maladministration, those recommendations are recommendations with respect to action which, in the Local Commissioner's opinion, the authority concerned should take—
  (a) to remedy any injustice sustained by the person affected in consequence of the maladministration, and
  (b) to prevent injustice being caused in the future in consequence of similar maladministration in connection with the exercise of the authority's administrative functions.

(2BA) Where the report relates to a failure in, or to provide, a service which it was the function of the authority to provide, those recommendations are recommendations with respect to action which, in the Local Commissioner's opinion, the authority concerned should take—
  (a) to remedy any injustice sustained by the person affected in consequence of the failure, and
  (b) to prevent injustice being caused in the future in consequence of a similar failure in, or to provide, a service which it is the function of the authority to provide.]

(2C) Section 30 above, with any necessary modifications, and subsection (2) above shall apply to a report under subsection (2A) above as they apply to a report under that section.

(2D) If the Local Commissioner—
  (a) does not receive the notification required by subsection (2) above as applied by subsection (2C) above within the period allowed by or under that subsection or is satisfied before the period allowed by that subsection has expired that the authority concerned have decided to take no action, or

(b) is not satisfied with the action which the authority concerned have taken or propose to take, or

(c) does not within a period of three months beginning with the end of the period allowed by or under subsection (2) above as applied by subsection (2C) above, or such longer period as the Local Commissioner may agree in writing, receive confirmation from the authority concerned that they have taken action, as proposed, to the satisfaction of the Local Commissioner,

he may, by notice to the authority, require them to arrange for a statement to be published in accordance with subsections (2E) and (2F) below.

(2E) The statement referred to in subsection (2D) above is a statement, in such form as the authority concerned and the Local Commissioner may agree, consisting of—

(a) details of any action recommended by the Local Commissioner in his further report which the authority have not taken;

(b) such supporting material as the Local Commissioner may require; and

(c) if the authority so require, a statement of the reasons for their having taken no action on, or not the action recommended in, the report.]

(2F)–(2H) *****

[(3) In any case where—

(a) a report is laid before an authority under subsection [(2) or (2C)] above, and

(b) on consideration of the report, it appears to the authority that a payment should be made to, or some other benefit should be provided for, a person who has suffered injustice in consequence of [the maladministration or failure] [to which the report relates],

the authority may incur such expenditure as appears to them to be appropriate in making such a payment or providing such a benefit.]

(4) *****

31A–33A *****

34 Interpretation of Part III

(1), (2) *****

(3) It is hereby declared that nothing in this Part of this Act authorises or requires a Local Commissioner to question the merits of a decision taken without maladministration by an authority in the exercise of a discretion vested in that authority.

*****

Section 26

SCHEDULE 5

MATTERS NOT SUBJECT TO INVESTIGATION

1. The commencement or conduct of civil or criminal proceedings before any court of law.

2. Action taken by [or on behalf of] any [local policing body] in connection with the investigation or prevention of crime.

[3.—(1) Action taken in matters relating to contractual or other commercial transactions of any authority to which Part 3 of this Act Applies relating to—

(a) the operation of public passenger transport;

(b) the carrying on of a dock or harbour undertaking;

(c) the provision of entertainment;

(d) the provision and operation of industrial establishments;

(e) the provision and operation of markets.

(2) Sub-paragraph (1) does not include transactions for or relating to—

(a) the acquisition or disposal of land;

(b) the acquisition or disposal of moorings which are not moorings provided in connection with a dock or harbour undertaking.

(3) Sub-paragraph (1)(a) does not include action taken by or on behalf of the London Transport Users Committee in operating a procedure for examining complaints or reviewing decisions.

(4) Sub-paragraph (1)(e) does not include transactions relating to—

    (a) the grant, renewal or revocation of a licence to occupy a pitch or stall in a fair or market, or

    (b) the attachment of any condition to such a licence.]

4. Action taken in respect of appointments or removals, pay, discipline, superannuation or other personnel matters.

5.–8. *****

*****

House of Commons Disqualification Act 1975

(1975, c. 24)

An Act to consolidate certain enactments relating to disqualification for membership of the House of Commons. [8th May 1975]

Territorial extent: United Kingdom

1 Disqualification of holders of certain offices and places

(1) Subject to the provisions of this Act, a person is disqualified for membership of the House of Commons who for the time being—

    [(za) is a Lord Spiritual;]

    (a) holds any of the judicial offices specified in Part I of Schedule 1 to this Act;

    (b) is employed in the civil service of the Crown, whether in an established capacity or not, and whether for the whole or part of his time;

    (c) is a member of any of the regular armed forces of the Crown...

    (d) is a member of any police force maintained by [a local policing body or] a police authority;

    [(da) ...]

    (e) is a member of the legislature of any country or territory outside the Commonwealth [other than Ireland]; or

    (f) holds any office described in Part II or Part III of Schedule 1.

(2), (3) *****

(4) Except as provided by this Act, a person shall not be disqualified for membership of the House of Commons by reason of his holding an office or place of profit under the Crown or any other office or place; and a person shall not be disqualified for appointment to or for holding any office or place by reason of his being a member of that House.

2 Ministerial offices

(1) Not more than ninety-five persons being the holders of offices specified in Schedule 2 to this Act (in this section referred to as Ministerial offices) shall be entitled to sit and vote in the House of Commons at any one time.

(2) If at any time the number of members of the House of Commons who are holders of Ministerial offices exceeds the number entitled to sit and vote in that House under subsection (1) above, none except any who were both members of that House and holders of Ministerial offices before the excess occurred shall sit or vote therein until the number has been reduced, by death, resignation or otherwise, to the number entitled to sit and vote as aforesaid.

(3) A person holding a Ministerial office is not disqualified by this Act by reason of any office held by him ex officio as the holder of that Ministerial office.

3 *****

4 Stewardship of Chiltern Hundreds, etc

For the purposes of the provisions of this Act relating to the vacation of the seat of a member of the House of Commons who becomes disqualified by this Act for membership of that House, the office of steward or bailiff of Her Majesty's three Chiltern Hundreds of Stoke, Desborough and Burnham, or of the Manor of Northstead, shall be treated as included among the offices described in Part III of Schedule 1 to this Act.

5 Power to amend Schedule 1

(1) If at any time it is resolved by the House of Commons that Schedule 1 to this Act be amended, whether by the addition or omission of any office or the removal of any office from one Part of the Schedule to another, or by altering the description of any office specified therein, Her Majesty may by Order in Council amend that Schedule accordingly.

(2) *****

6 Effects of disqualification and provision for relief

(1) Subject to any order made by the House of Commons under this section,—

(a) if any person disqualified by this Act for membership of that House, or for membership for a particular constituency, is elected as a member of that House, or as a member for that constituency, as the case may be, his election shall be void; and

(b) if any person being a member of that House becomes disqualified by this Act for membership for the constituency for which he is sitting, his seat shall be vacated.

(2) If, in a case falling or alleged to fall within subsection (1) above, it appears to the House of Commons that the grounds of disqualification or alleged disqualification under this Act which subsisted or arose at the material time have been removed, and that it is otherwise proper so to do, that House may by order direct that any such disqualification incurred on those grounds at that time shall be disregarded for the purposes of this section.

(3), (4) *****

7 Jurisdiction of Privy Council as to disqualification

(1) Any person who claims that a person purporting to be a member of the House of Commons is disqualified by this Act, or has been so disqualified at any time since his election, may apply to Her Majesty in Council, in accordance with such rules as Her Majesty in Council may prescribe, for a declaration to that effect.

(2) Section 3 of the Judicial Committee Act 1833 (reference to the Judicial Committee of the Privy Council of appeals to Her Majesty in Council) shall apply to any application under this section as it applies to an appeal to Her Majesty in Council from a court.

(3)–(5) *****

8, 9 *****

10 ...

*****

Section 2   SCHEDULE 2

MINISTERIAL OFFICE

Prime Minister and First Lord of the Treasury.
Lord President of the Council.
Lord Privy Seal.
Chancellor of the Duchy of Lancaster.
Paymaster General.
Secretary of State.
Chancellor of the Exchequer.
...
President of the Board of Trade.
Minister of State.

Chief Secretary to the Treasury.
Minister in charge of a public department of Her Majesty's Government in the United Kingdom (if not within the other provisions of this Schedule).
Attorney General.
...
Solicitor General.
[Advocate General for Scotland.]
...
Parliamentary Secretary to the Treasury.
Financial Secretary to the Treasury.
Parliamentary Secretary in a Government Department other than the Treasury, or not in a department.
Junior Lord of the Treasury.
Treasurer of Her Majesty's Household.
Comptroller of Her Majesty's Household.
Vice-Chamberlain of Her Majesty's Household.
Assistant Government Whip.
*****

Ministerial and Other Salaries Act 1975

(1975, c. 27)

An Act to consolidate the enactments relating to the salaries of Ministers and Opposition Leaders and Chief Whips and to other matters connected therewith.   [8th May 1975]

Territorial extent: United Kingdom

1   Salaries

(1) Subject to the provisions of this Act—
  (a) there shall be paid to the holder of any Ministerial office specified in Schedule 1 to this Act such salary as is provided for by that Schedule; and
  (b) there shall be paid to the Leaders and Whips of the Opposition such salaries as are provided for by Schedule 2 to this Act.

(2) There shall be paid to the Lord Chancellor a salary (which shall be charged on and paid out of the Consolidated Fund of the United Kingdom) [of—
  (a) £68,827, where the Lord Chancellor is a member of the House of Commons;
  (b) otherwise, £101,038].

(3) There shall be paid to the Speaker of the House of Commons a salary (which shall be charged on and paid out of the Consolidated Fund of the United Kingdom) of [£75,766] a year; and on a dissolution of Parliament the Speaker of the House of Commons at the time of the dissolution shall for this purpose be deemed to remain Speaker until a Speaker is chosen by the New Parliament.

[(3A) There shall be paid to the Speaker of the House of Lords a salary (which shall be paid out of money provided by Parliament) of £101,038 a year.]

(4) ...

(5)–[(7)] *****

1A, 1B   *****

2   Opposition Leaders and Whips

(1) In this Act 'Leader of the Opposition' means, in relation to either House of Parliament, that Member of that House who is for the time being the Leader in that House of the party in opposition

to Her Majesty's Government having the greatest numerical strength in the House of Commons; and 'Chief Opposition Whip' means, in relation to either House of Parliament, the person for the time being nominated as such by the Leader of the Opposition in that House; and 'Assistant Opposition Whip', in relation to the House of Commons, means a person for the time being nominated as such, and to be paid as such, by the Leader of the Opposition in the House of Commons.

(2) If any doubt arises as to which is or was at any material time the party in opposition to Her Majesty's Government having the greatest numerical strength in the House of Commons, or as to who is or was at any material time the leader in that House of such a party, the question shall be decided for the purposes of this Act by the Speaker of the House of Commons, and his decision, certified in writing under his hand, shall be final and conclusive.

(3) If any doubt arises as to who is or was at any material time the Leader in the House of Lords of the said party, the question shall be decided for the purposes of this Act by [the Speaker of the House of Lords] and his decision, certified in writing under his hand, shall be final and conclusive.

3   *****

4   Interpretation

(1) In this Act—

'Junior Lord of the Treasury' means any Lord Commissioner of the Treasury other than the First Lord and the Chancellor of the Exchequer;

'Minister of State' and 'Parliamentary Secretary' have the same meanings as in the House of Commons Disqualification Act 1975.

(2) *****

British Nationality Act 1981

(1981, c. 61)

An Act to make fresh provision about citizenship and nationality, and to amend the Immigration Act 1971 as regards the right of abode in the United Kingdom.   [30th October 1981]

Territorial extent: United Kingdom

PART I BRITISH CITIZENSHIP

Acquisition after commencement

1   Acquisition by birth or adoption

(1) A person born in the United Kingdom after commencement [, or in a qualifying territory on or after the appointed day] shall be a British citizen if at the time of the birth his father or mother is—

(a) a British citizen; or

(b) settled in the United Kingdom [or that territory].

[(1A) A person born in the United Kingdom or a qualifying territory on or after the relevant day shall be a British citizen if at the time of the birth his father or mother is a member of the armed forces.]

(2) A new-born infant who, after commencement, is found abandoned in the United Kingdom [, or on or after the appointed day is found abandoned in a qualifying territory] shall, unless the contrary is shown, be deemed for the purposes of subsection (1)—

(a) to have been born in the United Kingdom after commencement [or in that territory on or after the appointed day]; and

(b) to have been born to a parent who at the time of the birth was a British citizen or settled in the United Kingdom [or that territory].

(3) A person born in the United Kingdom after commencement who is not a British citizen by virtue of subsection (1), [1A] or (2) [or section 10A] shall be entitled to be registered as a British citizen if, while he is a minor—

(a) his father or mother becomes a British citizen or becomes settled in the United Kingdom; and

(b) an application is made for his registration as a British citizen.

[(3A) A person born in the United Kingdom on or after the relevant day who is not a British citizen by virtue of subsection (1), (1A) or (2) [or section 10A] shall be entitled to be registered as a British citizen if, while he is a minor—

(a) his father or mother becomes a member of the armed forces; and

(b) an application is made for his registration as a British citizen.]

(4) A person born in the United Kingdom after commencement who is not a British citizen by virtue of subsection (1), [1A] or (2) [or section 10A] shall be entitled, on an application for his registration as a British citizen made at any time after he has attained the age of ten years, to be registered as such a citizen if, as regards each of the first ten years of that person's life, the number of days on which he was absent from the United Kingdom in that year does not exceed 90.

(5)–(9) *****

2   Acquisition by descent

(1) A person born outside the United Kingdom [and the qualifying territories] after commencement shall be a British citizen if at the time of the birth his father or mother—

(a) is a British citizen otherwise than by descent; or

(b) is a British citizen and is serving outside the United Kingdom [and the qualifying territories] in service to which this paragraph applies, his or her recruitment for that service having taken place in the United Kingdom [or a qualifying territory]; or

(c) is a British citizen and is serving outside the United Kingdom [and the qualifying territories] in service under [an] [EU] institution, his or her recruitment for that service having taken place in a country which at the time of the recruitment was a member of the [European Union].

(2) Paragraph (b) of subsection (1) applies to—

(a) Crown service under the government of the United Kingdom [or of a qualifying territory]; and

(b) service of any description for the time being designated under subsection (3).

(3) For the purposes of this section the Secretary of State may by order made by statutory instrument designate any description of service which he considers to be closely associated with the activities outside the United Kingdom [and the qualifying territories] of Her Majesty's government in the United Kingdom [or in a qualifying territory].

(4) Any order made under subsection (3) shall be subject to annulment in pursuance of a resolution of either House of Parliament.

3   Acquisition by registration: minors

(1) If while a person is a minor an application is made for his registration as a British citizen, the Secretary of State may, if he thinks fit, cause him to be registered as such a citizen.

(2) A person born outside the United Kingdom [and the qualifying territories] shall be entitled, on an application for his registration as a British citizen made [while he is a minor], to be registered as such a citizen if the requirements specified in subsection (3) or, in the case of a person born stateless, the requirements specified in paragraphs (a) and (b) of that subsection, are fulfilled in the case of either that person's father or his mother ('the parent in question').

(3) The requirements referred to in subsection (2) are—

(a) that the parent in question was a British citizen by descent at the time of the birth; and

(b) that the father or mother of the parent in question—

(i)   was a British citizen otherwise than by descent at the time of the birth of the parent in question; or

(ii) became a British citizen otherwise than by descent at commencement, or would have become such a citizen otherwise than by descent at commencement but for his or her death; and

(c) that, as regards some period of three years ending with a date not later than that date of the birth—

(i) the parent in question was in the United Kingdom [or a qualifying territory] at the beginning of that period; and

(ii) the number of days on which the parent in question was absent from the United Kingdom [and the qualifying territories] in the period does not exceed 270.

(4) ...

(5) A person born outside the United Kingdom [and the qualifying territories] shall be entitled, on an application for his registration as a British citizen made while he is a minor, to be registered as such a citizen if the following requirements are satisfied, namely—

(a) that at the time of that person's birth his father or mother was a British citizen by descent; and

(b) subject to subsection (6), that that person and his father and mother were in the United Kingdom [or a qualifying territory] at the beginning of the period of three years ending with the date of the application and that, in the case of each of them, the number of days on which the person in question was absent from the United Kingdom [and the qualifying territories] in that period does not exceed 270; and

(c) subject to subsection (6), that the consent of his father and mother to the registration has been signified in the prescribed manner.

(6) In the case of an application under subsection (5) of the registration of a person as a British citizen—

(a) if his father or mother died, or their marriage [or civil partnership] was terminated, on or before the date of the application, or his father and mother were legally separated on that date, the references to his father and mother in paragraph (b) of that subsection shall be read either as references to his father or as references to his mother; [and]

(b) if his father or mother died on or before that date, the reference to his father and mother in paragraph (c) of that subsection shall be read as a reference to either of them.

(c) ...

4, [4A–4J] *****

[5 Acquisition by registration: British overseas territories citizens having connection with Gibraltar

A person who is a British overseas territories citizen by virtue of a connection with Gibraltar is entitled to be registered as a British citizen if an application is made for their registration as such as citizen.]

6 Acquisition by naturalisation

(1) If, on an application for naturalisation as a British citizen made by a person of full age and capacity, the Secretary of State is satisfied that the applicant fulfils the requirements of Schedule 1 for naturalisation as such a citizen under this subsection, he may, if he thinks fit, grant to him a certificate of naturalisation as such a citizen.

(2) If, on an application for naturalisation as a British citizen made by a person of full age and capacity who on the date of the application is married to a British citizen or is the civil partner of a British citizen, the Secretary of State is satisfied that the applicant fulfils the requirements of Schedule 1 for naturalisation as such a citizen under this subsection, he may, if he thinks fit, grant to him a certificate of naturalisation as such a citizen.

(3), (4) *****

7–9 ...

10–36 *****

37   Commonwealth citizenship

(1) Every person who—

  (a) under [the British Nationality Acts 1981 and 1983] [or the British Overseas Territories Act 2002] is a British citizen, a [British overseas territories citizen], [a British National (Overseas),] a British Overseas citizen or a British subject; or

  (b) is a citizen of that country,

shall have the status of a Commonwealth citizen.

(2) Her Majesty may by Order in Council amend Schedule 3* by the alteration of any entry, the removal of any entry, or the insertion of any additional entry.

(3) Any Order in Council made under this section shall be subject to annulment in pursuance of a resolution of either House of Parliament.

(4) After commencement no person shall have the status of a Commonwealth citizen or the status of a British subject otherwise than under this Act.

38, 39   *****

[40   Deprivation of citizenship

(1) In this section a reference to a person's 'citizenship status' is a reference to his status as—

  (a) a British citizen,

  (b) a British overseas territories citizen,

  (c) a British Overseas citizen,

  (d) a British National (Overseas),

  (e) a British protected person, or

  (f) a British subject.

[(2) The Secretary of State may by order deprive a person of a citizenship status if the Secretary of State is satisfied that deprivation is conducive to the public good.]

(3) The Secretary of State may by order deprive a person of a citizenship status which results from his registration or naturalisation if the Secretary of State is satisfied that the registration or naturalisation was obtained by means of—

  (a) fraud,

  (b) false representation, or

  (c) concealment of a material fact.

(4) The Secretary of State may not make an order under subsection (2) if he is satisfied that the order would make a person stateless.

[(4A) But that does not prevent the Secretary of State from making an order under subsection (2) to deprive a person of a citizenship status if—

  (a) the citizenship status results from the person's naturalisation,

  (b) the Secretary of State is satisfied that the deprivation is conducive to the public good because the person, while having that citizenship status, has conducted him or herself in a manner which is seriously prejudicial to the vital interests of the United Kingdom, any of the Islands, or any British overseas territory, and

  (c) the Secretary of State has reasonable grounds for believing that the person is able, under the law of a country or territory outside the United Kingdom, to become a national of such a country or territory.]

(5) Before making an order under this section in respect of a person the Secretary of State must give the person written notice specifying—

  (a) that the Secretary of State has decided to make an order,

  (b) the reasons for the order, and

  (c) the person's right of appeal under section 40A(1) or under section 2B of the Special Immigration Appeals Commission Act 1997.]

(6) *****

---

* **Editor's Note:** Schedule 3 (not printed) lists those countries currently members of the Commonwealth.

[40A   Deprivation of citizenship: appeal

(1) A person who is given notice under section 40(5) of a decision to make an order in respect of him under section 40 may appeal against the decision to [the First-tier Tribunal].

(2) Subsection (1) shall not apply to a decision if the Secretary of State certifies that it was taken wholly or partly in reliance on information which in his opinion should not be made public—

(a) in the interests of national security,

(b) in the interests of the relationship between the United Kingdom and another country, or

(c) otherwise in the public interest.]

(3) *****

(4)–(8) …

[40B]–41A *****

[42   Registration and naturalisation: citizenship ceremony, oath and pledge

(1) A person of full age shall not be registered under this Act as a British citizen unless he has made the relevant citizenship oath and pledge specified in Schedule 5 at a citizenship ceremony.

(2) A certificate of naturalisation as a British citizen shall not be granted under this Act to a person of full age unless he has made the relevant citizenship oath and pledge specified in Schedule 5 at a citizenship ceremony.

(3) A person of full age shall not be registered under this Act as a British overseas territories citizen unless he has made the relevant citizenship oath and pledge specified in Schedule 5.

(4) A certificate of naturalisation as a British overseas territories citizen shall not be granted under this Act to a person of full age unless he has made the relevant citizenship oath and pledge specified in Schedule 5.

(5) A person of full age shall not be registered under this Act as a British Overseas citizen or a British subject unless he has made the relevant citizenship oath specified in Schedule 5.

(6) Where the Secretary of State thinks it appropriate because of the special circumstances of a case he may—

(a) disapply any of subsections (1) to (5), or

(b) modify the effect of any of those subsections.

(7) Sections 5 and 6 of the Oaths Act 1978 (c. 19) (affirmation) apply to a citizenship oath; and a reference in this Act to a citizenship oath includes a reference to a citizenship affirmation.]

42A …

42B, 43 *****

44   Decisions involving exercise of discretion

(1) Any discretion vested by or under this Act in the Secretary of State, a Governor or a Lieutenant-Governor shall be exercised without regard to the race, colour or religion of any person who may be affected by its exercise.

(2), (3) …

44A–48 *****

49 …

50   Interpretation

(1) In this Act, unless the context otherwise requires—

'the 1948 Act' means the British Nationality Act 1948:

'alien' means a person who is neither a Commonwealth citizen nor a British protected person nor a citizen of the Republic of Ireland;

*****

['British National (Overseas)' means a person who is a British National (Overseas) under the Hong Kong (British Nationality) Order 1986, and 'status of a British National (Overseas)' shall be construed accordingly;

'British Overseas citizen' includes a person who is a British Overseas citizen under the Hong Kong (British Nationality) Order 1986;]

['British overseas territory' means a territory mentioned in Schedule 6;]

'British protected person' means a person who is a member of any class of person declared to be British protected persons by an Order in Council for the time being in force under section 38 or is a British protected person by virtue of the Solomon Islands Act 1978;

*****

'foreign country' means a country other than the United Kingdom, a [British overseas territory], a country mentioned in Schedule 3 and the Republic of Ireland;

*****

'immigration laws'—

    (a) in relation to the United Kingdom, means the Immigration Act 1971 and any law for purposes similar to that Act which is for the time being or has at any time been in force in any part of the United Kingdom;

    (b) in relation to a [British overseas territory], means any law for purposes similar to the Immigration Act 1971 which is for the time being or has at any time been in force in that territory;

*****

(1A), (1B) *****

(2) Subject to subsection (3), references in this Act to a person being settled in the United Kingdom or in a [British overseas territory] are references to his being ordinarily resident in the United Kingdom or, as the case may be, in that territory without being subject under the immigration laws to any restriction on the period for which he may remain.

(3), (4) *****

(5) It is hereby declared that a person is not to be treated for the purpose of any provision of this Act as ordinarily resident in the United Kingdom or in a [British overseas territory] at a time when he is in the United Kingdom or, as the case may be, in that territory in breach of the immigration laws.

(6)–(14) *****

50A–53 *****

Sections 6, 18   **SCHEDULE 1**

REQUIREMENTS FOR NATURALISATION*

Naturalisation as a British citizen under section 6(1)

1.—(1) Subject to paragraph 2, the requirements for naturalisation as a British citizen under section 6(1) are, in the case of any person who applies for it—

    (a)   the requirements specified in sub-paragraph (2) of this paragraph, or the alternative requirement specified in sub-paragraph (3) of this paragraph; and

    (b)   that he is of good character; and

    (c)   that he has a sufficient knowledge of the English, Welsh or Scottish Gaelic language; and

  [(ca) that he has sufficient knowledge about life in the United Kingdom; and]

---

*   **Editor's Note:** Paras 3 and 4 lay down in similar terms to the material reproduced here requirements for naturalisation of married persons but have been omitted to save space.

(d)   that either—
(i)   his intentions are such that, in the event of a certificate of naturalisation as a British citizen being granted to him, his home or (if he has more than one) his principal home will be in the United Kingdom; or
(ii)   he intends, in the event of such a certificate being granted to him, to enter into, or continue in, Crown service under the government of the United Kingdom, or service under an international organisation of which the United Kingdom or Her Majesty's government therein is a member, or service in the employment of a company or association established in the United Kingdom.

(2) The requirements referred to in sub-paragraph (1)(a) of this paragraph are—
(a)   that the applicant was in the United Kingdom at the beginning of the period of five years ending with the date of the application, and that the number of days on which he was absent from the United Kingdom in that period does not exceed 450; and
(b)   that the number of days on which he was absent from the United Kingdom in the period of twelve months so ending does not exceed 90; and
(c)   that he was not at any time in the period of twelve months so ending subject under the immigration laws to any restriction on the period for which he might remain in the United Kingdom; and
(d)   that he was not at any time in the period of five years so ending in the United Kingdom in breach of the immigration laws.

(3) …
2.–4. *****
*****

[SCHEDULE 5 CITIZENSHIP OATH AND PLEDGE

1. The form of citizenship oath and pledge is as follows for registration of or naturalisation as a British citizen—

Oath

'I, *[name]*, swear by Almighty God that, on becoming a British citizen, I will be faithful and bear true allegiance to Her Majesty Queen Elizabeth the Second, Her Heirs and Successors according to law.'

Pledge

'I will give my loyalty to the United Kingdom and respect its rights and freedoms. I will uphold its democratic values. I will observe its laws faithfully and fulfil my duties and obligations as a British citizen.']
*****

Contempt of Court Act 1981

(1981, c. 49)

An Act to amend the law relating to contempt of court and related matters.   [27th July 1981]

Territorial extent: United Kingdom (ss. 1–6, 8–11, Sch. 1); England and Wales (ss. 12–14); Scotland (s. 15); England, Wales and Northern Ireland (s. 7). For additional provisions applying to Northern Ireland see Sch. 4.

Strict liability

1   The strict liability rule

In this Act 'the strict liability rule' means the rule of law whereby conduct may be treated as a contempt of court as tending to interfere with the course of justice in particular legal proceedings regardless of intent to do so.

2   Limitation of scope of strict liability

(1) The strict liability rule applies only in relation to publications, and for this purpose 'publication' includes any speech, writing, [programme included in a programme service] or other communication in whatever form, which is addressed to the public at large or any section of the public.

(2) The strict liability rule applies only to a publication which creates a substantial risk that the course of justice in the proceedings in question will be seriously impeded or prejudiced.

(3) The strict liability rule applies to a publication only if the proceedings in question are active within the meaning of this section at the time of the publication.

(4) Schedule 1 applies for determining the times at which proceedings are to be treated as active within the meaning of this section.

[(5) In this section, 'programme service' has the same meaning as in the Broadcasting Act 1990.]

3   Defence of innocent publication or distribution

(1) A person is not guilty of contempt of court under the strict liability rule as the publisher of any matter to which that rule applies if at the time of publication (having taken all reasonable care) he does not know and has no reason to suspect that relevant proceedings are active.

(2) A person is not guilty of contempt of court under the strict liability rule as the distributor of a publication containing any such matter if at the time of distribution (having taken all reasonable care) he does not know that it contains such matter and has no reason to suspect that it is likely to do so.

(3) The burden of proof of any fact tending to establish a defence afforded by this section to any person lies upon that person.

(4) ...

4   Contemporary reports of proceedings

(1) Subject to this section a person is not guilty of contempt of court under the strict liability rule in respect of a fair and accurate report of legal proceedings held in public, published contemporaneously and in good faith.

(2) In any such proceedings the court may, where it appears to be necessary for avoiding a substantial risk of prejudice to the administration of justice in those proceedings, or in any other proceedings pending or imminent, order that the publication of any report of the proceedings, or any part of the proceedings, be postponed for such period as the court thinks necessary for that purpose.

(2A), (3) *****

(4) ...

5   Discussion of public affairs

A publication made as or as part of a discussion in good faith of public affairs or other matters of general public interest is not to be treated as a contempt of court under the strict liability rule if the risk of impediment or prejudice to particular legal proceedings is merely incidental to the discussion.

6   Savings

Nothing in the foregoing provisions of this Act—

    (a) prejudices any defence available at common law to a charge of contempt of court under the strict liability rule;

    (b) implies that any publication is punishable as contempt of court under that rule which would not be so punishable apart from those provisions;

(c) restricts liability for contempt of court in respect of conduct intended to impede or prejudice the administration of justice.

7　Consent required for institution of proceedings

Proceedings for a contempt of court under the strict liability rule (other than Scottish proceedings) shall not be instituted except by or with the consent of the Attorney General or on the motion of a court having jurisdiction to deal with it.

Other aspects of law and procedure

8　...

9　Use of tape recorders

(1) Subject to subsection (4) below, it is a contempt of court—

    (a) to use in court, or bring into court for use, any tape recorder or other instrument for recording sound, except with the leave of the court;

    (b) to publish a recording of legal proceedings made by means of any such instrument, or any recording derived directly or indirectly from it, by playing it in the hearing of the public or any section of the public, or to dispose of it or any recording so derived, with a view to such publication;

    (c) to use any such recording in contravention of any conditions of leave granted under paragraph (a);

    [(d) to publish or dispose of any recording in contravention of any conditions of leave granted under subsection (1A)].

[(1A) In the case of a recording of Supreme Court proceedings, subsection (1)(b) does not apply to its publication or disposal with the leave of the Court.]

(2) Leave under paragraph (a) of subsection (1) [, or under subsection (1A),] may be granted or refused at the discretion of the court, and [if granted—

    (a) may, in the case of leave under subsection (1)(a),] be granted subject to such conditions as the court thinks proper with respect to the use of any recording made pursuant to the leave; and

    (b) may, in the case of leave under subsection (1A), be granted subject to such conditions as the Supreme Court thinks proper with respect to publication or disposal of any recording to which the leave relates;

and] where leave has been granted the court may at the like discretion withdraw or amend it either generally or in relation to any particular part of the proceedings.

(3)–[(5)] *****

10　Sources of information

No court may require a person to disclose, nor is any person guilty of contempt of court for refusing to disclose, the source of information contained in a publication for which he is responsible, unless it be established to the satisfaction of the court that disclosure is necessary in the interests of justice or national security or for the prevention of disorder or crime.

11　Publication of matters exempted from disclosure in court

In any case where a court (having power to do so) allows a name or other matter to be withheld from the public in proceedings before the court, the court may give such directions prohibiting the publication of that name or matter in connection with the proceedings as appear to the court to be necessary for the purpose of which it was so withheld.

12　Offences of contempt of magistrates' courts

(1) A magistrates' court has jurisdiction under this section to deal with any person who—

    (a) wilfully insults the justice or justices, any witness before or officer of the court or any solicitor or counsel having business in the court, during his or their sitting or attendance in court or in going to or returning from the court; or

    (b) wilfully interrupts the proceedings of the court or otherwise misbehaves in court.

(2) In any such case the court may order any officer of the court, or any constable, to take the offender into custody and detain him until the rising of the court; and the court may, if it thinks fit, commit the offender to custody for a specified period not exceeding one month or impose on him a fine not exceeding [£2,500], or both.

(2A), (4), (5) *****

(3) …

13 …

Penalties for contempt and kindred offences

14 Proceedings in England and Wales

(1) In any case where a court has power to commit a person to prison for contempt of court and (apart from this provision) no limitation applies to the period of committal, the committal shall (without prejudice to the power of the court to order his earlier discharge) be for a fixed term, and that term shall not on any occasion exceed two years in the case of committal by a superior court, or one month in the case of committal by an inferior court.

(2) In any case where an inferior court has power to fine a person for contempt of court and (apart from the provision) no limit applies to the amount of the fine, the fine shall not on any occasion exceed [£2,500].

(2A)–(4A) *****

[(4A) For the purposes of the preceding provisions of this section [the county court] shall be treated as a superior court and not as an inferior court.]*

[(4B)], (5) *****

15 Penalties for contempt of court in Scottish proceedings

(1) In Scottish proceedings, when a person is committed to prison for contempt of court the committal shall (without prejudice to the power of the court to order his earlier discharge) be for a fixed term.

(2) The maximum penalty which may be imposed by way of imprisonment or fine for contempt of court in Scottish proceedings shall be two years' imprisonment or a fine or both, except that—

(a) where the contempt is dealt with by the sheriff in the course of or in connection with proceedings other than criminal proceedings on indictment, such penalty shall not exceed three months' imprisonment or a fine [of level 4 on the standard scale] or both; and

(b) where the contempt is dealt with by the district court, such penalty shall not exceed sixty days' imprisonment or a fine of [level 4 on the standard scale] or both.

(3)–(5) *****

(6) …

16–21 ***

Section 2   **SCHEDULE 1**

TIMES WHEN PROCEEDINGS ARE ACTIVE FOR PURPOSES OF SECTION 2

Preliminary

1. In this Schedule 'criminal proceedings' means proceedings against a person in respect of an offence, not being appellate proceedings or proceedings commenced by motion for committal or attachment in England and Wales or Northern Ireland; and 'appellate proceedings' means proceedings on appeal from or for the review of the decision of a court in any proceedings.

---

* **Editor's Note:** This section, as amended, contains two subsections both (4A).

[1ZA. Proceedings under the Double Jeopardy (Scotland) Act 2011 (asp 16) are criminal proceedings for the purposes of this Schedule.]

[1A. In paragraph 1 the reference to an offence includes a service offence within the meaning of the Armed Forces Act 2006.]

2. Criminal, appellate and other proceedings are active within the meaning of section 2 at the times respectively prescribed by the following paragraphs of this Schedule; and in relation to proceedings in which more than one of the steps described in any of those paragraphs is taken, the reference in that paragraph is a reference to the first of those steps.

Criminal proceedings

3. Subject to the following provisions of this Schedule, criminal proceedings are active from the relevant initial step specified in paragraph 4 [or 4A] until concluded as described in paragraph 5.

4. The initial steps of criminal proceedings are:—
    (a) arrest without warrant;
    (b) the issue, or in Scotland the grant, of a warrant for arrest;
    (c) the issue of a summons to appear, or in Scotland the grant of a warrant to cite;
    (d) the service of an indictment or other document specifying the charge;
    (e) except in Scotland, oral charge.
    [(f) the making of an application under section 2(2) (tainted acquittals), 3(3)(b) (admission made or becoming known after acquittal), 4(3)(b) (new evidence), 11(3) (eventual death of injured person) or 12(3) (nullity of previous proceedings) of the Double Jeopardy (Scotland) Act 2011 (asp 16).]

[4A. Where as a result of an order under section 54 of the Criminal Procedure and Investigations Act 1996 (acquittal tainted by administration of justice offence) proceedings are brought against a person for an offence of which he has previously been acquitted, the initial step of the proceedings is a certification under subsection (2) of that section; and paragraph 4 has effect subject to this.]

5. Criminal proceedings are concluded—
    (a) by acquittal or, as the case may be, by sentence;
    (b) by any other verdict, finding, order or decision which puts an end to the proceedings;
    (c) by discontinuance or by operation of law;
    [(d) where the initial steps of the proceedings are as mentioned in paragraph 4(f)—
        (i) by refusal of the application;
        (ii) if the application is granted and within the period of 2 months mentioned in section 6(3) of the Double Jeopardy (Scotland) Act 2011 (asp 16) a new prosecution is brought, by acquittal or, as the case may be, by sentence in the new prosecution.]

6. The reference in paragraph 5(a) to sentence includes any order or decision consequent on conviction or finding of guilt which disposes of the case, either absolutely or subject to future events, and a deferment of sentence under [Chapter 1 of Part 2 of the Sentencing Code], section 219 or 432 of the Criminal Procedure (Scotland) Act 1975 or Article 14 of the Treatment of Offenders (Northern Ireland) Order 1976.

7. *****

8. ...

9.–10. *****

11. Criminal proceedings against a person which become active on the issue or the grant of a warrant for his arrest cease to be active at the end of the period of twelve months beginning with the date of the warrant unless he has been arrested within that period, but become active again if he is subsequently arrested.

Other proceedings at first instance

12. Proceedings other than criminal proceedings and appellate proceedings are active from the time when arrangements for the hearing are made or, if no such arrangements are previously made, from the time the hearing begins, until the proceedings are disposed of or discontinued or withdrawn; and for the purposes of this paragraph any motion or application made in or for the purposes of any proceedings, and any pre-trial review in the county court, is to be treated as a distinct proceeding.

13. In England and Wales or Northern Ireland arrangements for the hearing of proceedings to which paragraph 12 applies are made within the meaning of that paragraph—

    (a) in the case of proceedings in the High Court for which provision is made by rules of court for setting down for trial, when the case is set down;

    (b) in the case of any proceedings, when a date for the trial or hearing is fixed.

14. In Scotland arrangements for the hearing of proceedings to which paragraph 12 applies are made within the meaning of that paragraph—

    (a) in the case of an ordinary action in the Court of Session or in the sheriff court, when the record is closed;

    (b) in the case of a motion or application, when it is enrolled or made;

    (c) in any other case, when the date for a hearing is fixed or a hearing is allowed.

Appellate proceedings

15. Appellate proceedings are active from the time when they are commenced—

    (a) by application for leave to appeal or apply for review, or by notice of such an application;

    (b) by notice of appeal or of application for review;

    (c) by other originating process,

until disposed of or abandoned, discontinued or withdrawn.

16. Where, in appellate proceedings relating to criminal proceedings, the court—

    (a) remits the case to the court below; or

    (b) orders a new trial or a *venire de novo*, or in Scotland grants authority to bring a new prosecution,

any further or new proceedings which result shall be treated as active from the conclusion of the appellate proceedings.

*****

Senior Courts Act 1981

(1981, c. 54)

An Act to consolidate with amendments the Supreme Court of Judicature (Consolidation) Act 1925 and other enactments relating to the [Senior Courts] in England and Wales and the administration of justice therein; to repeal certain obsolete or unnecessary enactments so relating; to amend Part VIII of the Mental Health Act 1959, the Courts-Martial (Appeals) Act 1968, the Arbitration Act 1979 and the law relating to county courts; and for connected purposes.   [28 July 1981]

Territorial extent: England and Wales

1–3 *****

The High Court

4 **The High Court**

    (1) The High Court shall consist of—

        (a)   ...

        (b)   the Lord Chief Justice;

        [(ba)   the President of the Queen's Bench Division;

(c)   the President of the Family Division;

(d)   the Chancellor of the High Court;]

[(dd)   the Senior Presiding Judge;]

[(ddd)   the vice-president of the Queen's Bench Division;] and

[(e)   the puisne judges of that court, of whom the maximum full-time equivalent number is 108].

(2) The puisne judges of the High Court shall be styled 'Justices of the High Court'.

(3) All the judges of the High Court shall, except where this Act expressly provides otherwise, have in all respects equal power, authority and jurisdiction.

(4)–(6) *****

5–9   *****

10   Appointment of judges of [Senior Courts]

(1) Whenever the office of Lord Chief Justice, Master of the Rolls, [President of the Queen's Bench Division, President of the Family Division or Chancellor of the High Court] is vacant, Her Majesty may [on the recommendation of the Lord Chancellor] by letters patent appoint a qualified person to that office.

(2) Subject to the limits on [full-time equivalent] numbers for the time being imposed by sections 2(1) and 4(1), Her Majesty may [on the recommendation of the Lord Chancellor] from time to time by letters patent appoint qualified persons as Lords Justices of Appeal or as puisne judges of the High Court.

(3) No person shall be qualified for appointment—

(a) as Lord Chief Justice, Master of the Rolls, [President of the Queen's Bench Division, President of the Family Division or Chancellor of High Court], unless he is qualified for appointment as a Lord Justice of Appeal or is a judge of the Court of Appeal;

(b) as a Lord Justice of Appeal, [unless—

(i)   [he satisfies the judicial-appointment eligibility condition on a 7 year basis]; or

(ii) he is a judge of the High Court;] or

(c) as a puisne judge of the High Court, [unless—

(i)   [he satisfies the judicial-appointment eligibility condition on a 7 year basis]; or

(ii) he is a Circuit Judge who has held that office for at least 2 years.]

(4)–(8) *****

11   Tenure of office of judges of [Senior Courts]

(1) This section applies to the office of any judge of the [Senior Courts] ...

(2) A person appointed to an office to which this section applies shall vacate it on the day on which he attains the age of [75] unless by virtue of this section he has ceased to hold it before then.

(3) A person appointed to an office to which this section applies shall hold that office during good behaviour, subject to a power of removal by Her Majesty on an address presented to Her by both Houses of Parliament.

[(3A) It is for the Lord Chancellor to recommend to Her Majesty the exercise of the power of removal under subsection (3).]

(4)–(6) *****

(7) A person who holds an office to which this section applies may at any time resign it by giving the Lord Chancellor notice in writing to that effect.

(8) The Lord Chancellor, if satisfied by means of a medical certificate that a person holding an office to which this section applies—

(a) is disabled by permanent infirmity from the performance of the duties of his office; and

(b) is for the time being incapacitated from resigning his office,

may, subject to subsection (9), by instrument under his hand declare that person's office to have been vacated; and the instrument shall have the like effect for all purposes as if that person had on the date of the instrument resigned his office.

(9) A declaration under subsection (8) with respect to a person shall be of no effect unless it is made—

    (a) in the case of any of the Lord Chief Justice, the Master of the Rolls, [the President of the Queen's Bench Division, the President of the Family Division and the Chancellor of the High Court], with the concurrence of two others of them;

    (b) in the case of a Lord Justice of Appeal, with the concurrence of the Master of the Rolls;

    (c) in the case of a puisne judge of any Division of the High Court, with the concurrence of the senior judge of that Division.

(10) ...

12 Salaries etc of judges of [Senior Courts]

(1) Subject to subsections (2) and (3), there shall be paid to judges of the [Senior Courts] ... such salaries as may be determined by the Lord Chancellor with the concurrence of the Minister for the Civil Service.

(2) Until otherwise determined under this section, there shall be paid to the judges mentioned in subsection (1) the same salaries as at the commencement of this Act.

(3) Any salary payable under this section may be increased, but not reduced, by a determination or further determination under this section.

(4) ...

(5)–(7) *****

13–18 *****

PART II JURISDICTION

The High Court

General jurisdiction

19 General jurisdiction

(1) The High Court shall be a superior court of record.

(2) Subject to the provisions of this Act, there shall be exercisable by the High Court—

    (a) all such jurisdiction (whether civil or criminal) as is conferred on it by this or any other Act; and

    (b) all such other jurisdiction (whether civil or criminal) as was exercisable by it immediately before the commencement of this Act (including jurisdiction conferred on a judge of the High Court by any statutory provision).

(3), (4) *****

20–[28A] *****

Other particular fields of jurisdiction

29 [Mandatory, prohibiting and quashing orders]

[(1) The orders of mandamus, prohibition and certiorari shall be known instead as mandatory, prohibiting and quashing orders respectively.

(1A) The High Court shall have jurisdiction to make mandatory, prohibiting and quashing orders in those classes of case in which, immediately before 1st May 2004, it had jurisdiction to make orders of mandamus, prohibition and certiorari respectively.]

(2) Every such order shall be final, subject to any right of appeal therefrom.

(3) In relation to the jurisdiction of the Crown Court, other than its jurisdiction in matters relating to trial on indictment, the High Court shall have all such jurisdiction to make [mandatory, prohibiting or quashing orders] as the High Court possesses in relation to the jurisdiction of an inferior court.

(3A) *****

(4) The power of the High Court under any enactment to require justices of the peace or a judge or officer of [the county court] to do any act relating to the duties of their respective offices, or to

require a magistrates' court to state a case for the opinion of the High Court, in any case where the High Court formerly had by virtue of any enactment jurisdiction to make a rule absolute, or an order, for any of those purposes, shall be exercisable by [mandatory order].

[(5) In any statutory provision—

    (a) references to mandamus or to a writ or order of mandamus shall be read as references to a mandatory order;

    (b) references to prohibition or to a writ or order of prohibition shall be read as references to a prohibiting order;

    (c) references to certiorari or to a writ or order of certiorari shall be read as references to a quashing order; and

    (d) references to the issue or award of a writ of mandamus, prohibition or certiorari shall be read as references to the making of the corresponding mandatory, prohibiting or quashing order.]

(6) *****

30 *****

31 Application for judicial review

(1) An application to the High court for one or more of the following forms of relief, namely—

    [(a) a mandatory, prohibiting or quashing order;]

    (b) a declaration or injunction under subsection (2); or

    (c) an injunction under section 30 restraining a person not entitled to do so from acting in an office to which that section applies,

shall be made in accordance with rules of court by a procedure to be known as an application for judicial review.

(2) A declaration may be made or an injunction granted under this subsection in any case where an application for judicial review, seeking that relief, has been made and the High Court considers that, having regard to—

    (a) the nature of the matters in respect of which relief may be granted by [mandatory, prohibiting or quashing orders;]

    (b) the nature of the persons and bodies against whom relief may be granted by such orders; and

    (c) all the circumstances of the case,

it would be just and convenient for the declaration to be made or for the injunction to be granted, as the case may be.

[(2A) The High Court—

    (a) must refuse to grant relief of an application for judicial review, and

    (b) may not make an award under subsection (4) on such an application,

if it appears to the court to be highly likely that the outcome for the applicant would not have been substantially different if the conduct complained of had not occurred.

(2B) The court may disregard the requirements of subsection (2A)(a) and (b) if it considers that it is appropriate to do so for reasons of exceptional public interest.

(2C) If the court gains relief or makes an award in reliance on subsection (2B), the court must certify that the condition in subsection (2B) is satisfied.]

(3) No application for judicial review shall be made unless the leave of the High Court has been obtained in accordance with rules of court; and the court shall not grant leave to make such an application unless[—

    (a)] it considers that the applicant has a sufficient interest in the matter to which the application relates[, and

    (b) the applicant has provided the court with any information about the financing of the application that is specified in rules of court for the purposes of this paragraph].

[(3A)–(3B)] *****

[(3C) When considering whether to grant leave to make an application for judicial review, the High Court—

(a) may of its own motion consider whether the outcome for the applicant would have been substantially different if the conduct complained of had not occurred, and

(b) must consider that question if the defendant asks it to do so.

(3D) If, on considering that question, it appears to the High Court to be highly likely that the outcome for the applicant would not have been substantially different, the court must refuse to grant leave.

(3E) The court may disregard the requirement in subsection (3D) if it considers that it is appropriate to do so for reasons of exceptional public interest.

(3F) If the court grants leave in reliance on subsection (3E), the court must certify that the condition in subsection (3E) is satisfied.]

[(4) On an application for judicial review the High Court may award to the applicant damages, restitution or the recovery of a sum due if—

(a) the application includes a claim for such an award arising from any matter to which the application relates; and

(b) the court is satisfied that such an award would have been made if the claim had been made in an action begun by the applicant at the time of making the application.]

[(5) If, on an application for judicial review, the High Court [makes a quashing order in respect of] the decision to which the application relates, it may in addition—

(a) remit the matter to the court, tribunal or authority which made the decision, with a direction to reconsider the matter and reach a decision in accordance with the findings of the High Court, or

(b) substitute its own decision for the decision in question.

(5A) But the power conferred by subsection (5)(b) is exercisable only if—

(a) the decision in question was made by a court or tribunal,

(b) the [quashing order is made] on the ground that there has been an error of law, and

(c) without the error, there would have been only one decision which the court or tribunal could have reached.

(5B) Unless the High Court otherwise directs, a decision substituted by it under subsection (5)(b) has effect as if it were a decision of the relevant court or tribunal.]

(6) Where the High Court considers that there has been undue delay in making an application for judicial review, the court may refuse to grant—

(a) leave for the making of the application; or

(b) any relief sought on the application,

if it considers that the granting of the relief sought would be likely to cause substantial hardship to, or substantially prejudice the rights of, any person or would be detrimental to good administration.

(7) Subsection (6) is without prejudice to any enactment or rule of court which has the effect of limiting the time within which an application for judicial review may be made.

[(8) In this section 'the conduct complained of', in relation to an application for judicial review, means the conduct (or alleged conduct) of the defendant that the applicant claims justifies the High Court in granting relief.]

*****

Canada Act 1982

(1982, c. 11)

An Act to give effect to a request by the Senate and House of Commons of Canada.   [29th March 1982]

Territorial extent: Canada

Whereas Canada has requested and consented to the enactment of an Act of the Parliament of the United Kingdom to give effect to the provisions hereinafter set forth and the Senate and the House of Commons of Canada in Parliament assembled have submitted an address to Her Majesty requesting that Her Majesty may graciously be pleased to cause a Bill to be laid before the Parliament of the United Kingdom for that purpose:

Be it therefore enacted by the Queen's Most Excellent Majesty, by and with the advice and consent of the Lords Spiritual and Temporal, and Commons, in this present Parliament assembled, and by the authority of the same, as follows:

1   Constitution Act 1982 enacted

The Constitution Act 1982 set out in Schedule B to this Act is hereby enacted for and shall have the force of law in Canada and shall come into force as provided in that Act.

2   Termination of power to legislate for Canada

No Act of the Parliament of the United Kingdom passed after the Constitution Act 1982 comes into force shall extend to Canada as part of its law.

3   French version

So far as it is not contained in Schedule B, the French version of this Act is set out in Schedule A to this Act and has the same authority in Canada as the English version thereof.

4   Short title

This Act may be cited as the Canada Act 1982.

*****

SCHEDULE B CONSTITUTION ACT 1982*

PART I CANADIAN CHARTER OF RIGHTS AND FREEDOMS

Whereas Canada is founded upon principles that recognize the supremacy of God and the rule of law:

Guarantee of rights and freedoms

1   Rights and freedoms in Canada

The *Canadian Charter of Rights and Freedoms* guarantees the rights and freedoms set out in it subject only to such reasonable limits prescribed by law as can be demonstrably justified in a free and democratic society.

Fundamental freedoms

2   Fundamental freedoms

Everyone has the following fundamental freedoms:
- (a) freedom of conscience and religion;
- (b) freedom of thought, belief, opinion and expression, including freedom of the press and other media of communication;
- (c) freedom of peaceful assembly; and
- (d) freedom of association.

Democratic rights

3   Democratic rights of citizens

Every citizen of Canada has the right to vote in an election of members of the House of Commons or of a legislative assembly and to be qualified for membership therein.

4   Maximum duration of legislative bodies

(1) No House of Commons and no legislative assembly shall continue for longer than five years from the date fixed for the return of the writs at a general election of its members.

---

* **Editor's Note:** Schedule A to this Act is a French language version of the Act, and Sch. B is also printed in English and French. Both texts have equal status.

Continuation in special circumstances

(2) In time of real or apprehended war, invasion or insurrection, a House of Commons may be continued by Parliament and a legislative assembly may be continued by the legislature beyond five years if such continuation is not opposed by the votes of more than one-third of the members of the House of Commons or the legislative assembly, as the case may be.

5 Annual sitting of legislative bodies

There shall be a sitting of Parliament and of each legislature at least once every twelve months.

Mobility rights

6 Mobility of citizens

(1) Every citizen of Canada has the right to enter, remain in and leave Canada.

Rights to move and gain livelihood

(2) Every citizen of Canada and every person who has the status of a permanent resident of Canada has the right

   (a) to move to and take up residence in any province; and

   (b) to pursue the gaining of a livelihood in any province.

Limitation

(3) The rights specified in subsection (2) are subject to

   (a) any laws or practices of general application in force in a province other than those that discriminate among persons primarily on the basis of province of present or previous residence; and

   (b) any laws providing for reasonable residency requirements as a qualification for the receipt of publicly provided social services.

Affirmative action programs

(4) Subsections (2) and (3) do not preclude any law, program or activity that has as its object the amelioration in a province of conditions of individuals in that province who are socially or economically disadvantaged if the rate of employment in that province is below the rate of employment in Canada.

Legal rights

7 Life, liberty and security of person

Everyone has the right to life, liberty and security of the person and the right not to be deprived thereof except in accordance with the principles of fundamental justice.

8 Search or seizure

Everyone has the right to be secure against unreasonable search or seizure.

9 Detention or imprisonment

Everyone has the right not to be arbitrarily detained or imprisoned.

10 Arrest or detention

Everyone has the right on arrest or detention

   (a) to be informed promptly of the reasons therefor;

   (b) to retain and instruct counsel without delay and to be informed of that right; and

   (c) to have the validity of the detention determined by way of *habeas corpus* and to be released if the detention is not lawful.

11 Proceedings in criminal and penal matters

Any person charged with an offence has the right

   (a) to be informed without unreasonable delay of the specific offence;

   (b) to be tried within a reasonable time;

(c) not to be compelled to be a witness in proceedings against that person in respect of the offence;

(d) to be presumed innocent until proven guilty according to law in a fair and public hearing by an independent and impartial tribunal;

(e) not to be denied reasonable bail without just cause;

(f) except in the case of an offence under military law tried before a military tribunal, to the benefit of trial by jury where the maximum punishment for the offence is imprisonment for five years or a more severe punishment;

(g) not to be found guilty on account of any act or omission unless, at the time of the act or omission, it constituted an offence under Canadian or international law or was criminal according to the general principles of law recognized by the community of nations;

(h) if finally acquitted of the offence, not to be tried for it again and, if finally found guilty and punished for the offence, not to be tried or punished for it again; and

(i) if found guilty of the offence and if the punishment for the offence has been varied between the time of commission and the time of sentencing, to the benefit of the lesser punishment.

12   Treatment or punishment
Everyone has the right not to be subjected to any cruel and unusual treatment or punishment.

13   Self-crimination
A witness who testifies in any proceedings has the right not to have any incriminating evidence so given used to incriminate that witness in any other proceedings, except in a prosecution for perjury or for the giving of contradictory evidence.

14   Interpreter
A party or witness in any proceedings who does not understand or speak the language in which the proceedings are conducted or who is deaf has the right to the assistance of an interpreter.

Equality rights

15   Equality before and under law and equal protection and benefit of law
(1) Every individual is equal before and under the law and has the right to the equal protection and equal benefit of the law without discrimination and, in particular, without discrimination based on race, national or ethnic origin, colour, religion, sex, age or mental or physical disability.

Affirmative action programs
(2) Subsection (1) does not preclude any law, program or activity that has as its object the amelioration of conditions of disadvantaged individuals or groups including those that are disadvantaged because of race, national or ethnic origin, colour, religion, sex, age or mental or physical disability.

Official languages of Canada

16   Official languages of Canada
(1) English and French are the official languages of Canada and have equality of status and equal rights and privileges as to their use in all institutions of the Parliament and government of Canada.

(2), (3) *****

17–23   *****

Enforcement

24   Enforcement of guaranteed rights and freedoms
(1) Anyone whose rights or freedoms, as guaranteed by this Charter, have been infringed or denied may apply to a court of competent jurisdiction to obtain such remedy as the court considers appropriate and just in the circumstances.

Exclusion of evidence bringing administration of justice into disrepute

(2) Where, in proceedings under subsection (1), a court concludes that evidence was obtained in a manner that infringed or denied any rights or freedoms guaranteed by this Charter, the evidence shall be excluded if it is established that, having regard to all the circumstances, the admission of it in the proceedings would bring the administration of justice into disrepute.

General

25 Aboriginal rights and freedoms not affected by Charter

The guarantee in this Charter of certain rights and freedoms shall not be construed so as to abrogate or derogate from any aboriginal, treaty or other rights or freedoms that pertain to the aboriginal peoples of Canada including

(a) any rights or freedoms that have been recognised by the Royal Proclamation of October 7, 1763; and

(b) any rights or freedoms that may be acquired by the aboriginal peoples of Canada by way of land claims settlement.

26 Other rights and freedoms not affected by Charter

The guarantee in this Charter of certain rights and freedoms shall not be construed as denying the existence of any other rights or freedoms that exist in Canada.

27 Multicultural heritage

This Charter shall be interpreted in a manner consistent with the preservation and enhancement of the multicultural heritage of Canadians.

28 Rights guaranteed equally to both sexes

Notwithstanding anything in this Charter, the rights and freedoms referred to in it are guaranteed equally to male and female persons.

29 Rights respecting certain schools preserved

Nothing in this Charter abrogates or derogates from any rights or privileges guaranteed by or under the Constitution of Canada in respect of denominational, separate or dissentient schools.

30 *****

31 Legislative powers not extended

Nothing in this Charter extends the legislative powers of any body or authority.

Application of Charter

32 Application of Charter

(1) This Charter applies

(a) to the Parliament and government of Canada in respect of all matters within the authority of Parliament including all matters relating to the Yukon Territory and Northwest Territories; and

(b) to the legislature and government of each province in respect of all matters within the authority of the legislature of each province.

Exception

(2) Notwithstanding subsection (1), section 15 shall not have effect until three years after this section comes into force.

33 Exceptions where express declaration

(1) Parliament or the legislature of a province may expressly declare in an Act of Parliament or of the legislature, as the case may be, that the Act or a provision thereof shall operate notwithstanding a provision included in section 2 or sections 7 to 15 of this Charter.

Operation of exception

(2) An Act or a provision of an Act in respect of which a declaration made under this section is in effect shall have such operation as it would have but for the provision of this Charter referred to in the declaration.

Five year limitation

(3) A declaration made under subsection (1) shall cease to have effect five years after it comes into force or on such earlier date as may be specified in the declaration.

Re-enactment

(4) Parliament or the legislature of a province may re-enact a declaration made under subsection (1).

Five year limitation

(5) Subsection (3) applies in respect of a re-enactment made under subsection (4).

Citation

34   Citation

This Part may be cited as the *Canadian Charter of Rights and Freedoms*.
*****

Representation of the People Act 1983

(1983, c. 2)

An Act to consolidate the Representation of the People Acts of 1949, 1969, 1977, 1978 and 1980, the Electoral Registers Acts of 1949 and 1953, the Elections (Welsh Forms) Act 1964, Part III of the Local Government Act 1972, sections 6 to 10 of the Local Government (Scotland) Act 1973, the Representation of the People (Armed Forces) Act 1976, the Returning Officers (Scotland) Act 1977, section 3 of the Representation of the People Act 1981, section 62 of and Schedule 2 to the Mental Health (Amendment) Act 1982, and connected provisions; and to repeal as obsolete the Representation of the People Act 1979 and other enactments related to the Representation of the People Acts.   [8th February 1983]

Territorial extent: United Kingdom

PART I PARLIAMENTARY AND LOCAL GOVERNMENT FRANCHISE AND ITS EXERCISE

Parliamentary and local government franchise

[1   Parliamentary electors

(1) A person is entitled to vote as an elector at a parliamentary election in any constituency if on the date of the poll he—

    (a) is registered in the register of parliamentary electors for that constituency;

    (b) is not subject to any legal incapacity to vote (age apart);

    (c) is either a Commonwealth citizen or a citizen of the Republic of Ireland; and

    (d) is of voting age (that is, 18 years or over).

(2) A person is not entitled to vote as an elector—

    (a) more than once in the same constituency at any parliamentary election; or

    (b) in more than one constituency at a general election.]
*****

PART II THE ELECTION CAMPAIGN

75 Prohibition of expenses not authorised by election agent

[(1) No expenses shall, with a view to promoting or procuring the election of a candidate [(or, in the case of an election of the London members of the London Assembly at an ordinary election, a registered political party or candidates of that party)] at an election, be incurred [after he becomes a candidate at that election] by any person other than the candidate, his election agent and persons authorised in writing by the election agent on account—

    (a) of holding public meetings or organising any public display; or

    (b) of issuing advertisements, circulars or publications; or

    (c) of otherwise presenting to the electors the candidate or his views or the extent or nature of his backing or disparaging another candidate; [or

    (d) in the case of an election of the London members of the London Assembly at an ordinary election, of otherwise presenting to the electors the candidate's registered political party (if any) or the views of that party or the extent or nature of that party's backing or disparaging any other registered political party],

...

[(1ZZA) Paragraph (c) or (d) of subsection (1) above does not restrict the publication of any matter relating to the election in—

    (a) a newspaper or other periodical,

    (b) a broadcast made by the British Broadcasting Corporation or by Sianel Pedwar Cymru, or

    (c) a programme included in any service licensed under Part 1 or 3 of the Broadcasting Act 1990 or Part 1 or 2 of the Broadcasting Act 1996.

(1ZZB) Subsection (1) above does not apply to any expenses incurred by any person—

    (a) which do not exceed in the aggregate the permitted sum (and are not incurred by that person as part of a concerted plan of action), or

    (b) in travelling or in living away from home or similar personal expenses.]

[(1ZA) For the purposes of [subsection (1ZZB)(a)] above, 'the permitted sum' means—

    (a) in respect of a candidate at a parliamentary election, [£700];

    (b) in respect of a candidate at a local government election, £50 together with an additional 0.5p for every entry in the register of local government electors for the electoral area in question as it has effect on the last day for publication of notice of the election;

and expenses shall be regarded as incurred by a person 'as part of a concerted plan of action' if they are incurred by that person in pursuance of any plan or other arrangement whereby that person and one or more other persons are to incur, with a view to promoting or procuring the election of the same candidate, expenses which (disregarding [subsection (1ZZB)(a)]) fall within subsection (1) above.]

[(1A)] *****

[(1B), (1C) ...]]

(2)–(4C) *****

(5) If a person—

    (a) incurs, or aids, abets, counsels or procures any other person to incur, any expenses in contravention of this section, or

    (b) knowingly makes the declaration required by subsection (2) falsely,

he shall be guilty of a corrupt practice; and if a person fails to [deliver or] send any declaration or return or a copy of it as required by this section he shall be guilty of an illegal practice, but—

    (i) the court before whom a person is convicted under this subsection may, if they think it just in the special circumstances of the case, mitigate or entirely remit any incapacity imposed by virtue of section 173 below; and

    (ii) a candidate shall not be liable, nor shall his election be avoided, for a corrupt or illegal practice under this subsection committed by an agent without his consent or connivance.

*****

92   Broadcasting from outside United Kingdom

[(1) No person shall, with intent to influence persons to give or refrain from giving their votes at a parliamentary or local government election, include, or aid, abet, counsel or procure the inclusion of, any matter relating to the election in any programme service (within the meaning of the Broadcasting Act 1990) provided from a place outside the United Kingdom otherwise than in pursuance of arrangements made with—

  (a) the British Broadcasting Corporation;
  (b) Sianel Pedwar Cymru; or
  (c) the holder of any licence granted by [the Office of Communications].

for the reception and re-transmission of that matter by that body or the holder of that licence.]

(2) An offence under this section shall be an illegal practice, but the court before whom a person is convicted of an offence under this section may, if they think it just in the special circumstances of the case, mitigate or entirely remit any incapacity imposed by virtue of section 173 below.

(3) *****

[93   Broadcasting of local items during election period

(1) Each broadcasting authority shall adopt a code of practice with respect to the participation of candidates at a parliamentary or local government election in items about the constituency or electoral area in question which are included in relevant services during the election period.

(2) The code for the time being adopted by a broadcasting authority under this section shall be either—

  (a) a code drawn up by that authority, whether on their own or jointly with one or more other broadcasting authorities, or
  (b) a code drawn up by one or more other such authorities;

and a broadcasting authority shall from time to time consider whether the code for the time being so adopted by them should be replaced by a further code falling within paragraph (a) or (b).

(3) Before drawing up a code under this section a broadcasting authority shall have regard to any views expressed by the Electoral Commission for the purposes of this subsection; and any such code may make different provision for different cases.

(4) The [Office of Communications shall] do all that they can to secure that the code for the time being adopted by them under this section is observed in the provision of relevant services; and the British Broadcasting Corporation and Sianel Pedwar Cymru shall each observe in the provision of relevant services the code so adopted by them.

(5) For the purposes of subsection (1) 'the election period', in relation to an election, means the period beginning—

  (a) (if a parliamentary general election) with the date of the dissolution of Parliament...
  (b) (if a parliamentary by-election) with the date of the issue of the writ for the election or any earlier date on which a certificate of the vacancy is notified in the London Gazette in accordance with the Recess Elections Act 1975, or
  (c) (if a local government election) with the last date for publication of notice of the election, and ending with the close of the poll.]

(6) *****

94–96   *****

97   Disturbances at election meetings

(1) A person who at a lawful public meeting to which this section applies acts, or incites others to act, in a disorderly manner for the purpose of preventing the transaction of the business for which the meeting was called together shall be guilty of an illegal practice.

(2) *****

(3) If a constable reasonably suspects any person of committing an offence under subsection (1) above, he may if requested so to do by the chairman of the meeting require that person to declare

to him immediately his name and address and, if that person refuses or fails so to declare his name and address or gives a false name and address, he shall be liable on summary conviction to a fine not exceeding [level 1 on the standard scale,] ...

This subsection does not apply in Northern Ireland.

98 ...

99 *****

100 Illegal canvassing by police officers

(1) No member of a police force shall by word, message, writing or in any other manner, endeavour to persuade any person to give, or dissuade any person from giving, his vote, whether as an elector or as proxy—

(a) at any parliamentary election for a constituency, or

(b) at any local government election for any electoral area, wholly or partly within the police area.

(2) A person acting in contravention of subsection (1) above shall be liable [on summary conviction to a fine not exceeding level 3 on the standard scale, but] nothing in that subsection shall subject a member of a police force to any penalty for anything done in the discharge of his duty as a member of the force.

(3) In this section references to a member of a police force and to a police area are to be taken in relation to Northern Ireland as references to a member of the [Police Service of Northern Ireland] and to Northern Ireland.

*****

Police and Criminal Evidence Act 1984

(1984, c. 60)

An Act to make further provision in relation to the powers and duties of the police, persons in police detention, criminal evidence, police discipline and complaints against the police; to provide for arrangements for obtaining the views of the community on policing and for a rank of deputy chief constable; to amend the law relating to the Police Federations and Police Forces and Police Cadets in Scotland; and for connected purposes.   [31st October 1984]

Territorial extent: England and Wales

PART I POWERS TO STOP AND SEARCH

1 Power of constable to stop and search persons, vehicles etc

(1) A constable may exercise any power conferred by this section—

(a) in any place to which at the time when he proposes to exercise the power the public or any section of the public has access, on payment or otherwise, as of right or by virtue of express or implied permission; or

(b) in any other place to which people have ready access at the time when he proposes to exercise the power but which is not a dwelling.

(2) Subject to subsection (3) to (5) below, a constable—

(a) may search—

(i)   any person or vehicle;

(ii) anything which is in or on a vehicle,

for stolen or prohibited articles [any article to which subsection (8A) below applies[, any substance to which subsection (8AA) below applies] or any firework to which subsection (8B) below applies]; and

(b) may detain a person or vehicle for the purpose of such a search.

(3) This section does not give a constable power to search a person or vehicle or anything in or on a vehicle unless he has reasonable grounds for suspecting that he will find stolen or prohibited

articles [any article to which subsection (8A) below applies[, any substance to which subsection (8AA) below applies] or any firework to which subsection (8B) below applies].

(4), (5) *****

(6) If in the course of such a search a constable discovers an article which he has reasonable grounds for suspecting to be a stolen or prohibited article[, an article to which subsection (8A) below applies[, a substance to which subsection (8AA) below applies] or a firework to which subsection (8B) applies], he may seize it.

(7) An article is prohibited for the purposes of this Part of this Act if it is—

(a) an offensive weapon; or
(b) an article—
  (i) made or adapted for use in the course of or in connection with an offence to which this sub-paragraph applies; or
  (ii) intended by the person having it with him for such use by him or by some other person.

(8) The offences to which subsection (7)(b)(i) above applies are—

(a) burglary;
(b) theft;
(c) offences under section 12 of the Theft Act 1968 (taking motor vehicle or other conveyance without authority); . . .
[(d) fraud (contrary to section 1 of the Fraud Act 2006)] [; and
(e) offences under section 1 of the Criminal Damage Act 1971 (destroying or damaging property).]

[(8A) This subsection applies to any article in relation to which a person has committed, or is committing or is going to commit an offence under section 139 [or 139AA] of the Criminal Justice Act 1988.]

[(8AA) This subsection applies to any substance in relation to which a person has committed, or is committing or is going to commit an offence under section 6 of the Offensive Weapons Act 2019 (offence of having a corrosive substance in a public place).

(8AB) In this section references to such a substance include an article which contains such a substance.]

(8B), (8C) *****

(9) In this Part of this Act 'offensive weapon' means any article—

(a) made or adapted for use for causing injury to persons; or
(b) intended by the person having it with him for such use by him or by some other person.

2 Provisions relating to search under section 1 and other powers

(1) A constable who detains a person or vehicle in the exercise—

(a) of the power conferred by section 1 above; or
(b) of any other power—
  (i) to search a person without first arresting him; or
  (ii) to search a vehicle without making an arrest,

need not conduct a search if it appears to him subsequently—

  (i) that no search is required; or
  (ii) that a search is impracticable.

(2) If a constable contemplates a search, other than a search of an unattended vehicle, in the exercise—

(a) of the power conferred by section 1 above; or
(b) of any other power, except the power conferred by section 6 below and the power conferred by section 27(2) of the Aviation Security Act 1982—
  (i) to search a person without first arresting him; or
  (ii) to search a vehicle without making an arrest,

it shall be his duty, subject to subsection (4) below, to take reasonable steps before he commences the search to bring to the attention of the appropriate person—

  (i) if the constable is not in uniform, documentary evidence that he is a constable; and
  (ii) whether he is in uniform or not, the matters specified in subsection (3) below;

and the constable shall not commence the search until he has performed that duty.

(3) The matters referred to in subsection (2)(ii) above are—
   (a) the constable's name and the name of the police station to which he is attached;
   (b) the object of the proposed search;
   (c) the constable's grounds for proposing to make it; and
   (d) the effect of section 3(7) or (8) below, as may be appropriate.

(4) A constable need not bring the effect of section 3(7) or (8) below to the attention of the appropriate person if it appears to the constable that it will not be practicable to make the record in section 3(1) below.

(5) In this section 'the appropriate person' means—
   (a) if the constable proposes to search a person, that person; and
   (b) if he proposes to search a vehicle, or anything in or on a vehicle, the person in charge of the vehicle.

(6) On completing a search of an unattended vehicle or anything in or on such a vehicle in the exercise of any such power as is mentioned in subsection (2) above a constable shall leave a notice—
   (a) stating that he has searched it;
   (b) giving the name of the police station to which he is attached;
   (c) stating that an application for compensation for any damage caused by the search may be made to that police station; and
   (d) stating the effect of section 3(8) below.

(7) *****

(8) The time for which a person or vehicle may be detained for the purposes of such a search is such time as is reasonably required to permit a search to be carried out either at the place where the person or vehicle was first detained or nearby.

(9) Neither the power conferred by section 1 above nor any other power to detain and search a person without first arresting him or to detain and search a vehicle without making an arrest is to be construed—
   (a) as authorising a constable to require a person to remove any of his clothing in public other than an outer coat, jacket or gloves; or
   (b) as authorising a constable not in uniform to stop a vehicle.

(10) *****

3   Duty to make records concerning searches

(1) Where a constable has carried out a search in the exercise of any such power as is mentioned in section 2(1) above, other than a search—
   (a) under section 6 below; or
   (b) under section 27(2) of the Aviation Security Act 1982,
[a record of the search shall be made] in writing unless it is not practicable to do so.

   [(2) If a record of a search is required to be made by subsection (1) above—
   (a) in a case where the search results in a person being arrested and taken to a police station, the constable shall secure that the record is made as part of the person's custody record;
   (b) in any other case, the constable shall make the record on the spot, or, if that is not practicable, as soon as practicable after the completion of the search.]

(3)–(5) ...

(6) The record of a search of a person or a vehicle—
   (a) shall state—
      (i)   the object of the search;
      (ii)   the grounds for making it;
      (iii) the date and time when it was made;
      (iv)   the place where it was made;
      [(v)   except in the case of a search of an unattended vehicle, the ethnic origins of the person searched or the person in charge of the vehicle searched (as the case may be; and;]

(vi) ...

(b) shall identify the constable [who carried out the search].

[(6A) The requirement in subsection (6)(a)(v) above for a record to state a person's ethnic origins is a requirement to state—

(a) the ethnic origins of the person as described by the person, and

(b) if different, the ethnic origins of the person as perceived by the constable.]

(7) [If a record of a search of a person has been made under this section,] the person who was searched shall be entitled to a copy of the record if he asks for one before the end of the period specified in subsection (9) below.

(8) If—

(a) the owner of a vehicle which has been searched or the person who was in charge of the vehicle at the time when it was searched asks for a copy of the record of the search before the end of the period specified in subsection (9) below; and

[(b) a record of the search of the vehicle has been made under this section,]

the person who made the request shall be entitled to a copy.

(9) The period mentioned in subsections (7) and (8) above is the period of [3 months] beginning with the date on which the search was made.

(10) *****

4 Road checks

(1) This section shall have effect in relation to the conduct of road checks by police officers for the purpose of ascertaining whether a vehicle is carrying—

(a) a person who has committed an offence other than a road traffic offence or a [vehicle] excise offence;

(b) a person who is a witness to such an offence;

(c) a person intending to commit such an offence; or

(d) a person who is unlawfully at large.

(2) For the purposes of this section a road check consists of the exercise in a locality of the power conferred by [section 163 of the Road Traffic Act 1988] in such a way as to stop during the period for which its exercise in that way in that locality continues all vehicles or vehicles selected by any criterion.

(3) Subject to subsection (5) below, there may only be such a road check if a police officer of the rank of superintendent or above authorises it in writing.

(4) An officer may only authorise a road check under subsection (3) above—

(a) for the purpose specified in subsection (1)(a) above, if he has reasonable grounds—

(i) for believing that the offence is [an indictable offence]; and

(ii) for suspecting that the person is, or is about to be, in the locality in which vehicles would be stopped if the road check were authorised;

(b) for the purpose specified in subsection (1)(b) above, if he has reasonable grounds for believing that the offence is [an indictable offence];

(c) for the purpose specified in subsection (1)(c) above, if he has reasonable grounds—

(i) for believing that the offence would be [an indictable offence]; and

(ii) for suspecting that the person is, or is about to be, in the locality in which vehicles would be stopped if the road check were authorised;

(d) for the purpose specified in subsection (1)(d) above, if he has reasonable grounds for suspecting that the person is, or is about to be, in that locality.

(5) An officer below the rank of superintendent may authorise such a road check if it appears to him that it is required as a matter of urgency for one of the purposes specified in subsection (1) above.

(6)–(14) *****

(15) Where a vehicle is stopped in a road check, the person in charge of the vehicle at the time when it is stopped shall be entitled to obtain a written statement of the purpose of the road check if he applies for such a statement not later than the end of the period of twelve months from the day on which the vehicle was stopped.

(16) Nothing in this section affects the exercise by police officers of any power to stop vehicles for purposes other than those specified in subsection (1) above.

5–7 *****

PART II POWERS OF ENTRY, SEARCH AND SEIZURE

Search warrants

8 Power of justice of the peace to authorise entry and search of premises

(1) If on an application made by a constable a justice of the peace is satisfied that there are reasonable grounds for believing—

(a) that [an indictable offence] has been committed; and

(b) that there is material on premises [mentioned in subsection (1A) below] which is likely to be of substantial value (whether by itself or together with other material) to the investigation of the offence; and

(c) that the material is likely to be relevant evidence; and

(d) that it does not consist of or include items subject to legal privilege, excluded material or special procedure material; and

(e) that any of the conditions specified in subsection (3) below applies, [in relation to each set of premises specified in the application,]

he may issue a warrant authorising a constable to enter and search the premises.

[(1A) The premises referred to in subsection (1)(b) above are—

(a) one or more sets of premises specified in the application (in which case the application is for a 'specific premises warrant'); or

(b) any premises occupied or controlled by a person specified in the application, including such sets of premises as are so specified (in which case the application is for an 'all premises warrant').

(1B) If the application is for an all premises warrant, the justice of the peace must also be satisfied—

(a) that because of the particulars of the offence referred to in paragraph (a) of subsection (1) above, there are reasonable grounds for believing that it is necessary to search premises occupied or controlled by the person in question which are not specified in the application in order to find the material referred to in paragraph (b) of that subsection; and

(b) that it is not reasonably practicable to specify in the application all the premises which he occupies or controls and which might need to be searched.]

[(1C) The warrant may authorise entry to and search of premises on more than one occasion if, on the application, the justice of the peace is satisfied that it is necessary to authorise multiple entries in order to achieve the purpose for which he issues the warrant.

(1D) If it authorises multiple entries, the number of entries authorised may be unlimited, or limited to a maximum.]

(2) A constable may seize and retain anything for which a search has been authorised under subsection (1) above.

(3) The conditions mentioned in subsection (1)(e) above are—

(a) that it is not practicable to communicate with any person entitled to grant entry to the premises;

(b) that it is practicable to communicate with a person entitled to grant entry to the premises but it is not practicable to communicate with any person entitled to grant access to the evidence;

(c) that entry to the premises will not be granted unless a warrant is produced;

(d) that the purpose of a search may be frustrated or seriously prejudiced unless a constable arriving at the premises can secure immediate entry to them.

(4) In this Act 'relevant evidence', in relation to an offence, means anything that would be admissible in evidence at a trial for the offence.

(5) The power to issue a warrant conferred by this section is in addition to any such power otherwise conferred.

(6), (7) *****

9 Special provisions as to access

(1) A constable may obtain access to excluded material or special procedure material for the purposes of a criminal investigation by making an application under Schedule 1 below and in accordance with that Schedule.

(2), (2A) *****

10 Meaning of 'items subject to legal privilege'

(1) Subject to subsection (2) below, in this Act 'items subject to legal privilege' means—

  (a) communications between a professional legal adviser and his client or any person representing his client made in connection with the giving of legal advice to the client;

  (b) communications between a professional legal adviser and his client or any person representing his client or between such an adviser or his client or any such representative and any other person made in connection with or in contemplation of legal proceedings and for the purposes of such proceedings; and

  (c) items enclosed with or referred to in such communications and made—

    (i) in connection with the giving of legal advice; or

    (ii) in connection with or in contemplation of legal proceedings and for the purposes of such proceedings,

when they are in the possession of a person who is entitled to possession of them.

(2) Items held with the intention of furthering a criminal purpose are not items subject to legal privilege.

11 Meaning of 'excluded material'

(1) Subject to the following provisions of this section, in this Act 'excluded material' means—

  (a) personal records which a person has acquired or created in the course of any trade, business, profession or other occupation or for the purposes of any paid or unpaid office and which he holds in confidence;

  (b) human tissue or tissue fluid which has been taken for the purposes of diagnosis or medical treatment and which a person holds in confidence;

  (c) journalistic material which a person holds in confidence and which consists—

    (i) of documents; or

    (ii) of records other than documents.

(2), (3) *****

12 Meaning of 'personal records'

In this Part of this Act 'personal records' means documentary and other records concerning an individual (whether living or dead) who can be identified from them and relating—

  (a) to his physical or mental health;

  (b) to spiritual counselling or assistance given or to be given to him; or

  (c) to counselling or assistance given or to be given to him, for the purposes of his personal welfare, by any voluntary organisation or by any individual who—

    (i) by reason of his office or occupation has responsibilities for his personal welfare; or

    (ii) by reason of an order of a court has responsibilities for his supervision.

13 Meaning of 'journalistic material'

(1) Subject to subsection (2) below, in this Act 'journalistic material' means material acquired or created for the purposes of journalism.

(2)   Material is only journalistic material for the purposes of this Act if it is in the possession of a person who acquired or created it for the purposes of journalism.

(3)   A person who receives material from someone who intends that the recipient shall use it for the purposes of journalism is to be taken to have acquired it for those purposes.

14   Meaning of 'special procedure material'

(1)   In this Act 'special procedure material' means—

    (a)   material to which subsection (2) below applies; and

    (b)   journalistic material, other than excluded material.

(2)   Subject to the following provisions of this section, this subsection applies to material, other than items subject to legal privilege and excluded material, in the possession of a person who—

    (a)   acquired or created it in the course of any trade, business, profession or other occupation or for the purposes of any paid or unpaid office; and

    (b)   holds it subject—

        (i)   to an express or implied undertaking to hold it in confidence; or

        (ii)   to a restriction or obligation such as is mentioned in section 11(2)(b) above.

(3)–(6)   *****

15   Search warrants—safeguards

(1)   This section and section 16 below have effect in relation to the issue to constables under any enactment, including an enactment contained in an Act passed after this Act, of warrants to enter and search premises; and an entry on or search of premises under a warrant is unlawful unless it complies with this section and section 16 below.

(2)   Where a constable applies for any such warrant, it shall be his duty—

    (a)   to state—

        (i)   the ground on which he makes the application; ...

        (ii)   the enactment under which the warrant would be issued; [and]

        [(iii)   if the application is for a warrant authorising entry and search on more than one occasion, the ground on which he applies for such a warrant, and whether he seeks a warrant authorising an unlimited number of entries, or (if not) the maximum number of entries desired;]

    [(b)   to specify the matters set out in subsection (2A) below; and]

    (c)   to identify, so far as is practicable, the articles or persons to be sought.

(2A)   *****

(3)   An application for such a warrant shall be made ex parte and supported by an information in writing.

(4)   The constable shall answer on oath any question that the justice of the peace or judge hearing the application asks him.

(5)   A warrant shall authorise an entry on one occasion only [unless it specifies that it authorises multiple entries].

[(5A)   If it specifies that it authorises multiple entries, it must also specify whether the number of entries authorised is unlimited, or limited to a specified maximum.]

(6)   A warrant—

    (a)   shall specify—

        (i)   the name of the person who applies for it;

        (ii)   the date on which it is issued;

        (iii)   the enactment under which it is issued; and

        [(iv)   each set of premises to be searched, or (in the case of an all premises warrant) the person who is in occupation or control of premises to be searched, together with any premises under his occupation or control which can be specified and which are to be searched; and]

    (b)   shall identify, so far as is practicable, the articles or persons to be sought.

(7), (8)   *****

16   Execution of warrants

(1) A warrant to enter and search premises may be executed by any constable.

(2) Such a warrant may authorise persons to accompany any constable who is executing it.

[(2A) A person so authorised has the same powers as the constable whom he accompanies in respect of—

(a) the execution of the warrant, and

(b) the seizure [or detention] of anything to which the warrant relates.

(2B) But he may exercise those powers only in the company, and under the supervision, of a constable.]

(3) Entry and search under a warrant must be within [three months] from the date of its issue.

(3A), (3B) *****

(4) Entry and search under a warrant must be at a reasonable hour unless it appears to the constable executing it that the purpose of a search may be frustrated on an entry at a reasonable hour.

(5) Where the occupier of premises which are to be entered and searched is present at the time when a constable seeks to execute a warrant to enter and search them, the constable—

(a) shall identify himself to the occupier and, if not in uniform, shall produce to him documentary evidence that he is a constable;

(b) shall produce the warrant to him; and

(c) shall supply him with a copy of it.

(6) Where—

(a) the occupier of such premises is not present at the time when a constable seeks to execute such a warrant; but

(b) some other person who appears to the constable to be in charge of the premises is present,

subsection (5) above shall have effect as if any reference to the occupier were a reference to that other person.

(7) If there is no person present who appears to the constable to be in charge of the premises, he shall leave a copy of the warrant in a prominent place on the premises.

(8) A search under a warrant may only be a search to the extent required for the purpose for which the warrant was issued.

(9) A constable executing a warrant shall make an endorsement on it stating—

(a) whether the articles or persons sought were found; and

(b) whether any articles were seized, other than articles which were sought [and, unless the warrant is a . . . warrant specifying one set of premises only, he shall do so separately in respect of each set of premises entered and searched which he shall in each case stated in the endorsement.]

(10)–(12) *****

Entry and search without search warrant

17   Entry for purpose of arrest etc

(1) Subject to the following provisions of this section, and without prejudice to any other enactment, a constable may enter and search any premises for the purpose—

(a) of executing—

(i) a warrant of arrest issued in connection with or arising out of criminal proceedings; or

(ii) a warrant of commitment issued under section 76 of the Magistrates' Courts Act 1980;

(b) of arresting a person for an [indictable] offence;

(c) of arresting a person for an offence under—

(i) section 1 (prohibition of uniforms in connection with political objects) . . . of the Public Order Act 1936;

(ii) any enactment contained in sections 6 to 8 or 10 of the Criminal Law Act 1977 (offences relating to entering and remaining on property);

[(iii)   section 4 of the Public Order Act 1986 (fear or provocation of violence);]

[(iiia)   section 4 (driving etc when under influence of drink or drugs) or 163 (failure to stop when required to do so by constable in uniform) of the Road Traffic Act 1988;

(iiib)   section 27 of the Transport and Works Act 1992 (which relates to offences involving drink or drugs);]

[(iv)   section 76 of the Criminal Justice and Public Order Act 1994 (failure to comply with interim possession order);]

[(v)   any of sections 4, 5, 6(1) and (2), 7 and 8(1) and (2) of the Animal Welfare Act 2006 (offences relating to the prevention of harm to animals);]

[(vi)   section 144 of the Legal Aid, Sentencing and Punishment of Offenders Act 2012 (squatting in a residential building);]

[(ca)   of arresting, in pursuance of section 32(1A) of the Children and Young Persons Act 1969, any child or young person who has been remanded [to local authority accommodation or youth detention accommodation under section 91 of the Legal Aid, Sentencing and Punishment of Offenders Act 2012];

[(caa) of arresting a person for an offence to which section 61 of the Animal Health Act 1981 applies;]

[(cab) of arresting a person under any of the following provisions—

(i)   section 30D(1) or (2A);

(ii)   section 46A(1) or (1A);

(iii)   section 5B(7) of the Bail Act 1976 (arrest where a person fails to surrender to custody in accordance with a court order);

(iv)   section 7(3) of the Bail Act 1976 (arrest where a person is not likely to surrender to custody etc);

(v)   section 97(1) of the Legal Aid, Sentencing and Punishment of Offenders Act 2012 (arrest where a child is suspected of breaking conditions of remand);]

(cb)   of recapturing any person who is, or is deemed for any purpose to be, unlawfully at large while liable to be detained—

(i)   in a prison, [young offender institution, secure training centre or secure college], or

(ii)   in pursuance of [section 92 of the Powers of Criminal Courts (Sentencing) Act 2000] [or section 260 of the Sentencing Code] (dealing with children and young persons guilty of grave crimes), in any other place;]

(d)   of recapturing [any person whatever] who is unlawfully at large and whom he is pursuing; or

(e)   of saving life or limb or preventing serious damage to property.

(2) Except for the purpose specified in paragraph (e) of subsection (1) above, the powers of entry and search conferred by this section—

(a) are only exercisable if the constable has reasonable grounds for believing that the person whom he is seeking is on the premises; and

(b) are limited, in relation to premises consisting of two or more separate dwellings, to powers to enter and search—

(i)   any parts of the premises which the occupiers of any dwelling comprised in the premises use in common with the occupiers of any other such dwelling; and

(ii)   any such dwelling in which the constable has reasonable grounds for believing that the person whom he is seeking may be.

(3) The powers of entry and search conferred by this section are only exercisable for the purposes specified in subsection (1)(c)(ii) [, (iv) or (vi)] above by a constable in uniform.

(4) The power of search conferred by this section is only a power to search to the extent that is reasonably required for the purpose for which the power of entry is exercised.

(5) Subject to subsection (6) below, all the rules of common law under which a constable has power to enter premises without a warrant are hereby abolished.

(6) Nothing in subsection (5) above affects any power of entry to deal with or prevent a breach of the peace.

18   Entry and search after arrest

(1) Subject to the following provisions of this section, a constable may enter and search any premises occupied or controlled by a person who is under arrest for an [indictable] offence, if he has reasonable grounds for suspecting that there is on the premises evidence, other than items subject to legal privilege, that relates—

> (a) to that offence; or
>
> (b) to some other [indictable] offence which is connected with or similar to that offence.

(2) A constable may seize and retain anything for which he may search under subsection (1) above.

(3) The power to search conferred by subsection (1) above is only a power to search to the extent that is reasonably required for the purpose of discovering such evidence.

(4)–(8) *****

Seizure etc

19   General power of seizure etc

(1) The powers conferred by subsections (2), (3) and (4) below are exercisable by a constable who is lawfully on any premises.

(2) The constable may seize anything which is on the premises if he has reasonable grounds for believing—

> (a) that it has been obtained in consequence of the commission of an offence; and
>
> (b) that it is necessary to seize it in order to prevent it being concealed, lost, damaged, altered or destroyed.

(3) The constable may seize anything which is on the premises if he has reasonable grounds for believing—

> (a) that it is evidence in relation to an offence which he is investigating or any other offence; and
>
> (b) that it is necessary to seize it in order to prevent the evidence being concealed, lost, altered or destroyed.

(4)–(6) *****

20   Extension of powers of seizure to computerised information

(1) Every power of seizure which is conferred by an enactment to which this section applies on a constable who has entered premises in the exercise of a power conferred by an enactment shall be construed as including a power to require any information [stored in any electronic form] and accessible from the premises to be produced in a form in which it can be taken away and in which it is visible and legible [or from which it can readily be produced in a visible and legible form].

(2) This section applies—

> (a) to any enactment contained in an Act passed before this Act;
>
> (b) to sections 8 and 18 above;
>
> (c) to paragraph 13 of Schedule 1 to this Act; and
>
> (d) to any enactment contained in an Act passed after this Act.

21   Access and copying

(1) A constable who seizes anything in the exercise of a power conferred by any enactment, including an enactment contained in an Act passed after this Act, shall, if so requested by a person showing himself—

> (a) to be the occupier of premises on which it was seized; or
>
> (b) to have had custody or control of it immediately before the seizure, provide that person with a record of what he seized.

(2) The officer shall provide the record within a reasonable time from the making of the request for it.

(3)–(10) *****

22 Retention

(1) Subject to subsection (4) below, anything which has been seized by a constable or taken away by a constable following a requirement made by virtue of section 19 or 20 above may be retained so long as is necessary in all the circumstances.

(2) Without prejudice to the generality of subsection (1) above—

    (a) anything seized for the purposes of a criminal investigation may be retained, except as provided by subsection (4) below—

        (i)   for use as evidence at a trial for an offence; or

        (ii) for forensic examination or for investigation in connection with an offence; and

    (b) anything may be retained in order to establish its lawful owner, where there are reasonable grounds for believing that it has been obtained in consequence of the commission of an offence.

(3) *****

(4) Nothing may be retained for either of the purposes mentioned in subsection (2)(a) above if a photograph or copy would be sufficient for that purpose.

(5)–(7) *****

23 *****

PART III ARREST

[24 Arrest without warrant: constables

(1) A constable may arrest without a warrant—

    (a) anyone who is about to commit an offence;

    (b) anyone who is in the act of committing an offence;

    (c) anyone whom he has reasonable grounds for suspecting to be about to commit an offence;

    (d) anyone whom he has reasonable grounds for suspecting to be committing an offence.

(2) If a constable has reasonable grounds for suspecting that an offence has been committed, he may arrest without a warrant anyone whom he has reasonable grounds to suspect of being guilty of it.

(3) If an offence has been committed, a constable may arrest without a warrant—

    (a) anyone who is guilty of the offence;

    (b) anyone whom he has reasonable grounds for suspecting to be guilty of it.

(4) But the power of summary arrest conferred by subsection (1), (2) or (3) is exercisable only if the constable has reasonable grounds for believing that for any of the reasons mentioned in subsection (5) it is necessary to arrest the person in question.

(5) The reasons are—

    (a) to enable the name of the person in question to be ascertained (in the case where the constable does not know, and cannot readily ascertain, the person's name, or has reasonable grounds for doubting whether a name given by the person as his name is his real name);

    (b) correspondingly as regards the person's address;

    (c) to prevent the person in question—

        (i)   causing physical injury to himself or any other person;

        (ii)   suffering physical injury;

        (iii) causing loss of or damage to property;

        (iv)   committing an offence against public decency (subject to subsection (6)); or

        (v)   causing an unlawful obstruction of the highway;

    (d) to protect a child or other vulnerable person from the person in question;

  (e) to allow the prompt and effective investigation of the offence or of the conduct of the person in question;

  (f) to prevent any prosecution for the offence from being hindered by the disappearance of the person in question.

(6) Subsection (5)(c)(iv) applies only where members of the public going about their normal business cannot reasonably be expected to avoid the person in question.]

[24A Arrest without warrant: other persons

(1) A person other than a constable may arrest without a warrant—

  (a) anyone who is in the act of committing an indictable offence;

  (b) anyone whom he has reasonable grounds for suspecting to be committing an indictable offence.

(2) Where an indictable offence has been committed, a person other than a constable may arrest without a warrant—

  (a) anyone who is guilty of the offence;

  (b) anyone whom he has reasonable grounds for suspecting to be guilty of it.

(3) But the power of summary arrest conferred by subsection (1) or (2) is exercisable only if—

  (a) the person making the arrest has reasonable grounds for believing that for any of the reasons mentioned in subsection (4) it is necessary to arrest the person in question; and

  (b) it appears to the person making the arrest that it is not reasonably practicable for a constable to make it instead.

(4) The reasons are to prevent the person in question—

  (a) causing physical injury to himself or any other person;

  (b) suffering physical injury;

  (c) causing loss of or damage to property; or

  (d) making off before a constable can assume responsibility for him.]

[(5) This section does not apply in relation to an offence under Part 3 or 3A of the Public Order Act 1986.]

25 ...

26, 27 *****

28 Information to be given on arrest

(1) Subject to subsection (5) below, where a person is arrested, otherwise than by being informed that he is under arrest, the arrest is not lawful unless the person arrested is informed that he is under arrest as soon as is practicable after his arrest.

(2) Where a person is arrested by a constable, subsection (1) above applies regardless of whether the fact of the arrest is obvious.

(3) Subject to subsection (5) below, no arrest is lawful unless the person arrested is informed of the ground for the arrest at the time of, or as soon as is practicable after, the arrest.

(4) Where a person is arrested by a constable, subsection (3) above applies regardless of whether the ground for the arrest is obvious.

(5) Nothing in this section is to be taken to require a person to be informed—

  (a) that he is under arrest; or

  (b) of the ground for the arrest,

if it was not reasonably practicable for him to be so informed by reason of his having escaped from arrest before the information could be given.

29 Voluntary attendance at police station etc

Where for the purpose of assisting with an investigation a person attends voluntarily at a police station or at any other place where a constable is present or accompanies a constable to a police station or any such other place without having been arrested—

  (a) he shall be entitled to leave at will unless he is placed under arrest;

  (b) he shall be informed at once that he is under arrest if a decision is taken by a constable to prevent him from leaving at will.

30 Arrest elsewhere than at police station

[(1) Subsection (1A) applies where a person is, at any place other than a police station—

(a) arrested by a constable for an offence, or

(b) taken into custody by a constable after being arrested for an offence by a person other than a constable.

(1A) The person must be taken by a constable to a police station as soon as practicable after the arrest.

(1B) Subsection (1A) has effect subject to section 30A (release on bail) and subsection (7) (release without bail).]

(2)–(6) *****

[(7) A person arrested by a constable at any place other than a police station must be released without bail if the condition in subsection (7A) is satisfied.

(7A) The condition is that, at any time before the person arrested reaches a police station, a constable is satisfied that there are no grounds for keeping him under arrest or releasing him on bail under section 30A.]

(8), (9) *****

[(10) Nothing in subsection (1A) or in section 30A prevents a constable delaying taking a person to a police station or releasing him [under section 30A] if the condition in subsection (10A) is satisfied.

(10A) The condition is that the presence of the person at a place (other than a police station) is necessary in order to carry out such investigations as it is reasonable to carry out immediately.

(11) Where there is any such delay the reasons for the delay must be recorded when the person first arrives at the police station or (as the case may be) is released [under section 30A].]

(12), (13) *****

[30A]–[30D] *****

31 *****

32 Search upon arrest

(1) A constable may search an arrested person, in any case where the person to be searched has been arrested at a place other than a police station, if the constable has reasonable grounds for believing that the arrested person may present a danger to himself or others.

(2) Subject to subsections (3) to (5) below, a constable shall also have power in any such case—

(a) to search the arrested person for anything—

(i) which he might use to assist him to escape from lawful custody; or

(ii) which might be evidence relating to an offence; and

(b) [if the offence for which he has been arrested is an indictable offence, to enter and search any premises in which he was when arrested or immediately before he was arrested for evidence relating to the offence].

(3) The power to search conferred by subsection (2) above is only a power to search to the extent that is reasonably required for the purpose of discovering any such thing or any such evidence.

(4) The powers conferred by this section to search a person are not to be construed as authorising a constable to require a person to remove any of his clothing in public other than an outer coat, jacket or gloves [but they do authorise a search of a person's mouth].

(5) A constable may not search a person in the exercise of the power conferred by subsection (2)(a) above unless he has reasonable grounds for believing that the person to be searched may have concealed on him anything for which a search is permitted under that paragraph.

(6) A constable may not search premises in the exercise of the power conferred by subsection (2)(b) above unless he has reasonable grounds for believing that there is evidence for which a search is permitted under that paragraph on the premises.

(7)–(10) *****

33 ...

PART IV DETENTION

Detention—conditions and duration

34 Limitations on police detention

(1) A person arrested for an offence shall not be kept in police detention except in accordance with the provisions of this Part of this Act.

(2) Subject to subsection (3) below, if at any time a custody officer—

(a) becomes aware, in relation to any person in police detention, that the grounds for the detention of that person have ceased to apply; and

(b) is not aware of any other grounds on which the continued detention of that person could be justified under the provisions of this Part of this Act,

it shall be the duty of the custody officer, subject to subsection (4) below, to order his immediate release from custody.

(3) No person in police detention shall be released except on the authority of a custody officer at the police station where his detention was authorised or, if it was authorised at more than one station, a custody officer at the station where it was last authorised.

(4) A person who appears to the custody officer to have been unlawfully at large when he was arrested is not to be released under subsection (2) above.

(5) A person whose release is ordered under subsection (2) must be released on bail if subsection (5A) applies.

(5A) This subsection applies if—

(a) it appears to the custody officer—

(i) that there is need for further investigation of any matter in connection with which the person was detained at any time during the period of the person's detention, or

(ii) that, in respect of any such matter, proceedings may be taken against the person or the person may be given a youth caution under section 66ZA of the Crime and Disorder Act 1998, and

(b) the pre-conditions for bail are satisfied.

(5AA) A person whose release is ordered under subsection (2) must be released without bail if subsection (5A) does not apply.

(5B)–(8) *****

35   *****

36 Custody officers at police stations

(1) One or more custody officers shall be appointed for each designated police station.

(2), [(2A)] *****

[(3) No officer may be appointed a custody officer unless the officer is at least of the rank of sergeant.]

(4) An officer of any rank may perform the functions of a custody officer at a designated police station if a custody officer is not readily available to perform them.

(5)–(10) *****

(11) ...

37 Duties of custody officer before charge

(1) Where—

(a) a person is arrested for an offence—

(i) without a warrant; or

(ii) under a warrant not endorsed for bail, ...

(b) ...

the custody officer at each police station where he is detained after his arrest shall determine whether he has before him sufficient evidence to charge that person with the offence for which he was arrested and may detain him at the police station for such period as is necessary to enable him to do so.

(2) If the custody officer determines that he does not have such evidence before him, the person arrested shall be released[—

    (a) without bail unless the pre-conditions for bail are satisfied, or

    (b) on bail if those pre-conditions are satisfied,

(subject to subsection (3))].

(3) If the custody officer has reasonable grounds for [believing that the person's detention without being charged is necessary to secure or preserve evidence relating to an offence for which the person is under arrest or to obtain such evidence by questioning the person], he may authorise the person arrested to be kept in police detention.

(4) Where a custody officer authorises a person who has not been charged to be kept in police detention, he shall, as soon as is practicable, make a written record of the grounds for the detention.

(5) Subject to subsection (6) below, the written record shall be made in the presence of the person arrested who shall at that time be informed by the custody officer of the grounds for his detention.

(6) Subsection (5) above shall not apply where the person arrested is, at the time when the written record is made—

    (a) incapable of understanding what is said to him;

    (b) violent or likely to become violent; or

    (c) in urgent need of medical attention.

[(6A) Subsection (6B) applies where—

    (a) a person is released under subsection (2), and

    (b) the custody officer determines that—

        (i)   there is not sufficient evidence to charge the person with an offence, or

        (ii) there is sufficient evidence to charge the person with an offence but the person should not be charged with an offence or given a caution in respect of an offence.

(6B) The custody officer must give the person notice in writing that the person is not to be prosecuted.

(6C) Subsection (6B) does not prevent the prosecution of the person for an offence if new evidence comes to light after the notice was given.]

(7)–(10), (15) *****

(11)–(14) …

37A–37D *****

38 Duties of custody officer after charge

(1) Where a person arrested for an offence otherwise than under a warrant endorsed for bail is charged with an offence, the custody officer shall [, subject to section 25 of the Criminal Justice and Public Order Act 1994,] order his release from police detention, either on bail or without bail, unless—

    (a) if the person arrested is not an arrested juvenile—

        (i)   his name or address cannot be ascertained or the custody officer has reasonable grounds for doubting whether a name or address furnished by him as his name or address is his real name or address;

        [(ii)   the custody officer has reasonable grounds for believing that the person arrested will fail to appear in court to answer to bail;

        (iii) in the case of a person arrested for an imprisonable offence, the custody officer has reasonable grounds for believing that the detention of the person arrested is necessary to prevent him from committing an offence;

        [(iiia) in a case where a sample may be taken from the person under section 63B below, the custody officer has reasonable grounds for believing that the detention of the person is necessary to enable a sample to be taken from him;]

        (iv)   in the case of a person arrested for an offence which is not an imprisonable offence, the custody officer has reasonable grounds for believing that the detention of the person arrested is necessary to prevent him from causing physical injury to any other person or from causing loss of or damage to property;

        (v)   the custody officer has reasonable grounds for believing that the detention of the person arrested is necessary to prevent him from interfering with the administration of justice or with the investigation of offences or of a particular offence; or

     (vi)   the custody officer has reasonable grounds for believing that the detention of the person arrested is necessary for his own protection;]

  (b) if he is an arrested juvenile—

     (i)   any of the requirements of paragraph (a) above is satisfied [(but, in the case of paragraph (a)(iiia) above only if the arrested juvenile has attained the minimum age)]; or

     (ii) the custody officer has reasonable grounds for believing that he ought to be detained in his own interests.

  [(c) the offence with which the person is charged is murder.]

(2) If the release of a person arrested is not required by subsection (1) above, the custody officer may authorise him to be kept in police detention [but may not authorise a person to be kept in police detention by virtue of subsection (1)(a)(iiia) after the end of the period of six hours beginning when he was charged with the offence].

(2A) *****

(3) Where a custody officer authorises a person who has been charged to be kept in police detention, he shall, as soon as practicable, make a written record of the grounds for the detention.

(4) Subject to subsection (5) below, the written record shall be made in the presence of the person charged who shall at that time be informed by the custody officer of the grounds for his detention.

(5) Subsection (4) above shall not apply where the person charged is, at the time when the written record is made—

  (a) incapable of understanding what is said to him;

  (b) violent or likely to become violent; or

  (c) in urgent need of medical attention.

(6)–(8)* *****

39　Responsibilities in relation to persons detained

(1) Subject to subsection (2) and (4) below, it shall be the duty of the custody officer at a police station to ensure—

  (a) that all persons in police detention at that station are treated in accordance with this Act and any code of practice issued under it and relating to the treatment of persons in police detention; and

  (b) that all matters relating to such persons which are required by this Act or by such codes of practice to be recorded are recorded in the custody records relating to such persons.

(2)–(6) *****

(7) …

40　Review of police detention

(1) Reviews of the detention of each person in police detention in connection with the investigation of an offence shall be carried out periodically in accordance with the following provisions of this section—

  (a) in the case of a person who has been arrested and charged, by the custody officer; and

  (b) in the case of a person who has been arrested but not charged, by an officer of at least the rank of inspector who has not been directly involved in the investigation.

(2) The officer to whom it falls to carry out a review is referred to in this section as a 'review officer'.

(3) Subject to subsection (4) below—

  (a) the first review shall be not later than six hours after the detention was first authorised;

  (b) the second review shall be not later than nine hours after the first;

  (c) subsequent reviews shall be at intervals of not more than nine hours.

(4) A review may be postponed—

  (a) if, having regard to all the circumstances prevailing at the latest time for it specified in subsection (3) above, it is not practicable to carry out the review at that time;

  (b) without prejudice to the generality of paragraph (a) above—

---

* **Editor's Note:** The 'minimum age' is 14 (subs. (6A)).

(i)   if at that time the person in detention is being questioned by a police officer and the review officer is satisfied that an interruption of the questioning for the purpose of carrying out the review would prejudice the investigation in connection with which he is being questioned; or

(ii)   if at that time no review officer is readily available.

(5)   If a review is postponed under subsection (4) above it shall be carried out as soon as practicable after the latest time specified for it in subsection (3) above.

(6)   If a review is carried out after postponement under subsection (4) above, the fact that it was so carried out shall not affect any requirement of this section as to the time at which any subsequent review is to be carried out.

(7)   The review officer shall record the reasons for any postponement of a review in the custody record.

(8)–(14) *****

40A *****

41   Limits on period of detention without charge

(1)   Subject to the following provisions of this section and to sections 42 and 43 below, a person shall not be kept in police detention for more than 24 hours without being charged.

(2)   The time from which the period of detention of a person is to be calculated (in this Act referred to as 'the relevant time')—

(a)   in the case of a person to whom this paragraph applies, shall be—
  (i)   the time at which that person arrives at the relevant police station; or
  (ii)   the time 24 hours after the time of that person's arrest,
  (iii)   whichever is the earlier;

(b)   in the case of a person arrested outside England and Wales, shall be—
  (i)   the time at which that person arrives at the first police station to which he is taken in the police area in England or Wales in which the offence for which he was arrested is being investigated; or
  (ii)   the time 24 hours after the time of that person's entry into England and Wales,
  (iii)   whichever is the earlier;

(c)   in the case of a person who—
  (i)   attends voluntarily at a police station; or
  (ii)   accompanies a constable to a police station without having been arrested, and is arrested at the police station, the time of his arrest;

[(ca)   in the case of a person who attends a police station to answer bail granted under section 30A, the time when he arrives at the police station;]

(d)   in any other case, except where subsection (5) below applies, shall be the time at which the person arrested arrives at the first police station to which he is taken after his arrest.

(3)–(6) *****

(7)   Subject to subsection (8) below, a person who at the expiry of 24 hours after the relevant time is in police detention and has not been charged shall be released at that time[—

(a)   [on bail, if the pre-conditions for bail are satisfied, or

(b)   without bail, if those pre-conditions are not satisfied]].

(8)   Subsection (7) above does not apply to a person whose detention for more than 24 hours after the relevant time has been authorised or is otherwise permitted in accordance with section 42 or 43 below.

(9)   A person released under subsection (7) above shall not be re-arrested without a warrant for the offence for which he was previously arrested unless[, since the person's release, new evidence has come to light or an examination or analysis of existing evidence has been made which could not reasonably have been made before] his release[; but this subsection does not prevent an arrest under section 46A below].

[(10)   Subsection (11) applies where—

(a)   a person is released under subsection (7), and

(b)   a custody officer determines that—

(i)   there is not sufficient evidence to charge the person with an offence, or

(ii) there is sufficient evidence to charge the person with an offence but the person should not be charged with an offence or given a caution in respect of an offence.

(11) The custody officer must give the person notice in writing that the person is not to be prosecuted.

(12) Subsection (11) does not prevent the prosecution of the person for an offence if new evidence comes to light after the notice was given.]

(13) *****

42   Authorisation of continued detention

(1) Where a police officer of the rank of superintendent or above who is responsible for the police station at which a person is detained has reasonable grounds for believing that—

(a) the detention of that person without charge is necessary to secure or preserve evidence relating to an offence for which he is under arrest or to obtain such evidence by questioning him;

[(b) an offence for which he is under arrest is an [indictable] offence; and]

(c) the investigation is being conducted diligently and expeditiously,

he may authorise the keeping of that person in police detention for a period expiring at or before 36 hours after the relevant time.

(2) Where an officer such as is mentioned in subsection (1) above has authorised the keeping of a person in police detention for a period expiring less than 36 hours after the relevant time, such an officer may authorise the keeping of that person in police detention for a further period expiring not more than 36 hours after that time if the conditions specified in subsection (1) above are still satisfied when he gives the authorisation.

(3) If it is proposed to transfer a person in police detention to another police area, the officer determining whether or not to authorise keeping him in detention under subsection (1) above shall have regard to the distance and the time the journey would take.

(4), (5) *****

(6) Before determining whether to authorise the keeping of a person in detention under subsection (1) or (2) above, an officer shall give—

(a) that person; or

(b) any solicitor representing him who is available at the time when it falls to the officer to determine whether to give the authorisation,

an opportunity to make representations to him about the detention.

(7)–(9) *****

(10) Where an officer has authorised the keeping of a person who has not been charged in detention under subsection (1) or (2) above, he shall be released from detention ..., not later than 36 hours after the relevant time[—

(a) [on bail, if the pre-conditions for bail are satisfied, or

(b) without bail, if those pre-conditions are not satisfied.

(subject to subsection (10A))]].

(10A) Subsection (10) does not apply if—

(a) the person has been charged with an offence, or

(b) the person's continued detention is authorised or otherwise permitted in accordance with section 43.

[(11)]–(14) *****

43   Warrants of further detention

(1) Where, on an application on oath made by a constable and supported by an information, a magistrate's court is satisfied that there are reasonable grounds for believing that the further detention of the person to whom the application relates is justified, it may issue a warrant of further detention authorising the keeping of that person in police detention.

(2) A court may not hear an application for a warrant of further detention unless the person to whom the application relates—

(a) has been furnished with a copy of the information; and

(b) has been brought before the court for the hearing.

(3) The person to whom the application relates shall be entitled to be legally represented at the hearing and, if he is not so represented but wishes to be so represented—

    (a) the court shall adjourn the hearing to enable him to obtain representation; and

    (b) he may be kept in police detention during the adjournment.

(4) A person's further detention is only justified for the purposes of this section or section 44 below if—

    (a) his detention without charge is necessary to secure or preserve evidence relating to an offence for which he is under arrest or to obtain such evidence by questioning him;

    (b) an offence for which he is under arrest is [an indictable offence]; and

    (c) the investigation is being conducted diligently and expeditiously.

(5)–(7) *****

(8) Where on an application such as is mentioned in subsection (1) above a magistrates' court is not satisfied that there are reasonable grounds for believing that the further detention of the person to whom the application relates is justified, it shall be its duty—

    (a) to refuse the application; or

    (b) to adjourn the hearing of it until a time not later than 36 hours after the relevant time.

(9) The person to whom the application relates may be kept in police detention during the adjournment.

(10) A warrant of further detention shall—

    (a) state the time at which it is issued;

    (b) authorise the keeping in police detention of the person to whom it relates for the period stated in it.

(11) Subject to subsection (12) below, the period stated in a warrant of further detention shall be such period as the magistrates' court thinks fit, having regard to the evidence before it.

(12) The period shall not be longer than 36 hours.

(13), (14) *****

(15) Where an application under this section is refused, the person to whom the application relates shall forthwith be charged or, subject to subsection (16) below, released[—

    (a) [on bail, if the pre-conditions for bail are satisfied, or

    (b) without bail, if those pre-conditions are not satisfied]].

(18)–[(22)] *****

44   Extension of warrants of further detention

(1) On an application on oath made by a constable and supported by an information a magistrates' court may extend a warrant of further detention issued under section 43 above if it is satisfied that there are reasonable grounds for believing that the further detention of the person to whom the application relates is justified.

(2) Subject to subsection (3) below, the period for which a warrant of further detention may be extended shall be such period as the court thinks fit, having regard to the evidence before it.

(3) The period shall not—

    (a) be longer than 36 hours; or

    (b) end later than 96 hours after the relevant time.

(4)–[(11)] *****

45, 45A *****

Detention—miscellaneous

46   Detention after charge

(1) Where a person—

    (a) is charged with an offence; and

    (b) after being charged—

        (i) is kept in police detention; or

        (ii) is detained by a local authority in pursuance of arrangements made under section 38(6) above,

he shall be brought before a magistrates' court in accordance with the provisions of this section.

(2) If he is to be brought before a magistrates' court [in the local justice] area in which the police station at which he was charged is situated, he shall be brought before such a court as soon as is practicable and in any event not later than the first sitting after he is charged with the offence.

(3) If no magistrates' court [in that area] is due to sit either on the day on which he is charged or on the next day, the custody officer for the police station at which he was charged shall inform the [designated officer] for the area that there is a person in the area to whom subsection (2) above applies.

(4) If the person charged is to be brought before a magistrates' court [in a local justice] area other than that in which the police station at which he was charged is situated, he shall be removed to that area as soon as is practicable and brought before such a court as soon as is practicable after this arrival in the area and in any event not later than the first sitting of a magistrates' court [in that area] after this arrival in the area.

(5)–(9) *****

46ZA–51 *****

52 ...

PART V QUESTIONING AND TREATMENT OF PERSONS BY POLICE

53 Abolition of certain powers of constables to search persons

(1) Subject to subsection (2) below, there shall cease to have effect any Act (including a local Act) passed before this Act in so far as it authorises—

(a) any search by a constable of a person in police detention at a police station; or

(b) an intimate search of a person by a constable; and any rule of common law which authorises a search such as is mentioned in paragraph (a) or (b) above is abolished.

(2) ...

54 Search of detained persons

(1) The custody officer at a police station shall ascertain ... everything which a person has with him when he is—

(a)   brought to the station after being arrested elsewhere or after being committed to custody by an order or sentence of a court; or

[(b)   arrested at the station or detained there [, as a person falling within section 34(7), under section 37 above] [or as a person to whom section 46ZA(4) or (5) applies]].

[(2) The custody officer may record or cause to be recorded all or any of the things which he ascertains under subsection (1).

(2A) In the case of an arrested person, any such record may be made as part of his custody record.]

(3) Subject to subsection (4) below, a custody officer may seize and retain any such thing or cause any such thing to be seized and retained.

(4) Clothes and personal effects may only be seized if the custody officer—

(a) believes that the person from whom they are seized may use them—

(i)   to cause physical injury to himself or any other person;

(ii) to damage property;

(iii) to interfere with evidence; or

(iv) to assist him to escape; or

(b) has reasonable grounds for believing that they may be evidence relating to an offence.

(5) Where anything is seized, the person from whom it is seized shall be told the reason for the seizure unless he is—

(a) violent or likely to become violent; or

(b) incapable of understanding what is said to him.

(6) Subject to subsection (7) below, a person may be searched if the custody officer considers it necessary to enable him to carry out his duty under subsection (1) above and to the extent that the custody officer considers necessary for that purpose.

[(6A) A person who is in custody at a police station or is in police detention otherwise than at a police station may at any time be searched in order to ascertain whether he has with him anything which he could use for any of the purposes specified in subsection (4)(a) above.

(6B) Subject to subsection (6C) below, a constable may seize and retain, or cause to be seized and retained, anything found on such a search.

(6C) A constable may only seize clothes and personal effects in the circumstances specified in subsection (4) above.]

(7) An intimate search may not be conducted under this section.

(8) A search under this section shall be carried out by a constable.

(9) The constable carrying out a search shall be of the same sex as the person searched.

[54A   Searches and examination to ascertain identity

(1) If an officer of at least the rank of inspector authorises it, a person who is detained in a police station may be searched or examined, or both—

    (a) for the purpose of ascertaining whether he has any mark that would tend to identify him as a person involved in the commission of an offence; or

    (b) for the purpose of facilitating the ascertainment of his identity.

(2) An officer may only give an authorisation under subsection (1) for the purpose mentioned in paragraph (a) of that subsection if—

    (a) the appropriate consent to a search or examination that would reveal whether the mark in question exists has been withheld; or

    (b) it is not practicable to obtain such consent.

(3) An officer may only give an authorisation under subsection (1) in a case in which subsection (2) does not apply if—

    (a) the person in question has refused to identify himself; or

    (b) the officer has reasonable grounds for suspecting that that person is not who he claims to be.

(4) An officer may give an authorisation under subsection (1) orally or in writing but, if he gives it orally, he shall confirm it in writing as soon as is practicable.

(5) Any identifying mark found on a search or examination under this section may be photographed—

    (a) with the appropriate consent; or

    (b) if the appropriate consent is withheld or it is not practicable to obtain it, without it.

(6) Where a search or examination may be carried out under this section, or a photograph may be taken under this section, the only persons entitled to carry out the search or examination, or to take the photograph, are [constables].

(7) A person may not under this section carry out a search or examination of a person of the opposite sex or take a photograph of any part of the body of a person of the opposite sex.

(8) An intimate search may not be carried out under this section.

(9) A photograph taken under this section—

    (a) may be used by, or disclosed to, any person for any purpose related to the prevention or detection of crime, the investigation of an offence or the conduct of a prosecution; and

    (b) after being so used or disclosed, may be retained but may not be used or disclosed except for a purpose so related.]

(10)–(13) *****

54B, 54C *****

55   Intimate searches

(1) Subject to the following provisions of this section, if an officer of at least the rank of [inspector] has reasonable grounds for believing—

    (a) that a person who has been arrested and is in police detention may have concealed on him anything which—

        (i)   he could use to cause physical injury to himself or others; and

        (ii) he might so use while he is in police detention or in the custody of a court; or

    (b) that such a person—

        (i)   may have a Class A drug concealed on him; and

        (ii) was in possession of it with the appropriate criminal intention before his arrest, he may authorise [an intimate] search of that person.

(2) An officer may not authorise an intimate search of a person for anything unless he has reasonable grounds for believing that it cannot be found without his being intimately searched.

(3)–(3B) *****

(4) An intimate search which is only a drug offence search shall be by way of examination by a suitably qualified person.

(5) Except as provided by subsection (4) above, an intimate search shall be by way of examination by a suitably qualified person unless an officer of at least the rank of [inspector] considers that this is not practicable.

(6) An intimate search which is not carried out as mentioned in subsection (5) above shall be carried out by a constable.

(7) A constable may not carry out an intimate search of a person of the opposite sex.

(8) No intimate search may be carried out except—

    (a) at a police station;

    (b) at a hospital;

    (c) at a registered medical practitioner's surgery; or

    (d) at some other place used for medical purposes.

(9) An intimate search which is only a drug offence search may not be carried out at a police station.

(10) If an intimate search of a person is carried out, the custody record relating to him shall state—

    (a) which parts of his body were searched; and

    (b) why they were searched.

(10A), (11) *****

(12) The custody officer at a police station may seize and retain anything which is found on an intimate search of a person, or cause any such thing to be seized and retained—

    (a) if he believes that the person from whom it is seized may use it—

        (i)   to cause physical injury to himself or any other person;

        (ii) to damage property;

        (iii) to interfere with evidence; or

        (iv) to assist him to escape; or

    (b) if he has reasonable grounds for believing that it may be evidence relating to an offence.

(13) Where anything is seized under this section, the person from whom it is seized shall be told the reason for the seizure unless he is—

    (a) violent or likely to become violent; or

    (b) incapable of understanding what is said to him.

(13A)–(16) *****

(17) In this section—

*****

'Class A drug' has the meaning assigned to it by section 2(1)(b) of the Misuse of Drugs Act 1971;

'drug offence search' means an intimate search for a Class A drug which an officer has authorised by virtue of subsection (1)(b) above; and

'suitably qualified person' means—

    (a) a registered medical practitioner; or

    (b) a registered nurse.

[55A] *****

56 Right to have someone informed when arrested

(1) Where a person has been arrested and is being held in custody in a police station or other premises, he shall be entitled, if he so requests, to have one friend or relative or other person who is

known to him or who is likely to take an interest in his welfare told, as soon as is practicable except to the extent that delay is permitted by this section, that he has been arrested and is being detained there.

(2) Delay is only permitted—

(a) in the case of a person who is in police detention for [an indictable offence]; and

(b) if an officer of at least the rank of [inspector] authorises it.

(3) In any case the person in custody must be permitted to exercise the right conferred by subsection (1) above within 36 hours from the relevant time as defined in section 41(2) above.

(4)–(5B) *****

(6) If a delay is authorised—

(a) the detained person shall be told the reason for it; and

(b) the reason shall be noted on his custody record.

(7)–(10) *****

57 ...

58 Access to legal advice

(1) A person arrested and held in custody in a police station or other premises shall be entitled, if he so requests, to consult a solicitor privately at any time.

(2) Subject to subsection (3) below, a request under subsection (1) above and the time at which it was made shall be recorded in the custody record.

(3) Such a request need not be recorded in the custody record of a person who makes it at a time while he is at a court after being charged with an offence.

(4) If a person makes such a request, he must be permitted to consult a solicitor as soon as is practicable except to the extent that delay is permitted by this section.

(5) In any case he must be permitted to consult a solicitor within 36 hours from the relevant time, as defined in section 41(2) above.

(6) Delay in compliance with a request is only permitted—

(a) in the case of a person who is in police detention for [an indictable offence]; and

(b) if an officer of at least the rank of superintendent authorises it.

(7)–(8B) *****

(9) If delay is authorised—

(a) the detained person shall be told the reason for it; and

(b) the reason shall be noted on his custody record.

(10) The duties imposed by subsection (9) above shall be performed as soon as is practicable.

(11) There may be no further delay in permitting the exercise of the right conferred by subsection (1) above once the reason for authorising delay ceases to subsist.

[(12) Nothing in this section applies to a person arrested or detained under the terrorism provisions [or detained under Part 1 of Schedule 3 to the Counter-Terrorism and Border Security Act 2019].]

59 ...

60 [Audio recording] of interviews

(1) It shall be the duty of the Secretary of State—

(a) to issue a code of practice in connection with the [audio recording] of interviews of persons suspected of the commission of criminal offences which are held by police officers at police stations; and

(b) to make an order requiring the [audio recording] of interviews of persons suspected of the commission of criminal offences, or of such descriptions of criminal offences as may be specified in the order, which are so held, in accordance with the code as it has effect for the time being.

(2) An order under subsection (1) above shall be made by statutory instrument and shall be subject to annulment in pursuance of a resolution of either House of Parliament.

[60A   Visual recording of interviews

(1) The Secretary of State shall have power—

(a) to issue a code of practice for the visual recording of interviews held by police officers at police stations; and

(b) to make an order requiring the visual recording of interviews so held, and requiring the visual recording to be in accordance with the code for the time being in force under this section.]

(2)–(4) *****

[60B]   ***

61   Fingerprinting

(1) Except as provided by this section no person's fingerprints may be taken without the appropriate consent.

(2) Consent to the taking of a person's fingerprints must be in writing if it is given at a time when he is at a police station.

[(3) The fingerprints of a person detained at a police station may be taken without the appropriate consent if—

(a) he is detained in consequence of his arrest for a recordable offence; and

(b) he has not had his fingerprints taken in the course of the investigation of the offence by the police.]

(3A) *****

[(4) The fingerprints of a person detained at a police station may be taken without the appropriate consent if—

(a) he has been charged with a recordable offence or informed that he will be reported for such an offence; and

(b) he has not had his fingerprints taken in the course of the investigation of the offence by the police.]

(4A)–(10) *****

61A–63C   ***

[63D   Destruction of fingerprints and DNA profiles]

[(1) This section applies to—

(a) fingerprints—

(i) taken from a person under any power conferred by this Part of this Act, or

(ii) taken by the police, with the consent of the person from whom they were taken, in connection with the investigation of an offence by the police, and

(b) a DNA profile derived from a DNA sample taken as mentioned in paragraph (a)(i) or (ii).

(2) Fingerprints and DNA profiles to which this section applies ('section 63D material') must be destroyed if it appears to the responsible chief officer of police that—

(a) the taking of the fingerprint or, in the case of a DNA profile, the taking of the sample from which the DNA profile was derived, was unlawful, or

(b) the fingerprint was taken, or, in the case of a DNA profile, was derived from a sample taken, from a person in connection with that person's arrest and the arrest was unlawful or based on mistaken identity.

(3) In any other case, section 63D material must be destroyed unless it is retained under any power conferred by sections 63E to 63O (including those sections as applied by section 63P).]

(4)–(5B) *****

[63E   Retention of section 63D material pending investigation or proceedings]

[(1) This section applies to section 63D material taken (or, in the case of a DNA profile, derived from a sample taken) in connection with the investigation of an offence in which it is suspected that the person to whom the material relates has been involved.

(2) The material may be retained until the conclusion of the investigation of the offence or, where the investigation gives rise to proceedings against the person for the offence, until the conclusion of those proceedings.]

[63F   Retention of section 63D material: persons arrested for or charged with a qualifying offence]

[(1) This section applies to section 63D material which—

(a) relates to a person who is arrested for, or charged with, a qualifying offence but is not convicted of that offence, and

(b) was taken (or, in the case of a DNA profile, derived from a sample taken) in connection with the investigation of the offence.

(2) If the person has previously been convicted of a recordable offence which is not an excluded offence, or is so convicted before the material is required to be destroyed by virtue of this section, the material may be retained indefinitely.

[(2A) In subsection (2), references to a recordable offence include an offence under the law of a country or territory outside England and Wales where the act constituting the offence would constitute a recordable offence if done in England and Wales (and, in the application of subsection (2) where a person has previously been convicted, this applies whether or not the act constituted such an offence when the person was convicted).]

(3) Otherwise, material falling within subsection (4)[, (5) or (5A)] may be retained until the end of the retention period specified in subsection (6).

(4) Material falls within this subsection if it—

(a) relates to a person who is charged with a qualifying offence but is not convicted of that offence, and

(b) was taken (or, in the case of a DNA profile, derived from a sample taken) in connection with the investigation of the offence.

(5) Material falls within this subsection if—

(a) it relates to a person who is arrested for a qualifying offence but is not charged with that offence,

(b) it was taken (or, in the case of a DNA profile, derived from a sample taken) in connection with the investigation of the offence, and

(c) the Commissioner for the Retention and Use of Biometric Material has consented under section 63G to the retention of the material.

[(5A) Material falls within this subsection if—

(a) it relates to a person who is arrested for a terrorism-related qualifying offence[, other than a terrorism-related qualifying offence,] but is not charged with that offence, and

(b) it was taken (or, in the case of a DNA profile, derived from a sample taken) in connection with the investigation of the offence.]

(6) The retention period is—

(a) in the case of fingerprints, the period of 3 years beginning with the date on which the fingerprints were taken, and

(b) in the case of a DNA profile, the period of 3 years beginning with the date on which the DNA sample from which the profile was derived was taken (or, if the profile was derived from more than one DNA sample, the date on which the first of those samples was taken).]

(7)–[(12)] *****

[63G   Retention of section 63D material by virtue of section 63F(5): consent of Commissioner]

[(1) The responsible chief officer of police may apply under subsection (2) or (3) to the Commissioner for the Retention and Use of Biometric Material for consent to the retention of section 63D material which falls within section 63F(5)(a) and (b).

(2) The responsible chief officer of police may make an application under this subsection if the responsible chief officer of police considers that the material was taken (or, in the case of a DNA

profile, derived from a sample taken) in connection with the investigation of an offence where any alleged victim of the offence was, at the time of the offence—

    (a) under the age of 18,

    (b) a vulnerable adult, or

    (c) associated with the person to whom the material relates.

    (3) The responsible chief officer of police may make an application under this subsection if the responsible chief officer of police considers that—

    (a) the material is not material to which subsection (2) relates, but

    (b) the retention of the material is necessary to assist in the prevention or detection of crime.

    (4) The Commissioner may, on an application under this section, consent to the retention of material to which the application relates if the Commissioner considers that it is appropriate to retain the material.

    (5) But where notice is given under subsection (6) in relation to the application, the Commissioner must, before deciding whether or not to give consent, consider any representations by the person to whom the material relates which are made within the period of 28 days beginning with the day on which the notice is given.

    (6) The responsible chief officer of police must give to the person to whom the material relates notice of—

    (a) an application under this section, and

    (b) the right to make representations.]

    (7)–(10) *****

[63H Retention of section 63D material: persons arrested for or charged with a minor offence]

    [(1) This section applies to section 63D material which—

    (a) relates to a person who—

        (i) is arrested for or charged with a recordable offence other than a qualifying offence,

        (ii) if arrested for or charged with more than one offence arising out of a single course of action, is not also arrested for or charged with a qualifying offence, and

        (iii) is not convicted of the offence or offences in respect of which the person is arrested or charged, and

    (b) was taken (or, in the case of a DNA profile, derived from a sample taken) in connection with the investigation of the offence or offences in respect of which the person is arrested or charged.

    (2) If the person has previously been convicted of a recordable offence which is not an excluded offence, the material may be retained indefinitely.]

    [(2A)], (3) *****

[63I Retention of material: persons convicted of a recordable offence]

    [(1) This section applies, subject to subsection (3), to—

    (a) section 63D material which—

        (i) relates to a person who is convicted of a recordable offence, and

        (ii) was taken (or, in the case of a DNA profile, derived from a sample taken) in connection with the investigation of the offence, or

    (b) material taken under section 61(6) or 63(3B) which relates to a person who is convicted of a recordable offence.

    (2) The material may be retained indefinitely.

    (3) This section does not apply to section 63D material to which section 63K applies.]

[63IA] *****

[63J   Retention of material: persons convicted of an offence outside England and Wales]

[(1) This section applies to material falling within subsection (2) relating to a person who is convicted of an offence under the law of any country or territory outside England and Wales.

(2) Material falls within this subsection if it is—

(a) fingerprints taken from the person under section 61(6D) (power to take fingerprints without consent in relation to offences outside England and Wales), or

(b) a DNA profile derived from a DNA sample taken from the person under section 62(2A) or 63(3E) (powers to take intimate and non-intimate samples in relation to offences outside England and Wales).

(3) The material may be retained indefinitely.]

[63K   Retention of section 63D material: exception for persons under 18 convicted of first minor offence]

[(1) This section applies to section 63D material which—

(a) relates to a person who—

(i)   is convicted of a recordable offence other than a qualifying offence,

(ii) has not previously been convicted of a recordable offence, and

(iii) is aged under 18 at the time of the offence, and

(b) was taken (or, in the case of a DNA profile, derived from a sample taken) in connection with the investigation of the offence.

[(1A) In subsection (1)(a)(ii), the reference to a recordable offence includes an offence under the law of a country or territory outside England and Wales where the act constituting the offence would constitute a recordable offence if done in England and Wales (whether or not it constituted such an offence when the person was convicted).]

(2) Where the person is given a relevant custodial sentence of less than 5 years in respect of the offence, the material may be retained until the end of the period consisting of the term of the sentence plus 5 years.

(3) Where the person is given a relevant custodial sentence of 5 years or more in respect of the offence, the material may be retained indefinitely.

(4) Where the person is given a sentence other than a relevant custodial sentence in respect of the offence, the material may be retained until—

(a) in the case of fingerprints, the end of the period of 5 years beginning with the date on which the fingerprints were taken, and

(b) in the case of a DNA profile, the end of the period of 5 years beginning with—

(i)   the date on which the DNA sample from which the profile was derived was taken, or

(ii) if the profile was derived from more than one DNA sample, the date on which the first of those samples was taken.

(5) But if, before the end of the period within which material may be retained by virtue of this section, the person is again convicted of a recordable offence, the material may be retained indefinitely.]

[(5A)], (6) *****

[63KA], [63L]   ***

[63M   Retention of section 63D material for purposes of national security]

[(1) Section 63D material may be retained for as long as a national security determination made by [a] chief officer of police has effect in relation to it.

(2) A national security determination is made if [a] chief officer of police determines that it is necessary for any section 63D material to be retained for the purposes of national security.

(3) A national security determination—

(a) must be made in writing,

(b) has effect for a maximum of [5 years] beginning with the date on which it is made, and

(c) may be renewed.]

[63N   Retention of section 63D material given voluntarily]

[(1) This section applies to the following section 63D material—

(a) fingerprints taken with the consent of the person from whom they were taken, and

(b) a DNA profile derived from a DNA sample taken with the consent of the person from whom the sample was taken.

(2) Material to which this section applies may be retained until it has fulfilled the purpose for which it was taken or derived.

(3) Material to which this section applies which relates to—

(a) a person who is convicted of a recordable offence, or

(b) a person who has previously been convicted of a recordable offence (other than a person who has only one exempt conviction),

may be retained indefinitely.]

(4)–[(6)] *****

[63O   Retention of section 63D material with consent]

[(1) This section applies to the following material—

(a) fingerprints (other than fingerprints taken under section 61(6A)) to which section 63D applies, and

(b) a DNA profile to which section 63D applies.

(2) If the person to whom the material relates consents to material to which this section applies being retained, the material may be retained for as long as that person consents to it being retained.

(3) Consent given under this section—

(a) must be in writing, and

(b) can be withdrawn at any time.]

[63P   Retention of 63D material in connection with different offence]

[(1) Subsection (2) applies if—

(a) section 63D material is taken (or, in the case of a DNA profile, derived from a sample taken) from a person in connection with the investigation of an offence, and

(b) the person is subsequently arrested for or charged with a different offence, or convicted of or given a penalty notice for a difference offence.

(2) Sections 63E to 63O and sections 63Q and 63T have effect in relation to the material as if the material were also taken (or, in the case of a DNA profile, derived from a sample taken)—

(a) in connection with the investigation of the offence mentioned in subsection (1)(b),

(b) on the date on which the person was arrested for that offence (or charged with it or given a penalty notice for it, if the person was not arrested.]

[63PA   Retention of further sets of fingerprints]

[(1) This section applies where section 63D material is or includes a person's fingerprints ('the original fingerprints').

(2) A constable may make a determination under this section in respect of any further fingerprints taken from the same person ('the further fingerprints') if any of conditions 1 to 3 are met.

(3) Condition 1 is met if—

(a) the further fingerprints are section 63D material, and

(b) the further fingerprints or the original fingerprints were taken in connection with a terrorist investigation.

(4) Condition 2 is met if the further fingerprints were taken from the person in England or Wales under—

(a) paragraph 10 of Schedule 8 to the Terrorism Act 2000,

(b) paragraph 1 of Schedule 6 to the Terrorism Prevention and Investigation Measures Act 2011, or

(c) paragraph 34 of Schedule 3 to the Counter-Terrorism and Border Security Act 2019.

(5) Condition 3 is met if the further fingerprints—

(a) are material to which section 18 of the Counter-Terrorism Act 2008 applies, and

(b) are held under the law of England and Wales.

(6) Where a determination under this section is made in respect of the further fingerprints—

(a) the further fingerprints may be retained for as long as the original fingerprints are retained under a power conferred by sections 63E to 63O (including those sections as applied by section 63P), and

(b) a requirement under any enactment to destroy the further fingerprints does not apply for as long as their retention is authorised by paragraph (a).

(7) Subsection (6)(a) does not prevent the further fingerprints being retained after the original fingerprints fall to be destroyed if the continued retention of the further fingerprints is authorised under any enactment.

(8) A written record must be made of a determination under this section.]

[63Q   Destruction of copies of section 63D material]

[(1) If fingerprints are required by section 63D to be destroyed, any copies of the fingerprints held by the police must also be destroyed.

(2) If a DNA profile is required by that section to be destroyed, no copy may be retained by the police except in a form which does not include information which identifies the person to whom the DNA profile relates.]

[63R   Destruction of samples]

[(1) This section applies to samples—

(a) taken from a person under any power conferred by this Part of this Act, or

(b) taken by the police, with the consent of the person from whom they were taken, in connection with the investigation of an offence by the police.

(2) Samples to which this section applies must be destroyed if it appears to the responsible chief officer of police that—

(a) the taking of the samples was unlawful, or

(b) the samples were taken from a person in connection with that person's arrest and the arrest was unlawful or based on mistaken identity.

(3) Subject to this, the rule in subsection (4) or (as the case may be) (5) applies.

(4) A DNA sample to which this section applies must be destroyed—

(a) as soon as a DNA profile has been derived from the sample, or

(b) if sooner, before the end of the period of 6 months beginning with the date on which the sample was taken.

(5) Any other sample to which this section applies must be destroyed before the end of the period of 6 months beginning with the date on which it was taken.

(6) The responsible chief officer of police may apply to a District Judge (Magistrates' Courts) for an order to retain a sample to which this section applies beyond the date on which the sample would otherwise be required to be destroyed by virtue of subsection (4) or (5) if—

(a) the sample was taken from a person in connection with the investigation of a qualifying offence, and

(b) the responsible chief officer of police considers that the condition in subsection (7) is met.

(7) The condition is that, having regard to the nature and complexity of other material that is evidence in relation to the offence, the sample is likely to be needed in any proceedings for the offence for the purposes of—

(a) disclosure to, or use by, a defendant, or

(b) responding to any challenge by a defendant in respect of the admissibility of material that is evidence on which the prosecution proposes to rely.]

(8)–(13) *****

[63S]   *****

[63T   Use of retained material]

[(1) Any material to which section 63D, 63R or 63S applies must not be used other than—

(a) in the interests of national security,

(b) for the purposes of a terrorist investigation,

(c) for purposes related to the prevention or detection of crime, the investigation of an offence or the conduct of a prosecution, or

(d) for purposes related to the identification of a deceased person or of the person to whom the material relates.

(2) Material which is required by section 63D, 63R or 63S to be destroyed must not at any time after it is required to be destroyed be used—

(a) in evidence against the person to whom the material relates, or

(b) for the purposes of the investigation of any offence.]

(3) *****

[63U]   *****

64 ...*

[64A   Photographing of suspects etc

(1) A person who is detained at a police station may be photographed—

(a) with the appropriate consent; or

(b) if the appropriate consent is withheld or it is not practicable to obtain it, without it.

(1A)–(1M) *****

(2) A person proposing to take a photograph of any person under this section—

(a) may, for the purpose of doing so, require the removal of any item or substance worn on or over the whole or any part of the head or face of the person to be photographed; and

(b) if the requirement is not complied with, may remove the item or substance himself.

(3) Where a photograph may be taken under this section, the only persons entitled to take the photograph are [constables].

(4) A photograph taken under this section—

(a) may be used by, or disclosed to, any person for any purpose related to the prevention or detection of crime, the investigation of an offence or the conduct of a prosecution [or to the enforcement of a sentence]; and

(b) after being so used or disclosed, may be retained but may not be used or disclosed except for a purpose so related.]

(5)–(7) *****

65   Part V—supplementary

(1) In this Part of this Act—

['analysis', in relation to a skin impression, includes comparison and matching;]

'appropriate consent' means—

(a) in relation to a person who [has attained the age of 18 years], the consent of that person;

(b) in relation to a person who has not attained that age but has attained the age of 14 years, the consent of that person and his parent or guardian; and

(c) in relation to a person who has not attained the age of 14 years, the consent of his parent or guardian;

['DNA profile' means any information derived from a DNA sample;

'DNA sample' means any material that has come from a human body and consists of or includes human cells;]

*****

---

* **Editor's Note:** Sections 64ZA–64ZN are not yet in force and not included here.

['fingerprints', in relation to any person, means a record (in any form and produced by any method) of the skin pattern and other physical characteristics or features of—

(a) any of that person's fingers; or

(b) either of his palms;]

['intimate sample' means—

(a) a sample of blood, semen or any other tissue fluid, urine or pubic hair;

(b) a dental impression;

(c) [a swab taken from any part of a person's genitals (including pubic hair) or from a person's body orifice other than the mouth];]

'intimate search' means a search which consists of the physical examination of a person's body orifices other than the mouth;

['non-intimate sample' means—

(a) a sample of hair other than pubic hair;

(b) a sample taken from a nail or from under a nail;

(c) [a swab taken from any part of a person's body other than a part from which a swab taken would be an intimate sample;]

(d) saliva;

(a) [(e) a skin impression;]]

*****

['the responsible chief officer of police', in relation to material to which section 63D or 63R applies, means the chief officer of police for the police area—

(a) in which the material concerned was taken, or

(b) in the case of a DNA profile, in which the sample from which the DNA profile was derived was taken;

'section 63D material' means fingerprints or DNA profiles to which section 63D applies;]

...

(1A)–(3) *****

65A *****

[65B 'Persons convicted of an offence']

[(1) For the purposes of this Part, any reference to a person who is convicted of an offence includes a reference to—

(a) a person who has been given a caution in respect of the offence which, at the time of the caution, the person has admitted,

(b) a person who has been warned or reprimanded under section 65 of the Crime and Disorder Act 1998 for the offence,

(c) a person who has been found not guilty of the offence by reason of insanity, or

(d) a person who has been found to be under a disability and to have done the act charged in respect of the offence.

(2) This Part, so far as it relates to persons convicted of an offence, has effect despite anything in the Rehabilitation of Offenders Act 1974.

(3) But a person is not to be treated as having been convicted of an offence if that conviction is a disregarded conviction or caution by virtue of section 92 of the Protection of Freedoms Act 2012.

(4) If a person is convicted of more than one offence arising out of a single course of action, those convictions are to be treated as a single conviction for the purposes of calculating under sections 63F, 63H and 63N whether the person has been convicted of only one offence.]

(5) *****

PART VI CODES OF PRACTICE—GENERAL

66 Codes of practice

(1) The Secretary of State shall issue codes of practice in connection with—

    (a) the exercise by police officers of statutory powers—

        (i)   to search a person without first arresting him; ...

        (ii) to search a vehicle without making an arrest; [or

        (iii) to arrest a person;]

    (b) the detention, treatment, questioning and indication of persons by police officers;

    (c) searches of premises by police officers; and

    (d) the seizure of property found by police officers on persons or premises.

[(2) Codes shall (in particular) include provisions in connection with the exercise by police officers of powers under section 63B, above.]

[(3) Nothing in this section requires the Secretary of State to issue a code of practice in relation to any matter falling within the code of practice issued under section 47AB(2) of the Terrorism Act 2000 (as that code is altered or replaced from time to time) (code of practice in relation to terrorism powers to search persons and vehicles and to stop and search in specified locations).]

67 Codes of practice—supplementary

[(1) In this section, 'code' means a code of practice under section 60, 60A or 66.]

(2) The Secretary of State may at any time revise the whole or any part of a code.

(3) A code may be made, or revised, so as to—

    (a) apply only in relation to one or more specified areas,

    (b) have effect only for a specified period,

    (c) apply only in relation to specified offences or descriptions of offender.

(4) Before issuing a code, or any revision of a code, the Secretary of State must consult—

    [[(a) such persons as appear to the Secretary of State to represent the views of police and crime commissioners,

    (aa) the Mayor's Office for Policing and Crime,

    (ab) the Common Council of the City of London,]

    [(b) the National Police Chiefs' Council,]

    (c) the General Council of the Bar,

    (d) the Law Society of England and Wales,

    (e) the Institute of Legal Executives, and

    (f) such other persons as he thinks fit.

[(4A) The duty to consult under subsection (4) does not apply to a revision of a code where the Secretary of State considers that—

    (a) the revision is necessary in consequence of legislation, and

    (b) the Secretary of State has no discretion as to the nature of the revision.

(4B) Where, in consequence of subsection (4A), a revision of a code is issued without prior consultation with the persons mentioned in subsection (4), the Secretary of State must (at the same time as issuing the revision) publish a statement that, in his or her opinion, paragraphs (a) and (b) of subsection (4A) apply to the revision.

(4C) In subsection (4A), 'legislation' means any provision of—

    (a) an Act,

    (b) subordinate legislation within the meaning of the Interpretation Act 1978.]

(5) A code, or a revision of a code, does not come into operation until the Secretary of State by order so provides.

(6) The power conferred by subsection (5) is exercisable by statutory instrument.

(7) An order bringing a code into operation may not be made unless a draft of the order has been laid before Parliament and approved by a resolution of each House.]

(7A)–(7D) *****

(8) ...

(9) Persons other than police officers who are charged with the duty of investigating offences or charging offenders shall in the discharge of that duty have regard to any relevant provision of ... a code.

[(9A) Persons on whom powers are conferred by—

(a) any designation under section 38 or 39 of the Police Reform Act 2002 (c. 30) (police powers for [civilian staff] [and volunteers]), or

(b) any accreditation under section 41 of that Act (accreditation under community safety accreditation schemes),

shall have regard to any relevant provision of a code ... in the exercise or performance of the powers and duties conferred or imposed on them by that designation or accreditation.]

(10) A failure on the part—

(a) of a police office to comply with any provision of ... a code; ...

(b) of any person other than a police officer who is charged with the duty of investigating offences or charging offenders to have regard to any relevant provision of ... a code in the discharge of that duty, [or

(c) of a person designated under section 38 or 39 or accredited under section 41 of the Police Reform Act 2002 (c. 30) to have regard to any relevant provision of ... a code in the exercise or performance of the powers and duties conferred or imposed on him by that designation or accreditation,]

shall not of itself render him liable to any criminal or civil proceedings.

(11) In all criminal and civil proceedings any ... code shall be admissible in evidence; and if any provision of ... a code appears to the court or tribunal conducting the proceedings to be relevant to any question arising in the proceedings it shall be taken into account in determining that question.

[(12), (13)] *****

68 ...

69–72 *****

PART VIII EVIDENCE IN CRIMINAL PROCEEDINGS—GENERAL

*****

Confessions

76 Confessions

(1) In any proceedings a confession made by an accused person may be given in evidence against him in so far as it is relevant to any matter in issue in the proceedings and is not excluded by the court in pursuance of this section.

(2) If, in any proceedings where the prosecution proposes to give in evidence a confession made by an accused person, it is represented to the court that the confession was or may have been obtained—

(a) by oppression of the person who made it; or

(b) in consequence of anything said or done which was likely, in the circumstances existing at the time, to render unreliable any confession which might be made by him in consequence thereof,

the court shall not allow the confession to be given in evidence against him except in so far as the prosecution proves to the court beyond reasonable doubt that the confession (notwithstanding that it may be true) was not obtained as aforesaid.

(3) In any proceedings where the prosecution proposes to give in evidence a confession made by an accused person, the court may of its own motion require the prosecution, as a condition of allowing it to do so, to prove that the confession was not obtained as mentioned in subsection (2) above.

(4) The fact that a confession is wholly or partly excluded in pursuance of this section shall not affect the admissibility in evidence—

(a) of any facts discovered as a result of the confession; or

(b) where the confession is relevant as showing that the accused speaks, writes or expresses himself in a particular way, of so much of the confession as is necessary to show that he does so.

(5) Evidence that a fact to which this subsection applies was discovered as a result of a statement made by an accused person shall not be admissible unless evidence of how it was discovered is given by him or on his behalf.

(6) Subsection (5) above applies—

(a) to any fact discovered as a result of a confession which is wholly excluded in pursuance of this section; and

(b) to any fact discovered as a result of a confession which is partly so excluded, if that fact is discovered as a result of the excluded part of the confession.

(7) Nothing in Part VII of this Act shall prejudice the admissibility of a confession made by an accused person.

(8) In this section 'oppression' includes torture, inhuman or degrading treatment, and the use or threat of violence (whether or not amounting to torture).

(9) …

[76A   Confessions may be given in evidence for co-accused

(1) In any proceedings a confession made by an accused person may be given in evidence for another person charged in the same proceedings (a co-accused) in so far as it is relevant to any matter in issue in the proceedings and is not excluded by the court in pursuance of this section.]

(2)–(7) *****

77   Confessions by mentally handicapped persons

(1) Without prejudice to the general duty of the court at a trial on indictment [with a jury] to direct the jury on any matter on which it appears to the court appropriate to do so, where at such a trial—

(a) the case against the accused depends wholly or substantially on a confession by him; and

(b) the court is satisfied—

(i)   that he is mentally handicapped; and

(ii)   that the confession was not made in the presence of an independent person,

the court shall warn the jury that there is special need for caution before convicting the accused in reliance on the confession, and shall explain that the need arises because of the circumstances mentioned in paragraphs (a) and (b) above.

(2) In any case where at the summary trial of a person for an offence it appears to the court that a warning under subsection (1) above would be required if the trial were on indictment [with a jury], the court shall treat the case as one in which there is a special need for caution before convicting the accused on his confession.

(2A), (3) *****

Miscellaneous

78   Exclusion of unfair evidence

(1) In any proceedings the court may refuse to allow evidence on which the prosecution proposes to rely to be given if it appears to the court that, having regard to all the circumstances, including the circumstances in which the evidence was obtained, the admission of the evidence would have such an adverse effect on the fairness of the proceedings that the court ought not to admit it.

(2) Nothing in this section shall prejudice any rule of law requiring a court to exclude evidence.

(3) …

79–81 *****

PART VIII SUPPLEMENTARY

82 Part VIII—interpretation

(1) In this Part of this Act—

'confession' includes any statement wholly or partly adverse to the person who made it, whether made to a person in authority or not and whether made in words or otherwise;

*****

83–106 ...

PART XI MISCELLANEOUS AND SUPPLEMENTARY

107, 111, 113–115 *****

108–110, 112, 116 ...

117 Power of constable to use reasonable force

Where any provision of this Act—

(a) confers a power on a constable; and

(b) does not provide that the power may only be exercised with the consent of some person, other than a police officer,

the officer may use reasonable force, if necessary, in the exercise of the power.

*****

Section 9   # SCHEDULE 1

SPECIAL PROCEDURE

Making of orders by [judge]

1. If on an application made by a constable a [judge] is satisfied that one or other of the sets of access conditions is fulfilled, he may make an order under paragraph 4 below.

2. The first set of access conditions is fulfilled if—

(a) there are reasonable grounds for believing—

(i) that [an indictable offence] has been committed;

(ii) that there is material which consists of special procedure material or includes special procedure material and does not also include excluded material on premises specified in the application [, or on premises occupied or controlled by a person specified in the application (including all such premises on which there are reasonable grounds for believing that there is such material as it is reasonably practicable so to specify)];

(iii) that the material is likely to be of substantial value (whether by itself or together with other material) to the investigation in connection with which the application is made; and

(iv) that the material is likely to be relevant evidence;

(b) other methods of obtaining the material—

(i) have been tried without success; or

(ii) have not been tried because it appeared that they were bound to fail; and

(c) it is in the public interest, having regard—

(i) to the benefit likely to accrue to the investigation if the material is obtained; and

(ii) to the circumstances under which the person in possession of the material holds it, that the material should be produced or that access to it should be given.

3. The second set of access conditions is fulfilled if—

    (a) there are reasonable grounds for believing that there is material which consists of or includes excluded material or special procedure material on premises specified in the application [, or on premises occupied or controlled by a person specified in the application (including all such premises on which there are reasonable grounds for believing that there is such material as it is reasonably practicable so to specify)];

    (b) but for section 9(2) above a search of [such premises] for that material could have been authorised by the issue of a warrant to a constable under an enactment other than this Schedule; and

    (c) the issue of such a warrant would have been appropriate.

4. An order under this paragraph is an order that the person who appears to the [judge] to be in possession of the material to which the application relates shall—

    [(a) produce it to a constable for him to take away; or]

    (b) give a constable access to it,

not later than the end of the period of seven days from the date of the order or the end of such longer period as the order may specify.

5. Where the material consists of information [stored in any electronic form]—

    (a) an order under paragraph 4(a) above shall have effect as an order to produce the material in a form in which it can be taken away and in which it is visible and legible [or from which it can readily be produced in a visible and legible form]; and

    (b) an order under paragraph 4(b) above shall have effect as an order to give a constable access to the material in a form in which it is visible and legible.

6. For the purposes of sections 21 and 22 above material produced in pursuance of an order under paragraph 4(a) above shall be treated as if it were material seized by a constable.

7.–11. *****

Issue of warrants by [judge]

12. If on an application made by a constable a [judge]—

    (a) is satisfied—

        (i) that either set of access conditions is fulfilled; and

        (ii) that any of the further conditions set out in paragraph 14 below is also fulfilled [in relation to each set of premises specified in the application]; or

    (b) is satisfied—

        (i) that the second set of access conditions is fulfilled; and

        (ii) that an order under paragraph 4 above relating to the material has not been complied with,

he may issue a warrant authorising a constable to enter and search the premises [or (as the case may be) all premises occupied or controlled by the person referred to in paragraph 2(a)(ii) or 3(a), including such sets of premises as are specified in the application (an 'all premises warrant')].

12A *****

13. A constable may seize and retain anything for which a search has been authorised under paragraph 12 above.

14. The further conditions mentioned in paragraph 12(a)(ii) above are—

    (a) that it is not practicable to communicate with any person entitled to grant entry to the premises…;

    (b) that it is practicable to communicate with a person entitled to grant entry to the premises but it is not practicable to communicate with any person entitled to grant access to the material;

    (c) that the material contains information which—

        (i) is subject to a restriction or obligation such as is mentioned in section 11(2)(b) above; and

        (ii) is likely to be disclosed in breach of it if a warrant is not issued;

    (d) that service of notice of an application for an order under paragraph 4 above may seriously prejudice the investigation.

15.—(1) If a person fails to comply with an order under paragraph 4 above, a [judge] may deal with him as if he had committed a contempt of the Crown Court.

(2) Any enactment relating to contempt of the Crown Court shall have effect in relation to such a failure as if it were such a contempt.

[15A.]–17. *****

*****

Prosecution of Offences Act 1985

(1985, c. 23)

An Act to provide for the establishment of a Crown Prosecution Service for England and Wales; to make provision as to costs in criminal cases; to provide for the imposition of time limits in relation to preliminary stages of criminal proceedings; to amend section 42 of the Supreme Court Act 1981 and section 3 of the Children and Young Persons Act 1969; to make provision with respect to consents to prosecutions; to re-peal section 9 of the Perjury Act 1911; and for connected purposes.   [23rd May 1985]

Territorial extent: England and Wales

PART I THE CROWN PROSECUTION SERVICE

Constitution and functions of Service

1   The Crown Prosecution Service

(1) There shall be a prosecuting service for England and Wales (to be known as the 'Crown Prosecution Service') consisting of—

   (a) the Director of Public Prosecutions, who shall be head of the Service;
   (b) the Chief Crown Prosecutors, designated under subsection (4) below, each of whom shall be the member of the Service responsible to the Director for supervising the operation of the service in his area; and
   (c) the other staff appointed by the Director under this section.

(2) The Director shall appoint such staff for the Service as, with the approval of the Treasury as to numbers, remuneration and other terms and conditions of service, he considers necessary for the discharge of his functions.

(3) The Director may designate any member of the Service [who has a general qualification (within the meaning of section 71 of the Courts and Legal Services Act 1990)] for the purposes of this subsection, and any person so designated shall be known as a Crown Prosecutor.

(4) The Director shall divide England and Wales into areas and, for each of those areas, designate a Crown Prosecutor for the purposes of this subsection and any person so designated shall be known as a Chief Crown Prosecutor.

(5) The Director may, from time to time, vary the division of England and Wales made for the purpose of subsection (4) above.

(6) Without prejudice to any functions which may have been assigned to him in his capacity as a member of the Service, every Crown Prosecutor shall have all the powers of the Director as to the institution and conduct of proceedings but shall exercise those powers under the direction of the Director.

(7) There any enactment (whenever passed)—

   (a) prevents any step from being taken without the consent of the Director or without his consent or the consent of another; or
   (b) requires any step to be taken by or in relation to the Director; any consent given by or, as the case may be, step taken by or in relation to, a Crown Prosecutor shall be treated, for the purposes of that enactment, as given by or, as the case may be, taken by or in relation to the Director.

2   The Director of Public Prosecutions

(1) The Director of Public Prosecutions shall be appointed by the Attorney General.

(2) The Director must be a [person who has a 10 year general qualification, within the meaning of section 71 of the Courts and Legal Services Act 1990.]

(3) *****

3   Functions of the Director

(1) The Director shall discharge his functions under this or any other enactment under the superintendence of the Attorney General.

(2) It shall be the duty of the Director [, subject to any provisions contained in the Criminal Justice Act 1987]—

(a)   to take over the conduct of all criminal proceedings, other than specified proceedings, instituted on behalf of a police force (whether by a member of that force or by any other person);

[(aa) to take over the conduct of any criminal proceedings instituted by an immigration officer (as defined for the purposes of the Immigration Act 1971) acting in his capacity as such an officer;]

[(ab) to take over the conduct of any criminal proceedings instituted in England and Wales by the Revenue and Customs;]

[(ac) to take over the conduct of any criminal proceedings instituted on behalf of the National Crime Agency;]

(b)   to institute and have the conduct of criminal proceedings in any case where it appears to him that—

(i)   the importance or difficulty of the case makes it appropriate that proceedings should be instituted by him; or

(ii)   it is otherwise appropriate for proceedings to be instituted by him;

[(ba) to institute and have the conduct of any criminal proceedings in any case where the proceedings relate to the subject matter of a report a copy of which has been sent to him under paragraph 23 or 24 of Schedule 3 to the Police Reform Act 2002 (reports or investigations into conduct of persons serving with the police);]

[(bb) where it appears to him appropriate to do so, to institute and have the conduct of any criminal proceedings in England and Wales relating to a criminal investigation by the Revenue and Customs;]

[(bc) where it appears to him appropriate to do so, to institute and have the conduct of any criminal proceedings relating to a criminal investigation by the National Crime Agency;]

(c)   to take over the conduct of all binding over proceedings instituted on behalf of a police force (whether by a member of that force or by any other person);

*****

(g)   to discharge such other functions as may from time to time be assigned to him by the Attorney General in pursuance of this paragraph.

(2A), (3), (4) *****

4   ...

5   *****

6   Prosecutions instituted and conducted otherwise than by the Service

(1) Subject to subsection (2) below, nothing in this Part shall preclude any person from instituting any criminal proceedings or conducting any criminal proceedings to which the Director's duty to take over the conduct of proceedings does not apply.

(2) Where criminal proceedings are instituted in circumstances in which the Director is not under a duty to take over their conduct, he may nevertheless do so at any stage.

7–9   *****

10   Guidelines for Crown Prosecutors

(1) The Director shall issue a Code for Crown Prosecutors giving guidance on general principles to be applied by them—

    (a) in determining, in any case—

        (i)   whether proceedings for an offence should be instituted or, where proceedings have been instituted, whether they should be discontinued; or

        (ii) what charges should be preferred; and

    (b) in considering, in any case, representations to be made by them to any magistrates' court about the mode of trial suitable for that case.

(2) The Director may from time to time make alterations in the Code.

(3) The provisions of the Code shall be set out in the Director's report under section 9 of this Act for the year in which the Code is issued; and any alteration in the Code shall be set out in his report under that section for the year in which the alteration is made.

*****

Public Order Act 1986

(1986, c. 64)

An Act to abolish the common law offences of riot, rout, unlawful assembly and affray and certain statutory offences relating to public order; to create new offences relating to public order; to control public processions and assemblies; to control the stirring up of racial hatred; to provide for the exclusion of certain offenders from sporting events; to create a new offence relating to the contamination of or interference with goods; to confer power to direct certain trespassers to leave land; to amend section 7 of the Conspiracy and Protection of Property Act 1875, section 1 of the Prevention of Crime Act 1953, Part V of the Criminal Justice (Scotland) Act 1980 and the Sporting Events (Control of Alcohol etc) Act 1985; to repeal certain obsolete or unnecessary enactments; and for connected purposes.   [7th November 1986]

Territorial extent: England and Wales (ss. 1–9, 13, 29A–N, 39, 40(4)); England and Wales, Scotland (remainder)

PART I   NEW OFFENCES

1   Riot

(1) Where 12 or more persons who are present together use or threaten unlawful violence for a common purpose and the conduct of them (taken together) is such as would cause a person of reasonable firmness present at the scene to fear for his personal safety, each of the persons using unlawful violence for the common purpose is guilty of riot.

(2) It is immaterial whether or not the 12 or more use or threaten unlawful violence simultaneously.

(3) The common purpose may be inferred from conduct.

(4) No person of reasonable firmness need actually be, or be likely to be, present at the scene.

(5) Riot may be committed in private as well as in public places.

(6) A person guilty of riot is liable on conviction on indictment to imprisonment for a term not exceeding ten years or a fine or both.

2   Violent disorder

(1) Where 3 or more persons who are present together use or threaten unlawful violence and the conduct of them (taken together) is such as would cause a person of reasonable firmness present

at the scene to fear for his personal safety, each of the persons using or threatening unlawful violence is guilty of violent disorder.

(2) It is immaterial whether or not the 3 or more use or threaten unlawful violence simultaneously.

(3) No person of reasonable firmness need actually be, or be likely to be, present at the scene.

(4) Violent disorder may be committed in private as well as in public places.

(5) A person guilty of violent disorder is liable on conviction on indictment to imprisonment for a term not exceeding 5 years or a fine or both, or on summary conviction to imprisonment for a term not exceeding 6 months or a fine not exceeding the statutory maximum or both.

3 Affray

(1) A person is guilty of affray if he uses or threatens unlawful violence towards another and his conduct is such as would cause a person of reasonable firmness present at the scene to fear for his personal safety.

(2) Where 2 or more persons use or threaten the unlawful violence, it is the conduct of them taken together that must be considered for the purposes of subsection (1).

(3) For the purposes of this section a threat cannot be made by the use of words alone.

(4) No person of reasonable firmness need actually be, or be likely to be, present at the scene.

(5) Affray may be committed in private as well as in public places.

(6) ...

(7) A person guilty of affray is liable on conviction on indictment to imprisonment for a term not exceeding 3 years or a fine or both, or on summary conviction to imprisonment for a term not exceeding 6 months or a fine not exceeding the statutory maximum or both.

4 Fear or provocation of violence

(1) A person is guilty of an offence if he—

(a) uses towards another person threatening, abusive or insulting words or behaviour, or

(b) distributes or displays to another person any writing, sign or other visible representation which is threatening, abusive or insulting,

with intent to cause that person to believe that immediate unlawful violence will be used against him or another by any person, or to provoke the immediate use of unlawful violence by that person or another, or whereby that person is likely to believe that such violence will be used or it is likely that such violence will be provoked.

(2) An offence under this section may be committed in a public or a private place, except that no offence is committed where the words or behaviour are used, or the writing, sign or other visible representation is distributed or displayed, by a person inside a dwelling and the other person is also inside that or another dwelling.

(3) ...

(4) A person guilty of an offence under this section is liable on summary conviction to imprisonment for a term not exceeding 6 months or a fine not exceeding level 5 on the standard scale or both.

[4A Intentional harassment, alarm or distress

(1) A person is guilty of an offence if, with intent to cause a person harassment, alarm or distress, he—

(a) uses threatening, abusive or insulting words or behaviour, or disorderly behaviour, or

(b) displays any writing, sign or other visible representation which is threatening, abusive or insulting,

thereby causing that or another person harassment, alarm or distress.

(2) An offence under this section may be committed in a public or a private place, except that no offence is committed where the words or behaviour are used, or the writing, sign or other visible representation is displayed, by a person inside a dwelling and the person who is harassed, alarmed or distressed is also inside that or another dwelling.

(3) It is a defence for the accused to prove—

    (a) that he was inside a dwelling and had no reason to believe that the words or behaviour used, or the writing, sign or other visible representation displayed, would be heard or seen by a person outside that or any other dwelling, or

    (b) that his conduct was reasonable.

(4) ...

(5) A person guilty of an offence under this section is liable on summary conviction to imprisonment for a term not exceeding 6 months or a fine not exceeding level 5 on the standard scale or both.]

5   Harassment, alarm or distress

(1) A person is guilty of an offence if he—

    (a) uses threatening [or abusive] words or behaviour, or disorderly behaviour, or

    (b) displays any writing, sign or other visible representation which is threatening [or abusive],

within the hearing or sight of a person likely to be caused harassment, alarm or distress thereby.

(2) An offence under this section may be committed in a public or a private place, except that no offence is committed where the words or behaviour are used, or the writing, sign or other visible representation is displayed, by a person inside a dwelling and the other person is also inside that or another dwelling.

(3) It is a defence for the accused to prove—

    (a) that he had no reason to believe that there was any person within hearing or sight who was likely to be caused harassment, alarm or distress, or

    (b) that he was inside a dwelling and had no reason to believe that the words or behaviour used, or the writing, sign or other visible representation displayed, would be heard or seen by a person outside that or any other dwelling, or

    (c) that his conduct was reasonable.

(4), (5) ...

(6) A person guilty of an offence under this section is liable on summary conviction to a fine not exceeding level 3 on the standard scale.

6   Mental element: miscellaneous

(1) A person is guilty of riot only if he intends to use violence or is aware that his conduct may be violent.

(2) A person is guilty of violent disorder or affray only if he intends to use or threaten violence or is aware that his conduct may be violent or threaten violence.

(3) A person is guilty of an offence under section 4 only if he intends his words or behaviour, or the writing, sign or other visible representation, to be threatening, abusive or insulting, or is aware that it may be threatening, abusive or insulting.

(4) A person is guilty of an offence under section 5 only if he intends his words or behaviour, or the writing, sign or other visible representation, to be threatening [or abusive], or is aware that it may be threatening [or abusive] or (as the case may be) he intends his behaviour to be or is aware that it may be disorderly.

(5) For the purposes of this section a person whose awareness is impaired by intoxication shall be taken to be aware of that of which he would be aware if not intoxicated, unless he shows either that his intoxication was not self-induced or that it was caused solely by the taking or administration of a substance in the course of medical treatment.

(6) In subsection (5) 'intoxication' means any intoxication, whether caused by drink, drugs or other means, or by a combination of means.

(7) Subsections (1) and (2) do not affect the determination for the purposes of riot or violent disorder of the number of persons who use or threaten violence.

7   Procedure: miscellaneous

(1) No prosecution for an offence of riot or incitement to riot may be instituted except by or with the consent of the Director of Public Prosecutions.

(2)–(4) *****

8 Interpretation
In this Part—
   'dwelling' means any structure or part of a structure occupied as a person's home or as other living accommodation (whether the occupation is separate or shared with others) but does not include any part not so occupied, and for this purpose 'structure' includes a tent, caravan, vehicle, vessel or other temporary or movable structure;
   'violence' means any violent conduct, so that—
   (a) except in the context of affray, it includes violent conduct towards property as well as violent conduct towards persons, and
   (b) it is not restricted to conduct causing or intended to cause injury or damage but includes any other violent conduct (for example, throwing at or towards a person a missile of a kind capable of causing injury which does not hit or falls short).

9 Offences abolished
(1) The Common Law offences of riot, rout, unlawful assembly and affray are abolished.
(2) ...

10 ...

PART II PROCESSIONS AND ASSEMBLIES

11 Advance notice of public processions
(1) Written notice shall be given in accordance with this section of any proposal to hold a public procession intended—
   (a) to demonstrate support for or opposition to the views or actions of any person or body of persons,
   (b) to publicise a cause or campaign, or
   (c) to mark or commemorate an event, unless it is not reasonably practicable to give any advance notice of the procession.
(2) Subsection (1) does not apply where the procession is one commonly or customarily held in the police area (or areas) in which it is proposed to be held or is a funeral procession organised by a funeral director acting in the normal course of his business.
(3) The notice must specify the date when it is intended to hold the procession, the time when it is intended to start it, its proposed route, and the name and address of the person (or of one of the persons) proposing to organise it.
(4) Notice must be delivered to a police station—
   (a) in the police area in which it is proposed the procession will start, or
   (b) where it is proposed the procession will start in Scotland and cross into England, in the first police area in England on the proposed route.
(5), (6) *****
(7) Where a public procession is held, each of the persons organising it is guilty of an offence if—
   (a) the requirements of this section as to notice have not been satisfied, or
   (b) the date when it is held, the time when it starts, or its route, differs from the date, time or route specified in the notice.
(8) It is a defence for the accused to prove that he did not know of, and neither suspected nor had reason to suspect, the failure to satisfy the requirements or (as the case may be) the difference of date, time or route.
(9) To the extent that an alleged offence turns on a difference of date, time or route, it is a defence for the accused to prove that the difference arose from circumstances beyond his control or from something done with the agreement of a police officer or by his direction.

(10) A person guilty of an offence under subsection (7) is liable on summary conviction to a fine not exceeding level 3 on the standard scale.

12   Imposing conditions on public processions

(1) If the senior police officer, having regard to the time or place at which and the circumstances in which any public procession is being held or is intended to be held and to its route or proposed route, reasonably believes that—

(a)   it may result in serious public disorder, serious damage to property or serious disruption to the life of the community,

[(aa) in the case of a procession in England and Wales, the noise generated by persons taking part in the procession may result in serious disruption to the activities of an organisation which are carried on in the vicinity of the procession,

(ab) in the case of a procession in England and Wales—

(i)   the noise generated by persons taking part in the procession may have a relevant impact on persons in the vicinity of the procession, and

(ii) that impact may be significant, or]

(b)   the purpose of the persons organising it is the intimidation of others with a view to compelling them not to do an act they have a right to do, or to do an act they have a right not to do,

he may give directions imposing on the persons organising or taking part in the procession such conditions as appear to him necessary to prevent such disorder, damage, disruption[, impact] or intimidation, including conditions as to the route of the procession or prohibiting it from entering any public place specified in the directions.

(2) In subsection (1) 'the senior police officer' means—

(a) in relation to a procession being held, or to a procession intended to be held in a case where persons are assembling with a view to taking part in it, the most senior in rank of the police officers present at the scene, and

(b) in relation to a procession intended to be held in a case where paragraph (a) does not apply, the chief officer of police.

[(2A) For the purposes of subsection (1)(a), the cases in which a public procession in England and Wales may result in serious disruption to the life of the community include, in particular, where—

(a) it may result in a significant delay to the delivery of a time-sensitive product to consumers of that product, or

(b) it may result in a prolonged disruption of access to any essential goods or any essential service, including, in particular, access to—

(i)   the supply of money, food, water, energy or fuel,

(ii) a system of communication,

(iii) a place of worship,

(iv) a transport facility,

(v)   an educational institution, or

(vi) a service relating to health.

(2B) In subsection (2A)(a) 'time-sensitive product' means a product whose value or use to its consumers may be significantly reduced by a delay in the supply of the product to them.

(2C) For the purposes of subsection (1)(aa), the cases in which the noise generated by persons taking part in a public procession may result in serious disruption to the activities of an organisation which are carried on in the vicinity of the procession include, in particular, where it may result in persons connected with the organisation not being reasonably able, for a prolonged period of time, to carry on in that vicinity the activities or any one of them.

(2D) For the purposes of subsection (1)(ab)(i), the noise generated by persons taking part in a public procession may have a relevant impact on persons in the vicinity of the procession if—

(a) it may result in the intimidation or harassment of persons of reasonable firmness with the characteristics of persons likely to be in the vicinity, or

(b) it may cause such persons to suffer alarm or distress.

(2E) In considering for the purposes of subsection (1)(ab)(ii) whether the noise generated by persons taking part in a public procession may have a significant impact on persons in the vicinity of the procession, the senior police officer must have regard to—

    (a) the likely number of persons of the kind mentioned in paragraph (a) of subsection (2D) who may experience an impact of the kind mentioned in paragraph (a) or (b) of that subsection,

    (b) the likely duration of that impact on such persons, and

    (c) the likely intensity of that impact on such persons.]

(3) A direction given by a chief officer of police by virtue of subsection (2)(b) shall be given in writing.

(4) [Subject to subsection (5A), a person] who organises a public procession and…fails to comply with a condition imposed under this section is guilty of an offence, but it is a defence for him to prove that the failure arose from circumstances beyond his control.

(5) [Subject to subsection (5A), a person] who takes part in a public procession and…fails to comply with a condition imposed under this section is guilty of an offence, but it is a defence for him to prove that the failure arose from circumstances beyond his control.

[(5A) A person is guilty of an offence under subsection (4) or (5) only if—

    (a) in the case of a public procession in England and Wales, at the time the person fails to comply with the condition the person knows or ought to know that the condition has been imposed;

    (b) in the case of a public procession in Scotland, the person knowingly fails to comply with the condition.]

(6) A person who incites another to commit an offence under subsection (5) is guilty of an offence.

(7) …

[(8) A person guilty of an offence under subsection (4) is liable on summary conviction—

    (a) in the case of a public procession in England and Wales, to imprisonment for a term not exceeding 51 weeks or a fine not exceeding level 4 on the standard scale or both;

    (b) in the case of a public procession in Scotland, to imprisonment for a term not exceeding 3 months or a fine not exceeding level 4 on the standard scale or both.

(9) A person guilty of an offence under subsection (5) is liable on summary conviction—

    (a) in the case of a public procession in England and Wales, to a fine not exceeding level 4 on the standard scale;

    (b) in the case of a public procession in Scotland, to a fine not exceeding level 3 on the standard scale.

(10) A person guilty of an offence under subsection (6) is liable on summary conviction—

    (a) in the case of a public procession in England and Wales, to imprisonment for a term not exceeding 51 weeks or a fine not exceeding level 4 on the standard scale or both;

    (b) in the case of a public procession in Scotland, to imprisonment for a term not exceeding 3 months or a fine not exceeding level 4 on the standard scale or both.

(10A) In relation to an offence committed before the coming into force of section 281(5) of the Criminal Justice Act 2003 (alteration of penalties for certain summary offences: England and Wales), the references in subsections (8)(a) and to (10)(a) to 51 weeks are to be read as references to 6 months.]

(11) In Scotland this section applies only in relation to a procession being held, and to a procession intended to be held in a case where persons are assembling with a view to taking part in it.

[(12) The Secretary of State may by regulations amend any of subsections (2A) to (2C) for the purposes of making provision about the meaning for the purposes of this section of—

    (a) serious disruption to the activities of an organisation which are carried on in the vicinity of a public procession, or

    (b) serious disruption to the life of the community.

(13) Regulations under subsection (12) may, in particular, amend any of those subsections for the purposes of—

    (a) defining any aspect of an expression mentioned in subsection (12)(a) or (b) for the purposes of this section;

(b) giving examples of cases in which a public procession is or is not to be treated as resulting in—

    (i) serious disruption to the activities of an organisation which are carried on in the vicinity of the procession, or

    (ii) serious disruption to the life of the community.

(14) Regulations under subsection (12)—

(a) are to be made by statutory instrument;

(b) may apply only in relation to public processions in England and Wales;

(c) may make incidental, supplementary, consequential, transitional, transitory or saving provision, including provision which makes consequential amendments to this Part.

(15) A statutory instrument containing regulations under subsection (12) may not be made unless a draft of the instrument has been laid before and approved by a resolution of each House of Parliament.]

13   Prohibiting public processions

(1) If at any time the chief officer of police reasonably believes that, because of particular circumstances existing in any district or part of a district, the powers under section 12 will not be sufficient to prevent the holding of public processions in that district or part from resulting in serious public disorder, he shall apply to the council of the district for an order prohibiting for such period not exceeding 3 months as may be specified in the application the holding of all public processions (or of any class of public procession so specified) in the district or part concerned.

(2) On receiving such an application, a council may with the consent of the Secretary of State make an order either in the terms of the application or with such modifications as may be approved by the Secretary of State.

(3) Subsection (1) does not apply in the City of London or the metropolitan police district.

(4) If at any time the Commissioner of Police for the City of London or the Commissioner of Police of the Metropolis reasonably believes that, because of particular circumstances existing in his police area or part of it, the powers under section 12 will not be sufficient to prevent the holding of public processions in that area or part from resulting in serious public disorder, he may with the consent of the Secretary of State make an order prohibiting for such period not exceeding 3 months as may be specified in the order the holding of all public processions (or of any class of public procession so specified) in the area or part concerned.

(5) An order made under this section may be revoked or varied by a subsequent order made in the same way, that is, in accordance with subsections (1) and (2) or subsection (4), as the case may be.

(6) An order under this section shall, if not made in writing, be recorded in writing as soon as practicable after being made.

(7) A person who organises a public procession the holding of which he knows is prohibited by virtue of an order under this section is guilty of an offence.

(8) A person who takes part in a public procession the holding of which he knows is prohibited by virtue of an order under this section is guilty of an offence.

(9) A person who incites another to commit an offence under subsection (8) is guilty of an offence.

(10) ...

(11) A person guilty of an offence under subsection (7) is liable on summary conviction to imprisonment for a term not exceeding 3 months or a fine not exceeding level 4 on the standard scale or both.

(12) A person guilty of an offence under subsection (8) is liable on summary conviction to a fine not exceeding level 3 on the standard scale.

(13) A person guilty of an offence under subsection (9) is liable on summary conviction to imprisonment for a term not exceeding 3 months or a fine not exceeding level 4 on the standard scale or both ...

14   Imposing conditions on public assemblies

(1) [Subsection (1A) applies if] the senior police officer, having regard to the time or place at which and the circumstances in which any public assembly is being held or is intended to be held, reasonably believes that—

(a)　it may result in serious public disorder, serious damage to property or serious disruption to the life of the community, or

[(aa)　in the case of an assembly in England and Wales, the noise generated by persons taking part in the assembly may result in serious disruption to the activities of an organisation which are carried on in the vicinity of the assembly,

(ab)　in the case of an assembly in England and Wales—

(i)　the noise generated by persons taking part in the assembly may have a relevant impact on persons in the vicinity of the assembly, and

(ii)　that impact may be significant, or]

(b)　the purpose of the persons organising it is the intimidation of others with a view to compelling them not to do an act they have a right to do, or to do an act they have a right not to do,

…

[(1A) The senior police officer may give directions imposing on the persons organising or taking part in the assembly—

(a)　in the case of an assembly in England and Wales, such conditions as appear to the officer necessary to prevent the disorder, damage, disruption, impact or intimidation mentioned in subsection (1);

(b)　in the case of an assembly in Scotland, such conditions as to the place at which the assembly may be (or continue to be) held, its maximum duration, or the maximum number of persons who may constitute it, as appear to the officer necessary to prevent the disorder, damage, disruption or intimidation mentioned in subsection (1)(a) or (b).]

(2)　In [this section] 'the senior police officer' means—

(a)　in relation to an assembly being held, the most senior in rank of the police officers present at the scene, and

(b)　in relation to an assembly intended to be held, the chief officer of police.

[(2A) For the purposes of subsection (1)(a), the cases in which a public assembly in England and Wales may result in serious disruption to the life of the community include, in particular, where—

(a)　it may result in a significant delay to the supply of a time-sensitive product to consumers of that product, or

(b)　it may result in a prolonged disruption of access to any essential goods or any essential service, including, in particular, access to—

(i)　the supply of money, food, water, energy or fuel,

(ii)　a system of communication,

(iii)　a place of worship,

(iv)　a transport facility,

(v)　an educational institution, or

(vi)　a service relating to health.

(2B) In subsection (2A)(a) 'time-sensitive product' means a product whose value or use to its consumers may be significantly reduced by a delay in the supply of the product to them.

(2C) For the purposes of subsection (1)(aa), the cases in which the noise generated by persons taking part in a public assembly may result in serious disruption to the activities of an organisation which are carried on in the vicinity of the assembly include, in particular, where it may result in persons connected with the organisation not being reasonably able, for a prolonged period of time, to carry on in that vicinity the activities or any one of them.

(2D) For the purposes of subsection (1)(ab)(i), the noise generated by persons taking part in an assembly may have a relevant impact on persons in the vicinity of the assembly if—

(a)　it may result in the intimidation or harassment of persons of reasonable firmness with the characteristics of persons likely to be in the vicinity, or

(b)　it may cause such persons to suffer alarm or distress.

(2E) In considering for the purposes of subsection (1)(ab)(ii) whether the noise generated by persons taking part in an assembly may have a significant impact on persons in the vicinity of the assembly, the senior police officer must have regard to—

    (a) the likely number of persons of the kind mentioned in paragraph (a) of subsection (2D) who may experience an impact of the kind mentioned in paragraph (a) or (b) of that subsection,

    (b) the likely duration of that impact on such persons, and

    (c) the likely intensity of that impact on such persons.]

(3) A direction given by a chief officer of police by virtue of subsection (2)(b) shall be given in writing.

(4) [Subject to subsection (5A), a person] who organises a public assembly and . . . fails to comply with a condition imposed under this section is guilty of an offence, but it is a defence for him to prove that the failure arose from circumstances beyond his control.

(5) [Subject to subsection (5A), a person] who takes part in a public assembly and … fails to comply with a condition imposed under this section is guilty of an offence, but it is a defence for him to prove that the failure arose from circumstances beyond his control.

[(5A) A person is guilty of an offence under subsection (4) or (5) only if—

    (a) in the case of a public assembly in England and Wales, at the time the person fails to comply with the condition the person knows or ought to know that the condition has been imposed;

    (b) in the case of a public assembly in Scotland, the person knowingly fails to comply with the condition.]

(6) A person who incites another to commit an offence under subsection (5) is guilty of an offence.

(7) …

[(8) A person guilty of an offence under subsection (4) is liable on summary conviction—

    (a) in the case of a public assembly in England and Wales, to imprisonment for a term not exceeding 51 weeks or a fine not exceeding level 4 on the standard scale or both;

    (b) in the case of a public assembly in Scotland, to imprisonment for a term not exceeding 3 months or a fine not exceeding level 4 on the standard scale or both.

(9) A person guilty of an offence under subsection (5) is liable on summary conviction—

    (a) in the case of a public assembly in England and Wales, to a fine not exceeding level 4 on the standard scale;

    (b) in the case of a public assembly in Scotland, to a fine not exceeding level 3 on the standard scale.

(10) A person guilty of an offence under subsection (6) is liable on summary conviction—

    (a) in the case of a public assembly in England and Wales, to imprisonment for a term not exceeding 51 weeks or a fine not exceeding level 4 on the standard scale or both;

    (b) in the case of a public assembly in Scotland, to imprisonment for a term not exceeding 3 months or a fine not exceeding level 4 on the standard scale or both.

(10A) In relation to an offence committed before the coming into force of section 281(5) of the Criminal Justice Act 2003 (alteration of penalties for certain summary offences: England and Wales), the references in subsections (8)(a) and to (10)(a) to 51 weeks are to be read as references to 6 months.]

[(11) The Secretary of State may by regulations amend any of subsections (2A) to (2C) for the purposes of making provision about the meaning for the purposes of this section of—

    (a) serious disruption to the activities of an organisation which are carried on in the vicinity of a public assembly, or

    (b) serious disruption to the life of the community.

(12) Regulations under subsection (11) may, in particular, amend any of those subsections for the purposes of—

    (a) defining any aspect of an expression mentioned in subsection (11)(a) or (b) for the purposes of this section;

    (b) giving examples of cases in which a public assembly is or is not to be treated as resulting in—

(i)   serious disruption to the activities of an organisation which are carried on in the vicinity of the assembly, or

(ii) serious disruption to the life of the community.

(13) Regulations under subsection (11)—

(a) are to be made by statutory instrument;

(b) may apply only in relation to public assemblies in England and Wales;

(c) may make incidental, supplementary, consequential, transitional, transitory or saving provision, including provision which makes consequential amendments to this Part.

(14) A statutory instrument containing regulations under subsection (11) may not be made unless a draft of the instrument has been laid before and approved by a resolution of each House of Parliament.]

[14ZA   Imposing conditions on one-person protests]

[(1) Subsection (2) applies if the senior police officer, having regard to the time or place at which and the circumstances in which any one-person protest in England and Wales is being carried on or is intended to be carried on, reasonably believes—

(a) that the noise generated by the person carrying on the protest may result in serious disruption to the activities of an organisation which are carried on in the vicinity of the protest, or

(b) that—

(i)   the noise generated by the person carrying on the protest may have a relevant impact on persons in the vicinity of the protest, and

(ii) that impact may be significant.

(2) The senior police officer may give directions imposing on the person organising or carrying on the protest such conditions as appear to the officer necessary to prevent such disruption or impact.

(3) Where the one-person protest is moving, or is intended to move, from place to place—

(a) the senior police officer must also have regard under subsection (1) to its route or proposed route, and

(b) the conditions which may be imposed under subsection (2) include conditions as to the route of the protest or prohibiting the person carrying on the protest from entering any public place specified in the direction while the person is carrying it on.

(4) In this section 'one-person protest' means a protest which, at any one time, is carried on by one person in a public place.

(5) In this section 'the senior police officer' means—

(a) in relation to a one-person protest being held or to a one-person protest intended to be held in a case where a person is in a place with a view to carrying on such a protest, the most senior in rank of the police officers present at the scene, and

(b) in relation to a one-person protest intended to be held in a case where paragraph (a) does not apply, the chief officer of police.

(6) For the purposes of subsection (1)(a), the cases in which the noise generated by a person taking part in a one-person protest may result in serious disruption to the activities of an organisation which are carried on in the vicinity of the protest include, in particular, where it may result in persons connected with the organisation not being reasonably able, for a prolonged period of time, to carry on in that vicinity the activities or any one of them.

(7) For the purposes of subsection (1)(b)(i), the noise generated by a person carrying on a one-person protest may have a relevant impact on persons in the vicinity of the protest if—

(a) it may result in the intimidation or harassment of persons of reasonable firmness with the characteristics of persons likely to be in the vicinity, or

(b) it may cause such persons to suffer alarm or distress.

(8) In considering for the purposes of subsection (1)(b)(ii) whether the noise generated by a person carrying on a one-person protest may have a significant impact on persons in the vicinity of the protest, the senior police officer must have regard to—

  (a) the likely number of persons of the kind mentioned in paragraph (a) of subsection (7) who may experience an impact of the kind mentioned in paragraph (a) or (b) of that subsection,

  (b) the likely duration of that impact on such persons, and

  (c) the likely intensity of that impact on such persons.

(9) A direction given by a chief officer of police by virtue of subsection (5)(b) must be given in writing.

(10) A person ('P') is guilty of an offence if—

  (a) P organises or carries on a one-person protest,

  (b) P fails to comply with a condition imposed under this section, and

  (c) at the time P fails to comply with the condition, P knows or ought to know that the condition has been imposed.

(11) It is a defence for a person charged with an offence under subsection (10) to prove that the failure arose from circumstances beyond the person's control.

(12) A person who incites another to commit an offence under subsection (10) is guilty of an offence.

(13) A person guilty of an offence under subsection (10) is liable on summary conviction to a fine not exceeding level 4 on the standard scale.

(14) A person guilty of an offence under subsection (12) is liable on summary conviction to imprisonment for a term not exceeding 51 weeks or a fine not exceeding level 4 on the standard scale or both.

(15) In relation to an offence committed before the coming into force of section 281(5) of the Criminal Justice Act 2003 (alteration of penalties for certain summary offences: England and Wales), the reference in subsection (14) to 51 weeks is to be read as a reference to 6 months.

(16) The Secretary of State may by regulations amend subsection (6) for the purposes of making provision about the meaning for the purposes of this section of serious disruption to the activities of an organisation which are carried on in the vicinity of a one-person protest.

(17) Regulations under subsection (16) may, in particular, amend that subsection for the purposes of—

  (a) defining any aspect of that expression for the purposes of this section;

  (b) giving examples of cases in which a one-person protest is or is not to be treated as resulting in serious disruption to the activities of an organisation which are carried on in the vicinity of the protest.

(18) Regulations under subsection (16)—

  (a) are to be made by statutory instrument;

  (b) may make incidental, supplementary, consequential, transitional, transitory or saving provision, including provision which makes consequential amendments to this Part.

(19) A statutory instrument containing regulations under subsection (16) may not be made unless a draft of the instrument has been laid before and approved by a resolution of each House of Parliament.]

[14A   Prohibiting trespassory assemblies

(1) If at any time the chief officer of police reasonably believes that an assembly is intended to be held in any district at a place on land to which the public has no right of access or only a limited right of access and that the assembly—

  (a) is likely to be held without the permission of the occupier of the land or to conduct itself in such a way as to exceed the limits of any permission of his or the limits of the public's right of access, and

  (b) may result—

    (i)   in serious disruption to the life of the community, or

    (ii) where the land, or a building or monument on it, is of historical, architectural, archaeological or scientific importance, in significant damage to the land, building or monument, he may apply to the council of the district for an order prohibiting for a specified period the holding of all trespassory assemblies in the district or a part of it, as specified.

(2) On receiving such an application, a council may—

(a) in England and Wales, with the consent of the Secretary of State make an order either in the terms of the application or with such modifications as may be approved by the Secretary of State; or

(b) in Scotland, make an order in the terms of the application.

(3), (4) *****

(5) An order prohibiting the holding of trespassory assemblies operates to prohibit any assembly which—

(a) is held on land to which the public has no right of access or only a limited right of access, and

(b) takes place in the prohibited circumstances, that is to say, without the permission of the occupier of the land or so as to exceed the limits of any permission of his or the limits of the public's right of access.

(6) No order under this section shall prohibit the holding of assemblies for a period exceeding 4 days or in an area exceeding an area represented by a circle with a radius of 5 miles from a specified centre.

(7) An order made under this section may be revoked or varied by a subsequent order made in the same way, that is, in accordance with subsection (1) and (2) or subsection (4), as the case may be.

(8) Any order under this section shall, if not made in writing, be recorded in writing as soon as practicable after being made.

(9) In this section and sections 14B and 14C—

'assembly' means an assembly of 20 or more persons;

'land', means land in the open air;

*****

(9A), (10), (11) *****

14B   Offences in connection with trespassory assemblies and arrest therefor

(1) A person who organises an assembly the holding of which he knows is prohibited by an order under section 14A is guilty of an offence.

(2) A person who takes part in an assembly which he knows is prohibited by an order under section 14A is guilty of an offence.

(3) In England and Wales, a person who incites another to commit an offence under subsection (2) is guilty of an offence.

(4) …

(5)–(8) *****

14C   Stopping persons from proceeding to trespassory assemblies

(1) If a constable in uniform reasonably believes that a person is on his way to an assembly within the area to which an order under section 14A applies which the constable reasonably believes is likely to be an assembly which is prohibited by that order, he may, subject to subsection (2) below—

(a) stop that person, and

(b) direct him not to proceed in the direction of the assembly.

(2) The power conferred by subsection (1) may only be exercised within the area to which the order applies.

(3) A person who fails to comply with a direction under subsection (1) which he knows has been given to him is guilty of an offence.

(4) …

(5) A person guilty of an offence under subsection (3) is liable on summary conviction to a fine not exceeding level 3 on the standard scale.]

15 *****

16   Interpretation

In this Part—

*****

'public assembly'* means an assembly of [2] or more persons in a public place which is wholly or partly open to the air;

'public place' means—

  (a) any highway, or in Scotland any road within the meaning of the Roads (Scotland) Act 1984, and

  (b) any place to which at the material time the public or any section of the public has access, on payment or otherwise, as of right or by virtue of express or implied permission;

'public procession' means a procession in a public place.

PART III RACIAL HATRED

Meaning of 'racial hatred'

17   Meaning of 'racial hatred'

In this Part 'racial hatred' means hatred against a group of persons . . . defined by reference to colour, race, nationality (including citizenship) or ethnic or national origins.

Acts intended or likely to stir up racial hatred

18   Use of words or behaviour or display of written material

  (1) A person who uses threatening, abusive or insulting words or behaviour, or displays any written material which is threatening, abusive or insulting, is guilty of an offence if—

  (a) he intends thereby to stir up racial hatred, or

  (b) having regard to all the circumstances racial hatred is likely to be stirred up thereby.

  (2) An offence under this section may be committed in a public or a private place, except that no offence is committed where the words or behaviour are used, or the written material is displayed, by a person inside a dwelling and are not heard or seen except by other persons in that or another dwelling.

  (3) ...

  (4) In proceedings for an offence under this section it is a defence for the accused to prove that he was inside a dwelling and had no reason to believe that the words or behaviour used, or the written material displayed, would be heard or seen by a person outside that or any other dwelling.

  (5) A person who is not shown to have intended to stir up racial hatred is not guilty of an offence under this section if he did not intend his words or behaviour, or the written material, to be, and was not aware that it might be, threatening, abusive or insulting.

  (6) This section does not apply to words or behaviour used, or written material displayed, solely for the purpose of being [included in a programme service].

19   Publishing or distributing written material

  (1) A person who publishes or distributes written material which is threatening, abusive or insulting is guilty of an offence if—

  (a) he intends thereby to stir up racial hatred, or

  (b) having regard to all the circumstances racial hatred is likely to be stirred up thereby.

  (2) In proceedings for an offence under this section it is a defence for an accused who is not shown to have intended to stir up racial hatred to prove that he was not aware of the content of

---

* **Editor's Note:** The amendment to the definition of 'public assembly' applies only to England and Wales; in Scotland the minimum number of persons remains 20: see the Anti-social Behaviour Act 2003, s. 57.

the material and did not suspect, and had no reason to suspect, that it was threatening, abusive or insulting.

(3) References in this Part to the publication or distribution of written material are to its publication or distribution to the public or a section of the public.

20 Public performance of play

(1) If a public performance of a play is given which involves the use of threatening, abusive or insulting words or behaviour, any person who presents or directs the performance is guilty of an offence if—

(a) he intends thereby to stir up racial hatred, or

(b) having regard to all the circumstances (and, in particular, taking the performance as a whole) racial hatred is likely to be stirred up thereby.

(2)–(6) *****

21, 22 *****

Racially inflammatory material

23 Possession of racially inflammatory material

(1) A person who has in his possession written material which is threatening, abusive or insulting, or a recording of visual images or sounds which are threatening, abusive or insulting, with a view to—

(a) in the case of written material, its being displayed, published, distributed, [or included in a programme service], whether by himself or another, or

(b) in the case of a recording, its being distributed, shown, played, [or included in a programme service], whether by himself or another,

is guilty of an offence if he intends racial hatred to be stirred up thereby or, having regard to all the circumstances, racial hatred is likely to be stirred up thereby.

(2) For this purpose regard shall be had to such display, publication, distribution, showing, playing, [or inclusion in a programme service] as he has, or it may reasonably be inferred that he has, in view.

(3) In proceedings for an offence under this section it is a defence for an accused who is not shown to have intended to stir up racial hatred to prove that he was not aware of the content of the written material or recording and did not suspect, and had no reason to suspect, that it was threatening, abusive or insulting.

(4) ...

24, 25 *****

Supplementary provisions

26 Savings for reports of parliamentary or judicial proceedings

(1) Nothing in this Part applies to a fair and accurate report of proceedings in Parliament [or in the Scottish Parliament] [or in the National Assembly for Wales].

(2) Nothing in this Part applies to a fair and accurate report of proceedings publicly heard before a court or tribunal exercising judicial authority where the report is published contemporaneously with the proceedings or, if it is not reasonably practicable or would be unlawful to publish a report of them contemporaneously, as soon as publication is reasonably practicable and lawful.

27 Procedure and punishment

(1) No proceedings for an offence under this Part may be instituted in England and Wales except by or with the consent of the Attorney General.

(2) For the purposes of the rules in England and Wales against charging more than one offence in the same count or information, each of sections 18 to 23 creates one offence.

(3) A person guilty of an offence under this Part is liable—

(a) on conviction on indictment to imprisonment for a term not exceeding [seven] years or a fine or both;

(b) on summary conviction to imprisonment for a term not exceeding six months or a fine not exceeding the statutory maximum or both.

28, 29   *****

[PART IIIA HATRED AGAINST PERSONS ON RELIGIOUS GROUNDS [OR GROUNDS OF SEXUAL ORIENTATION]]

Meaning of 'religious hatred' [and 'hatred on the grounds of sexual orientation']

[29A   Meaning of 'religious hatred'

In this Part 'religious hatred' means hatred against a group of persons defined by reference to religious belief or lack of religious belief.

[29AB   Meaning of 'hatred on the grounds of sexual orientation']

[In this Part 'hatred on the grounds of sexual orientation' means hatred against a group of persons defined by reference to sexual orientation (whether towards persons of the same sex, the opposite sex or both).]

Acts intended to stir up religious hatred [or hatred on the grounds of sexual orientation]

29B   Use of words or behaviour or display of written material

(1) A person who uses threatening words or behaviour, or displays any written material which is threatening, is guilty of an offence if he intends thereby to stir up religious hatred [or hatred on the grounds of sexual orientation].

(2) An offence under this section may be committed in a public or a private place, except that no offence is committed where the words or behaviour are used, or the written material is displayed, by a person inside a dwelling and are not heard or seen except by other persons in that or another dwelling.

(3) …

(4) In proceedings for an offence under this section it is a defence for the accused to prove that he was inside a dwelling and had no reason to believe that the words or behaviour used, or the written material displayed, would be heard or seen by a person outside that or any other dwelling.

(5) This section does not apply to words or behaviour used, or written material displayed, solely for the purpose of being included in a programme service.

29C   Publishing or distributing written material

(1) A person who publishes or distributes written material which is threatening is guilty of an offence if he intends thereby to stir up religious hatred [or hatred on the grounds of sexual orientation].

(2) References in this Part to the publication or distribution of written material are to its publication or distribution to the public or a section of the public.

29D   Public performance of play

(1) If a public performance of a play is given which involves the use of threatening words or behaviour, any person who presents or directs the performance is guilty of an offence if he intends thereby to stir up religious hatred [or hatred on the grounds of sexual orientation].

(2) This section does not apply to a performance given solely or primarily for one or more of the following purposes—

(a) rehearsal,

(b) making a recording of the performance, or

(c) enabling the performance to be included in a programme service;

but if it is proved that the performance was attended by persons other than those directly connected with the giving of the performance or the doing in relation to it of the things mentioned in paragraph (b) or (c), the performance shall, unless the contrary is shown, be taken not to have been given solely or primarily for the purpose mentioned above.

(3) For the purposes of this section—

(a) a person shall not be treated as presenting a performance of a play by reason only of his taking part in it as a performer,

(b) a person taking part as a performer in a performance directed by another shall be treated as a person who directed the performance if without reasonable excuse he performs otherwise than in accordance with that person's direction, and

(c) a person shall be taken to have directed a performance of a play given under his direction notwithstanding that he was not present during the performance;

and a person shall not be treated as aiding or abetting the commission of an offence under this section by reason only of his taking part in a performance as a performer.

(4), (5) *****

29E Distributing, showing or playing a recording

(1) A person who distributes, or shows or plays, a recording of visual images or sounds which are threatening is guilty of an offence if he intends thereby to stir up religious hatred [or hatred on the grounds of sexual orientation].

(2) In this Part 'recording' means any record from which visual images or sounds may, by any means, be reproduced; and references to the distribution, showing or playing of a recording are to its distribution, showing or playing to the public or a section of the public.

(3) This section does not apply to the showing or playing of a recording solely for the purpose of enabling the recording to be included in a programme service.

29F Broadcasting or including programme in programme service

(1) If a programme involving threatening visual images or sounds is included in a programme service, each of the persons mentioned in subsection (2) is guilty of an offence if he intends thereby to stir up religious hatred [or hatred on the grounds of sexual orientation].

(2) The persons are—

(a) the person providing the programme service,

(b) any person by whom the programme is produced or directed, and

(c) any person by whom offending words or behaviour are used.

Inflammatory material

29G Possession of inflammatory material

(1) A person who has in his possession written material which is threatening, or a recording of visual images or sounds which are threatening, with a view to—

(a) in the case of written material, its being displayed, published, distributed, or included in a programme service whether by himself or another, or

(b) in the case of a recording, its being distributed, shown, played, or included in a programme service, whether by himself or another,

is guilty of an offence if he intends [thereby to stir up religious hatred or hatred on the grounds of sexual orientation].

(2) For this purpose regard shall be had to such display, publication, distribution, showing, playing, or inclusion in a programme service as he has, or it may be reasonably be inferred that he has, in view.

29H, 29I *****

29J Protection of freedom of expression

Nothing in this Part shall be read or given effect in a way which prohibits or restricts discussion, criticism or expressions of antipathy, dislike, ridicule, insult or abuse of particular religions or the beliefs or practices of their adherents, or of any other belief system or the beliefs or practices of its adherents, or proselytising or urging adherents of a different religion or belief system to cease practising their religion or belief system.

[29JA   Protection of freedom of expression (sexual orientation)]

[(1)] [In this Part, for the avoidance of doubt, the discussion or criticism of sexual conduct or practices or the urging of persons to refrain from or modify such conduct or practices shall not be taken of itself to be threatening or intended to stir up hatred.

[(2) In this Part, for the avoidance of doubt, any discussion or criticism of marriage which concerns the sex of the parties to marriage shall not be taken of itself to be threatening or intended to stir up hatred.]]

Supplementary provisions

29K   Savings for reports of parliamentary or judicial proceedings

(1) Nothing in this Part applies to a fair and accurate report of proceedings in Parliament or in the Scottish Parliament [, in the Scottish Parliament or in the National Assembly for Wales].

(2) Nothing in this Part applies to a fair and accurate report of proceedings publicly heard before a court or tribunal exercising judicial authority where the report is published contemporaneously with the proceedings or, if it is not reasonably practicable or would be unlawful to publish a report of them contemporaneously, as soon as publication is reasonably practicable and lawful.

29L   Procedure and punishment

(1) No proceedings for an offence under this Part may be instituted . . . except by or with the consent of the Attorney General.

(2)–(4) *****

29M   Offences by corporations

(1) Where a body corporate is guilty of an offence under this Part and it is shown that the offence was committed with the consent or connivance of a director, manager, secretary or other similar officer of the body, or a person purporting to act in any such capacity, he as well as the body corporate is guilty of the offence and liable to be proceeded against and punished accordingly.

(2) Where the affairs of a body corporate are managed by its members, subsection (1) applies in relation to the acts and defaults of a member in connection with his functions of management as it applies to a director.

29N   Interpretation

In this Part—

'distribute', and related expressions, shall be construed in accordance with section 29C(2) (written material) and section 29E(2) (recordings);

'dwelling' means any structure or part of a structure occupied as a person's home or other living accommodation (whether the occupation is separate or shared with others) but does not include any part not so occupied, and for this purpose 'structure' includes a tent, caravan, vehicle, vessel or other temporary or movable structure;

['hatred on the grounds of sexual orientation' has the meaning given by section 29AB;]

'programme' means any item which [is included in a programme service];

['programme service' has the same meaning as in the Broadcasting Act 1990];

'publish', and related expressions, in relation to written material, shall be construed in accordance with section 29C(2);

'religious hatred' has the meaning given by section 29A;

'recording' has the meaning given by section 29E(2), and 'play' and 'show', and related expressions, in relation to a recording, shall be construed in accordance with that provision;

'written material' includes any sign or other visible representation.]

30–37, 39   ...

38   *****

40   Amendments repeals and savings

(1)–(3) *****

(4) Nothing in this Act affects the common law powers in England and Wales to deal with or prevent a breach of the peace.

(5) As respects Scotland, nothing in this Act affects any power of a constable under any rule of law.

*****

Criminal Justice Act 1988

(1988, c. 33)

An Act to make fresh provision for extradition; to amend the rules of evidence in criminal proceedings; to provide for the reference by the Attorney General of certain questions relating to sentencing to the Court of Appeal; to amend the law with regard to the jurisdiction and powers of criminal courts, the collection, enforcement and remission of fines imposed by coroners, juries, supervision orders, the detention of children and young persons, probation and the probation service, criminal appeals, anonymity in cases of rape and similar cases, orders under sections 4 and 11 of the Contempt of Court Act 1981 relating to trials on indictment, orders restricting the access of the public to the whole or any part of a trial on indictment or to any proceedings ancillary to such a trial and orders restricting the publication of any report of the whole or any part of a trial on indictment or any such ancillary proceedings, the alteration of names of petty sessions areas, officers of inner London magistrates' courts and the costs and expenses of prosecution witnesses and certain other persons; to make fresh provision for the payment of compensation by the Criminal Injuries Compensation Board; to make provision for the payment of compensation for a miscarriage of justice which has resulted in a wrongful conviction; to create an offence of torture and an offence of having an article with a blade or point in a public place; to create further offences relating to weapons; to create a summary offence of possession of an indecent photograph of a child; to amend the Police and Criminal Evidence Act 1984 in relation to searches, computer data about fingerprints and bail for persons in customs detention; to make provision in relation to the taking of body samples by the police in Northern Ireland; to amend the Bail Act 1976; to give a justice of the peace power to authorise entry and search of premises for offensive weapons; to provide for the enforcement of the Video Recordings Act 1984 by officers of a weights and measures authority and in Northern Ireland by Officers of the Department of Economic Development; to extend to the purchase of easements and other rights over land the power to purchase land conferred on the Secretary of State by section 36 of the Prison Act 1952; and for connected purposes. [29th July 1988]

Territorial extent: United Kingdom (sections printed)

*****

PART XI MISCELLANEOUS

Miscarriages of justice

133   Compensation for miscarriages of justice

(1) Subject to subsection (2) below, when a person has been convicted of a criminal offence and when subsequently his conviction has been reversed or he has been pardoned on the ground that a new or newly discovered fact shows beyond reasonable doubt that there has been a miscarriage of justice, the Secretary of State shall pay compensation for the miscarriage of justice to the person who has suffered punishment as a result of such conviction or, if he is dead, to his personal representatives, unless the non-disclosure of the unknown fact was wholly or partly attributable to the person convicted.

[1A], [1ZA] *****

(2) No payment of compensation under this section shall be made unless an application for such compensation has been made to the Secretary of State [before the end of the period of 2 years beginning with the date on which the conviction of the person concerned is reversed or he is pardoned.

[(2AA) Such an application requires to be made within the period of 3 years starting with—

    (a) in the case of compensation under subsection (1), the date on which the conviction is reversed or (as the case may be) the person is pardoned,

    (b) in the case of compensation under subsection (1A), whichever is relevant of—

       (i)   that date, or

      (ii)   the date on which the person is acquitted or the relevant decision is made known to the person.

(2AB) The Scottish Ministers may accept such an application outwith that time limit if they think it is appropriate in exceptional circumstances to do so.]

(2A) But the Secretary of State may direct that an application for compensation made after the end of that period is to be treated as if it had been made within that period if the Secretary of State considers that there are exceptional circumstances which justify doing so.]

(3) The question whether there is a right to compensation under this section shall be determined by the Secretary of State.

(4) If the Secretary of State determines that there is a right to such compensation, the amount of the compensation shall be assessed by an assessor appointed by the Secretary of State.

[(4A) Section 133A applies in relation to the assessment of the amount of the compensation.]

[(4B)]–(9) *****

[133A Miscarriages of justice: amount of compensation]

[(1) This section applies where an assessor is required to assess the amount of compensation payable to or in respect of a person under section 133 for a miscarriage of justice.

(2) In assessing so much of any compensation payable under section 133 as is attributable to suffering, harm to reputation or similar damage, the assessor must have regard in particular to—

    (a) the seriousness of the offence of which the person was convicted and the severity of the punishment suffered as a result of the conviction, and

    (b) the conduct of the investigation and prosecution of the offence.

(3) The assessor may make from the total amount of compensation that the assessor would otherwise have assessed as payable under section 133 any deduction or deductions that the assessor considers appropriate by reason of either or both of the following—

    (a) any conduct of the person appearing to the assessor to have directly or indirectly caused, or contributed to, the conviction concerned; and

    (b) any other convictions of the person and any punishment suffered as a result of them.

(4) If, having had regard to any matters falling within subsection (3)(a) or (b), the assessor considers that there are exceptional circumstances which justify doing so, the assessor may determine that the amount of compensation payable under section 133 is to be a nominal amount only.

(5) The total amount of compensation payable to or in respect of a person under section 133 for a particular miscarriage of justice must not exceed the overall compensation limit.

That limit is—

    (a) £1 million in a case to which section 133B applies, and

    (b) £500,000 in any other case.

(6) The total amount of compensation payable under section 133 for a person's loss of earnings or earnings capacity in respect of any one year must not exceed the earnings compensation limit.

That limit is an amount equal to 1.5 times the median annual gross earnings according to the latest figures published by the Office of National Statistics at the time of the assessment.

(7) The Secretary of State may by order made by statutory instrument amend subsection (5) or (6) so as to alter any amount for the time being specified as the overall compensation limit or the earnings compensation limit.

(8) No order may be made under subsection (7) unless a draft of the order has been laid before and approved by a resolution of each House of Parliament.]

[(9)–(12)] *****

[133B Cases where person has been detained for at least 10 years]

[(1) For the purposes of section 133A(5) this section applies to any case where the person concerned ('P') has been in qualifying detention for a period (or total period) of at least 10 years by the time when—

    (a) the conviction is reversed, or

    (b) the pardon is given,

as mentioned in section 133(1).

(2) P was 'in qualifying detention' at any time when P was detained in a prison, a hospital or at any other place, if P was so detained—

    (a) by virtue of a sentence passed in respect of the relevant offence,

    (b) under mental health legislation by reason of P's conviction of that offence (disregarding any conditions other than the fact of the conviction that had to be fulfilled in order for P to be so detained), or

    (c) as a result of P's having been remanded in custody in connection with the relevant offence or with any other offence the charge for which was founded on the same facts or evidence as that for the relevant offence.

(3) In calculating the period (or total period) during which P has been in qualifying detention as mentioned in subsection (1), no account is to be taken of any period of time during which P was both—

    (a) in qualifying detention, and

    (b) in excluded concurrent detention.

(4) P was 'in excluded concurrent detention' at any time when P was detained in a prison, a hospital or at any other place, if P was so detained—

    (a) during the term of a sentence passed in respect of an offence other than the relevant offence,

    (b) under mental health legislation by reason of P's conviction of any such other offence (disregarding any conditions other than the fact of the conviction that had to be fulfilled in order for P to be so detained), or

    (c) as a result of P's having been remanded in custody in connection with an offence for which P was subsequently convicted other than—

        (i) the relevant offence, or

        (ii) any other offence the charge for which was founded on the same facts or evidence as that for the relevant offence.

(5) But P was not 'in excluded concurrent detention' at any time by virtue of subsection (4)(a), (b) or (c) if P's conviction of the other offence mentioned in that provision was quashed on appeal, or a pardon was given in respect of it.

(6) In this section—

'mental health legislation' means—

    (a) Part 3 of the Mental Health Act 1983,

    (b) Part 3 of the Mental Health (Northern Ireland) Order 1986, or

    (c) the provisions of any earlier enactment corresponding to Part 3 of that Act or Part 3 of that Order;

'the relevant offence' means the offence in respect of which the conviction is quashed or the pardon is given (but see subsection (7));

'remanded in custody' is to be read in accordance with subsections (8) and (9);

'reversed' has the same meaning as in section 133 of this Act.

(7) If, as a result of the miscarriage of justice—

    (a) two or more convictions are reversed, or

    (b) a pardon is given in respect of two or more offences,

'the relevant offence' means any of the offences concerned.

(8) In relation to England and Wales, 'remanded in custody' has the meaning given by section 242(2) of the Criminal Justice Act 2003, but that subsection applies for the purposes of this section as if any reference there to a provision of the Mental Health Act 1983 included a reference to any corresponding provision of any earlier enactment.

(9) In relation to Northern Ireland, 'remanded in custody' means—

    (a) remanded in or committed to custody by an order of a court, or

    (b) remanded, admitted or removed to hospital under Article 42, 43, 45 or 54 of the Mental Health (Northern Ireland) Order 1986 or under any corresponding provision of any earlier enactment.]

Torture

134 Torture

(1) A public official or person acting in an official capacity, whatever his nationality, commits the offence of torture if in the United Kingdom or elsewhere he intentionally inflicts severe pain or suffering on another in the performance or purported performance of his official duties.

(2) A person not falling within subsection (1) above commits the offence of torture, whatever his nationality, if—

(a) in the United Kingdom or elsewhere he intentionally inflicts severe pain or suffering on another at the instigation or with the consent or acquiescence—

(i) of a public official; or

(ii) of a person acting in an official capacity; and

(b) the official or other person is performing or purporting to perform his official duties when he instigates the commission of the offence or consents to or acquiesces in it.

(3) It is immaterial whether the pain or suffering is physical or mental and whether it is caused by an act or an omission.

(4) It shall be a defence for a person charged with an offence under this section in respect of any conduct of his to prove that he had lawful authority, justification or excuse for that conduct.

(5), (6) *****

135 Requirement of Attorney General's consent for prosecutions

Proceedings for an offence under section 134 above shall not be begun—

(a) in England and Wales, except by, or with the consent of, the Attorney General; or

(b) in Northern Ireland, except by, or with the consent of, the [Advocate General for Northern Ireland].

136–137 ...

138–158 *****

159 Crown Court proceedings—orders restricting or preventing reports or restricting public access

(1) A person aggrieved may appeal to the Court of Appeal, if that court grants leave, against—

(a) an order under section 4 or 11 of the Contempt of Court Act 1981 made in relation to a trial on indictment;

[(aa) an order made by the Crown Court under [section 39(7) or (8) of the Sentencing Code or] section 58(7) or (8) of the Criminal Procedure and Investigations Act 1996 in a case where the court has convicted a person on a trial on indictment;]

(b) any order restricting the access of the public to the whole or any part of a trial on indictment or to any proceedings ancillary to such a trial; and

(c) any order restricting the publication of any report of the whole or any part of a trial on indictment or any such ancillary proceedings;

and the decision of the Court of Appeal shall be final.

(2)–(7) *****

*****

Official Secrets Act 1989

(1989, c. 6)

An Act to replace section 2 of the Official Secrets Act 1911 by provisions protecting more limited classes of official information. [11th May 1989]

Territorial extent: United Kingdom

1 Security and intelligence

(1) A person who is or has been—

(a) a member of the security and intelligence services; or

(b) a person notified that he is subject to the provisions of this subsection,

is guilty of an offence if without lawful authority he discloses any information, document or other article relating to security or intelligence which is or has been in his possession by virtue of his position as a member of any of those services or in the course of his work while the notification is or was in force.

(2) The reference in subsection (1) above to disclosing information relating to security or intelligence includes a reference to making any statement which purports to be a disclosure of such information or is intended to be taken by those to whom it is addressed as being such a disclosure.

(3) A person who is or has been a Crown Servant or government contractor is guilty of an offence if without lawful authority he makes a damaging disclosure of any information, document or other article relating to security or intelligence which is or has been in his possession by virtue of his position as such but otherwise than as mentioned in subsection (1) above.

(4) For the purposes of subsection (3) above a disclosure is damaging if—

(a) it causes damage to the work of, or of any part of, the security and intelligence service; or

(b) it is of information or a document or other article which is such that its unauthorised disclosure would be likely to cause such damage or which falls within a class or description of information, documents or articles the unauthorised disclosure of which would be likely to have that effect.

(5) It is a defence for a person charged with an offence under this section to prove that at the time of the alleged offence he did not know, and had no reasonable cause to believe, that the information, document or article in question related to security or intelligence or, in the case of an offence under subsection (3), that the disclosure would be damaging within the meaning of that subsection.

(6)–(8) *****

(9) In this section 'security or intelligence' means the work of, or in support of, the security and intelligence services or any part of them, and references to information relating to security or intelligence include references to information held or transmitted by those services or by persons in support of, or of any part of, them.

2   Defence

(1) A person who is or has been a Crown servant or government contractor is guilty of an offence if without lawful authority he makes a damaging disclosure of any information, document or other article relating to defence which is or has been in his possession by virtue of his position as such.

(2) For the purposes of subsection (1) above a disclosure is damaging if—

(a) it damages the capability of, or of any part of, the armed forces of the Crown to carry out their tasks or leads to loss of life or injury to members of those forces or serious damage to the equipment or installations of those forces; or

(b) otherwise than as mentioned in paragraph (a) above, it endangers the interests of the United Kingdom abroad, seriously obstructs the promotion or protection by the United Kingdom of those interests or endangers the safety of British citizens abroad; or

(c) it is of information or of a document or article which is such that its unauthorised disclosure would be likely to have any of those effects.

(3) It is a defence for a person charged with an offence under this section to prove that at the time of the alleged offence he did not know, and had no reasonable cause to believe, that the information, document or article in question related to defence or that its disclosure would be damaging within the meaning of subsection (1) above.

(4) *****

3   International relations

(1) A person who is or has been a Crown servant or government contractor is guilty of an offence if without lawful authority he makes a damaging disclosure of—

(a) any information, document or other article relating to international relations; or

(b) any confidential information, document or other article which was obtained from a State other than the United Kingdom or an international organisation,

being information or a document or article which is or has been in his possession by virtue of his position as a Crown servant or government contractor.

(2) For the purposes of subsection (1) above a disclosure is damaging if—

(a) it endangers the interests of the United Kingdom abroad, seriously obstructs the promotion or protection by the United Kingdom of those interests or endangers the safety of British citizens abroad; or

(b) it is of information or of a document or article which is such that its unauthorised disclosure would be likely to have any of those effects.

(3) In the case of information or a document or article within subsection (1)(b) above—

(a) the fact that it is confidential, or

(b) its nature or contents,

may be sufficient to establish for the purposes of subsection (2)(b) above that the information, document or article is such that its unauthorised disclosure would be likely to have any of the effects there mentioned.

(4) It is a defence for a person charged with an offence under this section to prove that at the time of the alleged offence he did not know, and had no reasonable cause to believe, that the information, document or article in question was such as is mentioned in subsection (1) above or that its disclosure would be damaging within the meaning of that subsection.

(5), (6) *****

4   Crime and special investigation powers

(1) A person who is or has been a Crown servant or government contractor is guilty of an offence if without lawful authority he discloses any information, document or other article to which this section applies and which is or has been in his possession by virtue of his position as such.

(2) This section applies to any information, document or other article—

(a) the disclosure of which—

(i)   results in the commission of an offence; or

(ii) facilitates an escape from legal custody or the doing of any other act prejudicial to the safekeeping of persons in legal custody; or

(iii) impedes the prevention or detection of offences or the apprehension or prosecution of suspected offenders; or

(b) which is such that its unauthorised disclosure would be likely to have any of those effects.

(3) This section also applies to—

(a) any information obtained by reason of the interception of any communication in obedience to a warrant issued under section 2 of the Interception of Communications Act 1985 [or under the authority of an interception warrant under section 5 of the Regulation of Investigatory Powers Act 2000], any information relating to the obtaining of information by reason of any such interception and any document or other article which is or has been used or held for use in, or has been obtained by reason of, any such interception; and

(b) any information obtained by reason of action authorised by a warrant issued under section 3 of the Security Service Act 1989 [or under section 5 of the Intelligence Services Act 1994 or by an authorisation given under section 7 of that Act], any information relating to the obtaining of information by reason of any such action and any document or other article which is or has been used or held for use in, or has been obtained by reason of, any such action[; and

(c) any information obtained under a warrant under Chapter 1 of Part 2 or Chapter 1 of Part 6 of the Investigatory Powers Act 2016, any information relating to the obtaining of information under such a warrant and any document or other article which is or has been used or held for use in, or has been obtained by reason of, the obtaining of information under such a warrant.]

(4) It is a defence for a person charged with an offence under this section in respect of a disclosure falling within subsection (2)(a) above to prove that at the time of the alleged offence he did not know, and had no reasonable cause to believe, that the disclosure would have any of the effects there mentioned.

(5) It is a defence for a person charged with an offence under this section in respect of any other disclosure to prove that at the time of the alleged offence he did not know, and had no reasonable cause to believe, that the information, document or article in question was information or a document or article to which this section applies.

(6) In this section 'legal custody' includes detention in pursuance of any enactment or any instrument made under an enactment.

5   Information resulting from unauthorised disclosures or entrusted in confidence

(1) Subsection (2) below applies where—

    (a) any information, document or other article protected against disclosure by the foregoing provisions of this Act has come into a person's possession as a result of having been—

        (i) disclosed (whether to him or another) by a Crown servant or government contractor without lawful authority; or

        (ii) entrusted to him by a Crown servant or government contractor on terms requiring it to be held in confidence or in circumstances in which the Crown servant or government contractor could reasonably expect that it would be so held; or

        (iii) disclosed (whether to him or another) without lawful authority by a person to whom it was entrusted as mentioned in sub-paragraph (ii) above; and

    (b) the disclosure without lawful authority of the information, document or article by the person into whose possession it has come is not an offence under any of those provisions.

(2) Subject to subsections (3) and (4) below, the person into whose possession the information, document or article has come is guilty of an offence if he discloses it without lawful authority knowing, or having reasonable cause to believe, that it is protected against disclosure by the foregoing provisions of this Act and that it has come into his possession as mentioned in subsection (1) above.

(3) In the case of information or a document or article protected against disclosure by sections 1 to 3 above, a person does not commit an offence under subsection (2) above unless—

    (a) the disclosure by him is damaging; and

    (b) he makes it knowing, or having reasonable cause to believe, that it would be damaging;

and the question whether a disclosure is damaging shall be determined for the purposes of this subsection as it would be in relation to a disclosure of that information, document or article by a Crown servant in contravention of section 1(3), 2(1) or 3(1) above.

(4) A person does not commit an offence under subsection (2) above in respect of information or a document or other article which has come into his possession as a result of having been disclosed—

    (a) as mentioned in subsection (1)(a)(i) above by a government contractor; or

    (b) as mentioned in subsection (1)(a)(iii) above,

unless that disclosure was by a British citizen or took place in the United Kingdom, in any of the Channel Islands or in the Isle of Man or a colony.

(5) For the purposes of this section information or a document or article is protected against disclosure by the foregoing provisions of this Act if—

    (a) it relates to security or intelligence, defence or international relations within the meaning of section 1, 2 or 3 above or is such as is mentioned in section 3(1)(b) above; or

    (b) it is information or a document or article to which section 4 above applies;

and information or a document or article is protected against disclosure by sections 1 to 3 above if it falls within paragraph (a) above.

(6) A person is guilty of an offence if without lawful authority he discloses any information, document or other article which he knows, or has reasonable cause to believe, to have come into his possession as a result of a contravention of section 1 of the Official Secrets Act 1911.

6   *****

7   Authorised disclosures

(1) For the purposes of this Act a disclosure by—

    (a) a Crown servant; or

    (b) a person, not being a Crown servant or government contractor, in whose case a notification for the purposes of section 1(1) above is in force,

is made with lawful authority if, and only if, it is made in accordance with his official duty.

(2) For the purposes of this Act a disclosure by a government contractor is made with lawful authority if, and only if, it is made—

    (a) in accordance with an official authorisation; or

    (b) for the purposes of the functions by virtue of which he is a government contractor and without contravening an official restriction.

(3) or the purposes of this Act a disclosure made by any other person is made with lawful authority if, and only if, it is made—

    (a) to a Crown servant for the purposes of his functions as such; or

    (b) in accordance with an official authorisation.

(4) It is a defence for a person charged with an offence under any of the foregoing provisions of this Act to prove that at the time of the alleged offence he believed that he had lawful authority to make the disclosure in question and had no reasonable cause to believe otherwise.

(5), (6) *****

8 Safeguarding of information

(1) Where a Crown servant or government contractor, by virtue of his position as such, has in his possession or under his control any document or other article which it would be an offence under any of the foregoing provisions of this Act for him to disclose without lawful authority he is guilty of an offence if—

    (a) being a Crown servant, he retains the document or article contrary to his official duty; or

    (b) being a government contractor, he fails to comply with an official direction for the return or disposal of the document or article,

or if he fails to take such care to prevent the unauthorised disclosure of the document or article as a person in his position may reasonably be expected to take.

(2) It is a defence for a Crown servant charged with an offence under subsection (1)(a) above to prove that at the time of the alleged offence he believed that he was acting in accordance with his official duty and had no reasonable cause to believe otherwise.

(3)–(9) *****

9 Prosecutions

(1) Subject to subsection (2) below, no prosecution for an offence under this Act shall be instituted in England and Wales or in Northern Ireland except by or with the consent of the Attorney General or, as the case may be, the Advocate General for Northern Ireland.

(2) *****

10 Penalties

(1) A person guilty of an offence under any provision of this Act other than section 8(1), (4) or (5) shall be liable—

    (a) on conviction on indictment, to imprisonment for a term not exceeding two years or a fine or both;

    (b) on summary conviction, to imprisonment for a term not exceeding six months or a fine not exceeding the statutory maximum or both.

(2) A person guilty of an offence under section 8(1), (4) or (5) above shall be liable on summary conviction to imprisonment for a term not exceeding three months or a fine not exceeding level 5 on the standard scale or both.

11 Arrest, search and trial

(1) ...

(2) *****

(3) Section 9(1) of the Official Secrets Act 1911 (search warrants) shall have effect as if references to offences under that Act included references to offences under any provision of this Act other

than section 8(1), (4) or (5); and the following provisions of the Police and Criminal Evidence Act 1984, that is to say—

    (a) section 9(2) (which excludes items subject to legal privilege and certain other material from powers of search conferred by previous enactments); and

    (b) paragraph 3(b) of Schedule 1 (which prescribes access conditions for the special procedure laid down in that Schedule),

shall apply to section 9(1) of the said Act of 1911 as extended by this subsection as they apply to that section as originally enacted.

(4) Section 8(4) of the Official Secrets Act 1920 (exclusion of public from hearing on grounds of national safety) shall have effect as if references to offences under that Act included references to offences under any provision of this Act other than section 8(1), (4) or (5).

(5) Proceedings for an offence under this Act may be taken in any place in the United Kingdom.

12 'Crown servant' and 'government contractor'

(1) In this Act 'Crown servant' means—

    (a)   a Minister of the Crown;

    [(aa) a member of the Scottish Executive or a Junior Scottish Minister;]

    [(ab) the First Minister for Wales, a Welsh Minister appointed under section 48 of the Government of Wales Act 2006, the Counsel General to the Welsh Assembly Government or a Deputy Welsh Minister;]

    (b)   ...

    (c)   any person employed in the civil service of the Crown, including Her Majesty's Diplomatic Service, Her Majesty's Overseas Civil Service, the civil service of Northern Ireland and the Northern Ireland Court Service;

    (d)   any member of the naval, military or air forces of the Crown, including any person employed by an association established for the purposes of [Part XI of the Reserve Forces Act 1996];

    (e)   any constable and any other person employed or appointed in or for the purposes of any police force [(including the Police Service of Northern Ireland and the Police Service of Northern Ireland Reserve)] [or] [an NCA special (within the meaning of Part 1 of the Crime and Courts Act 2013)];

    (f)   any person who is a member or employee of a prescribed body or a body of a prescribed class and either is prescribed for the purposes of this paragraph or belongs to a prescribed class of members or employees of any such body;

    (g)   any person who is the holder of a prescribed office or who is an employee of such a holder and either is prescribed for the purposes of this paragraph or belongs to a prescribed class of such employees.

(2) In this Act 'government contractor' means, subject to subsection (3) below, any person who is not a Crown servant but who provides, or is employed in the provision of, goods or services—

    (a)   For the purposes of any Minister or person mentioned in paragraph (a) [, (ab)] or (b) of subsection (1) above, [of any office-holder in the Scottish Administration,] of any of the services, forces or bodies mentioned in that subsection or of the holder of any office prescribed under that subsection;

    [(aa) ...] or

    (b)   under any agreement or arrangement certified by the Secretary of State as being one to which the government of a State other than the United Kingdom or an international organisation is a party or which is subordinate to, or made for the purposes of implementing, any such agreement or arrangement.

(3)–(5) *****

13 Other interpretation provisions

(1) In this Act—

'disclose' and 'disclosure', in relation to a document or other article, include parting with possession of it;

'international organisation' means, subject to subsections (2) and (3) below, an organisation of which only States are members and includes a reference to any organ of such an organisation;

'prescribed' means prescribed by an order made by the Secretary of State;

'State' includes the government of a State and any organ of its government and references to a State other than the United Kingdom include references to any territory outside the United Kingdom.

(2) In section 12(2)(b) above the reference to an international organisation includes a reference to any such organisation whether or not one of which only States are members and includes a commercial organisation.

(3) In determining for the purposes of subsection (1) above whether only States are members of an organisation, any member which is itself an organisation of which only States are members, or which is an organ of such an organisation, shall be treated as a State.

*****

Security Service Act 1989

(1989, c. 5)

An Act to place the Security Service on a statutory basis; to enable certain actions to be taken on the authority of warrants issued by the Secretary of State, with provision for the issue of such warrants to be kept under review by a Commissioner; to establish a procedure for the investigation by a Tribunal or, in some cases, by the Commissioner of complaints about the Service; and for connected purposes.   [27th April 1989]

Territorial extent: United Kingdom

1   The Security Service

(1) There shall continue to be a Security Service (in this Act referred to as 'the Service') under the authority of the Secretary of State.

(2) The function of the Service shall be the protection of national security and, in particular, its protection against threats from espionage, terrorism and sabotage, from the activities of agents of foreign powers and from actions intended to overthrow or undermine parliamentary democracy by political, industrial or violent means.

(3) It shall also be the function of the Service to safeguard the economic well-being of the United Kingdom against threats posed by the actions or intentions of persons outside the British Islands.

[(4) It shall also be the function of the Service to act in support of the activities of police forces [, the [National Crime Agency]] and other law enforcement agencies in the prevention and detection of serious crime.]

(5) *****

2   The Director-General

(1) The operations of the Service shall continue to be under the control of a Director-General appointed by the Secretary of State.

(2) The Director-General shall be responsible for the efficiency of the Service and it shall be his duty to ensure—

    (a) that there are arrangements for securing that no information is obtained by the Service except so far as necessary for the proper discharge of its functions or disclosed by it except so far as necessary for that purpose or for the purpose of [the prevention or detection of] serious crime [or for the purpose of any criminal proceedings]; and

    (b) that the Service does not take any action to further the interests of any political party [; and

    (c) that there are arrangements, agreed with [the [Director General of the National Crime Agency]], for co-ordinating the activities of the Service in pursuance of section 1(4) of this Act with the activities of police forces [, the [National Crime Agency]] and other law enforcement agencies.]

(3) The arrangements mentioned in subsection (2)(a) above shall be such as to ensure that information in the possession of the Service is not disclosed for use in determining whether a person

should be employed, or continue to be employed, by any person, or in any office or capacity, except in accordance with provisions in that behalf approved by the Secretary of State.

(3A) *****

(3B) ...

(4) The Director-General shall make an annual report on the work of the Service to the Prime Minister and the Secretary of State and may at any time report to either of them on any matter relating to its work.

*****

Criminal Justice and Public Order Act 1994

(1994, c. 33)

An Act to make further provision in relation to criminal justice (including employment in the prison service); to amend or extend the criminal law and powers for preventing crime and enforcing that law; to amend the Video Recordings Act 1984; and for purposes connected with those purposes.   [3rd November 1994]

Territorial extent: England and Wales, Scotland (ss. 61–66, 163), United Kingdom (ss. 68, 69), England and Wales (remaining provisions printed here). Sections 34–37 (below) have been applied, with modifications, to the armed forces by the Criminal Justice and Public Order Act 1994 (Application to the Armed Forces) Order 2009 (SI 2009/990)

*****

Inferences from accused's silence

34   Effect of accused's failure to mention facts when questioned or charged

(1) Where, in any proceedings against a person for an offence, evidence is given that the accused—

   (a) at any time before he was charged with the offence, on being questioned under caution by a constable trying to discover whether or by whom the offence had been committed, failed to mention any fact relied on in his defence in those proceedings; or

   (b) on being charged with the offence or officially informed that he might be prosecuted for it, failed to mention any such fact [; or

   (c) at any time after being charged with the offence, on being questioned under section 22 of the Counter-Terrorism Act 2008 (post-charge questioning), failed to mention any such fact],

being a fact which in the circumstances existing at the time the accused could reasonably have been expected to mention when so questioned, charged or informed, as the case may be, subsection (2) below applies.

(2) Where this subsection applies—
   *****

   (c) the court, in determining whether there is a case to answer; and

   (d) the court or jury, in determining whether the accused is guilty of the offence charged,

may draw such inferences from the failure as appear proper.

[(2A) Where the accused was at an authorised place of detention at the time of the failure, subsections (1) and (2) above do not apply if he had not been allowed an opportunity to consult a solicitor prior to being questioned, charged or informed as mentioned in subsection (1) above.]

(3) Subject to any directions by the court, evidence tending to establish the failure may be given before or after evidence tending to establish the fact which the accused is alleged to have failed to mention.

(4) This section applies in relation to questioning by persons (other than constables) charged with the duty of investigating offences or charging offenders as it applies in relation to questioning by constables; and in subsection (1) above 'officially informed' means informed by a constable or any such person.

(5) This section does not—

(a) prejudice the admissibility in evidence of the silence or other reaction of the accused in the face of anything said in his presence relating to the conduct in respect of which he is charged, in so far as evidence thereof would be admissible apart from this section; or

(b) preclude the drawing of any inference from any such silence or other reaction of the accused which could properly be drawn apart from this section.

(6) *****

(7) ...

35   Effect of accused's silence at trial

(1) At the trial of any person ... for an offence, subsections (2) and (3) below apply unless—

(a) the accused's guilt is not in issue; or

(b) it appears to the court that the physical or mental condition of the accused makes it un-desirable for him to give evidence;

but subsection (2) below does not apply if, at the conclusion of the evidence for the prosecution, his legal representative informs the court that the accused will give evidence or, where he is unrepresented, the court ascertains from him that he will give evidence.

(2) Where this subsection applies, the court shall, at the conclusion of the evidence for the prosecution, satisfy itself (in the case of proceedings on indictment [with a jury], in the presence of the jury) that the accused is aware that the stage has been reached at which evidence can be given for the defence and that he can, if he wishes, give evidence and that, if he chooses not to give evidence, or having been sworn, without good cause refuses to answer any question, it will be permissible for the court or jury to draw such inferences as appear proper from his failure to give evidence or his refusal, without good cause, to answer any question.

(3) Where this subsection applies, the court or jury, in determining whether the accused is guilty of the offence charged, may draw such inferences as appear proper from the failure of the accused to give evidence or his refusal, without good cause, to answer any question.

(4) This section does not render the accused compellable to give evidence on his own behalf, and he shall accordingly not be guilty of contempt of court by reason of a failure to do so.

(5) For the purposes of this section a person who, having been sworn, refuses to answer any question shall be taken to do so without good cause unless—

(a) he is entitled to refuse to answer the question by virtue of any enactment, whenever passed or made, or on the ground of privilege; or

(b) the court in the exercise of its general discretion excuses him from answering it.

(6) ...

(7) *****

36   Effect of accused's failure or refusal to account for objects, substances or marks

(1) Where—

(a) a person is arrested by a constable, and there is—

(i) on his person; or

(ii) in or on his clothing or footwear; or

(iii) otherwise in his possession; or

(iv) in any place in which he is at the time of his arrest,

any object, substance or mark, or there is any mark on any such object; and

(b) that or another constable investigating the case reasonably believes that the presence of the object, substance or mark may be attributable to the participation of the person arrested in the commission of an offence specified by the constable; and

(c) the constable informs the person arrested that he so believes, and requests him to account for the presence of the object, substance or mark; and

(d) the person fails or refuses to do so, then if, in any proceedings against the person for the offence so specified, evidence of those matters is given,

subsection (2) below applies.

(2) Where this subsection applies—

*****

    (c) the court, in determining whether there is a case to answer, and

    (d) the court or jury, in determining whether the accused is guilty of the offence charged,

may draw such inferences from the failure or refusal as appear proper.

(3) Subsections (1) and (2) above apply to the condition of clothing or footwear as they apply to a substance or mark thereon.

(4) Subsections (1) and (2) above do not apply unless the accused was told in ordinary language by the constable when making the request mentioned in subsection (1)(c) above what the effect of this section would be if he failed or refused to comply with the request.

(4A)–(7) *****

(8) …

37 Effect of accused's failure or refusal to account for presence at a particular place

(1) Where—

    (a) a person arrested by a constable was found by him at a place at or about the time the offence for which he was arrested is alleged to have been committed; and

    (b) that or another constable investigating the offence reasonably believes that the presence of the person at that place and at that time may be attributable to his participation in the commission of the offence; and

    (c) the constable informs the person that he so believes, and requests him to account for that presence; and

    (d) the person fails or refuses to do so,

then if, in any proceedings against the person for the offence, evidence of those matters is given, subsection (2) below applies.

(2) Where this subsection applies—

*****

    (c) the court, in determining whether there is a case to answer; and

    (d) the court or jury, in determining whether the accused is guilty of the offence charged,

may draw such inferences from the failure or refusal as appear proper.

(3) Subsections (1) and (2) do not apply unless the accused was told in ordinary language by the constable when making the request mentioned in subsection (1)(c) above what the effect of this section would be if he failed or refused to comply with the request.

(3A)–(6) *****

(7) …

38–59 *****

Powers of police to stop and search

60 Powers to stop and search in anticipation of [, or after,] violence

[(1) If a police officer of or above the rank of inspector reasonably believes—

    (a)   that incidents involving serious violence may take place in any locality in his police area, and that it is expedient to give an authorisation under this section to prevent their occurrence,

[(aa) that—

    (i)   an incident involving serious violence has taken place in England and Wales in his police area;

    (ii)   a dangerous instrument or offensive weapon used in the incident is being carried in any locality in his police area by a person; and

    (iii)   it is expedient to give an authorisation under this section to find the instrument or weapon;] or

    (b)   that persons are carrying dangerous instruments or offensive weapons in any locality in his police area without good reason,

he may give an authorisation that the powers conferred by this section are to be exercisable at any place within that locality for a specified period not exceeding 24 hours.]

    (2)   ...

    (3)   If it appears to [an officer of or above the rank of] superintendent that it is expedient to do so, having regard to offences which have, or are reasonably suspected to have, been committed in connection with any [activity] falling within the authorisation, he may direct that the authorisation shall continue in being for a further [24] hours.

    (3A) *****

    (4)   This section confers on any constable in uniform power—

    (a)   to stop any pedestrian and search him or anything carried by him for offensive weapons or dangerous instruments,

    (b)   to stop any vehicle and search the vehicle, its driver and any passenger for offensive weapons or dangerous instruments.

    (4A) ... (not repealed in Scotland)

    (5)   A constable may, in the exercise of [the powers conferred by subsection (4) above], stop any person or vehicle and make any search he thinks fit whether or not he has any grounds for suspecting that the person or vehicle is carrying weapons or articles of that kind.

    (6)   If in the course of a search under this section a constable discovers a dangerous instrument or an article which he has reasonable grounds for suspecting to be an offensive weapon, he may seize it.

    (7)–(10A) *****

    (11) In this section—

  *****

'dangerous instruments' means instruments which have a blade or are sharply pointed;

'offensive weapon' has the meaning given by section 1(9) of the Police and Criminal Evidence Act 1984 [or, in relation to Scotland, section 47(4) of the Criminal Law (Consolidation) (Scotland) Act 1995]; [but in subsections (1)(aa), (4), (5) and (6) above and subsection (11A) below includes, in the case of an incident of the kind mentioned in subsection (1)(aa)(i) above, any article used in the incident to cause or threaten injury to any person or otherwise to intimidate]; ... and

'vehicle' includes a caravan as defined in section 29(1) of the Caravan Sites and Control of Development Act 1960.

    [(11A) For the purposes of this section, a person carries a dangerous instrument or an offensive weapon if he has it in his possession.]

    (12) The powers conferred by this section are in addition to, and not in derogation of, any power otherwise conferred.

[60AA   Powers to require removal of disguises

    (1)   Where—

    (a)   an authorisation under section 60 is for the time being in force in relation to any locality for any period, or

    (b)   an authorisation under subsection (3) that the powers conferred by subsection (2) shall be exercisable at any place in a locality is in force for any period,

those powers shall be exercisable at any place in that locality at any time in that period.

    (2)   This subsection confers power on any constable in uniform—

    (a)   to require any person to remove any item which the constable reasonably believes that person is wearing wholly or mainly for the purpose of concealing his identity;

    (b)   to seize any item which the constable reasonably believes any person intends to wear wholly or mainly for that purpose.

    (3)   If a police officer of or above the rank of inspector reasonably believes—

    (a)   that activities may take place in any locality in his police area that are likely (if they take place) to involve the commission of offences, and

    (b)   that it is expedient, in order to prevent or control the activities, to give an authorisation under this subsection, he may give an authorisation that the powers conferred by this section shall be exercisable at any place within that locality for a specified period not exceeding twenty-four hours.

(4)–[(6B)] *****

(7) A person who fails to remove an item worn by him when required to do so by a constable in the exercise of his power under this section shall be liable, on summary conviction, to imprisonment for a term not exceeding one month or to a fine not exceeding level 3 on the standard scale or both.

(8), (9) *****

(10) The powers conferred by this section are in addition to, and not in derogation of, any power otherwise conferred.

(11) This section does not extend to Scotland.]

60A–60E *****

PART V PUBLIC ORDER: COLLECTIVE TRESPASS OR NUISANCE ON LAND

Powers to remove trespassers on land

61   Power to remove trespassers on land

(1) If the senior police officer present at the scene reasonably believes that two or more persons are trespassing on land and are present there with the common purpose of residing there for any period, that reasonable steps have been taken by or on behalf of the occupier to ask them to leave and—

(a) that any of those persons[—

(i)   in the case of persons trespassing on land in England and Wales, has caused damage, disruption or distress (see subsection (10));

(ii) in the case of persons trespassing on land in Scotland,]

has caused damage to the land or to property on the land or used threatening, abusive or insulting words or behaviour towards the occupier, a member of his family or an employee or agent of his, or

(b) [in either case] that those persons have between them six or more vehicles on the land,

he may direct those persons, or any of them, to leave the land and to remove any vehicles or other property they have with them on the land.

(2) Where the persons in question are reasonably believed by the senior police officer to be persons who were not originally trespassers but have become trespassers on the land, the officer must reasonably believe that the other conditions specified in subsection (1) are satisfied after those persons become trespassers before he can exercise the power conferred by that subsection.

(3) A direction under subsection (1) above, if not communicated to the persons referred to in subsection (1) by the police officer giving the direction, may be communicated to them by any constable at the scene.

(4) If a person knowing that a direction under subsection (1) above has been given which applies to him—

(a) fails to leave the land as soon as reasonably practicable, or

(b) having left again enters the land as a trespasser within the [prohibited period],

he commits an offence and is liable on summary conviction to imprisonment for a term not exceeding three months or a fine not exceeding level 4 on the standard scale, or both.

[(4ZA) The prohibited period is—

(a) in the case of a person trespassing on land in England and Wales, the period of twelve months beginning with the day on which the direction was given;

(b) in the case of a person trespassing on land in Scotland, the period of three months beginning with the day on which the direction was given.]

(4A), (4B) *****

(5) ...

(6) In proceedings for an offence under this section it is a defence for the accused to show—

    (a) that he was not trespassing on the land, or

    (b) that he had a reasonable excuse for failing to leave the land as soon as reasonably practicable or, as the case may be, for again entering the land as a trespasser.

(7)–(9) *****

62   Supplementary powers of seizure

(1) If a direction has been given under section 61 and a constable reasonably suspects that any person to whom the direction applies has, without reasonable excuse—

    (a) failed to remove any vehicle on the land which appears to the constable to belong to him or to be in his possession or under his control; or

    (b) entered the land as a trespasser with a vehicle within the [prohibited period],

the constable may seize and remove that vehicle.

[(1A) The prohibited period is—

    (a) in the case of a person trespassing on land in England and Wales, the period of twelve months beginning with the day on which the direction was given;

    (a)* in the case of a person trespassing on land in Scotland, the period of three months beginning with the day on which the direction was given.]

(2) *****

[62A   Power to remove trespassers: alternative site available

(1) If the senior police officer present at a scene reasonably believes that the conditions in subsection (2) are satisfied in relation to a person and land, he may direct the person—

    (a) to leave the land;

    (b) to remove any vehicle and other property he has with him on the land.

(2) The conditions are—

    (a) that the person and one or more others ('the trespassers') are trespassing on the land;

    (b) that the trespassers have between them at least one vehicle on the land;

    (c) that the trespassers are present on the land with the common purpose of residing there for any period;

    (d) if it appears to the officer that the person has one or more caravans in his possession or under his control on the land, that there is a suitable pitch on a relevant caravan site for that caravan or each of those caravans;

    (e) that the occupier of the land or a person acting on his behalf has asked the police to remove the trespassers from the land.

(3) A direction under subsection (1) may be communicated to the person to whom it applies by any constable at the scene

(4)–(8) *****

62B   Failure to comply with direction under section 62A: offences

(1) A person commits an offence if he knows that a direction under section 62A(1) has been given which applies to him and—

    (a) he fails to leave the relevant land as soon as reasonably practicable, or

    (b) he enters any land in the area of the relevant local authority as a trespasser before the end of the relevant period with the intention of residing there.

(2) The relevant period is the period of [twelve] months starting with the day on which the direction is given.

(3) A person guilty of an offence under this section is liable on summary conviction to imprisonment for a term not exceeding three months or a fine not exceeding level 4 on the standard scale or both.

(4) ...

(5) In proceedings for an offence under this section it is a defence for the accused to show—

* **Editor's Note:** This is an error in the legislation.

(a) that he was not trespassing on the land in respect of which he is alleged to have committed the offence, or

(b) that he had a reasonable excuse—

    (i) for failing to leave the relevant land as soon as reasonably practicable, or

    (ii) for entering land in the area of the relevant local authority as a trespasser with the intention of residing there, or

(c) that, at the time the direction was given, he was under the age of 18 years and was residing with his parent or guardian.

62C–67 *****

68   Offence of aggravated trespass

(1) A person commits the offence of aggravated trespass if he trespasses on land…and, in relation to any lawful activity which persons are engaging in or are about to engage in on that or adjoining land…, does there anything which is intended by him to have the effect—

(a) of intimidating those persons or any of them so as to deter them or any of them from engaging in that activity,

(b) of obstructing that activity, or

(c) of disrupting that activity.

(1A) *****

(2) Activity on any occasion on the part of a person or persons on land is 'lawful' for the purposes of this section if he or they may engage in the activity on the land on that occasion without committing an offence or trespassing on the land.

(3) A person guilty of an offence under this section is liable on summary conviction to imprisonment for a term not exceeding the three months or a fine not exceeding level 4 on the standard scale, or both.

(4) …

(5) *****

69   Powers to remove persons committing or participating in aggravated trespass

(1) If the senior police officer present at the scene reasonably believes—

(a) that a person is committing, has committed or intends to commit the offence of aggravated trespass on land…; or

(b) that two or more persons are trespassing on land…and are present there with the common purpose of intimidating persons so as to deter them from engaging in a lawful activity or of obstructing or disrupting a lawful activity,

he may direct that person or (as the case may be) those persons (or any of them) to leave the land.

(2) A direction under subsection (1) above, if not communicated to the persons referred to in subsection (1) by the police officer giving the direction, may be communicated to them by any constable at the scene.

(3) If a person knowing that a direction under subsection (1) above has been given which applies to him—

(a) fails to leave the land as soon as practicable, or

(b) having left again enters the land as a trespasser within the period of three months beginning with the day on which the direction was given,

he commits an offence and is liable on summary conviction to imprisonment for a term not exceeding three months or a fine not exceeding level 4 on the standard scale, or both.

(4) In proceedings for an offence under subsection (3) it is a defence for the accused to show—

(a) that he was not trespassing on the land, or

(b) that he had a reasonable excuse for failing to leave the land as soon as practicable or, as the case may be, for again entering the land as a trespasser.

(5) …

(6) In this section 'lawful activity' and 'land' have the same meaning as in section 68.

*****

Intelligence Services Act 1994

(1994, c. 13)

An Act to make provision about the Secret Intelligence Service and the Government Communications Headquarters, including provision for the issue of warrants and authorisations enabling certain actions to be taken and for the issue of such warrants and authorisations to be kept under review; to make further provision about warrants issued on applications by the Security Service; to establish a procedure for the investigation of complaints about the Secret Intelligence Service and the Government Communications Headquarters; to make provision for the establishment of an Intelligence and Security Committee to scrutinise all three of those bodies; and for connected purposes. [26th May 1994]

Territorial extent: United Kingdom. Sections 5(1) and 11(1) also apply to the Colonies listed in the Intelligence Services Act 1994 (Dependent Territories) Order 1995 (SI 1995/752)

The Secret Intelligence Service

1 The Secret Intelligence Service

(1) There shall continue to be a Secret Intelligence Service (in this Act referred to as 'the Intelligence Service') under the authority of the Secretary of State; and, subject to subsection (2) below, its functions shall be—

(a) to obtain and provide information relating to the actions or intentions of persons outside the British Islands; and

(b) to perform other tasks relating to the actions or intentions of such persons.

(2) The functions of the Intelligence Service shall be exercisable only—

(a) in the interests of national security, with particular reference to the defence and foreign policies of Her Majesty's Government in the United Kingdom; or

(b) in the interests of the economic well-being of the United Kingdom; or

(c) in support of the prevention or detection of serious crime.

2 The Chief of the Intelligence Service

(1) The operations of the Intelligence Service shall continue to be under the control of a Chief of that Service appointed by the Secretary of State.

(2) The Chief of the Intelligence Service shall be responsible for the efficiency of that Service and it shall be his duty to ensure—

(a) that there are arrangements for securing that no information is obtained by the Intelligence Service except so far as necessary for the proper discharge of its functions and that no information is disclosed by it except so far as necessary—

(i) for that purpose;

(ii) in the interests of national security;

(iii) for the purpose of the prevention or detection of serious crime; or

(iv) for the purpose of any criminal proceedings; and

(b) that the Intelligence Service does not take any action to further the interests of any United Kingdom political party.

(3), (4) *****

GCHQ

3 The Government Communications Headquarters

(1) There shall continue to be a Government Communications Headquarters under the authority of the Secretary of State; and, subject to subsection (2) below, its functions shall be—

(a) to monitor[, make use of] or interfere with electromagnetic, acoustic and other emissions and any equipment producing such emissions and to obtain and provide information derived from or related to such emissions or equipment and from encrypted material; and

(b) to provide advice and assistance about—
  (i) languages, including terminology used for technical matters, and
  (ii) cryptography and other matters relating to the protection of information and other material,

to the armed forces of the Crown, to Her Majesty's Government in the United Kingdom or to a Northern Ireland Department [or, in such cases as it considers appropriate, to other organisations or persons, or to the general public, in the United Kingdom or elsewhere].

(2) The functions referred to in subsection (1)(a) above shall be exercisable only—
  (a) in the interests of national security, with particular reference to the defence and foreign policies of Her Majesty's Government in the United Kingdom; or
  (b) in the interests of the economic well-being of the United Kingdom in relation to the actions or intentions of persons outside the British Islands; or
  (c) in support of the prevention or detection of serious crime.

(3) In this Act the expression 'GCHQ' refers to the Government Communications Headquarters and to any unit or part of a unit of the armed forces of the Crown which is for the time being required by the Secretary of State to assist the Government Communications Headquarters in carrying out its functions.

4 The Director of GCHQ

(1) The operations of GCHQ shall continue to be under the control of a Director appointed by the Secretary of State.

(2) The Director shall be responsible for the efficiency of GCHQ and it shall be his duty to ensure—
  (a) that there are arrangements for securing that no information is obtained by GCHQ except so far as necessary for the proper discharge of its functions and that no information is disclosed by it except so far as necessary for that purpose or for the purpose of any criminal proceedings; and
  (b) that GCHQ does not take any action to further the interests of any United Kingdom political party.

(3), (4) *****

Authorisation of certain actions

5 Warrants: general

(1) No entry on or interference with property or with wireless telegraphy shall be unlawful if it is authorised by a warrant issued by the Secretary of State under this section.

(2) The Secretary of State may, on an application made by the Security Service, the Intelligence Service or GCHQ, issue a warrant under this section authorising the taking...of such action as is specified in the warrant in respect of any property so specified or in respect of wireless telegraphy so specified if the Secretary of State—
  (a) thinks it necessary for the action to be taken [for the purpose of] assisting, as the case may be,—
    (i) the Security Service in carrying out any of its functions under the 1989 Act; or
    (ii) the Intelligence Service in carrying out any of its functions under section 1 above; or
    (iii) GCHQ in carrying out any function which falls within section 3(1)(a) above; and
  [(b) is satisfied that the taking of the action is proportionate to what the action seeks to achieve;] and
  (c) is satisfied that satisfactory arrangements are in force under section 2(2)(a) of the 1989 Act (duties of the Director-General of the Security Service), section 2(2)(a) above or section 4(2)(a) above with respect to the disclosure of information obtained by virtue of this section and that any information obtained under the warrant will be subject to those arrangements.

[(2A) The matters to be taken into account in considering whether the requirements of subsection (2)(a) and (b) and satisfied in the case of any warrant shall include whether what it is thought necessary to achieve by the conduct authorised by the warrant could reasonably be achieved by other means.]

[(3) ...

(3A) A warrant issued on the application of the Security Service for the purposes of the exercise of their function under section 1(4) of the Security Service Act 1989[, or on the application of the Intelligence Service or GCHQ for the purposes of the exercise of their functions by virtue of section 1(2)(c) or 3(2)(c),] may not relate to property in the British Islands unless it authorises the taking of action in relation to conduct within subsection (3B) below.

(3B) Conduct is within this subsection if it constitutes (or, if it took place in the United Kingdom, would constitute) one or more offences, and either—

(a) it involves the use of violence, results in substantial financial gain or is conduct by a large number of persons in pursuit of a common purpose; or

(b) the offence or one of the offences is an offence for which a person who has attained the age of twenty-one and has no previous convictions could reasonably be expected to be sentenced to imprisonment for a term of three years or more.]

(4), (5) *****

6 *****

7 Authorisation of acts outside the British Islands

(1) If, apart from this section, a person would be liable in the United Kingdom for any act done outside the British Islands, he shall not be so liable if the act is one which is authorised to be done by virtue of an authorisation given by the Secretary of State under this section.

(2) In subsection (1) above 'liable in the United Kingdom' means liable under the criminal or civil law of any part of the United Kingdom.

(3) The Secretary of State shall not give an authorisation under this section unless he is satisfied—

(a) that any acts which may be done in reliance on the authorisation or, as the case may be, the operation in the course of which the acts may be done will be necessary for the proper discharge of a function of the Intelligence Service [or GCHQ]; and

(b) that there are satisfactory arrangements in force to secure—

(i) that nothing will be done in reliance on the authorisation beyond what is necessary for the proper discharge of a function of the Intelligence Service [or GCHQ]; and

(ii) that, in so far as any act may be done in reliance on the authorisation, their nature and likely consequences will be reasonable, having regard to the purposes for which they are carried out; and

(c) that there are satisfactory arrangements in force under section 2(2)(a) [or 4(2)(a)] above with respect to the disclosure of information obtained by virtue of this section and that any information obtained by virtue of anything done in reliance on the authorisation will be subject to those arrangements.

(4)–(14) *****

*****

Defamation Act 1996

(1996, c. 31)

An Act to amend the law of defamation and to amend the law of limitation with respect to actions for defamation or malicious falsehood. [4th July 1996]

Territorial extent: United Kingdom

*****

13 ...

Statutory privilege

14 Reports of court proceedings absolutely privileged

(1) A fair and accurate report of proceedings in public before a court to which this section applies, if published contemporaneously with the proceedings, is absolutely privileged.

(2) A report of proceedings which by an order of the court, or as a consequence of any statutory provision, is required to be postponed shall be treated as published contemporaneously if it is published as soon as practicable after publication is permitted.

[(3) This section applies to—

(a) any court in the United Kingdom;

(b) any court established under the law of a country or territory outside the United Kingdom;

(c) any international court or tribunal established by the Security Council of the United Nations or by an international agreement;

and in paragraphs (a) and (b) 'court' includes any tribunal or body exercising the judicial power of the State.]

(4) ...

15 Reports, &c. protected by qualified privilege

(1) The publication of any report or other statement mentioned in Schedule 1 to this Act is privileged unless the publication is shown to be made with malice, subject as follows.

(2) In defamation proceedings in respect of the publication of a report or other statement mentioned in Part II of that Schedule, there is no defence under this section if the plaintiff shows that the defendant—

(a) was requested by him to publish in a suitable manner a reasonable letter or statement by way of explanation or contradiction, and

(b) refused or neglected to do so.

For this purpose 'in a suitable manner' means in the same manner as the publication complained of or in a manner that is adequate and reasonable in the circumstances.

(3) This section does not apply to the publication to the public, or a section of the public, of matter which is not of [public interest] and the publication of which is not for the public benefit.

(4) Nothing in this section shall be construed—

(a) as protecting the publication of matter the publication of which is prohibited by law, or

(b) as limiting or abridging any privilege subsisting apart from this section.

16–20 *****

Section 15 SCHEDULE 1 QUALIFIED PRIVILEGE

PART I STATEMENTS HAVING QUALIFIED PRIVILEGE WITHOUT EXPLANATION OR CONTRADICTION

1. A fair and accurate report of proceedings in public of a legislature anywhere in the world.

2. A fair and accurate report of proceedings in public before a court anywhere in the world.

3. A fair and accurate report of proceedings in public of a person appointed to hold a public inquiry by a government or legislature anywhere in the world.

4. A fair and accurate report of proceedings in public anywhere in the world of an international organisation or an international conference.

5. A fair and accurate copy of or extract from any register or other document required by law to be open to public inspection.

6. A notice or advertisement published by or on the authority of a court, or of a judge or officer of a court, anywhere in the world.

7. A fair and accurate copy of or extract from matter published by or on the authority of a government or legislature anywhere in the world.

8. A fair and accurate copy of or extract from matter published anywhere in the world by an international organisation or an international conference.

PART II STATEMENTS PRIVILEGED SUBJECT TO EXPLANATION OR CONTRADICTION

[9.—(1) A fair and accurate copy of, extract from or summary of a notice or other matter issued for the information of the public by or on behalf of—

(a) a legislature or government anywhere in the world;

(b) an authority anywhere in the world performing governmental functions;

(c) an international organisation or international conference.

(2) In this paragraph 'governmental functions' includes police functions.

10. A fair and accurate copy of, extract from or summary of a document made available by a court anywhere in the world, or by a judge or officer of such a court.]

11.—(1) A fair and accurate report of proceedings at any public meeting or sitting in the United Kingdom of—

(a)   a local authority or local authority committee;

[(aa) in the case of a local authority which are operating executive arrangements, the executive of that authority or a committee of that executive];

(b)   a justice or justices of the peace acting otherwise than as a court exercising judicial authority;

(c)   a commission, tribunal, committee or person appointed for the purposes of any inquiry by any statutory provision, by Her Majesty or by a Minister of the Crown [a member of the Scottish Executive] [, the Welsh Ministers or the Counsel General to the Welsh Assembly Government] or a Northern Ireland Department;

(d)   a person appointed by a local authority to hold a local inquiry in pursuance of any statutory provision;

(e)   any other tribunal, board, committee or body constituted by or under, and exercising functions under, any statutory provision.

(1A)–(3) *****

*****

Police Act 1996

(1996, c. 16)

An Act to consolidate the Police Act 1964, Part IX of the Police and Criminal Evidence Act 1984, Chapter I of Part I of the Police and Magistrates' Courts Act 1994 and certain other enactments relating to the police.
[22nd May 1996]

Territorial extent: England and Wales (and in the case of Part III (ss. 59–64) Scotland)

PART I ORGANISATION OF POLICE FORCES

Police areas [and police forces]

1 Police areas

(1) England and Wales shall be divided into police areas.

(2) The police areas referred to in subsection (1) shall be—

    (a) those listed in Schedule 1 (subject to [any amendment made to the first column of that Schedule by regulations under section 31A or any amendment made to the second column, or to the first and second columns, by an order] under section 32 below, [section 45 of the Local Government Act (Democracy) (Wales) Act 2013,] or [section 17 of the Local Government Act 1992 or Part 1 of the Local Government and Public Involvement in Health Act 2007]),

    (b) the metropolitan police district, and

    (c) the City of London police area.

(3) References in Schedule 1 to any local government area are to that area as it is for the time being...

2 Maintenance of police forces

[(1)] A police force shall be maintained for every police area for the time being listed in Schedule 1.

[(2) For further provision about the maintenance of those police forces, see Chapter 1 of Part 1 of the Police Reform and Social Responsibility Act 2011.]

3–5 ...

[The metropolitan police force]

5A Maintenance of the metropolitan police force

[(1) A police force shall be maintained for the metropolitan police district.]

[(2) For further provision about the maintenance of the metropolitan police force, see Chapter 2 of Part 1 of the Police Reform and Social Responsibility Act 2011.]

5B–6 ...

[The City of London]

[6AZA Common Council to remain police authority for City]

[The Common Council of the City of London is to continue to be the police authority for the City of London police area.]

6ZA–17 ...

18 *****

19–21 ...

General provisions

22 Reports by chief constables to police authorities

(1) [The Commissioner of Police for the City of London] shall, as soon as possible after the end of each financial year, submit to the [Common Council] a general report on the policing during that year of [the City of London Police area].

(2) [The Chief Constable] shall arrange for a report submitted by him under subsection (1) to be published in such manner as appears to him to be appropriate.

(3) [The Commissioner of Police for the City of London] shall, whenever so required by the [Common Council], submit to [the Common Council] a report on such matters as may be

specified in the requirement, being matters connected with [the policing of the City of London Police area].

(4) A report submitted under subsection (3) shall be in such form as the [Common Council] may specify.

(5) If it appears to [the Commissioner of Police for the City of London] that a report in compliance with subsection (3) would contain information which in the public interest ought not to be disclosed, or is not needed for the discharge of the functions of the [Common Council], he may request [the Common Council] to refer the requirement to submit the report to the Secretary of State; and in any such case the requirement shall be of no effect unless it is confirmed by the Secretary of State.

(6) The [Common Council] may arrange, or require the [chief officer] to arrange, for a report submitted under subsection (3) to be published in such manner as appears to the [Common Council] to be appropriate.

(7) ...

[22A   Collaboration agreements]

[(1) A collaboration agreement may be made by—
  (a) two or more policing bodies; or
  (b) the chief officers of police of one or more police forces [and—
    (i)   one or more policing bodies together with one or more other persons, or
    (ii) if no other person is a party to the agreement, two or more policing bodies].

(2) A collaboration agreement is an agreement containing one or more of the following—
  (a) provision about the discharge of functions of members of a police force ('force collaboration provision');
  (b) provision about support by a policing body for another policing body ('policing body collaboration provision');
  (c) provision about support by a policing body for the police force which another policing body is responsible for maintaining ('policing body & force collaboration provision').

(3) A collaboration agreement may not contain force collaboration provision unless the parties to the agreement consist of, or include,—
  (a) the chief officer of police of each police force to which the provision relates, and
  (b) the policing body that is responsible for maintaining each such police force.

(4) A collaboration agreement may not contain policing body collaboration provision unless the parties to the agreement consist of, or include, each policing body to which the provision relates.

(5) A collaboration agreement may not contain policing body & force collaboration provision unless the parties to the agreement consist of, or include—
  (a) the policing body, or each policing body, to which the provision relates;
  (b) the chief officer of police of the police force, or each police force, to which the provision relates; and
  (c) the policing body that is responsible for maintaining each such police force.

(6) Subsection [(1)(a)] does not prevent other persons from being parties to collaboration agreements.

(7) Subsection (2) does not prevent a collaboration agreement from including other kinds of provision.

(8) For the purposes of subsections (3) and (5), the circumstances in which force collaboration provision, or policing body & force collaboration provision, is to be taken to relate to a police force include the cases where provision relates—

(a) to functions of a kind which are or may be exercisable by members of that police force, or

(b) to the police area for which that police force is established.

(9) For the purposes of subsections (4) and (5), the circumstances in which policing body collaboration provision, or policing body & force collaboration provision, is to be taken to relate to a policing body include the cases where provision relates—

(a) to functions of a kind which are or may be exercisable by that policing body or members of the staff of that body, or

(b) to the police area for which that policing body is established.]

22B–23I   *****

24   Aid of one police force by another

(1) The chief officer of police of any police force may, on the application of the chief officer of police of any other police force, provide constables or other assistance for the purpose of enabling the other force to meet any special demand on its resources.

(2) If it appears to the Secretary of State to be expedient in the interests of public safety or order that any police force should be reinforced or should receive other assistance for the purpose of enabling it to meet any special demand on its resources, and that satisfactory arrangements under subsection (1) cannot be made, or cannot be made in time, he may direct the chief officer of police of any police force to provide such constables or other assistance for that purpose as may be specified in the direction.

(3) While a constable is provided under this section for the assistance of another police force he shall, notwithstanding [sections 2 and 4 of the Police Reform and Social Responsibility Act 2011 ('the 2011 Act')], be under the direction and control of the chief officer of police of that other force.

[(3A) While a member of the civilian staff of a police force maintained under section 2, or a member of the civilian staff of the metropolitan police force, is provided under this section for the assistance of another police force, that member of staff is, notwithstanding section 2 or 4 of the 2011 Act, under the direction and control of the chief officer of police of that other force.]

(4) The [local policing body] maintaining a police force for which assistance is provided under this section shall pay to the [local policing body] maintaining the force from which that assistance is provided such contribution as may be agreed upon between [those bodies] or, in the absence of any such agreement, as may be provided by any agreement subsisting at the time between all [local policing bodies] generally, or, in the absence of such general agreement, as may be determined by the Secretary of State.

[(4A) This section shall apply in relation to the British Transport Police Authority, the British Transport Police Force and the Chief Constable of that Force as it applies to a [local policing body], a police force and a chief officer of police respectively; and for that purpose the reference in subsection (3) to [sections 2 and 4 of the 2011 Act] shall be construed as including a reference to section 24(2) of the Railways and Transport Safety Act 2003.]

[(5) ...]

25   Provision of special services

(1) The chief officer of police of a police force may provide, at the request of any person, special police services at any premises or in any locality in the police area for which the force is maintained, subject to the payment to the [local policing body] of charges on such scales as may be determined by [that body].

(1A) *****

(2) ...

26   Provision of advice and assistance to international organisations etc

(1) Subject to the provisions of this section, a [local policing body] may provide advice and assistance—

(a) to an international organisation or institution, or

(b) to any other person or body which is engaged outside the United Kingdom in the carrying on of activities similar to any carried on by [the body] or the chief officer of police for its area.

(2) The power conferred on a [local policing body] by subsection (1) includes a power to make arrangements under which a member of the police force maintained by [the body] is engaged for a period of temporary service with a person or body within paragraph (a) or (b) of that subsection.

(3) The power conferred by subsection (1) shall not be exercised except with the consent of the Secretary of State or in accordance with a general authorisation given by him.

(4) A consent or authorisation under subsection (3) may be given subject to such conditions as appear to the Secretary of State to be appropriate.

(5) Nothing in this section authorises a [local policing body] to provide any financial assistance by—

(a) making a grant or loan,

(b) giving a guarantee or indemnity, or

(c) investing by acquiring share or loan capital.

(6) A [local policing body] may make charges for advice or assistance provided by it under this section.

(7) ...

(8) The provisions of this section are without prejudice to the Police (Overseas Service) Act 1945 ...

27–28   *****

29   Attestation of constables

Every member of a police force maintained for a police area and every special constable appointed for a police area shall, on appointment, be attested as a constable by making a declaration in the form set out in Schedule 4—

(a) ...

(b) ... before a justice of the peace having jurisdiction within the police area.

30   Jurisdiction of constables

(1) A member of a police force shall have all the powers and privileges of a constable throughout England and Wales and the adjacent United Kingdom waters.

[(2) A special constable shall have all the powers and privileges of a constable throughout England and Wales and the adjacent United Kingdom waters.]

(3) ...

[(3A) A member of the British Transport Police Force who is for the time being required by virtue of [section 22A] to serve with a police force maintained by a [local policing body] shall have all the powers and privileges of a member of that police force.]

[(3B) Where a member of the British Transport Police Force is for the time being under the direction and control of the chief officer of another police force by virtue of a [collaboration agreement under section 22A], the member shall have all the powers and privileges of a member of that other force.]

[(3C) In subsection (3B), 'police force' and 'chief officer' have the meanings given by section 23I.]

(4) ...

(5), (6) *****

31, 31A   *****

32   Power to alter police areas by order

(1) The Secretary of State may by order make alterations in police areas in England and Wales other than the City of London police area.

(2) The alterations that may be made by an order under this section include alterations that result in a reduction or an increase in the number of police areas, but not alterations that result in the abolition of the metropolitan police district.

(3) The Secretary of State shall not exercise his power under this section to make alterations unless either—

(a) he has received a request to make the alterations from the [local policing body] for each of the areas ... affected by them, or

(b) it appears to him to be expedient to make the alterations in the interests of efficiency or effectiveness.

(4) The Secretary of State shall exercise his power to make orders under this section in such a way as to ensure that [no police area falls partly in England and partly in Wales and that] none of the following areas—

(a) a county in which there are no district councils,

(b) a district in any other county,

(c) a county borough in Wales, and

(d) a London borough,

is divided between two or more police areas.

(5) ...

33–35   *****

PART II CENTRAL SUPERVISION, DIRECTION AND FACILITIES

Functions of Secretary of State

36   General duty of Secretary of State

(1) The Secretary of State shall exercise his powers under the provisions of this Act referred to in subsection (2) in such manner and to such extent as appears to him to be best calculated to promote the efficiency and effectiveness of the police.

(2) The provisions of this Act mentioned in subsection (1) are—

(a) Part I;

(b) this Part;

(c) Part III ...;

(d) in Chapter II of Part IV, [sections 84 and 85] and Schedule 6; and

(e) in Part V, section 95.

36A, 37   ...

37A   *****

38–39   ...

39A   *****

[40   Power to give directions in relation to police force]

[(1) Where the Secretary of State is satisfied that the whole or any part of a police force is failing to discharge any of its functions in an effective manner, whether generally or in particular respects, he may direct the [local policing body] responsible for maintaining the force to take specified measures for the purpose of remedying the failure.

(2) Where the Secretary of State is satisfied that the whole or a part of a police force will fail to discharge any of its functions in an effective manner, whether generally or in particular respects, unless remedial measures are taken, he may direct the [local policing body] responsible for maintaining the force to take specified measures in order to prevent such a failure occurring.

(3) The measures that may be specified in a direction under subsection (1) or (2) include the submission to the Secretary of State of an action plan setting out the measures which the person or persons submitting the plan propose to take for the purpose of remedying the failure in question or (as the case may be) preventing such a failure occurring.

(4) The Secretary of State shall not give a direction under this section in relation to any police force unless—

(a) the [local policing body] responsible for maintaining the force and the chief officer of police of that force have each been given such information about the Secretary of State's grounds for proposing to give that direction as he considers appropriate for enabling them to make representations or proposals under the following paragraphs of this subsection;

(b) that [local policing body] and chief officer have each been given an opportunity of making representations about those grounds;

(c) that [local policing body] and chief officer have each had an opportunity of making proposals for the taking of remedial measures that would make the giving of the direction unnecessary; and

(d) the Secretary of State has considered any such representations and any such proposals.

(5) Subsection (4) does not apply if the Secretary of State is satisfied that—

(a) the [local policing body] responsible for maintaining the force and the chief officer of police of that force have already been made aware of the matters constituting the Secretary of State's grounds for proposing to give a direction under this section;

(b) the information they had about those matters was sufficient to enable them to identify remedial measures that would have made the giving of the direction unnecessary; and

(c) they have each had a reasonable opportunity to take such measures.

(6) The Secretary of State shall not give a direction under this section unless Her Majesty's Chief Inspector of Constabulary has been given—

(a) the same information about the grounds for proposing to give that direction as is required to be given under subsection (4)(a) (or would be so required but for subsection (5)); and

(b) an opportunity of making written observations about those grounds.

The Secretary of State shall publish any such observations in such manner as appears to him to be appropriate.

(7) A [local policing body] that is given a direction under this section shall comply with it.]

[40A   Power to give directions in relation to [local policing body]]

[(1) Where the Secretary of State is satisfied that a [local policing body] is failing to discharge any of its functions in an effective manner, whether generally or in particular respects, he may direct the [local policing body] to take specified measures for the purpose of remedying the failure.

(2) Where the Secretary of State is satisfied that a [local policing body] will fail to discharge any of its functions in an effective manner, whether generally or in particular respects, unless remedial measures are taken, he may direct the [local policing body] to take specified measures in order to prevent such a failure occurring.

(3)–(7) *****

(8) Nothing in this section or in section 40 prevents the Secretary of State from exercising (whether in relation to the same matter or different matters or at the same time or at different times) both his powers under this section and his powers under section 40.]

[40B–41   *****]

41A, 41B   ...

42   [Metropolitan police: suspension or removal of Commissioner or Deputy Commissioner]

[(1) The Secretary of State may require the Mayor's Office for Policing & Crime to exercise its power under section 48 of the Police Reform and Social Responsibility Act 2011 (the '2011 Act') to call upon the Commissioner of Police of the Metropolis or Deputy Commissioner of Police of the Metropolis, to retire or to resign.

(1A) The Secretary of State may also require the Mayor's Office for Policing & Crime to exercise the power under section 48 of the 2011 Act to suspend the Commissioner of Police of the Metropolis, or the Deputy Commissioner of the Police of the Metropolis, if the Secretary of State considers that it is necessary for the maintenance of public confidence in the metropolitan police force for that police officer to be suspended.]

(2) [Before requiring the Mayor's Office for Policing & Crime to exercise its power to call upon the Commissioner of Police of the Metropolis or Deputy Commissioner of Police of the Metropolis to retire or to resign, the Secretary of State shall—]

   (a) give the officer concerned a notice in writing—
       (i) informing him of the Secretary of State's intention to require the exercise of that power; and
       (ii) explaining the Secretary of State's grounds for requiring the exercise of that power; and
   (b) give that officer an opportunity to make representations to the Secretary of State.

(2A) Where the Secretary of State gives a notice under subsection (2)(a), he shall send a copy of the [notice to the Mayor's Office for Policing & Crime.]

(2B) The Secretary of State shall consider any representations made to him under subsection (2).]

(3) [Where the Secretary of State proposes to require the exercise of a power mentioned in subsection (1), he] shall, appoint one or more persons (one at least of whom shall be a person who is not an officer of police or of a Government department) to hold an inquiry and report to him and shall consider any report made under this subsection.

[(3A) At an inquiry held under subsection (3)—

   (a) the Commissioner [or Deputy Commissioner] shall be entitled, in accordance with any regulations under section 42A, to make representations to the inquiry;
   (b) the [Mayor's Office of Policing & Crime] shall be entitled, in accordance with any regulations made under section 42A, to make representations to the inquiry.

(3B) The entitlement of the Commissioner [or Deputy Commissioner] to make representations shall include the entitlement to make them in person.]

(4) The costs incurred by the Commissioner [or Deputy Commissioner] in respect of an inquiry under this section, taxed in such manner as the Secretary of State may direct, shall be defrayed out of the police fund.

(4A)–(4B) *****
(4C)–(5) ...

42A–45   *****

46 Police grant

(1) Subject to the following provisions of this section, the Secretary of State shall—

[(a) make grants to police and crime commissioners for the purposes of their functions;

(b) make grants to the Common Council for the purposes of its functions as policy authority, and

(c) make grants to the Greater London Authority for the purposes of the functions of the Mayor's Office for Policing and Crime].

(2) For each financial year the Secretary of State shall with the approval of the Treasury determine—

(a) the aggregate amount of grants to be made under this section, and

(b) the amount of the grant to be made to each [grant recipient];

and any determination may be varied by further determinations under this subsection.

(3) The Secretary of State shall prepare a report setting out any determination under subsection (2), and stating the considerations which he took into account in making the determination.

(4) In determining the allocation among [grant recipients] of the whole or any part of the aggregate amount of grants, the Secretary of State may exercise his discretion by applying such formulae or other rules as he considers appropriate.

(5) The considerations which the Secretary of State takes into account in making a determination under subsection (2), and the formulae and other rules referred to in subsection (4), may be different for different authorities or [different grant recipients or different classes of grant recipient].

(6)–(9) *****

47, 48 *****

49 ...

50 Regulations for police forces

(1) Subject to the provisions of this section, the Secretary of State may make regulations as to the government, administration and conditions or service of police forces.

(2) Without prejudice to the generality of subsection (1), regulations under this section may make provision with respect to—

(a) ...

(b) the qualifications for appointment and promotion of members of police forces;

(c) periods of service on probation;

(d) voluntary retirement of members of police forces;

(e) the conduct, efficiency and effectiveness of members of police forces and the maintenance of discipline;

(f) the suspension of members of a police force from membership of that force and from their office as constable;

(g) the maintenance of personal records of members of police forces;

(h) the duties which are or are not to be performed by members of police forces;

(i) the treatment as occasions of police duty of attendance at meetings of the Police Federations and of any body recognised by the Secretary of State for the purposes of section 64;

(j) the hours of duty, leave, pay and allowances of members of police forces; and

(k) the issue, use and return of police clothing, personal equipment and accoutrements.

[(2ZA)]–(5) *****

(6) Regulations under this section as to conditions of service shall secure that appointments for fixed terms are not made except where the person appointed holds the rank of superintendent or a higher rank.

(6A)–(8) *****

[50A]–[53F] *****

Inspectors of constabulary

54 Appointment and functions of inspectors of constabulary

(1) Her Majesty may appoint such number of inspectors (to be known as 'Her Majesty's Inspectors of Constabulary') as the Secretary of State may with the consent of the Treasury determine, and of the persons so appointed one may be appointed as chief inspector of constabulary.

(2) The inspectors of constabulary shall inspect, and report… on the efficiency and effectiveness of, every police force maintained for a police area […]

(2A) …

(2B)–(6) *****

55–58 *****

PART III POLICE REPRESENTATIVE INSTITUTIONS

59–[60A] *****

61, 62 …

63 *****

64 Membership of trade unions

(1) Subject to the following provisions of this section, a member of a police force shall not be a member of any trade union, or of any association having for its objects, or one of its objects, to control or influence the pay, pensions or conditions of service of any police force.

(2) Where a person was a member of a trade union before becoming a member of a police force, he may, with the consent of the chief officer of police, continue to be a member of that union during the time of his service in the police force.

(3), (4A), (4B) …

(4), (4C)–(4F), (5) *****

[64A], [64B] *****

PART IV COMPLAINTS, DISCIPLINARY PROCEEDINGS ETC

65–83 …

Chapter II Disciplinary and other proceedings

84 Representation etc at disciplinary and other proceedings

[(1) The Secretary of State shall by regulations make provision for or in connection with—

(a) enabling the officer concerned or a relevant authority to be represented in proceedings conducted under regulations made in pursuance of section 50(3) [or (3A)] or section 51(2A) [or (2B)];

(b) enabling the panel conducting such proceedings to receive advice from a relevant lawyer or another person falling within any prescribed description of persons.

(2) Regulations under this section may in particular make provision—

(a) specifying the circumstances in which the officer concerned or a relevant authority is entitled to be legally represented (by a relevant lawyer);

(b) specifying the circumstances in which the officer concerned or a relevant authority is entitled to be represented by a person (other than a relevant lawyer) who falls within any prescribed description of persons;

(c) for securing that—

    (i) a relevant authority may be legally represented, and

    (ii) the panel conducting the proceedings may receive advice from a relevant lawyer,

whether or not the officer concerned is legally represented.

(3) Without prejudice to the powers conferred by this section, regulations under this section shall, in relation to cases where the officer concerned is entitled to legal or other representation, make provision—

    (a) for securing that the officer is notified of his right to such representation;

    (b) specifying when the officer is to be so notified;

    (c) for securing that proceedings at which the officer may be dismissed are not to take place unless the officer has been notified of his right to such representation.]

(4)–(9) *****

85 Appeals against dismissal etc

[(1) The Secretary of State shall by rules make provision specifying the cases in which a member of a police force or a special constable[, or a former member of a police force or a former special constable,] may appeal to a police appeals tribunal.

(2) A police appeals tribunal may, on the determination of an appeal under this section, make an order dealing with the appellant in any way in which he could have been dealt with by the person who made the decision appealed against.]

(3) The Secretary of State may make rules as to the procedure on appeals to police appeals tribunals under this section.

(4)–(6) *****

86 ...

87–[87A] *****

88 Liability for wrongful acts of constables

(1) The chief officer of police for a police area shall be liable in respect of [any unlawful conduct of] constables under his direction and control in the performance or purported performance of their functions in like manner as a master is liable in respect of [any unlawful conduct of] his servants in the course of their employment, and accordingly shall [, in the case of a tort,] be treated for all purposes as a joint tortfeasor.

(2) There shall be paid out of the police fund—

    (a) any damages or costs awarded against the chief officer of police in any proceedings brought against him by virtue of this section and any costs incurred by him in any such proceedings so far as not recovered by him in the proceedings; and

    (b) any sum required in connection with the settlement of any claim made against the chief officer of police by virtue of this section, if the settlement is approved by the [local policing body].

(3) Any proceedings in respect of a claim made by virtue of this section shall be brought against the chief officer of police for the time being or, in the case of a vacancy in that office, against the person for the time being performing the functions of the chief officer of police; and references in subsections (1) and (2) to the chief officer of police shall be construed accordingly.

(4) A [local policing body] may, in such cases and to such extent as appear to it to be appropriate, pay out of the police fund—

    (a) any damages or costs awarded against a person to whom this subsection applies in proceedings for [any lawful conduct of] that person,

    (b) any costs incurred and not recovered by such a person in such proceedings, and

    (c) any sum required in connection with the settlement of a claim that has or might have given rise to such proceedings.

(5) Subsection (4) applies to a person who is—

    (a) a member of the police force maintained by the [local policing body],

    (b) a constable for the time being required to serve with that force by virtue of section 24 or 98 [of this Act . . .], or

    (c) a special constable appointed for the [local policing body's] police area.

(5A)–(8) *****

[88A]–[88M] *****

PART V MISCELLANEOUS AND GENERAL

Offences

89   Assaults on constables

(1) Any person who assaults a constable in the execution of his duty, or a person assisting a constable in the execution of his duty, shall be guilty of an offence and liable on summary conviction to imprisonment for a term not exceeding six months or to a fine not exceeding level 5 on the standard scale, or to both.

(2) Any person who resists or wilfully obstructs a constable in the execution of his duty, or a person assisting a constable in the execution of his duty, shall be guilty of an offence and liable on summary conviction to imprisonment for a term not exceeding one month or to a fine not exceeding level 3 on the standard scale, or to both.

(3)–(6) *****

90   Impersonation, etc

(1) Any person who with intent to deceive impersonates a member of a police force or special constable, or makes any statement or does any act calculated falsely to suggest that he is such a member or constable, shall be guilty of an offence and liable on summary conviction to imprisonment for a term not exceeding six months or to a fine not exceeding level 5 on the standard scale, or to both.

(2) Any person who, not being a constable, wears any article of police uniform in circumstances where it gives him an appearance so nearly resembling that of a member of a police force as to be calculated to deceive shall be guilty of an offence and liable on summary conviction to a fine not exceeding level 3 on the standard scale.

(3) Any person who, not being a member of a police force or special constable, has in his possession any article of police uniform shall, unless he proves that he obtained possession of that article lawfully and has possession of it for a lawful purpose, be guilty of an offence and liable on summary conviction to a fine not exceeding level 1 on the standard scale.

(4) *****

91   Causing disaffection

(1) Any person who causes, or attempts to cause, or does any act calculated to cause, disaffection amongst the members of any police force, or induces or attempts to induce, or does any act calculated to induce, any member of a police force to withhold his services, [or to commit breaches of discipline], shall be guilty of an offence and liable—

    (a) on summary conviction, to imprisonment for a term not exceeding six months or to a fine not exceeding the statutory maximum, or to both;

    (b) on conviction on indictment, to imprisonment for a term not exceeding two years or to a fine, or to both.

[(2) This section applies in the case of—

    (a)   special constables appointed for a police area,

    [(aa) . . .]

    (b)   members of the Civil Nuclear Constabulary, and

(c)   members of the British Transport Police Force,

as it applies in the case of members of a police force.]

[(3) Liability under subsection (1) for any behaviour is in addition to any civil liability for that behaviour.]

92   ***

93   Acceptance of gifts and loans

(1) A [local policing body] may, in connection with the discharge of any of its functions, accept gifts of money, and gifts or loans of other property, on such terms as appear to [the body] to be appropriate.

(2) The terms on which gifts or loans are accepted under subsection (1) may include terms providing for the commercial sponsorship of any activity of the [local policing body] or of the police force maintained by it.

(3) ...

*****

SCHEDULE 4 FORM OF DECLARATION

[I,...................... of........................ do solemnly and sincerely declare and affirm that I will well and truly serve the Queen in the office of constable, with fairness, integrity, diligence and impartiality, upholding fundamental human rights and according equal respect to all people; and that I will, to the best of my power, cause the peace to be kept and preserved, and prevent all offences against people and property; and that while I continue to hold the said office I will to the best of my skill and knowledge discharge all the duties thereof faithfully according to law.]

*****

Police Act 1997

(1997, c. 50)

An Act to make provision for the National Criminal Intelligence Service and the National Crime Squad; to make provision about entry on and interference with property and with wireless telegraphy in the course of the prevention or detection of serious crime; to make provision for the Police Information Technology Organisation; to provide for the issue of certificates about criminal records; to make provision about the administration and organisation of the police; to repeal certain enactments about rehabilitation of offenders; and for connected purposes.   [21st March 1997]

Territorial extent: United Kingdom (sections printed)

1–87, 89, 90 ...

88   ***

PART III AUTHORISATION OF ACTION IN RESPECT OF PROPERTY

91 ...

Authorisations

92   Effect of authorisation under Part III

No entry on or interference with property or with wireless telegraphy shall be unlawful if it is authorised by an authorisation having effect under this Part.

93   Authorisations to interfere with property etc

(1) Where subsection (2) applies, an authorising officer may authorise—

    (a)   the taking of such action, in respect of such property in the relevant area, as he may specify,

    [(ab) the taking of such action falling within subsection (1A) in respect of property outside the relevant area, as he may specify, or]

    (b)   the taking of such action in the relevant area as he may specify, in respect of wireless telegraphy.

[(1A) The action falling within this subsection is action for maintaining or retrieving any equipment, apparatus or device the placing or use of which in the relevant area has been authorised under this Part or Part II of the Regulation of Investigatory Powers Act 2000 or under any enactment contained in or made under an Act of the Scottish Parliament which makes provision equivalent to that made by Part II of that Act of 2000.

(1B) Subsection (1) applies where the authorising officer is a [National Crime Agency officer], [giving an authorisation on an application made by virtue of subsection (3)(b)(i)],] [an officer of Revenue and Customs] [, an immigration officer] [or the chair of the Competition and Markets Authority] with the omission of—

    (a) the words 'in the relevant area' in each place where they occur; and

    (b) paragraph (ab).]

(2) This subsection applies where the authorising officer believes—

    (a) that it is necessary for the action specified to be taken [for the purpose of preventing or detecting][—

        (i)   serious crime, or

        (ii) the use of an unmanned aircraft in the commission of a relevant offence], and

    (b) [that the taking of the action is proportionate to what the action seeks to achieve.]]

[(2A)–(2B)], (3), [(3A)] *****

[(3B)–(3E)] ...

(4) For the purposes of subsection (2), conduct which constitutes one or more offences shall be regarded as serious crime if, and only if,—

    (a) it involves the use of violence, results in substantial financial gain or is conduct by a large number of persons in pursuit of a common purpose, or

    (b) the offence or one of the offences is an offence for which a person who has attained the age of twenty-one and has no previous convictions could reasonably be expected to be sentenced to imprisonment for a term of three years or more,

and, where the authorising officer is within subsection (5)(h), [the conduct] relates to an assigned matter within the meaning of section 1(1) of the Customs and Excise Management Act 1979 [or, where the authorizing officer is within subsection (5)(ha), any of the offences is an immigration or nationality offence].

[(4A)–(4C)] *****

(5) In this section 'authorising officer' means—

    (a)   the chief constable of a police force maintained under section 2 of the Police Act 1996 (maintenance of police forces for areas in England and Wales except London);

    (b)   the Commissioner, or an Assistant Commissioner, of Police of the Metropolis;

    (c)   the Commissioner of Police for the City of London;

    (d)   the Chief Constable of the Police Service of Scotland, or any Deputy Chief Constable or Assistance Chief Constable of the Police Service of Scotland who is designated for the purposes of this paragraph by the Chief Constable;]

    (e)   the Chief Constable or a Deputy Chief Constable of the [Police Service of Northern Ireland];

    [(ea) the Chief Constable of the Ministry of Defence Police;

    [(eb) the Provost Marshal of the [Royal Navy Police];

    [(ec) the Provost Marshal of the Royal Military Police;

    [(ed) the Provost Marshal of the Royal Air Force Police;

    [(eda) the Provost Marshal for serious crime;]

    [(ee) the Chief Constable of the British Transport Police;]

    [(ef) the Chief Constable of the Civil Nuclear Constabulary;]

[(f) the Director General of the National Crime Agency, or any other National Crime Agency officer who is designated for the purposes of this paragraph by that Director General;] ...

(h) [an officer of Revenue and Customs who is a senior official within the meaning of the Regulation of Investigatory Powers Act 2000 and who is designated for the purposes of this paragraph by the Commissioners of Her Majesty's Revenue and Customs] [; ...

[(ha) an immigration officer who is a senior official within the meaning of the Regulation of Investigatory Powers Act 2000 and who is designated for the purposes of this paragraph by the Secretary of State;]

[(hb) a member of senior management for prisons in England and Wales—

(i) whose duties as a member of senior management for prisons in England and Wales are exercisable in relation to the relevant England and Wales institution, and

(ii) who is designated for the purposes of this paragraph by the Secretary of State;

(hc) a member of senior management for prisons in Northern Ireland whose duties as a member of senior management for prisons in Northern Ireland are exercisable in relation to the relevant Northern Ireland institution;

(hd) a member of senior management for penal institutions in Scotland—

(i) whose duties as a member of senior management for penal institutions in Scotland are exercisable in relation to the relevant Scottish penal institution, and

(ii) who is designated for the purposes of this paragraph by the Scottish Ministers];

(i) [the chair of the Competition and Markets Authority];

[(ia) the Police Investigations and Review Commissioner];

[(j) ...]

(6), (6A), (6B) *****

(7) The powers conferred by, or by virtue of, this section are additional to any other powers which a person has as a constable either at common law or under or by virtue of any other enactment and are not to be taken to affect any of those other powers.

(8) *****

94 *****

95 Authorisations: form and duration etc

(1) An authorisation shall be in writing, except that in an urgent case an authorisation (other than one given by virtue of section 94) may be given orally.

(2) An authorisation shall, unless renewed under subsection (3), cease to have effect—

(a) if given orally or by virtue of section 94, at the end of the period of 72 hours beginning with the time when it took effect;

(b) in any other case, at the end of the period of three months beginning with the day on which it took effect.

(3) If at any time before an authorisation would cease to have effect the authorising officer who gave the authorisation, or in whose absence it was given, considers it necessary for the authorisation to continue to have effect for the purpose for which it was issued, he may, in writing, renew it for a period of three months beginning with the day on which it would cease to have effect.

(4) A person shall cancel an authorisation given by him if satisfied that [the authorisation is one in relation to which the requirement of paragraphs (a) to (b) of section 93(2) are no longer satisfied.]

(5)–(7) *****

96 *****

Authorisations requiring approval

97 Authorisations requiring approval

(1) An authorisation to which this section applies shall not take effect until—

(a) it has been approved in accordance with this section by [a Judicial Commissioner], appointed under section 91(1)(b), and

(b) the person who gave the authorisation has been notified under subsection (4).

(2) Subject to subsection (3), this section applies to an authorisation if, at the time it is given, the person who gives it believes—

    (a) that any of the property specified in the authorisation—

        (i)　is used wholly or mainly as a dwelling or as a bedroom in a hotel, or

        (ii)　constitutes office premises, or

    (b) that the action authorised by it is likely to result in any person acquiring knowledge of—

        (i)　matters subject to legal privilege,

        (ii)　confidential personal information, or

        (iii)　confidential journalistic material.

(3) This section does not apply to an authorisation where the person who gives it believes that the case is one of urgency.

(4) Where [a Judicial Commissioner] receives a notice under section 96 which specifies that this section applies to the authorisation, he shall as soon as is reasonably practicable—

    (a) decide whether to approve the authorisation or refuse approval, and

    (b) give written notice of his decision to the person who gave the authorisation.

(5) [A Judicial Commissioner] shall approve an authorisation if, and only if, he is satisfied that there are reasonable grounds for believing the matters specified in section 93(2).

    (6)–(8) *****

98 Matters subject to legal privilege

(1) Subject to subsection (5) below, in section 97 'matters subject to legal privilege' means matters to which subsection (2), (3) or (4) below applies.

(2) This subsection applies to communications between a professional legal adviser and—

    (a) his client, or

    (b) any person representing his client, which are made in connection with the giving of legal advice to the client.

(3) This subsection applies to communications—

    (a) between a professional legal adviser and his client or any person representing his client, or

    (b) between a professional legal adviser or his client or any such representative and any other person,

which are made in connection with or in contemplation of legal proceedings and for the purposes of such proceedings.

(4) This subsection applies to items enclosed with or referred to in communications of the kind mentioned in subsection (2) or (3) and made—

    (a) in connection with the giving of legal advice, or

    (b) in connection with or in contemplation of legal proceedings and for the purposes of such proceedings.

(5) For the purposes of section 97—

    (a) communications and items are not matters subject to legal privilege when they are in the possession of a person who is not entitled to possession of them, and

    (b) communications and items held, or oral communications made, with the intention of furthering a criminal purpose are not matters subject to legal privilege.

99 Confidential personal information

(1) In section 97 'confidential personal information' means—

    (a) personal information which a person has acquired or created in the course of any trade, business, profession or other occupation or for the purposes of any paid or unpaid office, and which he holds in confidence, and

    (b) communications as a result of which personal information—

        (i)　is acquired or created as mentioned in paragraph (a), and

        (ii)　is held in confidence.

(2) For the purposes of this section 'personal information' means information concerning an individual (whether living or dead) who can be identified from it and relating—

(a) to his physical or mental health, or

(b) to spiritual counselling or assistance given or to be given to him.

(3) A person holds information in confidence for the purposes of this section if he holds it subject—

(a) to an express or implied undertaking to hold it in confidence, or

(b) to a restriction on disclosure or an obligation of secrecy contained in any enactment (including an enactment contained in an Act passed after this Act).

100   Confidential journalistic material

(1) In section 97 'confidential journalistic material' means—

(a) material acquired or created for the purposes of journalism which—

(i)   is in the possession of persons who acquired or created it for those purposes,

(ii)   is held subject to an undertaking, restriction or obligation of the kind mentioned in section 99(3), and

(iii) has been continuously held (by one or more persons) subject to such an undertaking, restriction or obligation since it was first acquired or created for the purposes of journalism, and

(b) communications as a result of which information is acquired for the purposes of journalism and held as mentioned in paragraph (a)(ii).

(2) For the purposes of subsection (1), a person who receives material, or acquires information, from someone who intends that the recipient shall use it for the purposes of journalism is to be taken to have acquired it for those purposes.

101, 102 ...

103   Quashing of authorisations etc

(1) Where, at any time, [a Judicial Commissioner] is satisfied that, at the time an authorisation was given or renewed, there were no reasonable grounds for believing the matters specified in section 93(2), he may quash the authorisation or, as the case may be, renewal.

(2) Where, in the case of an authorisation or renewal to which section 97 does not apply, [a Judicial Commissioner] is at any time satisfied that, at the time the authorisation was given or, as the case may be, renewed,—

(a) there were reasonable grounds for believing any of the matters specified in subsection (2) of section 97, and

(b) there were no reasonable grounds for believing the case to be one of urgency for the purposes of subsection (3) of that section,

he may quash the authorisation or, as the case may be, renewal.

(3) Where [a Judicial Commissioner] quashes an authorisation or renewal under subsection (1) or (2), he may order the destruction of any records relating to information obtained by virtue of the authorisation (or, in the case of a renewal, relating wholly or partly to information so obtained after the renewal) other than records required for pending criminal or civil proceedings.

(4)–(9) *****

*****

Civil Procedure Rules 1998

*****

PART 54 JUDICIAL REVIEW AND STATUTORY REVIEW

54.1 Scope and interpretation

(1) This [section of this] Part contains rules about judicial review.

(2) In this [section]—

    (a) a 'claim for judicial review' means a claim to review the lawfulness of—
        (i)   an enactment; or
        (ii) a decision, action or failure to act in relation to the exercise of a public function;
    (b)–(d) ...
    (e) 'the judicial review procedure' means the Part 8 procedure as modified by this [section];
    (f) 'interested party' means any person (other than the claimant and defendant) who is directly affected by the claim; and
    (g) 'court' means the High Court, unless otherwise stated.

(Rule 8.1(6)(b) provides that a rule or practice direction may, in relation to a specified type of proceedings, disapply or modify any of the rules set out in Part 8 as they apply to those proceedings)

[54.1A   Who may exercise the powers of the High Court]

    [(1) A court officer assigned to the Administrative Court office who is—
    (a) a barrister; ...
    (b) a solicitor[; or]
    (c) a Fellow of the Chartered Institute of Legal Executives [or a CILEX lawyer],]

may exercise the jurisdiction of the High Court with regard to the matters set out in paragraph (2) with the consent of the President of the [King's] Bench Division.

    (2) The matters referred to in paragraph (1) are—
    (a) any matter incidental to any proceedings in the High Court;
    (b) any other matter where there is no substantial dispute between the parties; and
    (c) the dismissal of an appeal or application where a party has failed to comply with any order, rule or practice direction.

    (3) A court officer may not decide an application for—
    (a) permission to bring judicial review proceedings;
    (b) an injunction;
    (c) a stay of any proceedings, other than a temporary stay of any order or decision of the lower court over a period when the High Court is not sitting or cannot conveniently be convened, unless the parties seek a stay by consent.

    (4) Decisions of a court officer may be made without a hearing.

    (5) A party may request any decision of a court officer to be reviewed by a judge of the High Court.

    (6) At the request of a party, a hearing will be held to reconsider a decision of a court officer, made without a hearing.

    (7) A request under paragraph (5) or (6) must be filed within 7 days after the party is served with notice of the decision.]

54.2   When this [section] must be used

The judicial review procedure must be used in a claim for judicial review where the claimant is seeking—
    (a) a mandatory order;
    (b) a prohibiting order;
    (c) a quashing order; or
    (d) an injunction under section 30 of the [Senior Courts Act 1981] (restraining a person from acting in any office in which he is not entitled to act).

54.3   When this [section] may be used

    (1) The judicial review procedure may be used in a claim for judicial review where the claimant is seeking—
    (a) a declaration; or
    (b) an injunction.

(Section 31(2) of the [Senior Courts Act 1981] sets out the circumstances in which the court may grant a declaration or injunction in a claim for judicial review)

    (Where the claimant is seeking a declaration or injunction in addition to one of the remedies listed in rule 54.2, the judicial review procedure must be used)

(2) A claim for judicial review may include a claim for damages [, restitution or the recovery of a sum due] but may not seek [such a remedy] alone.

(Section 31(4) of the [Senior Courts Act 1981] sets out the circumstances in which the court may award damages [, restitution or a sum due] on a claim for judicial review)

54.4   Permission required

The court's permission to proceed is required in a claim for judicial review whether started under this [section] or transferred to the Administrative Court.

54.5   Time limit for filing claim form

[[(A1) In this rule—

'the planning acts' has the same meaning as in section 336 of the Town and Country Planning Act 1990;

'decision governed by the Public Contracts Regulations 2006' means any decision the legality of which is or may be affected by a duty owed to an economic operator by virtue of regulation 47A of those Regulations (and for this purpose it does not matter that the claimant is not an economic operator); and

'economic operator' has the same meaning as in [regulation 2(1) of the Public Contracts Regulations 2015].]

(1) The claim form must be filed—

    (a) promptly; and

    (b) in any event not later than 3 months after the grounds to make the claim first arose.

(2) The time [limits] in this rule may not be extended by agreement between the parties.

(3) This rule does not apply when any other enactment specifies a shorter time limit for making the claim for judicial review.

[(4) Paragraph (1) does not apply in the cases specified in paragraphs (5) and (6).

(5) Where the application for judicial review relates to a decision made by the Secretary of State or local planning authority under the planning acts, the claim form must be filed not later than six weeks after the grounds to make the claim first arose.

(6) Where the application for judicial review relates to a decision governed by [the Public Contracts Regulations 2015], the claim form must be filed within the time within which an economic operator would have been required by [regulation 92(2)] of those Regulations (and disregarding the rest of that regulation) to start any proceedings under those Regulations in respect of that decision.]]

54.6   Claim form

(1) In addition to the matters set out in rule 8.2 (contents of the claim form) the claimant must also state—

    (a) the name and address of any person he considers to be an interested party;

    (b) that he is requesting permission to proceed with a claim for judicial review; ...

    (c) any remedy (including any interim remedy) he is claiming [; and

    (d) where appropriate, the grounds on which it is contended that the claim is an Aarhus Convention claim].

[(Rules 45.41 to 45.44 make provision about costs in Aarhus Convention claims.)] (Part 25 sets out how to apply for an interim remedy)

(2) The claim form must be accompanied by the documents required by [Practice Direction 54A].

54.7   Service of claim form

The claim form must be served on—

    (a) the defendant; and

    (b) unless the court otherwise directs, any person the claimant considers to be an interested party,

within 7 days after the date of issue.

[54.7A   Judicial review of decisions of the Upper Tribunal]

[(1) Where the Upper Tribunal has refused permission to appeal against a decision of the First-tier Tribunal, no application for judicial review of the Upper Tribunal's decision, or which relates to the First-tier Tribunal's decision, may be made except where the question in the judicial review application is—

    (a) whether the application for permission to appeal was validly made to the Upper Tribunal;

    (b) whether the Upper Tribunal when refusing permission to appeal was properly constituted; or

    (c) whether the Upper Tribunal is acting or has acted in bad faith or in such a procedurally defective way as amounts to a fundamental breach of the principles of natural justice.

(2) The claim form and the supporting documents must be filed no later than 16 days after the date on which notice of the Upper Tribunal's decision was sent to the applicant.]

54.8–54.16   *****

54.17   Court's powers to hear any person

(1) Any person may apply for permission—

    (a) to file evidence; or

    (b) make representations at the hearing of the judicial review.

(2) An application under paragraph (1) should be made promptly.

54.18   Judicial review may be decided without a hearing

The court may decide the claim for judicial review without a hearing where all the parties agree.

54.19   Court's powers in respect of quashing orders

(1) This rule applies where the court makes a quashing order in respect of the decision to which the claim relates.

[(2) The court may—

    (a)

        (i)   remit the matter to the decision-maker; and

        (ii)   direct it to reconsider the matter and reach a decision in accordance with the judgment of the court; or

    (b) in so far as any enactment permits, substitute its own decision for the decision to which the claim relates.

(Section 31 of the Supreme Court Act 1981 enables the High Court, subject to certain conditions, to substitute its own decision for the decision in question.)]

    (3) …

54.20   Transfer

The court may—

    (a) order a claim to continue as if it had not been started under this [section] and

    (b) where it does so, give directions about the future management of the claim.

(Part 30 (transfer) applies to transfers to and from the Administrative Court.)

*****

Crime and Disorder Act 1998

(1998, c. 37)

An Act to make provision for preventing crime and disorder; to create certain racially-aggravated offences; to abolish the rebuttable presumption that a child is doli incapax and to make provision as to the effect of a child's failure to give evidence at his trial; to abolish the death penalty for treason and piracy; to make changes to the criminal justice system; to make further provision for dealing with offenders; to make further provision with respect to remands and committals for trial and the release and recall of prisoners; to amend Chapter I of Part II of the Crime (Sentences) Act 1997 and to repeal Chapter I of Part III of the Crime and Punishment (Scotland) Act 1997; to make amendments designed to facilitate, or otherwise desirable in connection with, the consolidation of certain enactments; and for connected purposes. [31st July 1998]

Territorial extent: England and Wales; ss. 12 and following, and 33, make equivalent provisions for Scotland to those reproduced. Certain provisions (not reproduced here) concerning the abolition of the death penalty for treason and piracy apply to Scotland and Northern Ireland.

PART I PREVENTION OF CRIME AND DISORDER

Crime and disorder: general

1–10 *****

11 Child safety orders

(1) Subject to subsection (2) below, if [the family court], on the application of a local authority, is satisfied that one or more of the conditions specified in subsection (3) below are fulfilled with respect to a child under the age of 10, it may make an order (a 'child safety order') which—

(a) places the child, for a period (not exceeding the permitted maximum) specified in the order, under the supervision of the responsible officer; and

(b) requires the child to comply with such requirements as are so specified.

(2) A court shall not make a child safety order unless it has been notified by the Secretary of State that arrangements for implementing such orders are available in the area in which it appears that the child resides or will reside and the notice has not been withdrawn.

(3) The conditions are—

(a) that the child has committed an act which, if he had been aged 10 or over, would have constituted an offence;

(b) that a child safety order is necessary for the purpose of preventing the commission by the child of such an act as is mentioned in paragraph (a) above;

(c) … and

(d) that the child has acted in a manner that caused or was likely to cause harassment, alarm or distress to one or more persons not of the same household as himself.

(4) The maximum period permitted for the purposes of subsection (1)(a) above is [twelve months].

(5) The requirements that may be specified under subsection (1)(b) above are those which the court considers desirable in the interests of—

(a) securing that the child receives appropriate care, protection and support and is subject to proper control; or

(b) preventing any repetition of the kind of behaviour which led to the child safety order being made.

(6) Proceedings under this section or section 12 below shall be family proceedings for the purposes of the 1989 Act … and the standard of proof applicable to such proceedings shall be that applicable to civil proceedings.

(7), (8) *****

12–27 *****

PART II CRIMINAL LAW

Racially [or religiously] aggravated offences: England and Wales

28 Meaning of [racially or religiously] aggravated

(1) An offence is racially [or religiously] aggravated for the purposes of sections 29 to 32 below if—

(a) at the time of committing the offence, or immediately before or after doing so, the offender demonstrates towards the victim of the offence hostility based on the victim's membership (or presumed membership) of a [racial or religious group]; or

(b) the offence is motivated (wholly or partly) by hostility towards members of a [racial or religious group] based on their membership of that group.

(2) In subsection (1)(a) above—

'membership', in relation to a [racial or religious group], includes association with members of that group;

'presumed' means presumed by the offender.

(3) It is immaterial for the purposes of paragraph (a) or (b) of subsection (1) above whether or not the offender's hostility is also based, to any extent, on [any other factor not mentioned in that paragraph.]

(4) In this section 'racial group' means a group of persons defined by reference to race, colour, nationality (including citizenship) or ethnic or national origins.

[(5) In this section 'religious group' means a group of persons defined by reference to religious belief or lack of religious belief.]

29 [Racially or religiously aggravated] assaults

(1) A person is guilty of an offence under this section if he commits—

(a)   an offence under section 20 of the Offences Against the Person Act 1861 (malicious wounding or grievous bodily harm);

(b)   an offence under section 47 of that Act (actual bodily harm);

[(ba) an offence under section 75A of the Serious Crime Act 2015 (strangulation or suffocation);] or

(c)   common assault,

which is [racially or religiously aggravated] for the purposes of this section.

(2) A person guilty of an offence falling within subsection (1)(a)[, (b) or (ba)] above shall be liable—

(a) on summary conviction, to imprisonment for a term not exceeding six months or to a fine not exceeding the statutory maximum, or to both;

(b) on conviction on indictment, to imprisonment for a term not exceeding seven years or to a fine, or to both.

(3) A person guilty of an offence falling within subsection (1)(c) above shall be liable—

(a) on summary conviction, to imprisonment for a term not exceeding six months or to a fine not exceeding the statutory maximum, or to both;

(b) on conviction on indictment, to imprisonment for a term not exceeding two years or to a fine, or to both.

30 [Racially or religiously aggravated] criminal damage

(1) A person is guilty of an offence under this section if he commits an offence under section 1(1) of the Criminal Damage Act 1971 (destroying or damaging property belonging to another) which is [racially or religiously aggravated] for the purposes of this section.

(2) A person guilty of an offence under this section shall be liable—

(a) on summary conviction, to imprisonment for a term not exceeding six months or to a fine not exceeding the statutory maximum, or to both;

(b) on conviction on indictment, to imprisonment for a term not exceeding fourteen years or to a fine, or to both.

(3) *****

31 [Racially or religiously aggravated] public order offences

(1) A person is guilty of an offence under this section if he commits—

(a) an offence under section 4 of the Public Order Act 1986 (fear or provocation of violence);

(b) an offence under section 4A of that Act (intentional harassment, alarm or distress); or

(c) an offence under section 5 of that Act (harassment, alarm or distress),

which is [racially or religiously aggravated] for the purposes of this section.

(2), (3) ...

(4) A person guilty of an offence falling within subsection (1)(a) or (b) above shall be liable—

(a) on summary conviction, to imprisonment for a term not exceeding six months or to a fine not exceeding the statutory maximum, or to both;

(b) on conviction on indictment, to imprisonment for a term not exceeding two years or to a fine, or to both.

(5) A person guilty of an offence falling within subsection (1)(c) above shall be liable on summary conviction to a fine not exceeding level 4 on the standard scale.

(6), (7) *****

32   [Racially or religiously aggravated] harassment etc

(1) A person is guilty of an offence under this section if he commits—

(a) an offence under section 2 [or 2A] of the Protection from Harassment Act 1997 ([offences of harassment and stalking]); or

(b) an offence under section 4 [or 4A] of that Act (putting people in fear of violence [and stalking involving fear of violence or serious alarm or distress]),

which is [racially or religiously aggravated] for the purposes of this section.

(2) ...

(3) A person guilty of an offence falling within subsection (1)(a) above shall be liable—

(a) on summary conviction, to imprisonment for a term not exceeding six months or to a fine not exceeding the statutory maximum, or to both;

(b) on conviction on indictment, to imprisonment for a term not exceeding two years or to a fine, or to both.

(4) A person guilty of an offence falling within subsection (1)(b) above shall be liable—

(a) on summary conviction, to imprisonment for a term not exceeding six months or to a fine not exceeding the statutory maximum, or to both;

(b) on conviction on indictment, to imprisonment for a term not exceeding [14 years] or to a fine, or to both.

(5)–(6) *****

(7) ...

*****

Human Rights Act 1998

(1998, c. 42)

An Act to give further effect to rights and freedoms guaranteed under the European Convention on Human Rights; to make provision with respect to holders of certain judicial offices who become judges of the European Court of Human Rights; and for connected purposes.   [9th November 1998]

Territorial extent: United Kingdom

Introduction

1   The Convention Rights

(1) In this Act 'the Convention rights' means the rights and fundamental freedoms set out in—

(a) Articles 2 to 12 and 14 of the Convention,

(b) Articles 1 to 3 of the First Protocol, and

(c) [Article 1 of the Thirteenth Protocol,]

as read with Articles 16 to 18 of the Convention.

(2) Those Articles are to have effect for the purposes of this Act subject to any designated derogation or reservation (as to which see sections 14 and 15).

(3) The Articles are set out in Schedule 1.*

(4) The [Secretary of State] may by order make such amendments to this act as he considers appropriate to reflect the effect, in relation to the United Kingdom, of a protocol.

(5) In subsection (4) 'protocol' means a protocol to the Convention—

    (a) which the United Kingdom has ratified; or

    (b) which the United Kingdom has signed with a view to ratification.

(6) No amendment may be made by an order under subsection (4) so as to come into force before the protocol concerned is in force in relation to the United Kingdom.

2 Interpretation of Convention rights

(1) A court or tribunal determining a question which has arisen in connection with a Convention right must take into account any—

    (a) judgment, decision, declaration or advisory opinion of the European Court of Human Rights,

    (b) opinion of the Commission given in a report adopted under Article 31 of the Convention,

    (c) decision of the Commission in connection with Article 26 or 27(2) of the Convention, or

    (d) decision of the Committee of Ministers taken under Article 46 of the Convention,

whenever made or given, so far as, in the opinion of the court or tribunal, it is relevant to the proceedings in which that question has arisen.

(2), (3) *****

Legislation

3 Interpretation of legislation

(1) So far as it is possible to do so, primary legislation and subordinate legislation must be read and given effect in a way which is compatible with Convention rights.

(2) This section—

    (a) applies to primary legislation and subordinate legislation whenever enacted;

    (b) does not affect the validity, continuing operation or enforcement of any incompatible primary legislation; and

    (c) does not affect the validity, continuing operation or enforcement of any incompatible subordinate legislation if (disregarding any possibility of revocation) primary legislation prevents removal of the incompatibility.

4 Declaration of incompatibility

(1) Subsection (2) applies in any proceedings in which a court determines whether a provision of primary legislation is compatible with a Convention right.

(2) If the court is satisfied that the provision is incompatible with a Convention right, it may make a declaration of that incompatibility.

(3) Subsection (4) applies in any proceedings in which a court determines whether a provision of subordinate legislation, made in the exercise of a power conferred by primary legislation, is compatible with a Convention right.

(4) If the court is satisfied—

    (a) that the provision is incompatible with a Convention right, and

    (b) that (disregarding any possibility of revocation) the primary legislation concerned prevents removal of the incompatibility,

it may make a declaration of that incompatibility.

(5) In this section 'court' means—

    [(a) the Supreme Court;]

    (b) the Judicial Committee of the Privy Council;

    (c) the [Court-Martial Appeal Court];

---

* **Editor's Note:** Schedule 1 is omitted, as the relevant Articles of and Protocols to the Convention are printed as part of the Convention in Part III. Note that Art. 13 of the Convention (effective remedy) is not incorporated by s. 1.

(d) in Scotland, the High Court of Justiciary sitting otherwise than as a trial court or the Court of Session;

(e) in England and Wales or Northern Ireland, the High Court or the Court of Appeal;

[(f) the Court of Protection, in any matter being dealt with by the President of the Family Division, the [Chancellor of the High Court] or a puisne judge of the High Court.]

(6) A declaration under this section ('a declaration of incompatibility')—

(a) does not affect the validity, continuing operation or enforcement of the provision in respect of which it is given; and

(b) is not binding on the parties to the proceedings in which it is made.

5 *********

Public authorities

6 Acts of public authorities

(1) It is unlawful for a public authority to act in a way which is incompatible with a Convention right.

(2) Subsection (1) does not apply to an act if—

(a) as the result of one or more provisions of primary legislation, the authority could not have acted differently; or

(b) in the case of one or more provisions of, or made under, primary legislation which cannot be read or given effect in a way which is compatible with the Convention rights, the authority was acting so as to give effect to or enforce those provisions.

(3) In this section 'public authority' includes—

(a) a court or tribunal, and

(b) any person certain of whose functions are functions of a public nature,

but does not include either House of Parliament or a person exercising functions in connection with proceedings in Parliament.

(4) ...

(5) In relation to a particular act, a person is not a public authority by virtue only of subsection (3)(b) if the nature of the act is private.

(6) 'An act' includes a failure to act but does not include a failure to—

(a) introduce in, or lay before, Parliament a proposal for legislation; or

(b) make any primary legislation or remedial order.

7 Proceedings

(1) A person who claims that a public authority has acted (or proposes to act) in a way which is made unlawful by section 6(1) may—

(a) bring proceedings against the authority under this Act in the appropriate court or tribunal, or

(b) rely on the convention right or rights concerned in any legal proceedings,

but only if he is (or would be) a victim of the unlawful act.

(2) In subsection (1)(a) 'appropriate court or tribunal' means such court or tribunal as may be determined in accordance with rules; and proceedings against an authority include a counterclaim or similar proceedings.

(3) If the proceedings are brought on an application for judicial review, the applicant is to be taken to have a sufficient interest in relation to the unlawful act only if he is, or would be, a victim of that act.

(4) If the proceedings are made by way of a petition for judicial review in Scotland, the applicant shall be taken to have title and interest to sue in relation to the unlawful act only if he is, or would be, a victim of that act.

(5) Proceedings under subsection (1)(a) must be brought before the end of—

(a) the period of one year beginning with the date on which the act complained of took place; or

(b) such longer period as the court or tribunal considers equitable having regard to all the circumstances, but that is subject to any rule imposing a stricter time limit in relation to the procedure in question.

(6) In subsection (1)(b) 'legal proceedings' includes—

(a) proceedings brought by or at the instigation of a public authority; and

(b) an appeal against the decision of a court or tribunal.

(7) For the purposes of this section, a person is a victim of an unlawful act only if he would be a victim for the purposes of Article 34 of the Convention if proceedings were brought in the European Court of Human Rights in respect of that act.

(8) Nothing in this Act creates a criminal offence.

(9)–(13) *****

[7A Limitation: overseas armed forces proceedings]

[(1) A court or tribunal exercising its discretion under section 7(5)(b) in respect of overseas armed forces proceedings must do so—

(a) in accordance with subsection (2), and

(b) subject to the rule in subsection (4).

(2) The court or tribunal must have particular regard to—

(a) the effect of the delay in bringing proceedings on the cogency of evidence adduced or likely to be adduced by the parties, with particular reference to—

(i) the likely impact of the operational context on the ability of individuals who are (or, at the time of the events to which the proceedings relate, were) members of Her Majesty's forces to remember relevant events or actions fully or accurately, and

(ii) the extent of dependence on the memories of such individuals, taking into account the effect of the operational context on the ability of such individuals to record, or to retain records of, relevant events or actions;

(b) the likely impact of the proceedings on the mental health of any witness or potential witness who is (or, at the time of the events to which the proceedings relate, was) a member of Her Majesty's forces.

(3) In subsection (2) references to 'the operational context' are to the fact that the events to which the proceedings relate took place in the context of overseas operations, and include references to the exceptional demands and stresses to which members of Her Majesty's forces are subject.

(4) The rule referred to in subsection (1)(b) is that overseas armed forces proceedings must be brought before the later of—

(a) the end of the period of 6 years beginning with the date on which the act complained of took place;

(b) the end of the period of 12 months beginning with the date of knowledge.

(5) In subsection (4), the 'date of knowledge' means the date on which the person bringing the proceedings first knew, or first ought to have known, both—

(a) of the act complained of, and

(b) that it was an act of the Ministry of Defence or the Secretary of State for Defence.

(6) 'Overseas armed forces proceedings' means proceedings—

(a) against the Ministry of Defence or the Secretary of State for Defence, and

(b) in connection with overseas operations.

(7) 'Overseas operations' means any operations outside the British Islands, including peace-keeping operations and operations for dealing with terrorism, civil unrest or serious public disorder, in the course of which members of Her Majesty's forces come under attack or face the threat of attack or violent resistance.

(8) In this section the reference to the British Islands includes the territorial sea adjacent to the United Kingdom and the territorial sea adjacent to any of the Channel Islands or the Isle of Man.

(9) In this section 'Her Majesty's forces' has the same meaning as in the Armed Forces Act 2006 (see section 374 of that Act).]

8 Judicial remedies

(1) In relation to any act (or proposed act) of a public authority which the court finds is (or would be) unlawful, it may grant such relief or remedy, or make such order, within its powers as it considers just and appropriate.

(2) But damages may be awarded only by a court which has power to award damages, or to order the payment of compensation, in civil proceedings.

(3) No award of damages is to be made unless, taking account of all the circumstances of the case, including—

(a) any other relief or remedy granted, or order made, in relation to the act in question (by that or any other court), and

(b) the consequences of any decision (of that or any other court) in respect of that act, the court is satisfied that the award is necessary to afford just satisfaction to the person in whose favour it is made.

(4) In determining—

(a) whether to award damages, or

(b) the amount of an award,

the court must take into account the principles applied by the European Court of Human Rights in relation to the award of compensation under Article 41 of the Convention.

(5), (6) *****

9   Judicial acts

(1) Proceedings under section 7(1)(a) in respect of a judicial act may be brought only—

(a) by exercising a right of appeal;

(b) on an application (in Scotland a petition) for a judicial review; or

(c) in such other forum as may be prescribed by rules.

(2) That does not affect any rule of law which prevents a court from being the subject of judicial review.

[(3) In proceedings under this Act in respect of a judicial act done in good faith, damages may not be awarded otherwise than

(a) to compensate a person to the extent required by Article 5(5) of the Convention, or

(b) to compensate a person for a judicial act that is incompatible with Article 6 of the Convention in circumstances where the person is detained and, but for the incompatibility, the person would not have been detained or would not have been detained for so long.]

(4) An award of damages permitted by subsection (3) is to be made against the Crown; but no award may be made unless the appropriate person, if not a party to the proceedings, is joined.

(5) In this section—

'appropriate person' means the minister responsible for the court concerned or a person or government department nominated by him;

'court' includes a tribunal;

'judge' includes a member of a tribunal, a justice of the peace [(or, in Northern Ireland, a lay magistrate)] and a clerk or other officer entitled to exercise the jurisdiction of a court;

'judicial act' means a judicial act of a court and includes an act done on the instructions, or on behalf, of a judge; and

'rules' has the same meaning as in section 7(9).

Remedial action

10   Power to take remedial action

(1) This section applies if—

(a) a provision of legislation has been declared under section 4 to be incompatible with a Convention right and, if an appeal lies—

(i) all persons who may appeal have stated in writing that they do not intend to do so;

(ii) the time for bringing an appeal has expired and no appeal has been brought within that time; or

(iii) an appeal brought within that time has been determined or abandoned; or

(b) it appears to a Minister of the Crown or Her Majesty in Council that, having regard to a finding of the European Court of Human Rights made after the coming into force of this section in proceedings against the United Kingdom, a provision of legislation is incompatible with an obligation of the United Kingdom arising from the Convention.

(2) If a Minister of the Crown considers that there are compelling reasons for proceedings under this section, he may by order make such amendments to the legislation as he considers necessary to remove the incompatibility.

(3) If, in the case of subordinate legislation, a Minister of the Crown considers—

(a) that it is necessary to amend the primary legislation under which the subordinate legislation in question was made, in order to enable the incompatibility to be removed, and

(b) that there are compelling reasons for proceeding under this section,

he may by order make such amendments to the primary legislation as he considers necessary.

(4)–(7) *****

Other rights and proceedings

11 Safeguard for existing human rights

A person's reliance on a Convention right does not restrict—

(a) any other right or freedom conferred on him by or under any law having effect in any part of the United Kingdom; or

(b) his right to make any claim or bring any proceedings which he could make or bring apart from sections 7 to 9.

12 Freedom of expression

(1) This section applies if a court is considering whether to grant any relief which, if granted, might affect the exercise of the Convention right to freedom of expression.

(2) If the person against whom the application for relief is made ('the respondent') is neither present nor represented, no such relief is to be granted unless the court is satisfied—

(a) that the applicant has taken all practicable steps to notify the respondent; or

(b) that there are compelling reasons why the respondent should not be notified.

(3) No such relief is to be granted so as to restrain publication before trial unless the court is satisfied that the applicant is likely to establish that publication should not be allowed.

(4) The court must have particular regard to the importance of the Convention right to freedom of expression and, where the proceedings relate to material which the respondent claims, or which appears to the court, to be journalistic, literary or artistic material (or to conduct connected with such material), to—

(a) the extent to which—

(i) the material has, or is about to, become available to the public; or

(ii) it is, or would be, in the public interest for the material to be published;

(b) any relevant privacy code.

(5) In this section—

'court' includes a tribunal; and

'relief' includes any remedy or order (other than in criminal proceedings).

13 Freedom of thought, conscience and religion

(1) If a court's determination of any question arising under this Act might affect the exercise by a religious organisation (itself or its members collectively) of the Convention right to freedom of thought, conscience and religion, it must have particular regard to the importance of that right.

(2) In this section 'court' includes a tribunal.

14 Derogations

(1) In this Act 'designated derogation' means . . . any derogation by the United Kingdom from an Article of the Convention, or of any protocol to the Convention, which is designated for the purposes of this Act in an order made by the [Secretary of State].

(2) ...

(3)–(6) *****

15–18 *****

19 Statements of compatibility

(1) A Minister of the Crown in charge of a Bill in either House of Parliament must, before Second Reading of the Bill—

    (a) make a statement to the effect that in his view the provisions of the Bill are compatible with the Convention rights ('a statement of compatibility'); or

    (b) make a statement to the effect that although he is unable to make a statement of compatibility the government nevertheless wishes the House to proceed with the Bill.

(2) The statement must be in writing and be published in such manner as the Minister making it considers appropriate.

    *****

Northern Ireland Act 1998

(1998, c. 47)

An Act to make new provision for the government of Northern Ireland for the purpose of implementing the agreement reached at multi-party talks on Northern Ireland set out in Command Paper 3883.   [19th November 1998]

Territorial extent: Northern Ireland

PART I   PRELIMINARY

1 Status of Northern Ireland

(1) It is hereby declared that Northern Ireland in its entirety remains part of the United Kingdom and shall not cease to be so without the consent of a majority of the people of Northern Ireland voting in a poll held for the purposes of this section in accordance with Schedule 1.

(2) But if the wish expressed by a majority in such a poll is that Northern Ireland should cease to be part of the United Kingdom and form part of a united Ireland, the Secretary of State shall lay before Parliament such proposals to give effect to that wish as may be agreed between Her Majesty's Government in the United Kingdom and the Government of Ireland.

2–3 *****

4 Transferred, excepted and reserved matters

(1) In this Act—

'excepted matter' means any matter falling within a description specified in Schedule 2;

'reserved matter' means any matter falling within a description specified in Schedule 3;

'transferred matter' means any matter which is not an excepted or reserved matter.

(2) If at any time after the appointed day it appears to the Secretary of State—

    (a) that any reserved matter should become a transferred matter; or

    (b) that any transferred matter should become a reserved matter,

he may, subject to [subsections (2A)] [to (3D)], lay before Parliament the draft of an Order in Council amending Schedule 3 so that the matter ceases to be or, as the case may be, becomes a reserved matter with effect from such date as may be specified in the Order.

[(2A) The Secretary of State shall not lay before Parliament under subsection (2) the draft of an Order amending Schedule 3 so that a [policing and justice matter] ceases to be a reserved matter unless—

    (a) a motion for a resolution praying that the matter should cease to be a reserved matter is tabled by the First Minister and the deputy First Minister acting jointly; and

(b) the resolution is passed by the Assembly with the support of a majority of the members voting on the motion, a majority of the designated Nationalists voting and a majority of the designated Unionists voting.]

(3) The Secretary of State shall not lay [before Parliament under subsection (2) the draft of any other Order] unless the Assembly has passed with cross-community support a resolution praying that the matter concerned should cease to be or, as the case may be, should become a reserved matter.

[(3A) The Secretary of State shall not lay before Parliament under subsection (2) the draft of an Order amending paragraph 16 of Schedule 3 (Civil Service Commissioners for Northern Ireland) unless the Secretary of State has, at least three months before laying the draft, laid a report before Parliament.

(3B) The report under subsection (3A) must set out the Secretary of State's view of the effect (if any) that the Order would have on—

(a) the independence of the Civil Service Commissioners for Northern Ireland;
(b) the application of the principle that persons should be selected for appointment to the Northern Ireland Civil Service on merit on the basis of fair and open competition; and
(c) the impartiality of the Northern Ireland Civil Service.]

[(3C) The Secretary of State shall not lay before Parliament under subsection (2) the draft of an Order amending paragraph 42(aa) of Schedule 3 (Northern Ireland Human Rights Commission) unless the Secretary of State has, at least three months before laying the draft, laid a report before Parliament.

(3D) The report under subsection (3C) must set out the Secretary of State's view of the effect (if any) that the Order would have on—

(a) the independence of the Northern Ireland Human Rights Commission;
(b) the application of internationally accepted principles relating to national human rights institutions; and
(c) the relationship between the Northern Ireland Human Rights Commission and the Assembly.]

(4) If the draft of an Order laid before Parliament under subsection (2) is approved by resolution of each House of Parliament, the Secretary of State shall submit it to Her Majesty in Council and Her Majesty in Council may make the Order.

(5)–(6) *****

PART II   LEGISLATIVE POWERS

General

5 Acts of the Northern Ireland Assembly

(1) Subject to sections 6 to 8, the Assembly may make laws, to be known as Acts.

(2) A Bill shall become an Act when it has been passed by the Assembly and has received Royal Assent.

(3) A Bill receives Royal Assent at the beginning of the day on which Letters Patent under the Great Seal of Northern Ireland signed with Her Majesty's own hand signifying Her Assent are notified to the Presiding Officer.

(4) The date of Royal Assent shall be written on the Act by the Presiding Officer, and shall form part of the Act.

(5) The validity of any proceedings leading to the enactment of an Act of the Assembly shall not be called into question in any legal proceedings.

(6) This section does not affect the power of the Parliament of the United Kingdom to make laws for Northern Ireland, but an Act of the Assembly may modify any provision made by or under an Act of Parliament in so far as it is part of the law of Northern Ireland.

6   Legislative competence

(1) A provision of an Act is not law if it is outside the legislative competence of the Assembly.

(2) A provision is outside that competence if any of the following paragraphs apply—

    (a)   it would form part of the law of a country or territory other than Northern Ireland, or confer or remove functions exercisable otherwise than in or as regards Northern Ireland;

    (b)   it deals with an excepted matter and is not ancillary to other provisions (whether in the Act or previously enacted) dealing with reserved or transferred matters;

    (c)   it is incompatible with any of the Convention rights;

    [(ca) it is incompatible with Article 2(1) of the Protocol on Ireland/Northern Ireland in the EU withdrawal agreement (rights of individuals);]

    (d)   ...

    (e)   it discriminates against any person or class of person on the ground of religious belief or political opinion;

    (f)   it modifies an enactment in breach of section 7.

(3)–(5) *****

6A ...

7   Entrenched enactments

(1) Subject to [subsection (2A)], the following enactments shall not be modified by an Act of the Assembly or subordinate legislation made, confirmed or approved by a Minister or Northern Ireland department—

    (a) ...

    (b) the Human Rights Act 1998; ...

    (c) section 43(1) to (6) and (8), section 67, sections 84 to [86B], section 95(3) and (4) and section 98; [...

    (d) section 1 and section 84 of the Justice (Northern Ireland) Act 2002][;

    (e) the European Union (Withdrawal) Act 2018][; and

    (f) the United Kingdom Internal Market Act 2020].

(2) ...

[(2A) For the purposes of subsection (2A)(ba), the following are excluded provisions of the European Union (Withdrawal) Act 2018—

    (a) section 1B(3) and (4),

    (b) sections 8A to 8C,

    (c) section 10(3) and (4),

    (d) sections 13A and 13B,

    (e) sections 15A to 15C,

    (f) Parts 1A to 1C of Schedule 2,

    (g) paragraphs 1(11) and (12), 2(12) and (13) and 8A to 8G of Schedule 8, and

    (h) paragraph 21 of Schedule 8.]

(3) In this Act 'Minister', unless the context otherwise requires, means the First Minister, the deputy First Minister or a Northern Ireland Minister.

8–15   ***

PART III   EXECUTIVE AUTHORITIES

Authorities

16 ...

[16A   Appointment of First Minister, deputy First Minister and Northern Ireland Ministers following Assembly election]

[(1) This section applies where an Assembly is elected under section 31 or 32.

(2) ...

(3) [Before the end of the period for filling Ministerial offices—]
  (a) the offices of First Minister and deputy First Minister shall be filled by applying subsections (4) to (7); and
  (b) the Ministerial offices to be held by Northern Ireland Ministers shall be filled by applying section 18(2) to (6).

[[(3A) In this section 'the period for filling Ministerial offices' means the period beginning with 13 May 2022 and ending with 18 January 2024.]

(3B) An extension period is excluded if, before it begins, the Assembly resolves that the period for filling Ministerial offices should not be extended (or further extended).

(3C) The Assembly may not pass a resolution under subsection (3B) without cross-community support.]

(4) The nominating officer of the largest political party of the largest political designation shall nominate a member of the Assembly to be the First Minister.

(5) The nominating officer of the largest political party of the second largest political designation shall nominate a member of the Assembly to be the deputy First Minister.

(6) If the persons nominated do not take up office within a period specified in standing orders, further nominations shall be made under subsections (4) and (5).

(7) Subsections (4) to (6) shall be applied as many times as may be necessary to secure that the offices of First Minister and deputy First Minister are filled.

(8) But no person may take up office as First Minister, deputy First Minister or Northern Ireland Minister by virtue of this section after the end of the period mentioned in subsection (3) (see further section 32(3)).

(9) The persons nominated under subsections (4) and (5) shall not take up office until each of them has affirmed the terms of the pledge of office.

(10) Subject to the provisions of this Part, the First Minister[, the deputy First Minister and the Northern Ireland Ministers] shall hold office until immediately before those offices are next filled by virtue of this section.

(11) The holder of the office of First Minister or deputy First Minister may by notice in writing to the Presiding Officer designate a Northern Ireland Minister to exercise the functions of that office—
  (a) during any absence or incapacity of the holder; or
  (b) during any vacancy in that office arising otherwise than under section 16B(2),
but a person shall not have power to act by virtue of paragraph (a) for a continuous period exceeding six weeks.

[(11A) The First Minister and deputy First Minister cease to hold office if the period of 24 weeks beginning with the day on which an Assembly first meets expires without those offices having been filled by virtue of this section.]

(12) This section shall be construed in accordance with, and is subject to, section 16C]

[16B Vacancies in the office of First Minister or deputy First Minister]

[(1) The First Minister or the deputy First Minister—
  (a) may at any time resign by notice in writing to the Presiding Officer; and
  (b) shall cease to hold office if he ceases to be a member of the Assembly otherwise than by virtue of a dissolution.

(2) If either the First Minister or the deputy First Minister ceases to hold office at any time, whether by resignation or otherwise, the other—
  (a) shall also cease to hold office at that time; but
  (b) may continue to exercise the functions of his office until immediately before those offices are filled in accordance with this section.

[(3) Where at any time the offices of First Minister and deputy First Minister become vacant otherwise than by virtue of section 16A(11A), they shall be filled by applying subsections (4) to (7) before the end of the period for filling the offices of First Minister and deputy First Minister.

(3A) In this section 'the period for filling the offices of First Minister and deputy First Minister' means the period comprising—

(a) the period of six weeks beginning with the day on which the offices of First Minister and deputy First Minister become vacant, and

(b) the next three successive periods of six weeks (each referred to as an 'extension period'), except for any period that is excluded by subsection (3B).

(3B) An extension period is excluded if, before it begins, the Assembly resolves that the period for filling the offices of First Minister and deputy First Minister should not be extended (or further extended).

(3C) The Assembly may not pass a resolution under subsection (3B) without cross-community support.]

(4) The nominating officer of the largest political party of the largest political designation shall nominate a member of the Assembly to be the First Minister.

(5) The nominating officer of the largest political party of the second largest political designation shall nominate a member of the Assembly to be the deputy First Minister.

(6) If the persons nominated do not take up office within a period specified in standing orders, further nominations shall be made under subsections (4) and (5).

(7) Subsections (4) to (6) shall be applied as many times as may be necessary to secure that the offices of First Minister and deputy First Minister are filled.

(8) But no person may take up office as First Minister or deputy First Minister under this section after the end of the period mentioned in subsection (3) (see further section 32(3)).

(9) The persons nominated under subsections (4) and (5) shall not take up office until each of them has affirmed the terms of the pledge of office.

(10) This section shall be construed in accordance with, and is subject to, section 16C.]

[16C   Sections 16A and 16B: supplementary]

[(1) In sections 16A and 16B and this section 'nominating officer', in relation to a party, means—

(a) the person registered under Part 2 of the Political Parties, Elections and Referendums Act 2000 as the party's nominating officer; or

(b) a member of the Assembly nominated by him for the purposes of this section.

(2) For the purposes of sections 16A and 16B and this section—

(a) the size of a political party is to be determined by reference to the number of seats in the Assembly which were held by members of the party on the day on which the Assembly first met following its election; but

(b) if two or more parties are taken by virtue of paragraph (a) to be of the same size, the respective sizes of those parties is to be determined by reference to the number of first preference votes cast for the parties at the last general election of members of the Assembly;

(this is subject to subsections (7) and (8)).

(3) For the purposes of sections 16A and 16B and this section, a political party to which one or more members of the Assembly belong is to be taken—

(a) to be of the political designation 'Nationalist' if, at the relevant time (see subsection (11)), more than half of the members of the Assembly who belonged to the party were designated Nationalists;

(b) to be of the political designation 'Unionist' if, at the relevant time, more than half of the members of the Assembly who belonged to the party were designated Unionists;

(c) otherwise, to be of the political designation 'Other'.

(4) For the purposes of sections 16A and 16B and this section—

(a) the size of the political designation 'Nationalist' is to be taken to be equal to the number of members of the Assembly who, at the relevant time, were designated Nationalists;

(b) the size of the political designation 'Unionist' is to be taken to be equal to the number of members of the Assembly who, at the relevant time, were designated Unionists;

(c) the size of the political designation 'Other' is to be taken to be equal to the number of members of the Assembly who, at the relevant time, were neither designated Nationalists nor designated Unionists.

(5) But if two or more political designations are taken by virtue of subsection (4) to be of the same size, the respective sizes of those designations is to be determined by reference to the aggregate number of first preference votes cast, at the last general election of members of the Assembly, for members of the Assembly who, at the relevant time, were—

(a) designated Nationalists (in the case of the political designation 'Nationalist');

(b) designated Unionists (in the case of the political designation 'Unionist'); or

(c) neither designated Nationalists nor designated Unionists (in the case of the political designation 'Other').

(6) If at any time the party which is the largest political party of the largest political designation is not the largest political party—

(a) any nomination to be made at that time under section 16A(4) or 16B(4) shall instead be made by the nominating officer of the largest political party; and

(b) any nomination to be made at that time under section 16A(5) or 16B(5) shall instead be made by the nominating officer of the largest political party of the largest political designation.

(7) Where—

(a) the Assembly has resolved under section 30(2) that a political party does not enjoy its confidence; and

(b) the party's period of exclusion (see subsection (12)) under that provision has not come to an end,

subsection (2)(a) above shall have effect as if the number of seats in the Assembly which were held by members of the party on the day on which the Assembly first met following its election was nil.

(8) ...

(9) Where—

(a) a person nominated by the nominating officer of a political party ceased to hold office as First Minister or deputy First Minister as a result of a resolution of the Assembly under section 30(2)...; and

(b) the party's period of exclusion under section 30(2)...subsequently comes to an end otherwise than by virtue of the dissolution of the Assembly,

the First Minister and the deputy First Minister shall cease to hold office when the party's period of exclusion under that provision comes to an end...

(10) ...

(11) In this section 'the relevant time' means the end of the day on which the Assembly first met following its election.

(12) In this section, a reference to a period of exclusion...is, in the case of a period of exclusion...which has been extended, a reference to that period as extended.

(13) Standing orders may make further provision in connection with the making of nominations under sections 16A and 16B.

(14) In this Act 'the pledge of office' means the pledge of office which, together with the code of conduct to which it refers, is set out in Schedule 4.]

17 Ministerial offices

(1) The First Minister and the deputy First Minister acting jointly may at any time, and shall where subsection (2) applies, determine—

(a) the number of Ministerial offices to be held by Northern Ireland Ministers; and

(b) the functions to be exercisable by the holder of each such office.

(2) This subsection applies where provision is made by an Act of the Assembly for establishing a new Northern Ireland department or dissolving an existing one.

(3) In making a determination under subsection (1), the First Minister and the deputy First Minister shall ensure that the functions exercisable by those in charge of the different Northern Ireland departments existing at the date of the determination are exercisable by the holders of different Ministerial offices.

(4) The number of Ministerial offices shall not exceed 10 or such greater number as the Secretary of State may by order provide.

(5) A determination under subsection (1) shall not have effect unless it is approved by a resolution of the Assembly passed with cross-community support.

18–19A   *****

20   The Executive Committee

(1) There shall be an Executive Committee of each Assembly consisting of the First Minister, the deputy First Minister and the Northern Ireland Ministers.

(2) The First Minister and the deputy First Minister shall be chairmen of the Committee.

(3) The Committee shall have the functions set out in paragraphs 19 and 20 of Strand One of the Belfast Agreement.

[(4) The Committee shall also have the function of discussing and agreeing upon—

    [(a) where the agreed programme referred to in paragraph 20 of Strand One of that Agreement has been approved by the Assembly and is in force, any significant or controversial matters that are clearly outside the scope of that programme;

    (aa) where no such programme has been approved by the Assembly, any significant or controversial matters;]

    (b) significant or controversial matters that the First Minister and deputy First Minister acting jointly have determined to be matters that should be considered by the Executive Committee.]

[(5) Subsections (3) and (4) are subject to [subsections (6) to (9)].

(6) Quasi-judicial decisions may be made by the Department of Justice or the Minister in charge of that Department without recourse to the Executive Committee.]

[(7) *****

(8) Nothing in subsection (3) requires a Minister to have recourse to the Executive Committee in relation to any matter unless that matter affects the exercise of the statutory responsibilities of one or more other Ministers more than incidentally.

(9) A matter does not affect the exercise of the statutory responsibilities of a Minister more than incidentally only because there is a statutory requirement to consult that Minister.]

21–[21C]   *****

Functions

22   Statutory functions

(1) An Act of the Assembly or other enactment may confer functions on a Minister (but not a junior Minister) or a Northern Ireland department by name.

(2) Functions conferred on a Northern Ireland department by an enactment passed or made before the appointed day shall, except as provided by an Act of the Assembly or other subsequent enactment, continue to be exercisable by that department.

23   Prerogative and executive powers

(1) The executive power in Northern Ireland shall continue to be vested in Her Majesty.

(2) As respects transferred matters, the prerogative and other executive powers of Her Majesty in relation to Northern Ireland shall, subject to [subsections (2A) and (3)], be exercisable on Her Majesty's behalf by any Minister or Northern Ireland department.

[(2A) So far as the Royal prerogative of mercy is exercisable on Her Majesty's behalf under subsection (2), it is exercisable only by the Minister in charge of the Department of Justice.]

(3) As respects the Northern Ireland Civil Service and the Commissioner for Public Appointments for Northern Ireland, the prerogative and other executive powers of Her Majesty in relation to Northern Ireland shall be exercisable on Her Majesty's behalf by the First Minister and the deputy First Minister acting jointly.

(4) The First Minister and deputy First Minister acting jointly may by prerogative order under subsection (3) direct that such of the powers mentioned in that subsection as are specified in the order shall be exercisable on Her Majesty's behalf by a Northern Ireland Minister or Northern Ireland department so specified.

24 ... Convention rights ... etc

(1) A Minister or Northern Ireland department has no power to make, confirm or approve any subordinate legislation, or to do any act, so far as the legislation or act—

    (a)   is incompatible with any of the Convention rights;

    [(aa) is incompatible with Article 2(1) of the Protocol on Ireland/Northern Ireland in the EU withdrawal agreement (rights of individuals);]

    (b)   ...

    (c)   discriminates against a person or class of person on the ground of religious belief or political opinion;

    (d)   in the case of an act, aids or incites another person to discriminate against a person or class of person on that ground; or

    (e)   in the case of legislation, modifies an enactment in breach of section 7.

(2) Subsection (1)(c) and (d) does not apply in relation to any act which is unlawful by virtue of the [Fair Employment and Treatment (Northern Ireland) Order 1998], or would be unlawful but for some exception made by virtue of [Part VIII of that Order].

    [(3)]–[15] ...

25 Excepted and reserved matters

(1) If any subordinate legislation made, confirmed or approved by a Minister or Northern Ireland department contains a provision dealing with an excepted or reserved matter, the Secretary of State may by order revoke the legislation.

(2) An order made under subsection (1) shall recite the reasons for revoking the legislation and may make provision having retrospective effect.

26 International obligations

(1) If the Secretary of State considers that any action proposed to be taken by a Minister or Northern Ireland department would be incompatible with any international obligations, with the interests of defence or national security or with the protection of public safety or public order, he may by order direct that the proposed action shall not be taken.

(2) If the Secretary of State considers that any action capable of being taken by a Minister or Northern Ireland department is required for the purpose of giving effect to any international obligations, of safeguarding the interests of defence or national security or of protecting public safety or public order, he may by order direct that the action shall be taken.

(3) In subsections (1) and (2), 'action' includes making, confirming or approving subordinate legislation and, in subsection (2), includes introducing a Bill in the Assembly.

    (4)–(5) *****

27–38 *****

Presiding Officer and Commission

39 Presiding Officer

(1) Each Assembly shall as its first business elect from among its members a Presiding Officer and deputies.

    (2)–(6) *****

(7) A person shall not be elected under subsections (1) to (3) without cross-community support.

40, [40A] *****

Proceedings etc

41   Standing orders

(1) The proceedings of the Assembly shall be regulated by standing orders.

(2) Standing orders shall not be made, amended or repealed without cross-community support.

(3) *****

42   Petitions of concern

[(1) If a petition expressing concern about a matter which is to be voted on by the Assembly is—

     (a) presented to the Assembly by 30 members, and

     (b) on the day after the consideration period, confirmed by 30 members,

the vote on that matter requires cross-community support.

(2) If such a petition is presented, the vote on the matter to which it relates may not take place until after the day mentioned in subsection (1)(b).

(3) The members presenting or confirming a petition must include—

     (a) one member who belongs to a political party and one member who belongs to a different political party,

     (b) one member who belongs to a political party and one member who does not belong to a political party and did not belong to a political party when returned as a member of the Assembly, or

     (c) two members who do not belong to a political party and did not belong to a political party when returned as members of the Assembly.

(4) A matter may not be the subject of a petition if it—

     (a) concerns a sanction in relation to the conduct of a Minister or other member of the Assembly;

     (b) concerns the vote on the general principles of a Bill referred to in section 13(1)(a);

     (c) is a matter specified in standing orders made under subsection (6)(c).

(5) A petition under this section may not be presented or confirmed by the Presiding Officer or a deputy Presiding Officer.

(6) Standing orders must—

     (a) make provision with respect to the procedure to be followed in presenting and confirming a petition under this section (which may include provision specifying a minimum period between the presentation of the petition and the time when the vote on the matter to which it relates would take place if not postponed by the petition);

     (b) provide that the matter to which a petition under this section relates may be referred, in accordance with paragraphs 11 and 13 of Strand One of the Belfast Agreement, to the committee established under section 13(3)(a);

     (c) specify further matters that may not be the subject of a petition under this section, for the purposes of fully implementing paragraph 2.2.4 of Annex B of Part 2 of The New Decade, New Approach Deal;

     (d) make provision for such steps to be taken during the consideration period as may be necessary for the purposes of fully implementing paragraph 2.2.7 of Annex B of Part 2 of The New Decade, New Approach Deal.

(7) If the day mentioned in paragraph (b) of subsection (1) is not a working day that paragraph is to be read as referring to the next day that is a working day.

(8) In this section—

'the consideration period' means the period of 14 days beginning with the day on which the petition is presented;

'working day' means any day other than a Saturday, a Sunday, Christmas Day, Good Friday or a day which is a bank holiday in Northern Ireland.]

43   Members' interests

(1) Standing orders shall include provision for a register of interests of members of the Assembly, and for—

     (a) registrable interests (as defined in standing orders) to be registered in it; and

  (b) the register to be published and made available for public inspection.
  (2)–(8) *****

44–49 *****

50 Privilege
  (1) For the purposes of the law of defamation, absolute privilege shall attach to—
    (a) the making of a statement in proceedings of the Assembly; and
    (b) the publication of a statement under the Assembly's authority.
  (2), (3) *****

51–[51D] *****

PART V   NSMC, BIC, BIIC ETC

52 ...

[52A   North-South Ministerial Council and British-Irish Council]
  [(1) The First Minister and the deputy First Minister acting jointly shall, as far in advance of each meeting of the North-South Ministerial Council or the British-Irish Council as is reasonably practicable, give to the Executive Committee and to the Assembly the following information in relation to the meeting—
    (a) the date;
    (b) the agenda; and
    (c) (once determined under this section) the names of the Ministers or junior Ministers who are to attend the meeting.
  (2) Each Minister or junior Minister who has responsibility (whether or not with another Minister or junior Minister) in relation to any matter included in the agenda for a meeting of either Council ('appropriate Minister') shall be entitled—
    (a) to attend the meeting; and
    (b) to participate (see section 52C) in the meeting so far as it relates to that matter.]
  (3)–(10) *****

[52B]–67 *****

PART VII   HUMAN RIGHTS AND EQUAL OPPORTUNITIES

Human rights

68 The Northern Ireland Human Rights Commission
  (1) There shall be a body corporate to be known as the Northern Ireland Human Rights Commission.
  (2) The Commission shall consist of a Chief Commissioner and other Commissioners appointed by the Secretary of State.
  (3) In making appointments under this section, the Secretary of State shall as far as practicable secure that the Commissioners, as a group, are representative of the community in Northern Ireland.
  (4) Schedule 7 (which makes supplementary provision about the Commission) shall have effect.

69 The Commission's functions
  (1) The Commission shall keep under review the adequacy and effectiveness in Northern Ireland of law and practice relating to the protection of human rights.
  (2) The Commission shall, before the end of the period of two years beginning with the commencement of this section, make to the Secretary of State such recommendations as it thinks fit for improving—
    (a) its effectiveness;

(b) the adequacy and effectiveness of the functions conferred on it by this Part; and

(c) the adequacy and effectiveness of the provisions of this Part relating to it.

(3) The Commission shall advise the Secretary of State and the Executive Committee of the Assembly of legislative and other measures which ought to be taken to protect human rights—

(a) as soon as reasonably practicable after receipt of a general or specific request for advice; and

(b) on such other occasions as the Commission thinks appropriate.

(4) The Commission shall advise the Assembly whether a Bill is compatible with human rights—

(a) as soon as reasonably practicable after receipt of a request for advice; and

(b) on such other occasions as the Commission thinks appropriate.

(5) The Commission may—

(a) give assistance to individuals in accordance with section 70; and

(b) bring proceedings involving law or practice relating to the protection of human rights.

(6) The Commission shall promote understanding and awareness of the importance of human rights in Northern Ireland; and for this purpose it may undertake, commission or provide financial or other assistance for—

(a) research; and

(b) educational activities.

(7)–(11) *****

[69A]–79 *****

80 Legislative power to remedy ultra vires acts

(1) The Secretary of State may by order make such provision as he considers necessary or expedient in consequence of—

(a) any provision of an Act of the Assembly which is not, or may not be, within the legislative competence of the Assembly; or

(b) any purported exercise by a Minister or Northern Ireland department of his or its functions which is not, or may not be, a valid exercise of those functions.

(2) An order under this section may—

(a) make provision having retrospective effect;

(b) make consequential or supplementary provision, including provision amending or repealing any Northern Ireland legislation, or any instrument made under such legislation;

(c) make transitional or saving provision.

81 Powers of courts or tribunals to vary retrospective decisions

(1) This section applies where any court or tribunal decides that—

(a) any provision of an Act of the Assembly is not within the legislative competence of the Assembly; or

(b) a Minister or Northern Ireland department does not have the power to make, confirm or approve a provision of subordinate legislation that he or it has purported to make, confirm or approve.

(2) The court or tribunal may make an order—

(a) removing or limiting any retrospective effect of the decision; or

(b) suspending the effect of the decision for any period and on any conditions to allow the defect to be corrected.

(3) In deciding whether to make an order under this section, the court or tribunal shall (among other things) have regard to the extent to which persons who are not parties to the proceedings would otherwise be adversely affected.

(4)–(7) *****

82 ...

83 Interpretation of Acts of the Assembly etc

(1) This section applies where—

(a) any provision of an Act of the Assembly, or of a Bill for such an Act, could be read either—
   (i) in such a way as to be within the legislative competence of the Assembly; or
   (ii) in such a way as to be outside that competence; or
(b) any provision of subordinate legislation made, confirmed or approved, or purporting to be made, confirmed or approved, by a Northern Ireland authority could be read either—
   (i) in such a way as not to be invalid by reason of section 24 or, as the case may be, section 76; or
   (ii) in such a way as to be invalid by reason of that section.

(2) The provision shall be read in the way which makes it within that competence or, as the case may be, does not make it invalid by reason of that section, and shall have effect accordingly.

(3) In this section 'Northern Ireland authority' means a Minister, a Northern Ireland department or a public authority (within the meaning of section 76) carrying out functions relating to Northern Ireland.

*****

Section 4(1)   **SCHEDULE 2**

                    EXCEPTED MATTERS

1. The Crown, including the succession to the Crown and a regency, but not—
   (a) functions of the First Minister and deputy First Minister, the Northern Ireland Ministers or the Northern Ireland departments, or functions in relation to Northern Ireland of any Minister of the Crown;
   (b) property belonging to Her Majesty in right of the Crown or belonging to a government department or held in trust for Her Majesty for the purposes of a government department (other than property used for the purposes of the armed forces of the Crown or the Ministry of Defence Police);
   (c) the foreshore or the sea bed or subsoil or their natural resources so far as vested in Her Majesty in right of the Crown.

2. The Parliament of the United Kingdom; parliamentary elections, including the franchise; disqualifications for membership of that Parliament.

3. International relations, including relations with territories outside the United Kingdom, the [European Union] (and their institutions) and other international organisations [and extradition], and international development assistance and co-operation, but not—
   (a) ...
   (aa) *****
   (b) the exercise of legislative powers so far as required for giving effect to any agreement or arrangement entered into—
      (i) by a Minister or junior Minister participating, by reason of [any provision of section 52A or 52B], in a meeting of the North-South Ministerial Council or the British-Irish Council; or
      (ii) by, or in relation to the activities of, any body established for implementing, on the basis mentioned in paragraph 11 of Strand Two of the Belfast Agreement, policies agreed in the North-South Ministerial Council;
   (c) observing and implementing international obligations [and obligations under the Human Rights Convention].
   *****

4. The defence of the realm; trading with the enemy; the armed forces of the Crown but not any matter within paragraph 10 of Schedule 3; war pensions; the Ministry of Defence Police.

5. Control of nuclear, biological and chemical weapons and other weapons of mass destruction.

6. Dignities and titles of honour.

7. Treason but not powers of arrest or criminal procedure.

8. Nationality; immigration, including asylum and the status and capacity of persons in the United Kingdom who are not British citizens; free movement of persons within the European Economic Area; issue of travel documents.

9. The following matters—

(a) taxes or duties under any law applying to the United Kingdom as a whole;

(b) stamp duty levied in Northern Ireland before the appointed day; and

(c) taxes or duties substantially of the same character as those mentioned in sub-paragraph (a) or (b).

[9A., 9C., 9D.] *****

9B....

10. The following matters—

(a) national insurance contributions;

(b) the control and management of the Northern Ireland National Insurance Fund and payments into and out of that Fund;

(c) reductions in and deductions from national insurance contributions;

(d) national insurance rebates;

(e) payments out of public money to money purchase pension schemes;

(f) contributions equivalent premiums;

(g) rights to return to the state pension scheme.

Sub-paragraph (a) includes the determination, payment, collection and return of national insurance contributions and matters incidental to those matters.

Sub-paragraph (b) does not include payments out of the Northern Ireland National Insurance Fund which relate to—

(i) the benefits mentioned in section 143(1) of the Social Security Administration (Northern Ireland) Act 1992, or benefits substantially of the same character as those benefits; or

(ii) administrative expenses incurred in connection with matters not falling within sub-paragraphs (a) to (g).

Sub-paragraphs (b) and (e) do not include payments out of or into the Northern Ireland National Insurance Fund under—

(i) section 172(1)(b), (2)(a) or (7)(c) of the Pension Schemes (Northern Ireland) Act 1993; or

(ii) Article 202, 227, 234 or 252 of the Employment Rights (Northern Ireland) Order 1996.

In this paragraph 'contributions equivalent premium' has the meaning given by section 51(2) of the Pension Schemes (Northern Ireland) Act 1993.

[10A.]–11. *****

[11A. The Supreme Court[, but not rights of appeal to the Supreme Court or legal aid for appeals to the Supreme Court].]

12. [(1)] Elections, including the franchise, in respect of the Northern Ireland Assembly ... and district councils.

[(2) This paragraph does not apply to—

(a) the division of local government districts into areas ('district electoral areas') for the purposes of elections to the councils of those districts,

(b) the determination of the names of district electoral areas, or

(c) the determination of the number of councillors to be elected for a district electoral area or a local government district.]

13. The subject-matter of the Political Parties, Elections and Referendums Act 2000 with the exception of Part IX (political donations etc by companies).

This paragraph does not include the funding of political parties for the purpose of assisting members of the Northern Ireland Assembly connected with such parties to perform their Assembly duties.]

14.–[16A.] *****

17. National security (including the Security Service, the Secret Intelligence Service and the Government Communications Headquarters); special powers and other provisions for dealing with terrorism or subversion; [the Technical Advisory Board provided for by section 245 of the Investigatory Powers Act 2016;] the subject-matter of—

    (a)   the Official Secrets Acts 1911 and 1920;

    [(b) the subject-matter of sections 3 to 10, Schedule 1, Part 2 and Chapter 1 of Part 6 of the Investigatory Powers Act 2016, except so far as relating to the prevention or detection of serious crime (within the meaning of that Act);] and

    (c)   the Official Secrets Act 1989, except so far as relating to any information, document or other article protected against disclosure by section 4(2) (crime) and not by any other provision of sections 1 to 4.

18. Nuclear energy and nuclear installations, including nuclear safety, security and safeguards, and liability for nuclear occurrences, but not the subject-matter of—

    (a)   section 3(5) to (7) of the Environmental Protection Act 1990 (emission limits); or

    (b) the Radioactive Substances Act 1993.

19. Regulation of sea fishing outside the Northern Ireland zone (except in relation to Northern Ireland fishing boats).

In this paragraph 'Northern Ireland fishing boat' means a fishing vessel which is registered in the register maintained under section 8 of the Merchant Shipping Act 1995 and whose entry in the register specifies a port in Northern Ireland as the port to which the vessel is to be treated as belonging.

20. Regulation of activities in outer space.

[20A. Regulation of activities in Antarctica (which for these purposes has the meaning given by section 1 of the Antarctic Act 1994).]

21.–22. *****

Section 4(1)   # SCHEDULE 3

RESERVED MATTERS

1. The conferral of functions in relation to Northern Ireland on any Minister of the Crown [apart from the Advocate General for Northern Ireland].

2. Property belonging to Her Majesty in right of the Crown or belonging to a department of the Government of the United Kingdom or held in trust for Her Majesty for the purposes of such a department (other than property used for the purposes of the armed forces of the Crown or the Ministry of Defence Police).

3.–[7.] *****

[7A. The alteration of the number of members of the Assembly returned for each constituency. This paragraph does not include—

    (a)   the alteration of that number to a number lower than five or higher than six, or

    (b) the provision of different numbers for different constituencies.]

8. Disqualification for membership of the Assembly; privileges, powers and immunities of the Assembly, its members and committees greater than those conferred by section 50.

[9.] *****

[9A. ...]

[10.—(1) The subject-matter of the Public Processions (Northern Ireland) Act 1998.

(2) In relation to the maintenance of public order, the armed forces of the Crown (including the conferring of powers, authorities, privileges or immunities on members of the armed forces for the purposes of the maintenance of public order).

(3) *****].

[11.]–14 .*****

[14A.]–[15A.] ...

16. *****
17. ...
18., 19. *****
20. Import and export controls and trade with any place outside the United Kingdom but not—
    (a) the furtherance of the trade of Northern Ireland or the protection of traders in Northern Ireland against fraud;
    (b) services in connection with, or the regulation of, the quality, insurance, transport, marketing or identification of agricultural or food products, including livestock;
    (c) the prevention of disease or the control of weeds and pests;
    (d) aerodromes and harbours;
    (e) any matter within paragraph 4 of Schedule 2.
21.–28. *****
29. Telecommunications; wireless telegraphy; the provision of programme services (within the meaning of the Broadcasting Act 1990); internet services; electronic encryption; the subject matter of Part II of the Wireless Telegraphy Act 1949 (electromagnetic disturbance).
30.–42. *****

Scotland Act 1998

(1998, c. 46)

An Act to provide for the establishment of a Scottish Parliament and Administration and other changes in the government of Scotland; to provide for changes in the constitution and functions of certain public authorities; to provide for the variation of the basic rate of income tax in relation to income of Scottish taxpayers in accordance with a resolution of the Scottish Parliament; to amend the law about parliamentary constituencies in Scotland; and for connected purposes.   [19th November 1998]

Territorial extent: United Kingdom (although many of the provisions apply only in Scotland) except for s. 25 which extends to Scotland alone

PART I   THE SCOTTISH PARLIAMENT

The Scottish Parliament

1 The Scottish Parliament
    (1) There shall be a Scottish Parliament.
    (2) One member of the Parliament shall be returned for each constituency (under the simple majority system) at an election held in the constituency.
    (3) Members of the Parliament for each region shall be returned at a general election under the additional member system of proportional representation provided for in this part and vacancies among such members shall be filled in accordance with this Part.
    (4) The validity of any proceedings of the Parliament is not affected by any vacancy in its membership.
    (5) Schedule 1 (which makes provision for the constituencies and regions for the purposes of this Act and the number of regional members) shall have effect.

General elections

2 Ordinary general elections
    (1) ...
    (2) [The day on which the poll at an ordinary general election for membership of the Parliament is to be held is the first Thursday in May in the fifth] calendar year following that in which the previous ordinary general election was held, unless[—
        (a) subsection (2A) prevents the poll being held on that day, or

(b)   the day of the poll is determined by a proclamation under subsection (5).]

[(2A) The poll shall not be held on the same date as the date of the poll at—

(a)   a parliamentary general election ..., ...

(b)   ...

(2B) Where subsection (2A) prevents the poll being held on the day specified in subsection (2), the poll shall be held on such day, subject to subsection (2A), as the Scottish Ministers may by order specify, unless the day of the poll is determined by a proclamation under subsection (5) as modified by subsection (5ZA).]

(3)–(6) *****

3   Extraordinary general elections

(1) The Presiding Officer shall propose a day for the holding of a poll if—

(a)   the Parliament resolves that it should be dissolved and, if the resolution is passed on a division, the number of members voting in favour of it is not less than two-thirds of the total number of seats for members of the Parliament, or

(b)   any period during which the Parliament is required under section 46 to nominate one of its members for appointment as First Minister ends without such a nomination being made.

(2) If the Presiding Officer makes such a proposal, Her Majesty may by proclamation under the Scottish Seal—

(a)   dissolve the Parliament and require an extraordinary general election to be held,

(b)   require the poll at the election to be held on the day proposed, and

(c)   require the Parliament to meet within the period of seven days beginning immediately after the day of the poll.

[(2A) Subsection (2B) applies if a proclamation is made under subsection (2).

(2B) If the Presiding Officer proposes another day for the holding of the poll at the extraordinary general election which is not more than one month later than the day on which the poll is required to be held under the proclamation, Her Majesty may by further proclamation under the Scottish Seal—

(a)   require the poll at the election to be held instead on the day proposed under this subsection, and

(b)   require the Parliament to meet within the period of seven days beginning immediately after the day of the poll.

(2C) Before proposing a day for the holding of the poll under subsection (2B), the Presiding Officer must consult the Electoral Commission.]

(3) If a poll is held under this section within the period of six months ending with the day on which the poll at the next ordinary general election would be held (disregarding section 2(5)), that ordinary general election shall not be held.

(4) Subsection (3) does not affect the year in which the subsequent ordinary general election is to be held.

4   *****

5   Candidates

(1) At a general election, the candidates may stand for return as constituency members or regional members.

(2) A person may not be a candidate to be a constituency member for more than one constituency.

(3) The candidates to be regional members shall be those included in a list submitted under subsection (4) or individual candidates.

(4) Any registered political party may submit to the regional returning officer a list of candidates to be regional members for a particular region (referred to in this Act, in relation to the region, as the party's 'regional list').

(5) A registered political party's regional list has effect in relation to the general election and any vacancy occurring among the regional members after that election and before the next general election.

(6) Not more than twelve persons may be included in the list (but the list may include only one person).

(7)–(9) *****

6   Poll for regional members

(1) This section and sections 7 and 8 are about the return of regional members at a general election.

(2) In each of the constituencies for the Parliament, a poll shall be held at which each person entitled to vote as elector may give a vote (referred to in this Act as a 'regional vote') for—

(a) a registered political party which has submitted a regional list, or

(b) an individual candidate to be a regional member for the region.

(3) The right conferred on a person by subsection (2) is in addition to any right the person may have to vote in any poll for the return of a constituency member.

7   Calculation of regional figures

(1) The persons who are to be returned as constituency members for constituencies included in the region must be determined before the persons who are to be returned as the regional members for the region.

(2) For each registered political party which has submitted a regional list, the regional figure for the purposes of section 8 is—

(a) the total number of regional votes given for the party in all the constituencies included in the region, divided by

(b) the aggregate of one plus the number of candidates of the party returned as constituency members for any of those constituencies.

(3) Each time a seat is allocated to the party under section 8, that figure shall be recalculated by increasing (or further increasing) the aggregate in subsection (2)(b) by one.

(4) For each individual candidate to be a regional member for the region, the regional figure for the purposes of section 8 is the total number of regional votes given for him in all the constituencies included in the region.

8   Allocation of seats to regional members

(1) The first regional member seat shall be allocated to the registered political party or individual candidate with the highest regional figure.

(2) The second and subsequent regional member seats shall be allocated to the registered political party or individual candidate with the highest regional figure, after any recalculation required by section 7(3) has been carried out.

(3) An individual candidate already returned as a constituency or regional member shall be disregarded.

(4) Seats for the region which are allocated to a registered political party shall be filled by the persons in the party's regional list in the order in which they appear in the list.

(5) For the purposes of this section and section 10, a person in a registered political party's regional list who is returned as a member of the Parliament shall be treated as ceasing to be in the list (even if his return is void).

(6) Once a party's regional list has been exhausted (by the return of persons included in it as constituency members or by the previous application of subsection (1) or (2)) the party shall be disregarded.

(7)–(9) *****

Vacancies

9   Constituency vacancies

(1) Where the seat of a constituency member is vacant, an election shall be held to fill the vacancy (subject to subsection (4)).

(2) The date of the poll shall be fixed by the Presiding Officer.

(3) The date shall fall within the period of three months—

(a) beginning with the occurrence of the vacancy, or

(b) if the vacancy does not come to the notice of the Presiding Officer within the period of one month beginning with its occurrence, beginning when it does come to his notice.

(4) The election shall not be held if the latest date for holding the poll would fall within the period of three months ending with the day on which the poll at the next ordinary general election would be held (disregarding section 2(5)).

(5), (6) *****

10   Regional vacancies

(1) This section applies where the seat of a regional member is vacant.

(2) If the regional member was returned as an individual candidate, or the vacancy is not filled in accordance with the following provisions, the seat shall remain vacant until the next general election.

(3) If the regional member was returned (under section 8 or this section) from a registered political party's regional list, the regional returning officer shall notify the Presiding Officer of the name of the person who is to fill the vacancy.

(4)–(7) *****

Franchise and conduct of elections

11   Electors

(1) The persons entitled to vote as electors at an election for membership of the parliament held in any constituency are those who on the day of the poll—

   (a) would be entitled to vote as electors at a local government election in an electoral area falling wholly or partly within the constituency, and

   (b) are registered in the register of local government electors at an address within the constituency.

(2) A person is not entitled to vote as elector in any constituency—

   (a) more than once at a poll for the return of a constituency member, or

   (b) more than once at a poll for the return of regional members,

or to vote as elector in more than one constituency at a general election.

12–18   *****

Presiding Officer and administration

19   Presiding Officer

(1) The Parliament shall,... following a general election, elect from among its members a Presiding Officer and two deputies.

[(1A) The Parliament must do so—

   (a) before it conducts any other proceedings, except the taking by its members of the oath of allegiance (see section 84), and

   (b) in any event, within the period of 14 days beginning immediately after the day of the poll at the election.

(1B) The Parliament may, at any time, elect from among its members one or more additional deputies.]

(2) A person elected Presiding Officer or deputy shall hold office until the conclusion of the next election for Presiding Officer under subsection (1) unless he previously resigns, ceases to be a member of the Parliament otherwise than by virtue of a dissolution or is removed from office by resolution of the Parliament.

[(2A) But standing orders may make provision for additional deputies to hold office for a shorter time than provided by subsection (2).]

(3) If the Presiding Officer or a deputy [elected under subsection (1)] ceases to hold office before the Parliament is dissolved, the Parliament shall elect another from among its members to fill his place.

(4)–(7) *****

20   Clerk of the Parliament

(1) There shall be a Clerk of the Parliament.

(2) The Clerk shall be appointed by the Scottish Parliamentary Corporate Body (established under section 21).

(3), (4) *****

21 Scottish Parliamentary Corporate Body

(1) There shall be a body corporate to be known as 'the Scottish Parliamentary Corporate Body' (referred to in this Act as the Parliamentary corporation) to perform the functions conferred on the corporation by virtue of this Act or any other enactment.

(2) The members of the corporation shall be—

(a) the Presiding Officer, and

(b) [at least] four members of the Parliament appointed in accordance with standing orders.

(3) The corporation shall provide the Parliament, or ensure that the Parliament is provided, with the property, staff and services required for the Parliament's purposes.

(4) The Parliament may give special or general directions to the corporation for the purpose of or in connection with the exercise of the corporation's functions.

(5)–(8) *****

Proceedings etc

22 Standing orders

(1) The proceedings of the Parliament shall be regulated by standing orders.

(2) *****

23–27 *****

Legislation

28 Acts of the Scottish Parliament

(1) Subject to section 29, the Parliament may make laws, to be known as Acts of the Scottish Parliament.

(2) Proposed Acts of the Scottish Parliament shall be known as Bills; and a Bill shall become an Act of the Scottish Parliament when it has been passed by the Parliament and has received Royal Assent.

(3) A Bill receives Royal Assent at the beginning of the day on which Letters Patent under the Scottish Seal signed with Her Majesty's own hand signifying Her Assent are recorded in the Register of the Great Seal.

(4) The date of Royal Assent shall be written on the Act of the Scottish Parliament by the Clerk, and shall form part of the Act.

(5) The validity of an Act of the Scottish Parliament is not affected by any invalidity in the proceedings of the Parliament leading to its enactment.

(6) Every Act of the Scottish Parliament shall be judicially noticed.

(7) This section does not affect the power of the Parliament of the United Kingdom to make laws for Scotland.

[(8) But it is recognised that the Parliament of the United Kingdom will not normally legislate with regard to devolved matters without the consent of the Scottish Parliament.]

29 Legislative competence

(1) An Act of the Scottish Parliament is not law so far as any provision of the Act is outside the legislative competence of the Parliament.

(2) A provision is outside the competence so far as any of the following paragraphs apply—

(a) it would form part of the law of a country or territory other than Scotland, or confer or remove functions exercisable otherwise than in or as regards Scotland,

(b) it relates to reserved matters,

(c) it is in breach of the restrictions in Schedule 4.

(d) it is incompatible with any of the Convention rights . . .,

(e) it would remove the Lord Advocate from his position as head of the systems of criminal prosecution and investigation of deaths in Scotland.

(3) For the purposes of this section, the question whether a provision of an Act of the Scottish Parliament relates to a reserved matter is to be determined, subject to subsection (4), by

reference to the purpose of the provision, having regard (among other things) to its effect in all the circumstances.

(4)–[(5)] *****

30   Legislative competence: supplementary

(1) Schedule 5 (which defines reserved matters) shall have effect.

(2)–[(6)] *****

[30A]   ...

31   Scrutiny of Bills [for legislative competence and protected subject-matter]

(1) [A person] in charge of a Bill shall, on or before introduction of the Bill in the Parliament state that in his view the provisions of the Bill would be within the legislative competence of the Parliament.

(2) The Presiding Officer shall, on or before the introduction of a Bill in the Parliament, decide whether or not in his view the provisions of the Bill would be within the legislative competence of the Parliament and state his decision.

[(2A) The Presiding Officer shall, after the last time when a Bill may be amended but before the decision whether to pass or reject it, decide whether or not in his view any provision of the Bill relates to a protected subject-matter and state his decision.]

(3) The form of any statement, and the manner in which it is to be made, shall be determined under standing orders, and standing orders may provide for any statement to be published.

[(4) For the purposes of this Part a provision of a Bill relates to a protected subject-matter if it would modify, or confer power to modify, any of the matters listed in subsection (5) (but not if the provision is incidental to or consequential on another provision of the Bill).

(5) The matters are—

    (a) the persons entitled to vote as electors at an election for membership of the Parliament,

    (b) the system by which members of the Parliament are returned,

    (c) the number of constituencies, regions or any equivalent electoral area, and

    (d) the number of members to be returned for each constituency, region or equivalent electoral area.]

[31A   Two-thirds majority for Bills relating to a protected subject-matter

If the Presiding Officer states under section 31(2A) that in his view any provision of a Bill relates to a protected subject-matter, the Bill is not passed unless the number of members voting in favour of it at the final stage is at least two-thirds of the total number of seats for members of the Parliament.]

32   Submission of Bills for Royal Assent

(1) It is for the Presiding Officer to submit Bills for Royal Assent.

(2) The Presiding Officer shall not submit a Bill for Royal Assent at any time when—

    (a) the Advocate General, the Lord Advocate or the Attorney General is entitled to make a reference in relation to the Bill under section [32A or] 33,

    (b) any such reference has been made but has not been decided or otherwise disposed of by the [Supreme Court], or

    (c) an order may be made in relation to the Bill under section 35.

[(2A) The Presiding Officer shall not submit a Bill for Royal Assent if the Supreme Court has decided on a reference made in relation to the Bill under section 32A(2)(b) that any provision of the Bill relates to a protected subject-matter, unless since the decision the Bill has been approved in accordance with standing orders made by virtue of section 36(5).]

(3) The Presiding Officer shall not submit a Bill in its unamended form for Royal Assent if—

    (a) the [Supreme Court has] decided that the Bill or any provision of it would not be within the legislative competence of the Parliament, ...

    (b) ...

(4) *****

[32A   Scrutiny of Bills by the Supreme Court (protected subject-matter)

(1) The Advocate General, the Lord Advocate or the Attorney General may refer the question of whether a Bill or any provision of a Bill relates to a protected subject-matter to the Supreme Court for decision.

(2) Subject to subsection (3), he may make a reference in relation to a Bill—

    (a) at any time during the period of four weeks beginning with the rejection of the Bill, if the Presiding Officer has made a statement under section 31(2A) that in his view any provision of the Bill relates to a protected subject-matter, and

    (b) at any time during the period of four weeks beginning with the passing of the Bill, if the Presiding Officer has made a statement under section 31(2A) that in his view no provision of the Bill relates to a protected subject-matter, unless the number of members voting in favour of the Bill at its passing is at least two-thirds of the total number of seats for members of the Parliament.

(3) He shall not make a reference in relation to a Bill if he has notified the Presiding Officer that he does not intend to make a reference in relation to the Bill, unless since the notification the Bill has been approved or rejected in accordance with standing orders made by virtue of section 36(5).]

33   Scrutiny of Bills by the Supreme Court [(legislative competence)]

(1) The Advocate General, the Lord Advocate or the Attorney General may refer the question of whether a Bill or any provision of a Bill would be within the legislative competence of the Parliament to the [Supreme Court] for decision.

(2), (3) *****

34   ...

35   Power to intervene in certain cases

(1) If a Bill contains provisions—

    (a) which the Secretary of State has reasonable grounds to believe would be incompatible with any international obligations or the interests of defence or national security, or

    (b) which make modifications of the law as it applies to reserved matters and which the Secretary of State has reasonable grounds to believe would have an adverse effect on the operation of the law as it applies to reserved matters,

he may make an order prohibiting the Presiding Officer from submitting the Bill for Royal Assent.

(2)–(5) *****

36   *****

Other provisions

37   Acts of Union

The Union with Scotland Act 1706 and the Union with England Act 1707 have effect subject to this Act.

38   *****

39   Members' interests

(1) Provision shall be made for a register of interests of members of the Parliament and for the register to be published and made available for public inspection.

(2) Provision shall be made—

    (a) requiring members of the Parliament to register in that register financial interests (including benefits in kind), as defined for the purposes of this paragraph,

    (b) requiring that any member of the Parliament who has a financial interest (including benefits in kind), as defined for the purposes of this paragraph, in any matter declares that interest before taking part in any proceedings of the Parliament relating to that matter.

(3) Provision made in pursuance of subsection (2) shall include any provision which the Parliament considers appropriate for preventing or restricting the participation in proceedings of the Parliament of a member with an interest defined for the purposes of subsection (2)(a) or (b) in a matter to which the proceedings relate.

(4) Provision shall be made prohibiting a member of the Parliament from—

    (a) advocating or initiating any cause or matter on behalf of any person, by any means specified in the provision, in consideration of any payment or benefit in kind of a description so specified, or

    (b) urging, in consideration of any such payment or benefit in kind, any other member on behalf of any person by any such means.

[(4A) Any requirement or prohibition (however expressed) imposed by provision made in pursuance of subsections (2) to (4) may be subject to such exceptions as are specified in the provision.]

(5) Provision may be made for—

    (a) excluding a member from the proceedings of the Parliament,

    (b) imposing on a member such other sanctions as the Parliament considers appropriate,

if the member fails to comply with, or contravenes, any provision made in pursuance of subsections (2) to (4) of this subsection.

[(5A) Provision made under subsection (5) may include provision that a sanction is not to be imposed in such circumstances as are specified in the provision.]

(6)–(8) *****

Legal issues

40 *****

41 Defamatory statements

(1) For the purposes of the law of defamation—

    (a) any statement made in proceedings of the Parliament, and

    (b) the publication under the authority of the Parliament of any statement, shall be absolutely privileged.

(2) In subsection (1), 'statement' has the same meaning as in the Defamation Act 1996.

42 Contempt of court

(1) The strict liability rule shall not apply in relation to any publication—

    (a) made in proceedings of the Parliament in relation to a Bill or subordinate legislation, or

    (b) to the extent that it consists of a fair and accurate report of such proceedings made in good faith.

(2) In subsection (1), 'the strict liability rule' and 'publication' have the same meanings as in the Contempt of Court Act 1981.

43 ...

PART II THE SCOTTISH ADMINISTRATION

Ministers and their staff

44 The [Scottish Government]

(1) There shall be a [Scottish Government], whose members shall be—

    (a) the First Minister,

    (b) such Ministers as the First Minister may appoint under section 47, and

    (c) the Lord Advocate and the Solicitor General for Scotland.

(2) The members of the [Scottish Government] are referred to collectively as the Scottish Ministers.

(3) A person who holds a Ministerial office may not be appointed a member of the [Scottish Government]; and if a member of the [Scottish Government] is appointed to a Ministerial office he shall cease to hold office as a member of the [Scottish Government].

(4) In subsection (3), references to a member of the [Scottish Government] include a junior Scottish Minister and 'Ministerial office' has the same meaning as in section 2 of the House of Commons Disqualification Act 1975.

45   The First Minister

(1) The First Minister shall be appointed by Her Majesty from among the members of the Parliament and shall hold office at Her Majesty's pleasure.

(2) The First Minister may at any time tender his resignation to Her Majesty and shall do so if the Parliament resolves that the [Scottish Government] no longer enjoys the confidence of the Parliament.

(3) The First Minister shall cease to hold office if a person is appointed in his place.

(4) If the office of First Minister is vacant or he is for any reason unable to act, the functions exercisable by him shall be exercisable by a person designated by the Presiding Officer.

(5)–(7) *****

46   Choice of the First Minister

(1) If one of the following events occurs, the Parliament shall within the period allowed nominate one of its members for appointment as First Minister.

(2) The events are—
    (a) the holding of a poll at a general election,
    (b) the First Minister tendering his resignation to Her Majesty,
    (c) the office of First Minister becoming vacant (otherwise than in consequence of his so tendering his resignation),
    (d) the First Minister ceasing to be a member of the Parliament otherwise than by virtue of a dissolution.

(3) The period allowed is the period of 28 days which begins with the day on which the event in question occurs; but—
    (a) if another of those events occurs within the period allowed, that period shall be extended (subject to paragraph (b)) so that it ends with the period of 28 days beginning with the day on which that other event occurred, and
    (b) the period shall end if the Parliament passes a resolution under section 3(1)(a) or when Her Majesty appoints a person as First Minister.

(4) The Presiding Officer shall recommend to Her Majesty the appointment of any member of the Parliament who is nominated by the Parliament under this section.

47   Ministers

(1) The First Minister may, with the approval of Her Majesty, appoint Ministers from among the members of the Parliament.

(2) The First Minister shall not seek Her Majesty's approval for any appointment under this section without the agreement of the Parliament.

(3) A Minister appointed under this section—
    (a) shall hold office at her Majesty's pleasure,
    (b) may be removed from office by the First Minister,
    (c) may at any time resign and shall do so if the Parliament resolves that the [Scottish Government] no longer enjoys the confidence of the Parliament,
    (d) if he resigns, shall cease to hold office immediately, and
    (e) shall cease to hold office if he ceases to be a member of the Parliament otherwise than by virtue of a dissolution.

48–50 *****

51   The Civil Service

(1) The Scottish Ministers may appoint persons to be members of the staff of the Scottish Administration.

(2) Service as—

(a) the holder of any office in the Scottish Administration which is not a ministerial office, or

(b) a member of the staff of the Scottish Administration,

shall be service in the [civil service of the State].

(3)–(8) *****

(9) ...

Ministerial functions

52 *****

53   General transfer of functions

(1) The functions mentioned in subsection (2) shall, so far as they are exercisable within devolved competence, be exercisable by the Scottish Ministers instead of by a Minister of the Crown.

(2) Those functions are—

(a) those of Her Majesty's prerogative and other executive functions which are exercisable on behalf of Her Majesty by a Minister of the Crown,

(b) other functions conferred on a Minister of the Crown by a prerogative instrument, and

(c) functions conferred on a Minister of the Crown by any pre-commencement enactment,

but do not include any retained functions of the Lord Advocate.

(3), (4) *****

54–56 *****

57   ... Convention rights ...

(1) ...

(2) A member of the [Scottish Government] has no power to make any subordinate legislation, or to do any other act, so far as the legislation or act is incompatible with any of the Convention rights ...

(3) Subsection (2) does not apply to an act of the Lord Advocate—

(a) in prosecuting any offence, or

(b) in his capacity as head of the systems of criminal prosecution and investigation of deaths in Scotland, ...

(4)–(15) ...

58   Power to prevent or require action

(1) If the Secretary of State has reasonable grounds to believe that any action proposed to be taken by a member of the [Scottish Government] would be incompatible with any international obligations, he may by order direct that the proposed action shall not be taken.

(2) If the Secretary of State has reasonable grounds to believe that any action capable of being taken by a member of the [Scottish Government] is required for the purpose of giving effect to any such obligations, he may by order direct that the action shall be taken.

(3) In subsections (1) and (2), 'action' includes making, confirming or approving subordinate legislation and, in subsection (2), includes introducing a Bill in the Parliament.

(4) If any subordinate legislation made or which could be revoked by a member of the [Scottish Government] contains provisions—

(a) which the Secretary of State has reasonable grounds to believe to be incompatible with any international obligations or the interests of defence or national security, or

(b) which make modifications of the law as it applies to reserved matters and which the Secretary of State has reasonable grounds to believe to have an adverse effect on the operation of the law as it applies to reserved matters,

the Secretary of State may by order revoke the legislation.

(5) An order under this section must state the reasons for making the order.

59–63 *****

[PART IIA PERMANENCE OF THE SCOTTISH PARLIAMENT AND SCOTTISH GOVERNMENT

63A Permanence of the Scottish Parliament and Scottish Government

(1) The Scottish Parliament and the Scottish Government are a permanent part of the United Kingdom's constitutional arrangements.

(2) The purpose of this section is, with regard to the other provisions of this Act, to signify the commitment of the Parliament and Government of the United Kingdom to the Scottish Parliament and the Scottish Government.

(3) In view of that commitment it is declared that the Scottish Parliament and the Scottish Government are not to be abolished except on the basis of a decision of the people of Scotland voting in a referendum.]

64–72 *****

73–80 ...

[Chapter 1 Introductory]

[80A Overview of Part 4A]

[(1) In this Part—

(a) Chapter 2 confers on the Scottish Parliament power to set a rate [or rates] of income tax to be paid by Scottish taxpayers, and

(b) [The remaining Chapters] specify the taxes about which the Scottish Parliament may make provision in the exercise of the power conferred by section 28(1).

(2) The power to make provision about a devolved tax is subject to the restrictions imposed by—

(a) subsection (3), and

(b) the other provisions of this Part.

(3) A devolved tax may not be imposed where to do so would be incompatible with any international obligations.

(4) In this Act 'devolved tax' means a tax specified in this Part as a devolved tax.]

[80B Power to add new devolved taxes]

[(1) Her Majesty may by Order in Council amend this Part so as to—

(a) specify, as an additional devolved tax, a tax of any description, or

(b) make any other modifications of the provisions relating to devolved taxes which She considers necessary or expedient.

(2) An Order in Council under this section may also make such modifications of—

(a) any enactment or prerogative instrument (including any enactment comprised in or made under this Act), or

(b) any other instrument or document,

as Her Majesty considers necessary or expedient in connection with other provision made by the Order.]

[80C   Power to set Scottish [rates]

[(1) The Scottish Parliament may by resolution (a 'Scottish rate resolution') set [the Scottish basic rate, and any other rates, for the purposes of section 11A of the Income Tax Act 2007 (which provides for the income of Scottish taxpayers which is charged at those rates).]

[(2A) Where a Scottish rate resolution sets more than one rate it must also set limits or make other provision to enable it to be ascertained, for the purposes of that section, which rates apply in relation to a Scottish taxpayer.

(2B) But a Scottish rate resolution may not provide for different rates to apply in relation to different types of income.

(2C) In this Chapter a 'Scottish rate' means a rate set by a Scottish rate resolution.]

(3) A Scottish rate resolution applies—

    (a) for only one tax year, and

    (b) for the whole of that year.

(4) …

(5) [A] Scottish rate must be a whole number or half a whole number [, or zero].

(6) A Scottish rate resolution—

    (a) must specify the tax year for which it applies,

    (b) must be made before the start of that tax year, and

    (c) must not be made more than 12 months before the start of that year.

(7) If a Scottish rate resolution is cancelled before the start of the tax year for which it is to apply—

    (a) the Income Tax Acts have effect for that year as if the resolution had never been passed, and

    (b) the resolution may be replaced by another Scottish rate resolution.

(8) Standing orders must provide that only a member of the Scottish Government may move a motion for a Scottish rate resolution.]

[80D–90C]   *****

Miscellaneous

91   Maladministration

(1) The Parliament shall make provision for the investigation of relevant complaints made to its members in respect of any action taken by or on behalf of—

    (a) a member of the [Scottish Government] in the exercise of functions conferred on the Scottish Ministers, or

    (b) any other office-holder in the Scottish Administration.

(2) For the purposes of subsection (1), a complaint is a relevant complaint if it is a complaint of a kind which could be investigated under the Parliamentary Commissioner Act 1967 if it were made to a member of the House of Commons in respect of a government department or other authority to which that Act applies.

(3)–(6) *****

92–94   *****

95   Appointment and removal of judges

(1) It shall continue to be for the Prime Minister to recommend to Her Majesty the appointment of a person as Lord President of the Court of Session or Lord Justice Clerk.

(2) The Prime Minister shall not recommend to Her Majesty the appointment of any person who has not been nominated by the First Minister for such appointment.

(3) Before nominating persons for such appointment the First Minister shall consult the Lord President and the Lord Justice Clerk (unless, in either case, the office is vacant).

(4) It is for the First Minister, after consulting the Lord President, to recommend to Her Majesty the appointment of a person as—

    (a) a judge of the Court of Session (other than the Lord President or the Lord Justice Clerk), or

(b) a sheriff principal or a sheriff.

(5) The First Minister shall comply with any requirement in relation to—

    (a) a nomination under subsection (2), or

    (b) a recommendation under subsection (4),

imposed by virtue of any enactment.

(6) A judge of the Court of Session and the Chairman of the Scottish Land Court may be removed from office only by Her Majesty; and any recommendation to Her Majesty for such removal shall be made by the First Minister.

(7) The First Minister shall make such a recommendation if (and only if) the Parliament, on a motion made by the First Minister, resolves that such a recommendation should be made.

(8) Provision shall be made for a tribunal constituted by the First Minister to investigate and report on whether a judge of the Court of Session or the Chairman of the Scottish Land Court is unfit for office by reason of inability, neglect of duty or misbehaviour and for the report to be laid before the Parliament.

(9)–(11) *****

96–97 *****

Juridical

98 Devolution issues

Schedule 6 (which makes provision in relation to devolution issues) shall have effect.

99 *****

100 Human rights

(1) This Act does not enable a person—

    (a) to bring any proceedings in a court or tribunal on the ground that an act is incompatible with the Convention rights, or

    (b) to rely on any of the Convention rights in any such proceedings,

unless he would be a victim for the purposes of Article 34 of the Convention (within the meaning of the Human Rights Act 1998) if proceedings in respect of the act were brought in the European Court of Human Rights.

(2) Subsection (1) does not apply to the Lord Advocate, the Advocate General, the Attorney General [, the Advocate General for Northern Ireland] or the Attorney General for Northern Ireland.

(3) This Act does not enable a court or tribunal to award any damages in respect of an act which is incompatible with any of the Convention rights which it could not award if section 8(3) and (4) of the Human Rights Act 1998 applied.

[(3A)–(3E)] ...

(4) [Subject to subsection (3D),] [...] in this section 'act' means—

    (a) making any legislation,

    (b) any other act or failure to act, if it is the act or failure of a member of the... [Scottish Government].

101 Interpretation of Acts of the Scottish Parliament etc

(1) This section applies to—

    (a) any provision of an Act of the Scottish Parliament, or of a Bill for such an Act, and

    (b) any provision of subordinate legislation made, confirmed or approved, or purporting to be made, confirmed or approved, by a member of the [Scottish Government],

which could be read in such a way as to be outside competence.

(2) Such a provision is to be read as narrowly as is required for it to be within competence, if such a reading is possible, and is to have effect accordingly.

(3) In this section 'competence'—

    (a) in relation to an Act of the Scottish Parliament, or a Bill for such an Act, means the legislative competence of the Parliament, and

    (b) in relation to subordinate legislation, means the powers conferred by virtue of this Act.

102 Powers of courts or tribunals to vary retrospective decisions

(1) This section applies where any court or tribunal decides that—

 (a) an Act of the Scottish Parliament or any provision of such an Act is not within the legislative competence of the Parliament, or

 (b) a member of the [Scottish Government] does not have the power to make, confirm or approve a provision of subordinate legislation that he has purported to make, confirm or approve [, or

 (c) any other purported exercise of a function by a member of the Scottish Government was outside devolved competence].

(2) The court or tribunal may make an order—

 (a) removing or limiting any retrospective effect of the decision, or

 (b) suspending the effect of the decision for any period and on any conditions to allow the defect to be corrected.

(3) In deciding whether to make an order under this section, the court or tribunal shall (among other things) have regard to the extent to which persons who are not parties to the proceedings would otherwise be adversely affected.

(4)–(7) *****

*****

Sections 29 and 53(4)   SCHEDULE 4

ENACTMENTS ETC PROTECTED FROM MODIFICATION

PART I THE PROTECTED PROVISIONS

Particular enactments

1.—(1) An Act of the Scottish Parliament cannot modify, or confer power by subordinate legislation to modify, any of the following provisions.

(2) The provisions are—

 (a) Articles 4 and 6 of the Union with Scotland Act 1706 and of the Union with England Act 1707 so far as they relate to freedom of trade,

 (b) the Private Legislation Procedure (Scotland) Act 1936,

 (c) ...

 (d) paragraphs 5(3)(b) and 15(4)(b) of Schedule 32 to the Local Government, Planning and Land Act 1980 (designation of enterprise zones),

 (e) sections 140A to 140G of the Social Security Administration Act 1992 (rent rebate and rent allowance subsidy and council tax benefit),

 (f) the Human Rights Act 1998.

 (g) the European Union (Withdrawal) Act 2018 (other than [any excluded provision of] that Act and any regulations made under that Act)][, and

 (h) the United Kingdom Internal Market Act 2020].

[(3) For the purposes of sub-paragraph (2)(g), the following are excluded provisions of the European Union (Withdrawal) Act 2018—

 (a) section 1B(3) and (4),

 (b) sections 8A to 8C,

 (c) section 10(3) and (4),

 (d) sections 13A and 13B,

 (e) sections 15A to 15C,

 (f) Parts 1A to 1C of Schedule 2,

 (g) paragraphs 8A to 8G of Schedule 7, and

 (h) paragraphs 31 to 35 of Schedule 8.]

The law on reserved matters

2.—(1) An Act of the Scottish Parliament cannot modify, or confer power by subordinate legislation to modify, the law on reserved matters.

(2) In this paragraph, 'the law on reserved matters' means—

(a) any enactment the subject-matter of which is a reserved matter and which is comprised
in an Act of Parliament or subordinate legislation under an Act of Parliament, and

(b) any rule of law which is not contained in an enactment and the subject-matter of which
is a reserved matter,

and in this sub-paragraph 'Act of Parliament' does not include this Act.

(3)–[(5)] *****

3.—(1) Paragraph 2 does not apply to modifications which—

(a) are incidental to, or consequential on, provision made (whether by virtue of the Act in
question or another enactment) which does not relate to reserved matters, and

(b) do not have a greater effect on reserved matters than is necessary to give effect to the
purpose of the provision.

(2) In determining for the purposes of sub-paragraph (1)(b) what is necessary to give effect to
the purpose of a provision, any power to make laws other than the power of the Parliament is to be
disregarded.

[(3)] *****

This Act

4.—(1) An Act of the Scottish Parliament cannot modify, or confer power by subordinate legislation to modify, this Act.

[(2) This paragraph does not apply to modifying—

(a) the following sections in Part 1 (the Scottish Parliament)—

(i) section 1(2) to (5),

(ii) section 2(1), (2), (2B) and (3) to (6),

(iii) sections 3 to 12,

(iv) sections 13 to 22,

(v) sections 24 to 26,

(vi) section 27(1) and (2),

(vii) section 28(4) and (5),

(viii) section 31(3),

(ix) section 36(1)(a) and (b), and (2) and (3), and

(x) sections 38 to 42,

(b) the following sections in Part 2 (the Scottish Administration)—

(i) section 44(1)(a) to (c) and (2),

(ii) section 45(3) to (7),

(iii) section 46(1) to (3),

(iv) section 47(2) and (3)(b) to (e),

(v) section 48(2) to (4),

(vi) section 49(2), (3) and (4)(b) to (e), and

(vii) section 50,

(c) in Part 3 (financial provisions)—

(i) section 69(2) to (5), and

(ii) section 70(1) to (5) and (7) to (9),

(d) in Part 5 (miscellaneous and general), sections 81 to 83, 85, 91, 92(1), (2) and (4) to (6),
93, 94 and 97,

(e) the following provisions in Part 6 (supplementary)—

(i) section 112(1) and (3) to (5), section 113 (except the application of subsection (9)),
section 115 and Schedule 7 (so far as those sections and that Schedule apply to any
power exercisable within devolved competence to make subordinate legislation),

(ii)   sections 118, 120 and 121, and

(iii) section 124 (so far as that section applies to any power exercisable within devolved competence to make subordinate legislation),

(f) Schedule 1 (constituencies, regions and regional members),

(g) paragraphs 1, 2(1) and 3 to 6 of Schedule 2 (Scottish Parliamentary corporate body), and

(h) paragraphs 1 to 6 of Schedule 3 (standing orders—further provision).]

[(2A)–(2C)] ...

(3)–(5) *****

[4A] ...

5.–14. *****

Section 30   **SCHEDULE 5**

RESERVED MATTERS

PART I GENERAL RESERVATIONS

The Constitution

1. The following aspects of the constitution are reserved matters, that is—

(a) the Crown, including succession to the Crown and a regency,

(b) the Union of the Kingdoms of Scotland and England,

(c) the Parliament of the United Kingdom,

(d) the continued existence of the High Court of Justiciary as a criminal court of first instance and of appeal,

(e) the continued existence of the Court of Session as a civil court of first instance and of appeal.

2.–[5.] *****

[5A.] ...

Political parties

6. The registration and funding of political parties is a reserved matter [but this paragraph does not reserve making payments to any political party for the purpose of assisting members of the Parliament who are connected with the party to perform their Parliamentary duties].

Foreign affairs etc

7.—(1) International relations, including relations with territories outside the United Kingdom, the [European Union] (and their institutions) and other international organisations, regulation of international trade, and international development assistance and co-operation are reserved matters.

(2) Sub-paragraph (1) does not reserve—

(a) observing and implementing international obligations, obligations under the Human Rights Convention and obligations under [EU] law,

(b) assisting Ministers of the Crown in relation to any matter to which that sub-paragraph applies.

Public service

8.—(1) The Civil Service of the State is a reserved matter.

(2) Sub-paragraph (1) does not reserve the subject-matter of—

(a) Part I of the Sheriff Courts and Legal Officers (Scotland) Act 1927 (appointment of sheriff clerks and procurators fiscal etc),

(b) Part III of the Administration of Justice (Scotland) Act 1933 (officers of the High Court of Justiciary and of the Court of Session).

Defence

9.—(1) The following are reserved matters—
  (a) the defence of the realm,
  (b) the naval, military or air forces of the Crown, including reserve forces,
  (c) visiting forces,
  (d) international headquarters and defence organisations,
  (e) trading with the enemy and enemy property.

(2) Sub-paragraph (1) does not reserve—
  (a) the exercise of civil defence functions by any person otherwise than as a member of any force or organisation referred to in sub-paragraph (1)(b) to (d) or any other force or organisation reserved by virtue of sub-paragraph (1)(a),
  (b) the conferral of enforcement powers in relation to sea fishing.

Treason

10. Treason (including constructive treason), treason felony and misprision of treason are reserved matters.

PART II SPECIFIC RESERVATIONS

Preliminary

1. The matters to which any of the Sections in this Part apply are reserved matters for the purposes of this Act.

2. A Section applies to any matter described or referred to in it when read with any illustrations, exceptions or interpretation provisions in that Section.

3. Any illustrations, exceptions or interpretation provisions in a Section relate only to that Section (so that an entry under the heading 'exceptions' does not affect any other Section).

Reservations

Head A—Financial and Economic Matters

Section A1

A1. Fiscal, economic and monetary policy
Fiscal, economic and monetary policy, including the issue and circulation of money, taxes and excise duties, government borrowing and lending, control over United Kingdom public expenditure, the exchange rate and the Bank of England.

[Exceptions]

[Devolved taxes, including their collection and management.]
  Local taxes to fund local authority expenditure (for example, council tax and non-domestic rates).

Section A2

A2. The currency
Coinage, legal tender and bank notes.

Section A3

A3. Financial services
Financial services, including investment business, banking and deposit-taking, collective investment schemes and insurance.

Exception

The subject-matter of section 1 of the Banking and Financial Dealings Act 1971 (bank holidays).

Section A4

A4. Financial markets
Financial markets, including listing and public offers of securities and investments, transfer of securities and insider dealing.

Section A5

A5. Money laundering
The subject-matter of the Money Laundering Regulations 1993, but in relation to any type of business.*
*****

Section 98   **SCHEDULE 6**

DEVOLUTION ISSUES

PART I PRELIMINARY

1. In this Schedule 'devolution issue' means—
    (a) a question whether an Act of the Scottish Parliament or any provision of an Act of the Scottish Parliament is within the legislative competence of the Parliament,
    (b) a question whether any function (being a function which any person has purported, or is proposing, to exercise) is a function of the Scottish Ministers, the First Minister or the Lord Advocate,
    (c) a question whether the purported or proposed exercise of a function by a member of the [Scottish Government] is, or would be, within devolved competence,
    (d) a question whether a purported or proposed exercise of a function by a member of the [Scottish Government] is, or would be incompatible with any of the Convention rights . . .,
    (e) a question whether a failure to act by a member of the [Scottish Government] is incompatible with any of the Convention rights . . .,
    (f) any other question about whether a function is exercisable within devolved competence or in or as regards Scotland and any other question arising by virtue of this Act about reserved matters.
[But a question arising in criminal proceedings in Scotland that would, apart from this paragraph, be a devolution issue is not a devolution issue if (however formulated) it relates to [a compatibility issue (within the meaning given by section 288ZA(2) of the Criminal Procedure (Scotland) Act 1995)].]
    2. A devolution issue shall not be taken to arise in any proceedings merely because of any contention of a party to the proceedings which appears to the court or tribunal before which the proceedings take place to be frivolous or vexatious.

---

* **Editor's Note:** The text of the remaining headings is omitted for reasons of space. The other headings are categorised as follows:
Head B—Home Affairs
Head C—Trade and Industry
Head D—Energy
Head E—Transport
Head F—Social Security
Head G—Regulation of the Professions
Head H—Employment
Head J—Health and Medicines
Head K—Media and Culture
Head L—Miscellaneous

PART II PROCEEDINGS IN SCOTLAND

Application of Part II

3. This Part of this Schedule applies in relation to devolution issues in proceedings in Scotland.

Institution of proceedings

4.—(1) Proceedings for the determination of a devolution issue may be instituted by the Advocate General or the Lord Advocate.

(2) The Lord Advocate may defend any such proceedings instituted by the Advocate General.

(3) This paragraph is without prejudice to any power to institute or defend proceedings exercisable apart from this paragraph by any person.

Intimation of devolution issue

5. Intimation of any devolution issue which arises in any proceedings before a court or tribunal shall be given to the Advocate General and the Lord Advocate (unless the person to whom the intimation would be given is a party to the proceedings).

6. A person to whom intimation is given in pursuance of paragraph 5 may take part as a party in the proceedings, so far as they relate to a devolution issue.

Reference of devolution issue to higher court

7. A court, other than the [Supreme Court] or any court consisting of three or more judges of the Court of Session, may refer any devolution issue which arises in proceedings (other than criminal proceedings) before it to the Inner House of the Court of Session.

8. A tribunal from which there is no appeal shall refer any devolution issue which arises in proceedings before it to the Inner House of the Court of Session; and any other tribunal may make such a reference.

9. A court, other than any court consisting of two or more judges of the High Court of Justiciary, may refer any devolution issue which arises in criminal proceedings before it to the High Court of Justiciary.

References from superior courts to [Supreme Court]

10. Any court consisting of three or more judges of the Court of Session may refer any devolution issue which arises in proceedings before it (otherwise than on a reference under paragraph 7 or 8) to the [Supreme Court].

11. Any court consisting of two or more judges of the High Court of Justiciary may refer any devolution issue which arises in proceedings before it (otherwise than on a reference under paragraph 9) to the [Supreme Court].

Appeals from superior courts to [Supreme Court]

12. An appeal against a determination of a devolution issue by the Inner House of the Court of Session on a reference under paragraph 7 or 8 shall lie to the [Supreme Court].

13. An appeal against a determination of a devolution issue by—

    (a) a court of two or more judges of the High Court of Justiciary (whether in the ordinary course of proceedings or on a reference under paragraph 9), or

    (b) a court of three or more judges of the Court of Session from which there is no appeal to the [Supreme Court apart from this paragraph],

shall lie to the [Supreme Court], but only with [permission] of the court [from which the appeal lies] or, failing such [permission], with [permission] of the [Supreme Court].

[13A. In criminal proceedings, an application to the High Court for permission under paragraph 13 must be made—

(a) within 28 days of the date of the determination against which the appeal lies, or

(b) within such longer period as the High Court considers equitable having regard to all the circumstances.

13B. In criminal proceedings, an application to the Supreme Court for permission under paragraph 13 must be made—

(a) within 28 days of the date on which the High Court refused permission under that paragraph, or

(b) within such longer period as the Supreme Court considers equitable having regard to all the circumstances.]

PART III PROCEEDINGS IN ENGLAND AND WALES

Application of Part III

14. This Part of this Schedule applies in relation to devolution issues in proceedings in England and Wales.

Institution of proceedings

15.—(1) Proceedings for the determination of a devolution issue may be instituted by the Attorney General.

(2) The Lord Advocate may defend any such proceedings.

(3) This paragraph is without prejudice to any power to institute or defend proceedings exercisable apart from this paragraph by any person.

Notice of devolution issue

16. A court or tribunal shall order notice of any devolution issue which arises in any proceedings before it to be given to the Attorney General and the Lord Advocate (unless the person to whom the notice would be given is a party to the proceedings).

17. A person to whom notice is given in pursuance of paragraph 16 may take part as a party in the proceedings, so far as they relate to a devolution issue.

Reference of devolution issue to High Court or Court of Appeal

18. A magistrates' court may refer any devolution issue which arises in proceedings (other than criminal proceedings) before it to the High Court.

19.—(1) A court may refer any devolution issue which arises in proceedings (other than criminal proceedings) before it to the Court of Appeal.

(2) Sub-paragraph (1) does not apply to—

(a) a magistrates' court, the Court of Appeal or the [Supreme Court], or

(b) the High Court if the devolution issue arises in proceedings on a reference under paragraph 18.

20. A tribunal from which there is no appeal shall refer any devolution issue which arises in proceedings before it to the Court of Appeal; and any other tribunal may make such a reference.

21. A court, other than the [Supreme Court] or the Court of Appeal, may refer any devolution issue which arises in criminal proceedings before it to—

(a) the High Court (if the proceedings are summary proceedings), or

(b) the Court of Appeal (if the proceedings are proceedings on indictment).

References from Court of Appeal to [Supreme Court]

22. The Court of Appeal may refer any devolution issue which arises in proceedings before it (otherwise than on a reference under paragraph 19, 20 or 21) to the [Supreme Court].

Appeals from superior courts to [Supreme Court]

23. An appeal against a determination of a devolution issue by the High Court or the Court of Appeal on a reference under paragraph 18, 19, 20 or 21 shall lie to the [Supreme Court] but only with

[permission] of the High Court or (as the case may be) the Court of Appeal or, failing such [permission], with [permission] of the [Supreme Court].

24.–31. *****

(Equivalent provisions for issues arising in Northern Ireland)

PART V GENERAL

32. ...

Direct references to [Supreme Court]

33. The Lord Advocate, the Advocate General, the Attorney General or the [Advocate General for Northern Ireland] may require any court or tribunal to refer to the [Supreme Court] any devolution issue which has arisen in proceedings before it to which he is a party.

34. The Lord Advocate, the Attorney General, the Advocate General or the [Advocate General for Northern Ireland] may refer to the [Supreme Court] any devolution issue which is not the subject of proceedings.

35.–38. *****

*****

Greater London Authority Act 1999

(1999, c. 29)

An Act to establish and make provision about the Greater London Authority, the Mayor of London and the London Assembly; to make provision in relation to London borough councils and the Common Council of the City of London with respect to matters consequential or the establishment of the Greater London Authority; to make provision with respect to the functions of other local authorities and statutory bodies exercising functions in Greater London; to make provision about transport and road traffic in and around Greater London; to make provision about policing in Greater London and to make an adjustment of the metropolitan police district; and for connected purposes.   [11th November 1999]

Territorial extent: England, Scotland and Wales (but necessarily the substantive provisions apply only to London)

PART I THE GREATER LONDON AUTHORITY

The Authority

1   The Authority

(1) There shall be an authority for Greater London, to be known as the Greater London Authority.

(2) The Authority shall be a body corporate.

(3) The Authority shall have the functions which are transferred to, or conferred or imposed on, the Authority by or under this Act or any other Act.

Membership

2   Membership of the Authority and the Assembly

(1) The Authority shall consist of—

(a) the Mayor of London; and

(b) an Assembly for London, to be known as the London Assembly.

(2) The Assembly shall consist of twenty five members, of whom—

(a) fourteen shall be members of Assembly constituencies ('constituency members'); and

(b) eleven shall be members for the whole of Greater London ('London Members').

(3) There shall be one constituency member for each Assembly constituency.

(4) The Assembly constituencies shall be the areas, and shall be known by the names, specified in an order made by [statutory instrument by [the Local Government Boundary Commission for England]].

(5)–(11) *****

3–19 *****

Qualifications and disqualifications

20 Qualification to be the Mayor or an Assembly member

(1) Subject to any disqualification by virtue of this Act or any other enactment, a person is qualified to be elected and to be the Mayor or an Assembly member if he satisfies the requirements of subsections (2) to (4) below.

(2) The person must be—

(a) a [qualifying] Commonwealth citizen;

(b) a citizen of the Republic of Ireland; or

(c) a relevant citizen of the Union.

(3) On the relevant day, the person must have attained the age of [18] years.

(4) The person must satisfy at least one of the following conditions—

(a) on the relevant day he is, and from that day continues to be, a local government elector for Greater London;

(b) he has, during the whole of the twelve months preceding that day, occupied as owner or tenant any land or other premises in Greater London;

(c) his principal or only place of work during that twelve months has been in Greater London;

(d) he has during the whole of that twelve months resided in Greater London.

(5)–(8) *****

21–29 *****

PART II GENERAL FUNCTIONS AND PROCEDURE

The general and subsidiary powers of the Authority

30 The general power of the Authority

(1) The Authority shall have power to do anything which it considers will further any one or more of its principal purposes.

(2) Any reference in this Act to the principal purposes of the Authority is a reference to the purposes of—

(a) promoting economic development and wealth creation in Greater London;

(b) promoting social development in Greater London; and

(c) promoting the improvement of the environment in Greater London.

(3) In determining whether or how to exercise the power conferred by subsection (1) above to further any one or more of its principal purposes, the Authority shall have regard to the desirability of so exercising that power as to—

(a) further the remaining principal purpose or purposes, so far as reasonably practicable to do so; and

(b) secure, over a period of time, a reasonable balance between furthering each of its principal purposes.

(4) In determining whether or how to exercise the power conferred by subsection (1) above, the Authority shall have regard to the effect which the proposed exercise of the power would have on [each of the following]—

(a) the health of persons in Greater London;

[(aa) health inequalities between persons living in Greater London;]

(b)   the achievement of sustainable development in the United Kingdom;

[(c)   climate change and the consequences of climate change.]

(5) Where the Authority exercises the power conferred by subsection (1) above, it shall do so in the way which it considers best calculated—

(a)   to promote improvements in the health of persons in Greater London,

[(aa) to promote the reduction of health inequalities between persons living in Greater London . . .]

(b)   to contribute towards the achievement of sustainable development in the United Kingdom, [and]

[(c)   to contribute towards the mitigation of, or adaptation to, climate change in the United Kingdom,]

except to the extent that the Authority considers that any action that would need to be taken by virtue of paragraph (a) [, (aa),] (b) [or (c)] above is not reasonably practicable in all the circumstances of the case.

(6)–(11) *****

*****

House of Lords Act 1999

(1999, c. 34)

An Act to restrict membership of the House of Lords by virtue of a hereditary peerage; to make related provision about disqualifications for voting at elections to and for membership of the House of Commons; and for connected purposes.   [11th November 1999]

Territorial extent: United Kingdom

1   Exclusion of hereditary peers

No-one shall be a member of the House of Lords by virtue of a hereditary peerage.

2   Exception from section 1

(1) Section 1 shall not apply in relation to anyone excepted from it by or in accordance with Standing Orders of the House.

(2) At any time 90 people shall be excepted from section 1; but anyone excepted as holder of the office of Earl Marshal, or as performing the office of Lord Great Chamberlain, shall not count towards that limit.

(3) Once excepted from section 1, a person shall continue to be so throughout his life (until an Act of Parliament provides to the contrary).

(4) Standing Orders shall make provision for filling vacancies among the people excepted from section 1; and in any case where—

(a) the vacancy arises on a death occurring after the end of the first Session of the next Parliament after that in which this Act is passed, and

(b) the deceased person was excepted in consequence of an election,

that provision shall require the holding of a by-election.

(5) A person may be excepted from section 1 by or in accordance with Standing Orders made in anticipation of the enactment or commencement of this section.

(6) Any question whether a person is excepted from section 1 shall be decided by the Clerk of the Parliaments, whose certificate shall be conclusive.

3   Removal of disqualifications in relation to the House of Commons

(1) The holder of a hereditary peerage shall not be disqualified by virtue of that peerage for—

(a) voting at elections to the House of Commons, or

(b) being, or being elected as, a member of that House.

(2) Subsection (1) shall not apply in relation to anyone excepted from section 1 by virtue of section 2.

4 *******

5 Commencement and transitional provision

(1) Sections 1 to 4 (including Schedules 1 and 2) shall come into force at the end of the Session of Parliament in which this Act is passed.

(2) Accordingly, any writ of summons issued for the present Parliament in right of a hereditary peerage shall not have effect after that Session unless it has been issued to a person who, at the end of the Session, is excepted from section 1 by virtue of section 2.

(3), (4) *******

6 Interpretation and short title

(1) In this Act 'hereditary peerage' includes the principality of Wales and the earldom of Chester.

(2) This Act may be cited as the House of Lords Act 1999.

*****

Freedom of Information Act 2000

(2000, c. 36)

An Act to make provision for the disclosure of information held by public authorities or by persons providing services for them and to amend the Data Protection Act 1998 and the Public Records Act 1958; and for connected purposes.   [30th November 2000]

Territorial extent: England and Wales, Northern Ireland. The Act applies also to a limited extent to public bodies which operate also in Scotland, but not to purely Scottish public authorities such as the Scottish Parliament or Executive (which are covered by the Freedom of Information (Scotland) Act 2002)

PART I ACCESS TO INFORMATION HELD BY PUBLIC AUTHORITIES

Right to information

1 General right of access to information held by public authorities

(1) Any person making a request for information to a public authority is entitled—

(a) to be informed in writing by the public authority whether it holds information of the description specified in the request, and

(b) if that is the case, to have that information communicated to him.

(2) Subsection (1) has effect subject to the following provisions of this section and to the provisions of sections 2, 9, 12 and 14.

(3) Where a public authority—

(a) reasonably requires further information in order to identify and locate the information requested, and

(b) has informed the applicant of that requirement,

the authority is not obliged to comply with subsection (1) unless it is supplied with that further information.

(4) The information—

(a) in respect of which the applicant is to be informed under subsection (1)(a), or

(b) which is to be communicated under subsection (1)(b),

is the information in question held at the time when the request is received, except that account may be taken of any amendment or deletion made between that time and the time when the information is to be communicated under subsection (1)(b), being an amendment or deletion that would have been made regardless of the receipt of the request.

(5) A public authority is to be taken to have complied with subsection (1)(a) in relation to any information if it has communicated the information to the applicant in accordance with subsection (1)(b).

(6) In this Act, the duty of a public authority to comply with subsection (1)(a) is referred to as 'the duty to confirm or deny'.

2 Effect of the exemptions in Part II

(1) Where any provision of Part II states that the duty to confirm or deny does not arise in relation to any information, the effect of the provision is that where either—

(a) the provision confers absolute exemption, or

(b) in all the circumstances of the case, the public interest in maintaining the exclusion of the duty to confirm or deny outweighs the public interest in disclosing whether the public authority holds the information,

section 1(1)(a) does not apply.

(2) In respect of any information which is exempt information by virtue of any provision of Part II, section 1(1)(b) does not apply if or to the extent that—

(a) the information is exempt information by virtue of a provision conferring absolute exemption, or

(b) in all the circumstances of the case, the public interest in maintaining the exemption outweighs the public interest in disclosing the information.

(3) For the purposes of this section, the following provisions of Part II (and no others) are to be regarded as conferring absolute exemption—

(a)   section 21,

(b)   section 23,

(c)   section 32,

(d)   section 34,

(e)   section 36 so far as relating to information held by the House of Commons or the House of Lords,

[(ea) in section 37, paragraphs (a) to (ab) of subsection (1), and subsection (2) so far as relating to those paragraphs,]

[(f)   in section 40(1),

(fa)   section 40(2) so far as relating to cases where the first condition referred to in that subsection is satisfied,]

(g)   section 41, and

(h)   section 44.

3 Public authorities

(1) In this Act 'public authority' means—

(a) subject to section 4(4), any body which, any other person who, or the holder of any office which—

(i)   is listed in Schedule 1, or

(ii)   is designated by order under section 5, or

(b) a publicly-owned company as defined by section 6.

(2) For the purposes of this Act, information is held by a public authority if—

(a) it is held by the authority, otherwise than on behalf of another person, or

(b) it is held by another person on behalf of the authority.

4–7 *****

8 Request for information

(1) In this Act any reference to a 'request for information' is a reference to such a request which—

(a) is in writing,

(b) states the name of the applicant and an address for correspondence, and

(c) describes the information requested.

(2) For the purposes of subsection (1)(a), a request is to be treated as made in writing where the text of the request—

(a) is transmitted by electronic means,

(b) is received in legible form, and

(c) is capable of being used for subsequent reference.

9 Fees

(1) A public authority to whom a request for information is made may, within the period for complying with section 1(1), give the applicant a notice in writing (in this Act referred to as a 'fees notice') stating that a fee of an amount specified in the notice is to be charged by the authority for complying with section 1(1).

(2) Where a fees notice has been given to the applicant, the public authority is not obliged to comply with section 1(1) unless the fee is paid within the period of three months beginning with the day on which the fees notice is given to the applicant.

(3) Subject to subsection (5), any fee under this section must be determined by the public authority in accordance with regulations made by the [Minister of the Cabinet Office].

(4), (5) *****

10 Time for compliance with request

(1) Subject to subsections (2) and (3), a public authority must comply with section 1(1) promptly and in any event not later than the twentieth working day following the date of receipt.

(2) Where the authority has given a fees notice to the applicant and the fee is paid in accordance with section 9(2), the working days in the period beginning with the day on which the fees notice is given to the applicant and ending with the day on which the fee is received by the authority are to be disregarded in calculating for the purposes of subsection (1) the twentieth working day following the date of receipt.

(3)–(6) *****

11 Means by which communication to be made

(1) Where, on making his request for information, the applicant expresses a preference for communication by any one or more of the following means, namely—

    (a) the provision to the applicant of a copy of the information in permanent form or in another form acceptable to the applicant,

    (b) the provision to the applicant of a reasonable opportunity to inspect a record containing the information, and

    (c) the provision to the applicant of a digest or summary of the information in permanent form or in another form acceptable to the applicant,

the public authority shall so far as reasonably practicable give effect to that preference.

[(1A) Where—

    (a) an applicant makes a request for information to a public authority in respect of information that is, or forms part of, a dataset held by the public authority, and

    (b) on making the request for information, the applicant expresses a preference for communication by means of the provision to the applicant of a copy of the information in electronic form,

the public authority must, so far as reasonably practicable, provide the information to the applicant in an electronic form which is capable of re-use.]

(2) In determining for the purposes of this section whether it is reasonably practicable to communicate information by particular means, the public authority may have regard to all the circumstances, including the cost of doing so.

(3) Where the public authority determines that it is not reasonably practicable to comply with any preference expressed by the applicant in making his request, the authority shall notify the applicant of the reasons for its determination.

(4) Subject to subsection (1) [and (1A)], a public authority may comply with a request by communicating information by any means which are reasonable in the circumstances.

[(5) In this Act 'dataset' means information comprising a collection of information held in electronic form where all or most of the information in the collection—

    (a) has been obtained or recorded for the purpose of providing a public authority with information in connection with the provision of a service by the authority or the carrying out of any other function of the authority,

(b) is factual information which—
    (i)   is not the product of analysis or interpretation other than calculation, and
    (ii) is not an official statistic (within the meaning given by section 6(1) of the Statistics and Registration Service Act 2007), and
(c) remains presented in a way that (except for the purpose of forming part of the collection) has not been organised, adapted or otherwise materially altered since it was obtained or recorded.]

[11A], [11B] *****

12   Exemption where cost of compliance exceeds appropriate limit

(1) Section 1(1) does not oblige a public authority to comply with a request for information if the authority estimates that the cost of complying with the request would exceed the appropriate limit.

(2) Subsection (1) does not exempt the public authority from its obligation to comply with paragraph (a) of section 1(1) unless the estimated cost of complying with that paragraph alone would exceed the appropriate limit.

(3) In subsections (1) and (2) 'the appropriate limit' means such amount as may be prescribed, and different amounts may be prescribed in relation to different cases.

(4) The [Minister of the Cabinet Office] may by regulations provide that, in such circumstances as may be prescribed, where two or more requests for information are made to a public authority—
(a) by one person, or
(b) by different persons who appear to the public authority to be acting in concert or in pursuance of a campaign,
the estimated cost of complying with any of the requests is to be taken to be the estimated total cost of complying with all of them.

(5) The [Minister of the Cabinet Office] may by regulations make provision for the purposes of this section as to the costs to be estimated and as to the manner in which they are to be estimated.

13–16 *****

Refusal of request

17   Refusal of request

(1) A public authority which, in relation to any request for information, is to any extent relying on a claim that any provision of Part II relating to the duty to confirm or deny is relevant to the request or on a claim that information is exempt information must, within the time for complying with section 1(1), give the applicant a notice which—
(a) states that fact,
(b) specifies the exemption in question, and
(c) states (if that would not otherwise be apparent) why the exemption applies.

(2) *****

(3) A public authority which, in relation to any request for information, is to any extent relying on a claim that subsection (1)(b) or (2)(b) of section 2 applies must, either in the notice under subsection (1) or in a separate notice given within such time as is reasonable in the circumstances, state the reasons for claiming—
(a) that, in all the circumstances of the case, the public interest in maintaining the exclusion of the duty to confirm or deny outweighs the public interest in disclosing whether the authority holds the information, or
(b) that, in all the circumstances of the case, the public interest in maintaining the exemption outweighs the public interest in disclosing the information.

(4) A public authority is not obliged to make a statement under subsection (1)(c) or (3) if, or to the extent that, the statement would involve the disclosure of information which would itself be exempt information.

(5) A public authority which, in relation to any request for information, is relying on a claim that section 12 or 14 applies must, within the time for complying with section 1(1), give the applicant a notice stating that fact.

(6), (7) *****

18 *****

Publication schemes

19 Publication schemes

(1) It shall be the duty of every public authority—

    (a) to adopt and maintain a scheme which relates to the publication of information by the authority and is approved by the Commissioner (in this Act referred to as a 'publication scheme'),

    (b) to publish information in accordance with its publication scheme, and

    (c) from time to time to review its publication scheme.

(2) A publication scheme must—

    (a) specify classes of information which the public authority publishes or intends to publish,

    (b) specify the manner in which information of each class is, or is intended to be, published, and

    (c) specify whether the material is, or is intended to be, available to the public free of charge or on payment.

[(2A) A publication scheme must, in particular, include a requirement for the public authority concerned—

    (a) to publish—

      (i) any dataset held by the authority in relation to which a person makes a request for information to the authority, and

      (ii) any up-dated version held by the authority of such a dataset,

      unless the authority is satisfied that it is not appropriate for the dataset to be published,

    (b) where reasonably practicable, to publish any dataset the authority publishes by virtue of paragraph (a) in an electronic form which is capable of re-use,

    (c) [subject to subsections (2AA) and (2AB)] where any information in a dataset published by virtue of paragraph (a) is a relevant copyright work in relation to which the authority is the only owner, to make the information available for re-use in accordance with the terms of the specified licence.]

[(2AA) If the whole of the relevant copyright work is a document to which the Re-use of Public Sector Information Regulations 2015 apply, subsections (2A)(c) and (2B) to (2F) do not apply to the relevant copyright work.

(2AB) If part of the relevant copyright work is a document to which those Regulations apply—

    (a) subsections (2A)(c) and (2B) to (2F) do not apply to that part, but

    (b) those provisions do apply to the part to which the Regulations do not apply (and references in the following provisions of this section to the relevant copyright work are to be read as references to that part).]

[(2B)–(2F)] *****

(3) In adopting or reviewing a publication scheme, a public authority shall have regard to the public interest—

    (a) in allowing public access to information held by the authority, and

    (b) in the publication of reasons for decisions made by the authority.

(4) A public authority shall publish its publication scheme in such manner as it thinks fit.

(5)–[(8)] *****

20 *****

PART II EXEMPT INFORMATION

21 Information accessible to applicant by other means

(1) Information which is reasonably accessible to the applicant otherwise than under section 1 is exempt information.

(2) For the purposes of subsection (1)—

(a) information may be reasonably accessible to the applicant even though it is accessible only on payment, and

(b) information is to be taken to be reasonably accessible to the applicant if it is information which the public authority or any other person is obliged by or under any enactment to communicate (otherwise than by making the information available for inspection) to members of the public on request, whether free of charge or on payment.

(3) *****

22, [22A] *****

23 Information supplied by, or relating to, bodies dealing with security matters

(1) Information held by a public authority is exempt information if it was directly or indirectly supplied to the public authority by, or relates to, any of the bodies specified in subsection (3).

(2) A certificate signed by a Minister of the Crown certifying that the information to which it applies was directly or indirectly supplied by, or relates to, any of the bodies specified in subsection (3) shall, subject to section 60, be conclusive evidence of that fact.

(3) The bodies referred to in subsections (1) and (2) are—

(a)   the Security Service,

(b)   the Secret Intelligence Service,

(c)   the Government Communications Headquarters,

(d)   the special forces,

(e)   the Tribunal established under section 65 of the Regulation of Investigatory Powers Act 2000,

(f)   the Tribunal established under section 7 of the Interception of Communications Act 1985,

(g)   the Tribunal established under section 5 of the Security Service Act 1989,

(h)   the Tribunal established under section 9 of the Intelligence Services Act 1994,

(i)   the Security Vetting Appeals Panel,

(j)   the Security Commission,

(k)   the National Criminal Intelligence Service, ...

(l)   the Service Authority for the National Criminal Intelligence Service,

[(m)   the Serious Organised Crime Agency;]

[(n)   the National Crime Agency;]

[(o)   the Intelligence and Security Committee of Parliament.]

(4), (5) *****

24 National security

(1) Information which does not fall within section 23(1) is exempt information if exemption from section 1(1)(b) is required for the purpose of safeguarding national security.

(2) The duty to confirm or deny does not arise if, or to the extent that, exemption from section 1(1)(a) is required for the purpose of safeguarding national security.

(3) A certificate signed by a Minister of the Crown certifying that exemption from section 1(1)(b), or from section 1(1)(a) and (b), is, or at any time was, required for the purpose of safeguarding national security shall, subject to section 60, be conclusive evidence of that fact.

(4) A certificate under subsection (3) may identify the information to which it applies by means of a general description and may be expressed to have prospective effect.

25　******

26　Defence

(1)　Information is exempt information if its disclosure under this Act would, or would be likely to, prejudice—

    (a)　the defence of the British Islands or of any colony, or

    (b)　the capability, effectiveness or security of any relevant forces.

(2)　In subsection (1)(b) 'relevant forces' means—

    (a)　the armed forces of the Crown, and

    (b)　any forces co-operating with those forces,

or any part of any of those forces.

(3)　The duty to confirm or deny does not arise if, or to the extent that, compliance with section 1(1)(a) would, or would be likely to, prejudice any of the matters mentioned in subsection (1).

27　International relations

(1)　Information is exempt information if its disclosure under this Act would, or would be likely to, prejudice—

    (a)　relations between the United Kingdom and any other State,

    (b)　relations between the United Kingdom and any international organisation or international court,

    (c)　the interests of the United Kingdom abroad, or

    (d)　the promotion or protection by the United Kingdom of its interests abroad.

(2)　Information is also exempt information if it is confidential information obtained from a State other than the United Kingdom or from an international organisation or international court.

(3)　For the purposes of this section, any information obtained from a State, organisation or court is confidential at any time while the terms on which it was obtained require it to be held in confidence or while the circumstances in which it was obtained make it reasonable for the State, organisation or court to expect that it will be so held.

(4)　The duty to confirm or deny does not arise if, or to the extent that, compliance with section 1(1)(a)—

    (a)　would, or would be likely to, prejudice any of the matters mentioned in subsection (1), or

    (b)　would involve the disclosure of any information (whether or not already recorded) which is confidential information obtained from a State other than the United Kingdom or from an international organisation or international court.

    (5)　******

28　Relations within the United Kingdom

(1)　Information is exempt information if its disclosure under this Act would, or would be likely to, prejudice relations between any administration in the United Kingdom and any other such administration.

(2)　In subsection (1) 'administration in the United Kingdom' means—

    (a)　the government of the United Kingdom,

    (b)　the Scottish Administration,

    (c)　the Executive Committee of the Northern Ireland Assembly, or

    [(d) the Welsh Assembly Government].

(3)　The duty to confirm or deny does not arise if, or to the extent that, compliance with section 1(1)(a) would, or would be likely to, prejudice any of the matters mentioned in subsection (1).

29　The economy

(1)　Information is exempt information if its disclosure under this Act would, or would be likely to, prejudice—

    (a)　the economic interests of the United Kingdom or of any part of the United Kingdom, or

    (b)　the financial interests of any administration in the United Kingdom, as defined by section 28(2).

(2) The duty to confirm or deny does not arise if, or to the extent that, compliance with section 1(1)(a) would, or would be likely to, prejudice any of the matters mentioned in subsection (1).

30   Investigations and proceedings conducted by public authorities

(1) Information held by a public authority is exempt information if it has at any time been held by the authority for the purposes of—

    (a) any investigation which the public authority has a duty to conduct with a view to it being ascertained—

        (i)   whether a person should be charged with an offence, or

        (ii) whether a person charged with an offence is guilty of it,

    (b) any investigation which is conducted by the authority and in the circumstances may lead to a decision by the authority to institute criminal proceedings which the authority has power to conduct, or

    (c) any criminal proceedings which the authority has power to conduct.

(2) *****

(3) The duty to confirm or deny does not arise in relation to information which is (or if it were held by the public authority would be) exempt information by virtue of subsection (1) or (2).

(4)–(6) *****

31   Law enforcement

(1) Information which is not exempt information by virtue of section 30 is exempt information if its disclosure under this Act would, or would be likely to, prejudice—

    (a) the prevention or detection of crime,

    (b) the apprehension or prosecution of offenders,

    (c) the administration of justice,

    (d) the assessment or collection of any tax or duty or of any imposition of a similar nature,

    (e) the operation of the immigration controls,

    (f) the maintenance of security and good order in prisons or in other institutions where persons are lawfully detained,

    (g) the exercise by any public authority of its functions for any of the purposes specified in subsection (2),

    (h) any civil proceedings which are brought by or on behalf of a public authority and arise out of an investigation conducted, for any of the purposes specified in subsection (2), by or on behalf of the authority by virtue of Her Majesty's prerogative or by virtue of powers conferred by or under an enactment, or

    (i) any inquiry held under the [Inquiries into Fatal Accidents and Sudden Deaths etc (Scotland) Act 2016] to the extent that the inquiry arises out of an investigation conducted, for any of the purposes specified in subsection (2), by or on behalf of the authority by virtue of Her Majesty's prerogative or by virtue of powers conferred by or under an enactment.

(2) The purposes referred to in subsection (1)(g) to (i) are—

    (a) the purpose of ascertaining whether any person has failed to comply with the law,

    (b) the purpose of ascertaining whether any person is responsible for any conduct which is improper,

    (c) the purpose of ascertaining whether circumstances which would justify regulatory action in pursuance of any enactment exist or may arise,

    (d) the purpose of ascertaining a person's fitness or competence in relation to the management of bodies corporate or in relation to any profession or other activity which he is, or seeks to become, authorised to carry on,

    (e) the purpose of ascertaining the cause of an accident,

    (f) the purpose of protecting charities against misconduct or mismanagement (whether by trustees or other persons) in their administration,

    (g) the purpose of protecting the property of charities from loss or misapplication,

(h) the purpose of recovering the property of charities,

(i) the purpose of securing the health, safety and welfare of persons at work, and

(j) the purpose of protecting persons other than persons at work against risk to health or safety arising out of or in connection with the actions of persons at work.

(3) The duty to confirm or deny does not arise if, or to the extent that, compliance with section 1(1)(a) would, or would be likely to, prejudice any of the matters mentioned in subsection (1).

32, 33 *****

34 Parliamentary privilege

(1) Information is exempt information if exemption from section 1(1)(b) is required for the purpose of avoiding an infringement of the privileges of either House of Parliament.

(2) The duty to confirm or deny does not apply if, or to the extent that, exemption from section 1(1)(a) is required for the purpose of avoiding an infringement of the privileges of either House of Parliament.

(3) A certificate signed by the appropriate authority certifying that exemption from section 1(1)(b), or from section 1(1)(a) and (b), is, or at any time was, required for the purpose of avoiding an infringement of the privileges of either House of Parliament shall be conclusive evidence of that fact.

(4) In subsection (3) 'the appropriate authority' means—

(a) in relation to the House of Commons, the Speaker of that House, and

(b) in relation to the House of Lords, the Clerk of the Parliaments.

35 Formulation of government policy, etc

(1) Information held by a government department or by the [Welsh Assembly Government] is exempt information if it relates to—

(a) the formulation or development of government policy,

(b) Ministerial communications,

(c) the provision of advice by any of the Law Officers or any request for the provision of such advice, or

(d) the operation of any Ministerial private office.

(2) Once a decision as to government policy has been taken, any statistical information used to provide an informed background to the taking of the decision is not to be regarded—

(a) for the purposes of subsection (1)(a), as relating to the formulation or development of government policy, or

(b) for the purposes of subsection (1)(b), as relating to ministerial communications.

(3) The duty to confirm or deny does not arise in relation to information which is (or if it were held by the public authority would be) exempt information by virtue of subsection (1).

(4), (5) *****

36 Prejudice to effective conduct of public affairs

(1) This section applies to—

(a) information which is held by a government department or by the [Welsh Assembly Government] and is not exempt information by virtue of section 35, and

(b) information which is held by any other public authority.

(2) Information to which this section applies is exempt information if, in the reasonable opinion of a qualified person, disclosure of the information under this Act—

(a) would, or would be likely to, prejudice—

(i) the maintenance of the convention of the collective responsibility of Ministers of the Crown, or

(ii) the work of the Executive Committee of the Northern Ireland Assembly, or

[(iii) the work of the Cabinet of the Welsh Assembly Government],

(b) would, or would be likely to, inhibit—

(i) the free and frank provision of advice, or

(ii) the free and frank exchange of views for the purposes of deliberation, or

(c)   would otherwise prejudice, or would be likely otherwise to prejudice, the effective conduct of public affairs.

(3) The duty to confirm or deny does not arise in relation to information to which this section applies (or would apply if held by the public authority) if, or to the extent that, in the reasonable opinion of a qualified person, compliance with section 1(1)(a) would, or would be likely to, have any of the effects mentioned in subsection (2).

(4)–(7) *****

37   Communications with Her Majesty, etc and honours

(1) Information is exempt information if it relates to—

[(a)   communications with the Sovereign,

(aa)   communications with the heir to, or the person who is for the time being second in line of succession to, the Throne,

(ab)   communications with a person who has subsequently acceded to the Throne or become heir to, or second in line to, the Throne,

(ac)   communications with other members of the Royal Family (other than communications which fall within any of paragraphs (a) to (ab) because they are made or received on behalf of a person falling within any of those paragraphs), and

(ad)   communications with the Royal Household (other than communications which fall within any of paragraphs (a) to (ac) because they are made or received on behalf of a person falling within any of those paragraphs), or]

(b)   the conferring by the Crown of any honour or dignity.

(2) The duty to confirm or deny does not arise in relation to information which is (or if it were held by the public authority would be) exempt information by virtue of subsection (1).

38–41 *****

42   Legal professional privilege

(1) Information in respect of which a claim to legal professional privilege or, in Scotland, to confidentiality of communications could be maintained in legal proceedings is exempt information.

(2) The duty to confirm or deny does not arise if, or to the extent that, compliance with section 1(1)(a) would involve the disclosure of any information (whether or not already recorded) in respect of which such a claim could be maintained in legal proceedings.

43, 44 *****

PART III GENERAL FUNCTIONS OF . . . [[MINISTER FOR THE CABINET OFFICE], SECRETARY OF STATE] AND INFORMATION COMMISSIONER

45   Issue of code of practice [by the Minister for the Cabinet Office] . . .

(1) The [Minister for the Cabinet Office] shall issue, and may from time to time revise, a code of practice providing guidance to public authorities as to the practice which it would, in his opinion, be desirable for them to follow in connection with the discharge of the authorities' functions under Part I.

(2), [(2A)], (3) *****

(4) Before issuing or revising any code under this section, the [Minister for the Cabinet Office] shall consult the Commissioner.

(5) The [Minister for the Cabinet Office] shall lay before each House of Parliament any code or revised code made under this section.

46–49 *****

PART IV ENFORCEMENT

50 Application for decision by Commissioner

(1) Any person (in this section referred to as 'the complainant') may apply to the Commissioner for a decision whether, in any specified respect, a request for information made by the complainant to a public authority has been dealt with in accordance with the requirements of Part I.

(2) In receiving an application under this section, the Commissioner shall make a decision unless it appears to him—

(a) that the complainant has not exhausted any complaints procedure which is provided by the public authority in conformity with the code of practice under section 45,

(b) that there has been undue delay in making the application,

(c) that the application is frivolous or vexatious, or

(d) that the application has been withdrawn or abandoned.

(3) Where the Commissioner has received an application under this section, he shall either—

(a) notify the complainant that he has not made any decision under this section as a result of the application and of his grounds for not doing so, or

(b) serve notice of his decision (in this Act referred to as a 'decision notice') on the complainant and the public authority.

(4) Where the Commissioner decides that a public authority—

(a) has failed to communicate information, or to provide confirmation or denial, in a case where it is required to do so by section 1(1), or

(b) has failed to comply with any of the requirements of sections 11 and 17,

the decision notice must specify the steps which must be taken by the authority for complying with that requirement and the period within which they must be taken.

(5) A decision notice must contain particulars of the right of appeal conferred by section 57.

(6), (7) *****

51, 52 *****

53 Exception from duty to comply with decision notice or enforcement notice

(1) This section applies to a decision notice or enforcement notice which—

(a) is served on—

(i) a government department,

[(ii) the Welsh Assembly Government, or]

(iii) any public authority designated for the purposes of this section by an order made by the [Minister for the Cabinet Office], and

(b) relates to a failure, in respect of one or more requests for information—

(i) to comply with section 1(1)(a) in respect of information which falls within any provision of Part II stating that the duty to confirm or deny does not arise, or

(ii) to comply with section 1(1)(b) in respect of exempt information.

(2) A decision notice or enforcement notice to which this section applies shall cease to have effect if, not later than the twentieth working day following the effective date, the accountable person in relation to that authority gives the Commissioner a certificate signed by him stating that he has on reasonable grounds formed the opinion that, in respect of the request or requests concerned, there was no failure falling within subsection (1)(b).

(3) Where the accountable person gives a certificate to the Commissioner under subsection (2) he shall as soon as practicable thereafter lay a copy of the certificate before—

(a) each House of Parliament,

(b) the Northern Ireland Assembly, in any case where the certificate relates to a decision notice or enforcement notice which has been served on a Northern Ireland department or any Northern Ireland public authority, or

[(c) the National Assembly for Wales, in any case where the certificate relates to a decision notice or enforcement notice which has been served on—

(i)   the Welsh Assembly Government,

(ii)   the National Assembly for Wales, or

(iii)   any Welsh public authority].

(4)   In subsection (2) 'the effective date', in relation to a decision notice or enforcement notice, means—

(a)   the day on which the notice was given to the public authority, or

(b)   where an appeal under section 57 is brought, the day on which that appeal (or any further appeal arising out of it) is determined or withdrawn.

(5)   Before making an order under subsection (1)(a)(iii), the [Minister for the Cabinet Office] shall—

(a)   if the order relates to a Welsh public authority, consult [the Welsh Ministers],

[(aa)   if the order relates to the National Assembly for Wales, consult the Presiding Officer of that Assembly,]

(b)   if the order relates to the Northern Ireland Assembly, consult the Presiding Officer of that Assembly, and

(c)   if the order relates to a Northern Ireland public authority, consult the First Minister and deputy First Minister in Northern Ireland.

(6)   Where the accountable person gives a certificate to the Commissioner under subsection (2) in relation to a decision notice, the accountable person shall, on doing so or as soon as reasonably practicable after doing so, inform the person who is the complainant for the purposes of section 50 of the reasons for his opinion.

(7)   The accountable person is not obliged to provide information under subsection (6) if, or to the extent that, compliance with that subsection would involve the disclosure of exempt information.

(8)   In this section 'the accountable person'—

(a)   in relation to a Northern Ireland department or any Northern Ireland public authority, means the First Minister and deputy First Minister in Northern Ireland acting jointly,

[(b)   in relation the Welsh Assembly Government, the National Assembly for Wales or any Welsh public authority, means the First Minister for Wales, and]

(c)   in relation to any other public authority, means—

(i)   a Minister of the Crown who is a member of the Cabinet, or

(ii)   the Attorney General, the Advocate General for Scotland or the Attorney General for Northern Ireland.

(9)   In this section 'working day' has the same meaning as in section 10.

*****

Political Parties, Elections and Referendums Act 2000

(2000, c. 41)

*An Act to establish an Electoral Commission; to make provision about the registration and finances of political parties; to make provision about donations and expenditure for political purposes; to make provision about election and referendum campaigns and the conduct of referendums; to make provision about election petitions and other legal proceedings in connection with elections; to reduce the qualifying periods set out in sections 1 and 3 of the Representation of the People Act 1985; to make pre-consolidation amendments relating to European Parliamentary Elections; and for connected purposes.** [30th November 2000]

Territorial extent: United Kingdom, except that ss. 50–69 do not apply to Northern Ireland (see SI 2001/446)

1   Establishment of the Electoral Commission

(1)   There shall be a body corporate to be known as the Electoral Commission or, in Welsh, Comisiwn Etholiadol (in this Act referred to as 'the Commission').

(2)   The Commission shall consist of members to be known as Electoral Commissioners.

* **Editor's Note:** Changes made by Political Parties and Elections Act 2009 which are not yet in force are not included here.

(3) There shall be [nine or ten] Electoral Commissioners.

(4) The Electoral Commissioners shall be appointed by Her Majesty (in accordance with section 3).

(5) Her Majesty shall (in accordance with section 3 [but subject to section 3A(6)]) appoint one of the Electoral Commissioners to be the chairman of the Commission.

(6) Schedule 1, which makes further provision in relation to the Commission, shall have effect.

2   Speaker's Committee

(1) There shall be a Committee (to be known as 'the Speaker's Committee') to perform the functions conferred on the Committee by this Act.

(2) The Speaker's Committee shall consist of the Speaker of the House of Commons, who shall be the chairman of the Committee, and the following other members, namely—

  (a)   the Member of the House of Commons who is for the time being the Chairman of the Home Affairs Select Committee of the House of Commons;

  [(b)   the [Secretary of State for Levelling Up, Housing and Communities];]

  (c)   a Member of the House of Commons who is a Minister of the Crown with responsibilities in relation to local government; and

  (d)   five Members of the House of Commons who are not Ministers of the Crown.

(3) The member of the Committee mentioned in subsection (2)(c) shall be appointed to membership of the Committee by the Prime Minister.

(4) The members of the Committee mentioned in subsection (2)(d) shall be appointed to membership of the Committee by the Speaker of the House of Commons.

(5), (6) *****

3–[13A] *****

14–20 ...

[20A]–21 *****

22   Parties to be registered in order to field candidates at elections

(1) Subject to subsection (4), no nomination may be made in relation to a relevant election unless the nomination is in respect of—

  (a) a person who stands for election in the name of a qualifying registered party; or

  (b) a person who does not purport to represent any party; or

  (c) a qualifying registered party, where the election is one for which registered parties may be nominated.

(2) For the purposes of subsection (1) a party (other than a minor party) is a 'qualifying registered party' in relation to a relevant election if—

  (a) the constituency, [police area,] local government area or electoral region in which the election is held—

    (i)   is in England, Scotland or Wales, or

    (ii)   is the electoral region of Scotland or Wales,

    and the party was, [on the day ('the relevant day') which is two days before the last day for the delivery of nomination papers at that election], registered in respect of that part of Great Britain in the Great Britain register maintained by the Commission under section 23, or

  (b) the constituency, district electoral area or electoral region in which the election is held—

    (i)   is in Northern Ireland, or

    (ii)   is the electoral region of Northern Ireland,

    and the party was, [on the relevant day], registered in the Northern Ireland register maintained by the Commission under that section.

  [(2A)] *****

(3) For the purposes of subsection (1) a person does not purport to represent any party if either—

(a) the description of the candidate given in his nomination paper, is—
    (i) 'Independent', or
    (ii) where the candidate is the Speaker of the House of Commons seeking re-election, 'The Speaker seeking re-election'; or
(b) no description of the candidate is given in his nomination paper.
(4) Subsection (1) does not apply in relation to any parish or community election.
(5) The following elections are relevant elections for the purposes of this Part—
    (a)   parliamentary elections,
    (b)   elections to the European Parliament,
    (c)   elections to the Scottish Parliament,
    (d)   elections to the National Assembly for Wales,
    (e)   elections to the Northern Ireland Assembly,
    [(ea) elections of police and crime commissioners,]
    (f)   local government elections, and
    (g)   local elections in Northern Ireland.
(6) For the purposes of this Act a person stands for election in the name of a registered party if his nomination paper includes a description authorised by a certificate issued by or on behalf of the registered nominating officer of the party.

23   The new registers
(1) In place of the register of political parties maintained by the registrar of companies under the Registration of Political Parties Act 1998, there shall be the new registers of political parties mentioned in subsection (2) which—
    (a) shall be maintained by the Commission, and
    (b) (subject to the provisions of this section) shall be so maintained in such form as the Commission may determine.
(2)–(6) *****

24–36   *****

37   Party political broadcasts
(1) A broadcaster shall not include in its broadcasting services any party political broadcast made on behalf of a party which is not a registered party.
(2) In this Act 'broadcaster' means—
    (a) the holder of a licence under the Broadcasting Act 1990 or 1996,
    (b) the British Broadcasting Corporation, or
    (c) Sianel Pedwar Cymru.
(3) ...

38–53   *****

54   Permissible donors
(1) A donation received by a registered party must not be accepted by the party if—
    (a)   the person by whom the donation would be made is not, at the time of its receipt by the party, a permissible donor; or
    [(aa) in the case of a donation of an amount exceeding £7,500, the party has not been given a declaration as required be section 54A; or]
    (b)   the party is (whether because the donation is given anonymously or by reason of any deception or concealment or otherwise) unable to ascertain the identity of that person.
(2) For the purposes of this Part the following are permissible donors—
    (a) an individual registered in an electoral register;
    (b) a company—
        (i)   [registered under the Companies Act 2006], and
        (ii) incorporated within the United Kingdom or another member State, which carries on business in the United Kingdom;

(c) a registered party [, other than a Gibraltar party whose entry in the register includes a statement that it intends to contest one or more elections to the European Parliament in the combined region];

(d) a trade union entered in the list kept under the Trade Union and Labour Relations (Consolidation) Act 1992 or the Industrial Relations (Northern Ireland) Order 1992;

(e) a building society (within the meaning of the Building Societies Act 1986);

(f) a limited liability partnership registered under the Limited Liability Partnerships Act … which carries on business in the United Kingdom;

(g) a friendly society registered under the Friendly Societies Act 1974 [, a registered society within the meaning of the Co-operative and Community Benefit Societies Act 2014 or a society registered (or deemed to be registered) under] the Industrial and Provident Societies Act 1965 or the Industrial and Provident Societies Act (Northern Ireland) 1969; and

(h) any unincorporated association of two or more persons which does not fall within any of the preceding paragraphs but which carries on business or other activities wholly or mainly in the United Kingdom and whose main office is there.

(2A)–(8) *****

55 *****

56 Acceptance or return of donations: general

(1) Where—

(a) a donation is received by a registered party, and

(b) it is not immediately decided that the party should (for whatever reason) refuse the donation,

all reasonable steps must be taken forthwith by or on behalf of the party to verify (or, so far as any of the following is not apparent, ascertain) the identity of the donor, whether he is a permissible donor, and (if that appears to be the case) all such details in respect of him as are required by virtue of paragraph 2 [or 2A] of Schedule 6 to be given in respect of the donor of a recordable donation.

(2) if a registered party receives a donation which it is prohibited from accepting by virtue of section 54(1), or which it is decided that the party should for any other reason refuse, then—

(a) unless the donation falls within section 54(1)(b), the donation, or a payment of an equivalent amount, must be sent back to the person who made the donation or any person appearing to be acting on his behalf,

(b) if the donation falls within that provision, the required steps (as defined by section 57(1)) must be taken in relation to the donation,

within the period of 30 days beginning with the date when the donation is received by the party.

(3) Where—

(a) subsection (2)(a) applies in relation to a donation, and

(b) the donation is not dealt with in accordance with that provision,

the party and the treasurer of the party are each guilty of an offence.

[(3A) Where a party or its treasurer is charged with an offence under subsection (3), it shall be a defence to prove that—

(a) all reasonable steps were taken by or on behalf of the party to verify (or ascertain) whether the donor was a permissible donor, and

(b) as a result, the treasurer believed the donor to be a permissible donor.]

[(3B)] …

(4) Where—

(a) subsection (2)(b) applies in relation to a donation, and

(b) the donation is not dealt with in accordance with that provision,

the treasurer of the party is guilty of an offence.

(5), (6) *****

57 Return of donations where donor unidentifiable

(1) For the purposes of section 56(2)(b) the required steps are as follows—

(a) if the donation mentioned in that provision was transmitted by a person other than the donor, and the identity of that person is apparent, to return the donation to that person;

(b) if paragraph (a) does not apply but it is apparent that the donor has, in connection with the donation, used any facility provided by an identifiable financial institution, to return the donation to that institution; and

(c) in any other case, to send the donation to the Commission.

(2) In subsection (1) any reference to returning or sending a donation to any person or body includes a reference to sending a payment of an equivalent amount to that person or body.

(3) Any amount sent to the Commission in pursuance of subsection (1)(c) shall be paid by them into the Consolidated Fund.

57A ...

58 Forfeiture of donations made by impermissible or unidentifiable donors

(1) This section applies to any donation received by a registered party—

(a) which, by virtue of section 54(1)(a) or (b), the party are prohibited from accepting, but

(b) which has been accepted by the party.

(2) The court may, on an application made by the Commission, order the forfeiture by the party of an amount equal to the value of the donation.

(3)–(5) *****

*****

Terrorism Act 2000

(2000, c. 11)

An Act to make provision about terrorism; and to make temporary provision for Northern Ireland about the prosecution and punishment of certain offences, the preservation of peace and the maintenance of order.   [20th July 2000]

Territorial extent: United Kingdom (with certain limited exceptions)

PART I INTRODUCTORY

1 Terrorism: interpretation

(1) In this Act 'terrorism' means the use or threat of action where—

(a) the action falls within subsection (2),

(b) the use or threat is designed to influence the government [or an international governmental organisation] or to intimidate the public or a section of the public, and

(c) the use or threat is made for the purpose of advancing a political, religious [, racial] or ideological cause.

(2) Action falls within this subsection if it—

(a) involves serious violence against a person,

(b) involves serious damage to property,

(c) endangers a person's life, other than that of the person committing the action,

(d) creates a serious risk to the health or safety of the public or a section of the public, or

(e) is designed seriously to interfere with or seriously to disrupt an electronic system.

(3) The use or threat of action falling within subsection (2) which involves the use of firearms or explosives is terrorism whether or not subsection (1)(b) is satisfied.

(4) In this section—

(a) 'action' includes action outside the United Kingdom,

(b) a reference to any person or to property is a reference to any person, or to property, wherever situated,

(c) a reference to the public includes a reference to the public of a country other than the United Kingdom, and

(d) 'the government' means the government of the United Kingdom, of a Part of the United Kingdom or of a country other than the United Kingdom.

(5) In this Act a reference to action taken for the purposes of terrorism includes a reference to action taken for the benefit of a proscribed organisation.

2 *****

PART II PROSCRIBED ORGANISATIONS

Procedure

3 Proscription

(1) For the purposes of this Act an organisation is proscribed if—

(a) it is listed in Schedule 2, or

(b) it operates under the same name as an organisation listed in that Schedule.

(2) Subsection (1)(b) shall not apply in relation to an organisation listed in Schedule 2 if its entry is the subject of a note in that Schedule.

(3) The Secretary of State may by order—

(a) add an organisation to Schedule 2;

(b) remove an organisation from that Schedule,

(c) amend that Schedule in some other way.

(4) The Secretary of State may exercise his power under subsection (3)(a) in respect of an organisation only if he believes that it is concerned in terrorism.

(5) For the purposes of subsection (4) an organisation is concerned in terrorism if it—

(a) commits or participates in acts of terrorism,

(b) prepares for terrorism,

(c) promotes or encourages terrorism, or

(d) is otherwise concerned in terrorism.

(5A)–(9) *****

4 Deproscription: application

(1) [An application may be made to the Secretary of State for an order under section 3(3) or (8)—

(a) removing an organisation from Schedule 2, or

(b) providing for a name to cease to be treated as a name for an organisation listed in that Schedule].

(2) An application may be made by—

(a) the organisation, or

(b) any person affected by the organisation's proscription [or by the treatment of the name as a name for the organisation].

(3) The Secretary of State shall make regulations prescribing the procedure for applications under this section.

(4) The regulations shall, in particular—

(a) require the Secretary of State to determine an application within a specified period of time, and

(b) require an application to state the grounds on which it is made.

5 Deproscription: appeal

(1) There shall be a commission, to be known as the Proscribed Organisations Appeal Commission.

(2) Where an application under section 4 has been refused, the applicant may appeal to the Commission.

(3) The Commission shall allow an appeal against a refusal to deproscribe an organisation [or to provide for a name to cease to be treated as a name for an organisation] if it considers that the decision to refuse was flawed when considered in the light of the principles applicable on an application for judicial review.

(4)–(6) *****

6 Further appeal

(1) A party to an appeal under section 5 which the Proscribed Organisations Appeal Commission has determined may bring a further appeal on a question of law to—

(a) the Court of Appeal, if the first appeal was heard in England and Wales,

(b) the Court of Session, if the first appeal was heard in Scotland, or

(c) the Court of Appeal in Northern Ireland, if the first appeal was heard in Northern Ireland.

(2) An appeal under subsection (1) may be brought only with the permission—

(a) of the Commission, or

(b) where the Commission refuses permission, of the court to which the appeal would be brought.

(3) An order under section 5(4) shall not require the Secretary of State to take any action until the final determination or disposal of an appeal under this section (including any appeal to the [Supreme Court]).

7–10 *****

Offences

11   Membership

(1) A person commits an offence if he belongs or professes to belong to a proscribed organisation.

(2) It is a defence for a person charged with an offence under subsection (1) to prove—

(a) that the organisation was not proscribed on the last (or only) occasion on which he became a member or began to profess to be a member, and

(b) that he has not taken part in the activities of the organisation at any time while it was proscribed.

(3) A person guilty of an offence under this section shall be liable—

(a) on conviction on indictment, to imprisonment for a term not exceeding [14] years, to a fine or to both, or

(b) on summary conviction, to imprisonment for a term not exceeding six months, to a fine not exceeding the statutory maximum or to both.

(4) *****

12   Support

(1) A person commits an offence if—

(a) he invites support for a proscribed organisation, and

(b) the support is not, or is not restricted to, the provision of money or other property (within the meaning of section 15).

[(1A) A person commits an offence if the person—

(a) expresses an opinion or belief that is supportive of a proscribed organisation, and

(b) in doing so is reckless as to whether a person to whom the expression is directed will be encouraged to support a proscribed organisation.]

(2) A person commits an offence if he arranges, manages or assists in arranging or managing a meeting which he knows is—

(a) to support a proscribed organisation,

(b) to further the activities of a proscribed organisation, or

(c) to be addressed by a person who belongs or professes to belong to a proscribed organisation.

(3) A person commits an offence if he addresses a meeting and the purpose of his address is to encourage support for a proscribed organisation or to further its activities.

(4) Where a person is charged with an offence under subsection (2)(c) in respect of a private meeting it is a defence for him to prove that he had no reasonable cause to believe that the address mentioned in subsection (2)(c) would support a proscribed organisation or further its activities.

(5) In subsections (2) to (4)—

  (a) 'meeting' means a meeting of three or more persons, whether or not the public are admitted, and

  (b) a meeting is private if the public are not admitted.

(6) A person guilty of an offence under this section shall be liable—

  (a) on conviction on indictment, to imprisonment for a term not exceeding [14] years, to a fine or to both, or

  (b) on summary conviction, to imprisonment for a term not exceeding six months, to a fine not exceeding the statutory maximum or to both.

13 Uniform [and publication of images]

(1) A person in a public place commits an offence if he—

  (a) wears an item of clothing, or

  (b) wears, carries or displays an article,

in such a way or in such circumstances as to arouse reasonable suspicion that he is a member or supporter of a proscribed organisation.

[(1A) A person commits an offence if the person publishes an image of—

  (a) an item of clothing, or

  (b) any other article,

in such a way or in such circumstances as to arouse reasonable suspicion that the person is a member or supporter of a proscribed organisation.

(1B) In subsection (1A) the reference to an image is a reference to a still or moving image (produced by any means)].

(2) …

(3) A person guilty of an offence under this section shall be liable on summary conviction to—

  (a) imprisonment for a term not exceeding six months,

  (b) a fine not exceeding level 5 on the standard scale, or

  (c) both.

[(4) A constable may seize an item of clothing or any other article if the constable—

  (a) reasonably suspects that it is evidence in relation to an offence under subsection (1), and

  (b) is satisfied that it is necessary to seize it in order to prevent the evidence being concealed, lost, altered or destroyed.

(5) In connection with exercising the power in subsection (4), a constable may require a person to remove the item of clothing or other article if the person is wearing it.

(6) But the powers conferred by subsections (4) and (5) may not be exercised so as to seize, or require a person to remove, an item of clothing being worn next to the skin or immediately over a garment being worn as underwear.]

14 *****

Offences

15 Fund-raising

(1) A person commits an offence if he—

  (a) invites another to provide money or other property, and

  (b) intends that it should be used, or has reasonable cause to suspect that it may be used, for the purposes of terrorism.

(2) A person commits an offence if he—

    (a) receives money or other property, and

    (b) intends that it should be used, or has reasonable cause to suspect that it may be used, for the purposes of terrorism.

(3) A person commits an offence if he—

    (a) provides money or other property, and

    (b) knows or has reasonable cause to suspect that it will or may be used for the purposes of terrorism.

(4) In this section a reference to the provision of money or other property is a reference to its being given, lent or otherwise made available, whether or not for consideration.

16–18 *****

19 Disclosure of information: duty

(1) This section applies where a person—

    (a) believes or suspects that another person has committed an offence under any of sections 15 to 18, and

    (b) bases his belief or suspicion on information which [comes to his attention—

        (i) in the course of a trade, profession or business, or

        (ii) in the course of his employment (whether or not in the course of a trade, profession or business)].

[(1A) But this section does not apply if the information came to the person in the course of a business in the regulated sector.]

(2) The person commits an offence if he does not disclose to a constable as soon as is reasonably practicable—

    (a) his belief or suspicion, and

    (b) the information on which it is based.

(3) It is a defence for a person charged with an offence under subsection (2) to prove that he had a reasonable excuse for not making the disclosure.

(4) Where—

    (a) a person is in employment,

    (b) his employer has established a procedure for the making of disclosures of the matters specified in subsection (2), and

    (c) he is charged with an offence under that subsection,

it is a defence for him to prove that he disclosed the matters specified in that subsection in accordance with the procedure.

(5) Subsection (2) does not require disclosure by a professional legal adviser of—

    (a) information which he obtains in privileged circumstances, or

    (b) a belief or suspicion based on information which he obtains in privileged circumstances.

(6) For the purpose of subsection (5) information is obtained by an adviser in privileged circumstances if it comes to him, otherwise than with a view to furthering a criminal purpose—

    (a) from a client or a client's representative, in connection with the provision of legal advice by the adviser to the client,

    (b) from a person seeking legal advice from the adviser, or from the person's representative, or

    (c) from any person, for the purpose of actual or contemplated legal proceedings.

(7)–(8) *****

20–23 *****

24–31 ...

32–39 *****

PART V COUNTER-TERRORIST POWERS

Suspected terrorists [etc]

40 Terrorist: interpretation

(1) In this Part 'terrorist' means a person who—

    (a) has committed an offence under any of sections 11, 12, 15 to 18, 54 and 56 to 63, or

    (b) is or has been concerned in the commission, preparation or instigation of acts of terrorism.

(2) The reference in subsection (1)(b) to a person who has been concerned in the commission, preparation or instigation of acts of terrorism includes a reference to a person who has been, whether before or after the passing of this Act, concerned in the commission, preparation or instigation of acts of terrorism within the meaning given by section 1.

41 Arrest without warrant

(1) A constable may arrest without a warrant a person whom he reasonably suspects to be a terrorist.

(2) Where a person is arrested under this section the provisions of Schedule 8 (detention: treatment, review and extension) shall apply.

(3) Subject to subsections (4) to (7), a person detained under this section shall (unless detained under any other power) be released not later than the end of the period of 48 hours beginning—

    (a) with the time of his arrest under this section, or

    (b) if he was being detained under Schedule 7[, or under Part 1 of Schedule 3 to the Counter-Terrorism and Border Security Act 2019,] when he was arrested under this section, with the time when his examination under that Schedule began.

(4) If on a review of a person's detention under Part II of Schedule 8 the review officer does not authorise continued detention, the person shall (unless detained in accordance with subsection (5) or (6) or under any other power) be released.

(5) Where a police officer intends to make an application for a warrant under paragraph 29 of Schedule 8 extending a person's detention, the person may be detained pending the making of the application.

(6) Where an application has been made under paragraph 29 or 36 of Schedule 8 in respect of a person's detention, he may be detained pending the conclusion of proceedings on the application.

(7) Where an application under paragraph 29 or 36 of Schedule 8 is granted in respect of a person's detention, he may be detained, subject to paragraph 37 of that Schedule, during the period specified in the warrant.

(8) The refusal of an application in respect of a person's detention under paragraph 29 or 36 of Schedule 8 shall not prevent his continued detention in accordance with this section.

[(8A) If a person detained under this section, including by virtue of a warrant under Part 3 of Schedule 8, is removed to hospital because the person needs medical treatment—

    (a) any time during which the person is being questioned in hospital or on the way there or back for the purpose of obtaining relevant evidence is to be included in calculating any period which falls to be calculated for the purposes of this section or Part 3 of Schedule 8, but

    (b) any other time when the person is in hospital or on the way there or back is not to be included.

(8B) In subsection (8A), 'relevant evidence' means, in relation to the detained person, evidence which—

    (a) relates to the person's commission of an offence under any of the provisions mentioned in section 40(1)(a), or

    (b) indicates that the person is a person falling within section 40(1)(b).]

(9) A person who has the powers of a constable in one Part of the United Kingdom may exercise the power under subsection (1) in any Part of the United Kingdom.

42   Search of premises

(1) A justice of the peace may on the application of a constable issue a warrant in relation to specified premises if he is satisfied that there are reasonable grounds for suspecting that a person whom the constable reasonably suspects to be a person falling within section 40(1)(b) is to be found there.

(2) A warrant under this section shall authorise any constable to enter and search the specified premises for the purpose of arresting the person referred to in subsection (1) under section 41.

(3) In the application of subsection (1) to Scotland—

    (a) 'justice of the peace' includes the sheriff, and

    (b) the justice of the peace or sheriff can be satisfied as mentioned in that subsection only by having heard evidence on oath.

43   Search of persons

(1) A constable may stop and search a person whom he reasonably suspects to be a terrorist to discover whether he has in his possession anything which may constitute evidence that he is a terrorist.

(2) A constable may search a person arrested under section 41 to discover whether he has in his possession anything which may constitute evidence that he is a terrorist.

(3) ...

(4) A constable may seize and retain anything which he discovers in the course of a search of a person under subsection (1) or (2) and which he reasonably suspects may constitute evidence that the person is a terrorist.

[(4A) Subsection (4B) applies if a constable, in exercising the power under subsection (1) to stop a person whom the constable reasonably suspects to be a terrorist, stops a vehicle (see section 116(2)).

(4B) The constable—

    (a) may search the vehicle and anything in or on it to discover whether there is anything which may constitute evidence that the person concerned is a terrorist, and

    (b) may seize and retain anything which the constable—

        (i)   discovers in the course of such a search, and

        (ii) reasonably suspects may constitute evidence that the person is a terrorist.

(4C) Nothing in subsection (4B) confers a power to search any person but the power to search in that subsection is in addition to the power in subsection (1) to search a person whom the constable reasonably suspects to be a terrorist.]

(5) A person who has the powers of a constable in one Part of the United Kingdom may exercise a power under this section in any Part of the United Kingdom.

[43A   Search of vehicles]

[(1) Subsection (2) applies if a constable reasonably suspects that a vehicle is being used for the purposes of terrorism.

(2) The constable may stop and search—

    (a) the vehicle;

    (b) the driver of the vehicle;

    (c) a passenger in the vehicle;

    (d) anything in or on the vehicle or carried by the driver or a passenger;

to discover whether there is anything which may constitute evidence that the vehicle is being used for the purposes of terrorism.

(3) A constable may seize and retain anything which the constable—

    (a) discovers in the course of a search under this section, and

    (b) reasonably suspects may constitute evidence that the vehicle is being used for the purposes of terrorism.

(4) A person who has the powers of a constable in one Part of the United Kingdom may exercise a power under this section in any Part of the United Kingdom.

(5) In this section 'driver', in relation to an aircraft, hovercraft or vessel, means the captain, pilot or other person with control of the aircraft, hovercraft or vessel or any member of its crew and, in relation to a train, includes any member of its crew.]

44–47 ...

[47A]–58A ***

[Entering or remaining in designated areas overseas]

[58B   Entering or remaining in a designated area
(1) Subject to subsections (3) and (4), a person commits an offence if—
  (a) the person enters, or remains in, a designated area, and
  (b) the person is a United Kingdom national, or a United Kingdom resident, at the time of entering the area or at any time during which the person remains there.
(2) It is a defence for a person charged with an offence under this section to prove that the person had a reasonable excuse for entering, or remaining in, the designated area.
(3) A person does not commit an offence under this section of entering, or remaining in, a designated area if—
  (a) the person is already travelling to, or is already in, the area on the day on which it becomes a designated area, and
  (b) the person leaves the area before the end of the period of one month beginning with that day.
(4) A person does not commit an offence under this section of entering, or remaining in, a designated area if—
  (a) the person enters, or remains in, a designated area involuntarily, or
  (b) the person enters, or remains in, a designated area for or in connection with one or more of the purposes mentioned in subsection (5).
(5) The purposes are—
  (a) providing aid of a humanitarian nature;
  (b) satisfying an obligation to appear before a court or other body exercising judicial power;
  (c) carrying out work for the government of a country other than the United Kingdom (including service in or with the country's armed forces);
  (d) carrying out work for the United Nations or an agency of the United Nations;
  (e) carrying out work as a journalist;
  (f) attending the funeral of a relative or visiting a relative who is terminally ill;
  (g) providing care for a relative who is unable to care for themselves without such assistance.
(6) But a person does not commit an offence of entering or remaining in a designated area by virtue of subsection (4)(b) only if—
  (a) the person enters or remains in the area exclusively for or in connection with one or more of the purposes mentioned in subsection (5), or
  (b) in a case where the person enters or remains in the area for or in connection with any other purpose or purposes (in addition to one or more of the purposes mentioned in subsection (5)), the other purpose or purposes provide a reasonable excuse for doing so under subsection (2).
(7) The Secretary of State may by regulations add a purpose to or remove a purpose from subsection (5).
(8) For the purposes of subsection (5)—
  (a) the reference to the provision of aid of a humanitarian nature does not include the provision of aid in contravention of internationally recognised principles and standards applicable to the provision of humanitarian aid;
  (b) references to the carrying out of work do not include the carrying out of any act which constitutes an offence in a part of the United Kingdom or would do so if the act occurred in a part of the United Kingdom;
  (c) a person is 'terminally ill' at any time if at that time the person suffers from a progressive disease and the person's death in consequence of that disease can reasonably be expected within 6 months.
(9) A person guilty of an offence under this section is liable on conviction on indictment to imprisonment for a term not exceeding 10 years, or to a fine, or to both.

(10) In this section—

'designated area' means an area outside the United Kingdom that is for the time being designated for the purposes of this section in regulations under section 58C;

'relative' means spouse or civil partner, brother, sister, ancestor or lineal descendant;

'United Kingdom national' means an individual who is—

    (a) a British citizen, a British overseas territories citizen, a British National (Overseas) or a British Overseas citizen,

    (b) a person who under the British Nationality Act 1981 is a British subject, or

    (c) a British protected person within the meaning of that Act;

'United Kingdom resident' means an individual who is resident in the United Kingdom.

(11) The reference in subsection (3) to the day on which an area becomes a designated area is a reference to the day on which regulations under section 58C come into force designating the area for the purposes of this section.

(12) Nothing in this section imposes criminal liability on any person acting on behalf of, or holding office under, the Crown.]

[58C   Section 58B: designated areas

(1) The Secretary of State may by regulations designate an area outside the United Kingdom as a designated area for the purposes of section 58B if the following condition is met.

(2) The condition is that the Secretary of State is satisfied that it is necessary, for the purpose of protecting members of the public from a risk of terrorism, to restrict United Kingdom nationals and United Kingdom residents from entering, or remaining in, the area.

(3) The reference in subsection (2) to the public includes a reference to the public of a country other than the United Kingdom.

(4) Where an area is designated by regulations under this section, the Secretary of State must—

    (a) keep under review whether the condition in subsection (2) continues to be met in relation to the area, and

    (b) if the Secretary of State determines that the condition is no longer met, revoke the regulations (or revoke them so far as they have effect in relation to that area if the regulations designate more than one area).

(5) Regulations under this section cease to have effect at the end of the period of 3 years beginning with the day on which they are made (unless they cease to have effect at an earlier time as a result of their revocation or by virtue of section 123(6ZA)(b)).

(6) Subsection (5) does not prevent the making of new regulations to the same or similar effect.

(7) In this section 'designated area', 'United Kingdom national' and 'United Kingdom resident' have the same meaning as in section 58B.]

Inciting terrorism overseas

59   England and Wales*

(1) A person commits an offence if—

    (a) he incites another person to commit an act of terrorism wholly or partly outside the United Kingdom, and

    (b) the act would, if committed in England and Wales, constitute one of the offences listed in subsection (2).

(2) Those offences are—

    (a) murder,

    (b) an offence under section 18 of the Offences against the Person Act 1861 (wounding with intent),

    (c) an offence under section 23 or 24 of that Act (poison),

---

* **Editor's Note:** There is equivalent provision for Northern Ireland in s. 60 and for Scotland in s. 61.

(d) an offence under section 28 or 29 of that Act (explosions), and

(e) an offence under section 1(2) of the Criminal Damage Act 1971 (endangering life by damaging property).

(3) A person guilty of an offence under this section shall be liable to any penalty to which he would be liable on conviction of the offence listed in subsection (2) which corresponds to the act which he incites.

(4) For the purposes of subsection (1) it is immaterial whether or not the person incited is in the United Kingdom at the time of the incitement.

(5) Nothing in this section imposes criminal liability on any person acting on behalf of, or holding office under, the Crown.

60, 61   ******

Terrorist bombing and finance offences

62   Terrorist bombing: jurisdiction

(1) If—

(a) a person does anything outside the United Kingdom as an act of terrorism or for the purposes of terrorism, and

(b) his action would have constituted the commission of one of the offences listed in subsection (2) if it had been done in the United Kingdom,

he shall be guilty of the offence.

(2) The offences referred to in subsection (1)(b) are—

(a) an offence under section 2, 3 or 5 of the Explosive Substances Act 1883 (causing explosions, &c.),

(b) an offence under section 1 of the Biological Weapons Act 1974 (biological weapons), and

(c) an offence under section 2 of the Chemical Weapons Act 1996 (chemical weapons).

63   ******

[63A   Other terrorist offences under this Act: jurisdiction]

[(1) If—

(a) a United Kingdom national or a United Kingdom resident does anything outside the United Kingdom, and

(b) his action, if done in any part of the United Kingdom, would have constituted an offence under ... any of sections 56 to 61,

he shall be guilty in that part of the United Kingdom of the offence.

(2) For the purposes of this section and sections 63B and 63C a 'United Kingdom national' means an individual who is—

(a) a British citizen, a British overseas territories citizen, a British National (Overseas) or a British Overseas citizen.

(b) a person who under the British Nationality Act 1981 is a British subject, or

(c) a British protected person within the meaning of that Act.

(3) For the purposes of this section and sections 63B and 63C a 'United Kingdom resident' means an individual who is resident in the United Kingdom.]

[63B   Terrorist attacks abroad by UK nationals or residents: jurisdiction]

[(1) If—

(a) a United Kingdom national or a United Kingdom resident does anything outside the United Kingdom as an act of terrorism or for the purposes of terrorism, and

(b) his action, if done in any part of the United Kingdom, would have constituted an offence listed in subsection (2).

he shall be guilty in that part of the United Kingdom of the offence.

(2) These are the offences—

(a) murder, manslaughter, culpable homicide, rape, assault causing injury, assault to injury, kidnapping, abduction or false imprisonment,

(b) an offence under section 4, 16, 18, 20, 21, 22, 23, 24, 28, 29, 30 or 64 of the Offences against the Person Act 1861,

(c) an offence under any of sections 1 to 5 of the Forgery and Counterfeiting Act 1981,

(d) the uttering of a forged document or an offence under section 46A of the Criminal Law (Consolidation) (Scotland) Act 1995,

(e) an offence under section 1 or 2 of the Criminal Damage Act 1971,

(f) an offence under Article 3 or 4 of the Criminal Damage (Northern Ireland) Order 1977,

(g) malicious mischief,

(h) wilful fire-raising.]

63C–113   ***

PART VIII   GENERAL

114   Police powers

(1) A power conferred by virtue of this Act on a constable—

(a) is additional to powers which he has at common law or by virtue of any other enactment, and

(b) shall not be taken to affect those powers.

(2) A constable may if necessary use reasonable force for the purpose of exercising a power conferred on him by virtue of this Act (apart from paragraphs 2 and 3 of Schedule 7).

(3) Where anything is seized by a constable under a power conferred by virtue of this Act, it may (unless the contrary intention appears) be retained for so long as is necessary in all the circumstances.

*****

SCHEDULE 2   PROSCRIBED ORGANISATIONS*

The Irish Republican Army

Cumann na mBan

Fianna na hEireann

The Red Hand Commando

*****

SCHEDULES 3–8** *****

Anti-terrorism, Crime and Security Act 2001

(2001, c. 24)

An Act to amend the Terrorism Act 2000; to make further provision about terrorism and security; to provide for the freezing of assets; to make provision about immigration and asylum; to amend or extend the criminal law and powers for preventing crime and enforcing that law: to make provision about the control of pathogens and toxins; to provide for the retention of communications data; to provide for implementation of Title VI of the Treaty on European Union; and for connected purposes.   [14th December 2001]

Territorial extent: United Kingdom (provisions reproduced here)

1–3   ***

---

* **Editor's Note:** The full list is available at: https://www.gov.uk/government/publications/proscribed-terror-groups-or-organisations--2.

** **Editor's Note:** Schedule 8 (not reproduced) contains provisions for the detention and treatment of persons arrested under this Act, equivalent to provisions for persons arrested under s. 24 Police and Criminal Evidence Act 1984 contained in that Act. The Terrorism Act 2006 amends Sch. 8, and allows for a maximum period of detention following arrest of 28 days (para. 36).

PART 2 FREEZING ORDERS

Orders

4 Power to make order

(1) The Treasury may make a freezing order if the following two conditions are satisfied.

(2) The first condition is that the Treasury reasonably believe that—

    (a) action to the detriment of the United Kingdom's economy (or part of it) has been or is likely to be taken by a person or persons, or

    (b) action constituting a threat to the life or property of one or more nationals of the United Kingdom or residents of the United Kingdom has been or is likely to be taken by a person or persons.

(3) If one person is believed to have taken or to be likely to take the action the second condition is that the person is—

    (a) the government of a country or territory outside the United Kingdom, or

    (b) a resident of a country or territory outside the United Kingdom.

(4) If two or more persons are believed to have taken or to be likely to take the action the second condition is that each of them falls within paragraph (a) or (b) of subsection (3); and different persons may fall within different paragraphs.

5 Contents of order

(1) A freezing order is an order which prohibits persons from making funds available to or for the benefit of a person or persons specified in the order.

(2) The order must provide that these are the persons who are prohibited—

    (a) all persons in the United Kingdom, and

    (b) all persons elsewhere who are nationals of the United Kingdom or are bodies incorporated under the law of any part of the United Kingdom or are Scottish partnerships.

(3) The order may specify the following (and only the following) as the person or persons to whom or for whose benefit funds are not to be made available—

    (a) the person or persons reasonably believed by the Treasury to have taken or to be likely to take the action referred to in section 4;

    (b) any person the Treasury reasonably believe has provided or is likely to provide assistance (directly or indirectly) to that person or any of those persons.

(4) A person may be specified under subsection (3) by—

    (a) being named in the order, or

    (b) falling within a description of persons set out in the order.

(5) The description must be such that a reasonable person would know whether he fell within it.

(6) Funds are financial assets and economic benefits of any kind.

6 *****

7 Review of order

The Treasury must keep a freezing order under review.

8 Duration of order

A freezing order ceases to have effect at the end of the period of 2 years starting with the day on which it is made.

9 *****

Orders: procedure etc

10 Procedure for making freezing orders

(1) A power to make a freezing order is exercisable by statutory instrument.

(2) A freezing order—

    (a) must be laid before Parliament after being made;

(b) ceases to have effect at the end of the relevant period unless before the end of that period the order is approved by a resolution of each House of Parliament (but without that affecting anything done under the order or the power to make a new order).

(3) The relevant period is a period of 28 days starting with the day on which the order is made.

(4), (5) *****

11–14 *****

15   The Crown

(1) A freezing order binds the Crown, subject to the following provisions of this section.

(2) No contravention by the Crown of a provision of a freezing order makes the Crown criminally liable; but the High Court or in Scotland the Court of Session may, on the application of a person appearing to the Court to have an interest, declare unlawful any act or omission of the Crown which constitutes such a contravention.

(3) Nothing in this section affects Her Majesty in her private capacity; and this is to be construed as if section 38(3) of the Crown Proceedings Act 1947 (meaning of Her Majesty in her private capacity) were contained in this Act.

16–20 *****

21–33, 37, 38 ...

34–36, 39–46 *****

PART 6 WEAPONS OF MASS DESTRUCTION

Nuclear weapons

47   Use etc of nuclear weapons

(1) A person who—

(a) knowingly causes a nuclear weapon explosion;

(b) develops or produces, or participates in the development or production of, a nuclear weapon;

(c) has a nuclear weapon in his possession;

(d) participates in the transfer of a nuclear weapon; or

(e) engages in military preparations, or in preparations of a military nature, intending to use, or threaten to use, a nuclear weapon,

is guilty of an offence.

(2) Subsection (1) has effect subject to the exceptions and defences in sections 48 and 49.

(3)–(9) *****

48   Exceptions

(1) Nothing in section 47 applies—

(a) to an act which is authorised under subsection (2); or

(b) to an act done in the course of an armed conflict.

(2) The Secretary of State may—

(a) authorise any act which would otherwise contravene section 47 in such manner and on such terms as he thinks fit; and

(b) withdraw or vary any authorisation given under this subsection.

(3) Any question arising in proceedings for an offence under section 47 as to whether anything was done in the course of an armed conflict shall be determined by the Secretary of State.

(4) *****

49   Defences

(1) In proceedings for an offence under section 47(1)(c) or (d) relating to an object it is a defence for the accused to show that he did not know and had no reason to believe that the object was a nuclear weapon.

(2) But he shall be taken to have shown that fact if—

 (a) sufficient evidence is adduced to raise an issue with respect to it; and

 (b) the contrary is not proved by the prosecution beyond reasonable doubt.

(3) In proceedings for such an offence it is also a defence for the accused to show that he knew or believed that the object was a nuclear weapon but, as soon as reasonably practicable after he first knew or believed that fact, he took all reasonable steps to inform the Secretary of State or a constable of his knowledge or belief.

*****

Criminal Justice and Police Act 2001

(2001, c. 16)

An Act to make provision for combating crime and disorder; to make provision about the disclosure of information relating to criminal matters and about powers of search and seizure; to amend the Police and Criminal Evidence Act 1984, the Police and Criminal Evidence (Northern Ireland) Order 1989 and the Terrorism Act 2000; to make provision about the police, the National Criminal Intelligence Service, and the National Crime Squad; to make provision about the powers of the Courts in relation to criminal matters; and for connected purposes. [11th May 2001]

Territorial extent: England and Wales, but Parts 2, 5 (National Criminal Intelligence Service) extend to the United Kingdom

1–37 *****

38 . . .

39 Intimidation of witnesses

(1) A person commits an offence if—

 (a) he does an act which intimidates, and is intended to intimidate, another person ('the victim');

 (b) he does the act—

  (i)   knowing or believing that the victim is or may be a witness in any relevant proceedings; and

  (ii) intending, by his act, to cause the course of justice to be obstructed, perverted or interfered with;

  and

 (c) the act is done after the commencement of those proceedings.

(2) For the purposes of subsection (1) it is immaterial—

 (a) whether or not the act that is done is done in the presence of the victim;

 (b) whether that act is done to the victim himself or to another person; and

 (c) whether or not the intention to cause the course of justice to be obstructed, perverted or interfered with is the predominating intention of the person doing the act in question.

(3) If, in proceedings against a person for an offence under this section, it is proved—

 (a) that he did any act that intimidated, and was intended to intimidate, another person, and

 (b) that he did that act knowing or believing that that other person was or might be a witness in any relevant proceedings that had already commenced,

he shall be presumed, unless the contrary is shown, to have done the act with the intention of causing the course of justice to be obstructed, perverted or interfered with.

(4) A person guilty of an offence under this section shall be liable—

 (a) on conviction on indictment, to imprisonment for a term not exceeding five years or to a fine, or to both;

(b) on summary conviction, to imprisonment for a term not exceeding six months or to a fine not exceeding the statutory maximum, or to both.

(5)–(7) *****

40   Harming witnesses etc

(1) A person commits an offence if, in circumstances falling within subsection (2)—

    (a) he does an act which harms, and is intended to harm, another person; or

    (b) intending to cause another person to fear harm, he threatens to do an act which would harm that other person.

(2) The circumstances fall within this subsection if—

    (a) the person doing or threatening to do the act does so knowing or believing that some person (whether or not the person harmed or threatened or the person against whom harm is threatened) has been a witness in relevant proceedings; and

    (b) he does or threatens to do that act because of that knowledge or belief.

(3) If, in proceedings against a person for an offence under this section, it is proved that, within the relevant period—

    (a) he did an act which harmed, and was intended to harm, another person, or

    (b) intending to cause another person to fear harm, he threatened to do an act which would harm that other person,

and that he did the act, or (as the case may be) threatened to do the act, with the knowledge or belief required by paragraph (a) of subsection (2), he shall be presumed, unless the contrary is shown, to have done the act, or (as the case may be) threatened to do the act, because of that knowledge or belief.

(4) For the purposes of this section it is immaterial—

    (a) whether or not the act that is done or threatened, or the threat that is made, is or would be done or is made in the presence of the person who is or would be harmed or of the person who is threatened;

    (b) whether or not the motive mentioned in subsection (2)(b) is the predominating motive for the act or threat; and

    (c) whether the harm that is done or threatened is physical or financial or is harm to a person or to his property.

(5) A person guilty of an offence under this section shall be liable—

    (a) on conviction on indictment, to imprisonment for a term not exceeding five years or to a fine, or to both;

    (b) on summary conviction, to imprisonment for a term not exceeding six months or to a fine not exceeding the statutory maximum, or to both.

(6) In this section 'the relevant period', in relation to an act done, or threat made, with the knowledge or belief that a person has been a witness in any relevant proceedings, means the period that begins with the commencement of those proceedings and ends one year after they are finally concluded.

(7), (8) *****

41   Relevant proceedings

(1) A reference in section 39 or 40 to relevant proceedings is a reference to any proceedings in or before the Court of Appeal, the High Court, the Crown Court or any county court or magistrates' court which—

    (a) are not proceedings for an offence; and

    (b) were commenced after the coming into force of that section.

(2)–(5) *****

42   Police directions stopping the harassment etc of a person in his home

(1) Subject to the following provisions of this section, a constable who is at the scene may give a direction under this section to any person if—

(a) that person is present outside or in the vicinity of any premises that are used by any individual ('the resident') as his dwelling;

(b) that constable believes, on reasonable grounds, that that person is present there for the purpose (by his presence or otherwise) of representing to the resident or another individual (whether or not one who uses the premises as his dwelling), or of persuading the resident or such another individual—

(i) that he should not do something that he is entitled or required to do; or

(ii) that he should do something that he is not under any obligation to do; and

(c) that constable also believes, on reasonable grounds, that the presence of that person (either alone or together with that of any other persons who are also present)—

(i) amounts to, or is likely to result in, the harassment of the resident; or

(ii) is likely to cause alarm or distress to the resident.

(2) A direction under this section is a direction requiring the person to whom it is given to do all such things as the constable giving it may specify as the things he considers necessary to prevent one or both of the following—

(a) the harassment of the resident; or

(b) the causing of any alarm or distress to the resident.

(3) A direction under this section may be given orally; and where a constable is entitled to give a direction under this section to each of several persons outside, or in the vicinity of, any premises, he may give that direction to those persons by notifying them of his requirements either individually or all together.

[(4) The requirements that may be imposed by a direction under this section include—

(a) a requirement to leave the vicinity of the premises in question, and

(b) a requirement to leave that vicinity, and not to return to it within such period as the constable may specify, not being longer than 3 months;

and (in either case) the requirement to leave the vicinity may be to do so immediately or after a specified period of time.]

(5) A direction under this section may make exceptions to any requirement imposed by the direction, and may make any such exception subject to such conditions as the constable giving the direction thinks fit; and those conditions may include—

(a) conditions as to the distance from the premises in question at which, or otherwise as to the location where, persons who do not leave their vicinity must remain; and

(b) conditions as to the number or identity of the persons who are authorised by the exception to remain in the vicinity of those premises.

(6) The power of a constable to give a direction under this section shall not include—

(a) any power to give a direction at any time when there is a more senior-ranking police officer at the scene; or

(b) any power to direct a person to refrain from conduct that is lawful under section 220 of the Trade Union and Labour Relations (Consolidation) Act 1992 (c. 52) (right peacefully to picket a work place);

but it shall include power to vary or withdraw a direction previously given under this section.

(7) Any person who knowingly [fails to comply with a requirement in a direction given to him under this section (other than a requirement under subsection (4)(b))] shall be guilty of an offence and liable, on summary conviction, to imprisonment for a term not exceeding three months or to a fine not exceeding level 4 on the standard scale, or to both.

[(7A) Any person to whom a constable has given a direction including a requirement under subsection (4)(b) commits an offence if he—

(a) returns to the vicinity of the premises in question within the period specified in the direction beginning with the date on which the direction is given; and

(b) does so for the purpose described in subsection (1)(b).

(7B) A person guilty of an offence under subsection (7A) shall be liable, on summary conviction, to imprisonment for a term not exceeding six months or to a fine not exceeding level 4 on the standard scale, or to both.]

(7C) *****

(8) ...

(9) In this section 'dwelling' has the same meaning as in Part 1 of the Public Order Act 1986 (c. 64).

42A–47 *****

48, 49 ...

PART 2 POWERS OF SEIZURE

Additional powers of seizure

50 Additional powers of seizure from premises

(1) Where—

    (a) a person who is lawfully on any premises finds anything on those premises that he has reasonable grounds for believing may be or may contain something for which he is authorised to search on those premises,

    (b) a power of seizure to which this section applies or the power conferred by subsection (2) would entitle him, if he found it, to seize whatever it is that he has grounds for believing that thing to be or to contain, and

    (c) in all the circumstances, it is not reasonably practicable for it to be determined, on those premises—

        (i) whether what he has found is something that he is entitled to seize, or

        (ii) the extent to which what he has found contains something that he is entitled to seize,

    that person's powers of seizure shall include power under this section to seize so much of what he has found as it is necessary to remove from the premises to enable that to be determined.

(2) Where—

    (a) a person who is lawfully on any premises finds anything on those premises ('the seizable property') which he would be entitled to seize but for its being comprised in something else that he has (apart from this subsection) no power to seize,

    (b) the power under which that person would have power to seize the seizable property is a power to which this section applies, and

    (c) in all the circumstances it is not reasonably practicable for the seizable property to be separated, on those premises, from that in which it is comprised,

that person's powers of seizure shall include power under this section to seize both the seizable property and that from which it is not reasonably practicable to separate it.

(3)–(6) *****

51 Additional powers of seizure from the person

(1) Where—

    (a) a person carrying out a lawful search of any person finds something that he has reasonable grounds for believing may be or may contain something for which he is authorised to search,

    (b) a power of seizure to which this section applies or the power conferred by subsection (2) would entitle him, if he found it, to seize whatever it is that he has grounds for believing that thing to be or to contain, and

    (c) in all the circumstances it is not reasonably practicable for it to be determined, at the time and place of the search—

        (i) whether what he has found is something that he is entitled to seize, or

        (ii) the extent to which what he has found contains something that he is entitled to seize, that person's powers of seizure shall include power under this section to seize so much of what he has found as it is necessary to remove from that place to enable that to be determined.

(2)–(5) *****

52–58 *****

Remedies and safeguards

59 Application to the appropriate judicial authority

(1) This section applies where anything has been seized in exercise, or purported exercise, of a relevant power of seizure.

(2) Any person with a relevant interest in the seized property may apply to the appropriate judicial authority, on one or more of the grounds mentioned in subsection (3), for the return of the whole or a part of the seized property.

(3) Those grounds are—

(a) that there was no power to make the seizure;

(b) that the seized property is or contains an item subject to legal privilege that is not comprised in property falling within section 54(2);

(c) that the seized property is or contains any excluded material or special procedure material which—

(i) has been seized under a power to which section 55 applies;

(ii) is not comprised in property falling within section 55(2) or (3); and

(iii) is not property the retention of which is authorised by section 56;

(d) that the seized property is or contains something seized under section 50 or 51 which does not fall within section 53(3);

and subsections (5) and (6) of section 55 shall apply for the purposes of paragraph (c) as they apply for the purposes of that section.

(4) Subject to subsection (6), the appropriate judicial authority, on an application under subsection (2), shall—

(a) if satisfied as to any of the matters mentioned in subsection (3), order the return of so much of the seized property as is property in relation to which the authority is so satisfied; and

(b) to the extent that that authority is not so satisfied, dismiss the application.

(5)–[(13)] *****
*****

Civil Contingencies Act 2004

(2004, c. 36)

An Act to make provision about civil contingencies   [18th November 2004]

Territorial extent: United Kingdom

1–18 *****

PART 2 EMERGENCY POWERS

19 Meaning of 'emergency'

(1) In this Part 'emergency' means—

(a) an event or situation which threatens serious damage to human welfare in the United Kingdom or in a Part or region,

(b) an event or situation which threatens serious damage to the environment of the United Kingdom or of a Part or region, or

      (c) war, or terrorism, which threatens serious damage to the security of the United Kingdom.

(2) For the purposes of subsection (1)(a) an event or situation threatens damage to human welfare only if it involves, causes or may cause—

      (a) loss of human life,

      (b) human illness or injury,

      (c) homelessness,

      (d) damage to property,

      (e) disruption of a supply of money, food, water, energy or fuel,

      (f) disruption of a system of communication,

      (g) disruption of facilities for transport, or

      (h) disruption of services relating to health.

(3) For the purposes of subsection (1)(b) an event or situation threatens damage to the environment only if it involves, causes or may cause—

      (a) contamination of land, water or air with biological, chemical or radio-active matter, or

      (b) disruption or destruction of plant life or animal life.

(4)–(6) *****

20 Power to make emergency regulations

(1) Her Majesty may by Order in Council make emergency regulations if satisfied that the conditions in section 21 are satisfied.

(2) A senior Minister of the Crown may make emergency regulations if satisfied—

      (a) that the conditions in section 21 are satisfied, and

      (b) that it would not be possible, without serious delay, to arrange for an Order in Council under subsection (1).

(3) In this Part 'senior Minister of the Crown' means—

      (a) the First Lord of the Treasury (the Prime Minister),

      (b) any of Her Majesty's Principal Secretaries of State, and

      (c) the Commissioners of Her Majesty's Treasury.

(4) In this Part 'serious delay' means a delay that might—

      (a) cause serious damage, or

      (b) seriously obstruct the prevention, control or mitigation of serious damage.

(5) *****

21 Conditions for making emergency regulations

(1) This section specifies the conditions mentioned in section 20.

(2) The first condition is that an emergency has occurred, is occurring or is about to occur.

(3) The second condition is that it is necessary to make provision for the purpose of preventing, controlling or mitigating an aspect or effect of the emergency.

(4) The third condition is that the need for provision referred to in subsection (3) is urgent.

(5), (6) *****

22 Scope of emergency regulations

(1) Emergency regulations may make any provision which the person making the regulations is satisfied is appropriate for the purpose of preventing, controlling or mitigating an aspect or effect of the emergency in respect of which the regulations are made.

(2) In particular, emergency regulations may make any provision which the person making the regulations is satisfied is appropriate for the purpose of—

      (a) protecting human life, health or safety,

      (b) treating human illness or injury,

      (c) protecting or restoring property,

      (d) protecting or restoring a supply of money, food, water, energy or fuel,

(e) protecting or restoring a system of communication,

(f) protecting or restoring facilities for transport,

(g) protecting or restoring the provision of services relating to health,

(h) protecting or restoring the activities of banks or other financial institutions,

(i) preventing, containing or reducing the contamination of land, water or air,

(j) preventing, reducing or mitigating the effects of disruption or destruction of plant life or animal life,

(k) protecting or restoring activities of Parliament, of the Scottish Parliament, of the Northern Ireland Assembly or of the National Assembly for Wales, or

(l) protecting or restoring the performance of public functions.

(3) Emergency regulations may make provision of any kind that could be made by Act of Parliament or by the exercise of the Royal Prerogative; in particular, regulations may—

(a) confer a function on a Minister of the Crown, on the Scottish Ministers, on the National Assembly for Wales, on a Northern Ireland department, on a coordinator appointed under section 24 or on any other specified person (and a function conferred may, in particular, be—

(i) a power, or duty, to exercise a discretion;

(ii) a power to give directions or orders, whether written or oral);

(b) provide for or enable the requisition or confiscation of property (with or without compensation);

(c) provide for or enable the destruction of property, animal life or plant life (with or without compensation);

(d) prohibit, or enable the prohibition of, movement to or from a specified place;

(e) require, or enable the requirement of, movement to or from a specified place;

(f) prohibit, or enable the prohibition of, assemblies of specified kinds, at specified places or at specified times;

(g) prohibit, or enable the prohibition of, travel at specified times;

(h) prohibit, or enable the prohibition of, other specified activities;

(i) create an offence of—

(i) failing to comply with a provision of the regulations;

(ii) failing to comply with a direction or order given or made under the regulations;

(iii) obstructing a person in the performance of a function under or by virtue of the regulations;

(j) disapply or modify an enactment or a provision made under or by virtue of an enactment;

(k) require a person or body to act in performance of a function (whether the function is conferred by the regulations or otherwise and whether or not the regulations also make provision for remuneration or compensation);

(l) enable the Defence Council to authorise the deployment of Her Majesty's armed forces;

(m) make provision (which may include conferring powers in relation to property) for facilitating any deployment of Her Majesty's armed forces;

(n) confer jurisdiction on a court or tribunal (which may include a tribunal established by the regulations);

(o) make provision which has effect in relation to, or to anything done in—

(i) an area of the territorial sea,

(ii) an area within British fishery limits, or

(iii) an area of the continental shelf;

(p) make provision which applies generally or only in specified circumstances or for a specified purpose;

(q) make different provision for different circumstances or purposes.

(4) In subsection (3) 'specified' means specified by, or to be specified in accordance with, the regulations.

(5) A person making emergency regulations must have regard to the importance of ensuring that Parliament, the High Court and the Court of Session are able to conduct proceedings in connection with—

    (a) the regulations, or

    (b) action taken under the regulations.

23   Limitations of emergency regulations

(1) Emergency regulations may make provision only if and in so far as the person making the regulations is satisfied—

    (a) that the provision is appropriate for the purpose of preventing, controlling or mitigating an aspect or effect of the emergency in respect of which the regulations are made, and

    (b) that the effect of the provision is in due proportion to that aspect or effect of the emergency.

(2) Emergency regulations must specify the Parts of the United Kingdom or regions in relation to which the regulations have effect.

(3) Emergency regulations may not—

    (a) require a person, or enable a person to be required, to provide military service, or

    (b) prohibit or enable the prohibition of participation in, or any activity in connection with, a strike or other industrial action.

(4) Emergency regulations may not—

    (a) create an offence other than one of the kind described in section 22(3)(i),

    (b) create an offence other than one which is triable only before a magistrates' court or, in Scotland, before a sheriff under summary procedure,

    (c) create an offence which is punishable—

        (i)   with imprisonment for a period exceeding three months, or

        (ii)   with a fine exceeding level 5 on the standard scale, or

    (d) alter procedure in relation to criminal proceedings.

(5) Emergency regulations may not amend—

    (a) this Part of this Act, or

    (b) the Human Rights Act 1998 (c. 42).

24   *****

25   ...

26   Duration

(1) Emergency regulations shall lapse—

    (a) at the end of the period of 30 days beginning with the date on which they are made, or

    (b) at such earlier time as may be specified in the regulations.

(2) Subsection (1)—

    (a) shall not prevent the making of new regulations, and

    (b) shall not affect anything done by virtue of the regulations before they lapse.

27   Parliamentary scrutiny

(1) Where emergency regulations are made—

    (a) a senior Minister of the Crown shall as soon as is reasonably practicable lay the regulations before Parliament, and

    (b) the regulations shall lapse at the end of the period of seven days beginning with the date of laying unless during that period each House of Parliament passes a resolution approving them.

(2) If each House of Parliament passes a resolution that emergency regulations shall cease to have effect, the regulations shall cease to have effect—

    (a) at such time, after the passing of the resolutions, as may be specified in them, or

(b) if no time is specified in the resolutions, at the beginning of the day after that on which the resolutions are passed (or, if they are passed on different days, at the beginning of the day after that on which the second resolution is passed).

(3) If each House of Parliament passes a resolution that emergency regulations shall have effect with a specified amendment, the regulations shall have effect as amended, with effect from—

(a) such time, after the passing of the resolutions, as may be specified in them, or

(b) if no time is specified in the resolutions, the beginning of the day after that on which the resolutions are passed (or, if they are passed on different days, the beginning of the day after that on which the second resolution is passed).

(4) Nothing in this section—

(a) shall prevent the making of new regulations, or

(b) shall affect anything done by virtue of regulations before they lapse, cease to have effect or are amended under this section.

*****

Constitutional Reform Act 2005

(2005, c. 4)

An Act to make provision for modifying the office of Lord Chancellor, and to make provision relating to the functions of that office; to establish a Supreme Court of the United Kingdom, and to abolish the appellate jurisdiction of the [Supreme Court]; to make provision about the jurisdiction of the Judicial Committee of the Privy Council and the judicial functions of the President of the Council; to make other provision about the judiciary, their appointment and discipline; and for connected purposes. [24th March 2005]

Territorial extent: United Kingdom

PART 1 THE RULE OF LAW

1   The rule of law

This Act does not adversely affect—

(a) the existing constitutional principle of the rule of law, or

(b) the Lord Chancellor's existing constitutional role in relation to that principle.

PART 2 ARRANGEMENTS TO MODIFY THE OFFICE OF LORD CHANCELLOR

Qualifications for office of Lord Chancellor

2   Lord Chancellor to be qualified by experience

(1) A person may not be recommended for appointment as Lord Chancellor unless he appears to the Prime Minister to be qualified by experience.

(2) The Prime Minister may take into account any of these—

(a) experience as a Minister of the Crown;

(b) experience as a member of either House of Parliament;

(c) experience as a qualifying practitioner;

(d) experience as a teacher of law in a university;

(e) other experience that the Prime Minister considers relevant.

(3) In this section 'qualifying practitioner' means any of these—

(a) a person who has a Senior Courts qualification, within the meaning of section 71 of the Courts and Legal Services Act 1990 (c. 41);

(b) an advocate in Scotland or a solicitor entitled to appear in the Court of Session and the High Court of Justiciary;

(c) a member of the Bar of Northern Ireland or a solicitor of the Court of Judicature of Northern Ireland.

Continued judicial independence

3 Guarantee of continued judicial independence

(1) The Lord Chancellor, other Ministers of the Crown and all with responsibility for matters relating to the judiciary or otherwise to the administration of justice must uphold the continued independence of the judiciary.

(2) Subsection (1) does not impose any duty which it would be within the legislative competence of the Scottish Parliament to impose.

(3) A person is not subject to the duty imposed by subsection (1) if he is subject to the duty imposed by section 1(1) of the Justice (Northern Ireland) Act 2002 (c. 26).

(4) The following particular duties are imposed for the purpose of upholding that independence.

(5) The Lord Chancellor and other Ministers of the Crown must not seek to influence particular judicial decisions through any special access to the judiciary.

(6) The Lord Chancellor must have regard to—

(a) the need to defend that independence;

(b) the need for the judiciary to have the support necessary to enable them to exercise their functions;

(c) the need for the public interest in regard to matters relating to the judiciary or otherwise to the administration of justice to be properly represented in decisions affecting those matters.

(7) In this section 'the judiciary' includes the judiciary of any of the following—

(a) the Supreme Court;

(b) any other court established under the law of any part of the United Kingdom;

(c) any international court.

[(7A) In this section 'the judiciary' also includes every person who—

(a) holds an office listed in Schedule 14 or holds an office listed in subsection (7B), and

(b) but for this subsection would not be a member of the judiciary for the purposes of this section.

(7B) The offices are those of—

(a) Senior President of Tribunals;

(b) President of Employment Tribunals (Scotland);

(c) Vice President of Employment Tribunals (Scotland);

(d) member of a panel of [Employment Judges] (Scotland);

(e) member of a panel of members of employment tribunals that is not a panel of [Employment Judges];

(f) ...]

(8) *****

4 *****

Representations by senior judges

5 Representations to Parliament

[(A1) The President of the Supreme Court may lay before Parliament written representations on matters that appear to the President to be matters of importance relating to the Supreme Court or to the jurisdiction it exercises.]

(1) The chief justice of any part of the United Kingdom may lay before Parliament written representations on matters that appear to him to be matters of importance relating to the judiciary, or otherwise to the administration of justice, in that part of the United Kingdom.

(2)–(4) *****

(5) In this section 'chief justice' means—

(a) in relation to England and Wales or Northern Ireland, the Lord Chief Justice of that part of the United Kingdom;

(b) in relation to Scotland, the Lord President of the Court of Session.

6–16 *****

17 Lord Chancellor's oath

(1) In the Promissory Oaths Act 1868 (c. 72) after section 6 insert—

'6A Lord Chancellor's Oath

(1) The oath set out in subsection (2) shall be tendered to and taken by the Lord Chancellor, after and in the same manner as the official oath, as soon as may be after his acceptance of office.

(2) The oath is—

"I,   , do swear that in the office of Lord High Chancellor of Great Britain I will respect the rule of law, defend the independence of the judiciary and discharge my duty to ensure the provision of resources for the efficient and effective support of the courts for which I am responsible.   So help me God.".'

(2) The section inserted by subsection (1) does not apply in the case of acceptance of office before the coming into force of this section.

18 *****

Functions subject to transfer, modification or abolition

19 Transfer, modification or abolition of functions by order

(1) The Lord Chancellor may by order make provision for any of these purposes—

(a) to transfer an existing function of the Lord Chancellor to another person;

(b) to direct that an existing function of the Lord Chancellor is to be exercisable concurrently with another person;

(c) to direct that an existing function of the Lord Chancellor exercisable concurrently with another person is to cease to be exercisable by the Lord Chancellor;

(d) to modify an existing function of the Lord Chancellor;

(e) to abolish an existing function of the Lord Chancellor.

(2)–(8) *****

20–22 *****

PART 3 THE SUPREME COURT

The Supreme Court

23 The Supreme Court

(1) There is to be a Supreme Court of the United Kingdom.

(2) The Court consists of [the persons appointed as its judges] by Her Majesty by letters patent [, but no appointment may cause the full-time equivalent number of judges of the Court at any time to be more than 12].

(3) Her Majesty may from time to time by Order in Council amend subsection (2) so as to increase the [maximum full-time equivalent] number of judges of the Court.

(4) No recommendation may be made to Her Majesty in Council to make an Order under subsection (3) unless a draft of the Order has been laid before and approved by resolution of each House of Parliament.

(5) Her Majesty may by letters patent appoint one of the judges to be President and one to be Deputy President of the Court.

(6) The judges other than the President and Deputy President are to be styled 'Justices of the Supreme Court'.

(7) The Court is to be taken to be duly constituted despite any vacancy...in the office of President or Deputy President.

[(8) For the purposes of this section, the full-time equivalent number of judges of the Court is to be calculated by taking the number of full-time judges and adding, for each judge who is not a full-time judge, such fraction as is reasonable.]

24   First members of the Court
On the commencement of section 23—
    (a) the persons who immediately before that commencement are Lords of Appeal in Ordinary become judges of the Supreme Court,
    (b) the person who immediately before that commencement is the senior Lord of Appeal in Ordinary becomes the President of the Court, and
    (c) the person who immediately before that commencement is the second senior Lord of Appeal in Ordinary becomes the Deputy President of the Court.

25–[27B]   *****

28–31   ...

32   *****

33   Tenure
A judge of the Supreme Court holds that office during good behaviour, but may be removed from it on the address of both Houses of Parliament.

34–39   *****

Jurisdiction, relation to other courts etc

40   Jurisdiction
(1) The Supreme Court is a superior court of record.

(2) An appeal lies to the Court from any order or judgment of the Court of Appeal in England and Wales in civil proceedings.

(3) ...

(4), (5)   *****

(6) An appeal under subsection (2) lies only with the permission of the Court of Appeal or the Supreme Court; but this is subject to provision under any other enactment restricting such an appeal.

41   Relation to other courts etc
(1) Nothing in this Part is to affect the distinctions between the separate legal systems of the parts of the United Kingdom.

(2) A decision of the Supreme Court on appeal from a court of any part of the United Kingdom, other than a decision on a devolution matter, is to be regarded as the decision of a court of that part of the United Kingdom.

(3) A decision of the Supreme Court on a devolution matter—
    (a) is not binding on that Court when making such a decision;
    (b) otherwise, is binding in all legal proceedings.

(4) In this section 'devolution matter' means—
    (a) a question referred to the Supreme Court under [section...99 or 112 of the Government of Wales Act 2006,] section 33 of the Scotland Act 1998 (c. 46) or section 11 of the Northern Ireland Act 1998 (c. 47);
    (b) a devolution issue as defined in [Schedule 9 to the Government of Wales Act 2006], Schedule 6 to the Scotland Act 1998 or Schedule 10 to the Northern Ireland Act 1998.

42–60   *****

PART 4 JUDICIAL APPOINTMENTS AND DISCIPLINE

Chapter 1 Commission and Ombudsman

61 The Judicial Appointments Commission

(1) There is to be a body corporate called the Judicial Appointments Commission.

(2) Schedule 12* is about the Commission.

62 Judicial Appointments and Conduct Ombudsman

(1) There is to be a Judicial Appointments and Conduct Ombudsman.

(2) Schedule 13** is about the Ombudsman.

Chapter 2 Appointments

General provisions

63 Merit and good character

(1) Subsections (2) [to (4)] apply to any selection under this Part by the Commission or a selection panel ('the selecting body').

(2) Selection must be solely on merit.

(3) A person must not be selected unless the selecting body is satisfied that he is of good character.

[(4) Neither 'solely' in subsection (2), nor Part 5 of the Equality Act 2010 (public appointments etc), prevents the selecting body, where two persons are of equal merit, from preferring one of them over the other for the purpose of increasing diversity within—

    (a) the group of persons who hold offices for which there is selection under this Part, or

    (b) a sub-group of that group.]

64 Encouragement of diversity

(1) The Commission, in performing its functions under this Part, must have regard to the need to encourage diversity in the range of persons available for selection for appointments.

(2) This section is subject to section 63.

65 Guidance about procedures

(1) The Lord Chancellor may issue guidance about procedures for the performance by the Commission or a selection panel of its functions of—

    (a) identifying persons willing to be considered for selection under this Part, and

    (b) assessing such persons for the purposes of selection.

(2) The guidance may, among other things, relate to consultation or other steps in determining such procedures.

(3) The purposes for which guidance may be issued under this section include the encouragement of diversity in the range of persons available for selection.

(4) The Commission and any selection panel must have regard to the guidance in matters to which it relates.

66–98 *****

Complaints and references

99 Complaints: interpretation

(1) This section applies for the purposes of this Part.

(2) A Commission complaint is a complaint by a qualifying complainant of maladministration by the Commission or a committee of the Commission.

---

* **Editor's Note:** Schedule 12 is not reproduced.

** **Editor's Note:** Schedule 13 is not reproduced.

(3) A departmental complaint is a complaint by a qualifying complainant of maladministration by the Lord Chancellor or his department in connection with any of the following—

(a) selection under this Part;

(b) recommendation for or appointment to an office listed in Schedule 14.

[(3A), (3B)] *****

(4) A qualifying complainant is a complainant who claims to have been adversely affected, as an applicant for selection or as a person selected under this Part, by the maladministration complained of.

100 Complaints to the Commission or the Lord Chancellor

(1) The Commission must make arrangements for investigating any Commission complaint made to it.

(2) The Lord Chancellor must make arrangements for investigating any departmental complaint made to him.

[(2A), (2B)], (3) *****

101 Complaints to the Ombudsman

(1) Subsections (2) and (3) apply to a complaint which the complainant—

(a) has made to the Commission [, the Lord Chancellor, the Lord Chief Justice or the Senior President of Tribunals] in accordance with arrangements under section 100, and

(b) makes to the Ombudsman not more than 28 days after being notified of the [decision of the Commission, the Lord Chancellor, the Lord Chief Justice or the Senior President of Tribunals] on the complaint.

(2) If the Ombudsman considers that investigation of the complaint is not necessary, he must inform the complainant.

(3) Otherwise he must investigate the complaint.

(4) The Ombudsman may investigate a complaint which the complainant—

(a) has made to the Commission [, the Lord Chancellor, the Lord Chief Justice or the Senior President of Tribunals] in accordance with arrangements under section 100, and

(b) makes to the Ombudsman at any time.

(5) The Ombudsman may investigate a transferred complaint made to him, and no such complaint may be made under the Judicial Appointments Order after the commencement of this section.

(6) The Judicial Appointments Order is the Judicial Appointments Order in Council 2001, which sets out the functions of Her Majesty's Commissioners for Judicial Appointments.

(7) A transferred complaint is a complaint that lay to those Commissioners (whether or not it was made to them) in respect of the application of appointment procedures before the commencement of this section, but not a complaint that those Commissioners had declined to investigate or on which they had concluded their investigation.

(8) Any complaint to the Ombudsman under this section must be in a form approved by him.

102 Report and recommendations

(1) The Ombudsman must prepare a report on any complaint he has investigated under section 101.

(2) The report must state—

(a) what findings the Ombudsman has made;

(b) whether he considers the complaint should be upheld in whole or part;

(c) if he does, what if any action he recommends should be taken by the Commission [, the Lord Chancellor, the Lord Chief Justice or the Senior President of Tribunals] as a result of the complaint.

(3) The recommendations that may be made under subsection (2)(c) include recommendations for the payment of compensation.

(4) Such a recommendation must relate to loss which appears to the Ombudsman to have been suffered by the complainant as a result of maladministration and not as a result of any failure to be appointed to an office [, or selected for membership of a pool,] to which the complaint related.

103   *****

104   References by the Lord Chancellor

(1) If the Lord Chancellor [, the Lord Chief Justice or the Senior President of Tribunals] refers to the Ombudsman any matter relating to the procedures of the Commission or a committee of the Commission, the Ombudsman must investigate it.

(2) The matter may relate to such procedures generally or in a particular case.

(3) The Ombudsman must report to the Lord Chancellor [, the Lord Chief Justice and the Senior President of Tribunals] on any investigation under this section.

(4) The report must state—

(a) what findings the Ombudsman has made;

(b) what if any action he recommends should be taken by any person in relation to the matter.

(5) The report must be signed by the Ombudsman.

105   Information

The Commission [, the Lord Chief Justice, the Senior President of Tribunals] and the Lord Chancellor must provide the Ombudsman with such information as he may reasonably require relating to the subject matter of any investigation by him under section 101 or 104.

106, 107   *****

Chapter 3 Discipline

Disciplinary powers

108   Disciplinary powers

(1) Any power of the Lord Chancellor to remove a person from an office listed in Schedule 14 is exercisable only after the Lord Chancellor has complied with prescribed procedures (as well as any other requirements to which the power is subject).

(2) The Lord Chief Justice may exercise any of the following powers but only with the agreement of the Lord Chancellor and only after complying with prescribed procedures.

(3) The Lord Chief Justice may give a judicial office holder formal advice, or a formal warning or reprimand, for disciplinary purposes (but this section does not restrict what he may do informally or for other purposes or where any advice or warning is not addressed to a particular office holder).

(4) He may suspend a person from a judicial office for any period during which any of the following applies—

(a) the person is subject to criminal proceedings;

(b) the person is serving a sentence imposed in criminal proceedings;

(c) the person has been convicted of an offence and is subject to prescribed procedures in relation to the conduct constituting the offence.

(5) He may suspend a person from a judicial office for any period if—

(a) the person has been convicted of a criminal offence,

(b) it has been determined under prescribed procedures that the person should not be removed from office, and

(c) it appears to the Lord Chief Justice with the agreement of the Lord Chancellor that the suspension is necessary for maintaining confidence in the judiciary.

(6) He may suspend a person from office as a senior judge for any period during which the person is subject to proceedings for an Address.

(7) He may suspend the holder of an office listed in Schedule 14* for any period during which the person—

(a) is under investigation for an offence, or

(b) is subject to prescribed procedures.

---

* **Editor's Note:** Schedule 14 is not reproduced.

(8) While a person is suspended under this section from any office he may not perform any of the functions of the office (but his other rights as holder of the office are not affected).

109 *****

Applications for review and references

110 Applications to the Ombudsman

(1) This section applies if an interested party makes an application to the Ombudsman for the review of the exercise by any person of a regulated disciplinary function, on the grounds that there has been—

(a) a failure to comply with prescribed procedures, or

(b) some other maladministration.

(2) The Ombudsman must carry out a review if the following three conditions are met.

(3) The first condition is that the Ombudsman considers that a review is necessary.

(4) The second condition is that—

(a) the application is made within the permitted period,

(b) the application is made within such longer period as the Ombudsman considers appropriate in the circumstances, or

(c) the application is made on grounds alleging undue delay and the Ombudsman considers that the application has been made within a reasonable time.

(5) The third condition is that the application is made in a form approved by the Ombudsman.

(6) But the Ombudsman may not review the merits of a decision made by any person.

(7) If any of the conditions in subsections (3) to (5) is not met, or if the grounds of the application relate only to the merits of a decision, the Ombudsman—

(a) may not carry out a review, and

(b) must inform the applicant accordingly.

(8)–(10) *****

*****

Inquiries Act 2005

(2005, c. 12)

An Act to make provision about the holding of inquiries. [7th April 2005]

Territorial extent: United Kingdom

Constitution of inquiry

1 Power to establish inquiry

(1) A Minister may cause an inquiry to be held under this Act in relation to a case where it appears to him that—

(a) particular events have caused, or are capable of causing, public concern, or

(b) there is public concern that particular events may have occurred.

(2) In this Act 'Minister' means—

(a) a United Kingdom Minister;

(b) the Scottish Ministers;

[(ba) the Welsh Ministers;]

(c) a Northern Ireland Minister;

...

(3) References in this Act to an inquiry, except where the context requires otherwise, are to an inquiry under this Act.

2   No determination of liability

(1) An inquiry panel is not to rule on, and has no power to determine, any person's civil or criminal liability.

(2) But an inquiry panel is not to be inhibited in the discharge of its functions by any likelihood of liability being inferred from facts that it determines or recommendations that it makes.

3   The inquiry panel

(1)   An inquiry is to be undertaken either—

    (a) by a chairman alone, or

    (b) by a chairman with one or more other members.

(2) References in this Act to an inquiry panel are to the chairman and any other member or members.

4   Appointment of inquiry panel

(1) Each member of an inquiry panel is to be appointed by the Minister by an instrument in writing.

(2) The instrument appointing the chairman must state that the inquiry is to be held under this Act.

(3) Before appointing a member to the inquiry panel (otherwise than as chairman) the Minister must consult the person he has appointed, or proposes to appoint, as chairman.

5   Setting-up date and terms of reference

(1) In the instrument under section 4 appointing the chairman, or by a notice given to him within a reasonable time afterwards, the Minister must—

    (a) specify the date that is to be the setting-up date for the purposes of this Act; and

    (b) before that date—

      (i) set out the terms of reference of the inquiry;

      (ii) state whether or not the Minister proposes to appoint other members to the inquiry panel, and if so how many.

(2) An inquiry must not begin considering evidence before the setting-up date.

(3) The Minister may at any time after setting out the terms of reference under this section amend them if he considers that the public interest so requires.

(4) Before setting out or amending the terms of reference the Minister must consult the person he proposes to appoint, or has appointed, as chairman.

(5) Functions conferred by this Act on an inquiry panel, or a member of an inquiry panel, are exercisable only within the inquiry's terms of reference.

(6) In this Act 'terms of reference', in relation to an inquiry under this Act, means—

    (a) the matters to which the inquiry relates;

    (b) any particular matters as to which the inquiry panel is to determine the facts;

    (c) whether the inquiry panel is to make recommendations;

    (d) any other matters relating to the scope of the inquiry that the Minister may specify.

6   Minister's duty to inform Parliament or Assembly

(1) A Minister who proposes to cause an inquiry to be held, or who has already done so without making a statement under this section, must as soon as is reasonably practicable make a statement to that effect to the relevant Parliament or Assembly.

(2) A statement under subsection (1) must state—

    (a) who is to be, or has been, appointed as chairman of the inquiry;

    (b) whether the Minister has appointed, or proposes to appoint, any other members to the inquiry panel, and if so how many;

    (c) what are to be, or are, the inquiry's terms of reference.

(3) Where the terms of reference of an inquiry are amended under section 5(3), the Minister must, as soon as is reasonably practicable, make a statement to the relevant Parliament or Assembly setting out the amended terms of reference.

(4) A statement under this section may be oral or written.

7–12 *****

13 Power to suspend inquiry

(1) The Minister may at any time, by notice to the chairman, suspend an inquiry for such period as appears to him to be necessary to allow for—

    (a) the completion of any other investigation relating to any of the matters to which the inquiry relates, or

    (b) the determination of any civil or criminal proceedings (including proceedings before a disciplinary tribunal) arising out of any of those matters.

(2) The power conferred by subsection (1) may be exercised whether or not the investigation or proceedings have begun.

(3) Before exercising that power the Minister must consult the chairman.

(4) A notice under subsection (1) may suspend the inquiry until a specified day, until the happening of a specified event or until the giving by the Minister of a further notice to the chairman.

(5)–(7) *****

14 End of inquiry

(1) For the purposes of this Act an inquiry comes to an end—

    (a) on the date, after the delivery of the report of the inquiry, on which the chairman notifies the Minister that the inquiry has fulfilled its terms of reference, or

    (b) on any earlier date specified in a notice given to the chairman by the Minister.

(2) The date specified in a notice under subsection (1)(b) may not be earlier than the date on which the notice is sent.

(3) Before exercising his power under subsection (1)(b) the Minister must consult the chairman.

(4) Where the Minister gives a notice under subsection (1)(b) he must—

    (a) set out in the notice his reasons for bringing the inquiry to an end;

    (b) lay a copy of the notice, as soon as is reasonably practicable, before the relevant Parliament or Assembly.

15–20 *****

21 Powers of chairman to require production of evidence etc

(1) The chairman of an inquiry may by notice require a person to attend at a time and place stated in the notice—

    (a) to give evidence;

    (b) to produce any documents in his custody or under his control that relate to a matter in question at the inquiry;

    (c) to produce any other thing in his custody or under his control for inspection, examination or testing by or on behalf of the inquiry panel.

(2) The chairman may by notice require a person, within such period as appears to the inquiry panel to be reasonable—

    (a) to provide evidence to the inquiry panel in the form of a written statement;

    (b) to provide any documents in his custody or under his control that relate to a matter in question at the inquiry;

    (c) to produce any other thing in his custody or under his control for inspection, examination or testing by or on behalf of the inquiry panel.

(3) A notice under subsection (1) or (2) must—

    (a) explain the possible consequences of not complying with the notice;

    (b) indicate what the recipient of the notice should do if he wishes to make a claim within subsection (4).

(4) A claim by a person that—

    (a) he is unable to comply with a notice under this section, or

    (b) it is not reasonable in all the circumstances to require him to comply with such a notice,

is to be determined by the chairman of the inquiry, who may revoke or vary the notice on that ground.

(5) In deciding whether to revoke or vary a notice on the ground mentioned in subsection (4)(b), the chairman must consider the public interest in the information in question being obtained by the inquiry, having regard to the likely importance of the information.

(6) For the purposes of this section a thing is under a person's control if it is in his possession or if he has a right to possession of it.

*****

Serious Organised Crime and Police Act 2005

(2005, c. 15)

An Act to provide for the establishment and functions of the Serious Organised Crime Agency; to make provision about investigations, prosecutions, offenders and witnesses in criminal proceedings and the protection of persons involved in investigations or proceedings; to provide for the implementation of certain international obligations relating to criminal matters; to amend the proceeds of Crime Act 2002; to make further provision for combating crime and disorder, including new provision about powers of arrest and search warrants and about parental compensation orders; to make further provision about the police and policing and persons supporting the police; to make provision for protecting certain organisations from interference with their activities; to make provision about criminal records; to provide for the Private Security Industry Act 2001 to extend to Scotland; and for connected purposes. [7th April 2005]

Territorial extent: See s. 179 (reproduced below)

1–59   ...

PART 2 INVESTIGATIONS, PROSECUTIONS, PROCEEDINGS AND PROCEEDS OF CRIME

Chapter 1 Investigatory powers of DPP, etc

Introductory

60   Investigatory powers of DPP etc

(1) This Chapter confers powers on—

    (a) the Director of Public Prosecutions,

    (b) ...

    (c) the Lord Advocate, [and

    (d) the Director of Public Prosecutions for Northern Ireland,]

in relation to the giving of disclosure notices in connection with the investigation of offences to which this Chapter applies [or in connection with a terrorist investigation].

(2)–(6) *****

[(7) In this Chapter 'terrorist investigation' means an investigation of—

    (a) the commission, preparation or instigation of acts of terrorism,

    (b) any act or omission which appears to have been for the purposes of terrorism and which consists in or involves the commission, preparation or instigation of an offence, or

    (c) the commission, preparation or instigation of an offence under the Terrorism Act 2000 (c. 11) or under Part 1 of the Terrorism Act 2006 other than an offence under section 1 or 2 of that Act.]

61   Offences to which this Chapter applies

(1) This Chapter applies to the following offences—

    (a)   any offence listed in Schedule 2 to the Proceeds of Crime Act 2002 (c. 29) (lifestyle offences: England and Wales);

(b)   any offence listed in Schedule 4 to that Act (lifestyle offences: Scotland);

[(ba) any offence listed in Schedule 5 to that Act (lifestyle offences: Northern Ireland);]

(c)   any offence under sections 15 to 18 of the Terrorism Act 2000 (c. 11) (offences relating to fund-raising, money laundering etc);

(d)   any offence under section 170 of the Customs and Excise Management Act 1979 (c. 2) (fraudulent evasion of duty) or section 72 of the Value Added Tax Act 1994 (c. 23) (offences relating to VAT) which is a qualifying offence;

(e)   any offence under section 17 of the Theft Act 1968 (c. 60) [or section 17 of the Theft Act (Northern Ireland) 1969] (false accounting), or any offence at common law of cheating in relation to the public revenue, which is a qualifying offence;

(f)   any offence under section 1 of the Criminal Attempts Act 1981 (c. 47) [or Article 3 of the Criminal Attempts and Conspiracy (Northern Ireland) Order 1983], or in Scotland at common law, of attempting to commit any offence in paragraph (c) or any offence in paragraph (d) or (e) which is a qualifying offence;

(g)   any offence under section 1 of the Criminal Law Act 1977 (c. 45) [or Article 9 of the Criminal Attempts and Conspiracy (Northern Ireland) Order 1983], or in Scotland at common law, of conspiracy to commit any offence in paragraph (c) or any offence in paragraph (d) or (e) which is a qualifying offence;

[(h) any offence under the Bribery Act 2010].

[(i)   any offence under section 45 or 46 of the Criminal Finances Act 2017 (failure to prevent the facilitation of UK tax evasion offences in foreign tax evasion offences)].

[(j)   any offence under regulations under section 1 of the Sanctions and Anti-Money Laundering Act 2018 (sanctions regulations) which is specified by those regulations by virtue of section 17(8) of that Act].

(2) For the purposes of subsection (1) an offence in paragraph (d) or (e) of that subsection is a qualifying offence if the Investigating Authority certifies that in his opinion—

(a) in the case of an offence in paragraph (d) or an offence of cheating the public revenue, the offence involved or would have involved a loss, or potential loss, to the public revenue of an amount not less than £5,000;

(b) in the case of an offence under section 17 of the Theft Act 1968 (c. 60) [or section 17 of the Theft Act (Northern Ireland) 1969], the offence involved or would have involved a loss or gain, or potential loss or gain, of an amount not less than £5,000.

(3)–(5) *****

Disclosure notices

62 Disclosure notices

(1) If it appears to the Investigating Authority—

(a) that there are reasonable grounds for suspecting that an offence to which this Chapter applies has been committed,

(b) that any person has information (whether or not contained in a document) which relates to a matter relevant to the investigation of that offence, and

(c) that there are reasonable grounds for believing that information which may be provided by that person in compliance with a disclosure notice is likely to be of substantial value (whether or not by itself) to that investigation,

he may give, or authorise an appropriate person to give, a disclosure notice to that person.

(1A) *****

(2) In this Chapter 'appropriate person' means—

(a) a constable,

[(b) a National Crime Agency officer who is for the time being designated under section 9 or 10 of the Crime and Courts Act 2013, or]

(c) an officer of Revenue and Customs.

[But in the application of this Chapter to Northern Ireland, this subsection has effect as if paragraph (b) were omitted.]

(3) In this Chapter 'disclosure notice' means a notice in writing requiring the person to whom it is given to do all or any of the following things in accordance with the specified requirements, namely—

    (a) answer questions with respect to any matter relevant to the investigation;

    (b) provide information with respect to any such matter as is specified in the notice;

    (c) produce such documents, or documents of such descriptions, relevant to the investigation as are specified in the notice.

(4)–(6) *****

63 Production of documents

(1) This section applies where a disclosure notice has been given under section 62.

(2) An authorised person may—

    (a) take copies of or extracts from any documents produced in compliance with the notice, and

    (b) require the person producing them to provide an explanation of any of them.

(3) Documents so produced may be retained for so long as the Investigating Authority considers that it is necessary to retain them (rather than copies of them) in connection with the investigation for the purposes of which the disclosure notice was given.

(4)–(7) *****

64 Restrictions on requiring information etc

(1) A person may not be required under section 62 or 63—

    (a) to answer any privileged question,

    (b) to provide any privileged information, or

    (c) to produce any privileged document,

except that a lawyer may be required to provide the name and address of a client of his.

(2) A 'privileged question' is a question which the person would be entitled to refuse to answer on grounds of legal professional privilege in proceedings in the High Court.

(3) 'Privileged information' is information which the person would be entitled to refuse to provide on grounds of legal professional privilege in such proceedings.

(4) A 'privileged document' is a document which the person would be entitled to refuse to produce on grounds of legal professional privilege in such proceedings.

(5) A person may not be required under section 62 to produce any excluded material (as defined by section 11 of the Police and Criminal Evidence Act 1984 (c. 60) [or, in relation to Northern Ireland, Article 13 of the Police and Criminal Evidence (Northern Ireland) Order 1989]).

(6), (7) *****

(8) A person may not be required under section 62 or 63 to disclose any information or produce any document in respect of which he owes an obligation of confidence by virtue of carrying on any banking business, unless—

    (a) the person to whom the obligation of confidence is owed consents to the disclosure or production, or

    (b) the requirement is made by, or in accordance with a specific authorisation given by, the Investigating Authority.

(9) Subject to the preceding provisions, any requirement under section 62 or 63 has effect despite any restriction on disclosure (however imposed).

65 *****

Enforcement

66 Power to enter and seize documents

(1) A justice of the peace may issue a warrant under this section if, on an information on oath laid by the Investigating Authority, he is satisfied—

    (a) that any of the conditions mentioned in subsection (2) is met in relation to any documents of a description specified in the information, and

    (b) that the documents are on premises so specified.

(2) The conditions are—

    (a) that a person has been required by a disclosure notice to produce the documents but has not done so;

    (b) that it is not practicable to give a disclosure notice requiring their production;

    (c) that giving such a notice might seriously prejudice the investigation of an offence to which this Chapter applies.

(3) A warrant under this section is a warrant authorising an appropriate person named in it—

    (a) to enter and search the premises, using such force as is reasonably necessary;

    (b) to take possession of any documents appearing to be documents of a description specified in the information, or to take any other steps which appear to be necessary for preserving, or preventing interference with, any such documents;

    (c) in the case of any such documents consisting of information recorded otherwise than in legible form, to take possession of any computer disk or other electronic storage device which appears to contain the information in question, or to take any other steps which appear to be necessary for preserving, or preventing interference with, that information;

    (d) to take copies of or extracts from any documents or information falling within paragraph (b) or (c);

    (e) to require any person on the premises to provide an explanation of any such documents or information or to state where any such documents or information may be found;

    (f) to require any such person to give the appropriate person such assistance as he may reasonably require for the taking of copies or extracts as mentioned in paragraph (d).

(4) A person executing a warrant under this section may take other persons with him, if it appears to him to be necessary to do so.

(5) A warrant under this section must, if so required, be produced for inspection by the owner or occupier of the premises or anyone acting on his behalf.

(6) If the premises are unoccupied or the occupier is temporarily absent, a person entering the premises under the authority of a warrant under this section must leave the premises as effectively secured against trespassers as he found them.

(7)–(11) *****

67–70 *****

Chapter 2 Offenders assisting investigations and prosecutions

71 Assistance by offender: immunity from prosecution

(1) If a specified prosecutor thinks that for the purposes of the investigation or prosecution of [an indictable offence or an offence triable either way] it is appropriate to offer any person immunity from prosecution [for any offence] he may give the person a written notice under this subsection (an 'immunity notice').

(2) If a person is given an immunity notice, no proceedings for an offence of a description specified in the notice may be brought against that person in England and Wales or Northern Ireland except in circumstances specified in the notice.

(3) An immunity notice ceases to have effect in relation to the person to whom it is given if the person fails to comply with any conditions specified in the notice.

(4) Each of the following is a specified prosecutor—

    (a)   the Director of Public Prosecutions;

    (b)   ...;

    (c)   the Director of the Serious Fraud Office;

    (d)   the Director of Public Prosecutions for Northern Ireland;

    [[(da) the Financial Conduct Authority;

    (daa) the Prudential Regulation Authority;

    (dab) the Bank of England, where the indictable offence or offence triable either way which is being investigated or prosecuted is an offence under the Financial Services and Markets Act 2000;]

    (db)   the Secretary of State for Business, Innovation and Skills, acting personally;]

    (e)   a prosecutor designated for the purposes of this section by a prosecutor mentioned in paragraphs (a) to [(db)].

(5)–(7) *****

72 Assistance by offender: undertakings as to use of evidence

(1) If a specified prosecutor thinks that for the purposes of the investigation or prosecution of [an indictable offence or an offence triable either way] it is appropriate to offer any person an undertaking that information of any description will not be used against the person in any proceedings to which this section applies he may give the person a written notice under this subsection (a 'restricted use undertaking').

(2) This section applies to—

    (a) [any] criminal proceedings;

    (b) proceedings under Part 5 of the Proceeds of Crime Act 2002 (c. 29).

(3) If a person is given a restricted use undertaking the information described in the undertaking must not be used against that person in any proceedings to which this section applies brought in England and Wales or Northern Ireland except in the circumstances specified in the undertaking.

(4) A restricted use undertaking ceases to have effect in relation to the person to whom it is given if the person fails to comply with any conditions specified in the undertaking.

(5)–(7) *****

73, 74 ...

75–127 *****

Trespass on designated site

128 Offence of trespassing on designated site

(1) A person commits an offence if he enters, or is on, any [protected] site in England and Wales or Northern Ireland as a trespasser.

[(1A) In this section 'protected site' means—

    (a) a nuclear site; or

    (b) a designated site.]

(1B), (1C) *****

(2) A 'designated site' means a site

    (a) specified or described (in any way) in an order made by the Secretary of State, and

    (b) designated for the purposes of this section by the order.

(3) The Secretary of State may only designate a site for the purposes of this section if—

    (a) it is comprised in Crown land; or

    (b) it is comprised in land belonging to Her Majesty in Her private capacity or to the immediate heir to the Throne in his private capacity; or

    (c) it appears to the Secretary of State that it is appropriate to designate the site in the interests of national security.

(4) It is a defence for a person charged with an offence under this section to prove that he did not know, and had no reasonable cause to suspect, that the site in relation to which the offence is alleged to have been committed was a [protected] site.

(5) A person guilty of an offence under this section is liable on summary conviction—

    (a) to imprisonment for a term not exceeding 51 weeks, or

    (b) to a fine not exceeding level 5 on the standard scale, or to both.

(6)–(10) *****

129 Corresponding Scottish offence

(1) A person commits an offence if he enters, or is on, any [protected] Scottish site without lawful authority.

[(1A) In this section 'protected Scottish site' means—

    (a) a nuclear site in Scotland; or

    (b) a designated Scottish site.]

(1B), (1C) *****

(2) A 'designated Scottish site' means a site in Scotland—

(a) specified or described (in any way) in an order made by the Secretary of State, and

(b) designated for the purposes of this section by the order.

(3) The Secretary of State may only designate a site for the purposes of this section if it appears to him that it is appropriate to designate the site in the interests of national security.

(4)–(7) *****

130–178 *****

179 Short title and extent

(1) This Act may be cited as the Serious Organised Crime and Police Act 2005.

(2) Subject to the following provisions, this Act extends to England and Wales only.

(3) The following extend also to Scotland—

(a) sections 1 to 54, [and 56 to] 58,

(b) sections 60 to 68, 70, 82 to 96, 98 to 106, 107(1) and (4) and 108,

(c) section 123,

(d) section 131,

(e) sections 150 to 153, 156(6), 158, 163(1) and (2), 164, 165(1) and (2), 166(2), 167 and 171(1),

(f) sections 172, 173, 176 to 178 and this section,

(g) Schedules 1, 3, 5 and 15.

(4) The following extend to Scotland only—

(a) section 107(3),

(b) sections 129 and 130(3),

(c) sections 156(1) to (5), 166(1) and 171(2).

(5) The following extend also to Northern Ireland—

(a) sections 1 to 54 [and 56 to] 58,

(b) sections [60] to 75, 82 to 106, 107(1), (2) and (4) and 108,

(c) section 123(1),

(d) sections 128, 131 and 144,

(e)–(g) *****

(6)–(10) *****

*****

Equality Act 2006

(2006, c. 3)

An Act to make provision for the establishment of the Commission for Equality and Human Rights; to dissolve the Equal Opportunities Commission, the Commission for Racial Equality and the Disability Rights Commission; to make provision about discrimination on grounds of religion or belief; to enable provision to be made about discrimination on grounds of sexual orientation; to impose duties relating to sex discrimination on persons performing public functions; to amend the Disability Discrimination Act 1995; and for connected purposes.   [16th February 2006]

Territorial extent: England and Wales, Scotland

PART 1 THE COMMISSION FOR EQUALITY AND HUMAN RIGHTS

The Commission

1 Establishment

There shall be a body corporate known as the Commission for Equality and Human Rights.

2 *****

mnop library.

3 General duty

The Commission shall exercise its functions under this Part with a view to encouraging and supporting the development of a society in which—

(a) people's ability to achieve their potential is not limited by prejudice or discrimination,
(b) there is respect for and protection of each individual's human rights,
(c) there is respect for the dignity and worth of each individual,
(d) each individual has an equal opportunity to participate in society, and
(e) there is mutual respect between groups based on understanding and valuing of diversity and on shared respect for equality and human rights.

4–7 *****

8 Equality and diversity

(1) The Commission shall, by exercising the powers conferred by this Part—

(a) promote understanding of the importance of equality and diversity,
(b) encourage good practice in relation to equality and diversity,
(c) promote equality of opportunity,
(d) promote awareness and understanding of rights under the [Equality Act 2010],
(e) enforce [that Act],
(f) work towards the elimination of unlawful discrimination, and
(g) work towards the elimination of unlawful harassment.

(2) In subsection (1)—

'diversity' means the fact that individuals are different,
'equality' means equality between individuals, and
'unlawful' is to be construed in accordance with section 34.

(3) In promoting equality of opportunity between disabled persons and others, the Commission may, in particular, promote the favourable treatment of disabled persons.

(4) In this Part 'disabled person' means a person who—

(a) is a disabled person within the meaning of the [Equality Act 2010], or
(b) has been a disabled person within that meaning (whether or not at a time when that Act had effect).

9 Human rights

(1) The Commission shall, by exercising the powers conferred by this Part—

(a) promote understanding of the importance of human rights,
(b) encourage good practice in relation to human rights,
(c) promote awareness, understanding and protection of human rights, and
(d) encourage public authorities to comply with section 6 of the Human Rights Act 1998 (c. 42) (compliance with Convention rights).

(2) In this Part 'human rights' means—

(a) the Convention rights within the meaning given by section 1 of the Human Rights Act 1998, and
(b) other human rights.

(3) In determining what action to take in pursuance of this section the Commission shall have particular regard to the importance of exercising the powers conferred by this Part in relation to the Convention rights.

(4) In fulfilling a duty under section 8 ... the Commission shall take account of any relevant human rights.

(5) A reference in this Part (including this section) to human rights does not exclude any matter by reason only of its being a matter to which section 8 ... relates.

10 Groups

(1) ...

(2) In this Part 'group' means a group or class of persons who share a common attribute in respect of any of the following matters—

(a) age,

(b) disability,

(c) gender,

[(d) gender reassignment (within the meaning of section 7 of the Equality Act 2010)].

(e) race,

(f) religion or belief, and

(g) sexual orientation.

(3) *****

(4)–(7) …

11 Monitoring the law

(1) The Commission shall monitor the effectiveness of the equality and human rights enactments.

(2) The Commission may—

(a) advise central government about the effectiveness of any of the equality and human rights enactments;

(b) recommend to central government the amendment, repeal, consolidation (with or without amendments) or replication (with or without amendments) of any of the equality and human rights enactments;

(c) advise central or devolved government about the effect of an enactment (including an enactment in or under an Act of the Scottish Parliament);

(d) advise central or devolved government about the likely effect of a proposed change of law.

(3) *****

12 Monitoring progress

(1) The Commission shall from time to time identify—

(a) changes in society that have occurred or are expected to occur and are relevant to [the duties specified in sections 8 and 9],

(b) results at which to aim for the purpose of encouraging and supporting [changes in society that are consistent with those duties] ('outcomes'), and

(c) factors by reference to which progress towards those results may be measured ('indicators').

(2)–(5) *****

13 *****

14 Codes of practice

(1) The Commission may issue a code of practice in connection with a matter addressed by [the Equality Act 2010].

(2) A code of practice under subsection (1) shall contain provision designed—

(a) to ensure or facilitate compliance with [the Equality Act 2010 or an enactment made under that Act], or

(b) to promote equality of opportunity.

(3), (4) *****

(5) The Commission shall comply with a direction of the [Secretary of State] to issue a code under this section in connection with a specified matter if—

(a) the matter is not [a matter addressed by the Equality Act 2010], but

(b) the [Secretary of State] expects to add it by order under section 15(6).

(6) Before issuing a code under this section the Commission shall—

(a) publish proposals, and

(b) consult such persons as it thinks appropriate.

(7) Before issuing a code under this section the Commission shall submit a draft to the [Secretary of State], who shall—

(a) if he approves the draft—

(i) notify the Commission, and

(ii) lay a copy before Parliament, or

(b) otherwise, give the Commission written reasons why he does not approve the draft.

(8) Where a draft is laid before Parliament under subsection (7)(a)(ii), if neither House passes a resolution disapproving the draft within 40 days—

(a) the Commission may issue the code in the form of the draft, and

(b) it shall come into force in accordance with provision made by the [Secretary of State] by order.

(9), (10) *****

15 *****

16 Inquiries

(1) The Commission may conduct an inquiry into a matter relating to any of the Commission's duties under sections 8 [and 9].

(2) If in the course of an inquiry the Commission begins to suspect that a person may have committed an unlawful act—

(a) in continuing the inquiry the Commission shall, so far as possible, avoid further consideration of whether or not the person has committed an unlawful act,

(b) the Commission may commence an investigation into that question under section 20,

(c) the Commission may use information or evidence acquired in the course of the inquiry for the purpose of the investigation, and

(d) the Commission shall so far as possible ensure (whether by aborting or suspending the inquiry or otherwise) that any aspects of the inquiry which concern the person investigated, or may require his involvement, are not pursued while the investigation is in progress.

(3) The report of an inquiry—

(a) may not state (whether expressly or by necessary implication) that a specified or identifiable person has committed an unlawful act, and

(b) shall not otherwise refer to the activities of a specified or identifiable person unless the Commission thinks that the reference—

(i) will not harm the person, or

(ii) is necessary in order for the report adequately to reflect the results of the inquiry.

(4) Subsections (2) and (3) shall not prevent an inquiry from considering or reporting a matter relating to human rights (whether or not a necessary implication arises in relation to the [Equality Act 2010]).

(5) Before settling a report of an inquiry which records findings which in the Commission's opinion are of an adverse nature and relate (whether expressly or by necessary implication) to a specified or identifiable person the Commission shall—

(a) send a draft of the report to the person,

(b) specify a period of at least 28 days during which he may make written representations about the draft, and

(c) consider any representations made.

(6) *****

17, 18 *****

19 ...

20 Investigations

(1) The Commission may investigate whether or not a person—

(a) has committed an unlawful act,

(b) has complied with a requirement imposed by an unlawful act notice under section 21, or

(c) has complied with an undertaking given under section 23.

(2) The Commission may conduct an investigation under subsection (1)(a) only if it suspects that the person concerned may have committed an unlawful act.

(3) A suspicion for the purposes of subsection (2) may (but need not) be based on the results of, or a matter arising during the course of, an inquiry under section 16.

(4), (5) *****

21   Unlawful act notice

(1) The Commission may give a person a notice under this section (an 'unlawful act notice') if—

(a) he is or has been the subject of an investigation under section 20(1)(a), and

(b) the Commission is satisfied that he has committed an unlawful act.

(2) A notice must specify—

(a) the unlawful act, and

(b) the provision of the [Equality Act 2010] by virtue of which the act is unlawful.

(3) A notice must inform the recipient of the effect of—

(a) subsections (5) to (7),

(b) section 20(1)(b), and

(c) section 24(1).

(4) A notice may—

(a) require the person to whom the notice is given to prepare an action plan for the purpose of avoiding repetition or continuation of the unlawful act;

(b) recommend action to be taken by the person for that purpose.

(5) A person who is given a notice may, within the period of six weeks beginning with the day on which the notice is given, appeal to the appropriate court or tribunal on the grounds—

(a) that he has not committed the unlawful act specified in the notice, or

(b) that a requirement for the preparation of an action plan imposed under subsection (4)(a) is unreasonable.

(6) An appeal under subsection (5) the court or tribunal may—

(a) affirm a notice;

(b) annul a notice;

(c) vary a notice;

(d) affirm a requirement;

(e) annul a requirement;

(f) vary a requirement;

(g) make an order for costs or expenses.

(7) In subsection (5) 'the appropriate court or tribunal' means—

(a) an employment tribunal, if a claim in respect of the alleged unlawful act could be made to it, or

(b) the county court (in England and Wales) or the sheriff (in Scotland), if a claim in respect of the alleged unlawful act could be made to it or to him.

22   ***

23   Agreements

(1) The Commission may enter into an agreement with a person under which—

(a) the person undertakes—

(i)   not to commit an unlawful act of a specified kind, and

(ii)   to take, or refrain from taking, other specified action (which may include the preparation of a plan for the purpose of avoiding an unlawful act), and

(b) the Commission undertakes not to proceed against the person under section 20 or 21 in respect of any unlawful act of the kind specified under paragraph (a)(i).

(2) The Commission may enter into an agreement with a person under this section only if it thinks that the person has committed an unlawful act.

(3) But a person shall not be taken to admit to the commission of an unlawful act by reason only of entering into an agreement under this section.

(4), (5) *****

24   Applications to court

(1) If the Commission thinks that a person is likely to commit an unlawful act, it may apply—

(a) in England and Wales, to the [county court] for an injunction restraining the person from committing the act, or

(b) in Scotland, to the sheriff for an interdict prohibiting the person from committing the act.

(2) Subsection (3) applies if the Commission thinks that a party to an agreement under section 23 has failed to comply, or is likely not to comply, with an undertaking under the agreement.

(3) The Commission may apply to the [county court] (in England and Wales) or to the sheriff (in Scotland) for an order requiring the person—

(a) to comply with his undertaking, and

(b) to take such other action as the court or the sheriff may specify.

[24A] *****

25–29 ...

30 Judicial review and other legal proceedings

(1) The Commission shall have capacity to institute or intervene in legal proceedings, whether for judicial review or otherwise, if it appears to the Commission that the proceedings are relevant to a matter in connection with which the Commission has a function.

(2) The Commission shall be taken to have title and interest in relation to the subject matter of any legal proceedings in Scotland which it has capacity to institute, or in which it has capacity to intervene, by virtue of subsection (1).

(3)–(4) *****

31–42 *****

43–81 ...

82 *****

83–90 ...

91–95 *****

SCHEDULE 1   *****

SCHEDULE 2 INQUIRIES, INVESTIGATIONS AND ASSESSMENTS

Introduction

1. This Schedule applies to—

    (a) inquiries under section 16,

    (b) investigations under section 20, and

    (c) assessments under section 31.

Terms of reference

2. Before conducting an inquiry the Commission shall—

    (a) publish the terms of reference of the inquiry in a manner that the Commission thinks is likely to bring the inquiry to the attention of persons whom it concerns or who are likely to be interested in it, and

    (b) in particular, give notice of the terms of reference to any persons specified in them.

3. Before conducting an investigation the Commission shall—

    (a) prepare terms of reference specifying the person to be investigated and the nature of the unlawful act which the Commission suspects,

    (b) give the person to be investigated notice of the proposed terms of reference,

    (c) give the person to be investigated an opportunity to make representations about the proposed terms of reference,

    (d) consider any representations made, and

    (e) publish the terms of reference once settled.

4. Before conducting an assessment of a person's compliance with a duty the Commission shall—

    (a) prepare terms of reference,

    (b) give the person notice of the proposed terms of reference,

(c) give the person an opportunity to make representations about the proposed terms of reference,

(d) consider any representations made, and

(e) publish the terms of reference once settled.

5. Paragraphs 2 to 4 shall apply in relation to revised terms of reference as they apply in relation to original terms of reference.

Representations

6.—(1) The Commission shall make arrangements for giving persons an opportunity to make representations in relation to inquiries, investigations and assessments.

(2) In particular, in the course of an investigation, inquiry or assessment the Commission must give any person specified in the terms of reference an opportunity to make representations.

7. Arrangements under paragraph 6 may (but need not) include arrangements for oral representations.

8.—(1) The Commission shall consider representations made in relation to an inquiry, investigation or assessment.

(2) But the Commission may, where they think it appropriate, refuse to consider representations—

(a) made neither by nor on behalf of a person specified in the terms of reference, or

(b) made on behalf of a person specified in the terms of reference by a person who is not a [relevant lawyer].

[(2A) 'Relevant lawyer' means—

(a) an advocate or solicitor in Scotland, or

(b) a person who, for the purposes of the Legal Services Act 2007, is an authorised person in relation to an activity which constitutes the exercise of a right of audience or the conduct of litigation (within the meaning of that Act).]

(3) If the Commission refuse to consider representations in reliance on sub-paragraph (2) they shall give the person who makes them written notice of the Commission's decision and the reasons for it.

Evidence

9. In the course of an inquiry, investigation or assessment the Commission may give a notice under this paragraph to any person.

10.—(1) A notice given to a person under paragraph 9 may require him—

(a) to provide information in his possession,

(b) to produce documents in his possession, or

(c) to give oral evidence.

(2) A notice under paragraph 9 may include provision about—

(a) the form of information, documents or evidence;

(b) timing.

(3) A notice under paragraph 9—

(a) may not require a person to provide information that he is prohibited from disclosing by virtue of an enactment,

(b) may not require a person to do anything that he could not be compelled to do in proceedings before the High Court or the Court of Session, and

(c) may not require a person to attend at a place unless the Commission undertakes to pay the expenses of his journey.

11. The recipient of a notice under paragraph 9 may apply to the [county court] (in England and Wales) or to the sheriff (in Scotland) to have the notice cancelled on the grounds that the requirement imposed by the notice is—

(a) unnecessary having regard to the purpose of the inquiry, investigation or assessment to which the notice relates, or

(b) otherwise unreasonable.

12.–20. *****

*****

Government of Wales Act 2006

(2006, c. 32)

An Act to make provision about the government of Wales.   [25th July 2006]

[PART A1 PERMANENCE OF THE SENEDD]

[A1   Permanence of the [Senedd] and Welsh Government]

[(1) The [Senedd] established by Part 1 and the Welsh Government established by Part 2 are a permanent part of the United Kingdom's constitutional arrangements.

(2) The purpose of this section is, with due regard to the other provisions of this Act, to signify the commitment of the Parliament and Government of the United Kingdom to the [Senedd] and the Welsh Government.

(3) In view of that commitment it is declared that the [Senedd] and the Welsh Government are not to be abolished except on the basis of a decision of the people of Wales voting in a referendum.]

[A2   Recognition of Welsh law]

[(1) The law that applies in Wales includes a body of Welsh law made by the [Senedd] and the Welsh Ministers.

(2) The purpose of this section is, with due regard to the other provisions of this Act, to recognise the ability of the [Senedd] and the Welsh Ministers to make law forming part of the law of England and Wales.]

PART 1 [SENEDD CYMRU]

The [Senedd]

1   The [Senedd]

(1)   There is to be [a parliament] for Wales to be known as [Senedd Cymru or the Welsh Parliament (referred to in this Act as 'the Senedd')].

(2) The [Senedd] is to consist of—

   (a) one member for each [Senedd] constituency (referred to in this Act as '[Senedd] constituency members'), and

   (b) members for each [Senedd] electoral region (referred to in this Act as '[Senedd] regional members').

[(2A) Members of the Senedd are to be known by that name or as Aelodau o'r Senedd.]

(3) [Members of the Senedd] are to be returned in accordance with the provision made by and under this Act for—

   (a) the holding of general elections of [Members of the Senedd] (for the return of the entire [Senedd]), and

   (b) the filling of vacancies in [Senedd] seats.

(4) The validity of any [Senedd] proceedings is not affected by any vacancy in its membership.

(5) In this Act '[Senedd] proceedings' means any proceedings of—

   (a) the [Senedd],

   (b) committees of the [Senedd], or

   (c) sub-committees of such committees.

2   [Senedd] constituencies and electoral regions

[(1) The [Senedd] constituencies are the constituencies specified in the Parliamentary Constituencies and [Senedd] Electoral Regions (Wales) Order 2006 (SI 2006/1041) as amended by—

(a) the Parliamentary Constituencies and [Senedd] Electoral Regions (Wales) (Amendment) Order 2008 (SI 2008/1791), and

(b) any Order in Council under the Parliamentary Constituencies Act 1986 giving effect (with or without modifications) to a report falling within section 13(3) or (4) of the Parliamentary Voting System and Constituencies Act 2011.]

(2) There are five [Senedd] electoral regions.

(3) The [Senedd] electoral regions are as specified in the Parliamentary Constituencies and [Senedd] Electoral Regions (Wales) Order 2006.

(4) There are four seats for each [Senedd] electoral region.

(5), (6) …

3   Ordinary general elections

(1) The poll at an ordinary general election is to be held on the first Thursday in May in the [fifth] calendar year following that in which the previous ordinary general election was held, [unless—

(a) subsection (1A) prevents the poll being held on that day, or

(b) the day of the poll is determined by a proclamation under section 4].

[(1A) The poll is not to be held on the same date as the date of the poll at—

(a) a parliamentary general election …, …

(b) …

(1B) Where subsection (1A) prevents the poll being held on the day specified in subsection (1), the poll is to be held on such day, subject to subsection (1A), as the Welsh Ministers may by order specify unless the day of the poll is determined by a proclamation under section 4(2) as modified by section 4(2A).]

(2) If the poll is to be held on the first Thursday in May [or on the day specified by an order under subsection (1B)], the [Senedd]—

(a) is dissolved by virtue of this section at the beginning of the minimum period which ends with that day, and

(b) must meet within the period of [fourteen] days beginning immediately after the day of the poll.

(3) In subsection (2) 'the minimum period' means the period determined in accordance with an order under section 13.

(4) *****

[(5) No order is to be made under subsection (1B) unless a draft of the statutory instrument containing it has been laid before, and approved by a resolution of, the [Senedd].]

4   Power to vary date of ordinary general election

[(1) Subject to section 3(1A), the Presiding Officer may propose, for the holding of the poll at an ordinary general election, a day which is not more than one month earlier, nor more than one month later, than the first Thursday in May.

(2) If the Presiding Officer proposes a day under subsection (1), Her Majesty may by proclamation under the Welsh Seal—

(a) dissolve the [Senedd],

(b) require the poll at the election to be held on the day proposed, and

(c) require the [Senedd] to meet within the period of [fourteen] days beginning immediately after the day of the poll.

(2A) Where a day is specified by an order under section 3(1B), subsection (1) applies as if the reference to the first Thursday in May were a reference to that day.]

(3) *****

(4) [The Welsh Ministers may by order] make provision for-—

(a) any provision of, or made under, the Representation of the People Acts, or

(b) any other enactment relating to the election of [Members of the Senedd],

to have effect with such modifications or exceptions as the [Welsh Ministers consider] appropriate in connection with the alteration of the day of the poll [under this section].

(5) …

(6) A statutory instrument containing an order under this section is subject to annulment in pursuance of a resolution of [the] [Senedd].

5–24 *****

25 Presiding Officer etc

(1) The [Senedd] must, at its first meeting following a general election, elect from among the [Members of the Senedd]—

(a) a presiding officer (referred to in this Act as 'the Presiding Officer'), and

(b) a deputy presiding officer (referred to in this Act as 'the Deputy Presiding Officer').

(2) The person elected under paragraph (a) of subsection (1) is to be known as the Presiding Officer or by such other title as the standing orders may provide; and the person elected under paragraph (b) of that subsection is to be known as the Deputy Presiding Officer or by such other title as the standing orders may provide.

(3) The Presiding Officer holds office until the conclusion of the next election of a Presiding Officer under subsection (1).

(4) The Deputy Presiding Officer holds office until the [Senedd] is dissolved.

(5) But the Presiding Officer or Deputy Presiding Officer—

(a) may at any time resign,

(b) ceases to hold office on ceasing to be [a Member of the Senedd] otherwise than by reason of a dissolution, and

(c) may be removed from office by the [Senedd].

(6) If the Presiding Officer or the Deputy Presiding Officer ceases to hold office under subsection (5) (or dies), the [Senedd] must elect a replacement from among the [Members of the Senedd].

(7) Subject to subsection (9), the Presiding Officer and the Deputy Presiding Officer must not belong to—

(a) the same political group, or

(b) different political groups both of which are political groups with an executive role.

(8) For the purposes of this Act a political group is a political group with an executive role if the First Minister or one or more of the Welsh Ministers appointed under section 48 belong to it.

(9) The [Senedd] may resolve that subsection (7) is not to apply for so long as the resolution so provides; but if the motion for the resolution is passed on a vote it is of no effect unless at least two-thirds of the [Members of the Senedd] voting support it.

(10) The Presiding Officer's functions may be exercised by the Deputy Presiding Officer if—

(a) the office of Presiding Officer is vacant, or

(b) the Presiding Officer is for any reason unable to act.

(11) The Presiding Officer may (subject to the standing orders) authorise the Deputy Presiding Officer to exercise functions of the Presiding Officer.

(12) The standing orders may include provision for the Presiding Officer's functions to be exercisable by any person specified in, or determined in accordance with, the standing orders if—

(a) the office of Presiding Officer is vacant or the Presiding Officer is for any reason unable to act, and

(b) the office of Deputy Presiding Officer is vacant or the Deputy Presiding Officer is for any reason unable to act.

(13) The standing orders may include provision as to the participation (including voting) in [Senedd] proceedings of the Presiding Officer and Deputy Presiding Officer and any person acting by virtue of subsection (12).

(14) The validity of any act of a person as Presiding Officer or Deputy Presiding Officer, or of any person acting by virtue of subsection (12), is not affected by any defect in the person's appointment by the [Senedd].

(15) *****

26   *****

27   [Senedd] Commission

(1) There is to be a body corporate to be known as the [Senedd Commission or Comisiwn y Senedd] (referred to in this Act as 'the [Senedd] Commission').

(2) The members of the [Senedd] Commission are to be—

    (a) the Presiding Officer, and

    (b) four other [Members of the Senedd].

(3) The standing orders must make provision for the appointment of the four other [Members of the Senedd] as members of the [Senedd] Commission.

(4) The provision included in the standing orders in compliance with subsection (3) must (so far as it is reasonably practicable to do so) secure that not more than one of the members of the [Senedd] Commission (other than the Presiding Officer) belongs to any one political group.

(5) The [Senedd] Commission must—

    (a) provide to the [Senedd], or

    (b) ensure that the [Senedd] is provided with,

the property, staff and services required for the [Senedd's] purposes.

(6) The [Senedd] may give special or general directions to the [Senedd] Commission for the purpose of, or in connection with, the exercise of the [Senedd] Commission's functions.

(7), (8) *****

28   *****

29   ...

30   *****

Proceedings etc

31   Standing orders

(1) [Senedd] proceedings are to be regulated by standing orders (referred to in this Act as 'the standing orders').

(2) The standing orders must include provision for preserving order in [Senedd] proceedings, including provision for—

    (a) preventing conduct which would constitute a criminal offence or contempt of court, and

    (b) a sub judice rule.

(3) The standing orders may include provision for excluding [a Member of the Senedd] from [Senedd] proceedings.

(4) The standing orders may include provision for withdrawing from [a Member of the Senedd] any or all of the rights and privileges of membership of the [Senedd].

(5) The standing orders—

    (a) must include provision requiring the proceedings of the [Senedd] to be held in public, and for proceedings of a committee of the [Senedd] or a sub-committee of such a committee to be held in public except in circumstances provided for in the standing orders, and

    (b) may include provision as to the conditions to be complied with by members of the public attending the proceedings (including provision for excluding any member of the public who does not comply with the conditions).

(6) The standing orders must include provision—

    (a) for reporting the proceedings of the [Senedd], and for reporting proceedings of committees of the [Senedd] and sub-committees of such committees which are held in public, and

    (b) for publishing the reports of proceedings as soon as reasonably practicable after the proceedings take place.

(7) The [Senedd] may by resolution remake or revise the standing orders; but if the motion for a resolution to remake or revise the standing orders is passed on a vote, it has no effect unless at least two-thirds of the [Members of the Senedd] voting support it.

(8) The Clerk must from time to time publish the standing orders.

32–33 ...

34–43 *****

44 ...

PART 2 WELSH ... GOVERNMENT

Government

45 Welsh ... Government

(1) There is to be a Welsh ... Government, or Llywodraeth ... Cymru, whose members are—

  (a) the First Minister or Prif Weinidog (see sections 46 and 47),

  (b) the Welsh Ministers, or Gweinidogion Cymru, appointed under section 48,

  (c) the Counsel General to the Welsh ... Government or Cwnsler Cyffredinol i Lywodraeth ... Cymru (see section 49) (referred to in this Act as 'the Counsel General'), and

  (d) the Deputy Welsh Ministers or Dirprwy Weinidogion Cymru (see section 50).

(2) In this Act and in any other enactment or instrument the First Minister and the Welsh Ministers appointed under section 48 are referred to collectively as the Welsh Ministers.

46 The First Minister

(1) The First Minister is to be appointed by Her Majesty after nomination in accordance with section 47.

(2) The First Minister holds office at Her Majesty's pleasure.

(3) The First Minister may at any time tender resignation to Her Majesty and ceases to hold office as First Minister when it is accepted.

(4) A person ceases to hold office as the First Minister if another person is appointed to that office.

(5) The functions of the First Minister are exercisable by a person designated by the Presiding Officer if—

  (a) the office of the First Minister is vacant,

  (b) the First Minister is for any reason unable to act, or

  (c) the First Minister has ceased to be [a Member of the Senedd] [otherwise than by reason of dissolution].

(6) A person may not be designated to exercise the functions of the First Minister unless the person is—

  (a) [a Member of the Senedd], or

  (b) if the [Senedd] has been dissolved, a person who ceased to be [a Member of the Senedd] by reason of the dissolution.

(7) A person may be designated to exercise the functions of the First Minister only on the recommendation of the Welsh Ministers (unless there is no-one holding office as a Welsh Minister appointed under section 48).

(8) If a person is designated to exercise the functions of the First Minister, the designation continues to have effect even if the [Senedd] is dissolved.

47 Choice of First Minister

(1) If one of the following events occurs, the [Senedd] must, before the end of the relevant period, nominate [a Member of the Senedd] for appointment as First Minister.

(2) The events are—

  (a) the holding of a poll at a general election,

(b) the [Senedd] resolving that the Welsh Ministers no longer enjoy the confidence of the [Senedd],

(c) the First Minister tendering resignation to Her Majesty,

(d) the First Minister dying or becoming permanently unable to act and to tender resignation, and

(e) the First Minister ceasing to be [a Member of the Senedd] otherwise than by reason of a dissolution.

(3) The relevant period is the period of 28 days beginning with the day on which the event occurs; but—

(a) if another of those events occurs within that period, the relevant period is (subject to paragraph (b)) extended to end with the period of 28 days beginning with the day on which that other event occurs, and

(b) the relevant period ends if the [Senedd] passes a resolution under section 5(2)(a) or when Her Majesty appoints a person as the First Minister.

(4) The Presiding Officer must recommend to Her Majesty the appointment of the person nominated by the [Senedd] under subsection (1).

48   Welsh Ministers

(1) The First Minister may, with the approval of Her Majesty, appoint Welsh Ministers from among the [Members of the Senedd].

(2) A Welsh Minister appointed under this section holds office at Her Majesty's pleasure.

(3) A Welsh Minister appointed under this section may be removed from office by the First Minister.

(4) A Welsh Minister appointed under this section may at any time resign.

(5) A Welsh Minister appointed under this section must resign if the [Senedd] resolves that the Welsh Ministers no longer enjoy the confidence of the [Senedd].

(6) A Welsh Minister appointed under this section who resigns ceases to hold office immediately.

(7) A Welsh Minister appointed under this section ceases to hold office on ceasing to be [a Member of the Senedd] otherwise than by reason of a dissolution.

49–55   *****

56   Introduction

(1) The persons to whom this section applies have the functions conferred or imposed on them by or by virtue of this Act or any other enactment or prerogative instrument.

(2) This section applies to the Welsh Ministers, the First Minister and the Counsel General.

57   Exercise of functions

(1) Functions may be conferred or imposed on the Welsh Ministers by that name.

(2) Functions of the Welsh Ministers, the First Minister and the Counsel General are exercisable on behalf of Her Majesty.

(3) Functions of the Welsh Ministers are exercisable by the First Minister or any of the Welsh Ministers appointed under section 48.

(4) Any act or omission of, or in relation to, the First Minister or any of the Welsh Ministers appointed under section 48 is to be treated as an act or omission of, or in relation to, each of them.

(5) But subsection (4) does not apply in relation to the exercise of functions conferred or imposed on the First Minister alone.

(6) Where a function conferred or imposed on the Counsel General is (either generally or in particular circumstances) exercisable concurrently by the Welsh Ministers or the First Minister, subsection (4) applies in relation to the exercise of the function (or to its exercise in those circumstances) as if the Counsel General were included among the Welsh Ministers.

58   Transfer of Ministerial functions

(1) Her Majesty may by Order in Council—

(a) provide for the transfer to the Welsh Ministers, the First Minister or the Counsel General of any function so far as exercisable by a Minister of the Crown in relation to Wales [or the Welsh zone],

(b) direct that any function so far as so exercisable is to be exercisable by the Welsh Ministers, the First Minister or the Counsel General[—

   (i) concurrently with the Minister of the Crown, or

   (ii) only with the agreement of, or after consultation with, a Minister of the Crown,] or

(c) direct that any function so far as exercisable by a Minister of the Crown in relation to Wales [or the Welsh zone] is to be exercisable by the Minister of the Crown only with the agreement of, or after consultation with, the Welsh Ministers, the First Minister or the Counsel General.

(1A), (1B) *****

(2) An Order in Council under this section may, in particular, provide for any function exercisable by the Welsh Ministers, the First Minister or the Counsel General by virtue of an Order in Council under subsection (1)(a) or (b) to be exercisable either generally or in such circumstances as may be specified in the Order in Council, concurrently with any other of the Welsh Ministers, the First Minister or the Counsel General.

[(2A)], [(2B)] *****

(3) An Order in Council under this section may make such modifications of—

(a) any enactment (including any enactment comprised in or made under this Act) or prerogative instrument, or

(b) any other instrument or document,

as Her Majesty considers appropriate in connection with the provision made by the Order in Council.

(4) No recommendation is to be made to Her Majesty in Council to make an Order in Council under this section unless a draft of the statutory instrument containing the Order in Council—

(a) has been laid before, and approved by a resolution of, each House of Parliament, and

(b) has been approved by the Welsh Ministers.

(5) *****

[58A   Executive ministerial functions]

[(1) Executive ministerial functions, so far as exercisable within devolved competence, are exercisable by the Welsh Ministers.

(2) Executive ministerial functions that are ancillary to a function of the Welsh Ministers exercised outside devolved competence are also exercisable by the Welsh Ministers.

(3) Functions exercisable by the Welsh Ministers under subsection (1) or (2) are not exercisable by a Minister of the Crown unless they are functions to which subsection (4) applies.

If they are functions to which subsection (4) applies, they are exercisable by the Welsh Ministers concurrently with any relevant Minister of the Crown.

(4) This subsection applies to—

(a) functions ancillary to a function of the Welsh Ministers that is exercisable concurrently or jointly with a Minister of the Crown;

(b) functions ancillary to a function of a Minister of the Crown;

(c) functions that are not ancillary to another function;

(d) functions in relation to observing and implementing [retained EU obligations].

(5) In this section—

'executive ministerial function' means a function of Her Majesty of a kind that is exercisable on Her behalf by a Minister of the Crown (including a function involving expenditure or other financial matters), but not a function conferred or imposed by or by virtue of any legislation or the prerogative;

'within devolved competence' and 'outside devolved competence' are to be read in accordance with subsections (7) and (8).

(6) For the purposes of this section a function is 'ancillary to' another function if or to the extent that it is exercisable with a view to facilitating, or in a way that is conducive or incidental to, the exercise of the other function.

(7) It is outside devolved competence—

    (a) to make any provision by subordinate legislation that would be outside the legislative competence of the [Senedd] if it were included in an Act of the [Senedd] (see section 108A), or

    (b) to confirm or approve any subordinate legislation containing such provision.

(8) *****

58B–79   *****

80   [Retained] [EU] [obligations]

(1) [A retained EU obligation] of the United Kingdom is also an obligation of the Welsh Ministers if and to the extent that the obligation could be implemented (or enabled to be implemented) or complied with by the exercise by the Welsh Ministers of any of their functions.

(2) Subsection (1) does not apply in the case of [a retained EU obligation] of the United Kingdom if—

    (a) it is an obligation to achieve a result defined by reference to a quantity (whether expressed as an amount, proportion or ratio or otherwise), and

    (b) the quantity relates to the United Kingdom (or to an area including the United Kingdom or to an area consisting of a part of the United Kingdom which includes [the whole or part of Wales or of the Welsh zone]).

(3) But if such [a retained EU obligation] could (to any extent) be implemented (or enabled to be implemented) or complied with by the exercise by the Welsh Ministers of any of their functions, a Minister of the Crown may by order provide for the achievement by the Welsh Ministers (in the exercise of their functions) of so much of the result to be achieved under [the retained EU obligation] as is specified in the order.

(4) The order may specify the time by which any part of the result to be achieved by the Welsh Ministers is to be achieved.

(5) No order is to be made by a Minister of the Crown under subsection (3) unless the Minister of the Crown has consulted the Welsh Ministers.

(6) A statutory instrument containing an order under subsection (3) is subject to annulment in pursuance of a resolution of either House of Parliament.

(7) Where an order under subsection (3) is in force in relation to [a retained EU obligation], to the extent that [the retained EU obligation] involves achieving what is specified in the order it is also an obligation of the Welsh Ministers (enforceable as if it were an obligation of the Welsh Ministers under subsection (1)).

(8)–[8L] . . .

(9) [Subsection (1) applies] to the First Minister and the Counsel General as to the Welsh Ministers.

81–86   *****

Property, rights and liabilities

87   Property, rights and liabilities of Welsh Ministers etc

(1) Property, rights and liabilities may belong to—

    (a) the Welsh Ministers by that name,

    (b) the First Minister by that name, or

    (c) the Counsel General by that name.

(2) Property and rights acquired by or transferred to the Welsh Ministers belong to, and liabilities incurred by the Welsh Ministers are liabilities of, the Welsh Ministers for the time being.

(3) Property and rights acquired by or transferred to any of the Welsh Ministers appointed under section 48 belong to, and liabilities incurred by any of those Welsh Ministers are liabilities of, the Welsh Ministers for the time being.

(4) Property and rights acquired by or transferred to the First Minister belong to, and liabilities incurred by the First Minister are liabilities of, the First Minister for the time being.

(5) Property and rights acquired by or transferred to the Counsel General belong to, and liabilities incurred by the Counsel General are liabilities of, the Counsel General for the time being.

(6) In relation to property and rights acquired by or transferred to (or belonging to), or to liabilities incurred by—

(a) the Welsh Ministers or any of the Welsh Ministers appointed under section 48,

(b) the First Minister, or

(c) the Counsel General,

references to the Welsh Ministers, the First Minister or the Counsel General in any register or other document are to be read in accordance with this section.

88–92 *****

93–[106A] ...

Power

107   Acts of the [Senedd]

(1) The [Senedd] may make laws, to be known as Acts of [Senedd Cymru or Deddfau Senedd Cymru (referred to in this Act as 'Acts of the Senedd')].

(2) Proposed Acts of the [Senedd] are to be known as Bills; and a Bill becomes an Act of the [Senedd] when it has been passed by the [Senedd] and has received Royal Assent.

(3) The validity of an Act of the [Senedd] is not affected by any invalidity in the [Senedd] proceedings leading to its enactment.

(4) Every Act of the [Senedd] is to be judicially noticed.

(5) This Part does not affect the power of the Parliament of the United Kingdom to make laws for Wales.

[(6) But it is recognised that the Parliament of the United Kingdom will not normally legislate with regard to devolved matters without the consent of the [Senedd].]

108   ...

[108A   Legislative competence]

[(1) An Act of the [Senedd] is not law so far as any provision of the Act is outside the [Senedd's] legislative competence.

(2) A provision is outside that competence so far as any of the following paragraphs apply—

(a) it extends otherwise than only to England and Wales;

(b) it applies otherwise than in relation to Wales or confers, imposes, modifies or removes (or gives power to confer, impose, modify or remove) functions exercisable otherwise than in relation to Wales;

(c) it relates to reserved matters (see Schedule 7A);

(d) it breaches any of the restrictions in Part 1 of Schedule 7B, having regard to any exception in Part 2 of that Schedule from those restrictions;

(e) it is incompatible with the Convention rights ...

(3) But subsection (2)(b) does not apply to a provision that—

(a) is ancillary to a provision of any Act of the [Senedd] or Assembly Measure or to a devolved provision of an Act of Parliament, and

(b) has no greater effect otherwise than in relation to Wales, or in relation to functions exercisable otherwise than in relation to Wales, than is necessary to give effect to the purpose of that provision.

(4) For this purpose, a provision of an Act of Parliament is 'devolved' if it would be within the [Senedd's] legislative competence if it were contained in an Act of the [Senedd] (ignoring any requirement for consent or consultation imposed under paragraph 8, 10 or 11 of Schedule 7B or otherwise).

[(4A) References in subsections (2)(b) and (3) to Wales include, in relation to a relevant provision of an Act of the Senedd, the area of the Welsh zone beyond the seaward limit of the territorial sea.

A provision of an Act of the Senedd is 'relevant' if it relates to fishing, fisheries or fish health.]

(5) In determining what is necessary for the purposes of subsection (3), any power to make laws other than that of the [Senedd] is disregarded.

(6) The question whether a provision of an Act of the [Senedd] relates to a reserved matter is determined by reference to the purpose of the provision, having regard (among other things) to its effect in all the circumstances.

(7) For the purposes of this Act a provision is ancillary to another provision if it—

    (a) provides for the enforcement of the other provision or is otherwise appropriate for making that provision effective, or

    (b) is otherwise incidental to, or consequential on, that provision.]

109 Legislative competence: supplementary

(1) Her Majesty may by Order in Council amend [Schedule 7A or 7B].

(2) An Order in Council under this section may make such modifications of—

    (a) any enactment (including any enactment comprised in or made under this Act) or prerogative instrument, or

    (b) any other instrument or document, as Her Majesty considers appropriate in connection with the provision made by the Order in Council.

(3) An Order in Council under this section may make provision having retrospective effect.

(4), (5) *****

109A ...

110 Introduction of Bills

(1) A Bill may, subject to the standing orders, be introduced in the [Senedd] —

    (a) by the First Minister, any Welsh Minister appointed under section 48 any Deputy Welsh Minister or the Counsel General, or

    (b) by any other [Member of the Senedd].

(2) The person in charge of a Bill must, on or before the introduction of the Bill, state that, in that person's view, its provisions would be within the [Senedd's] legislative competence.

(3) The Presiding Officer must, on or before the introduction of a Bill in the [Senedd]—

    (a) decide whether or not, in the view of the Presiding Officer, the provisions of the Bill would be within the [Senedd's] legislative competence, and

    (b) state that decision.

(4) A statement under this section must be made in both English and Welsh; but, subject to that, the form of the statement and the manner in which it is to be made are to be determined under the standing orders.

(5) The standing orders—

    (a) may provide for a statement under this section to be published, and

    (b) if they do so, must provide for it to be published in both English and Welsh.

[110A Introduction of Bills: justice impact assessment]

[(1) The standing orders must include provision requiring the person in charge of a Bill, on or before the introduction of the Bill, to make a written statement setting out the potential impact (if any) on the justice system in England and Wales of the provisions of the Bill (a 'justice impact assessment').

(2) The form of the justice impact assessment and the manner in which it is to be made are to be determined under the standing orders.

(3) The standing orders must provide for the justice impact assessment to be published.]

111 Proceedings on Bills

(1) The standing orders must include provision—

    (a) for general debate on a Bill with an opportunity for [Members of the Senedd] to vote on its general principles,

    (b) for the consideration of, and an opportunity for [Members of the Senedd] to vote on, the details of a Bill, and

    (c) for a final stage at which a Bill can be passed or rejected.

(2) Subsection (1) does not prevent the standing orders making provision to enable the [Senedd] to expedite proceedings in relation to a particular Bill.

(3) The standing orders may make provision different from that required by subsection (1) for the procedure applicable to Bills of any of the following kinds—

(a) Bills which restate the law,

(b) Bills which repeal or revoke spent enactments, and

(c) private Bills.

(4) The standing orders must include provision for securing that the [Senedd] may only pass a Bill containing provisions which would, if contained in a Bill for an Act of Parliament, require the consent of Her Majesty or the Duke of Cornwall if such consent has been signified in accordance with the standing orders.

(5) The standing orders must include provision for securing that the [Senedd] may only pass a Bill if the text of the Bill is in both English and Welsh, unless the circumstances are such as are specified by the standing orders as any in which the text need not be in both languages.

(6) The standing orders must provide for an opportunity for the reconsideration of a Bill after its passing if (and only if)—

[(za) the Supreme Court decides on a reference made in relation to the Bill under section 111B(2)(b) (reference following Presiding Officer's decision that Bill does not contain protected subject-matter) that any provision of the Bill relates to a protected subject-matter,]

(a) the Supreme Court decides on a reference made in relation to the Bill under section 112 that the Bill or any provision of it would not be within the [Senedd's] legislative competence,

(b) ... or

(c) an order is made in relation to the Bill under section 114.

[(6A) The standing orders must provide for an opportunity for the reconsideration of a Bill after its rejection if (and only if), on a reference made in relation to the Bill under section 111B(2)(a) (reference following Presiding Officer's decision that Bill contains protected subject-matter), the Supreme Court decides that no provision that is subject to the reference relates to a protected subject-matter.]

[(7) The standing orders must, in particular, ensure that—

(a) any Bill amended on reconsideration in accordance with standing orders made by virtue of subsection (6)(a) ... or (c), and

(b) any Bill reconsidered in accordance with standing orders made by virtue of subsection (6)(za) or (6A),

is subject to a final stage at which it can be approved or rejected.]

(8) References in subsections (4), (5) and (6) of this section and sections 107(2), 109(5)[, 111A(3) and (4), 111B(2)(b)][, 116(3) and 116C(4)] to the passing of a Bill are, in the case of a Bill [to which subsection (7)(a) or (b) applies], to be read as references to its approval.

[111A   Bills with protected subject-matter: super-majority requirement]

[(1) For the purposes of this Part a provision of a Bill relates to a protected subject-matter if it would modify, or confer power to modify, any of the matters listed in subsection (2) (but not if the provision is incidental to or consequential on another provision of the Bill).

(2) The matters are—

(a) the name of the [Senedd],

(b) the persons entitled to vote as electors at an election for membership of the [Senedd],

(c) the system by which members of the [Senedd] are returned,

(d) the specification or number of constituencies, regions or any equivalent electoral area,

(e) the number of members to be returned for each constituency, region or equivalent electoral area, and

(f) the number of persons who may hold the office of Welsh Minister appointed under section 48 or the office of Deputy Welsh Minister.

(3) The Presiding Officer must, after the last time when a Bill may be amended but before the decision whether to pass or reject it—

(a) decide whether or not, in the view of the Presiding Officer, any provision of the Bill relates to a protected subject-matter, and

(b) state that decision.

(4) If the Presiding Officer decides that any provision of the Bill relates to a protected subject-matter, the Bill is not passed unless the number of [Members of the Senedd] voting in favour of it at the final stage is at least two-thirds of the total number of [Senedd] seats.]

[111B Scrutiny of Bills by the Supreme Court (protected subject-matter)]

[(1) The Counsel General or the Attorney General may refer the question whether any provision of a Bill relates to a protected subject-matter to the Supreme Court for decision.

(2) Subject to subsection (3), the Counsel General or the Attorney General may make a reference in relation to a Bill—

(a) at any time during the period of four weeks beginning with the rejection of the Bill, if the Presiding Officer has decided under section 111A(3) that a provision of the Bill relates to a protected subject-matter, or

(b) at any time during the period of four weeks beginning with the passing of the Bill, if the Presiding Officer has decided under section 111A(3) that no provision of the Bill relates to a protected subject-matter, unless the number of [Members of the Senedd] voting in favour of the Bill at its passing is at least two-thirds of the total number of [Senedd] seats.

(3) No reference may be made in relation to a Bill—

(a) by the Counsel General if the Counsel General has notified the Presiding Officer that no reference is to be made in relation to it by the Counsel General, or

(b) by the Attorney General if the Attorney General has notified the Presiding Officer that no reference is to be made in relation to it by the Attorney General.

(4) But subsection (3) does not apply if the Bill has, since the notification, been approved or rejected in accordance with standing orders made by virtue of section 111(7).]

112 Scrutiny of Bills by Supreme Court [(legislative competence)]

(1) The Counsel General or the Attorney General may refer the question whether a Bill, or any provision of a Bill, would be within the [Senedd's] legislative competence to the Supreme Court for decision.

(2) Subject to subsection (3), the Counsel General or the Attorney General may make a reference in relation to a Bill at any time during—

(a) the period of four weeks beginning with the passing of the Bill, and

(b) any period of four weeks beginning with ... approval of the Bill in accordance with provision included in the standing orders in compliance with section 111(7).

(3) No reference may be made in relation to a Bill—

(a) by the Counsel General if the Counsel General has notified the [Presiding Officer] that no reference is to be made in relation to it by the Counsel General, or

(b) by the Attorney General if the Attorney General has notified the [Presiding Officer] that no reference is to be made in relation to it by the Attorney General.

(4) But subsection (3) does not apply if the Bill has been approved as mentioned in subsection (2)(b) since the notification.

113 ...

114 Power to intervene in certain cases

(1) This section applies if a Bill contains provisions which the Secretary of State has reasonable grounds to believe—

(a) would have an adverse effect on [a reserved matter],

(b) ...

(c) would have an adverse effect on the operation of the law as it applies in England, or

(d) would be incompatible with any international obligation or the interests of defence or national security.

(2) The Secretary of State may make an order prohibiting the [Presiding Officer] from submitting the Bill for Royal Assent.

(3) The order must identify the Bill and the provisions in question and state the reasons for making the order.

(4) The order may be made at any time during—

(a) the period of four weeks beginning with the passing of the Bill,

(b) any period of four weeks beginning with any approval of the Bill in accordance with provision included in the standing orders in compliance with section 111(7), or

(c) if a reference is made in relation to the Bill under section [111B or] 112, the period of four weeks beginning with the reference being decided or otherwise disposed of by the Supreme Court.

(5) The Secretary of State must not make an order in relation to a Bill if the Secretary of State has notified the [Presiding Officer] that no order is to be made in relation to the Bill.

(6) Subsection (5) does not apply if the Bill has been approved as mentioned in subsection (4)(b) since the notification.

(7) An order in force under this section at a time when such approval is given ceases to have effect.

(8) A statutory instrument containing an order under this section is subject to annulment in pursuance of a resolution of either House of Parliament.

115   Royal Assent

(1) It is for the [Presiding Officer] to submit Bills for Royal Assent.

(2) The [Presiding Officer] may not submit a Bill for Royal Assent at any time when—

(a) the Attorney General or the Counsel General is entitled to make a reference in relation to the Bill under section [111B or] 112,

(b) such a reference has been made but has not been decided or otherwise disposed of by the Supreme Court, or

(c) an order may be made in relation to the Bill under section 114.

(3) The [Presiding Officer] may not submit a Bill in its unamended form for Royal Assent if—

(a) the Supreme Court has decided on a reference made in relation to the Bill under section 112 that the Bill or any provision of it would not be within the [Senedd's] legislative competence, ...

(b) ...

[(3A) The Presiding Officer may not submit a Bill for Royal Assent if the Supreme Court has decided on a reference made in relation to the Bill under section 111B(2)(b) (reference following Presiding Officer's decision that Bill does not contain protected subject-matter) that any provision of the Bill relates to a protected subject-matter unless, since the decision, the Bill has been approved in accordance with standing orders made by virtue of section 111(7).]

(4) A Bill receives Royal Assent when Letters Patent under the Welsh Seal signed with Her Majesty's own hand signifying Her Assent are notified to the Clerk.

[(4A)]–(7) *****

116   *****

[PART 4A   TAXATION

Chapter 1   Introductory

116A   Overview of Part 4A

(1) In this Part[—

(a) Chapter 2 confers on the [Senedd] power to set rates of income tax to be paid by Welsh taxpayers, and

(b) Chapters 3 and 4 specify particular taxes as devolved about which the [Senedd] may make provision in the exercise of the power conferred by section 107(1).

(2) The power to make provision about a devolved tax is subject to the restrictions imposed by—

(a) subsection (3), and

(b) the other provisions of this Part.

(3) A devolved tax may not be imposed where to do so would be incompatible with any international obligations.

(4) In this Act 'devolved tax' means a tax specified in this Part as a devolved tax.]

[116B], [116C] *****

[Chapter 2   Income Tax]

[116D   Power to set Welsh rates for Welsh taxpayers

(1) The [Senedd] may be resolution (a 'Welsh rate resolution') set one or more of the following—

(a) a Welsh rate for the purpose of calculating the Welsh basic rate;

(b) a Welsh rate for the purpose of calculating the Welsh higher rate;

(c) a Welsh rate for the purpose of calculating the Welsh additional rate.

(2) See section 6B of the Income Tax Act 2007 for provision about the calculation of the Welsh basic, higher and additional rates and section 11B of that Act for provision about the income of Welsh taxpayers charged at those rates.

(3) A Welsh rate resolution applies—

(a) for only one tax year, and

(b) for the whole of that year.

(4) Any Welsh rate specified must be a whole number or half a whole number.

(5) A Welsh rate resolution—

(a) must specify the tax year for which it applies,

(b) must be made before the start of that tax year, and

(c) must not be made more than 12 months before the start of that year.

(6) If a Welsh rate resolution is cancelled before the start of the tax year for which it is to apply—

(a) The Income Tax Acts have effect for that year as if the resolution had never been made, and

(b) The resolution may be replaced by another Welsh rate resolution.

(7) The standing orders must provide that only the First Minister or a Welsh Minister appointed under section 48 may move a motion for a Welsh rate resolution.]

[116E]–166 *****

SCHEDULE 1 . . .

SCHEDULES [1A]–4 *****

SCHEDULE 5–7 . . .

Section 108A   ## SCHEDULE 7A

RESERVED MATTERS

PART 1*   GENERAL RESERVATIONS

The Constitution

1. The following aspects of the constitution are reserved matters—

(a) the Crown, including succession to the Crown and a regency;

(b) the union of the nations of Wales and England;

(c) the Parliament of the United Kingdom.

---

* **Editor's Note:** Part 2 of Sch. 7A contains a further list of exceptions which takes the number up to 200 but for reasons of space these are omitted here.

2.—(1) Paragraph 1 does not reserve—
    (a) Her Majesty's executive functions,
    (b) functions exercisable by any person acting on behalf of the Crown, or
    (c) the use of the Welsh Seal.

(2) Sub-paragraph (1) does not affect the reservation by paragraph 1 of the management (in accordance with any enactment regulating the use of land) of the Crown Estate.

(3) Sub-paragraph (1) does not affect the reservation by paragraph 1 of the functions of the Security Service, the Secret Intelligence Service and the Government Communications Headquarters.

(4) In this paragraph 'executive function' does not include a function conferred or imposed by or by virtue of any legislation or the prerogative.

3.—(1) Paragraph 1 does not reserve property belonging—
    (a) to Her Majesty in right of the Crown,
    (b) to Her Majesty in right of the Duchy of Lancaster, or
    (c) to the Duchy of Cornwall.

(2) Paragraph 1 does not reserve property belonging to any person acting on behalf of the Crown or held in trust for Her Majesty for the purposes of any person acting on behalf of the Crown.

(3) Sub-paragraphs (1) and (2) do not affect the reservation by paragraph 1 of—
    (a) the hereditary revenues of the Crown,
    (b) the royal arms and standard, or
    (c) the compulsory acquisition of property—
        (i)   belonging to Her Majesty in right of the Crown;
        (ii) belonging to Her Majesty in right of the Duchy of Lancaster;
        (iii) belonging to the Duchy of Cornwall;
        (iv) held or used by a Minister of the Crown or government department.

4.—(1) Paragraph 1 does not reserve property held by Her Majesty in Her private capacity.

(2) Sub-paragraph (1) does not affect the reservation by paragraph 1 of the subject-matter of the Crown Private Estates Acts 1800 to 1873.

Public service

5. The Civil Service of the State is a reserved matter.

Political parties

6. The following are reserved matters—
    (a) the registration of political parties;
    (b) funding of political parties and of their members and officers;
    (c) accounting requirements in relation to political parties;
but this is subject to paragraph 7.

7. Paragraph 6 does not reserve making payments to any political party for the purpose of assisting members of the [Senedd] who are connected with the party to perform their [Senedd] duties.

Single legal jurisdiction of England and Wales

8.—(1) The following are reserved matters—
    (a) courts (including, in particular, their creation and jurisdiction);
    (b) judges (including, in particular, their appointment and remuneration);
    (c) civil or criminal proceedings (including, in particular, bail, costs, custody pending trial, disclosure, enforcement of orders of courts, evidence, sentencing, limitation of actions, procedure, prosecutors and remedies);
    (d) pardons for criminal offences;
    (e) private international law;
    (f) judicial review of administrative action.
(See also paragraphs 3 and 4 of Schedule 7B (restrictions on modifying private law and criminal law).)

(2) The reference to prosecutors in sub-paragraph (1)(c) does not prevent an Act of the [Senedd] from making provision about responsibility for the prosecution of devolved offences.

(3) Sub-paragraph (1) does not reserve—

(a) welfare advice to courts in respect of family proceedings in which the welfare of children ordinarily resident in Wales is or may be in question;

(b) representation in respect of such proceedings;

(c) the provision of support (including information and advice), to children ordinarily resident in Wales and their families, in respect of such proceedings;

(d) Welsh family proceedings officers.

Tribunals

9.—(1) Tribunals, including—

(a) their membership,

(b) the appointment and remuneration of their members,

(c) their functions and procedure, and

(d) appeals against their decisions,

are a reserved matter.

(2) But this paragraph does not apply to a tribunal (a 'devolved tribunal') all of whose functions are functions that—

(a) are exercisable only in relation to Wales, and

(b) do not relate to reserved matters.

(3) In the case of a tribunal which has functions that do not relate to reserved matters, sub-paragraph (1) does not reserve any function of deciding an appeal or application which—

(a) relates to a matter that is not a reserved matter, and

(b) is not an appeal against the decision of a tribunal (other than a devolved tribunal),

but it does reserve the tribunal's procedure in relation to that function.

(4) In determining for the purposes of this paragraph whether functions of a tribunal are exercisable only in relation to Wales, no account is taken of any function that—

(a) is exercisable otherwise than in relation to Wales, and

(b) could (apart from paragraph 8 of Schedule 7B) be conferred or imposed by provision falling within the [Senedd's] legislative competence (by virtue of section 108A(3)).

[(4A) References in this paragraph to Wales include, in relation to a relevant function of a tribunal, the area of the Welsh zone beyond the seaward limit of the territorial sea.

A function of a tribunal is 'relevant' if it relates to fishing, fisheries or fish health.]

(5) Where the question whether this paragraph applies to a particular tribunal is relevant to determining whether a provision of an Act of the [Senedd] is within the [Senedd's] legislative competence, the time for deciding the question is the time when the Act is passed.

Foreign affairs etc

10.—(1) International relations, regulation of international trade, and international development assistance and co-operation are reserved matters.

(2) In sub-paragraph (1) 'international relations' includes—

(a) relations with territories outside the United Kingdom;

(b) relations with the EU and its institutions;

(c) relations with other international organisations.

(3) But sub-paragraph (1) does not reserve—

(a) observing and implementing international obligations [and] obligations under the Human Rights Convention . . . , or

(b) assisting Ministers of the Crown in relation to any matter to which that sub-paragraph applies.

(4) In this paragraph 'the Human Rights Convention' means—

(a) the Convention for the Protection of Human Rights and Fundamental Freedoms, agreed by the Council of Europe at Rome on 4th November 1950, and

(b) the Protocols to the Convention,

as they have effect for the time being in relation to the United Kingdom.

Defence

11. The following are reserved matters—
    (a) the defence of the realm;
    (b) the naval, military or air forces of the Crown, including reserve forces;
    (c) visiting forces;
    (d) international headquarters and defence organisations;
    (e) trading with the enemy and enemy property.

*****

Section 108A   **SCHEDULE 7B**

GENERAL RESTRICTIONS

PART 1   GENERAL RESTRICTIONS

The law on reserved matters

1.—(1) A provision of an Act of the [Senedd] cannot make modifications of, or confer power by subordinate legislation to make modifications of, the law on reserved matters.

(2) 'The law on reserved matters' means—
    (a) any enactment the subject-matter of which is a reserved matter and which is comprised in an Act of Parliament or subordinate legislation under an Act of Parliament, and
    (b) any rule of law which is not contained in an enactment and the subject-matter of which is a reserved matter,
and in this sub-paragraph 'Act of Parliament' does not include this Act.

2.—(1) Paragraph 1 does not apply to a modification that—
    (a) is ancillary to a provision made (whether by the Act in question or another enactment) which does not relate to reserved matters, and
    (b) has no greater effect on reserved matters than is necessary to give effect to the purpose of that provision.

(2) In determining what is necessary for the purposes of this paragraph, any power to make laws other than the power of the [Senedd] is disregarded.

Private law

3.—(1) A provision of an Act of the [Senedd] cannot make modifications of, or confer power by subordinate legislation to make modifications of, the private law.

(2) 'The private law' means the law of contract, agency, bailment, tort, unjust enrichment and restitution, property, trusts and succession.

(3) In sub-paragraph (2) the reference to the law of property does not include intellectual property rights relating to plant varieties or seeds but does include the compulsory acquisition of property.

(4) Sub-paragraph (1) does not apply to a modification that has a purpose (other than modification of the private law) which does not relate to a reserved matter.

Criminal law

4.—(1) A provision of an Act of the [Senedd] cannot—
    (a) make modifications of, or confer power by subordinate legislation to make modifications of, an offence in a listed category;
    (b) create, or confer power by subordinate legislation to create, an offence in a listed category.

(2) The listed categories of offences are—
    (a) treason and related offences;

(b) homicide offences (including offences relating to suicide) and other offences against the person (including offences involving violence or threats of violence) that are triable only on indictment;

(c) sexual offences (including offences relating to indecent or pornographic images);

(d) offences of a kind dealt with by the Perjury Act 1911.

(3) A provision of an Act of the [Senedd] cannot make modifications of, or confer power by subordinate legislation to make modifications of, the law about—

(a) criminal responsibility and capacity,

(b) the meaning of intention, recklessness, dishonesty and other mental elements of offences,

(c) inchoate and secondary criminal liability, or

(d) sentences and other orders and disposals in respect of defendants in criminal proceedings, or otherwise in respect of criminal conduct, and their effect and operation.

(4) For the purposes of this paragraph, a modification of the law relating to defences to an offence is a modification of the offence.

(5) This paragraph does not affect the reservation, by virtue of Schedule 7A, of the creation or modification of offences in relation to reserved matters.

(See also paragraph 8 of that Schedule (single legal jurisdiction of England and Wales).)

Enactments other than this Act

5.—(1) A provision of an Act of the [Senedd] cannot make modifications of, or confer power by subordinate legislation to make modifications of, any of the provisions listed in the table below—

Enactment	*Provisions protected from modification*
…	…
Government of Wales Act 1998	Section 144(7).
Human Rights Act 1998	The whole Act.
Civil Contingencies Act 2004	The whole Act.
Energy Act 2008	Section 100 and regulations under that section.
[The European Union (Withdrawal) Act 2018	The whole Act [other than any excluded provision].]
[The United Kingdom Internal Market Act 2020	The whole Act.]

[(1A) For the purposes of the entry in the table in sub-paragraph (1) for the European Union (Withdrawal) Act 2018, the following are excluded provisions of that Act—

(a) section 1B(3) and (4),

(b) sections 8A to 8C,

(c) section 10(3) and (4),

(d) sections 13A and 13B,

(e) sections 15A to 15C,

(f) Parts 1A to 1C of Schedule 2, and

(g) paragraphs 8A to 8G of Schedule 7.]

(2) A provision of an Act of the [Senedd] cannot, unless it is an oversight provision, make modifications of—

(a) section 146A(1) of the Government of Wales Act 1998, or

(b) sections 2(1) to (3), 3(2) to (4) or 6(2) and (3) of the Public Audit (Wales) Act 2013 (anaw 3),

or confer power by subordinate legislation to do so.

(3) A provision of an Act of the [Senedd] cannot, unless it is an oversight provision and also a non-governmental committee provision—

(a) make modifications of section 8(1) of the Public Audit (Wales) Act 2013 so far as that section relates to the Auditor General's exercise of functions free from the direction or control of the [Senedd] or Welsh Government, or

(b) confer power by subordinate legislation to do so.

(4) An 'oversight provision' is a provision of an Act of the [Senedd] that—

(a) relates to the oversight or supervision of the Auditor General or of the exercise of the Auditor General's functions, or

(b) is ancillary to a provision falling within paragraph (a).

(5) A 'non-governmental committee provision' is a provision conferring functions on a committee of the [Senedd] that—

(a) does not consist of or include members of the Welsh Government, and

(b) is not chaired by [a Member of the Senedd] who is a member of a political group with an executive role,

or a provision conferring power by subordinate legislation to do so.

(6) A person designated under section 46(5) to exercise the functions of the First Minister is treated as a member of the Welsh Government for the purposes of sub-paragraph (5)(a).

6.–12. *****

PART 2   GENERAL EXCEPTIONS FROM PART 1

Restatement

13.—(1) Part 1 does not prevent an Act of the [Senedd]—

(a) restating the law (or restating it with such modifications as are not prevented by that Part), or

(b) repealing or revoking any spent enactment,

or conferring power by subordinate legislation to do so.

(2) For the purposes of paragraph 1, the law on reserved matters includes any restatement in an Act of the [Senedd] or an [Senedd] Measure, or subordinate legislation under such an Act or Measure, of the law on reserved matters if the subject-matter of the restatement is a reserved matter.

Subordinate legislation

14. Part 1 does not prevent an Act of the [Senedd] making modifications of, or conferring power by subordinate legislation to make modifications of, an enactment for or in connection with any of the following purposes—

(a) making different provision about the document by which a power to make, confirm or approve subordinate legislation is to be exercised;

(b) making provision (or no provision) for the procedure, in relation to the [Senedd], to which legislation made in the exercise of such a power (or the instrument or other document in which it is contained) is to be subject;

(c) applying any enactment comprised in or made under an Act of the [Senedd] relating to the documents by which such powers may be exercised.

SCHEDULE 8 ...

SCHEDULE 9 DEVOLUTION ISSUES

PART 1 PRELIMINARY

1.—(1) In this Schedule 'devolution issue' means—

(a) a question whether [a Senedd] Measure or Act of the [Senedd], or any provision of [a Senedd] Measure or Act of the [Senedd], is within the [Senedd's] legislative competence,

(b) a question whether any function (being a function which any person has purported, or is proposing, to exercise) is exercisable by the Welsh Ministers, the First Minister or the Counsel General,

(c) a question whether the purported or proposed exercise of a function by the Welsh Ministers, the First Minister or the Counsel General is, or would be, within the powers of the Welsh Ministers, the First Minister or the Counsel General (including a question whether a purported or proposed exercise of a function is, or would be, outside those powers by virtue of section 80(8) or 81(1)),

(d) a question whether there has been any failure to comply with a duty imposed on the Welsh Ministers, the First Minister or the Counsel General (including any obligation imposed by virtue of section 80(1) or (7)), or

(e) a question of whether a failure to act by the Welsh Ministers, the First Minister or the Counsel General is incompatible with any of the Convention rights.

(2) *****

2. A devolution issue is not to be taken to arise in any proceedings merely because of any contention of a party to the proceedings which appears to the court or tribunal before which the proceedings take place to be frivolous or vexatious.

PART 2 PROCEEDINGS IN ENGLAND AND WALES

Application of Part 2

3. This Part applies in relation to devolution issues in proceedings in England and Wales.

Institution of proceedings

4.—(1) Proceedings for the determination of a devolution issue may be instituted by the Attorney General or the Counsel General.

(2) The Counsel General may defend any such proceedings instituted by the Attorney General.

(3) This paragraph does not limit any power to institute or defend proceedings exercisable apart from this paragraph by any person.

Notice of devolution issue

5.—(1) A court or tribunal must order notice of any devolution issue which arises in any proceedings before it to be given to the Attorney General and the Counsel General (unless a party to the proceedings).

(2) A person to whom notice is given in pursuance of sub-paragraph (1) may take part as a party in the proceedings, so far as they relate to a devolution issue.

Reference of devolution issue to High Court or Court of Appeal

6. A magistrates' court may refer any devolution issue which arises in civil proceedings before it to the High Court.

7.—(1) A court may refer any devolution issue which arises in civil proceedings before it to the Court of Appeal.

(2) Sub-paragraph (1) does not apply—

(a) to a magistrates' court, the Court of Appeal or the [Supreme Court], or

(b) to the High Court if the devolution issue arises in proceedings on a reference under paragraph 6.

8. A tribunal from which there is no appeal must refer any devolution issue which arises in proceedings before it to the Court of Appeal; and any other tribunal may make such a reference.

9. A court, other than the Court of Appeal or the [Supreme Court], may refer any devolution issue which arises in criminal proceedings before it to—

(a) the High Court if the proceedings are summary proceedings, or

(b) the Court of Appeal if the proceedings are proceedings on indictment.

References from Court of Appeal to [Supreme Court]

10. The Court of Appeal may refer any devolution issue which arises in proceedings before it (otherwise than on a reference under paragraph 7, 8 or 9) to the [Supreme Court].

Appeals from superior courts to [Supreme Court]

11. An appeal against a determination of a devolution issue by the High Court or the Court of Appeal on a reference under paragraph 6, 7, 8 or 9 lies to the [Supreme Court] but only—

    (a) with [permission] of the court from which the appeal lies, or

    (b) failing such [permission], with [permission] of the [Supreme Court].

*****

Immigration, Asylum and Nationality Act 2006

(2006, c. 13)

An Act to make provision about immigration, asylum and nationality; and for connected purposes.

[30th March 2006]

Territorial extent: United Kingdom

1–6 ...

7–14 *****

Employment

15 Penalty

(1) It is contrary to this section to employ an adult subject to immigration control if—

    (a) he has not been granted leave to enter or remain in the United Kingdom, or

    (b) his leave to enter or remain in the United Kingdom—

        (i) is invalid,

        (ii) has ceased to have effect (whether by reason of curtailment, revocation, cancellation, passage of time or otherwise), or

        (iii) is subject to a condition preventing him from accepting the employment.

(2) The Secretary of State may give an employer who acts contrary to this section a notice requiring him to pay a penalty of a specified amount not exceeding the prescribed maximum.

(3) An employer is excused from paying a penalty if he shows that he complied with any prescribed requirements in relation to the employment.

(4) But the excuse in subsection (3) shall not apply to an employer who knew, at any time during the period of the employment, that it was contrary to this section.

(5) The Secretary of State may give a penalty notice without having established whether subsection (3) applies.

(6) A penalty notice must—

    (a) state why the Secretary of State thinks the employer is liable to the penalty,

    (b) state the amount of the penalty,

    (c) specify a date, at least 28 days after the date specified in the notice as the date on which it is given, before which the penalty must be paid,

    (d) specify how the penalty must be paid,

    (e) explain how the employer may object to the penalty [or make an appeal against it], and

    (f) explain how the Secretary of State may enforce the penalty.

(7) An order prescribing requirements for the purposes of subsection (3) may, in particular—

    (a) require the production to an employer of a document of a specified description;

    (b) require the production to an employer of one document of each of a number of specified descriptions;

    (c) require an employer to take specified steps to verify, retain, copy or record the content of a document produced to him in accordance with the order;

    (d) require action to be taken before employment begins;

    (e) require action to be taken at specified intervals or on specified occasions during the course of employment.

16 Objection

(1) This section applies where an employer to whom a penalty notice is given objects on the ground that—

    (a) he is not liable to the imposition of a penalty,

    (b) he is excused payment by virtue of section 15(3), or

    (c) the amount of the penalty is too high.

(2) The employer may give a notice of objection to the Secretary of State.

(3) A notice of objection must—

    (a) be in writing,

    (b) give the objector's reasons,

    (c) be given in the prescribed manner, and

    (d) be given before the end of the prescribed period.

(4) Where the Secretary of State receives a notice of objection to a penalty he shall consider it and—

    (a) cancel the penalty,

    (b) reduce the penalty,

    (c) increase the penalty, or

    (d) determine to take no action.

(5) Where the Secretary of State considers a notice of objection he shall—

    (a) have regard to the code of practice under section 19 (in so far as the objection relates to the amount of the penalty),

    (b) inform the objector of his decision before the end of the prescribed period or such longer period as he may agree with the objector,

    (c) if he increases the penalty, issue a new penalty notice under section 15, and

    (d) if he reduces the penalty, notify the objector of the reduced amount.

17 Appeal

(1) An employer to whom a penalty notice is given may appeal to the court on the ground that—

    (a) he is not liable to the imposition of a penalty,

    (b) he is excused payment by virtue of section 15(3), or

    (c) the amount of the penalty is too high.

(2) The court may—

    (a) allow the appeal and cancel the penalty,

    (b) allow the appeal and reduce the penalty, or

    (c) dismiss the appeal.

(3) An appeal shall be a re-hearing of the Secretary of State's decision to impose a penalty and shall be determined having regard to—

    (a) the code of practice under section 19 that has effect at the time of the appeal (in so far as the appeal relates to the amount of the penalty), and

    (b) any other matters which the court thinks relevant (which may include matters of which the Secretary of State was unaware);

and this subsection has effect despite any provision of rules of court.

    (4)–(7) *****

18 *****

19 Code of practice

(1) The Secretary of State shall issue a code of practice specifying factors to be considered by him in determining the amount of a penalty imposed under section 15.

(2) The code—

    (a) shall not be issued unless a draft has been laid before Parliament, and

    (b) shall come into force in accordance with provision made by order of the Secretary of State.

(3) The Secretary of State shall from time to time review the code and may revise and re-issue it following a review; and a reference in this section to the code includes a reference to the code as revised.

20 *****

21 Offence

(1) A person commits an offence if he employs another ('the employee') knowing that the employee is [disqualified from employment by reason of the employee's immigration status].

[(1A) A person commits an offence if the person—

(a) employs another person ('the employee') who is disqualified from employment by reason of the employee's immigration status, and

(b) has reasonable cause to believe that the employee is disqualified from employment by reason of the employee's immigration status.

(1B) For the purposes of subsections (1) and (1A) a person is disqualified from employment by reason of the person's immigration status if the person is an adult subject to immigration control and—

(a) the person has not been granted leave to enter or remain in the United Kingdom, or

(b) the person's leave to enter or remain in the United Kingdom—

(i) is invalid,

(ii) has ceased to have effect (whether by reason of curtailment, revocation, cancellation, passage of time or otherwise), or

(iii) is subject to a condition preventing him from accepting the employment.]

(2)–(4) *****

22 Offence: bodies corporate, etc

(1) For the purposes of section 21(1) a body (whether corporate or not) shall be treated as knowing a fact about an employee if a person who has responsibility within the body for an aspect of the employment knows the fact.

[(1A) For the purposes of section 21(1A) a body (whether corporate or not) shall be treated as having reasonable cause to believe a fact about an employee if a person who has responsibility within the body for an aspect of the employment has reasonable cause to believe that fact.]

(2) If an offence under section 21(1) [or (1A)] is committed by a body corporate with the consent or connivance of an officer of the body, the officer, as well as the body, shall be treated as having committed the offence.

(3), (4) *****

23 Discrimination: code of practice

(1) The Secretary of State shall issue a code of practice specifying what an employer should or should not do in order to ensure that, while avoiding liability to a penalty under section 15 and while avoiding the commission of an offence under section 21, he also avoids contravening—

(a) [the Equality Act 2010, so far as relating to race], or

(b) the Race Relations (Northern Ireland) Order 1997 (S.I. 869 (N.I. 6)).

(2), (3) *****

(4) A breach of the code—

(a) shall not make a person liable to civil or criminal proceedings, but

(b) may be taken into account by a court or tribunal.

(5) The Secretary of State shall from time to time review the code and may revise and re-issue it following a review; and a reference in this section to the code includes a reference to the code as revised.

(6) *****

24–31 *****

32 Passenger and crew information: police powers

(1) This section applies to ships and aircraft which are—

(a) arriving, or expected to arrive, in the United Kingdom, or

(b) leaving, or expected to leave, the United Kingdom.

(2) The owner or agent of a ship or aircraft shall comply with any requirement imposed by a constable of the rank of superintendent or above to provide passenger or service information.

(3) A passenger or member of crew shall provide to the owner or agent of a ship or aircraft any information that he requires for the purpose of complying with a requirement imposed by virtue of subsection (2).

(4) A constable may impose a requirement under subsection (2) only if he thinks it necessary—

(a) in the case of a constable in England, Wales or Northern Ireland, for police purposes, or

(b) in the case of a constable in Scotland, for police purposes which are or relate to reserved matters.

(5), (6) *****

(7) The Secretary of State may make an order specifying a kind of information under subsection (5)(a) only if satisfied that the nature of the information is such that there are likely to be circumstances in which it can be required under subsection (2) without breaching Convention rights (within the meaning of the Human Rights Act 1998 (c. 42)).

(8) *****

[32A Regulations requiring information to be provided to police]

[(1) The Secretary of State may make regulations requiring responsible persons in relation to ships or aircraft—

(a) which have arrived, or are expected to arrive, in the United Kingdom, or

(b) which have left, or are expected to leave, the United Kingdom,

to provide information to the police.

(2) The following information may be required under subsection (1)—

(a) information about the persons on board;

(b) information about the voyage or flight.]

(3)–(7) *****

[32B] *****

33–35 *****

36 Duty to share information

(1) This section applies to—

[(a) designated customs officials,

(aa) immigration officers,

(ab) the Secretary of State in so far as the Secretary of State has general customs functions,

(ac) the Secretary of State in so far as the Secretary of State has functions relating to immigration, asylum or nationality,

(ad) the Director of Border Revenue and any person exercising functions of the Director,]

(b) a chief officer of police, and

(c) Her Majesty's Revenue and Customs.

(2) The persons specified in subsection (1) shall share information to which subsection (4) applies and which is obtained or held by them in the course of their functions to the extent that the information is likely to be of use for—

(a) immigration purposes,

(b) police purposes, or

(c) Revenue and Customs purposes.

(3) But a chief officer of police in Scotland shall share information under subsection (2) only to the extent that it is likely to be of use for—

(a) immigration purposes,

(b) police purposes, in so far as they are or relate to reserved matters within the meaning of the Scotland Act 1998, or

(c) Revenue and Customs purposes other than the prosecution of crime.

(4) This subsection applies to information which—

    (a) is obtained or held in the exercise of a power specified by the Secretary of State and the Treasury jointly by order and relates to—

        (i) passengers on a ship or aircraft,

        (ii) crew of a ship or aircraft,

        (iii) freight on a ship or aircraft, or

        (iv) flights or voyages, or

    (b) relates to such other matters in respect of travel or freight as the Secretary of State and the Treasury may jointly specify by order.

(5) The Secretary of State and the Treasury may make an order under subsection (4) which has the effect of requiring information to be shared only if satisfied that—

    (a) the sharing is likely to be of use for—

        (i) immigration purposes,

        (ii) police purposes, or

        (iii) Revenue and Customs purposes, and

    (b) the nature of the information is such that there are likely to be circumstances in which it can be shared under subsection (2) without breaching Convention rights (within the meaning of the Human Rights Act 1998 (c. 42)).

(6) Information shared in accordance with subsection (2)—

    (a) shall be made available to each of the persons [or descriptions of persons] specified in subsection (1), and

    (b) may be used for immigration purposes, police purposes or Revenue and Customs purposes (regardless of its source).

(7)–(10) *****

37 Information sharing: code of practice

(1) The Secretary of State and the Treasury shall jointly issue one or more codes of practice about—

    (a) the use of information shared in accordance with section 36(2), and

    (b) the extent to which, or form or manner in which, shared information is to be made available in accordance with section 36(6).

(2) A code—

    (a) shall not be issued unless a draft has been laid before Parliament, and

    (b) shall come into force in accordance with provision made by order of the Secretary of State and the Treasury jointly.

(3), (4) *****

38 ...
*****

Legislative and Regulatory Reform Act 2006

(2006, c. 51)

An Act to enable provision to be made for the purpose of removing or reducing burdens resulting from legislation and promoting regulatory principles; to make provision about the exercise of regulatory functions; to make provision about the interpretation of legislation relating to the European Communities and the European Economic Area; to make provision relating to section 2(2) of the European Communities Act 1972; and for connected purposes. [8th November 2006]

Territorial extent: United Kingdom

PART 1 ORDER-MAKING POWERS

Powers

1 Power to remove or reduce burdens

(1) A Minister of the Crown may by order under this section make any provision which he considers would serve the purpose in subsection (2).

(2) That purpose is removing or reducing any burden, or the overall burdens, resulting directly or indirectly for any person from any legislation.

(3) In this section 'burden' means any of the following—

(a) a financial cost;

(b) an administrative inconvenience;

(c) an obstacle to efficiency, productivity or profitability; or

(d) a sanction, criminal or otherwise, which affects the carrying on of any lawful activity.

(4) Provision may not be made under subsection (1) in relation to any burden which affects only a Minister of the Crown or government department, unless it affects the Minister or department in the exercise of a regulatory function.

(5) For the purposes of subsection (2), a financial cost or administrative inconvenience may result from the form of any legislation (for example, where the legislation is hard to understand).

(6) In this section 'legislation' means any of the following or a provision of any of the following—

(a)   a public general Act or local Act (whether passed before or after the commencement of this section), ...

[(aa) a Measure or Act of the Assembly, or]

(b)   any Order in Council, order, rules, regulations, scheme, warrant, byelaw or other subordinate instrument made at any time [under—

(a)   an Act referred to in paragraph (a), or

(b)   a Measure or Act of the Assembly],

but does not include any instrument which is, or is made under, Northern Ireland legislation.

(7) Subject to this Part, the provision that may be made under subsection (1) includes—

(a) provision abolishing, conferring or transferring, or providing for the delegation of, functions of any description,

(b) provision creating or abolishing a body or office,

and provision made by amending or repealing any enactment.

(8) An order under this section may contain such consequential, supplementary, incidental or transitional provision (including provision made by amending or repealing any enactment or other provision) as the Minister making it considers appropriate.

(9) An order under this section may bind the Crown.

(10) An order under this section must be made in accordance with this Part.

2 Power to promote regulatory principles

(1) A Minister of the Crown may by order under this section make any provision which he considers would serve the purpose in subsection (2).

(2) That purpose is securing that regulatory functions are exercised so as to comply with the principles in subsection (3).

(3) Those principles are that—

(a) regulatory activities should be carried out in a way which is transparent, accountable, proportionate and consistent;

(b) regulatory activities should be targeted only at cases in which action is needed.

(4) Subject to this Part, the provision that may be made under subsection (1) for the purpose in subsection (2) includes—

(a) provision modifying the way in which a regulatory function is exercised by any person,

(b) provision amending the constitution of a body exercising regulatory functions which is established by or under an enactment,

(c) provision transferring, or providing for the delegation of, the regulatory functions conferred on any person,

and provision made by amending or repealing any enactment.

(5) The provision referred to in subsection (4)(c) includes provision—

(a) to create a new body to which, or a new office to the holder of which, regulatory functions are transferred;

(b) to abolish a body from which, or office from the holder of which, regulatory functions are transferred.

(6) The provision that may be made under subsection (1) does not include provision conferring any new regulatory function or abolishing any regulatory function.

(7) An order under this section may contain such consequential, supplementary, incidental or transitional provision (including provision made by amending or repealing any enactment or other provision) as the Minister making it considers appropriate.

(8) An order under this section may bind the Crown.

(9) An order under this section must be made in accordance with this Part.

3 Preconditions

(1) A Minister may not make provision under section 1(1) or 2(1), other than provision which merely restates an enactment, unless he considers that the conditions in subsection (2), where relevant, are satisfied in relation to that provision.

(2) Those conditions are that—

(a) the policy objective intended to be secured by the provision could not be satisfactorily secured by non-legislative means;

(b) the effect of the provision is proportionate to the policy objective;

(c) the provision, taken as a whole, strikes a fair balance between the public interest and the interests of any person adversely affected by it;

(d) the provision does not remove any necessary protection;

(e) the provision does not prevent any person from continuing to exercise any right or freedom which that person might reasonably expect to continue to exercise;

(f) the provision is not of constitutional significance.

(3) A Minister may not make provision under section 1(1) or 2(1) which merely restates an enactment unless he considers that the condition in subsection (4) is satisfied in relation to that provision.

(4) That condition is that the provision made would make the law more accessible or more easily understood.

(5) In this section and sections 4 to 7, to 'restate' an enactment means to replace it with alterations only of form or arrangement (and for these purposes to remove an ambiguity is to make an alteration other than one of form or arrangement).

4 Subordinate legislation

(1) An order under this Part may only confer or transfer a function of legislating on or to—

(a) a Minister of the Crown;

(b) any person on or to whom functions are conferred or have been transferred by an enactment; or

(c) a body which, or the holder of an office which, is created by the order.

(2) An order under this Part may not make provision for the delegation of any function of legislating.

(3) An order under this Part may not make provision to confer a function of legislating on a Minister of the Crown (alone or otherwise) unless the conditions in subsections (4) and (5) are satisfied.

[(3A) An order under this Part may not make provision to confer a function of legislating on the Welsh Ministers, the First Minister for Wales or the Counsel General to the Welsh Assembly Government (alone or otherwise) unless the conditions in subsections (4) and (5A) are satisfied.]

(4) The condition in this subsection is that the function is exercisable by statutory instrument.

(5) The condition in this subsection is that such a statutory instrument—

(a) is an instrument to which section 5(1) of the Statutory Instruments Act 1946 (c. 36) applies (instruments subject to annulment by resolution of either House of Parliament); or

(b) is not to be made unless a draft of the statutory instrument has been laid before and approved by a resolution of each House of Parliament.

[(5A) The condition in this subsection is that such a statutory instrument—

(a) is an instrument to which section 5(1) of the Statutory Instruments Act 1946 applies (instruments subject to annulment); or

(b) is not to be made unless a draft of the statutory instrument has been laid before and approved by a resolution of the Assembly.]

(6) Subsections (1) to [(3A)] do not apply to provision which merely restates an enactment.

(7) For the purposes of this section a 'function of legislating' is a function of legislating by order, rules, regulations or other subordinate instrument.

5 Taxation

(1) An order under this Part may not make provision to impose, abolish or vary any tax.

(2)–(7) *****

6 Criminal penalties

(1) An order under this Part may not make provision to create a new offence that is punishable, or increase the penalty for an existing offence so that it is punishable—

(a) on indictment, with imprisonment for a term exceeding two years; or

(b) on summary conviction, with—

(i) imprisonment for a term exceeding the normal maximum term; or

(ii) a fine exceeding level 5 on the standard scale.

(2) In subsection (1)(b)(i), 'the normal maximum term' means—

(a) in relation to England and Wales—

(i) in the case of a summary offence, 51 weeks; and

(ii) in the case of an offence triable either way, twelve months; and

(b) in relation to Scotland or Northern Ireland, six months.

(3)–(6) *****

7 Forcible entry etc

(1) An order under this Part may not make provision to—

(a) authorise any forcible entry, search or seizure; or

(b) compel the giving of evidence.

(2) Subsection (1) does not prevent an order under this Part from extending any power for purposes similar to those to which the power applied before the order was made.

(3) Subsection (1) does not apply to provision which merely restates an enactment.

8 Excepted enactments

An order under this Part may not make provision amending or repealing any provision of—

(a) this Part; or

(b) the Human Rights Act 1998 (c. 42).

9 Scotland

An order under this Part may not, except by virtue of section 1(8) or 2(7), make provision which would be within the legislative competence of the Scottish Parliament if it were contained in an Act of that Parliament.

10   Northern Ireland

An order under this Part may not, except by virtue of section 1(8) or 2(7), make provision to amend or repeal any Northern Ireland legislation.

[11   Wales]

[(1) Except with the agreement of the Assembly, an order under this Part may not make provision which would be within the legislative competence of the Assembly if the provision were contained in—

   (a) an Assembly Measure (until the Assembly Act provisions of the Government of Wales Act 2006 come into force), or
   (b) an Act of the Assembly (after those provisions come into force).

(2) An order under this Part may not make any provision—

   (a) conferring a function on the Welsh Ministers, the First Minister for Wales or the Counsel General to the Welsh Assembly Government,
   (b) modifying or removing a function of the Welsh Ministers, the First Minister for Wales or the Counsel General to the Welsh Assembly Government,
   (c) restating any provision which confers a function on the Welsh Ministers, the First Minister for Wales or the Counsel General to the Welsh Assembly Government, or
   (d) that could be made by the Welsh Ministers, the First Minister for Wales or the Counsel General to the Welsh Assembly Government in the exercise of any of their functions,

except with the agreement of the Welsh Ministers.

(3) Subsections (1) and (2)(d) do not apply to any provision of an order under this Part falling within sections 1(8) or 2(7).]

Procedure

12   Procedure: introductory

(1) An order under this Part must be made by statutory instrument.

(2) A Minister may not make an order under this Part unless—

   (a) he has consulted in accordance with section 13;
   (b) following that consultation, he has laid a draft order and explanatory document before Parliament in accordance with section 14; and
   (c) the order is made, as determined under section 15, in accordance with—
      (i)   the negative resolution procedure (see section 16);
      (ii) the affirmative resolution procedure (see section 17); or
      (iii) the super-affirmative resolution procedure (see section 18).

13–19   *****

20 . . .

*****

Terrorism Act 2006

(2006, c. 11)

An Act to make provision for and about offences relating to conduct carried out, or capable of being carried out, for purposes connected with terrorism; to amend enactments relating to terrorism; to amend the Intelligence Services Act 1994 and the Regulation of Investigatory Powers Act 2000; and for connected purposes.   [30th March 2006]

Territorial extent: United Kingdom; for the application of the Act outside the United Kingdom, see s. 17

PART 1 OFFENCES

Encouragement etc of terrorism

1 Encouragement of terrorism

(1) This section applies to a statement that is likely to be understood by [a reasonable person] as a direct or indirect encouragement or other inducement [to some or all of the members of the public to whom it is published] to the commission, preparation or instigation of acts of terrorism or Convention offences.

(2) A person commits an offence if—

    (a) he publishes a statement to which this section applies or causes another to publish such a statement; and

    (b) at the time he publishes it or causes it to be published, he—

        (i) intends members of the public to be directly or indirectly encouraged or otherwise induced by the statement to commit, prepare or instigate acts of terrorism or Convention offences; or

        (ii) is reckless as to whether members of the public will be directly or indirectly encouraged or otherwise induced by the statement to commit, prepare or instigate such acts or offences.

(3) For the purposes of this section, the statements that are likely to be understood by [a reasonable person] as indirectly encouraging the commission or preparation of acts of terrorism or Convention offences include every statement which—

    (a) glorifies the commission or preparation (whether in the past, in the future or generally) of such acts or offences; and

    (b) is a statement from which ... members of the public could reasonably be expected to infer that what is being glorified is being glorified as conduct that should be emulated by them in existing circumstances.

(4) For the purposes of this section the questions how a statement is likely to be understood and what members of the public could reasonably be expected to infer from it must be determined having regard both—

    (a) to the contents of the statement as a whole; and

    (b) to the circumstances and manner of its publication.

(5) It is irrelevant for the purposes of subsections (1) to (3)—

    (a) whether anything mentioned in those subsections relates to the commission, preparation or instigation of one or more particular acts of terrorism or Convention offences, of acts of terrorism or Convention offences of a particular description or of acts of terrorism or Convention offences generally; and,

    (b) whether any person is in fact encouraged or induced by the statement to commit, prepare or instigate any such act or offence.

(6) In proceedings for an offence under this section against a person in whose case it is not proved that he intended the statement directly or indirectly to encourage or otherwise induce the commission, preparation or instigation of acts of terrorism or Convention offences, it is a defence for him to show—

    (a) that the statement neither expressed his views nor had his endorsement (whether by virtue of section 3 or otherwise); and

    (b) that it was clear, in all the circumstances of the statement's publication, that it did not express his views and (apart from the possibility of his having been given and failed to comply with a notice under subsection (3) of that section) did not have his endorsement.

(7) A person guilty of an offence under this section shall be liable—

    (a) on conviction on indictment, to imprisonment for a term not exceeding [15 years] or to a fine, or to both;

    (b) on summary conviction in England and Wales, to imprisonment for a term not exceeding [the general limit in a magistrates' court] or to a fine not exceeding the statutory maximum, or to both;

    (c) on summary conviction in Scotland or Northern Ireland, to imprisonment for a term not exceeding 6 months or to a fine not exceeding the statutory maximum, or to both.

  (8) In relation to an offence committed before [2 May 2022], the reference in subsection (7)(b) to [the general limit in a magistrates' court] is to be read as a reference to 6 months.

2   Dissemination of terrorist publications

  (1) A person commits an offence if he engages in conduct falling within subsection (2) and, at the time he does so—

    (a) he intends an effect of his conduct to be a direct or indirect encouragement or other inducement to the commission, preparation or instigation of acts of terrorism;

    (b) he intends an effect of his conduct to be the provision of assistance in the commission or preparation of such acts; or

    (c) he is reckless as to whether his conduct has an effect mentioned in paragraph (a) or (b).

  (2) For the purposes of this section a person engages in conduct falling within this subsection if he—

    (a) distributes or circulates a terrorist publication;

    (b) gives, sells or lends such a publication;

    (c) offers such a publication for sale or loan;

    (d) provides a service to others that enables them to obtain, read, listen to or look at such a publication, or to acquire it by means of a gift, sale or loan;

    (e) transmits the contents of such a publication electronically; or

    (f) has such a publication in his possession with a view to its becoming the subject of conduct falling within any of paragraphs (a) to (e).

  (3) For the purposes of this section a publication is a terrorist publication, in relation to conduct falling within subsection (2), if matter contained in it is likely—

    (a) to be understood, [by a reasonable person as a direct or indirect encouragement or other inducement, to some or all of the persons to whom it is or may become available as a result of that conduct], to the commission, preparation or instigation of acts of terrorism; or

    (b) to be useful in the commission or preparation of such acts and to be understood, by some or all of those persons, as contained in the publication, or made available to them, wholly or mainly for the purpose of being so useful to them.

  (4) For the purposes of this section matter that is likely to be understood by a [reasonable] person as indirectly encouraging the commission or preparation of acts of terrorism includes any matter which—

    (a) glorifies the commission or preparation (whether in the past, in the future or generally) of such acts; and

    (b) is matter from which [a person] could reasonably be expected to infer that what is being glorified is being glorified as conduct that should be emulated by him in existing circumstances.

  (5) For the purposes of this section the question whether a publication is a terrorist publication in relation to particular conduct must be determined—

    (a) as at the time of that conduct; and

    (b) having regard both to the contents of the publication as a whole and to the circumstances in which that conduct occurs.

  (6) In subsection (1) references to the effect of a person's conduct in relation to a terrorist publication include references to an effect of the publication on one or more persons to whom it is or may become available as a consequence of that conduct.

  (7) It is irrelevant for the purposes of this section whether anything mentioned in subsections (1) to (4) is in relation to the commission, preparation or instigation of one or more particular acts of terrorism, of acts of terrorism of a particular description or of acts of terrorism generally.

(8) For the purposes of this section it is also irrelevant, in relation to matter contained in any article whether any person—

    (a) is in fact encouraged or induced by that matter to commit, prepare or instigate acts of terrorism; or

    (b) in fact makes use of it in the commission or preparation of such acts.

(9) In proceedings for an offence under this section against a person in respect of conduct to which subsection (10) applies, it is a defence for him to show—

    (a) that the matter by reference to which the publication in question was a terrorist publication neither expressed his views nor had his endorsement (whether by virtue of section 3 or otherwise); and

    (b) that it was clear, in all the circumstances of the conduct, that that matter did not express his views and (apart from the possibility of his having been given and failed to comply with a notice under subsection (3) of that section) did not have his endorsement.

(10) This subsection applies to the conduct of a person to the extent that—

    (a) the publication to which his conduct related contained matter by reference to which it was a terrorist publication by virtue of subsection (3)(a); and

    (b) that person is not proved to have engaged in that conduct with the intention specified in subsection (1)(a).

(11) A person guilty of an offence under this section shall be liable—

    (a) on conviction on indictment, to imprisonment for a term not exceeding [15 years] or to a fine, or to both;

    (b) on summary conviction in England and Wales, to imprisonment for a term not exceeding [the general limit in a magistrates' court] or to a fine not exceeding the statutory maximum, or to both;

    (c) on summary conviction in Scotland or Northern Ireland, to imprisonment for a term not exceeding 6 months or to a fine not exceeding the statutory maximum, or to both.

(12) In relation to an offence committed before [2 May 2022], the reference in subsection (11)(b) to [the general limit in a magistrates' court] is to be read as a reference to 6 months.

(13) In this section—

'lend' includes let on hire, and 'loan' is to be construed accordingly;

'publication' means an article or record of any description that contains any of the following, or any combination of them—

    (a) matter to be read;

    (b) matter to be listened to;

    (c) matter to be looked at or watched.

3 Application of ss. 1 and 2 to internet activity etc

(1) This section applies for the purposes of sections 1 and 2 in relation to cases where—

    (a) a statement is published or caused to be published in the course of, or in connection with, the provision or use of a service provided electronically; or

    (b) conduct falling within section 2(2) was in the course of, or in connection with, the provision or use of such a service.

(2) The cases in which the statement, or the article or record to which the conduct relates, is to be regarded as having the endorsement of a person ('the relevant person') at any time include a case in which—

    (a) a constable has given him a notice under subsection (3);

    (b) that time falls more than 2 working days after the day on which the notice was given; and

    (c) the relevant person has failed, without reasonable excuse, to comply with the notice.

(3) A notice under this subsection is a notice which—

(a) declares that, in the opinion of the constable giving it, the statement or the article or record is unlawfully terrorism-related;

(b) requires the relevant person to secure that the statement or the article or record, so far as it is so related, is not available to the public or is modified so as no longer to be so related;

(c) warns the relevant person that a failure to comply with the notice within 2 working days will result in the statement, or the article or record, being regarded as having his endorsement; and

(d) explains how, under subsection (4), he may become liable by virtue of the notice if the statement, or the article or record, becomes available to the public after he has complied with the notice.

(4) Where—

(a) a notice under subsection (3) has been given to the relevant person in respect of a statement, or an article or record, and he has complied with it, but

(b) he subsequently publishes or causes to be published a statement which is, or is for all practical purposes, the same or to the same effect as the statement to which the notice related, or to matter contained in the article or record to which it related, (a 'repeat statement');

the requirements of subsection (2)(a) to (c) shall be regarded as satisfied in the case of the repeat statement in relation to the times of its subsequent publication by the relevant person.

(5)–(6) *****

(7) For the purposes of this section a statement or an article or record is unlawfully terrorism-related if it constitutes, or if matter contained in the article or record constitutes—

(a) something that is likely to be understood, by any one or more of the persons to whom it has or may become available, as a direct or indirect encouragement or other inducement to the commission, preparation or instigation of acts of terrorism or Convention offences; or

(b) information which—

(i) is likely to be useful to any one or more of those persons in the commission or preparation of such acts; and

(ii) is in a form or context in which it is likely to be understood by any one or more of those persons as being wholly or mainly for the purpose of being so useful.

(8) The reference in subjection (7) to something that is likely to be understood as an indirect encouragement to the commission or preparation of acts of terrorism or Convention offences includes anything which is likely to be understood as—

(a) the glorification of the commission or preparation (whether in the past, in the future or generally) of such acts or such offences; and

(b) a suggestion that what is being glorified as conduct that should be emulated in existing circumstances.

(9) *****

4 *****

Preparation of terrorist acts and terrorist training

5 Preparation of terrorist acts

(1) A person commits an offence if, with the intention of—

(a) committing acts of terrorism, or

(b) assisting another to commit such acts,

he engages in any conduct in preparation for giving effect to his intention.

(2) It is irrelevant for the purposes of subsection (1) whether the intention and preparations relate to one or more particular acts of terrorism, acts of terrorism of a particular description or acts of terrorism generally.

(3) A person guilty of an offence under this section shall be liable, on conviction on indictment, to imprisonment for life.

6 Training for terrorism

(1) A person commits an offence if—

    (a) he provides instruction or training in any of the skills mentioned in subsection (3); and

    (b) at the time he provides the instruction or training, he knows that a person receiving it intends to use the skills in which he is being instructed or trained—

        (i) for or in connection with the commission or preparation of acts of terrorism or Convention offences; or

        (ii) for assisting the commission or preparation by others of such acts or offences.

(2) A person commits an offence if—

    (a) he receives instruction or training in any of the skills mentioned in subsection (3); and

    (b) at the time of the instruction or training, he intends to use the skills in which he is being instructed or trained—

        (i) for or in connection with the commission or preparation of acts of terrorism or Convention offences; or

        (ii) for assisting the commission or preparation by others of such acts or offences.

(3) The skills are—

    (a) the making, handling or use of a noxious substance, or of substances of a description of such substances;

    (b) the use of any method or technique for doing anything else that is capable of being done for the purposes of terrorism, in connection with the commission or preparation of an act of terrorism or Convention offence or in connection with assisting the commission or preparation by another of such an act or offence; and

    (c) the design or adaptation for the purposes of terrorism, or in connection with the commission or preparation of an act of terrorism or Convention offence, of any method or technique for doing anything.

(4) It is irrelevant for the purposes of subsections (1) and (2)—

    (a) whether any instruction or training that is provided is provided to one or more particular persons or generally;

    (b) whether the acts or offences in relation to which a person intends to use skills in which he is instructed or trained consist of one or more particular acts of terrorism or Convention offences, acts of terrorism or Convention offences of a particular description or acts of terrorism or Convention offences generally; and

    (c) whether assistance that a person intends to provide to others is intended to be provided to one or more particular persons or to one or more persons whose identities are not yet known.

(5) A person guilty of an offence under this section shall be liable—

    (a) on conviction on indictment, to [imprisonment for life] or to a fine, or to both;

    (b) on summary conviction in England and Wales, to imprisonment for a term not exceeding [the general limit in a magistrates' court] or to a fine not exceeding the statutory maximum, or to both;

    (c) on summary conviction in Scotland or Northern Ireland, to imprisonment for a term not exceeding 6 months or to a fine not exceeding the statutory maximum, or to both.

(6) In relation to an offence committed before [2 May 2022], the reference in subsection (5)(b) to [the general limit in a magistrates' court] is to be read as a reference to 6 months.

(7) In this section—

'noxious substance' means—

    (a) a dangerous substance within the meaning of Part 7 of the Anti-terrorism, Crime and Security Act 2001 (c. 24); or

(b) any other substance which is hazardous or noxious or which may be or become hazardous or noxious only in certain circumstances;

'substance' includes any natural or artificial substance (whatever its origin or method of production and whether in solid or liquid form or in the form of a gas or vapour) and any mixture of substances.

7 Powers of forfeiture in respect of offences under s. 6

(1) A court before which a person is convicted of an offence under section 6 may order the forfeiture of anything the court considers to have been in the person's possession for purposes connected with the offence.

(2)–(7) *****

8 Attendance at a place used for terrorist training

(1) A person commits an offence if—

(a) he attends at any place, whether in the United Kingdom or elsewhere;

(b) while he is at that place, instruction or training of the type mentioned in section 6(1) of this Act or section 54(1) of the Terrorism Act 2000 (c. 11) (weapons training) is provided there;

(c) that instruction or training is provided there wholly or partly for purposes connected with the commission or preparation of acts of terrorism or Convention offences; and

(d) the requirements of subsection (2) are satisfied in relation to that person.

(2) The requirements of this subsection are satisfied in relation to a person if—

(a) he knows or believes that instruction or training is being provided there wholly or partly for purposes connected with the commission or preparation of acts of terrorism or Convention offences; or

(b) a person attending at that place throughout the period of that person's attendance could not reasonably have failed to understand that instruction or training was being provided there wholly or partly for such purposes.

(3) It is immaterial for the purposes of this section—

(a) whether the person concerned receives the instruction or training himself; and

(b) whether the instruction or training is provided for purposes connected with one or more particular acts of terrorism or Convention offences, acts of terrorism or Convention offences of a particular description or acts of terrorism or Convention offences generally.

(4) A person guilty of an offence under this section shall be liable—

(a) on conviction on indictment, to imprisonment for a term not exceeding [14] years or to a fine, or to both;

(b) on summary conviction in England and Wales, to imprisonment for a term not exceeding [the general limit in a magistrates' court] or to a fine not exceeding the statutory maximum, or to both;

(c) on summary conviction in Scotland or Northern Ireland, to imprisonment for a term not exceeding 6 months or to a fine not exceeding the statutory maximum, or to both.

(5) In relation to an offence committed before [2 May 2022], the reference in subsection (4)(b) to [the general limit in a magistrates' court] is to be read as a reference to 6 months.

(6) References in this section to instruction or training being provided include references to its being made available.

Offences involving radioactive devices and materials and nuclear facilities and sites

9 Making and possession of devices or materials

(1) A person commits an offence if—

(a) he makes or has in his possession a radioactive device, or

(b) he has in his possession radioactive material,

with the intention of using the device or material in the course of or in connection with the commission or preparation of an act of terrorism or for the purposes of terrorism, or of making it available to be so used.

(2) It is irrelevant for the purposes of subsection (1) whether the act of terrorism to which an intention relates is a particular act of terrorism, an act of terrorism of a particular description or an act of terrorism generally.

(3) A person guilty of an offence under this section shall be liable, on conviction on indictment, to imprisonment for life.

(4), (5) *****

10   Misuse of devices or material and misuse and damage of facilities

(1) A person commits an offence if he uses—

    (a) a radioactive device, or

    (b) radioactive material,

in the course of or in connection with the commission of an act of terrorism or for the purposes of terrorism.

(2) A person commits an offence if, in the course of or in connection with the commission of an act of terrorism or for the purposes of terrorism, he uses or damages a nuclear facility in a manner which—

    (a) causes a release of radioactive material; or

    (b) creates or increases a risk that such material will be released.

(3) A person guilty of an offence under this section shall be liable, on conviction on indictment, to imprisonment for life.

(4), (5) *****

11   Terrorist threats relating to devices, materials or facilities

(1) A person commits an offence if, in the course of or in connection with the commission of an act of terrorism or for the purposes of terrorism—

    (a) he makes a demand—

        (i)   for the supply to himself or to another of a radioactive device or of radioactive material;

        (ii) for a nuclear facility to be made available to himself or to another; or

        (iii) for access to such a facility to be given to himself or to another;

    (b) he supports the demand with a threat that he or another will take action if the demand is not met; and

    (c) the circumstances and manner of the threat are such that it is reasonable for the person to whom it is made to assume that there is real risk that the threat will be carried out if the demand is not met.

(2) A person also commits an offence if—

    (a) he makes a threat falling within subsection (3) in the course of or in connection with the commission of an act of terrorism or for the purposes of terrorism; and

    (b) the circumstances and manner of the threat are such that it is reasonable for the person to whom it is made to assume that there is real risk that the threat will be carried out, or would be carried out if demands made in association with the threat are not met.

(3) A threat falls within this subsection if it is—

    (a) a threat to use radioactive material;

    (b) a threat to use a radioactive device; or

    (c) a threat to use or damage a nuclear facility in a manner that releases radioactive material or creates or increases a risk that such material will be released.

(4) A person guilty of an offence under this section shall be liable, on conviction on indictment, to imprisonment for life.

(5) *****

[11A   Forfeiture of devices, materials or facilities]

[(1) A court by or before which a person is convicted of an offence under section 9 or 10 may order the forfeiture of any radioactive device or radioactive material, or any nuclear facility, made or used in committing the offence.

(2) A court by or before which a person is convicted of an offence under section 11 may order the forfeiture of any radioactive device or radioactive material, or any nuclear facility, which is the subject of—

(a) a demand under subsection (1) of that section, or

(b) a threat falling within subsection (3) of that section.

(3) Before making an order under this section, a court must give an opportunity to be heard to any person, other than the convicted person, who claims to be the owner or otherwise interested in anything which can be forfeited under this section.

(4) An order under this section does not come into force until there is no further possibility of it being varied, or set aside, on appeal (disregarding any power of a court to grant leave to appeal out of time).

(5)–(7) *****

12–16 *****

17   Commission of offences abroad

(1) If—

(a) a person does anything outside the United Kingdom, and

(b) his action, if done in a part of the United Kingdom, would constitute an offence falling within subsection (2),

he shall be guilty in that part of the United Kingdom of the offence.

(2) The offences falling within this subsection are—

(a)   an offence under section 1 [or 2] ... of this Act ...

(b)   an offence under [section 5 or 6 or] any of sections 8 to 11 of this Act;

(c)   an offence under section 11(1) of the Terrorism Act 2000 (c. 11) (membership of proscribed organisations);

[(ca) an offence under section 12(1) or (1A) of that Act (inviting or expressing support for proscribed organisation);

(cb) an offence under section 13 of that Act (uniform etc associated with proscribed organisation);]

(d)   an offence under section 54 of that Act (weapons training);

[(da) an offence under section 4 of the Explosive Substances Act 1883 (making or possessing explosives under suspicious circumstances) so far as committed for the purposes of an act of terrorism;]

(e)   conspiracy to commit an offence falling within this subsection;

(f)   inciting a person to commit such an offence;

(g)   attempting to commit such an offence;

(h)   aiding, abetting, counselling or procuring the commission of such an offence.

(3) Subsection (1) applies irrespective of whether the person is a British citizen [(subject to subsection (3A))] or, in the case of a company, a company incorporated in a part of the United Kingdom.

[(3A) Subsection (1) applies in the case of an offence falling within subsection (2)(ca) or (cb) only if at the time of committing the offence the person is a United Kingdom national or a United Kingdom resident.

(3B) In subsection (3A)—

'United Kingdom national' means an individual who is—

(a) a British citizen, a British overseas territories citizen, a British National (Overseas) or a British Overseas citizen,

(b) a person who under the British Nationality Act 1981 is a British subject, or

(c) a British protected person within the meaning of that Act;

'United Kingdom resident' means an individual who is resident in the United Kingdom.]

(4) In the case of an offence falling within subsection (2) which is committed wholly or partly outside the United Kingdom—

(a) proceedings for the offence may be taken at any place in the United Kingdom; and

(b) the offence may for all incidental purposes be treated as having been committed at any such place.

(5), (6) *****

18 *****

19 Consents to prosecutions

(1) Proceedings for an offence under this Part—

(a) may be instituted in England and Wales only with the consent of the Director of Public Prosecutions; and

(b) may be instituted in Northern Ireland only with the consent of the Director of Public Prosecutions for Northern Ireland.

(2) But if it appears to the Director of Public Prosecutions or the Director of Public Prosecutions for Northern Ireland that an offence under this Part has been committed [outside the United Kingdom or] for a purpose wholly or partly connected with the affairs of a country other than the United Kingdom, his consent for the purposes of this section may be given only with the permission—

(a) in the case of the Director of Public Prosecutions, of the Attorney General; and

(b) in the case of the Director of Public Prosecutions for Northern Ireland, of the Advocate General for Northern Ireland.

(3) In relation to any time before the coming into force of section 27(1) of the Justice (Northern Ireland) Act 2002 (c. 26), the reference in subsection (2)(b) to the Advocate General for Northern Ireland is to be read as a reference to the Attorney General for Northern Ireland.

Interpretation of Part 1

20 Interpretation of Part 1

(1) Expressions used in this Part and in the Terrorism Act 2000 (c. 11) have the same meanings in this Part as in that Act.

(2) In this Part—

'act of terrorism' includes anything constituting an action taken for the purposes of terrorism, within the meaning of the Terrorism Act 2000 (see section 1(5) of that Act);

'article' includes anything for storing data;

'Convention offence' means an offence listed in Schedule 1 or an equivalent offence under the law of a country or territory outside the United Kingdom; [and see subsection (2A)]

'glorification' includes any form of praise or celebration, and cognate expressions are to be construed accordingly;

'public' is to be construed in accordance with subsection (3);

'publish' and cognate expressions are to be construed in accordance with subsection (4);

'record' means a record so far as not comprised in an article, including a temporary record created electronically and existing solely in the course of, and for the purposes of, the transmission of the whole or a part of its contents;

'statement' is to be construed in accordance with subsection (6).

[(2A) Offences under any of the following paragraphs of Schedule 4 to the Space Industry Act 2018 are to be treated for the purposes of this Part as if they were Convention offences—

(a) paragraph 1 (hijacking of spacecraft);

(b) paragraph 2 (destroying, damaging or endangering safety of spacecraft);

(c) paragraph 3 (other acts endangering or likely to endanger safety of spacecraft);

(d) paragraph 4 (endangering safety at spaceports).]

(3) In this Part references to the public—

    (a) are references to the public of any part of the United Kingdom or of a country or territory outside the United Kingdom, or any section of the public; and

    (b) except in section 9(4), also include references to a meeting or other group of persons which is open to the public (whether unconditionally or on the making of a payment or the satisfaction of other conditions).

(4) In this Part references to a person's publishing a statement are references to—

    (a) his publishing it in any manner to the public;

    (b) his providing electronically any service by means of which the public have access to the statement; or

    (c) his using a service provided to him electronically by another so as to enable or to facilitate access by the public to the statement;

but this subsection does not apply to the references to a publication in section 2.

(5)–(11) *****

21–35 *****

PART 3 SUPPLEMENTAL PROVISIONS

36 Review of terrorism legislation

(1) The Secretary of State must appoint a person to review the operation of the provisions of the Terrorism Act 2000 and of Part 1 of this Act.

(2) That person may, from time to time, [carry out—

    (a) a review of the provisions of the Terrorism Act 2000, and

    (b) a review of the provisions of Part 1 of this Act,

and,] a review of those provisions and, where he does so, must send a report on the outcome of his review to the Secretary of State as soon as reasonably practicable after completing the review.

[(2A)] *****

(3) [The person appointed under subsection (1)] must carry out and report on his first review [under subsection (2)] before the end of the period of 12 months after the laying before Parliament of the last report to be so laid under section 126 of the Terrorism Act 2000 before the commencement of this section.

(4) That person must carry out and report on a review [subsection (2)(a)]] at least once in every twelve month period ending with an anniversary of the end of the twelve month period mentioned in subsection (3).

[(4A) The person appointed under subsection (1) must ensure that a review is carried out (whether by that person or another person) into any case where the period specified in a warrant of further detention issued under Part 3 of Schedule 8 of the Terrorism Act 2000 (extension of detention of terrorist suspects) is further extended by virtue of paragraph 36 of that Schedule to a time that is more than 14 days after the relevant time (within the meaning of that paragraph).

(4B) The person appointed under subsection (1) must ensure that a report on the outcome of the review is sent to the Secretary of State as soon as reasonably practicable after the completion of the review.]

[(4C) In each calendar year the person appointed under subsection (1) must, by 31 January, inform the Secretary of State what (if any) reviews under subsection (2)(b) the person intends to carry out in that year.

Those reviews must be completed during that year or as soon as reasonably practicable after the end of it.]

(5) On receiving a report under this section, the Secretary of State must lay a copy of it before Parliament [as soon as the Secretary of State is satisfied that doing so will not prejudice any criminal proceedings].

(6) The Secretary of State may, out of money provided by Parliament, pay a person appointed [under subsection (1)], both his expenses and also such allowances as the Secretary of State determines.

[(6A)] *****

37–39 *****

Section 20   # SCHEDULE 1

CONVENTION OFFENCES

Explosives offences

1.—(1) Subject to sub-paragraph (3), an offence under any of sections 28 to 30 of the Offences against the Person Act 1861 (c. 100) (causing injury by explosions, causing explosions and handling or placing explosives).

(2) Subject to sub-paragraph (3), an offence under any of the following provisions of the Explosive Substances Act 1883 (c. 3)—

(a) section 2 (causing an explosion likely to endanger life);

(b) section 3 (preparation of explosions);

(c) section 5 (ancillary offences).

(3) An offence in or as regards Scotland is a Convention offence by virtue of this paragraph only if it consists in—

(a) the doing of an act as an act of terrorism; or

(b) an action for the purposes of terrorism.

Biological weapons

2. An offence under section 1 of the Biological Weapons Act 1974 (c. 6) (development etc of biological weapons).

Offences against internationally protected persons

3.—(1) Subject to sub-paragraph (4), an offence mentioned in section 1(1)(a) of the Internationally Protected Persons Act 1978 (c. 17) (attacks against protected persons committed outside the United Kingdom) which is committed (whether in the United Kingdom or elsewhere) in relation to a protected person.

(2) Subject to sub-paragraph (4), an offence mentioned in section 1(1)(b) of that Act (attacks on relevant premises etc) which is committed (whether in the United Kingdom or elsewhere) in connection with an attack—

(a) on relevant premises or on a vehicle ordinarily used by a protected person, and

(b) at a time when a protected person is in or on the premises or vehicle.

(3) Subject to sub-paragraph (4), an offence under section 1(3) of that Act (threats etc in relation to protected persons).

(4) An offence in or as regards Scotland is a Convention offence by virtue of this paragraph only if it consists in—

(a) the doing of an act as an act of terrorism; or

(b) an action for the purposes of terrorism.

(5) Expressions used in this paragraph and section 1 of that Act have the same meanings in this paragraph as in that section.

Hostage-taking

4. An offence under section 1 of the Taking of Hostages Act 1982 (c. 28) (hostage-taking).

Hijacking and other offences against aircraft

5. Offences under any of the following provisions of the Aviation Security Act 1982 (c. 36)—

(a) section 1 (hijacking);

(b) section 2 (destroying, damaging or endangering safety of aircraft);

(c) section 3 (other acts endangering or likely to endanger safety of aircraft);

(d) section 6(2) (ancillary offences).

Offences involving nuclear material [or nuclear facilities]

6.—(1) An offence mentioned in section 1(1) [(a) to (d)] of the Nuclear Material (Offences) Act 1983 (c. 18) (offences in relation to nuclear material committed outside the United Kingdom) which is committed (whether in the United Kingdom or elsewhere) in relation to or by means of nuclear material.

[(2) An offence mentioned in section 1(1)(a) or (b) of that Act where the act making the person guilty of the offence (whether done in the United Kingdom or elsewhere)—

(a) is directed at a nuclear facility or interferes with the operation of such a facility, and

(b) causes death, injury or damage resulting from the emission of ionising radiation or the release of radioactive material.

(3) An offence under any of the following provisions of that Act—

(a) section 1B (offences relating to damage to environment);

(b) section 1C (offences of importing or exporting etc nuclear material: extended jurisdiction);

(c) section 2 (offences involving preparatory acts and threats).

(4) Expressions used in this paragraph and that Act have the same meanings in this paragraph as in that Act.]

[6A—(1) Any of the following offences under the Customs and Excise Management Act 1979—

(a) an offence under section 50(2) or (3) (improper importation of goods) in connection with a prohibition or restriction relating to the importation of nuclear material;

(b) an offence under section 68(2) (exportation of prohibited or restricted goods) in connection with a prohibition or restriction relating to the exportation or shipment as stores of nuclear material;

(c) an offence under section 170(1) or (2) (fraudulent evasion of duty etc) in connection with a prohibition or restriction relating to the importation, exportation or shipment as stores of nuclear material.

(2) In this paragraph 'nuclear material' has the same meaning as in the Nuclear Material (Offences) Act 1983 (see section 6 of that Act).]

Offences under the Aviation and Maritime Security Act 1990 (c. 31)

7. Offences under any of the following provisions of the Aviation and Maritime Security Act 1990—

(a) section 1 (endangering safety at aerodromes);

(b) section 9 (hijacking of ships);

(c) section 10 (seizing or exercising control of fixed platforms);

(d) section 11 (destroying ships or fixed platforms or endangering their safety);

(e) section 12 (other acts endangering or likely to endanger safe navigation);

(f) section 13 (offences involving threats relating to ships or fixed platforms);

(g) section 14 (ancillary offences).

Offences involving chemical weapons

8. An offence under section 2 of the Chemical Weapons Act 1996 (c. 6) (use, development etc of chemical weapons).

Terrorist funds

9. An offence under any of the following provisions of the Terrorism Act 2000 (c. 11)—

(a) section 15 (terrorist fund-raising);

(b) section 16 (use or possession of terrorist funds);

(c) section 17 (funding arrangements for terrorism);

(d) section 18 (money laundering of terrorist funds).

Directing terrorist organisations

10. An offence under section 56 of the Terrorism Act 2000 (directing a terrorist organisation).

Offences involving nuclear weapons

11. An offence under section 47 of the Anti-terrorism, Crime and Security Act 2001 (c. 24) (use, development etc of nuclear weapons).

Conspiracy etc

12. Any of the following offences—
    (a) conspiracy to commit a Convention offence;
    (b) inciting the commission of a Convention offence;
    (c) attempting to commit a Convention offence;
    (d) aiding, abetting, counselling or procuring the commission of a Convention offence.

*****

Tribunals, Courts and Enforcement Act 2007

(2007, c. 15)

An Act to make provision about tribunals and inquiries; to establish an Administrative Justice and Tribunals Council; to amend the law relating to judicial appointments and appointments to the Law Commission; to amend the law relating to the enforcement of judgments and debts; to make further provision about the management and relief of debt; to make provision protecting cultural objects from seizure or forfeiture in certain circumstances; to amend the law relating to the taking of possession of land affected by compulsory purchase; to alter the powers of the High Court in judicial review applications; and for connected purposes.   [19th July 2007]

Territorial extent: United Kingdom (provisions reproduced here)

PART 1 TRIBUNALS AND INQUIRIES

Chapter 1 Tribunal judiciary: independence and Senior President

1* *****

2   Senior President of Tribunals

(1) Her Majesty may, on the recommendation of the Lord Chancellor, appoint a person to the office of Senior President of Tribunals.

(2) Schedule 1 makes further provision about the Senior President of Tribunals and about recommendations for appointment under subsection (1).

(3) A holder of the office of Senior President of Tribunals must, in carrying out the functions of that office, have regard to—
    (a) the need for tribunals to be accessible,
    (b) the need for proceedings before tribunals—
        (i)   to be fair, and
        (ii) to be handled quickly and efficiently,
    (c) the need for members of tribunals to be experts in the subject-matter of, or the law to be applied in, cases in which they decide matters, and
    (d) the need to develop innovative methods of resolving disputes that are of a type that may be brought before tribunals.

---

* **Editor's Note:** Section 1 amends the Constitutional Reform Act 2005 by inserting s. 3(7A) and (7B).

(4) In subsection (3) 'tribunals' means—
  (a) the First-tier Tribunal,
  (b) the Upper Tribunal,
  (c) employment tribunals, [and]
  (d) the Employment Appeal Tribunal, ...
  (e) ...

Chapter 2 First-tier Tribunal and Upper Tribunal

Establishment

3 The First-tier Tribunal and the Upper Tribunal

(1) There is to be a tribunal, known as the First-tier Tribunal, for the purpose of exercising the functions conferred on it under or by virtue of this Act or any other Act.

(2) There is to be a tribunal, known as the Upper Tribunal, for the purpose of exercising the functions conferred on it under or by virtue of this Act or any other Act.

(3) Each of the First-tier Tribunal, and the Upper Tribunal, is to consist of its judges and other members.

(4) The Senior President of Tribunals is to preside over both of the First-tier Tribunal and the Upper Tribunal.

(5) The Upper Tribunal is to be a superior court of record.

Members and composition of tribunals

4 Judges and other members of the First-tier Tribunal

(1) A person is a judge of the First-tier Tribunal if the person—
  (a) is a judge of the First-tier Tribunal by virtue of appointment under paragraph 1(1) of Schedule 2,
  (b) is a transferred-in judge of the First-tier Tribunal (see section 31(2)),
  (c) is a judge of the Upper Tribunal,
  [(ca) is within section 6A,]
  (d) ... or
  (e) is a member of a panel of [Employment Judges].

(2) A person is also a judge of the First-tier Tribunal, but only as regards functions of the tribunal in relation to appeals such as are mentioned in subsection (1) of section 5 of the Criminal Injuries Compensation Act 1995 (c. 53), if the person is an adjudicator appointed under that section by the Scottish Ministers.

(3) A person is one of the other members of the First-tier Tribunal if the person—
  (a) is a member of the First-tier Tribunal by virtue of appointment under paragraph 2(1) of Schedule 2,
  (b) is a transferred-in other member of the First-tier Tribunal (see section 31(2)),
  (c) is one of the other members of the Upper Tribunal, or
  (d) is a member of a panel of members of employment tribunals that is not a panel of [Employment Judges].

(4) Schedule 2—
contains provision for the appointment of persons to be judges or other members of the First-tier Tribunal, and makes further provision in connection with judges and other members of the First-tier Tribunal.

5–[6A] *****

7 Chambers: jurisdiction and Presidents

(1) The Lord Chancellor may, with the concurrence of the Senior President of Tribunals, by order make provision for the organisation of each of the First-tier Tribunal and the Upper Tribunal into a number of chambers.

(2) There is—

(a) for each chamber of the First-tier Tribunal, and

(b) for each chamber of the Upper Tribunal,

to be a person, or two persons, to preside over that chamber.

[(3) A person may at any particular time-

(a) preside over more than one chamber of the First-tier Tribunal;

(b) preside over more than one chamber of the Upper Tribunal;

(c) preside over—

(i) one or more chambers of the First-tier Tribunal, and

(ii) one or more chambers of the Upper Tribunal.]

(4) A person appointed under this section to preside over a chamber is to be known as a Chamber President.

(5)–(9) *****

8–10 *****

Review of decisions and appeals

11 Right to appeal to Upper Tribunal

(1) For the purposes of subsection (2), the reference to a right of appeal is to a right to appeal to the Upper Tribunal on any point of law arising from a decision made by the First-tier Tribunal other than an excluded decision.

(2) Any party to a case has a right of appeal, subject to subsection (8).

(3) That right may be exercised only with permission (or, in Northern Ireland, leave).

(4) Permission (or leave) may be given by—

(a) the First-tier Tribunal, or

(b) the Upper Tribunal,

on an application by the party.

(5)–(8) *****

[11A Finality of decisions by Upper Tribunal about permission to appeal]

[(1) Subsections (2) and (3) apply in relation to a decision by the Upper Tribunal to refuse permission (or leave) to appeal further to an application under section 11(4)(b).

(2) The decision is final, and not liable to be questioned or set aside in any other court.

(3) In particular—

(a) the Upper Tribunal is not to be regarded as having exceeded its powers by reason of any error made in reaching the decision;

(b) the supervisory jurisdiction does not extend to, and no application or petition for judicial review may be made or brought in relation to, the decision.

(4) Subsections (2) and (3) do not apply so far as the decision involves or gives rise to any question as to whether—

(a) the Upper Tribunal has or had a valid application before it under section 11(4)(b),

(b) the Upper Tribunal is or was properly constituted for the purpose of dealing with the application, or

(c) the Upper Tribunal is acting or has acted—

(i) in bad faith, or

(ii) in such a procedurally defective way as amounts to a fundamental breach of the principles of natural justice.

(5) Subsections (2) and (3) do not apply so far as provision giving the First-tier Tribunal jurisdiction to make the first-instance decision could (if the Tribunal did not already have that jurisdiction) be made by—

(a) an Act of the Scottish Parliament, or

(b) an Act of the Northern Ireland Assembly the Bill for which would not require the consent of the Secretary of State.

(6) The court of supervisory jurisdiction is not to entertain any application or petition for judicial review in respect of a decision of the First-tier Tribunal that it would not entertain (whether as a matter of law or discretion) in the absence of this section.

(7) *****

12 Proceedings on appeal to Upper Tribunal

(1) Subsection (2) applies if the Upper Tribunal, in deciding an appeal under section 11, finds that the making of the decision concerned involved the making of an error on a point of law.

(2) The Upper Tribunal—

    (a) may (but need not) set aside the decision of the First-tier Tribunal, and

    (b) if it does, must either—

        (i)   remit the case to the First-tier Tribunal with directions for its reconsideration, or

        (ii) re-make the decision.

(3) In acting under subsection (2)(b)(i), the Upper Tribunal may also—

    (a) direct that the members of the First-tier Tribunal who are chosen to reconsider the case are not to be the same as those who made the decision that has been set aside;

    (b) give procedural directions in connection with the reconsideration of the case by the First-tier Tribunal.

(4) In acting under subsection (2)(b)(ii), the Upper Tribunal—

    (a) may make any decision which the First-tier Tribunal could make if the First-tier Tribunal were re-making the decision, and

    (b) may make such findings of fact as it considers appropriate.

13 Right to appeal to Court of Appeal etc

(1) For the purposes of subsection (2), the reference to a right of appeal is to a right to appeal to the relevant appellate court on any point of law arising from a decision made by the Upper Tribunal other than an excluded decision.

(2) Any party to a case has a right of appeal, subject to subsection (14).

(3) That right may be exercised only with permission (or, in Northern Ireland, leave).

(4) Permission (or leave) may be given by—

    (a) the Upper Tribunal, or

    (b) the relevant appellate court,

on an application by the party.

(5) An application may be made under subsection (4) to the relevant appellate court only if permission (or leave) has been refused by the Upper Tribunal.

(6) The Lord Chancellor may, as respects an application under subsection (4) that falls within subsection (7) and for which the relevant appellate court is the Court of Appeal in England and Wales or the Court of Appeal in Northern Ireland, by order make provision for permission (or leave) not to be granted on the application unless the Upper Tribunal or (as the case may be) the relevant appellate court considers—

    (a) that the proposed appeal would raise some important point of principle or practice, or

    (b) that there is some other compelling reason for the relevant appellate court to hear the appeal.

[(6A) Rules of court may make provision for permission not to be granted on an application under subsection (4) to the Court of Session that falls within subsection (7) unless the court considers—

    (a) that the proposed appeal would raise some important point of principle, or

    (b) that there is some other compelling reason for the court to hear the appeal.]

(7)–(15) *****

14–[14C] *****

'Judicial review'

15 Upper Tribunal's 'judicial review' jurisdiction

(1) The Upper Tribunal has power, in cases arising under the law of England and Wales or under the law of Northern Ireland, to grant the following kinds of relief—

      (a) a mandatory order;

      (b) a prohibiting order;

      (c) a quashing order;

      (d) a declaration;

      (e) an injunction.

  (2) The power under subsection (1) may be exercised by the Upper Tribunal if—

      (a) certain conditions are met (see section 18), or

      (b) the tribunal is authorised to proceed even though not all of those conditions are met (see section 19(3) and (4)).

  (3) Relief under subsection (1) granted by the Upper Tribunal—

      (a) has the same effect as the corresponding relief granted by the High Court on an application for judicial review, and

      (b) is enforceable as if it were relief granted by the High Court on an application for judicial review.

  (4) In deciding whether to grant relief under subsection (1)(a), (b) or (c), the Upper Tribunal must apply the principles that the High Court would apply in deciding whether to grant that relief on an application for judicial review.

  (5) In deciding whether to grant relief under subsection (1)(d) or (e), the Upper Tribunal must—

      (a) in cases arising under the law of England and Wales apply the principles that the High Court would apply in deciding whether to grant that relief under section 31(2) of the [Senior Courts Act 1981] (c. 54) on an application for judicial review, and

      (b) in cases arising under the law of Northern Ireland apply the principles that the High Court would apply in deciding whether to grant that relief on an application for judicial review.

  [(5A) In cases arising under the law of England and Wales, subsections (2A) and (2B) of section 31 of the Senior Courts Act 1981 apply to the Upper Tribunal when deciding whether to grant relief under subsection (1) as they apply to the High Court when deciding whether to grant relief on an application for judicial review.

  (5B) If the tribunal grants relief in reliance on section 31(2B) of the Senior Courts Act 1981 as applied by subsection (5A), the tribunal must certify that the condition in section 31(2B) as so applied is satisfied.]

  (6) *****

16 Application for relief under section 15(1)

  (1) This section applies in relation to an application to the Upper Tribunal for relief under section 15(1).

  (2) The application may be made only if permission (or, in a case arising under the law of Northern Ireland, leave) to make it has been obtained from the tribunal.

  (3) The tribunal may not grant permission (or leave) to make the application unless[—

      (a)] it considers that the applicant has a sufficient interest in the matter to which the application relates[, and

      (b) in cases arising under the law of England and Wales, the applicant has provided the tribunal with any information about the financing of the application that is specified in Tribunal Procedure Rules for the purposes of this paragraph].

  [(3A) The information that may be specified for the purposes of subsection (3)(b) includes—

      (a) information about the source, nature and extent of financial resources available, or likely to be available, to the applicant to meet liabilities arising in connection with the application, and

      (b) if the applicant is a body corporate that is unable to demonstrate that it is likely to have financial resources available to meet such liabilities, information about its members and about their ability to provide financial support for the purposes of the application.

  (3B) Tribunal Procedure Rules under subsection (3)(b) that specify information identifying those who are, or are likely to be, sources of financial support must provide that only a person whose financial support (whether direct or indirect) exceeds, or is likely to exceed, a level set out in the rules has to be identified.

This subsection does not apply to rules that specify information described in subsection (3A)(b).]

[(3C) In cases arising under the law of England and Wales, when considering whether to grant permission to make the application, the tribunal—

    (a) may of its own initiative consider whether the outcome for the applicant would have been substantially different if the conduct complained of had not occurred, and

    (b) must consider that question if the respondent asks it to do so.

(3D) In subsection (3C) 'the conduct complained of' means the conduct (or alleged conduct) of the respondent that the applicant claims justifies the tribunal in granting relief.

(3E) If, on considering the question mentioned in subsection (3C)(a) and (b), it appears to the tribunal to be highly likely that the outcome for the applicant would not have been substantially different, the tribunal must refuse to grant permission.

(3F) The tribunal may disregard the requirement in subsection (3E) if it considers that it is appropriate to do so for reasons of exceptional public interest.

(3G) If the tribunal grants permission in reliance on subsection (3F), the tribunal must certify that the condition in subsection (3F) is satisfied.]

(4) Subsection (5) applies where the tribunal considers—

    (a) that there has been undue delay in making the application, and

    (b) that granting the relief sought on the application would be likely to cause substantial hardship to, or substantially prejudice the rights of, any person or would be detrimental to good administration.

(5) The tribunal may—

    (a) refuse to grant permission (or leave) for the making of the application;

    (b) refuse to grant any relief sought on the application.

(6) The tribunal may award to the applicant damages, restitution or the recovery of a sum due if—

    (a) the application includes a claim for such an award arising from any matter to which the application relates, and

    (b) the tribunal is satisfied that such an award would have been made by the High Court if the claim had been made in an action begun in the High Court by the applicant at the time of making the application.

[(6A) In cases arising under the law of England and Wales, subsections (2A) and (2B) of section 31 of the Senior Courts Act 1981 apply to the Upper Tribunal as regards the making of an award under subsection (6) as they apply to the High Court as regards the making of an award under section 31(4) of the Senior Courts Act 1981.

(6B) If the tribunal makes an award in reliance on section 31(2B) of the Senior Courts Act 1981 as applied by subsection (6A), the tribunal must certify that the condition in section 31(2B) as so applied is satisfied.]

(7)–(9) *****

17–149 *****

SCHEDULE 1 *****

SCHEDULE 2 JUDGES AND OTHER MEMBERS OF THE FIRST-TIER TRIBUNAL

Power to appoint judges of First-tier Tribunal

1.—(1) The [Senior President of Tribunals] may appoint a person to be one of the judges of the First-tier Tribunal.

(2) A person is eligible for appointment under sub-paragraph (1) only if the person—

(a) satisfies the judicial-appointment eligibility condition on a 5-year basis,

(b) is an advocate or solicitor in Scotland of at least five years' standing,

(c) is a barrister or solicitor in Northern Ireland of at least five years' standing, or

(d) in the [opinion of the Senior President of Tribunals], has gained experience in law which makes the person as suitable for appointment as if the person satisfied any of paragraphs (a) to (c).

(3) Section 52(2) to (5) (meaning of 'gain experience in law') apply for the purposes of sub-paragraph (2)(d), but as if section 52(4)(i) referred to the [Senior President of Tribunals] instead of to the relevant decision-maker.

Power to appoint other members of First-tier Tribunal

2.—(1) The [Senior President of Tribunals] may appoint a person to be one of the members of the First-tier Tribunal who are not judges of the tribunal.

(2) A person is eligible for appointment under sub-paragraph (1) only if the person has qualifications prescribed in an order made by the Lord Chancellor with the concurrence of the Senior President of Tribunals.

Appointed and transferred-in judges and other members: removal from office

3.—(1) This paragraph applies to any power by which—

(a) a person appointed under paragraph 1(1) or 2(1),

(b) a transferred-in judge of the First-tier Tribunal, or

(c) a transferred-in other member of the First-tier Tribunal,

may be removed from office.

(2) If the person exercises functions wholly or mainly in Scotland, the power may be exercised only with the concurrence of the Lord President of the Court of Session.

(3) If the person exercises functions wholly or mainly in Northern Ireland, the power may be exercised only with the concurrence of the Lord Chief Justice of Northern Ireland.

(4) If neither of sub-paragraphs (2) and (3) applies, the power may be exercised only with the concurrence of the Lord Chief Justice of England and Wales.

Terms of appointment

4.—(1) This paragraph applies—

(a) to a person appointed under paragraph 1(1) or 2(1),

(b) to a transferred-in judge of the First-tier Tribunal, and

(c) to a transferred-in other member of the First-tier Tribunal.

(2) If the terms of the person's appointment provide that he is appointed on a salaried (as opposed to fee-paid) basis, the person may be removed from office—

(a) only by the Lord Chancellor (and in accordance with paragraph 3), and

(b) only on the ground of inability or misbehaviour.

[(2A) If the terms of the person's appointment provide that the person is appointed on a fee-paid basis, the person may be removed from office—

(a) only by the Lord Chancellor (and in accordance with paragraph 3), and

(b) only on—

(i) the ground of inability or misbehaviour, or

(ii) a ground specified in the person's terms of appointment.

(2B) If the period (or extended period) for which the person is appointed ends before—

(a) the day on which the person attains the age of [75]

(b) ...

then, subject to sub-paragraph (2C), the Lord Chancellor must extend the period of the person's appointment (including a period already extended under this sub-paragraph) before it ends.

(2C) Extension under sub-paragraph (2B)—

(a) requires the person's agreement,

(b) is to be for such period as the Lord Chancellor considers appropriate, and

(c) may be refused on—

(i) the ground of inability or misbehaviour, or

(ii) a ground specified in the person's terms of appointment,

but only with any agreement of a senior judge (see section 46(7)), or a nominee of a senior judge, that may be required by those terms.]

(3) Subject to [the preceding provisions of this paragraph (but subject in the first place] to the Judicial Pensions and Retirement Act 1993 (c. 8)), the person is to hold and vacate office in accordance with the terms of his appointment[, which are to be such as the Lord Chancellor may determine].

5.–9. *****

*****

UK Borders Act 2007

(2007, c. 30)

An Act to make provision about immigration and asylum; and for connected purposes.

[30th October 2007]

Territorial extent: England, Scotland Wales, Northern Ireland (ss. 1–3); United Kingdom (other provisions reproduced here)

Detention at ports

1 Designated immigration officers

(1) The Secretary of State may designate immigration officers for the purposes of section 2.

(2) The Secretary of State may designate only officers who the Secretary of State thinks are—

(a) fit and proper for the purpose, and

(b) suitably trained.

(3) A designation—

(a) may be permanent or for a specified period, and

(b) may (in either case) be revoked.

2 Detention

(1) A designated immigration officer at a port in England, Wales or Northern Ireland may detain an individual if the immigration officer thinks that the individual—

(a) may be liable to arrest by a constable under section 24(1), (2) or (3) of the Police and Criminal Evidence Act 1984 (c. 60) or Article 26(1), (2) or (3) of the Police and Criminal Evidence (Northern Ireland) Order 1989 (S.I. 1989/1341 (N.I. 12)),

[(aa) is the subject of a certificate under section 74B of the Extradition Act 2003,] or

(b) is subject to a warrant for arrest.

[(1A) A designated immigration officer at a port in Scotland may detain an individual if the immigration officer thinks that [the individual—

(a) may be liable to be [arrested by a constable under section 1 of the Criminal Justice (Scotland) Act 2016] in respect of an offence under section 10(1) of the Counter-Terrorism and Security Act 2015,

[(aa) is the subject of a certificate under section 74B of the Extradition Act 2003,] or

(b) is subject to a warrant for arrest].]

(2) A designated immigration officer who detains an individual—

(a) must arrange for a constable to attend as soon as is reasonably practicable,

(b) may search the individual for, and retain, anything that might be used to assist escape or to cause physical injury to the individual or another person,

    (c) must retain anything found on a search which the immigration officer thinks may be evidence of the commission of an offence, and

    (d) must, when the constable arrives, deliver to the constable the individual and anything retained on a search.

(3) An individual may not be detained under this section for longer than three hours.

(4) A designated immigration officer may use reasonable force for the purpose of exercising a power under this section.

(5) Where an individual whom a designated immigration officer has detained or attempted to detain under this section leaves the port, a designated immigration officer may—

    (a) pursue the individual, and

    (b) return the individual to the port.

(6) Detention under this section shall be treated as detention under the Immigration Act 1971 (c. 77) for the purposes of Part 8 of the Immigration and Asylum Act 1999 (c. 33) (detained persons).

3 Enforcement

(1) An offence is committed by a person who—

    (a) absconds from detention under section 2,

    (b) assaults an immigration officer exercising a power under section 2, or

    (c) obstructs an immigration officer in the exercise of a power under section 2.

(2) A person guilty of an offence under subsection (1)(a) or (b) shall be liable on summary conviction to—

    (a) imprisonment for a term not exceeding [51 weeks],

    (b) a fine not exceeding level 5 on the standard scale, or

    (c) both.

(3) A person guilty of an offence under subsection (1)(c) shall be liable on summary conviction to—

    (a) imprisonment for a term not exceeding [51 weeks],

    (b) a fine not exceeding level 3 on the standard scale, or

    (c) both.

(4)–(5) *****

4–31 *****

Deportation of criminals

32 Automatic deportation

(1) In this section 'foreign criminal' means a person—

    (a) who is not a British citizen [or an Irish citizen],

    (b) who is convicted in the United Kingdom of an offence, and

    (c) to whom Condition 1 or 2 applies.

(2) Condition 1 is that the person is sentenced to a period of imprisonment of at least 12 months.

(3) Condition 2 is that—

    (a) the offence is specified by order of the Secretary of State under section 72(4)(a) of the Nationality, Immigration and Asylum Act 2002 (c. 41) (serious criminal), and

    (b) the person is sentenced to a period of imprisonment.

(4) For the purpose of section 3(5)(a) of the Immigration Act 1971 (c. 77), the deportation of a foreign criminal is conducive to the public good.

(5) The Secretary of State must make a deportation order in respect of a foreign criminal (subject to section 33).

(6) The Secretary of State may not revoke a deportation order made in accordance with subsection (5) unless—

    (a) he thinks that an exception under section 33 applies,

(b) the application for revocation is made while the foreign criminal is outside the United Kingdom, or

(c) section 34(4) applies.

(7) Subsection (5) does not create a private right of action in respect of consequences of non-compliance by the Secretary of State.

33 Exceptions

(1) Section 32(4) and (5)—

(a) do not apply where an exception in this section applies (subject to subsection (7) below), and

(b) are subject to sections 7 and 8 of the Immigration Act 1971 (Commonwealth citizens, Irish citizens, crew and other exemptions).

(2) Exception 1 is where removal of the foreign criminal in pursuance of the deportation order would breach—

(a) a person's Convention rights, or

(b) the United Kingdom's obligations under the Refugee Convention.

(3) Exception 2 is where the Secretary of State thinks that the foreign criminal was under the age of 18 on the date of conviction.

(4) ...

(5) Exception 4 is where the foreign criminal—

(a) is the subject of a certificate under section 2 or 70 of the Extradition Act 2003 (c. 41),

(b) is in custody pursuant to arrest under section 5 of that Act,

(c) is the subject of a provisional warrant under section 73 of that Act,

[(ca) is the subject of a certificate under section 74B of that Act,]

(d) is the subject of an authority to proceed under section 7 of the Extradition Act 1989 (c. 33) or an order under paragraph 4(2) of Schedule 1 to that Act, or

(e) is the subject of a provisional warrant under section 8 of that Act or of a warrant under paragraph 5(1)(b) of Schedule 1 to that Act.

(6), (6A)–(6D), (7) *****

34 Timing

(1) Section 32(5) requires a deportation order to be made at a time chosen by the Secretary of State.

(2) A deportation order may not be made under section 32(5) while an appeal or further appeal against the conviction or sentence by reference to which the order is to be made—

(a) has been instituted and neither withdrawn nor determined, or

(b) could be brought.

(3) For the purpose of subsection (2)(b)—

(a) the possibility of an appeal out of time with permission shall be disregarded, and

(b) a person who has informed the Secretary of State in writing that the person does not intend to appeal shall be treated as being no longer able to appeal.

(4) *****

35 *****

36 Detention

(1) A person who has served a period of imprisonment may be detained under the authority of the Secretary of State—

(a) while the Secretary of State considers whether section 32(5) applies, and

(b) where the Secretary of State thinks that section 32(5) applies, pending the making of the deportation order.

(2) Where a deportation order is made in accordance with section 32(5) the Secretary of State shall exercise the power of detention under paragraph 2(3) of Schedule 3 to the Immigration Act

1971 (c. 77) (detention pending removal) [unless the person is granted immigration bail under Schedule 10 to the Immigration Act 2016].

[(2A) The detention under subsection (1) of a person to whom section 60 (limitation on detention of pregnant women) of the Immigration Act 2016 applies is subject to that section.]

(3) A court determining an appeal against conviction or sentence may [release a person on bail] from detention under subsection (1) or (2).

[(3A) The provisions of Schedule 10 to the Immigration Act 2016 that apply in relation to the grant of immigration bail by the First-tier Tribunal apply in relation to the grant of bail by the court under subsection (3).

(3B) If the court grants bail to a person under subsection (3), Schedule 10 to the Immigration Act 2016 applies in relation to that person as if the person had been granted immigration bail by the First-tier Tribunal under that Schedule.

(3C) A reference in any provision of, or made under, an enactment other than this section to immigration bail granted, or a condition imposed, under Schedule 10 to the Immigration Act 2016 includes bail granted by the court under subsection (3) or (as the case may be) a condition imposed by the court on the grant of such bail.]

(4) *****

(5) ...

37 Family

(1) Where a deportation order against a foreign criminal states that it is made in accordance with section 32(5) ('the automatic deportation order') this section shall have effect in place of the words from 'A deportation order' to 'after the making of the deportation order against him' in section 5(3) of the Immigration Act 1971 (period during which family members may also be deported).

(2) A deportation order may not be made against a person as belonging to the family of the foreign criminal after the end of the relevant period of 8 weeks.

(3) In the case of a foreign criminal who has not appealed in respect of the automatic deportation order, the relevant period begins when an appeal can no longer be brought (ignoring any possibility of an appeal out of time with permission).

(4) In the case of a foreign criminal who has appealed in respect of the automatic deportation order, the relevant period begins when the appeal is no longer pending (within the meaning of section 104 of the Nationality, Immigration and Asylum Act 2002 (c. 41)).

38 Interpretation

(1) In section 32(2) the reference to a person who is sentenced to a period of imprisonment of at least 12 months—

  (a) does not include a reference to a person who receives a suspended sentence (unless a court subsequently orders that the sentence or any part of it (of whatever length) is to take effect),

  (b) does not include a reference to a person who is sentenced to a period of imprisonment of at least 12 months only by virtue of being sentenced to consecutive sentences amounting in aggregate to more than 12 months,

  (c) includes a reference to a person who is sentenced to detention, or ordered or directed to be detained, in an institution other than a prison (including, in particular, a hospital or an institution for young offenders) for at least 12 months, and

  (d) includes a reference to a person who is sentenced to imprisonment or detention, or ordered or directed to be detained, for an indeterminate period (provided that it may last for 12 months).

(2)–(4) *****

*****

Counter-Terrorism Act 2008

(2008, c. 28)

An Act to confer further powers to gather and share information for counter-terrorism and other purposes; to make further provision about the detention and questioning of terrorist suspects and the prosecution and punishment of terrorist offences; to impose notification requirements on persons convicted of such offences; to confer further powers to act against terrorist financing, money laundering and certain other activities; to provide for review of certain Treasury decisions and about evidence in, and other matters connected with, review proceedings; to amend the law relating to inquiries; to amend the definition of 'terrorism'; to amend the enactments relating to terrorist offences, control orders and the forfeiture of terrorist cash; to provide for recovering the costs of policing at certain gas facilities; to amend provisions about the appointment of special advocates in Northern Ireland; and for connected purposes.

[26th November 2008]

Territorial extent: United Kingdom

1–15*   *********

16, 17   **...**

[18   Destruction of national security material not subject to existing statutory restrictions]

[(1)   This section applies to fingerprints, DNA samples and DNA profiles that—

    (a)   are held for the purposes of national security by a law enforcement authority under the law of England and Wales or Northern Ireland, and

    (b)   are not held subject to existing statutory restrictions.

(2)   Material to which this section applies ('section 18 material') must be destroyed if it appears to the responsible officer that the condition in subsection (3) is not met.

(3)   The condition is that the material has been—

    (a)   obtained by the law enforcement authority pursuant to an authorisation under Part 3 of the Police Act 1997 (authorisation of action in respect of property),

    (b)   obtained by the law enforcement authority in the course of surveillance, or use of a covert human intelligence source, authorised under Part 2 of the Regulation of Investigatory Powers Act 2000,

    (c)   supplied to the law enforcement authority by another law enforcement authority, or

    (d)   otherwise lawfully obtained or acquired by the law enforcement authority for any of the purposes mentioned in section 18D(1).

(4)   In any other case, section 18 material must be destroyed unless it is retained by the law enforcement authority under any power conferred by section 18A or 18B, but this is subject to subsection (5).

(5)   A DNA sample to which this section applies must be destroyed—

    (a)   as soon as a DNA profile has been derived from the sample, or

    (b)   if sooner, before the end of the period of 6 months beginning with the date on which it was taken.

(6)   Section 18 material which ceases to be retained under a power mentioned in subsection (4) may continue to be retained under any other such power which applies to it.

(7)   Nothing in this section prevents section 18 material from being checked against other fingerprints, DNA samples or DNA profiles held by a law enforcement authority within such time as may reasonably be required for the check, if the responsible officer considers the check to be desirable.

(8)   For the purposes of subsection (1), the following are 'existing statutory restrictions'—

    (a)   paragraph 18(2) of Schedule 2 to the Immigration Act 1971;

---

* **Editor's Note:** The early sections of this Act have been omitted as they are largely not yet in force (April 2023).

(b) sections 22, 63A and 63D to 63U of the Police and Criminal Evidence Act 1984 and any corresponding provision in an order under section 113 of that Act;

(c) Articles 24, 63A and 64 of the Police and Criminal Evidence (Northern Ireland) Order 1989 (SI 1989/1341 (NI 12));

(d) section 2(2) of the Security Service Act 1989;

(e) section 2(2) of the Intelligence Services Act 1994;

(f) paragraphs 20(3) and 20A to 20J of Schedule 8 to the Terrorism Act 2000;

(g) section 56 of the Criminal Justice and Police Act 2001;

(h) paragraph 8 of Schedule 4 to the International Criminal Court Act 2001;

(i) sections 73, 83, 87, 88 and 89 of the Armed Forces Act 2006 and any provision relating to the retention of material in an order made under section 74, 93 or 323 of that Act;

(j) paragraphs 5 to 14 of Schedule 6 to the Terrorism Prevention and Investigation Measures Act 2011.]

[(k) paragraphs 43 to 51 of Schedule 3 to the Counter-Terrorism and Border Security Act 2019.]

[18A   Retention of material: general]

[(1)   Section 18 material which is not a DNA sample and relates to a person who has no previous convictions or only one exempt conviction may be retained by the law enforcement authority until the end of the retention period specified in subsection (2), but this is subject to subsection (5).

(2)   The retention period is—

(a) in the case of fingerprints, the period of 3 years beginning with the date on which the fingerprints were taken, and

(b) in the case of a DNA profile, the period of 3 years beginning with the date on which the DNA sample from which the profile was derived was taken (or, if the profile was derived from more than one DNA sample, the date on which the first of those samples was taken).

(3)   Section 18 material which is not a DNA sample and relates to a person who has previously been convicted of a recordable offence (other than a single exempt conviction), or is so convicted before the material is required to be destroyed by virtue of this section, may be retained indefinitely.

(4)   Section 18 material which is not a DNA sample may be retained indefinitely if—

(a) it is held by the law enforcement authority in a form which does not include information which identifies the person to whom the material relates, and

(b) the law enforcement authority does not know, and has never known, the identity of the person to whom the material relates.

(5)   In a case where section 18 material is being retained by a law enforcement authority under subsection (4), if—

(a) the law enforcement authority comes to know the identity of the person to whom the material relates, and

(b) the material relates to a person who has no previous convictions or only one exempt conviction,

the material may be retained by the law enforcement authority until the end of the retention period specified in subsection (6).

(6)   The retention period is the period of 3 years beginning with the date on which the identity of the person to whom the material relates comes to be known by the law enforcement authority.]

[18B   Retention for purposes of national security]

[(1)   Section 18 material which is not a DNA sample may be retained for as long as a national security determination made by the responsible officer[, or by a chief officer of police,] has effect in relation to it.

(2)   A national security determination is made if the responsible officer[, or a chief officer of police,] determines that it is necessary for any such section 18 material to be retained for the purposes of national security.

(3)   A national security determination—

(a) must be made in writing,

(b) has effect for a maximum of [5 years] beginning with the date on which the determination is made, and

(c) may be renewed.]

[(4) In this section 'chief officer of police' means a person other than the responsible officer who is—

(a) the chief officer of police of a police force in England and Wales, or

(b) the Chief Constable of the Police Service of Northern Ireland.]

[18BA] *****

[18C Destruction of copies]

[(1) If fingerprints are required by section 18 to be destroyed, any copies of the fingerprints held by the law enforcement authority concerned must also be destroyed.

(2) If a DNA profile is required by that section to be destroyed, no copy may be retained by the law enforcement authority concerned except in a form which does not include information which identifies the person to whom the DNA profile relates.]

[18D Use of retained material]

[(1) Section 18 material must not be used other than—

(a) in the interests of national security,

(b) for the purposes of a terrorist investigation,

(c) for purposes related to the prevention or detection of crime, the investigation of an offence or the conduct of a prosecution, or

(d) for purposes related to the identification of a deceased person or of the person to whom the material relates.

(2) Subject to subsection (1), section 18 material may be checked against other fingerprints, DNA samples or DNA profiles held by a law enforcement authority or the Scottish Police Services Authority if the responsible officer considers the check to be desirable.

(3) Material which is required by section 18 to be destroyed must not at any time after it is required to be destroyed be used—

(a) in evidence against the person to whom the material relates, or

(b) for the purposes of the investigation of any offence.

(4) In this section—

(a) the reference to using material includes a reference to allowing any check to be made against it and to disclosing it to any person,

(b) the reference to crime includes a reference to any conduct which—

(i) constitutes one or more criminal offences (whether under the law of a part of the United Kingdom or of a country or territory outside the United Kingdom), or

(ii) is, or corresponds to, any conduct which, if it all took place in any one part of the United Kingdom, would constitute one or more criminal offences, and

(c) the references to an investigation and to a prosecution include references, respectively, to any investigation outside the United Kingdom of any crime or suspected crime and to a prosecution brought in respect of any crime in a country or territory outside the United Kingdom.]

[18E] *****

Disclosure of information and the intelligence services

19 Disclosure and the intelligence services

(1) A person may disclose information to any of the intelligence services for the purposes of the exercise by that service of any of its functions.

(2) Information obtained by any of the intelligence services in connection with the exercise of any of its functions may be used by that service in connection with the exercise of any of its other functions.

(3) Information obtained by the Security Service for the purposes of any of its functions may be disclosed by it—

(a) for the purpose of the proper discharge of its functions,

(b) for the purpose of the prevention or detection of serious crime, or

(c) for the purpose of any criminal proceedings.

(4) Information obtained by the Secret Intelligence Service for the purposes of any of its functions may be disclosed by it—

(a) for the purpose of the proper discharge of its functions,

(b) in the interests of national security,

(c) for the purpose of the prevention or detection of serious crime, or

(d) for the purpose of any criminal proceedings.

(5) Information obtained by GCHQ for the purposes of any of its functions may be disclosed by it—

(a) for the purpose of the proper discharge of its functions, or

(b) for the purpose of any criminal proceedings.

(6) A disclosure under this section does not breach—

(a) any obligation of confidence owed by the person making the disclosure, or

(b) any other restriction on the disclosure of information (however imposed).

(7) The provisions of this section are subject to section 20 (savings and other supplementary provisions).

20 Disclosure and the intelligence services: supplementary provisions

(1) The provisions of section 19 (disclosure and use of information) do not affect the duties with respect to the obtaining or disclosure of information imposed—

(a) on the Director-General of the Security Service, by section 2(2) of the Security Service Act 1989;

(b) on the Chief of the Intelligence Service, by section 2(2) of the Intelligence Services Act 1994;

(c) on the Director of GCHQ, by section 4(2) of that Act.

(2) Nothing in that section authorises a disclosure that—

(a) contravenes [the data protection legislation], or

(b) is prohibited by [any of Parts 1 to 7 or Chapter 1 of the Investigatory Powers Act 2016].

(3) The provisions of that section are without prejudice to any rule of law authorising the obtaining, use or disclosure of information by any of the intelligence services.

(4), [(5)] *****

21 Disclosure and the intelligence services: interpretation

(1) In sections 19 and 20 'the intelligence services' means the Security Service, the Secret Intelligence Service and GCHQ.

(2)–(4) *****

PART 2 POST-CHARGE QUESTIONING
OF TERRORIST SUSPECTS

22 Post-charge questioning: England and Wales*

(1) The following provisions apply in England and Wales.

(2) A judge of the Crown Court may authorise the questioning of a person about an offence—

(a) after the person has been charged with the offence or been officially informed that they may be prosecuted for it, or

(b) after the person has been sent for trial for the offence,

if the offence is a terrorism offence or it appears to the judge that the offence has a terrorist connection.

(3) The judge—

---

* **Editor's Note:** Sections 23 and 24 repeat these powers for the Sheriff (Scotland) and District Judge (Northern Ireland).

(a) must specify the period during which questioning is authorised, and

(b) may impose such conditions as appear to be necessary in the interests of justice, which may include conditions as to the place where the questioning is to be carried out.

(4) The period during which questioning is authorised—

(a) begins when questioning pursuant to the authorisation begins and runs continuously from that time (whether or not questioning continues), and

(b) must not exceed 48 hours.

This is without prejudice to any application for a further authorisation under this section.

(5) Where the person is in prison or otherwise lawfully detained, the judge may authorise the person's removal to another place and detention there for the purpose of being questioned.

(6) A judge must not authorise the questioning of a person under this section unless satisfied—

(a) that further questioning of the person is necessary in the interests of justice,

(b) that the investigation for the purposes of which the further questioning is proposed is being conducted diligently and expeditiously, and

(c) that what is authorised will not interfere unduly with the preparation of the person's defence to the charge in question or any other criminal charge.

(7) Codes of practice under section 66 of the Police and Criminal Evidence Act 1984 (c. 60) must make provision about the questioning of a person by a constable in accordance with this section.

(8) Nothing in this section prevents codes of practice under that section making other provision for the questioning of a person by a constable about an offence—

(a) after the person has been charged with the offence or been officially informed that they may be prosecuted for it, or

(b) after the person has been sent for trial for the offence.

(9), (10) *****

23, 24 *****

25 Recording of interviews

(1) This section applies to any interview of a person by a constable under section 22, 23 or 24 (post-charge questioning).

(2) Any such interview must be video recorded, and the video recording must be with sound.

(3) The Secretary of State must issue a code of practice about the video recording of interviews to which this section applies.

(4) The interview and video recording must be conducted in accordance with that code of practice.

(5) A code of practice under this section—

(a) may make provision in relation to a particular part of the United Kingdom, and

(b) may make different provision for different parts of the United Kingdom.

26 Issue and revision of code of practice

(1) This section applies to the code of practice under section 25 (recording of interviews).

(2) The Secretary of State must—

(a) publish a draft of the proposed code, and

(b) consider any representations made about the draft,

and may modify the draft in the light of the representations made.

(3) The Secretary of State must lay a draft of the code before Parliament.

(4) After laying the draft code before Parliament the Secretary of State may bring it into operation by order.

(5) The order is subject to affirmative resolution procedure.

(6) The Secretary of State may revise a code and issue the revised code, and subsections (2) to (5) apply to a revised code as they apply to an original code.

(7) Failure to observe a provision of a code does not of itself render a constable liable to criminal or civil proceedings.

(8) A code—
   (a) is admissible in evidence in criminal and civil proceedings, and
   (b) shall be taken into account by a court or tribunal in any case in which it appears to the court or tribunal to be relevant.

27   Meaning of 'terrorism offence'
   (1) For the purposes of sections 22 to 24 (post-charge questioning) the following are terrorism offences—
   (a) an offence under any of the following provisions of the Terrorism Act 2000 (c. 11)—sections 11 to 13 (offences relating to proscribed organisations), sections 15 to 19, 21A and 21D (offences relating to terrorist property), sections 38B and 39 (disclosure of and failure to disclose information about terrorism), section 54 (weapons training), sections 56 to 58A (directing terrorism, possessing things and collecting information for the purposes of terrorism), [section 58B (entering or remaining in a designated area)] sections 59 to 61 (inciting terrorism outside the United Kingdom), paragraph 14 of Schedule 5 (order for explanation of material: false or misleading statements), paragraph 1 of Schedule 6 (failure to provide customer information in connection with a terrorist investigation), paragraph 18 of Schedule 7 (offences in connection with port and border controls);
   (b) an offence in respect of which there is jurisdiction by virtue of any of sections 62 to 63D of that Act (extra-territorial jurisdiction in respect of certain offences committed outside the United Kingdom for the purposes of terrorism etc);
   (c) an offence under section 113 of the Anti-Terrorism, Crime and Security Act 2001 (c. 24) (use of noxious substances or things);
   (d) an offence under any of the following provisions of Part 1 of the Terrorism Act 2006 (c. 11)—sections 1 and 2 (encouragement of terrorism), sections 5, 6 and 8 (preparation and training for terrorism), sections 9, 10 and 11 (offences relating to radioactive devices and material and nuclear facilities);
   (e) an offence in respect of which there is jurisdiction by virtue of section 17 of that Act (extra-territorial jurisdiction in respect of certain offences committed outside the United Kingdom for the purposes of terrorism etc);
   (f) an offence under paragraph 8 or 9 of Schedule 3 to the Justice and Security (Northern Ireland) Act 2007 (c. 6) (offences in connection with searches for munitions and transmitters in Northern Ireland).
   (2) Any ancillary offence in relation to an offence listed in subsection (1) is a terrorism offence for the purposes of sections 22 to 24.
   (3) The Secretary of State may by order amend subsection (1).
   (4) Any such order is subject to affirmative resolution procedure.

PART 3 PROSECUTION AND PUNISHMENT OF TERRORIST OFFENCES

28   Jurisdiction to try offences committed in the UK
   (1) Where an offence to which this section applies is committed in the United Kingdom—
   (a) proceedings for the offence may be taken at any place in the United Kingdom, and
   (b) the offence may for all incidental purposes be treated as having been committed at any such place.
   (2) The section applies to—
   (a) an offence under any of the following provisions of the Terrorism Act 2000 (c. 11)—sections 11 to 13 (offences relating to proscribed organisations), sections 15 to 19, 21A and 21D (offences relating to terrorist property), sections 38B and 39 (disclosure of and failure to disclose information about terrorism), section 47 (offences relating to stop and search powers), section 51 (parking a vehicle in contravention of an authorisation or

restriction), section 54 (weapons training), sections 56 to 58A (directing terrorism and possessing things or collecting information for the purposes of terrorism), section 116 (failure to stop a vehicle when required to do so), paragraph 1 of Schedule 6 (failure to provide customer information in connection with a terrorist investigation), paragraph 18 of Schedule 7 (offences in connection with port and border controls);

(b) an offence under section 113 of the Anti-terrorism, Crime and Security Act 2001 (c. 24) (use of noxious substances or things to cause harm and intimidate);

(c) an offence under any of the following provisions of the Terrorism Act 2006 (c. 11)— sections 1 and 2 (encouragement of terrorism), sections 5, 6 and 8 (preparation and training for terrorism), sections 9, 10 and 11 (offences relating to radioactive devices etc).

[(d) an offence under any provision of Part 1 of the Terrorist Asset-Freezing etc Act 2010].

(3) The Secretary of State may by order amend subsection (2).

(4) Any such order is subject to affirmative resolution procedure.

(5) The power conferred by subsection (3) may be exercised so as to add offences to subsection (2) only if it appears to the Secretary of State necessary to do so for the purpose of dealing with terrorism.

(6) *****

29–31   *****

32, 33   ...

34–39   *****

PART 4 NOTIFICATION REQUIREMENTS

40 Scheme of this Part

(1) This Part imposes notification requirements on persons dealt with in respect of certain offences—

(a) sections 41 to 43 specify the offences to which this Part applies;

(b) sections 44 to 46 make provision as to the sentences or orders triggering the notification requirements;

(c) sections 47 to 52 contain the notification requirements; and

(d) section 53 makes provision as to the period for which the requirements apply.

(2) This Part also provides for—

(a) orders applying the notification requirements to persons dealt with outside the United Kingdom for corresponding foreign offences (see section 57 and Schedule 4); ...

(b) orders imposing restrictions on travel outside the United Kingdom on persons subject to the notification requirements (see section 58 and Schedule 5)[, and

[(c) warrants authorising entry and search of premises notified under this Part or where a person to whom the notification requirements apply resides or may be found].

(3) Schedule 6 provides for the application of this Part to service offences and related matters.

41 Offences to which this Part applies: terrorism offences

(1) This Part applies to—

(a) an offence under any of the following provisions of the Terrorism Act 2000 (c. 11)— section 11 or 12 (offences relating to proscribed organisations), sections 15 to 18 (offences relating to terrorist property), section 38B (failure to disclose information about acts of terrorism), section 54 (weapons training), sections 56 to 61 (directing terrorism, possessing things and collecting information for the purposes of terrorism [eliciting information about members of armed forces etc, entering or remaining in a designated area] and inciting terrorism outside the United Kingdom);

(b) an offence in respect of which there is jurisdiction by virtue of any of sections 62 to 63D of that Act (extra-territorial jurisdiction in respect of certain offences committed outside the United Kingdom for the purposes of terrorism etc);

(c) an offence under section 113 of the Anti-terrorism, Crime and Security Act 2001 (c. 24) (use of noxious substances or things);

(d) an offence under any of the following provisions of Part 1 of the Terrorism Act 2006 (c. 11)—sections 1 and 2 (encouragement of terrorism), sections 5, 6 and 8 (preparation and training for terrorism), sections 9, 10 and 11 (offences relating to radioactive devices and material and nuclear facilities);

(e) an offence in respect of which there is jurisdiction by virtue of section 17 of that Act (extra-territorial jurisdiction in respect of certain offences committed outside the United Kingdom for the purposes of terrorism etc).

[(f) an offence under section 23 of the Terrorism Prevention and Investigation Measures Act 2011 (breach of notice imposing terrorism prevention and investigation measures) dealt with on or after the day on which section 42 of the Counter-Terrorism and Sentencing Act 2021 comes into force;

(g) an offence under section 10(1) or (3) of the Counter-Terrorism and Security Act 2015 (breach of temporary exclusion order or related obligation) dealt with on or after that day.]

(2) This Part also applies to any ancillary offence in relation to an offence listed in subsection (1).

(3) The Secretary of State may by order amend subsection (1).

(4) Any such order is subject to affirmative resolution procedure.

(5) An order adding an offence applies only in relation to offences dealt with after the order comes into force.

(6) An order removing an offence has effect in relation to offences whenever dealt with, whether before or after the order comes into force.

(7) Where an offence is removed from the list, a person subject to the notification requirements by reason of that offence being listed (and who is not otherwise subject to those requirements) ceases to be subject to them when the order comes into force.

42 Offences to which this Part applies: offences having a terrorist connection

(1) This Part applies to—

(a) an offence as to which a court has determined under section 30 (sentences for offences with a terrorist connection: England and Wales [and Northern Ireland]) that the offence has a terrorist connection, and

(b) an offence in relation to which section 31 applies (sentences for offences with terrorist connection: Scotland).

(2) A person to whom the notification requirements apply by virtue of such a determination as is mentioned in subsection (1)(a) may appeal against it to the same court, and subject to the same conditions, as an appeal against sentence.

(3) If the determination is set aside on appeal, the notification requirements are treated as never having applied to that person in respect of the offence.

(4) Where an order is made under section 33 removing an offence from the list in Schedule 2, a person subject to the notification requirements by reason of that offence being so listed (and who is not otherwise subject to those requirements) ceases to be subject to them when the order comes into force.

43 *****

44 Persons to whom the notification requirements apply

The notification requirements apply to a person who—

(a) is aged 16 or over at the time of being dealt with for an offence to which this Part applies, and

(b) is made subject in respect of the offence to a sentence or order within section 45 (sentences or orders triggering notification requirements).

45 Sentences or orders triggering notification requirements

(1) The notification requirements apply to a person who in England and Wales—

(a) has been convicted of an offence to which this Part applies and sentenced in respect of the offence to—

    (i)   imprisonment or custody for life,

    (ii)   imprisonment or detention in a young offender institution for a term of 12 months or more,

    (iii)   imprisonment or detention in a young offender institution for public protection under section 225 of the Criminal Justice Act 2003 (c. 44),

    (iv)   detention for life or for a period of 12 months or more under section 91 of the Powers of Criminal Courts (Sentencing) Act 2000 (c. 6) [or section 250 of the Sentencing Code] (offenders under 18 convicted of certain serious offences),

    (v)   a detention and training order for a term of 12 months or more under section 100 [of the Powers of Criminal Courts (Sentencing) Act 2000 or under Chapter 2 of Part 10 of the Sentencing Code] (offenders under age of 18),

    (vi)   detention for public protection under section 226 of the Criminal Justice Act 2003 (serious offences committed by persons under 18),

    [(via)   detention under section 226B of that Act [or under section 254 of the Sentencing Code] (extended sentence of detention for certain dangerous offenders aged under 18),]

    [(vib)   detention under section 252A of the Sentencing Code (special sentence for terrorist offenders of particular concern aged under 18),] or

    (vii)   detention during Her Majesty's pleasure; or

(b) has been—

    (i)   convicted of an offence to which this Part applies carrying a maximum term of imprisonment of 12 months or more,

    (ii)   found not guilty by reason of insanity of such an offence, or

    (iii)   found to be under a disability and to have done the act charged against them in respect of such an offence,

and made subject in respect of the offence to a hospital order.

(2)–(5) *****

46 Power to amend specified terms or periods of imprisonment or detention

(1) The Secretary of State may by order amend the provisions of section 45 referring to a specified term or period of imprisonment or detention.

(2)–(4) *****

47 Initial notification

(1) A person to whom the notification requirements apply must notify the following information to the police within the period of three days beginning with the day on which the person is dealt with in respect of the offence in question.

(2) The information required is—

    (a)   date of birth;

    (b)   national insurance number;

    (c)   name on the date on which the person was dealt with in respect of the offence (where the person used one or more other names on that date, each of those names);

    (d)   home address on that date;

    [(da)   all contact details on that date;]

    (e)   name on the date on which notification is made (where the person uses one or more other names on that date, each of those names);

    (f)   home address on the date on which notification is made;

    [(fa)   all contact details on the date on which notification is made;]

    (g)   address of any other premises in the United Kingdom at which, at the time the notification is made, the person regularly resides or stays;

[(ga) identifying information of any motor vehicle of which the person is the registered keeper, or which the person has a right to use (whether routinely or on specific occasions or for specific purposes), on the date on which notification is made;

(gb) the financial information specified in paragraph 1 of Schedule 3A;

(gc) the information about identification documents specified in paragraph 2 of Schedule 3A;]

(h) any prescribed information.

(3) In subsection (2) 'prescribed' means prescribed by regulations made by the Secretary of State. Such regulations are subject to affirmative resolution procedure.

(4) In determining the period within which notification is to be made under this section, there shall be disregarded any time when the person is—

(a) remanded in or committed to custody by an order of a court,

(b) serving a sentence of imprisonment or detention,

(c) detained in a hospital, or

(d) detained under the Immigration Acts.

(5) This section does not apply to a person who—

(a) is subject to the notification requirements in respect of another offence (and does not cease to be so subject before the end of the period within which notification is to be made), and

(b) has complied with this section in respect of that offence.

(6) In the application of this section to a person dealt with for an offence before the commencement of this Part who, immediately before commencement—

(a) would be imprisoned or detained in respect of the offence but for being unlawfully at large, absent without leave, on temporary leave or leave of absence, or on bail pending an appeal, or

(b) is on licence, having served the custodial part of a sentence of imprisonment in respect of the offence,

the reference in subsection (1) to the day on which the person is dealt with in respect of the offence shall be read as a reference to the commencement of this Part.

48 Notification of changes [: general]

(1) A person to whom the notification requirements apply who uses a name that has not previously been notified to the police must notify the police of that name.

(2) If there is a change of the home address of a person to whom the notification requirements apply, the person must notify the police of the new home address.

(3) A person to whom the notification requirements apply who resides or stays at premises in the United Kingdom the address of which has previously not been notified to the police—

(a) for a period of 7 days, or

(b) for two or more periods, in any period of 12 months, that taken together amount to 7 days,

must notify the police of the address of those premises.

(4) A person to whom the notification requirements apply who is released—

(a) from custody pursuant to an order of a court,

(b) from imprisonment or detention pursuant to a sentence of a court,

(c) from detention in a hospital, or

(d) from detention under the Immigration Acts,

must notify the police of that fact.

This does not apply if the person is at the same time required to notify the police under section 47 (initial notification).

[(4A) If there is a change in the contact details of a person to whom the notification requirements apply, the person must notify the police of the new contact details.

(4B) If a person to whom the notification requirements apply ceases to use contact details which the person has previously notified under this Part, the person must notify the police of that fact.

(4C) If a person to whom the notification requirements apply becomes the registered keeper of, or acquires a right to use, a motor vehicle the identifying information of which has not previously been notified to the police, the person must notify the police of the identifying information of that motor vehicle.

(4D) If there is a change in the identifying information of a motor vehicle previously notified under this Part, the person must notify the police—

    (a) that there has been a change, and

    (b) of the new identifying information of the motor vehicle.

(4E) If a person to whom the notification requirements apply ceases to be the registered keeper of a motor vehicle the identifying information of which the person has notified, or ceases to have the right to use such a motor vehicle, the person must notify the police that the person is no longer the registered keeper of the motor vehicle or no longer has the right to use it.]

(5) A person who is required to notify information within section 47(2)(h) (prescribed information) must notify the police of the prescribed details of any prescribed changes in that information.

(6)–(10) *****

[48A Notification of changes: financial information and information about identification documents

(1) If there is a change in any of the financial information (see paragraph 1 of Schedule 3A), or information about identification documents (see paragraph 2 of that Schedule), in relation to a person to whom the notification requirements apply, the person must notify the police of the change.

(2) For the purposes of subsection (1) there is a change in the financial information if—

    (a) an account previously notified in accordance with this Part is closed;

    (b) a payment card previously notified in accordance with this Part is no longer held by the person notified as holding it;

    (c) an account is opened, or a payment card is obtained, which would have been required to be notified in accordance with section 47(2)(gb) if the account or card had been held at the time when notification was made under section 47(1);

    (d) any other financial information previously notified in accordance with this Part is altered or becomes inaccurate.

(3) For the purposes of subsection (1) there is a change in the information about identification documents if—

    (a) the person ceases to hold a passport or other document previously notified in accordance with this Part;

    (b) the person obtains a passport or other document which would have been required to be notified in accordance with section 47(2)(gc) if it had been held at the time when notification was made under section 47(1).

(4) Where a change required to be notified under subsection (1) relates to opening a new account or obtaining a new payment card as mentioned in subsection (2)(c), the person must in notifying the change include all the information (so far as relevant) specified in paragraph 1(2) of Schedule 3A in respect of the new account or card.

(5) Where a change required to be notified under subsection (1) relates to the holding of a new passport or other document as mentioned in subsection (3)(b), the person must in notifying the change include all the information (so far as relevant) specified in paragraph 2 of Schedule 3A in relation to the new passport or other document.

(6) Notification under this section must be made before the end of the period of three days beginning with the day on which the event in question occurs.

(7) In determining the period within which notification is to be made under this section, any time when the person is—

    (a) remanded in or committed to custody by any order of a court,

    (b) serving a sentence of imprisonment or detention,

    (c) detained in a hospital, or

(d) detained under the Immigration Acts, is to be ignored.

(8) Notification under this section must be accompanied by re-notification of the other information mentioned in section 47(2)]

49   Periodic re-notification

(1) A person to whom the notification requirements apply must, within the [applicable period] after last notifying the police in accordance with—

    (a)   section 47 (initial notification),

    (b)   section 48 (notification of change [general]),

    [(ba) section 48A (notification of changes: financial information and information about identification documents)]

    (c)   this section, or

    (d)   section 56 (notification on return after absence from UK),

re-notify to the police the information mentioned in section 47(2).

    [(1A) In this section the 'applicable period' means—

    (a)   in the case of a person who has no sole or main residence in the United Kingdom, the period of one week, and

    (b)   in any other case, the period of one year.]

(2) Subsection (1) does not apply if the [applicable period] referred to in that subsection ends at a time when the person is—

    (a) remanded in or committed to custody by an order of a court,

    (b) serving a sentence of imprisonment or detention,

    (c) detained in a hospital, or

    (d) detained under the Immigration Acts.

(3) In that case section 48(4) and (10) (duty to notify of release and to re-notify other information) apply when the person is released.

50   Method of notification and related matters

(1) This section applies to notification under—

    (a)   section 47 (initial notification),

    (b)   section 48 (notification of change[: general]),

    [(ba) section 48A (notification of changes: financial information and information about identification documents),]

    (c)   section 49 (periodic re-notification), or

    (d)   section 56 (notification on return after absence from UK).

(2) Notification must be made by the person—

    (a) attending at a police station in the person's local police area, and

    (b) making an oral notification to a police officer or to a person authorised for the purpose by the officer in charge of the station.

(3) A person making a notification under section 48 (notification of change) in relation to premises referred to in subsection (3) of that section may make the notification at a police station that would fall within subsection (2)(a) above if the address of those premises were the person's home address.

(4) The notification must be acknowledged.

(5) The acknowledgement must be in writing, and in such form as the Secretary of State may direct.

(6) The person making the notification must, if requested to do so by the police officer or person to whom the notification is made, allow the officer or person to—

    (a) take the person's fingerprints,

    (b) photograph any part of the person, or

    (c) do both these things,

for the purpose of verifying the person's identity.

    (7) *****

51   *****

52   Travel outside the United Kingdom

(1) The Secretary of State may by regulations make provision requiring a person to whom the notification requirements apply who leaves the United Kingdom—

(a) to notify the police of their departure before they leave, and

(b) to notify the police of their return if they subsequently return to the United Kingdom.

(2) Notification of departure must disclose—

(a) the date on which the person intends to leave the United Kingdom;

(b) the country (or, if there is more than one, the first country) to which the person will travel;

(c) the person's point of arrival (determined in accordance with the regulations) in that country;

(d) any other information required by the regulations.

(3) Notification of return must disclose such information as is required by the regulations about the person's return to the United Kingdom.

(4), (5) *****

53   Period for which notification requirements apply

(1) The period for which the notification requirements apply is—

(a) 30 years in the case of a person who—

(i)   is aged 18 or over at the time of conviction for the offence, and

(ii)   receives in respect of the offence a sentence within subsection (2);

(b) 15 years in the case of a person who—

(i)   is aged 18 or over at the time of conviction for the offence, and

(ii)   receives in respect of the offence a sentence within subsection (3);

(c) 10 years in any other case.

(2) The sentences in respect of which a 30 year period applies are—

(a) in England and Wales—

(i)   imprisonment or custody for life,

(ii)   imprisonment or detention in a young offender institution for a term of 10 years or more,

(iii) imprisonment or detention in a young offender institution for public protection under section 225 of the Criminal Justice Act 2003 (c. 44),

(iv)   detention during Her Majesty's pleasure;

(b) in Scotland—

(i)   imprisonment or detention in a young offenders institution for life,

(ii)   imprisonment or detention in a young offenders institution for a term of 10 years or more,

(iii) an order for lifelong restriction under section 210F of the Criminal Procedure (Scotland) Act 1995 (c. 46);

(c) in Northern Ireland—

(i)   imprisonment for life,

(ii)   imprisonment for a term of 10 years or more,

(iii) an indeterminate custodial sentence under Article 13 of the Criminal Justice (Northern Ireland) Order 2008 (S.I. 2008/1216 (N.I. 1)),

(iv)   an extended custodial sentence for a term of 10 years or more under Article 14(5) of that Order (offenders under 21 convicted of certain offences),

(v)   detention during the pleasure of the [Minister in charge of the Department of Justice] under Article 45(1) of the Criminal Justice (Children) (Northern Ireland) Order 1998 (S.I. 1998/1504 (N.I. 9)).

(3) The sentences in respect of which a 15 year period applies are—

(a) in England and Wales, imprisonment or detention in a young offender institution for a term of 5 years or more but less than 10 years;

(b) in Scotland, imprisonment or detention in a young offenders institution for a term of 5 years or more but less than 10 years;

(c) in Northern Ireland—

(i) imprisonment for a term of 5 years or more but less than 10 years,

(ii) an extended custodial sentence for a term of 5 years or more but less than 10 years under Article 14(5) of the Criminal Justice (Northern Ireland) Order 2008 (S.I. 2008/1216 (N.I. 1)) (offenders under 21 convicted of certain offences).

(4) The period begins with the day on which the person is dealt with for the offence.

(5) If a person who is the subject of a finding within section 45(1)(b)(iii), (2)(b)(iii) or (3)(b)(iii) (finding of disability, etc) is subsequently tried for the offence, the period resulting from that finding ends—

(a) if the person is acquitted, at the conclusion of the trial;

(b) if the person is convicted, when the person is again dealt with in respect of the offence.

(6) For the purposes of determining the length of the period—

(a) a person who has been sentenced in respect of two or more offences to which this Part applies to consecutive terms of imprisonment is treated as if sentenced, in respect of each of the offences, to a term of imprisonment equal to the aggregate of the terms; and

(b) a person who has been sentenced in respect of two or more such offences to concurrent terms of imprisonment (X and Y) that overlap for a period (Z) is treated as if sentenced, in respect of each of the offences, to a term of imprisonment equal to X plus Y minus Z.

(7) In determining whether the period has expired, there shall be disregarded any period when the person was—

(a) remanded in or committed to custody by an order of a court,

(b) serving a sentence of imprisonment or detention,

(c) detained in a hospital, or

(d) detained under the Immigration Acts.

54 Offences relating to notification

(1) A person commits an offence who—

(a) fails without reasonable excuse to comply with—section 47 (initial notification), section 48 (notification of changes [general]), [section 48A (notification of changes: financial information and information about identification documents]) section 49 (periodic re-notification), section 50(6) (taking of fingerprints or photographs), any regulations made under section 52(1) (travel outside United Kingdom), or section 56 (notification on return after absence from UK); or

(b) notifies to the police in purported compliance with—section 47 (initial notification), section 48 (notification of changes), section 49 (periodic re-notification), any regulations made under section 52(1) (travel outside United Kingdom), or section 56 (notification on return after absence from UK), any information that the person knows to be false.

(2), (3) *****

(4) A person—

(a) commits an offence under subsection (1)(a) above on the day on which the person first fails without reasonable excuse to comply with—section 47 (initial notification), section 48 (notification of changes [general]), [section 48A (notification of changes: financial information and information about identification documents]) section 49 (periodic re-notification), any regulations made under section 52(1) (travel outside United Kingdom), or section 56 (notification on return after absence from UK), and

(b) continues to commit it throughout any period during which the failure continues.

But a person must not be prosecuted under subsection (1) more than once in respect of the same failure.

(5) Proceedings for an offence under this section may be commenced in any court having jurisdiction in any place where the person charged with the offence resides or is found.

55 Effect of absence abroad

(1) If a person to whom the notification requirements apply is absent from the United Kingdom for any period the following provisions apply.

(2) During the period of absence the period for which the notification requirements apply continues to run.

(3) The period of absence does not affect the obligation under section 47 (initial notification). This is subject to subsection (4).

(4) Section 47 does not apply if—

    (a) the period of absence begins before the end of the period within which notification must be made under that section, and

    (b) the person's absence results from the person's removal from the United Kingdom.

(5) [Sections 48 and 48A] (notification of changes)—

    (a) [apply] in relation to an event that occurs before the period of absence, but

    (b) [do] not apply in relation to an event that occurs during the period of absence.

Paragraph (a) is subject to subsection (6).

(6) [Sections 48 and 48A do] not apply in relation to an event that occurs before the period of absence if—

    (a) the period of absence begins before the end of the period within which notification must be made under that section, and

    (b) the person's absence results from the person's removal from the United Kingdom.

(7) Section 49 (periodic re-notification) does not apply if [the applicable period] referred to in subsection (1) of that section ends during the period of absence.

(8) Section 53(7) (disregard of period of custody etc) applies in relation to the period of absence as if it referred to any period when the person was—

    (a) remanded in or committed to custody by an order of a court outside the United Kingdom,

    (b) serving a sentence of imprisonment or detention imposed by such a court,

    (c) detained in a hospital pursuant to an order of such a court that is equivalent to a hospital order, or

    (d) subject to a form of detention outside the United Kingdom that is equivalent to detention under the Immigration Acts.

(9) References in this section and section 56 to a person's removal from the United Kingdom include—

    (a) the person's removal from the United Kingdom in accordance with the Immigration Acts,

    (b) the person's extradition from the United Kingdom, or

    (c) the person's transfer from the United Kingdom to another country pursuant to a warrant under section 1 of the Repatriation of Prisoners Act 1984 (c. 47).

56 Notification on return after absence from UK

(1) This section applies if, before the end of the period for which the notification requirements apply, a person to whom the requirements apply returns to the United Kingdom after a period of absence and—

    (a) the person was not required to make a notification under section 47 (initial notification),

    (b) there has been a change to any of the information last notified to the police in accordance with—

        (i) section 47,

        (ii) section 48 (notification of changes [general]),

        [(iia) section 48A (notification of changes: financial information and information about identification documents)]

        (iii) section 49 (periodic re-notification), or

        (iv) this section, or

(c) the period referred to in section 49(1) (period after which re-notification required) ended during the period of absence.

(2) The person must notify or (as the case may be) re-notify to the police the information mentioned in section 47(2) within the period of three days beginning with the day of return.

(3) In determining the period within which notification is to be made under this section, there shall be disregarded any time when the person is—

(a) remanded in or committed to custody by an order of a court,

(b) serving a sentence of imprisonment or detention,

(c) detained in a hospital, or

(d) detained under the Immigration Acts.

(4) This section does not apply if—

(a) the person subsequently leaves the United Kingdom,

(b) the period of absence begins before the end of the period within which notification must be made under this section, and

(c) the person's absence results from the person's removal from the United Kingdom.

(5) The obligation under this section does not affect any obligation to notify information under section 52(3) (regulations requiring notification of return etc).

[Entry and search of home address

56A Power to enter and search home address

(1) If on an application made by a senior police officer of the relevant force a justice is satisfied that the requirements in subsection (2) are met, the justice may issue a warrant authorising a constable of that force—

(a) to enter premises specified in the warrant for the purpose of assessing the risks posed by the person to whom the warrant relates; and

(b) to search the premises for that purpose.

(2) The requirements are—

(a) that the person to whom the warrant relates—

(i) is a person to whom the notification requirements apply, and

(ii) is not a person to whom subsection (3) applies,

(b) that the address of each set of premises specified in the application is an address falling within subsection (4),

(c) that it is necessary for a constable to enter and search the premises for the purpose mentioned in subsection (1)(a), and

(d) that on at least two occasions a constable has sought entry to the premises in order to search them for that purpose and has been unable to gain entry for that purpose.

(3) This subsection applies to a person who is—

(a) remanded in or committed to custody by order of a court,

(b) serving a sentence of imprisonment or a term of service detention,

(c) detained in a hospital, or

(d) outside the United Kingdom.

(4) An address falls within this subsection if—

(a) it is the address which was last notified in accordance with the notification requirements by the person to whom the warrant relates, or

(b) there are reasonable grounds to believe that the person to whom the warrant relates resides there or may regularly be found there.

(5) A warrant issued under this section must specify each set of premises to which it relates.

(6) The warrant may authorise the constable executing it to use reasonable force if necessary to enter and search the premises.

(7) The warrant may authorise entry to and search of premises on more than one occasion if, on the application, the justice is satisfied that it is necessary to authorise multiple entries in order to achieve the purpose mentioned in subsection (1)(a).

(8) Where a warrant issued under this section authorises multiple entries, the number of entries authorised may be unlimited or limited to a maximum.

(9) In this section—

'justice' means—

(a) in the application of this section to England and Wales, a justice of the peace;

(b) in the application of this section to Northern Ireland, a lay magistrate;

(c) in the application of this section to Scotland, a sheriff or summary sheriff;

'the relevant force' means—

(a) in relation to premises in England or Wales, the police force maintained for the police area in which the premises in respect of which the application is made or the warrant is issued are situated;

(b) in relation to premises in Northern Ireland, the Police Service of Northern Ireland;

(c) in relation to premises in Scotland, the Police Service of Scotland;

'senior police officer' means a constable of the rank of superintendent or above;

'sentence of imprisonment' includes any form of custodial sentence (apart from service detention);

'service detention' has the meaning given by section 374 of the Armed Forces Act 2006.]

57 Notification orders

Schedule 4* makes provision for notification orders applying the notification requirements of this Part to persons who have been dealt with outside the United Kingdom in respect of a corresponding foreign offence.

58 Foreign travel restriction orders

Schedule 5** makes provision for foreign travel restriction orders prohibiting persons to whom the notification requirements apply from—

(a) travelling to a country outside the United Kingdom named or described in the order,

(b) travelling to any country outside the United Kingdom other than a country named or described in the order, or

(c) travelling to any country outside the United Kingdom.

59 Application of Part to service offences and related matters

Schedule 6*** makes provision for the application of this Part to service offences and related matters.

*****

Criminal Justice and Immigration Act 2008

(2008, c. 4)

An Act to make further provision about criminal justice (including provision about the police) and dealing with offenders and defaulters; to make further provision about the management of offenders; to amend the criminal law; to make further provision for combating crime and disorder; to make provision about the mutual recognition of financial penalties; to amend the Repatriation of Prisoners Act 1984; to make provision for a new immigration status in certain cases involving criminality; to make provision about the automatic deportation of criminals under the UK Borders Act 2007; to amend section 127 of the Criminal Justice and Public Order Act 1994 and to confer power to suspend the operation of that section; and for connected purposes. [8th May 2008]

Territorial extent: England, Wales and Northern Ireland (in the case of Part 5 below)

*****

---

* **Editor's Note:** Schedule 4 is not reproduced here.
** **Editor's Note:** Schedule 5 is not reproduced here.
*** **Editor's Note:** Schedule 6 is not reproduced here.

PART 5 CRIMINAL LAW

Pornography etc

63 Possession of extreme pornographic images

(1) It is an offence for a person to be in possession of an extreme pornographic image.

(2) An 'extreme pornographic image' is an image which is both—

(a) pornographic, and

(b) an extreme image.

(3) An image is 'pornographic' if it is of such a nature that it must reasonably be assumed to have been produced solely or principally for the purpose of sexual arousal.

(4) Where (as found in the person's possession) an image forms part of a series of images, the question whether the image is of such a nature as is mentioned in subsection (3) is to be determined by reference to—

(a) the image itself, and

(b) (if the series of images is such as to be capable of providing a context for the image) the context in which it occurs in the series of images.

(5) So, for example, where—

(a) an image forms an integral part of a narrative constituted by a series of images, and

(b) having regard to those images as a whole, they are not of such a nature that they must reasonably be assumed to have been produced solely or principally for the purpose of sexual arousal,

the image may, by virtue of being part of that narrative, be found not to be pornographic, even though it might have been found to be pornographic if taken by itself.

[(5A) In relation to possession of an image in England and Wales, an 'extreme image' is an image which—

(a) falls within subsection (7) or (7A), and

(b) is grossly offensive, disgusting or otherwise of an obscene character.]

(6) [In relation to possession of an image in Northern Ireland, an] 'extreme image' is an image which—

(a) falls within subsection (7), and

(b) is grossly offensive, disgusting or otherwise of an obscene character.

(7) An image falls within this subsection if it portrays, in an explicit and realistic way, any of the following—

(a) an act which threatens a person's life,

(b) an act which results, or is likely to result, in serious injury to a person's anus, breasts or genitals,

(c) an act which involves sexual interference with a human corpse, or

(d) a person performing an act of intercourse or oral sex with an animal (whether dead or alive),

and a reasonable person looking at the image would think that any such person or animal was real.

[(7A) An image falls within this subsection if it portrays, in an explicit and realistic way, either of the following—

(a) an act which involves the non-consensual penetration of a person's vagina, anus or mouth by another with the other person's penis, or

(b) an act which involves the non-consensual sexual penetration of a person's vagina or anus by another with a part of the other person's body or anything else,

and a reasonable person looking at the image would think that the persons were real.

(7B) For the purposes of subsection (7A)—

(a) penetration is a continuing act from entry to withdrawal;

(b) 'vagina' includes vulva.]

(8) In this section 'image' means—

(a) a moving or still image (produced by any means); or

(b) data (stored by any means) which is capable of conversion into an image within paragraph (a).

(9) In this section references to a part of the body include references to a part surgically constructed (in particular through gender reassignment surgery).

(10) Proceedings for an offence under this section may not be instituted—

(a) in England and Wales, except by or with the consent of the Director of Public Prosecutions; or

(b) in Northern Ireland, except by or with the consent of the Director of Public Prosecutions for Northern Ireland.

64 Exclusion of classified films etc

(1) Section 63 does not apply to excluded images.

(2) An 'excluded image' is an image which forms part of a series of images contained in a recording of the whole or part of a classified work.

(3) But such an image is not an 'excluded image' if—

(a) it is contained in a recording of an extract from a classified work, and

(b) it is of such a nature that it must reasonably be assumed to have been extracted (whether with or without other images) solely or principally for the purpose of sexual arousal.

(4) Where an extracted image is one of a series of images contained in the recording, the question whether the image is of such a nature as is mentioned in subsection (3)(b) is to be determined by reference to—

(a) the image itself, and

(b) (if the series of images is such as to be capable of providing a context for the image) the context in which it occurs in the series of images;

and section 63(5) applies in connection with determining that question as it applies in connection with determining whether an image is pornographic.

(5) In determining for the purposes of this section whether a recording is a recording of the whole or part of a classified work, any alteration attributable to—

(a) a defect caused for technical reasons or by inadvertence on the part of any person, or

(b) the inclusion in the recording of any extraneous material (such as advertisements), is to be disregarded.

(6) Nothing in this section is to be taken as affecting any duty of a designated authority to have regard to section 63 (along with other enactments creating criminal offences) in determining whether a video work is suitable for a classification certificate to be issued in respect of it.

(7) In this section—

'classified work' means (subject to subsection (8)) a video work in respect of which a classification certificate has been issued by a designated authority (whether before or after the commencement of this section);

'classification certificate' and 'video work' have the same meanings as in the Video Recordings Act 1984 (c. 39);

'designated authority' means an authority which has been designated by the Secretary of State under section 4 of that Act;

'extract' includes an extract consisting of a single image;

'image' and 'pornographic' have the same meanings as in section 63;

'recording' means any disc, tape or other device capable of storing data electronically and from which images may be produced (by any means).

(8) *****

65 Defences: general

(1) Where a person is charged with an offence under section 63, it is a defence for the person to prove any of the matters mentioned in subsection (2).

(2) The matters are—

(a) that the person had a legitimate reason for being in possession of the image concerned;

(b) that the person had not seen the image concerned and did not know, nor had any cause to suspect, it to be an extreme pornographic image;

(c) that the person—
  (i) was sent the image concerned without any prior request having been made by or on behalf of the person, and
  (ii) did not keep it for an unreasonable time.
(3) *****

66 Defence: participation in consensual acts

[(A1) Subsection (A2) applies where in England and Wales—
  (a) a person ('D') is charged with an offence under section 63, and
  (b) the offence relates to an image that portrays an act or acts within subsection (7)(a) to (c) or (7A) of that section (but does not portray an act within subsection (7)(d) of that section).
(A2) It is a defence for D to prove—
  (a) that D directly participated in the act or any of the acts portrayed, and
  (b) that the act or acts did not involve the infliction of any non-consensual harm on any person, and
  (c) if the image portrays an act within section 63(7)(c), that what is portrayed as a human corpse was not in fact a corpse, and
  (d) if the image portrays an act within section 63(7A), that what is portrayed as non-consensual penetration was in fact consensual.]
(1) [Subsection (2)] applies where [in Northern Ireland]—
  (a) a person ('D') is charged with an offence under section 63, and
  (b) the offence relates to an image that portrays an act or acts within paragraphs (a) to (c) (but none within paragraph (d)) of subsection (7) of that section.
(2) It is a defence for D to prove—
  (a) that D directly participated in the act or any of the acts portrayed, and
  (b) that the act or acts did not involve the infliction of any non-consensual harm on any person, and
  (c) if the image portrays an act within section 63(7)(c), that what is portrayed as a human corpse was not in fact a corpse.
(3) For the purposes of this section harm inflicted on a person is 'non-consensual' harm if—
  (a) the harm is of such a nature that the person cannot, in law, consent to it being inflicted on himself or herself; or
  (b) where the person can, in law, consent to it being so inflicted, the person does not in fact consent to it being so inflicted.

67 Penalties etc for possession of extreme pornographic images

(1) This section has effect where a person is guilty of an offence under section 63.
(2) [If the offence relates to an image that portrays any relevant act (with or without other acts)], the offender is liable—
  (a) on summary conviction, to imprisonment for a term not exceeding the relevant period or a fine not exceeding the statutory maximum or both;
  (b) on conviction on indictment, to imprisonment for a term not exceeding 3 years or a fine or both.
(3) If the offence relates to an image that does not portray any [relevant act], the offender is liable—
  (a) on summary conviction, to imprisonment for a term not exceeding the relevant period or a fine not exceeding the statutory maximum or both;
  (b) on conviction on indictment, to imprisonment for a term not exceeding 2 years or a fine or both.
(4) In subsection (2)(a) or (3)(a) 'the relevant period' means—
  (a) in relation to England and Wales, [the general limit in a magistrates' court];
  (b) in relation to Northern Ireland, 6 months.
*****

Parliamentary Standards Act 2009

(2009, c. 13)

An Act to make provision establishing a body corporate known as the Independent Parliamentary Standards Authority and an officer known as the Commissioner for Parliamentary Investigations; to make provision relating to salaries and allowances for members of the House of Commons and to their financial interests and conduct; and for connected purposes.   [21st July 2009]

Territorial extent: United Kingdom

Introductory

1   Bill of Rights
Nothing in this Act shall be construed by any court in the United Kingdom as affecting Article IX of the Bill of Rights 1689.

2   House of Lords
(1) Nothing in this Act shall affect the House of Lords.
(2) *****

Independent Parliamentary Standards Authority etc

3   Independent Parliamentary Standards Authority etc
(1) There is to be a body corporate known as the Independent Parliamentary Standards Authority ('IPSA').
(2) *****
(3) There is to be an officer known as the Compliance Officer for the Independent Parliamentary Standards Authority ('the Compliance Officer').
(4)–(6) *****

[3A   General duties of the IPSA]
[(1) In carrying out its functions the IPSA must have regard to the principle that it should act in a way which is efficient, cost-effective and transparent.
(2) In carrying out its functions the IPSA must have regard to the principle that members of the House of Commons should be supported in efficiently, cost-effectively and transparently carrying out their Parliamentary functions.]

Salaries and allowances for MPs

4   [MPs' salaries]
[(1) Members of the House of Commons are to receive a salary for the relevant period.
(2) The salaries are to be paid by the IPSA.
(3) Salaries are to be paid on a monthly basis in arrears.
(4) The amounts of the salaries are to be determined by the IPSA (see section 4A).
(5) 'Relevant period', in relation to a person who is a member of the House of Commons, means the period beginning with the day after the day of the poll for the parliamentary election at which the member was elected and ending with—
    (a) if the person is a member immediately before Parliament is dissolved, the day of the poll for the parliamentary general election which follows the dissolution;
    (b) otherwise, the day on which the person ceases to be a member.
(6) No payment of salary is to be made to a member before the member has made and subscribed the oath required by the Parliamentary Oaths Act 1866 (or the corresponding affirmation).
(7) The duty of the IPSA to pay a salary to a member is subject to anything done in relation to the member in the exercise of the disciplinary powers of the House of Commons.]

[4A Determination of MPs' salaries]

[(1) This section is about determinations under section 4(4).

(2) A determination may provide for higher salaries to be payable to members while holding an office or position specified for the purposes of this subsection in a resolution of the House of Commons.

(3) A determination by virtue of subsection (2) may make different provision for different offices or positions or different classes of member (and may include exceptions).

(4) A determination may include a formula or other mechanism for adjusting salaries from time to time.

(5) A determination (other than the first determination) may have retrospective effect.

(6) The IPSA must review the current determination (and make a new determination as appropriate)—

    (a) in the first year of each Parliament;

    (b) at any other time it considers appropriate.

(7) In reviewing a determination (and before making the first determination) the IPSA must consult—

    (a) the Review Body on Senior Salaries,

    (b) persons appearing to the IPSA to represent persons likely to be affected by the determination or the review,

    (c) the Minister for the Civil Service,

    (d) the Treasury, and

    (e) any other person the IPSA considers appropriate.

(8) After making a determination, the IPSA must publish in a way it considers appropriate—

    (a) the determination, and

    (b) a statement of how it arrived at the determination.

(9) If the IPSA reviews the current determination but decides not to make a new determination, it must publish in a way it considers appropriate a statement of how it arrived at that decision.

(10) The IPSA may delegate to the Review Body on Senior Salaries its function of reviewing a determination (but not its function of deciding whether or not to make a new determination).]

5 MPs' allowances scheme

(1) The IPSA is to pay allowances to members of the House of Commons in accordance with the MPs' allowances scheme.

(2) In this Act 'the MPs' allowances scheme' means the scheme prepared under this section as it is in effect for the time being.

(3) The IPSA must—

    (a) prepare the scheme;

    (b) review the scheme regularly and revise it as appropriate.

(4) In preparing or revising the scheme, the IPSA must consult—

    (a) the Speaker of the House of Commons,

    (b) the Committee on Standards in Public Life,

    (c) the Leader of the House of Commons,

    (d) any committee of the House of Commons nominated by the Speaker,

    (e) members of the House of Commons,

    (f) the Review Body on Senior Salaries,

    (g) Her Majesty's Revenue and Customs,

    (h) the Treasury, and

    (i) any other person the IPSA considers appropriate.

(5) The Speaker must lay the scheme (or revision) before the House of Commons.

[(5A) When the scheme (or revision) is laid, the IPSA must publish in a way it considers appropriate—

    (a) the scheme (or revision), and

    (b) a statement of its reasons for adopting that scheme (or making that revision).]

(6) The scheme (or revision) comes into effect on the date specified in the scheme (or revision).

(7) The scheme may, for example—

    (a) provide for allowances to be payable in respect of specified kinds of expenditure or in specified circumstances;

    (b) provide for allowances to be payable only on specified conditions (such as a condition that claims for allowances must be supported by documentary evidence);

    (c) impose limits on the amounts that may be paid.

(8) The scheme may provide for allowances to be payable in connection with a person's ceasing to be a member of the House of Commons; [and in relation to any such allowances, references in this Act to a member of the House of Commons include a former member of that House].

[(8A) Any duty of the IPSA to pay an allowance to a member is subject to anything done in relation to the member in the exercise of the disciplinary powers of the House of Commons.]

(9), (10) *****

6 Dealing with claims under the scheme

(1) No allowance is to be paid to a member of the House of Commons under the MPs' allowances scheme unless a claim for the allowance has been made to the IPSA.

(2) The claim must be made by the member (except where the scheme provides otherwise).

(3) On receipt of a claim, the IPSA must—

    (a) determine whether to allow or refuse the claim, and

    (b) if it is allowed, determine how much of the amount claimed is to be allowed and pay it accordingly.

(4) ...

(5) ...

(6) The MPs' allowances scheme may include—

    (a) further provision about how claims are to be dealt with;

    [(b) provision for deducting amounts within subsection (6A) from allowances payable under the scheme or salaries payable under section 4;

    (c) provision about how such deductions, and deductions under paragraph 5 or 12 of Schedule 4, are to be made].

(6A)–(10) *****

[6A], 7 *****

8 ...

Investigation and enforcement

[9 Investigations]

[(1) The Compliance Officer may conduct an investigation if the Compliance Officer has reason to believe that a member of the House of Commons may have been paid an amount under the MPs' allowances scheme that should not have been allowed.

(2) An investigation may be conducted—

    (a) on the Compliance Officer's own initiative,

    (b) at the request of the IPSA,

    (c) at the request of the member, or

    (d) in response to a complaint by an individual.

(3) For the purposes of the investigation the member and the IPSA—
   (a) must provide the Compliance Officer with any information (including documents) the Compliance Officer reasonably requires, and
   (b) must do so within such period as the Compliance Officer reasonably requires.

(4) The Compliance Officer must, after giving the member and the IPSA an opportunity to make representations to the Compliance Officer, prepare a statement of the Compliance Officer's provisional findings.

(5) The Compliance Officer must, after giving the member and the IPSA an opportunity to make representations to the Compliance Officer about the provisional findings, prepare a statement of the Compliance Officer's findings (subject to subsection (7)).

(6) Provisional findings under subsection (4) and findings under subsection (5) may include—
   (a) a finding that the member failed to comply with subsection (3),
   (b) findings about the role of the IPSA in the matters under investigation, including findings that the member's being paid an amount under the MPs' allowances scheme that should not have been allowed was wholly or partly the IPSA's fault.

(7) If subsection (8) applies, the Compliance Officer need not make a finding under subsection (5) as to whether the member was paid an amount under the MPs' allowances scheme that should not have been allowed.

(8) This subsection applies if—
   (a) the member accepts a provisional finding that the member was paid an amount under the MPs' allowances scheme that should not have been allowed,
   (b) such other conditions as may be specified by the IPSA are, in the Compliance Officer's view, met in relation to the case, and
   (c) the member agrees to repay to the IPSA, in such manner and within such period as the Compliance Officer considers reasonable, such amount as the Compliance Officer considers reasonable (and makes the repayment accordingly).

(9) Before specifying conditions under subsection (8)(b) the IPSA must consult the persons listed in section 9A(6).

(10) References in this section (and section 9A) to a member of the House of Commons include a former member of that House.]

9A, 9B   *****

10   Offence of providing false or misleading information for allowances claims

(1) A member of the House of Commons commits an offence if the member—
   (a) makes a claim under the MPs' allowances scheme, and
   (b) provides information for the purposes of the claim that the member knows to be false or misleading in a material respect.

(2) A person guilty of an offence under subsection (1) is liable—
   (a) on summary conviction, to imprisonment for a term not exceeding 12 months or to a fine not exceeding the statutory maximum or to both;
   (b) on conviction on indictment, to imprisonment for a term not exceeding 12 months or to a fine or to both.

[(2A)], (3) *****

10A   *****

11   ...
*****

Bribery Act 2010

(2010, c. 23)

An Act to make provision about offences relating to bribery; and for connected purposes.   [8th April 2010]

Territorial extent: United Kingdom

General bribery offences

1   Offences of bribing another person

(1) A person ('P') is guilty of an offence if either of the following cases applies.

(2) Case 1 is where—

  (a) P offers, promises or gives a financial or other advantage to another person, and

  (b) P intends the advantage—

    (i)   to induce a person to perform improperly a relevant function or activity, or

    (ii)   to reward a person for the improper performance of such a function or activity.

(3) Case 2 is where—

  (a) P offers, promises or gives a financial or other advantage to another person, and

  (b) P knows or believes that the acceptance of the advantage would itself constitute the improper performance of a relevant function or activity.

(4) In case 1 it does not matter whether the person to whom the advantage is offered, promised or given is the same person as the person who is to perform, or has performed, the function or activity concerned.

(5) In cases 1 and 2 it does not matter whether the advantage is offered, promised or given by P directly or through a third party.

2   Offences relating to being bribed

(1) A person ('R') is guilty of an offence if any of the following cases applies.

(2) Case 3 is where R requests, agrees to receive or accepts a financial or other advantage intending that, in consequence, a relevant function or activity should be performed improperly (whether by R or another person).

(3) Case 4 is where—

  (a) R requests, agrees to receive or accepts a financial or other advantage, and

  (b) the request, agreement or acceptance itself constitutes the improper performance by R of a relevant function or activity.

(4) Case 5 is where R requests, agrees to receive or accepts a financial or other advantage as a reward for the improper performance (whether by R or another person) of a relevant function or activity.

(5) Case 6 is where, in anticipation of or in consequence of R requesting, agreeing to receive or accepting a financial or other advantage, a relevant function or activity is performed improperly—

  (a) by R, or

  (b) by another person at R's request or with R's assent or acquiescence.

(6) In cases 3 to 6 it does not matter—

  (a) whether R requests, agrees to receive or accepts (or is to request, agree to receive or accept) the advantage directly or through a third party,

  (b) whether the advantage is (or is to be) for the benefit of R or another person.

(7) In cases 4 to 6 it does not matter whether R knows or believes that the performance of the function or activity is improper.

(8) In case 6, where a person other than R is performing the function or activity, it also does not matter whether that person knows or believes that the performance of the function or activity is improper.

3   Function or activity to which bribe relates

(1) For the purposes of this Act a function or activity is a relevant function or activity if—

  (a) it falls within subsection (2), and

(b) meets one or more of conditions A to C.

(2) The following functions and activities fall within this subsection—

(a) any function of a public nature,

(b) any activity connected with a business,

(c) any activity performed in the course of a person's employment,

(d) any activity performed by or on behalf of a body of persons (whether corporate or unincorporate).

(3) Condition A is that a person performing the function or activity is expected to perform it in good faith.

(4) Condition B is that a person performing the function or activity is expected to perform it impartially.

(5) Condition C is that a person performing the function or activity is in a position of trust by virtue of performing it.

(6) A function or activity is a relevant function or activity even if it—

(a) has no connection with the United Kingdom, and

(b) is performed in a country or territory outside the United Kingdom.

(7) In this section 'business' includes trade or profession.

4 Improper performance to which bribe relates

(1) For the purposes of this Act a relevant function or activity—

(a) is performed improperly if it is performed in breach of a relevant expectation, and

(b) is to be treated as being performed improperly if there is a failure to perform the function or activity and that failure is itself a breach of a relevant expectation.

(2) In subsection (1) 'relevant expectation'—

(a) in relation to a function or activity which meets condition A or B, means the expectation mentioned in the condition concerned, and

(b) in relation to a function or activity which meets condition C, means any expectation as to the manner in which, or the reasons for which, the function or activity will be performed that arises from the position of trust mentioned in that condition.

(3) Anything that a person does (or omits to do) arising from or in connection with that person's past performance of a relevant function or activity is to be treated for the purposes of this Act as being done (or omitted) by that person in the performance of that function or activity.

5 Expectation test

(1) For the purposes of sections 3 and 4, the test of what is expected is a test of what a reasonable person in the United Kingdom would expect in relation to the performance of the type of function or activity concerned.

(2) In deciding what such a person would expect in relation to the performance of a function or activity where the performance is not subject to the law of any part of the United Kingdom, any local custom or practice is to be disregarded unless it is permitted or required by the written law applicable to the country or territory concerned.

(3) In subsection (2) 'written law' means law contained in—

(a) any written constitution, or provision made by or under legislation, applicable to the country or territory concerned, or

(b) any judicial decision which is so applicable and is evidenced in published written sources.

Bribery of foreign public officials

6 Bribery of foreign public officials

(1) A person ('P') who bribes a foreign public official ('F') is guilty of an offence if P's intention is to influence F in F's capacity as a foreign public official.

(2) P must also intend to obtain or retain—

(a) business, or

(b) an advantage in the conduct of business.

(3) P bribes F if, and only if—

    (a) directly or through a third party, P offers, promises or gives any financial or other advantage—

        (i)   to F, or

        (ii) to another person at F's request or with F's assent or acquiescence, and

    (b) F is neither permitted nor required by the written law applicable to F to be influenced in F's capacity as a foreign public official by the offer, promise or gift.

(4) References in this section to influencing F in F's capacity as a foreign public official mean influencing F in the performance of F's functions as such an official, which includes—

    (a) any omission to exercise those functions, and

    (b) any use of F's position as such an official, even if not within F's authority.

(5) 'Foreign public official' means an individual who—

    (a) holds a legislative, administrative or judicial position of any kind, whether appointed or elected, of a country or territory outside the United Kingdom (or any subdivision of such a country or territory),

    (b) exercises a public function—

        (i)   for or on behalf of a country or territory outside the United Kingdom (or any subdivision of such a country or territory), or

        (ii) for any public agency or public enterprise of that country or territory (or subdivision), or

    (c) is an official or agent of a public international organisation.

(6) 'Public international organisation' means an organisation whose members are any of the following—

    (a) countries or territories,

    (b) governments of countries or territories,

    (c) other public international organisations,

    (d) a mixture of any of the above.

(7) For the purposes of subsection (3)(b), the written law applicable to F is—

    (a) where the performance of the functions of F which P intends to influence would be subject to the law of any part of the United Kingdom, the law of that part of the United Kingdom,

    (b) where paragraph (a) does not apply and F is an official or agent of a public international organisation, the applicable written rules of that organisation,

    (c) where paragraphs (a) and (b) do not apply, the law of the country or territory in relation to which F is a foreign public official so far as that law is contained in—

        (i)   any written constitution, or provision made by or under legislation, applicable to the country or territory concerned, or

        (ii) any judicial decision which is so applicable and is evidenced in published written sources.

(8) For the purposes of this section, a trade or profession is a business.

Failure of commercial organisations to prevent bribery

7 Failure of commercial organisations to prevent bribery

(1) A relevant commercial organisation ('C') is guilty of an offence under this section if a person ('A') associated with C bribes another person intending—

    (a) to obtain or retain business for C, or

    (b) to obtain or retain an advantage in the conduct of business for C.

(2) But it is a defence for C to prove that C had in place adequate procedures designed to prevent persons associated with C from undertaking such conduct.

(3) For the purposes of this section, A bribes another person if, and only if, A—

    (a) is, or would be, guilty of an offence under section 1 or 6 (whether or not A has been prosecuted for such an offence), or

    (b) would be guilty of such an offence if section 12(2)(c) and (4) were omitted.

(4) See section 8 for the meaning of a person associated with C and see section 9 for a duty on the Secretary of State to publish guidance.

(5) In this section—

'partnership' means—

    (a) a partnership within the Partnership Act 1890, or

    (b) a limited partnership registered under the Limited Partnerships Act 1907,

or a firm or entity of a similar character formed under the law of a country or territory outside the United Kingdom,

'relevant commercial organisation' means—

    (a) a body which is incorporated under the law of any part of the United Kingdom and which carries on a business (whether there or elsewhere),

    (b) any other body corporate (wherever incorporated) which carries on a business, or part of a business, in any part of the United Kingdom,

    (c) a partnership which is formed under the law of any part of the United Kingdom and which carries on a business (whether there or elsewhere), or

    (d) any other partnership (wherever formed) which carries on a business, or part of a business, in any part of the United Kingdom,

and, for the purposes of this section, a trade or profession is a business.

8–11   *****

Other provisions about offences

12   Offences under this Act: territorial application

(1) An offence is committed under section 1, 2 or 6 in England and Wales, Scotland or Northern Ireland if any act or omission which forms part of the offence takes place in that part of the United Kingdom.

(2) Subsection (3) applies if—

    (a) no act or omission which forms part of an offence under section 1, 2 or 6 takes place in the United Kingdom,

    (b) a person's acts or omissions done or made outside the United Kingdom would form part of such an offence if done or made in the United Kingdom, and

    (c) that person has a close connection with the United Kingdom.

(3) In such a case—

    (a) the acts or omissions form part of the offence referred to in subsection (2)(a), and

    (b) proceedings for the offence may be taken at any place in the United Kingdom.

(4) For the purposes of subsection (2)(c) a person has a close connection with the United Kingdom if, and only if, the person was one of the following at the time the acts or omissions concerned were done or made—

    (a) a British citizen,

    (b) a British overseas territories citizen,

    (c) a British National (Overseas),

    (d) a British Overseas citizen,

    (e) a person who under the British Nationality Act 1981 was a British subject,

    (f) a British protected person within the meaning of that Act,

    (g) an individual ordinarily resident in the United Kingdom,

    (h) a body incorporated under the law of any part of the United Kingdom,

    (i) a Scottish partnership.

(5) An offence is committed under section 7 irrespective of whether the acts or omissions which form part of the offence take place in the United Kingdom or elsewhere.

(6) Where no act or omission which forms part of an offence under section 7 takes place in the United Kingdom, proceedings for the offence may be taken at any place in the United Kingdom.

(7)–(9) *****

13   Defence for certain bribery offences etc

(1) It is a defence for a person charged with a relevant bribery offence to prove that the person's conduct was necessary for—

(a) the proper exercise of any function of an intelligence service, or

(b) the proper exercise of any function of the armed forces when engaged on active service.

(2) The head of each intelligence service must ensure that the service has in place arrangements designed to ensure that any conduct of a member of the service which would otherwise be a relevant bribery offence is necessary for a purpose falling within subsection (1)(a).

(3) The Defence Council must ensure that the armed forces have in place arrangements designed to ensure that any conduct of—

(a) a member of the armed forces who is engaged on active service, or

(b) a civilian subject to service discipline when working in support of any person falling within paragraph (a),

which would otherwise be a relevant bribery offence is necessary for a purpose falling within subsection (1)(b).

(4)–(6) *****

14, 15 *****

Supplementary and final provisions

16   Application to Crown

This Act applies to individuals in the public service of the Crown as it applies to other individuals. *****

Constitutional Reform and Governance Act 2010

(2010, c. 25)

An Act to make provision relating to the civil service of the State; to make provision in relation to section 3 of the Act of Settlement; to make provision relating to the ratification of treaties; to make provision relating to the counting of votes in parliamentary elections; to amend the Parliamentary Standards Act 2009 and the European Parliament (Pay and Pensions) Act 1979 and to make provision relating to pensions for members of the House of Commons, Ministers and other office holders; to make provision for treating members of the House of Commons and members of the House of Lords as resident, ordinarily resident and domiciled in the United Kingdom for taxation purposes; to amend the Government Resources and Accounts Act 2000 and to make corresponding provision in relation to Wales; to amend the Public Records Act 1958 and the Freedom of Information Act 2000.   [8th April 2010]

Territorial extent: United Kingdom

PART 1 THE CIVIL SERVICE

Chapter 1 Statutory basis for management of the civil service

Application

1   Application of Chapter

(1) Subject to subsections (2) and (3), this Chapter applies to the civil service of the State.

(2) This Chapter does not apply to the following parts of the civil service of the State—

(a) the Secret Intelligence Service;

(b) the Security Service;

    (c) the Government Communications Headquarters;

    (d) the Northern Ireland Civil Service;

    (e) ...

(3) Further, this Chapter—

    (a) does not apply in relation to the making, outside the United Kingdom, of selections of persons who are not members of the civil service of the State for appointment to that service for the purpose only of duties to be carried out wholly outside the United Kingdom;

    (b) does not apply in relation to the appointment of a person to the civil service of the State who was selected for the appointment as mentioned in paragraph (a);

    (c) does not apply to the civil service of the State so far as it consists of persons—

        (i)   who were appointed to the civil service of the State as mentioned in paragraph (b), and

        (ii) all of whose duties are carried out wholly outside the United Kingdom.

(4) In this Chapter references to the civil service—

    (a) are to the civil service of the State excluding the parts mentioned in subsections (2) and (3)(c);

    (b) are to be read subject to subsection (3)(a) and (b);

and references to civil servants are to be read accordingly.

Civil Service Commission

2   Establishment of the Civil Service Commission

(1) There is to be a body corporate called the Civil Service Commission ('the Commission').

(2) Schedule 1 (which is about the Commission) has effect.

(3) The Commission has the role in relation to selections for appointments to the civil service set out in sections 11 to 14.

(4) See also—

    (a) section 9 (which sets out the Commission's role in dealing with conduct that conflicts with civil service codes of conduct);

    (b) section 17 (under which the Commission may be given additional functions).

Power to manage the civil service

3   Management of the civil service

(1) The Minister for the Civil Service has the power to manage the civil service (excluding the diplomatic service).

(2) The Secretary of State has the power to manage the diplomatic service.

(3) The powers in subsections (1) and (2) include (among other things) power to make appointments.

(4) But they do not cover national security vetting (and, accordingly, subsections (1) and (2) do not affect any power relating to national security vetting).

(5) The agreement of the Minister for the Civil Service is required for any exercise of the power in subsection (2) in relation to—

    (a) remuneration of civil servants (including compensation payable on leaving the civil service), or

    (b) the conditions on which a civil servant may retire.

(6) In exercising his power to manage the civil service, the Minister for the Civil Service shall have regard to the need to ensure that civil servants who advise Ministers are aware of the constitutional significance of Parliament and of the conventions governing the relationship between Parliament and Her Majesty's Government.

4   *****

Codes of conduct

5   Civil service code

(1) The Minister for the Civil Service must publish a code of conduct for the civil service (excluding the diplomatic service).

(2) For this purpose, the Minister may publish separate codes of conduct covering civil servants who serve the Scottish Executive or the Welsh Assembly Government.

(3) Before publishing a code (or any revision of a code) under subsection (2), the Minister must consult the First Minister for Scotland or the First Minister for Wales (as the case may be).

(4) In this Chapter 'civil service code' means a code of conduct published under this section as it is in force for the time being.

(5) The Minister for the Civil Service must lay any civil service code before Parliament.

(6) The First Minister for Scotland must lay before the Scottish Parliament any civil service code under subsection (2) that covers civil servants who serve the Scottish Executive.

(7) The First Minister for Wales must lay before the National Assembly for Wales any civil service code under subsection (2) that covers civil servants who serve the Welsh Assembly Government.

(8) A civil service code forms part of the terms and conditions of service of any civil servant covered by the code.

6–19   *****

PART 2 RATIFICATION OF TREATIES

20   Treaties to be laid before Parliament before ratification

(1) Subject to what follows, a treaty is not to be ratified unless—
- (a) a Minister of the Crown has laid before Parliament a copy of the treaty,
- (b) the treaty has been published in a way that a Minister of the Crown thinks appropriate, and
- (c) period A has expired without either House having resolved, within period A, that the treaty should not be ratified.

(2) Period A is the period of 21 sitting days beginning with the first sitting day after the date on which the requirement in subsection (1)(a) is met.

(3) Subsections (4) to (6) apply if the House of Commons resolved as mentioned in subsection (1)(c) (whether or not the House of Lords also did so).

(4) The treaty may be ratified if—
- (a) a Minister of the Crown has laid before Parliament a statement indicating that the Minister is of the opinion that the treaty should nevertheless be ratified and explaining why, and
- (b) period B has expired without the House of Commons having resolved, within period B, that the treaty should not be ratified.

(5) Period B is the period of 21 sitting days beginning with the first sitting day after the date on which the requirement in subsection (4)(a) is met.

(6) A statement may be laid under subsection (4)(a) in relation to the treaty on more than one occasion.

(7) Subsection (8) applies if—
- (a) the House of Lords resolved as mentioned in subsection (1)(c), but
- (b) the House of Commons did not.

(8) The treaty may be ratified if a Minister of the Crown has laid before Parliament a statement indicating that the Minister is of the opinion that the treaty should nevertheless be ratified and explaining why.

(9) 'Sitting day' means a day on which both Houses of Parliament sit.

21   Extension of 21 sitting day period

(1) A Minister of the Crown may, in relation to a treaty, extend the period mentioned in section 20(1)(c) by 21 sitting days or less.

(2)–(5) *****

22   Section 20 not to apply in exceptional cases

(1) Section 20 does not apply to a treaty if a Minister of the Crown is of the opinion that, exceptionally, the treaty should be ratified without the requirements of that section having been met.

(2) But a treaty may not be ratified by virtue of subsection (1) after either House has resolved, as mentioned in section 20(1)(c), that the treaty should not be ratified.

(3) If a Minister determines that a treaty is to be ratified by virtue of subsection (1), the Minister must, either before or as soon as practicable after the treaty is ratified—

(a) lay before Parliament a copy of the treaty,

(b) arrange for the treaty to be published in a way that the Minister thinks appropriate, and

(c) lay before Parliament a statement indicating that the Minister is of the opinion mentioned in subsection (1) and explaining why.

23   Section 20 not to apply to certain descriptions of treaties

(1) ...

(2) Section 20 does not apply to a treaty in relation to which an Order in Council may be made under one or more of the following—

(a) section 158 of the Inheritance Tax Act 1984 (double taxation conventions);

(b) section 2 of the Taxation (International and Other Provisions) Act 2010 (double taxation arrangements);

(c) section 173 of the Finance Act 2006 (international tax enforcement arrangements).

[(2A)–(2B)] *****

(3) Section 20 does not apply to a treaty concluded (under authority given by the government of the United Kingdom) by the government of a British overseas territory, of any of the Channel Islands or of the Isle of Man.

(4) Section 20 does not apply to a treaty a copy of which is presented to Parliament by command of Her Majesty before that section comes into force.

Equality Act 2010

(2010, c. 15)

An Act to make provision to require Ministers of the Crown and others when making strategic decisions about the exercise of their functions to have regard to the desirability of reducing socio-economic inequalities; to reform and harmonise equality law and restate the greater part of the enactments relating to discrimination and harassment related to certain personal characteristics; to enable certain employers to be required to publish information about the differences in pay between male and female employees; to prohibit victimisation in certain circumstances; to require the exercise of certain functions to be with regard to the need to eliminate discrimination and other prohibited conduct; to enable duties to be imposed in relation to the exercise of public procurement functions; to increase equality of opportunity; to amend the law relating to rights and responsibilities in family relationships; and for connected purposes. [8th April 2010]

Territorial extent: England and Wales

PART 1 SOCIO-ECONOMIC INEQUALITIES

1   Public sector duty regarding socio-economic inequalities

(1) An authority to which this section applies must, when making decisions of a strategic nature about how to exercise its functions, have due regard to the desirability of exercising them in a way that is designed to reduce the inequalities of outcome which result from socio-economic disadvantage.

(2) In deciding how to fulfil a duty to which it is subject under subsection (1), an authority must take into account any guidance issued in accordance with subsection (2A).

[(2A) The guidance to be taken into account under subsection (2) is—

(a)   in the case of a duty imposed on an authority in relation to devolved Scottish functions, guidance issued by the Scottish Ministers;

[(aa) in the case of a duty imposed on an authority in relation to devolved Welsh functions, guidance issued by the Welsh Ministers;]
(b)   in any other case, guidance issued by a Minister of the Crown.]
(3) The authorities to which this section applies are—
(a)   a Minister of the Crown;
(b)   a government department other than the Security Service, the Secret Intelligence Service or the Government Communications Headquarters;
[(ba) a corporate joint committee established by regulations made under Part 5 of the Local Government and Elections (Wales) Act 2021;]
(c)   a county council or district council in England;
(d)   the Greater London Authority;
(e)   a London borough council;
(f)   the Common Council of the City of London in its capacity as a local authority;
(g)   the Council of the Isles of Scilly;
(h)–(j)   ...
(k)   a [police and crime commissioner] established for an area in England.
[(3A) This section also applies to the following authorities—
(a) the Welsh Ministers;
(b) a county council or county borough council in Wales;
(c) a Local Health Board established under section 11 of the National Health Service (Wales) Act 2006;
(d) an NHS Trust established under section 18 of the National Health Service (Wales) Act 2006;
(e) a Special Health Authority established under section 22 of the National Health Service (Wales) Act 2006 other than a cross-border Special Health Authority (within the meaning of section 8A(5) of the National Health Service (Wales) Act 2006);
(f) a fire and rescue authority constituted by a scheme under section 2 of the Fire and Rescue Services Act 2004, or a scheme to which section 4 of that Act applies, for an area in Wales;
(g) a National Park authority established by an order under section 63 of the Environment Act 1995 for an area in Wales;
(h) the Welsh Revenue Authority or Awdurdod Cyllid Cymru.]
(4), (5) ...
(6) The reference to inequalities in subsection (1) does not include any inequalities experienced by a person as a result of being a person subject to immigration control within the meaning given by section 115(9) of the Immigration and Asylum Act 1999.

2   *****

3   Enforcement
A failure in respect of a performance of a duty under section 1 does not confer a cause of action at private law.

PART 2 EQUALITY: KEY CONCEPTS

Chapter 1 Protected characteristics

4   The protected characteristics
The following characteristics are protected characteristics—
age;
disability;
gender reassignment;
marriage and civil partnership;

pregnancy and maternity;

race;

religion or belief;

sex;

sexual orientation.

5   Age

  (1) In relation to the protected characteristic of age—

    (a) a reference to a person who has a particular protected characteristic is a reference to a person of a particular age group;

    (b) a reference to persons who share a protected characteristic is a reference to persons of the same age group.

  (2) A reference to an age group is a reference to a group of persons defined by reference to age, whether by reference to a particular age or to a range of ages.

6   Disability

  (1) A person (P) has a disability if—

    (a) P has a physical or mental impairment, and

    (b) the impairment has a substantial and long-term adverse effect on P's ability to carry out normal day-to-day activities.

  (2) A reference to a disabled person is a reference to a person who has a disability.

  (3) In relation to the protected characteristic of disability—

    (a) a reference to a person who has a particular protected characteristic is a reference to a person who has a particular disability;

    (b) a reference to persons who share a protected characteristic is a reference to persons who have the same disability.

  (4) This Act (except Part 12 and section 190) applies in relation to a person who has had a disability as it applies in relation to a person who has the disability; accordingly (except in that Part and that section)—

    (a) a reference (however expressed) to a person who has a disability includes a reference to a person who has had the disability, and

    (b) a reference (however expressed) to a person who does not have a disability includes a reference to a person who has not had the disability.

  (5), (6) *****

7   Gender reassignment

  (1) A person has the protected characteristic of gender reassignment if the person is proposing to undergo, is undergoing or has undergone a process (or part of a process) for the purpose of reassigning the person's sex by changing physiological or other attributes of sex.

  (2) A reference to a transsexual person is a reference to a person who has the protected characteristic of gender reassignment.

  (3) In relation to the protected characteristic of gender reassignment—

    (a) a reference to a person who has a particular protected characteristic is a reference to a transsexual person;

    (b) a reference to persons who share a protected characteristic is a reference to transsexual persons.

8   Marriage and civil partnership

  (1) A person has the protected characteristic of marriage and civil partnership if the person is married or is a civil partner.

  (2) In relation to the protected characteristic of marriage and civil partnership—

    (a) a reference to a person who has a particular protected characteristic is a reference to a person who is married or is a civil partner;

    (b) a reference to persons who share a protected characteristic is a reference to persons who are married or are civil partners.

9   Race

(1) Race includes—
   (a) colour;
   (b) nationality;
   (c) ethnic or national origins.

(2) In relation to the protected characteristic of race—
   (a) a reference to a person who has a particular protected characteristic is a reference to a person of a particular racial group;
   (b) a reference to persons who share a protected characteristic is a reference to persons of the same racial group.

(3) A racial group is a group of persons defined by reference to race; and a reference to a person's racial group is a reference to a racial group into which the person falls.

(4) The fact that a racial group comprises two or more distinct racial groups does not prevent it from constituting a particular racial group.

(5), (6) *****

10   Religion or belief

(1) Religion means any religion and a reference to religion includes a reference to a lack of religion.

(2) Belief means any religious or philosophical belief and a reference to belief includes a reference to a lack of belief.

(3) In relation to the protected characteristic of religion or belief—
   (a) a reference to a person who has a particular protected characteristic is a reference to a person of a particular religion or belief;
   (b) a reference to persons who share a protected characteristic is a reference to persons who are of the same religion or belief.

11   Sex

In relation to the protected characteristic of sex—
   (a) a reference to a person who has a particular protected characteristic is a reference to a man or to a woman;
   (b) a reference to persons who share a protected characteristic is a reference to persons of the same sex.

12   Sexual orientation

(1) Sexual orientation means a person's sexual orientation towards—
   (a) persons of the same sex,
   (b) persons of the opposite sex, or
   (c) persons of either sex.

(2) In relation to the protected characteristic of sexual orientation—
   (a) a reference to a person who has a particular protected characteristic is a reference to a person who is of a particular sexual orientation;
   (b) a reference to persons who share a protected characteristic is a reference to persons who are of the same sexual orientation.

Chapter 2 Prohibited conduct

Discrimination

13   Direct discrimination

(1) A person (A) discriminates against another (B) if, because of a protected characteristic, A treats B less favourably than A treats or would treat others.

(2) If the protected characteristic is age, A does not discriminate against B if A can show A's treatment of B to be a proportionate means of achieving a legitimate aim.

(3) If the protected characteristic is disability, and B is not a disabled person, A does not discriminate against B only because A treats or would treat disabled persons more favourably than A treats B.

(4) If the protected characteristic is marriage and civil partnership, this section applies to a contravention of Part 5 (work) only if the treatment is because it is B who is married or a civil partner.

(5) If the protected characteristic is race, less favourable treatment includes segregating B from others.

(6) If the protected characteristic is sex—

(a) less favourable treatment of a woman includes less favourable treatment of her because she is breast-feeding;

(b) in a case where B is a man, no account is to be taken of special treatment afforded to a woman in connection with pregnancy or childbirth.

(7) Subsection (6)(a) does not apply for the purposes of Part 5 (work).

(8) *****

14   Combined discrimination: dual characteristics

(1) A person (A) discriminates against another (B) if, because of a combination of two relevant protected characteristics, A treats B less favourably than A treats or would treat a person who does not share either of those characteristics.

(2) The relevant protected characteristics are—

(a) age;

(b) disability;

(c) gender reassignment;

(d) race

(e) religion or belief;

(f) sex;

(g) sexual orientation.

(3) For the purposes of establishing a contravention of this Act by virtue of subsection (1), B need not show that A's treatment of B is direct discrimination because of each of the characteristics in the combination (taken separately).

(4) But B cannot establish a contravention of this Act by virtue of subsection (1) if, in reliance on another provision of this Act or any other enactment, A shows that A's treatment of B is not direct discrimination because of either or both of the characteristics in the combination.

(5) Subsection (1) does not apply to a combination of characteristics that includes disability in circumstances where, if a claim of direct discrimination because of disability were to be brought, it would come within section 116 (special educational needs).

(6), (7) *****

15–18   *****

19   Indirect discrimination

(1) A person (A) discriminates against another (B) if A applies to B a provision, criterion or practice which is discriminatory in relation to a relevant protected characteristic of B's.

(2) For the purposes of subsection (1), a provision, criterion or practice is discriminatory in relation to a relevant protected characteristic of B's if—

(a) A applies, or would apply, it to persons with whom B does not share the characteristic,

(b) it puts, or would put, persons with whom B shares the characteristic at a particular disadvantage when compared with persons with whom B does not share it,

(c) it puts, or would put, B at that disadvantage, and

(d) A cannot show it to be a proportionate means of achieving a legitimate aim.

(3) The relevant protected characteristics are—

age;

disability;

gender reassignment;

marriage and civil partnership;
race;
religion or belief;
sex;
sexual orientation.

*****

Police Reform and Social Responsibility Act 2011

(2011, c. 13)

An Act to make provision about the administration and governance of police forces; about the licensing of, and for the imposition of a late night levy in relation to, the sale and supply of alcohol, and for the repeal of provisions about alcohol disorder zones; for the repeal of sections 132 to 138 of the Serious Organised Crime and Police Act 2005 and for the prohibition of certain activities in Parliament Square; to enable provision in local authority byelaws to include powers of seizure and forfeiture; about the control of dangerous or otherwise harmful drugs; to restrict the issue of arrest warrants for certain extra-territorial offences; and for connected purposes. [15th September 2011]

Territorial extent: England and Wales

PART 1 POLICE REFORM

Chapter 1 Police areas outside London

1 Police and crime commissioners

(1) There is to be a police and crime commissioner for each police area listed in Schedule 1 to the Police Act 1996 (police areas outside London).

(2) A police and crime commissioner is a corporation sole.

(3) [Unless subsection (3B) applies, the] name of the police and crime commissioner for a police area is 'the Police and Crime Commissioner for' with the addition of the name of the police area.

[(3A) Subsection (3B) applies if the person who is the police and crime commissioner for a police area is also the fire and rescue authority for the area which corresponds to, or an area which falls within, the police area.

(3B) In that case the name of the police and crime commissioner is 'the Police, Fire and Crime Commissioner for' with the addition of the name of the police area.]

(4) The police and crime commissioner for a police area is to be elected, and hold office, in accordance with Chapter 6.

(5) A police and crime commissioner has—

(a) the functions conferred by this section,

(b) the functions relating to community safety and crime prevention conferred by Chapter 3, and

(c) the other functions conferred by this Act and other enactments.

(6) The police and crime commissioner for a police area must—

(a) secure the maintenance of the police force for that area, and

(b) secure that the police force is efficient and effective.

(7) The police and crime commissioner for a police area must hold the relevant chief constable to account for the exercise of—

(a) the functions of the chief constable, and

(b) the functions of persons under the direction and control of the chief constable.

(8)–(10) *****

2 Chief constables

(1) Each police force is to have a chief constable.

(2) The chief constable of a police force is to be appointed, and hold office, in accordance with—

(a) section 38, and

(b) the terms and conditions of the appointment.

(3) A police force, and the civilian staff of a police force, are under the direction and control of the chief constable of the force.

(4) A chief constable has the other functions conferred by this Act and by other enactments.

(5) A chief constable must exercise the power of direction and control conferred by subsection (3) in such a way as is reasonable to assist the relevant police and crime commissioner to exercise the commissioner's functions.

(6)–(8) *****

Chapter 2 Metropolitan police district

3 Mayor's Office for Policing and Crime

(1) There is to be a body with the name 'The Mayor's Office for Policing and Crime' for the metropolitan police district.

(2) The Mayor's Office for Policing and Crime is a corporation sole.

(3) The person who is Mayor of London for the time being is to be the occupant for the time being of the Mayor's Office for Policing and Crime.

(4) Accordingly, where a person is the occupant of the Mayor's Office for Policing and Crime by virtue of a particular term of office as Mayor of London (the 'relevant mayoral term'), the person's term as the occupant of the Mayor's Office for Policing and Crime—

(a) begins at the same time as the relevant mayoral term, and

(b) ends at the same time as the relevant mayoral term.

(5) The Mayor's Office for Policing and Crime has—

(a) the functions conferred by this section,

(b) the functions relating to community safety and crime prevention conferred by Chapter 3, and

(c) the other functions conferred by this Act and other enactments.

(6) The Mayor's Office for Policing and Crime must—

(a) secure the maintenance of the metropolitan police force, and

(b) secure that the metropolitan police force is efficient and effective.

(7) The Mayor's Office for Policing and Crime must hold the Commissioner of Police of the Metropolis to account for the exercise of—

(a) the functions of the Commissioner, and

(b) the functions of persons under the direction and control of the Commissioner.

(8) The Mayor's Office for Policing and Crime must, in particular, hold the Commissioner to account for—

(a) the exercise of the duty imposed by section 8(4) (duty to have regard to police and crime plan);

(b) the exercise of the duty under section 37A(2) of the Police Act 1996 (duty to have re-gard to strategic policing requirement);

(c) the exercise of the duty imposed by section 39A(7) of the Police Act 1996 (duty to have regard to codes of practice issued by Secretary of State);

[(ca) the exercise of the Commissioner's functions under Part 2 of the Police Reform Act 2002 in relation to the handling of complaints;]

(d)   the effectiveness and efficiency of the Commissioner's arrangements for co-operating with other persons in the exercise of the Commissioner's functions (whether under section 22A of the Police Act 1996 or otherwise);
(e)   the effectiveness and efficiency of the Commissioner's arrangements under section 34 (engagement with local people);
(f)   the extent to which the Commissioner has complied with section 35 (value for money);
(g)   the exercise of duties relating to equality and diversity imposed on the Commissioner by any enactment;
(h)   the exercise of duties in relation to the safeguarding of children and the promotion of child welfare that are imposed on the Commissioner by sections 10 and 11 of the Children Act 2004.
(9)–(13) *****

4   Commissioner of Police of the Metropolis

(1) There is to be a corporation sole with the name 'the Commissioner of Police of the Metropolis'.

(2) The Commissioner of Police of the Metropolis is to be appointed, and hold office, in accordance with—
(a) sections 42 and 48, and
(b) the terms and conditions of the appointment.

(3) The metropolitan police force, and the civilian staff of the metropolitan police force, are under the direction and control of the Commissioner of Police of the Metropolis.

(4) The Commissioner of Police of the Metropolis has the other functions conferred by this Act and by other enactments.

(5) The Commissioner of Police of the Metropolis must exercise the power of direction and control conferred by subsection (3) in such a way as is reasonable to assist the Mayor's Office for Policing and Crime to exercise that Office's functions.

(6)–(7) *****

Chapter 3 Functions of elected local policing bodies etc

Community safety and crime prevention

5   Police and crime commissioners to issue police and crime plans

(1) The police and crime commissioner for a police area must issue a police and crime plan within the financial year in which each ordinary election is held.

(2) A police and crime commissioner must comply with the duty under subsection (1) as soon as practicable after the commissioner takes office.

(3) A police and crime commissioner may, at any time, issue a police and crime plan.

(4) A police and crime commissioner may vary a police and crime plan.

(5) In issuing or varying a police and crime plan, a police and crime commissioner must have regard to the strategic policing requirement issued by the Secretary of State under section 37A of the Police Act 1996.

[(5A) Subsections (5B) to (5E) apply to a police and crime commissioner for a police area—
(a) which corresponds to the area of a fire and rescue authority created by an order under section 4A, or
(b) within which the area of such a fire and rescue authority falls.

(5B) Subject to subsection (5E), in issuing or varying a police and crime plan, the police and crime commissioner must have regard to—
(a) the current Fire and Rescue National Framework prepared under section 21 of the Fire and Rescue Services Act 2004, and

(b) the last document prepared and published by the fire and rescue authority in accordance with that Framework which sets out the authority's priorities and objectives, for the period covered by the document, in connection with the discharge of the authority's functions.

(5C) A police and crime plan which the police and crime commissioner is required to prepare may be prepared jointly by the commissioner and the fire and rescue authority.

(5D) If the police and crime commissioner and the fire and rescue authority prepare a joint police and crime plan, the plan must also set out the fire and rescue authority's priorities and objectives, for the period of the plan, in connection with the discharge of the authority's functions.

(5E) Subsection (5B)(b) does not apply to a joint police and crime plan.]

(6)–(13) *****

6 Mayor's Office for Policing and Crime to issue police and crime plans

(1) The Mayor's Office for Policing and Crime must issue a police and crime plan within the financial year in which each ordinary election is held.

(2) The Mayor's Office for Policing and Crime must comply with the duty under subsection (1) as soon as practicable after the person elected in the ordinary election takes office.

(3) The Mayor's Office for Policing and Crime may, at any time, issue a police and crime plan.

(4) The Mayor's Office for Policing and Crime may vary a police and crime plan.

(5) In issuing or varying a police and crime plan, the Mayor's Office for Policing and Crime must have regard to the strategic policing requirement issued by the Secretary of State under section 37A of the Police Act 1996.

(6)–(15) *****

7 Police and crime plans

(1) A police and crime plan is a plan which sets out, in relation to the planning period, the following matters—

(a) the elected local policing body's police and crime objectives;

(b) the policing of the police area which the chief officer of police is to provide;

(c) the financial and other resources which the elected local policing body is to provide to the chief officer of police for the chief officer to exercise the functions of chief officer;

(d) the means by which the chief officer of police will report to the elected local policing body on the chief officer's provision of policing;

(e) the means by which the chief officer of police's performance in providing policing will be measured;

[(ea) the services which are to be provided by virtue of section 143 of the Anti-social Behaviour, Crime and Policing Act 2014;

(f) any grants which the elected local policy body is to make under that section, and the conditions (if any) subject to which any such grants are to be made.]

(2) The elected local policing body's police and crime objectives are the body's objectives for—

(a) the policing of the body's area,

(b) crime and disorder reduction in that area, and

(c) the discharge by the relevant police force of its national or international functions.

(3) A police and crime plan has effect from the start of the planning period until—

(a) the end of that planning period, or

(b) if another police and crime plan is issued in relation to the elected local policing body's area before the end of that planning period, the day when that other plan first has effect.

(4) The Secretary of State may give guidance to elected local policing bodies about the matters to be dealt with in police and crime plans.

(5) An elected local policing body must have regard to such guidance.

(6), (7) *****

8 Duty to have regard to police and crime plan

(1) A police and crime commissioner must, in exercising the functions of commissioner, have regard to the police and crime plan issued by the commissioner.

(2)–(7) *****

9–27 *****

Chapter 4 Accountability of elected local policing bodies

Scrutiny of police and crime commissioners

28 Police and crime panels outside London

(1) Each police area, other than the metropolitan police district, is to have a police and crime panel established and maintained in accordance with Schedule 6 (police and crime panels).

[(1A) Subsection (1B) applies if the person who is the police and crime commissioner for a police area is also the fire and rescue authority for the area which corresponds to, or an area which falls within, the police area.

(1B) The police and crime panel for the police area is to be known as 'the Police, Fire and Crime Panel'.]

(2) The functions of the police and crime panel for a police area must be exercised with a view to supporting the effective exercise of the functions of the police and crime commissioner for that police area.

(3) A police and crime panel must—

    (a) review the draft police and crime plan, or draft variation, given to the panel by the relevant police and crime commissioner in accordance with section 5(6)(c), and

    (b) make a report or recommendations on the draft plan or variation to the commissioner.

(4), (5) *****

(6) A police and crime panel must—

    (a) review or scrutinise decisions made, or other action taken, by the relevant police and crime commissioner in connection with the discharge of the commissioner's functions; and

    (b) make reports or recommendations to the relevant police and crime commissioner with respect to the discharge of the commissioner's functions,

insofar as the panel is not otherwise required to do so by subsection (3) or (4) or by Schedule 1, 5 or 8.

(7) A police and crime panel must publish any reports or recommendations made to the relevant police and crime commissioner.

(8)–(11) *****

29 Power to require attendance and information

(1) A police and crime panel may require the relevant police and crime commissioner, and members of that commissioner's staff, to attend before the panel (at reasonable notice) to answer any question which appears to the panel to be necessary in order for it to carry out its functions.

(2) Nothing in subsection (1) requires a member of the police and crime commissioner's staff to give any evidence, or produce any document, which discloses advice given to the commissioner by that person.

(3) A police and crime panel may require the relevant police and crime commissioner to respond in writing (within a reasonable period determined by the panel) to any report or recommendation made by the panel to the commissioner.

(4) The police and crime commissioner must comply with any requirement imposed by the panel under subsection (1) or (3).

(5) Members of the staff of the police and crime commissioner must comply with any requirement imposed on them under subsection (1).

(6) If a police and crime panel requires the relevant police and crime commissioner to attend before the panel, the panel may (at reasonable notice) request the relevant chief constable to attend before the panel on the same occasion to answer any question which appears to the panel to be necessary in order for it to carry out its functions.

30 Suspension of police and crime commissioner

(1) A police and crime panel may suspend the relevant police and crime commissioner if it appears to the panel that—

    (a) the commissioner has been charged in the United Kingdom, the Channel Islands or the Isle of Man with an offence, and

    (b) the offence is one which carries a maximum term of imprisonment exceeding two years.

(2) The suspension of the police and crime commissioner ceases to have effect upon the occurrence of the earliest of these events—

    (a) the charge being dropped;

    (b) the police and crime commissioner being acquitted of the offence;

    (c) the police and crime commissioner being convicted of the offence but not being disqualified under section 66 by virtue of the conviction;

    (d) the termination of the suspension by the police and crime panel.

(3) For the purposes of salary, pensions and allowances in respect of times during a period of suspension, the police and crime commissioner is to be treated as not holding that office during that suspension.

(4) *****

31–33 *****

Chapter 5 Police forces in areas with elected local policing bodies

Chief officers of police

34 Engagement with local people

(1) A chief officer of police must make arrangements for obtaining the views of persons within each neighbourhood in the relevant police area about crime and disorder in that neighbourhood.

(2) A chief officer of police must make arrangements for providing persons within each neighbourhood in the relevant police area with information about policing in that neighbourhood (including information about how policing in that neighbourhood is aimed at dealing with crime and disorder there).

(3)–(4) *****

35–37 *****

Police forces outside London

38 Appointment, suspension and removal of chief constables

(1) The police and crime commissioner for a police area is to appoint the chief constable of the police force for that area.

(2) The police and crime commissioner for a police area may suspend from duty the chief constable of the police force for that area.

(3) The police and crime commissioner for a police area may call upon the chief constable of the police force for that area to resign or retire.

(4) The chief constable must retire or resign if called upon to do so by the relevant police and crime commissioner in accordance with subsection (3).

(5)–(7) *****

*****

Terrorism Prevention and Investigation Measures Act 2011

(2011, c. 23)

An Act to abolish control orders and make provision for the imposition of terrorism prevention and investigation measures.   [14th December 2011]

Territorial extent: United Kingdom

New regime to protect the public from terrorism

1   *****

2   Imposition of terrorism prevention and investigation measures

(1) The Secretary of State may by notice (a 'TPIM notice') impose specified terrorism prevention and investigation measures on an individual if conditions A to E in section 3 are met.

(2) In this Act 'terrorism prevention and investigation measures' means requirements, restrictions and other provision which may be made in relation to an individual by virtue of Schedule 1 (terrorism prevention and investigation measures).

(3) In this section and Part 1 of Schedule 1 'specified' means specified in the TPIM notice.

[(4) Secretary of State must publish factors that he or she considers are appropriate to take into account when deciding whether to impose restrictions on an individual by virtue of paragraph 2 of Schedule 1 (travel measure).]

3   Conditions A to E

(1) Condition A is that the Secretary of State [reasonably believes,] that the individual is, or has been, involved in terrorism-related activity (the 'relevant activity').

(2) Condition B is that some or all of the relevant activity is new terrorism-related activity.

(3) Condition C is that the Secretary of State reasonably considers that it is necessary, for purposes connected with protecting members of the public from a risk of terrorism, for terrorism prevention and Investigation measures to be imposed on the individual.

(4) Condition D is that the Secretary of State reasonably considers that it is necessary, for purposes connected with preventing or restricting the individual's involvement in terrorism-related activity, for the specified terrorism prevention and investigation measures to be imposed on the individual.

(5) Condition E is that—

(a) the court gives the Secretary of State permission under section 6, or

(b) the Secretary of State reasonably considers that the urgency of the case requires terrorism prevention and investigation measures to be imposed without obtaining such permission.

(6) In this section 'new terrorism-related activity' means—

(a) if no TPIM notice relating to the individual has ever been in force, terrorism-related activity occurring at any time (whether before or after the coming into force of this Act);

(b) if only one TPIM notice relating to the individual has ever been in force, terrorism-related activity occurring after that notice came into force; or

(c) if two or more TPIM notices relating to the individual have been in force, terrorism-related activity occurring after such a notice came into force most recently.

4   Involvement in terrorism-related activity

(1) For the purposes of this Act, involvement in terrorism-related activity is any one or more of the following—

(a) the commission, preparation or instigation of acts of terrorism;

(b) conduct which facilitates the commission, preparation or instigation of such acts, or which is intended to do so;

(c) conduct which gives encouragement to the commission, preparation or instigation of such acts, or which is intended to do so;

(d) conduct which gives support or assistance to individuals who are known or believed by the individual concerned to be involved in conduct falling within [paragraph (a)];

and for the purposes of this Act it is immaterial whether the acts of terrorism in question are specific acts of terrorism or acts of terrorism in general.

(2) For the purposes of this Act, it is immaterial whether an individual's involvement in terrorism-related activity occurs before or after the coming into force of this Act.

[Duration of measures]

5 [Five] year limit for TPIM notices

(1) A TPIM notice—

(a) comes into force when the notice is served on the individual or, if later, at the time specified for this purpose in the notice; and

(b) is in force for the period of one year.

(2) The Secretary of State may by notice extend a TPIM notice for a period of one year beginning when the TPIM notice would otherwise expire.

(3) A TPIM notice—

(a) may be extended under subsection (2) only if conditions A, C and D are met; and

(b) may be so extended on [up to four occasions].

(4) *****

Court scrutiny of imposition of measures

6 Prior permission of the court

(1) This section applies if the Secretary of State—

(a) makes the relevant decisions in relation to an individual, and

(b) makes an application to the court for permission to impose measures on the individual.

(2) The application must set out a draft of the proposed TPIM notice.

(3) The function of the court on the application is—

(a) to determine whether the relevant decisions of the Secretary of State are obviously flawed, and

(b) to determine whether to give permission to impose measures on the individual and (where applicable) whether to exercise the power of direction under subsection (9).

(4) The court may consider the application—

(a) in the absence of the individual;

(b) without the individual having been notified of the application; and

(c) without the individual having been given an opportunity (if the individual was aware of the application) of making any representations to the court.

(5) But that does not limit the matters about which rules of court may be made.

(6) In determining the application, the court must apply the principles applicable on an application for judicial review.

(7) In a case where the court determines that a decision of the Secretary of State that condition A, condition B, or condition C is met is obviously flawed, the court may not give permission under this section.

(8) In any other case, the court may give permission under this section.

(9) If the court determines that the Secretary of State's decision that condition D is met is obviously flawed, the court may (in addition to giving permission under subsection (8)) give directions to the Secretary of State in relation to the measures to be imposed on the individual.

(10) In this section 'relevant decisions' means the decisions that the following conditions are met—

(a) condition A;

(b) condition B;

(c) condition C; and

(d) condition D.

7, 8 *****

9   Review hearing

(1) On a review hearing held in compliance with directions under section 8(4), the function of the court is to review the decisions of the Secretary of State that the relevant conditions were met and continue to be met.

(2) In doing so, the court must apply the principles applicable on an application for judicial review.

(3) The court—

(a) must discontinue the review hearing if the individual requests the court to do so; and

(b) may discontinue the review hearing in any other circumstances.

(4) The court may not discontinue the review hearing in accordance with subsection (3)(b) without giving the Secretary of State and the individual the opportunity to make representations.

(5) The court has the following powers (and only those powers) on a review hearing—

(a) power to quash the TPIM notice;

(b) power to quash measures specified in the TPIM notice;

(c) power to give directions to the Secretary of State for, or in relation to,—

(i) the revocation of the TPIM notice, or

(ii) the variation of measures specified in the TPIM notice.

(6) If the court does not exercise any of its powers under subsection (5), the court must decide that the TPIM notice is to continue in force.

(7) If the court exercises a power under subsection (5)(b) or (c)(ii), the court must decide that the TPIM notice is to continue in force subject to that exercise of that power.

(8) In this section 'relevant conditions' means—

(a) condition A;

(b) condition B;

(c) condition C; and

(d) condition D.

10   *****

Review of ongoing necessity

11   Review of ongoing necessity

During the period that a TPIM notice is in force, the Secretary of State must keep under review whether conditions C and D are met.

12–16   *****

17   Jurisdiction in relation to decisions under this Act

(1) TPIM decisions are not to be questioned in any legal proceedings other than—

(a) proceedings in the court; or

(b) proceedings on appeal from such proceedings.

(2) The court is the appropriate tribunal for the purposes of section 7 of the Human Rights Act 1998 in relation to proceedings all or any part of which call a TPIM decision into question.

(3) *****

*****

Protection of Freedoms Act 2012

(2012, c. 9)

An Act to provide for the destruction, retention, use and other regulation of certain evidential material; to impose consent and other requirements in relation to certain processing of biometric information relating to children; to provide for a code of practice about surveillance camera systems and for the appointment and role of the Surveillance Camera Commissioner; to provide for judicial approval in relation to certain authorisations and notices under the Regulation of Investigatory Powers Act 2000; to provide for the repeal or rewriting of powers of entry and associated powers and for codes of practice and other safeguards in relation to such powers; to make provision about vehicles left on land; to amend the maximum detention period for terrorist suspects; to replace certain stop and search powers and to provide for a related code of practice; to make provision about the safeguarding of vulnerable groups and about criminal records including provision for the establishment of the Disclosure and Barring Service and the dissolution of the Independent Safeguarding Authority; to disregard convictions and cautions for certain abolished offences; to make provision about the release and publication of datasets held by public authorities and to make other provision about freedom of information and the Information Commissioner; to make provision about the trafficking of people for exploitation and about stalking; to repeal certain enactments; and for con-nected purposes. [1st May 2012]

Territorial extent: England and Wales (Surveillance and Disregard of Offences); United Kingdom (Biometric Material and Powers of Entry)

1–19 *******

The Commissioner for the Retention and Use of Biometric Material

20 **Appointment and functions of Commissioner**

(1) The Secretary of State must appoint a Commissioner to be known as the Commissioner for the Retention and Use of Biometric Material (referred to in this section and section 21 as 'the Commissioner').

(2) It is the function of the Commissioner to keep under review—

    (a) every national security determination made or renewed under—

        (i) section 63M of the Police and Criminal Evidence Act 1984 (section 63D material retained for purposes of national security),

        (ii) paragraph 20E of Schedule 8 to the Terrorism Act 2000 (paragraph 20A material retained for purposes of national security),

        (iii) section 18B of the Counter-Terrorism Act 2008 (section 18 material retained for purposes of national security),

        (iv) paragraph 11 of Schedule 6 to the Terrorism Prevention and Investigation Measures Act 2011 (paragraph 6 material retained for purposes of national security),

        [(iva) paragraph 46 of Schedule 3 to the Counter-Terrorism and Border Security Act 2019]

        (v) section 18G of the Criminal Procedure (Scotland) Act 1995 (certain material retained for purposes of national security), and

        (vi) paragraph 7 of Schedule 1 to this Act (material subject to the Police and Criminal Evidence (Northern Ireland) Order 1989 retained for purposes of national security),

    (b) the uses to which material retained pursuant to a national security determination is being put.

(3) It is the duty of every person who makes or renews a national security determination under a provision mentioned in subsection (2)(a) to—

    (a) send to the Commissioner a copy of the determination or renewed determination, and the reasons for making or renewing the determination, within 28 days of making or renewing it, and

    (b) disclose or provide to the Commissioner such documents and information as the Commissioner may require for the purpose of carrying out the Commissioner's functions under subsection (2).

(4) If, on reviewing a national security determination made or renewed under a provision men-tioned in subsection (2)(a), the Commissioner concludes that it is not necessary for any material retained pursuant to the determination to be so retained, the Commissioner may order the destruc-tion of the material if the condition in subsection (5) is met.

(5) The condition is that the material retained pursuant to the national security determination is not otherwise capable of being lawfully retained.

(6) The Commissioner also has the function of keeping under review—

   (a) the retention and use in accordance with sections 63A and 63D to 63T of the Police and Criminal Evidence Act 1984 of—

      (i) any material to which section 63D or 63R of that Act applies (fingerprints, DNA profiles and samples), and

      (ii) any copies of any material to which section 63D of that Act applies (fingerprints and DNA profiles),

   (b) the retention and use in accordance with paragraphs 20A to 20J of Schedule 8 to the Terrorism Act 2000 of—

      (i) any material to which paragraph 20A or 20G of that Schedule applies (fingerprints, relevant physical data, DNA profiles and samples), and

      (ii) any copies of any material to which paragraph 20A of that Schedule applies (fingerprints, relevant physical data and DNA profiles),

   (c) the retention and use in accordance with sections 18 to 18E of the Counter-Terrorism Act 2008 of—

      (i) any material to which section 18 of that Act applies (fingerprints, DNA samples and DNA profiles), and

      (ii) any copies of fingerprints or DNA profiles to which section 18 of that Act applies,

   (d) the retention and use in accordance with paragraphs 5 to 14 of Schedule 6 to the Terrorism Prevention and Investigation Measures Act 2011 of—

      (i) any material to which paragraph 6 or 12 of that Schedule applies (fingerprints, relevant physical data, DNA profiles and samples), and

      (ii) any copies of any material to which paragraph 6 of that Schedule applies (fingerprints, relevant physical data and DNA profiles).

   [(e) the retention and use in accordance with paragraphs 43 to 51 of Schedule 3 to the Counter-Terrorism and Border Security Act 2019 of—

      (i) any material to which paragraph 43 or 49 of that Schedule applies (fingerprints, relevant physical data, DNA profiles and samples), and

      (ii) any copies of any material to which paragraph 43 of that Schedule applies (fingerprints, relevant physical data and DNA profiles).]

(7) But subsection (6) does not apply so far as the retention or use of the material falls to be reviewed by virtue of subsection (2).

(8) In relation to Scotland—

   (a) the reference in subsection (6)(b) to use of material, or copies of material, in accordance with paragraphs 20A to 20J of Schedule 8 to the Terrorism Act 2000 includes a reference to use of material, or copies of material, in accordance with section 19C(2)(c) and (d) of the Criminal Procedure (Scotland) Act 1995, . . .

   (b) the reference in subsection (6)(d) to use of material, or copies of material, in accordance with paragraphs 5 to 14 of Schedule 6 to the Terrorism Prevention and Investigation Measures Act 2011 is to be read as a reference to use only for a purpose mentioned in paragraph 13(1)(a) or (b) of that Schedule to that Act[, and

   (c) the reference in subsection (6)(e) to use of material, or copies of material, in accordance with paragraphs 43 to 51 of Schedule 3 to the Counter-Terrorism and Border Security Act 2019 includes a reference to use of material, or copies of material, in accordance with section 19C(2)(c) and (d) of the Criminal Procedure (Scotland) Act 1995.]

(9) The Commissioner also has functions under sections 63F(5)(c) and 63G (giving of consent in relation to the retention of certain section 63D material).

(10) The Commissioner is to hold office in accordance with the terms of the Commissioner's appointment; and the Secretary of State may pay in respect of the Commissioner any expenses, remuneration or allowances that the Secretary of State may determine.

(11) The Secretary of State may, after consultation with the Commissioner, provide the Commissioner with—

   (a) such staff, and

    (b) such accommodation, equipment and other facilities,

as the Secretary of State considers necessary for the carrying out of the Commissioner's functions.

21   Reports by Commissioner

    (1) The Commissioner must make a report to the Secretary of State about the carrying out of the Commissioner's functions as soon as reasonably practicable after the end of—

        (a) the period of 9 months beginning when this section comes into force, and

        (b) every subsequent 12 month period.

    (2) The Commissioner may also, at any time, make such report to the Secretary of State on any matter relating to the Commissioner's functions as the Commissioner considers appropriate.

    (3) The Secretary of State may at any time require the Commissioner to report on any matter relating to the Commissioner's functions.

    (4) On receiving a report from the Commissioner under this section, the Secretary of State must—

        (a) publish the report, and

        (b) lay a copy of the published report before Parliament.

    (5) The Secretary of State may, after consultation with the Commissioner, exclude from publication any part of a report under this section if, in the opinion of the Secretary of State, the publication of that part would be contrary to the public interest or prejudicial to national security.

Other provisions

22   Guidance on making national security determinations

    (1) The Secretary of State must give guidance about making or renewing national security determinations under a provision mentioned in section 20(2)(a).

    (2) Any person authorised to make or renew any such national security determination must have regard to any guidance given under this section.

    (3) The Secretary of State may give different guidance for different purposes.

    (4) In the course of preparing the guidance, or revising guidance already given, the Secretary of State must consult the Commissioner for the Retention and Use of Biometric Material and the Lord Advocate.

    (5) Before giving guidance under this section, or revising guidance already given, the Secretary of State must lay before Parliament—

        (a) the proposed guidance or proposed revisions, and

        (b) a draft of an order providing for the guidance, or revisions to the guidance, to come into force.

    (6) The Secretary of State must make the order, and issue the guidance or (as the case may be) make the revisions to the guidance, if the draft of the order is approved by a resolution of each House of Parliament.

    (7) Guidance, or revisions to guidance, come into force in accordance with an order under this section.

    (8) Such an order—

        (a) is to be a statutory instrument, and

        (b) may contain transitional, transitory or saving provision.

    (9) The Secretary of State must publish any guidance given or revised under this section.

23–25   *****

Chapter 2 Protection of biometric information of children in schools etc

26   Requirement to notify and obtain consent before processing biometric information

    (1) This section applies in relation to any processing of a child's biometric information by or on behalf of the relevant authority of—

(a) a school,

(b) a 16 to 19 Academy, or

(c) a further education institution.

(2) Before the first processing of a child's biometric information on or after the coming into force of subsection (3), the relevant authority must notify each parent of the child—

(a) of its intention to process the child's biometric information, and

(b) that the parent may object at any time to the processing of the information.

(3) The relevant authority must ensure that a child's biometric information is not processed unless—

(a) at least one parent of the child consents to the information being processed, and

(b) no parent of the child has withdrawn his or her consent, or otherwise objected, to the information being processed.

(4) Section 27 makes further provision about the requirement to notify parents and the obtaining and withdrawal of consent (including when notification and consent are not required).

(5) But if, at any time, the child—

(a) refuses to participate in, or continue to participate in, anything that involves the processing of the child's biometric information, or

(b) otherwise objects to the processing of that information,

the relevant authority must ensure that the information is not processed, irrespective of any consent given by a parent of the child under subsection (3).

(6) Subsection (7) applies in relation to any child whose biometric information, by virtue of this section, may not be processed.

(7) The relevant authority must ensure that reasonable alternative means are available by which the child may do, or be subject to, anything which the child would have been able to do, or be subject to, had the child's biometric information been processed.

27   Exceptions and further provision about consent and notification

(1) For the purposes of section 26(2) and (3), the relevant authority is not required to notify a parent, or obtain the consent of a parent, if the relevant authority is satisfied that—

(a) the parent cannot be found,

(b) the parent lacks capacity (within the meaning of the Mental Capacity Act 2005) to object or (as the case may be) consent to the processing of the child's biometric information,

(c) the welfare of the child requires that the parent is not contacted, or

(d) it is otherwise not reasonably practicable to notify the parent or (as the case may be) obtain the consent of the parent.

(2) A notification under section 26(2) must be given in writing, and any objection to the processing of a child's biometric information must be made in writing.

(3) Consent under section 26(3) may be withdrawn at any time.

(4) Consent under section 26(3) must be given, and (if withdrawn) withdrawn, in writing.

(5) Section 26 and this section are in addition to the requirements of [the data protection legislation].

[(6) In this section, 'the data protection legislation' has the same meaning as in the Data Protection Act 2018 (see section 3 of that Act).]

28   Interpretation: Chapter 2

(1) *****

(2) 'Biometric information' means information about a person's physical or behavioural characteristics or features which—

(a) is capable of being used in order to establish or verify the identity of the person, and

(b) is obtained or recorded with the intention that it be used for the purposes of a biometric recognition system.

(3) Biometric information may, in particular, include—

(a) information about the skin pattern and other physical characteristics or features of a person's fingers or palms,

(b) information about the features of an iris or any other part of the eye, and

(c) information about a person's voice or handwriting.

(4) In subsection (2) 'biometric recognition system' means a system which, by means of equipment operating automatically—

(a) obtains or records information about a person's physical or behavioural characteristics or features, and

(b) compares the information with stored information that has previously been so obtained or recorded, or otherwise processes the information, for the purpose of establishing or verifying the identity of the person, or otherwise determining whether the person is recognised by the system.

(5)–(10) *****

PART 2 REGULATION OF SURVEILLANCE

Chapter 1 Regulation of CCTV and other surveillance camera technology

Code of practice

29 Code of practice for surveillance camera systems

(1) The Secretary of State must prepare a code of practice containing guidance about surveillance camera systems.

(2) Such a code must contain guidance about one or more of the following—

(a) the development or use of surveillance camera systems,

(b) the use or processing of images or other information obtained by virtue of such systems.

(3) Such a code may, in particular, include provision about—

(a) considerations as to whether to use surveillance camera systems,

(b) types of systems or apparatus,

(c) technical standards for systems or apparatus,

(d) locations for systems or apparatus,

(e) the publication of information about systems or apparatus,

(f) standards applicable to persons using or maintaining systems or apparatus,

(g) standards applicable to persons using or processing information obtained by virtue of systems,

(h) access to, or disclosure of, information so obtained,

(i) procedures for complaints or consultation.

(4) Such a code—

(a) need not contain provision about every type of surveillance camera system,

(b) may make different provision for different purposes.

(5) In the course of preparing such a code, the Secretary of State must consult—

(a)   such persons appearing to the Secretary of State to be representative of the views of persons who are, or are likely to be, subject to the duty under section 33(1) (duty to have regard to the code) as the Secretary of State considers appropriate,

(b)   [the National Police Chiefs' Council],

(c)   the Information Commissioner,

[(d) the Investigatory Powers Commissioner,]

(e)   the Surveillance Camera Commissioner,

(f)   the Welsh Ministers, and

(g)   such other persons as the Secretary of State considers appropriate.

(6), (7) *****

Procedural requirements

30　Issuing of code

(1)　The Secretary of State must lay before Parliament—

(a)　a code of practice prepared under section 29, and

(b)　a draft of an order providing for the code to come into force.

(2)　The Secretary of State must make the order and issue the code if the draft of the order is approved by a resolution of each House of Parliament.

(3)　The Secretary of State must not make the order or issue the code unless the draft of the order is so approved.

(4)　The Secretary of State must prepare another code of practice under section 29 if—

(a)　the draft of the order is not so approved, and

(b)　the Secretary of State considers that there is no realistic prospect that it will be so approved.

(5)　A code comes into force in accordance with an order under this section.

(6)　Such an order—

(a)　is to be a statutory instrument, and

(b)　may contain transitional, transitory or saving provision.

(7)　If a draft of an instrument containing an order under this section would, apart from this subsection, be treated as a hybrid instrument for the purposes of the standing orders of either House of Parliament, it is to proceed in that House as if it were not a hybrid instrument.

31, 32　*****

Enforcement and Commissioner

33　Effect of code

(1)　A relevant authority must have regard to the surveillance camera code when exercising any functions to which the code relates.

(2)　A failure on the part of any person to act in accordance with any provision of the surveillance camera code does not of itself make that person liable to criminal or civil proceedings.

(3)　The surveillance camera code is admissible in evidence in any such proceedings.

(4)　A court or tribunal may, in particular, take into account a failure by a relevant authority to have regard to the surveillance camera code in determining a question in any such proceedings.

(5)　In this section 'relevant authority' means—

(a)　a local authority within the meaning of the Local Government Act 1972,

(b)　the Greater London Authority,

(c)　the Common Council of the City of London in its capacity as a local authority,

(d)　the Sub-Treasurer of the Inner Temple or the Under-Treasurer of the Middle Temple, in their capacity as a local authority,

(e)　the Council of the Isles of Scilly,

(f)　a parish meeting constituted under section 13 of the Local Government Act 1972,

(g)　a police and crime commissioner,

(h)　the Mayor's Office for Policing and Crime,

(i)　the Common Council of the City of London in its capacity as a police authority,

(j)　any chief officer of a police force in England and Wales,

(k)　any person specified or described by the Secretary of State in an order made by statutory instrument.

(6)　An order under subsection (5) may, in particular—

(a)　restrict the specification or description of a person to that of the person when acting in a specified capacity or exercising specified or described functions,

(b)　contain transitional, transitory or saving provision.

(7)　So far as an order under subsection (5) contains a restriction of the kind mentioned in subsection (6)(a) in relation to a person, the duty in subsection (1) applies only to the person in that capacity or (as the case may be) only in relation to those functions.

(8) Before making an order under subsection (5) in relation to any person or description of persons, the Secretary of State must consult—

    (a)   such persons appearing to the Secretary of State to be representative of the views of the person or persons in relation to whom the order may be made as the Secretary of State considers appropriate,

    (b)   [the National Police Chiefs' Council],

    (c)   the Information Commissioner,

    [(d)   the Investigatory Powers Commissioner,]

    (e)   the Surveillance Camera Commissioner,

    (f)   the Welsh Ministers, and

    (g)   such other persons as the Secretary of State considers appropriate.

(9) No instrument containing an order under subsection (5) is to be made unless a draft of it has been laid before, and approved by a resolution of, each House of Parliament.

(10) If a draft of an instrument containing an order under subsection (5) would, apart from this subsection, be treated as a hybrid instrument for the purposes of the standing orders of either House of Parliament, it is to proceed in that House as if it were not a hybrid instrument.

34   Commissioner in relation to code

(1) The Secretary of State must appoint a person as the Surveillance Camera Commissioner (in this Chapter 'the Commissioner').

(2) The Commissioner is to have the following functions—

    (a) encouraging compliance with the surveillance camera code,

    (b) reviewing the operation of the code, and

    (c) providing advice about the code (including changes to it or breaches of it).

(3) The Commissioner is to hold office in accordance with the terms of the Commissioner's appointment; and the Secretary of State may pay in respect of the Commissioner any expenses, remuneration or allowances that the Secretary of State may determine.

(4) The Secretary of State may, after consultation with the Commissioner, provide the Commissioner with—

    (a) such staff, and

    (b) such accommodation, equipment and other facilities,

as the Secretary of State considers necessary for the carrying out of the Commissioner's functions.

35–38   *****

PART 3   PROTECTION OF PROPERTY FROM DISPROPORTIONATE ENFORCEMENT ACTION

Chapter 1   Power of entry

Repealing, adding safeguards or rewriting powers of entry

39   Repealing etc unnecessary or inappropriate powers of entry

(1) The appropriate national authority may by order repeal any power of entry or associated power which the appropriate national authority considers to be unnecessary or inappropriate.

(2) Schedule 2 (which contains repeals etc of certain powers of entry) has effect.

40   Adding safeguards to powers of entry

(1) The appropriate national authority may by order provide for safeguards in relation to any power of entry or associated power.

(2) Such safeguards may, in particular, include—

    (a) restrictions as to the premises over which the power may be exercised,

(b) restrictions as to the times at which the power may be exercised,

(c) restrictions as to the number or description of persons who may exercise the power,

(d) a requirement for a judicial or other authorisation before the power may be exercised,

(e) a requirement to give notice within a particular period before the power may be exercised,

(f) other conditions which must be met before the power may be exercised,

(g) modifications of existing conditions which must be met before the power may be exercised,

(h) other restrictions on the circumstances in which the power may be exercised,

(i) new obligations on the person exercising the power which must be met before, during or after its exercise,

(j) modifications of existing obligations which must be met by the person exercising the power before, during or after its exercise,

(k) restrictions on any power to use force, or any other power, which may be exercised in connection with the power of entry or associated power.

41   Rewriting powers on entry

(1) The appropriate national authority may by order rewrite, with or without modifications—

(a) powers of entry, associated powers or any aspects of any such powers, or

(b) enactments relating to, or connected with, any such powers or aspects.

(2) The power under subsection (1) to rewrite a power of entry or associated power includes, in particular, the power to remove an aspect of such a power without replacing it.

(3) But no order under this section may alter the effect of—

(a) a power of entry,

(b) any associated power connected with it, or

(c) any safeguard relating to, but not forming part of, the power of entry or associated power,

unless, on and after the changes made by the order, the safeguards in relation to the power of entry and associated powers connected with it, taken together, provide a greater level of protection than any safeguards applicable immediately before the changes.

42   Duty to review certain existing powers of entry

(1) Each Minister of the Crown who is a member of the Cabinet must, within the relevant period—

(a) review relevant powers of entry, and relevant associated powers, for which the Minister is responsible with a view to deciding whether to make an order under section 39(1), 40 or 41 in relation to any of them,

(b) prepare a report of that review, and

(c) lay a copy of the report before Parliament.

(2) A failure by a Minister of the Crown to comply with a duty under subsection (1) in relation to a power of entry or associated power does not affect the validity of the power.

(3) In this section—

'relevant associated power' means any associated power in a public general Act or a statutory instrument made under such an Act,

'the relevant period' means the period of two years beginning with the day on which this Act is passed,

'relevant power of entry' means any power of entry in a public general Act or a statutory instrument made under such an Act.

43   Consultation requirements before modifying powers of entry

Before making an order under section 39(1), 40 or 41 in relation to a power of entry or associated power, the appropriate national authority must consult—

(a) such persons appearing to the appropriate national authority to be representative of the views of persons entitled to exercise the power of entry or associated power as the appropriate national authority considers appropriate, and

(b) such other persons as the appropriate national authority considers appropriate.

44 Procedural and supplementary provisions

(1) An order under section 39(1), 40 or 41—

(a) is to be made by statutory instrument,

(b) may modify any enactment,

(c) may include such incidental, consequential, supplementary, transitory, transitional or saving provision as the appropriate national authority considers appropriate (including provision modifying any enactment).

(2) Subject to subsection (4), no instrument containing an order of a Minister of the Crown under section 39(1), 40 or 41 is to be made unless a draft of it has been laid before, and approved by a resolution of, each House of Parliament.

(3) If a draft of an instrument containing an order of a Minister of the Crown under section 39(1), 40 or 41 would, apart from this subsection, be treated as a hybrid instrument for the purposes of the standing orders of either House of Parliament, it is to proceed in that House as if it were not a hybrid instrument.

(4) An instrument containing an order of a Minister of the Crown under section 39(1), 40 or 41 which neither amends nor repeals any provision of primary legislation is subject to annulment in pursuance of a resolution of either House of Parliament.

(5) In subsection (4) 'primary legislation' means—

(a) a public general Act,

(b) an Act of the Scottish Parliament,

(c) a Measure or Act of the National Assembly for Wales, and

(d) Northern Ireland legislation.

(6) Subject to subsection (7), no instrument containing an order of the Welsh Ministers under section 39(1), 40 or 41 is to be made unless a draft of it has been laid before, and approved by a resolution of, the National Assembly for Wales.

(7) An instrument containing an order of the Welsh Ministers under section 39(1), 40 or 41 which neither amends nor repeals any provision of primary legislation is subject to annulment in pursuance of a resolution of the National Assembly for Wales.

(8) In subsection (7) 'primary legislation' means—

(a) a public general Act, and

(b) a Measure or Act of the National Assembly for Wales.

45 Devolution: Scotland and Northern Ireland

(1) An order under section 39(1), 40 or 41 may not make provision which would be within the legislative competence of the Scottish Parliament if it were contained in an Act of the Scottish Parliament.

(2) An order under section 39(1), 40 or 41 may not make provision which, if it were contained in an Act of the Northern Ireland Assembly, would be within the legislative competence of the Northern Ireland Assembly and would deal with a transferred matter without being ancillary to other provision (whether in that Act or previously enacted) which deals with an excepted or reserved matter.

(3) In subsection (2) 'excepted matter', 'reserved matter' and 'transferred matter' have the meaning given by section 4(1) of the Northern Ireland Act 1998.

46 Sections 39 to 46: interpretation

In sections 39 to 45 and this section—

'appropriate national authority' means—

(a) in relation to the making of any provision which would be within the legislative competence of the National Assembly for Wales, the Welsh Ministers,

(b) in any other case, a Minister of the Crown,

'associated power' means any power which—

(a) is contained in an enactment,

(b) is connected with a power of entry, and

(c) is a power—
  (i) to do anything on, or in relation to, the land or other premises entered in pursuance of the power of entry,
  (ii) to do anything in relation to any person, or anything, found on the land or other premises entered in pursuance of the power of entry, or
  (iii) otherwise to do anything in connection with the power of entry,
  and includes any safeguard which forms part of the associated power;

*****

47–91   *****

Chapter 4 Disregarding certain convictions for buggery etc [: England and Wales]

General

92 Power of Secretary of State to disregard convictions or cautions

(1) A person who has been convicted of, or cautioned for, an offence under—
  (a) section 12 of the Sexual Offences Act 1956 (buggery),
  (b) section 13 of that Act (gross indecency between men), or
  (c) section 61 of the Offences against the Person Act 1861 or section 11 of the Criminal Law Amendment Act 1885 (corresponding earlier offences),
may apply to the Secretary of State for the conviction or caution to become a disregarded conviction or caution.

(2) A conviction or caution becomes a disregarded conviction or caution when conditions A and B are met.

(3) Condition A is that the Secretary of State decides that it appears that—
  (a) the other person involved in the conduct constituting the offence consented to it and was aged 16 or over, and
  (b) any such conduct now would not be an offence under section 71 of the Sexual Offences Act 2003 (sexual activity in a public lavatory).

(4) Condition B is that—
  (a) the Secretary of State has given notice of the decision to the applicant under section 94(4)(b), and
  (b) the period of 14 days beginning with the day on which the notice was given has ended.

(5) Sections 95 to 98 explain the effect of a conviction or caution becoming a disregarded conviction or caution.

[(6) Except in relation to service disciplinary proceedings, this section applies only in relation to persons convicted or cautioned in England and Wales.]

93 Applications to the Secretary of State

(1) An application under section 92 must be in writing.

(2) It must state—
  (a) the name, address and date of birth of the applicant,
  (b) the name and address of the applicant at the time of the conviction or caution,
  (c) so far as known to the applicant, the time when and the place where the conviction was made or the caution given and, for a conviction, the case number, and
  (d) such other information as the Secretary of State may require.

(3) It may include representations by the applicant or written evidence about the matters mentioned in condition A in section 92.

94 Procedure for decisions by the Secretary of State

(1) In considering whether to make a decision of the kind mentioned in condition A in section 92, the Secretary of State must, in particular, consider—

(a) any representations or evidence included in the application, and

(b) any available record of the investigation of the offence and of any proceedings relating to it that the Secretary of State considers to be relevant.

(2) The Secretary of State may not hold an oral hearing for the purpose of deciding whether to make a decision of the kind mentioned in condition A in section 92.

(3) Subsection (4) applies if the Secretary of State—

(a) decides that it appears as mentioned in condition A in section 92, or

(b) makes a different decision in relation to the matters mentioned in that condition.

(4) The Secretary of State must—

(a) record the decision in writing, and

(b) give notice of it to the applicant.

Effect of disregard

95 Effect of disregard on police and other records

(1) The Secretary of State must by notice direct the relevant data controller to delete details, contained in relevant official records, of a disregarded conviction or caution.

(2) A notice under subsection (1) may be given at any time after condition A in section 92 is met but no deletion may have effect before condition B in that section is met.

(3) Subject to that, the relevant data controller must delete the details as soon as reasonably practicable.

(4) Having done so, the relevant data controller must give notice to the person who has the disregarded conviction or caution that the details of it have been deleted.

(5), (6) *******

96 Effect of disregard for disclosure and other purposes

(1) A person who has a disregarded conviction or caution is to be treated for all purposes in law as if the person has not—

(a) committed the offence,

(b) been charged with, or prosecuted for, the offence,

(c) been convicted of the offence,

(d) been sentenced for the offence, or

(e) been cautioned for the offence.

(2) In particular—

(a) no evidence is to be admissible in any proceedings before a judicial authority exercising its jurisdiction or functions in England and Wales to prove that the person has done, or undergone, anything within subsection (1)(a) to (e), and

(b) the person is not, in any such proceedings, to be asked (and, if asked, is not to be required to answer) any question relating to the person's past which cannot be answered without acknowledging or referring to the conviction or caution or any circumstances ancillary to it.

(3) Where a question is put to a person, other than in such proceedings, seeking information with respect to the previous convictions, cautions, offences, conduct or circumstances of any person—

(a) the question is to be treated as not relating to any disregarded conviction or caution, or any circumstances ancillary to it (and the answer to the question may be framed accordingly), and

(b) the person questioned is not to be subjected to any liability or otherwise prejudiced in law by reason of any failure to acknowledge or disclose that conviction or caution or any circumstances ancillary to it in answering the question.

(4) Any obligation imposed on any person by any enactment or rule of law or by the provisions of any agreement or arrangement to disclose any matters to any other person is not to extend to requiring the disclosure of a disregarded conviction or caution or any circumstances ancillary to it.

(5) A disregarded conviction or caution, or any circumstances ancillary to it, is not a proper ground for—

(a) dismissing or excluding a person from any office, profession, occupation or employment, or

(b) prejudicing the person in any way in any office, profession, occupation or employment.

(6) This section is subject to section 97 but otherwise applies despite any enactment or rule of law to the contrary.

(7) See also section 98 (meaning of 'proceedings before a judicial authority' and 'circumstances ancillary to a conviction or caution').

97   Saving for Royal pardons etc

Nothing in section 96 affects any right of Her Majesty, by virtue of Her Royal prerogative or otherwise, to grant a free pardon, to quash any conviction or sentence, or to commute any sentence.
*****

Crime and Courts Act 2013

(2013, c. 22)

An Act to establish, and make provision about, the National Crime Agency; to abolish the Serious Organised Crime Agency and the National Policing Improvement Agency; to make provision about the judiciary and the structure, administration, proceedings and powers of courts and tribunals; to make provision about deferred prosecution agreements; to make provision about border control; to make provision about drugs and driving; and for connected purposes.   [25th April 2013]

Territorial extent: United Kingdom but England and Wales only in the case of s. 33

PART 1 THE NATIONAL CRIME AGENCY

The NCA and its officers

1   The National Crime Agency

(1) A National Crime Agency, consisting of the NCA officers, is to be formed.

(2) The NCA is to be under the direction and control of one of the NCA officers, who is to be known as the Director General of the National Crime Agency.

(3) The NCA is to have—

(a) the functions conferred by this section;

(b) the functions conferred by the Proceeds of Crime Act 2002; and

(c) the other functions conferred by this Act and by other enactments.

(4) The NCA is to have the function (the 'crime-reduction function') of securing that efficient and effective activities to combat organised crime and serious crime are carried out (whether by the NCA, other law enforcement agencies, or other persons).

(5) The NCA is to have the function (the 'criminal intelligence function') of gathering, storing, processing, analysing, and disseminating information that is relevant to any of the following—

(a) activities to combat organised crime or serious crime;

(b) activities to combat any other kind of crime;

(c) exploitation proceeds investigations (within the meaning of section 341(5) of the Proceeds of Crime Act 2002), exploitation proceeds orders (within the meaning of Part 7 of the Coroners and Justice Act 2009), and applications for such orders.

(6) The NCA must discharge the crime-reduction function in the following ways (in particular).

(7) The first way is by the NCA itself—

(a) preventing and detecting organised crime and serious crime,

(b) investigating offences relating to organised crime or serious crime, and

(c) otherwise carrying out activities to combat organised crime and serious crime, including by instituting criminal proceedings in England and Wales and Northern Ireland.

(8) The second way is by the NCA securing that activities to combat organised crime or serious crime are carried out by persons other than the NCA.

(9) The third way is by the NCA securing improvements—

(a) in co-operation between persons who carry out activities to combat organised crime or serious crime, and

(b) in co-ordination of activities to combat organised crime or serious crime.

(10)–(12) *****

2 Modification of NCA functions

(1) The Secretary of State may, by order, make—

(a) provision about NCA counter-terrorism functions (and, in particular, may make provision conferring, removing, or otherwise modifying such functions); and

(b) other provision which the Secretary of State considers necessary in consequence of provision made under paragraph (a) (and, in particular, may make provision about the functions of any person other than the NCA, including provision conferring or otherwise modifying, but not removing, such functions).

(2) If an order under this section confers an NCA counter-terrorism function, an NCA officer may only carry out activities in Northern Ireland for the purpose of the discharge of the function if the NCA officer does so with the agreement of the Chief Constable of the Police Service of Northern Ireland.

(3) That includes cases where an order under this section confers an NCA counterterrorism function by the modification of a function.

(4) An order under this section may amend or otherwise modify this Act or any other enactment.

(5), (6) *****

3 Strategic priorities

(1) The Secretary of the State must determine strategic priorities for the NCA.

(2) In determining strategic priorities for the NCA (including deciding whether there should be such priorities), the Secretary of State must consult—

(a) the strategic partners,

(b) the Director General, and

(c) any other persons whom the Secretary of State considers it is appropriate to consult.

4 Operations

(1) The Director General has (by virtue of the function of direction and control of the NCA) the power to decide—

(a) which particular operations are to be mounted by NCA officers, and

(b) how such operations are to be conducted.

(2) In exercising functions, the Director General must have regard to—

(a) any strategic priorities for the NCA (see section 3);

(b) the annual plan (see below); and

(c) the framework document (see Part 1 of Schedule 2).

(3) Before the beginning of each financial year, the Director General must issue a document (the 'annual plan') setting out how the Director General intends that NCA functions are to be exercised during that year (including how they are to be exercised in Scotland and Northern Ireland).

(4) The annual plan for a financial year must include—

(a) a statement of any strategic priorities for the NCA,

(b) a statement of the operational priorities for the NCA, and

(c) in relation to each of the strategic and operational priorities, an explanation of how the Director General intends that the priority will be given effect to.

(5) The Director General must determine operational priorities for the NCA; and those priorities may relate—

(a) to matters to which current strategic priorities also relate, or

(b) to other matters;

but operational priorities must, in any event, be framed so as to be consistent with the current strategic priorities.

(6) In preparing any annual plan, the Director General must consult—

(a) the strategic partners [and the Northern Ireland Policing Board], and

(b) any other persons whom the Director General considers it is appropriate to consult.

(7) The Director General is required by subsection (6)(a)—

(a) to consult the Scottish Ministers about the annual plan only as it relates to activities in Scotland; and

(b) to consult the Department of Justice in Northern Ireland [and the Northern Ireland Policing Board] about the annual plan only as it relates to activities in Northern Ireland.

(8) Before issuing any annual plan, the Director General must obtain—

(a) the consent of the Secretary of State to the plan,

(b) the consent of the Scottish Ministers to the plan as it relates to activities in Scotland, and

(c) the consent of the Department of Justice in Northern Ireland [and the Northern Ireland Policing Board] as it relates to activities in Northern Ireland.

(9) The Director General must arrange for each annual plan to be published in the manner which the Director General considers appropriate.

(10) Schedule 2 (the framework document & annual report) has effect.

Other functions etc

5 Relationships between NCA and other agencies: tasking etc

(1) Any of the following persons may perform a task if the Director General requests the person to perform it—

(a) the chief officer of a UK police force;

(b) a UK law enforcement agency.

(2) A request under subsection (1)—

(a) may be made only if the Director General considers that performance of the task would assist the NCA to exercise functions;

(b) must explain how performance of the requested task would so assist the exercise of functions.

(3) The Director General may perform a task if any of the following persons requests the Director General to perform it—

(a) the chief officer of a UK police force;

(b) a UK law enforcement agency.

(4) A request under subsection (3)—

(a) may be made only if the person making it considers that performance of the task would assist that person—or, in a case where that person is the chief officer of a police force, would assist that person or police force—to exercise functions;

(b) must explain how performance of the requested task would so assist the exercise of functions.

(5) The Director General may direct any of the following persons to perform a task specified in the direction—

(a) the chief officer of an England and Wales police force;

(b) the Chief Constable of the British Transport Police.

(6) The Director General may give a direction under subsection (5) only if the Director General considers that—

(a) performance of the task would assist the NCA to exercise functions;

(b) it is expedient for the directed person to perform that task; and

(c) satisfactory arrangements cannot be made, or cannot be made in time, under subsection (1).

(7) A person given a direction under this section must comply with it.

(8) If a person is requested or directed under this section to perform a task, the person may comply with that request or direction by securing that the task is performed by another person.

(9) The Director General may give a direction under this section to the Chief Constable of the British Transport Police only if the Secretary of State consents.

(10)–(12) *****

6 Duty to publish information

(1) The Director General must—

(a) make arrangements for publishing information about the exercise of NCA functions and other matters relating to the NCA, and

(b) publish information in accordance with those arrangements.

(2) The framework document may impose on the Director General requirements in relation to performance of the duties imposed by subsection (1) (including requirements about what information is not to be published).

(3) The Director General must comply with any such requirements in the framework document (and accordingly the duty in section 4(2)(c) to have regard to that document does not apply in relation to such requirements).

(4) This section is subject to Schedule 7 (information: restrictions on disclosure).

7 Information gateways

(1) A person may disclose information to the NCA if the disclosure is made for the purposes of the exercise of any NCA function.

(2) Subsection (1) does not authorise any of the following to disclose information to the NCA—

(a) a person serving in the Security Service;

(b) a person serving in the Secret Intelligence Service;

(c) a person serving in GCHQ;

but this does not affect the disclosures which such a person may make to the NCA in accordance with intelligence service disclosure arrangements.

(3) Information obtained by the NCA in connection with the exercise of any NCA functions may be used by the NCA in connection with the exercise of any other NCA function.

(4) An NCA officer may disclose information obtained by the NCA in connection with the exercise of any NCA function if the disclosure is for any permitted purpose.

(5) Subsection (4) authorises an NCA officer to disclose information for the purpose of the exercise of—

(a) the functions of the Lord Advocate under Part 3 of the Proceeds of Crime Act 2002 ('PCA 2002'), or

(b) the functions of the Scottish Ministers under, or in relation to, Part 5 of PCA 2002,

only where the information has been obtained by the NCA in connection with the exercise of a function under PCA 2002 (other than a function under Part 6 of that Act).

(6) Where information has been obtained by the NCA in connection with the exercise of a function under Part 6 of PCA 2002 (revenue functions), subsection (4) does not authorise an NCA officer to disclose the information.

(7) But an NCA officer may disclose the information if the disclosure is—

(a) to the Commissioners for Her Majesty's Revenue and Customs,

(b) to the Lord Advocate for the purposes of the exercise by the Lord Advocate of the Lord Advocate's functions under Part 3 of PCA 2002 (confiscation: Scotland),

(c) to any person for purposes relating to civil proceedings (whether or not in the United Kingdom) which relate to a matter in respect of which the NCA has functions, or

(d) to any person for the purposes of compliance with an order of a court or tribunal (whether or not in the United Kingdom).

(8) A disclosure of information which is authorised or required by this Part does not breach—

(a) an obligation of confidence owed by the person making the disclosure, or

(b) any other restriction on the disclosure of information (however imposed).

(9), (10) *****

8–10 *****

General

11 Inspections and complaints

(1) Her Majesty's Inspectors of Constabulary ('HMIC') must carry out inspections of the NCA.

(2) HMIC must also carry out an inspection of the NCA if requested to do so by the Secretary of State either—

(a) generally, or

(b) in respect of a particular matter.

[(2A) The Secretary of State must consult the Department of Justice in Northern Ireland before requesting HMIC to carry out an inspection in respect of a particular matter which relates only to the exercise of NCA functions in Northern Ireland.

(2B) The Department of Justice may request that HMIC carry out an inspection in respect of a particular matter that relates only to the exercise of NCA functions in Northern Ireland, but only with the consent of the Secretary of State.]

(3) Following an inspection under this section, HMIC must report to the Secretary of State on the efficiency and effectiveness of the NCA either—

(a) generally, or

(b) in the case of an inspection under subsection (2)(b), in respect of the matter to which the inspection related.

(4) HMIC must carry out such other duties for the purpose of furthering the efficiency and effectiveness of the NCA as the Secretary of State may from time to time direct.

(5)–(9) *****

12–14 *****

15 Abolition of SOCA and NPIA

(1) The Serious Organised Crime Agency is abolished.

(2) The National Policing Improvement Agency is abolished.

(3) *****

16–32 *****

33 Abolition of scandalising the judiciary as form of contempt of court

(1) Scandalising the judiciary (also referred to as scandalising the court or scandalising judges) is abolished as a form of contempt of court under the common law of England and Wales.

(2) That abolition does not prevent proceedings for contempt of court being brought against a person for conduct that immediately before that abolition would have constituted both scandalising the judiciary and some other form of contempt of court.

*****

Defamation Act 2013

(2013, c. 26)

An Act to amend the law of defamation.   [25th April 2013]

Territorial extent: England and Wales but s. 6 applies to Scotland

1–3   *****

4   Publication on matter of public interest

(1) It is a defence to an action for defamation for the defendant to show that—

    (a) the statement complained of was, or formed part of, a statement on a matter of public interest; and

    (b) the defendant reasonably believed that publishing the statement complained of was in the public interest.

(2) Subject to subsections (3) and (4), in determining whether the defendant has shown the matters mentioned in subsection (1), the court must have regard to all the circumstances of the case.

(3) If the statement complained of was, or formed part of, an accurate and impartial account of a dispute to which the claimant was a party, the court must in determining whether it was reasonable for the defendant to believe that publishing the statement was in the public interest disregard any omission of the defendant to take steps to verify the truth of the imputation conveyed by it.

(4) In determining whether it was reasonable for the defendant to believe that publishing the statement complained of was in the public interest, the court must make such allowance for editorial judgement as it considers appropriate.

(5) For the avoidance of doubt, the defence under this section may be relied upon irrespective of whether the statement complained of is a statement of fact or a statement of opinion.

(6) The common law defence known as the Reynolds defence is abolished.

5   Operators of websites

(1) This section applies where an action for defamation is brought against the operator of a website in respect of a statement posted on the website.

(2) It is a defence for the operator to show that it was not the operator who posted the statement on the website.

(3) The defence is defeated if the claimant shows that—

    (a) it was not possible for the claimant to identify the person who posted the statement,

    (b) the claimant gave the operator a notice of complaint in relation to the statement, and

    (c) the operator failed to respond to the notice of complaint in accordance with any provision contained in regulations.

(4) For the purposes of subsection (3)(a), it is possible for a claimant to 'identify' a person only if the claimant has sufficient information to bring proceedings against the person.

(5) Regulations may—

    (a) make provision as to the action required to be taken by an operator of a website in response to a notice of complaint (which may in particular include action relating to the identity or contact details of the person who posted the statement and action relating to its removal);

    (b) make provision specifying a time limit for the taking of any such action;

    (c) make provision conferring on the court a discretion to treat action taken after the expiry of a time limit as having been taken before the expiry;

    (d) make any other provision for the purposes of this section.

(6) Subject to any provision made by virtue of subsection (7), a notice of complaint is a notice which—

    (a) specifies the complainant's name,

(b) sets out the statement concerned and explains why it is defamatory of the complainant,

(c) specifies where on the website the statement was posted, and

(d) contains such other information as may be specified in regulations.

(7) Regulations may make provision about the circumstances in which a notice which is not a notice of complaint is to be treated as a notice of complaint for the purposes of this section or any provision made under it.

(8) Regulations under this section—

(a) may make different provision for different circumstances;

(b) are to be made by statutory instrument.

(9) A statutory instrument containing regulations under this section may not be made unless a draft of the instrument has been laid before, and approved by a resolution of, each House of Parliament.

(10) In this section 'regulations' means regulations made by the Secretary of State.

(11) The defence under this section is defeated if the claimant shows that the operator of the website has acted with malice in relation to the posting of the statement concerned.

(12) The defence under this section is not defeated by reason only of the fact that the operator of the website moderates the statements posted on it by others.

6 Peer-reviewed statement in scientific or academic journal etc

(1) The publication of a statement in a scientific or academic journal (whether published in electronic form or otherwise) is privileged if the following conditions are met.

(2) The first condition is that the statement relates to a scientific or academic matter.

(3) The second condition is that before the statement was published in the journal an independent review of the statement's scientific or academic merit was carried out by—

(a) the editor of the journal, and

(b) one or more persons with expertise in the scientific or academic matter concerned.

(4) Where the publication of a statement in a scientific or academic journal is privileged by virtue of subsection (1), the publication in the same journal of any assessment of the statement's scientific or academic merit is also privileged if—

(a) the assessment was written by one or more of the persons who carried out the independent review of the statement; and

(b) the assessment was written in the course of that review.

(5) Where the publication of a statement or assessment is privileged by virtue of this section, the publication of a fair and accurate copy of, extract from or summary of the statement or assessment is also privileged.

(6) A publication is not privileged by virtue of this section if it is shown to be made with malice.

(7) Nothing in this section is to be construed—

(a) as protecting the publication of matter the publication of which is prohibited by law;

(b) as limiting any privilege subsisting apart from this section.

(8) The reference in subsection (3)(a) to 'the editor of the journal' is to be read, in the case of a journal with more than one editor, as a reference to the editor or editors who were responsible for deciding to publish the statement concerned.

*****

Justice and Security Act 2013

(2013, c. 18)

An Act to provide for oversight of the Security Service, the Secret Intelligence Service, the Government Communications Headquarters and other activities relating to intelligence or security matters; to make provision about closed material procedure in relation to certain civil proceedings; to prevent the making of certain court orders for the disclosure of sensitive information; and for connected purposes.   [25th April 2013]

Territorial extent: United Kingdom

PART 1 OVERSIGHT OF INTELLIGENCE AND SECURITY ACTIVITIES

Oversight by the Intelligence and Security Committee of Parliament

1 The Intelligence and Security Committee of Parliament

(1) There is to be a body known as the Intelligence and Security Committee of Parliament (in this Part referred to as 'the ISC').

(2) The ISC is to consist of nine members who are to be drawn both from the members of the House of Commons and from the members of the House of Lords.

(3) Each member of the ISC is to be appointed by the House of Parliament from which the member is to be drawn.

(4) A person is not eligible to become a member of the ISC unless the person—

    (a) is nominated for membership by the Prime Minister, and

    (b) is not a Minister of the Crown.

(5) Before deciding whether to nominate a person for membership, the Prime Minister must consult the Leader of the Opposition.

(6), (7) *****

2 Main functions of the ISC

(1) The ISC may examine or otherwise oversee the expenditure, administration, policy and operations of—

    (a) the Security Service,

    (b) the Secret Intelligence Service, and

    (c) the Government Communications Headquarters.

(2) The ISC may examine or otherwise oversee such other activities of Her Majesty's Government in relation to intelligence or security matters as are set out in a memorandum of understanding.

(3) The ISC may, by virtue of subsection (1) or (2), consider any particular operational matter but only so far as—

    (a) the ISC and the Prime Minister are satisfied that the matter—

        (i)   is not part of any ongoing intelligence or security operation, and

        (ii) is of significant national interest,

    (b) the Prime Minister has asked the ISC to consider the matter, or

    (c) the ISC's consideration of the matter is limited to the consideration of information provided voluntarily to the ISC (whether or not in response to a request by the ISC) by—

        (i)   the Security Service,

        (ii)   the Secret Intelligence Service,

        (iii) the Government Communications Headquarters, or

        (iv)   a government department.

(4) The ISC's consideration of a particular operational matter under subsection (3)(a) or (b) must, in the opinion of the ISC and the Prime Minister, be consistent with any principles set out in, or other provision made by, a memorandum of understanding.

(5) A memorandum of understanding under this section—

    (a) may include other provision about the ISC or its functions which is not of the kind envisaged in subsection (2) or (4),

    (b) must be agreed between the Prime Minister and the ISC, and

    (c) may be altered (or replaced with another memorandum) with the agreement of the Prime Minister and the ISC.

(6) The ISC must publish a memorandum of understanding under this section and lay a copy of it before Parliament.

3 Reports of the ISC

(1) The ISC must make an annual report to Parliament on the discharge of its functions.

(2) The ISC may make such other reports to Parliament as it considers appropriate concerning any aspect of its functions.

(3) Before making a report to Parliament, the ISC must send it to the Prime Minister.

(4) The ISC must exclude any matter from any report to Parliament if the Prime Minister, after consultation with the ISC, considers that the matter would be prejudicial to the continued discharge of the functions of the Security Service, the Secret Intelligence Service, the Government Communications Headquarters or any person carrying out activities falling within section 2(2).

(5) A report by the ISC to Parliament must contain a statement as to whether any matter has been excluded from the report by virtue of subsection (4).

(6) The ISC must lay before Parliament any report made by it to Parliament.

(7) The ISC may make a report to the Prime Minister in relation to matters which would be excluded by virtue of subsection (4) if the report were made to Parliament.

4, 5   *****

PART 2 DISCLOSURE OF SENSITIVE MATERIAL

Closed material procedure: general

6 Declaration permitting closed material applications in proceedings

(1) The court seised of relevant civil proceedings may make a declaration that the proceedings are proceedings in which a closed material application may be made to the court.

(2) The court may make such a declaration—
   (a) on the application of—
      (i)   the Secretary of State (whether or not the Secretary of State is a party to the proceedings), or
      (ii) any party to the proceedings, or
   (b) of its own motion.

(3) The court may make such a declaration if it considers that the following two conditions are met.

(4) The first condition is that—
   (a) a party to the proceedings would be required to disclose sensitive material in the course of the proceedings to another person (whether or not another party to the proceedings), or
   (b) a party to the proceedings would be required to make such a disclosure were it not for one or more of the following—
      (i)   the possibility of a claim for public interest immunity in relation to the material,
      (ii)   the fact that there would be no requirement to disclose if the party chose not to rely on the material,
      (iii) section 17(1) of the Regulation of Investigatory Powers Act 2000 (exclusion for intercept material),
      (iv)   any other enactment that would prevent the party from disclosing the material but would not do so if the proceedings were proceedings in relation to which there was a declaration under this section.

(5) The second condition is that it is in the interests of the fair and effective administration of justice in the proceedings to make a declaration.

(6) The two conditions are met if the court considers that they are met in relation to any material that would be required to be disclosed in the course of the proceedings (and an application under subsection (2)(a) need not be based on all of the material that might meet the conditions or on material that the applicant would be required to disclose).

(7) The court must not consider an application by the Secretary of State under subsection (2)(a) unless it is satisfied that the Secretary of State has, before making the application, considered whether to make, or advise another person to make, a claim for public interest immunity in relation to the material on which the application is based.

(8) A declaration under this section must identify the party or parties to the proceedings who would be required to disclose the sensitive material ('a relevant person').

(9) Rules of court may—

    (a) provide for notification to the Secretary of State by a party to relevant civil proceedings, or by the court concerned, of proceedings to which a declaration under this section may be relevant,

    (b) provide for a stay or sist of relevant civil proceedings (whether on an application by a party to the proceedings or by the court concerned of its own motion) where a person is considering whether to apply for a declaration under this section,

    (c) provide for the Secretary of State, if not a party to proceedings in relation to which there is a declaration under this section or proceedings for or about such a declaration, to be joined as a party to the proceedings.

(10) Rules of court must make provision—

    (a) requiring a person, before making an application under subsection (2)(a), to give notice of the person's intention to make an application to every other person entitled to make such an application in relation to the relevant civil proceedings,

    (b) requiring the applicant to inform every other such person of the outcome of the application.

(11) In this section—

'closed material application' means an application of the kind mentioned in section 8(1)(a),

'relevant civil proceedings' means any proceedings (other than proceedings in a criminal cause or matter) before—

    (a) the High Court,

    (b) the Court of Appeal,

    (c) the Court of Session, or

    (d) the Supreme Court,

'sensitive material' means material the disclosure of which would be damaging to the interests of national security.

7   Review and revocation of declaration under section 6

(1) This section applies where a court seised of relevant civil proceedings has made a declaration under section 6.

(2) The court must keep the declaration under review, and may at any time revoke it if it considers that the declaration is no longer in the interests of the fair and effective administration of justice in the proceedings.

(3) The court must undertake a formal review of the declaration once the pre-trial disclosure exercise in the proceedings has been completed, and must revoke it if it considers that the declaration is no longer in the interests of the fair and effective administration of justice in the proceedings.

(4) The court may revoke a declaration under subsection (2) or (3)—

    (a) on the application of—

        (i) the Secretary of State (whether or not the Secretary of State is a party to the proceedings), or

        (ii) any party to the proceedings, or

    (b) of its own motion.

(5) In deciding for the purposes of subsection (2) or (3) whether a declaration continues to be in the interests of the fair and effective administration of justice in the proceedings, the court must consider all of the material that has been put before it in the course of the proceedings (and not just the material on which the decision to make the declaration was based).

(6) Rules of court must make provision—

    (a) as to how a formal review is to be conducted under subsection (3),

    (b) as to when the pre-trial disclosure exercise is to be considered to have been completed for the purposes of subsection (3).

(7) In relation to proceedings before the Court of Session—

(a) the reference in subsection (3) to the completion of the pre-trial disclosure exercise is a reference to the fixing of a hearing to determine the merits of the proceedings, and

(b) the reference in subsection (6)(b) to when the pre-trial disclosure exercise is to be considered to have been completed is a reference to what constitutes a hearing to determine the merits of the proceedings.

8   Determination by court of applications in section 6 proceedings

(1) Rules of court relating to any relevant civil proceedings in relation to which there is a declaration under section 6 ('section 6 proceedings') must secure—

(a) that a relevant person has the opportunity to make an application to the court for permission not to disclose material otherwise than to—

(i)   the court,

(ii)   any person appointed as a special advocate, and

(iii) where the Secretary of State is not the relevant person but is a party to the proceedings, the Secretary of State,

(b) that such an application is always considered in the absence of every other party to the proceedings (and every other party's legal representative),

(c) that the court is required to give permission for material not to be disclosed if it considers that the disclosure of the material would be damaging to the interests of national security,

(d) that, if permission is given by the court not to disclose material, it must consider requiring the relevant person to provide a summary of the material to every other party to the proceedings (and every other party's legal representative),

(e) that the court is required to ensure that such a summary does not contain material the disclosure of which would be damaging to the interests of national security.

(2) Rules of court relating to section 6 proceedings must secure that provision to the effect mentioned in subsection (3) applies in cases where a relevant person—

(a) does not receive the permission of the court to withhold material, but elects not to disclose it, or

(b) is required to provide another party to the proceedings with a summary of material that is withheld, but elects not to provide the summary.

(3) The court must be authorised—

(a) if it considers that the material or anything that is required to be summarised might adversely affect the relevant person's case or support the case of another party to the proceedings, to direct that the relevant person—

(i)   is not to rely on such points in that person's case, or

(ii)   is to make such concessions or take such other steps as the court may specify, or

(b) in any other case, to ensure that the relevant person does not rely on the material or (as the case may be) on that which is required to be summarised.

9   Appointment of special advocate

(1) The appropriate law officer may appoint a person to represent the interests of a party in any section 6 proceedings from which the party (and any legal representative of the party) is excluded.

(2) A person appointed under subsection (1) is referred to in this section as appointed as a 'special advocate'.

(3) The 'appropriate law officer' is—

(a) in relation to proceedings in England and Wales, the Attorney General,

(b) in relation to proceedings in Scotland, the Advocate General for Scotland, and

(c) in relation to proceedings in Northern Ireland, the Advocate General for Northern Ireland.

(4) A person appointed as a special advocate is not responsible to the party to the proceedings whose interests the person is appointed to represent.

(5) A person may be appointed as a special advocate only if—

    (a) in the case of an appointment by the Attorney General, the person has a general qualification for the purposes of section 71 of the Courts and Legal Services Act 1990,

    (b) in the case of an appointment by the Advocate General for Scotland, the person is an advocate or a solicitor who has rights of audience in the Court of Session or the High Court of Justiciary by virtue of section 25A of the Solicitors (Scotland) Act 1980, and

    (c) in the case of an appointment by the Advocate General for Northern Ireland, the person is a member of the Bar of Northern Ireland.

10   Saving for normal disclosure rules

Subject to sections 8, 9 and 11, rules of court relating to section 6 proceedings must secure that the rules of disclosure otherwise applicable to those proceedings continue to apply in relation to the disclosure of material by a relevant person.

11   General provision about section 6 proceedings

(1) A person making rules of court relating to section 6 proceedings must have regard to the need to secure that disclosures of information are not made where they would be damaging to the interests of national security.

(2) Rules of court relating to section 6 proceedings may make provision—

    (a) about the mode of proof and about evidence in the proceedings,

    (b) enabling or requiring the proceedings to be determined without a hearing,

    (c) about legal representation in the proceedings,

    (d) enabling the proceedings to take place without full particulars of the reasons for decisions in the proceedings being given to a party to the proceedings (or to any legal representative of that party),

    (e) enabling the court concerned to conduct proceedings in the absence of any person, including a party to the proceedings (or any legal representative of that party),

    (f) about the functions of a person appointed as a special advocate,

    (g) enabling the court to give a party to the proceedings a summary of evidence taken in the party's absence.

(3) In subsection (2) references to a party to the proceedings do not include the relevant person concerned and (if the Secretary of State is not the relevant person but is a party to the proceedings) the Secretary of State.

(4) The following proceedings are to be treated as section 6 proceedings for the purposes of sections 8 to 10, this section and sections 12 to 14—

    (a) proceedings on, or in relation to, an application for a declaration under section 6,

    (b) proceedings on, or in relation to, a decision of the court to make a declaration under that section of its own motion,

    (c) proceedings on, or in relation to, an application for a revocation under section 7, and

    (d) proceedings on, or in relation to, a decision of the court to make a revocation under that section of its own motion.

(5) In proceedings treated as section 6 proceedings by virtue of subsection (4), a relevant person, for the purposes of sections 8 to 10, this section and sections 12 to 14, is a person who would be required to disclose sensitive material in the course of the proceedings.

12   Reports on use of closed material procedure

(1) The Secretary of State must—

    (a) prepare a report on the matters mentioned in subsection (2) for—

        (i)   the period of twelve months beginning with the day on which section 6 comes into force, and

        (ii) every subsequent twelve month period, and

    (b) lay a copy of each such report before Parliament.

(2) The matters are—

  (a) the number of applications made during the reporting period—

    (i) by the Secretary of State under section 6(2)(a)(i) or 7(4)(a)(i), and

    (ii) by persons other than the Secretary of State under section 6(2)(a)(ii) or 7(4)(a)(ii),

  (b) the number of declarations made by the court under section 6(1), and the number of revocations made by the court under section 7(2) or (3), during the reporting period—

    (i) in response to applications made by the Secretary of State during the reporting period,

    (ii) in response to applications made by the Secretary of State during previous reporting periods,

    (iii) in response to applications made by persons other than the Secretary of State during the reporting period,

    (iv) in response to applications made by persons other than the Secretary of State during previous reporting periods, and

    (v) of the court's own motion,

  (c) the number of final judgments given in section 6 proceedings during the reporting period which are closed judgments, and

  (d) the number of such judgments which are not closed judgments.

(3) The report may also include such other matters as the Secretary of State considers appropriate.

(4) The duty under subsection (1) in relation to the preparation and laying of a report must be carried out as soon as reasonably practicable after the end of the twelve month period to which the report relates.

(5) In this section—

'closed judgment' means a judgment that is not made available, or fully available, to the public,

'final judgment', in relation to section 6 proceedings, means a final judgment to determine the proceedings.

13 Review of sections 6 to 11

(1) The Secretary of State must appoint a person to review the operation of sections 6 to 11 (the 'reviewer').

(2) The reviewer must carry out a review of the operation of sections 6 to 11 in respect of the period of five years beginning with the day on which section 6 comes into force.

(3) The review must be completed as soon as reasonably practicable after the end of the period to which the review relates.

(4) As soon as reasonably practicable after completing a review under this section, the reviewer must send to the Secretary of State a report on its outcome.

(5) On receiving a report under subsection (4), the Secretary of State must lay a copy of it before Parliament.

(6) Before laying a copy of a report before Parliament under subsection (5), the Secretary of State may, after consulting the reviewer, exclude from the copy any part of the report that would, in the opinion of the Secretary of State, be damaging to the interests of national security if it were included in the copy laid before Parliament.

(7) The Secretary of State may pay to the reviewer—

  (a) expenses incurred by the reviewer in carrying out functions under this section, and

  (b) such allowances as the Secretary of State determines.

14–16 *****

'Norwich Pharmacal' and similar jurisdictions

17 Disclosure proceedings

(1) This section applies where, by way of civil proceedings, a person ('A') seeks the disclosure of information by another person ('B') on the grounds that—

(a) wrongdoing by another person ('C') has, or may have, occurred,

(b) B was involved with the carrying out of the wrongdoing (whether innocently or not), and

(c) the disclosure is reasonably necessary to enable redress to be obtained or a defence to be relied on in connection with the wrongdoing.

(2) A court may not, in exercise of its residual disclosure jurisdiction, order the disclosure of information sought (whether that disclosure would be to A or to another person) if the information is sensitive information.

(3) 'Sensitive information' means information—

(a) held by an intelligence service,

(b) obtained from, or held on behalf of, an intelligence service,

(c) derived in whole or part from information obtained from, or held on behalf of, an intelligence service,

(d) relating to an intelligence service, or

(e) specified or described in a certificate issued by the Secretary of State, in relation to the proceedings, as information which B should not be ordered to disclose.

(4) The Secretary of State may issue a certificate under subsection (3)(e) only if the Secretary of State considers that it would be contrary to the public interest for B to disclose—

(a) the information,

(b) whether the information exists, or

(c) whether B has the information.

(5) For the purposes of subsection (4) a disclosure is contrary to the public interest if it would cause damage—

(a) to the interests of national security, or

(b) to the interests of the international relations of the United Kingdom.

(6) In this section—

'enactment' means an enactment whenever passed or made and includes an enactment contained in—

(a) an Act of the Scottish Parliament,

(b) Northern Ireland legislation, or

(c) a Measure or Act of the National Assembly for Wales,

'Her Majesty's forces' has the same meaning as in the Armed Forces Act 2006,

'information' includes—

(a) information contained in any form of document or stored in any other way, and

(b) alleged information,

'intelligence service' means—

(a) the Security Service,

(b) the Secret Intelligence Service,

(c) the Government Communications Headquarters, or

(d) any part of Her Majesty's forces, or of the Ministry of Defence, which engages in intelligence activities,

'obtained' means obtained directly or indirectly,

'residual disclosure jurisdiction' means any jurisdiction to order the disclosure of information which is not specifically conferred as such a jurisdiction by or under an enactment.

(7) This section—

(a) enables the Secretary of State to issue a certificate under subsection (3)(e) where the Secretary of State is B as it enables the Secretary of State to issue such a certificate where another person is B, and

(b) does not restrict any other right or privilege that the Secretary of State can claim in order to resist an application for the disclosure of information.

18 Review of certification

(1) Where the Secretary of State has issued a certificate under section 17(3)(e) in relation to proceedings, any party to the proceedings may apply to the relevant court to set aside the decision on the ground in subsection (2).

(2) That ground is that the Secretary of State ought not to have determined, in relation to the information specified or described in the certificate, that a disclosure by B as mentioned in section 17(4) would be contrary to the public interest.

(3) In determining whether the decision to issue the certificate should be set aside on the ground in subsection (2), the relevant court must apply the principles which would be applied in judicial review proceedings.

(4) Proceedings arising by virtue of this section are to be treated as section 6 proceedings for the purposes of sections 8 to 14.

(5) Sections 8 to 14 apply in relation to proceedings treated as section 6 proceedings by sub-section (4) as if—

(a) the Secretary of State were the relevant person, and

(b) the references to the interests of national security in sections 8, 11 and 13 were references to the interests of national security or the interests of the international relations of the United Kingdom.

(6) In this section 'relevant court' means—

(a) if the court seised of the proceedings in relation to which the certificate has been issued is a county court, the High Court,

(b) if the court seised of those proceedings is the sheriff, the Court of Session, and

(c) in any other case, the court seised of those proceedings.

*****

Marriage (Same Sex Couples) Act 2013

(2013, c. 30)

An Act to make provision for the marriage of same sex couples in England and Wales, about gender change by married persons and civil partners, about consular functions in relation to marriage, for the marriage of armed forces personnel overseas, for permitting marriages according to the usages of belief organisations to be solemnized on the authority of certificates of a superintendent registrar, for the review of civil partnership, for the review of survivor benefits under occupational pension schemes, and for connected purposes.   [17th July 2013]

Territorial extent: England and Wales

PART 1 MARRIAGE OF SAME SEX COUPLES IN ENGLAND AND WALES

Extension of marriage

1 Extension of marriage to same sex couples

(1) Marriage of same sex couples is lawful.

(2) The marriage of a same sex couple may only be solemnized in accordance with—

(a) Part 3 of the Marriage Act 1949,

(b) Part 5 of the Marriage Act 1949,

(c) the Marriage (Registrar General's Licence) Act 1970, or

(d) an Order in Council made under Part 1 or 3 of Schedule 6.

(3) No Canon of the Church of England is contrary to section 3 of the Submission of the Clergy Act 1533 (which provides that no Canons shall be contrary to the Royal Prerogative or the customs, laws or statutes of this realm) by virtue of its making provision about marriage being the union of one man with one woman.

(4) Any duty of a member of the clergy to solemnize marriages (and any corresponding right of persons to have their marriages solemnized by members of the clergy) is not extended by this Act to marriages of same sex couples.

(5) A 'member of the clergy' is—
(a) a clerk in Holy Orders of the Church of England, or
(b) a clerk in Holy Orders of the Church in Wales.

2–8 *******

Other provisions relating to marriages of same sex couples

9   Conversion of civil partnership into marriage

(1) The parties to an England and Wales civil partnership may convert their civil partnership into a marriage under a procedure established by regulations made by the Secretary of State.

(2) The parties to a civil partnership within subsection (3) may convert their civil partnership into a marriage under a procedure established by regulations made by the Secretary of State.

[(2A) Subsections (1) and (2) apply only where both parties to the civil partnership are of the same sex.]

(3) A civil partnership is within this subsection if—
(a) it was formed outside the United Kingdom under an Order in Council made under Chapter 1 of Part 5 of the Civil Partnership Act 2004 (registration at British consulates etc or by armed forces personnel), and
(b) the part of the United Kingdom that was relevant for the purposes of section 210(2)(b) or (as the case may be) section 211(2)(b) of that Act was England and Wales.

(4) Regulations under this section may in particular make—
(a) provision about the making by the parties to a civil partnership of an application to convert their civil partnership into a marriage;
(b) provision about the information to be provided in support of an application to convert;
(c) provision about the making of declarations in support of an application to convert;
(d) provision for persons who have made an application to convert to appear before any person or attend at any place;
(e) provision conferring functions in connection with applications to convert on relevant officials, relevant armed forces personnel, the Secretary of State, or any other persons;
(f) provision for fees, of such amounts as are specified in or determined in accordance with the regulations, to be payable in respect of—
(i)   the making of an application to convert;
(ii) the exercise of any function conferred by virtue of paragraph (e).

(5) Functions conferred by virtue of paragraph (e) of subsection (4) may include functions relating to—
(a)   the recording of information on the conversion of civil partnerships;
(b)   the issuing of certified copies of any information recorded;
[(ba) the carrying out, on request, of searches of any information recorded and the provision, on request, of records of any information recorded (otherwise than in the form of certified copies);]
(c)   the conducting of services or ceremonies (other than religious services or ceremonies) following the conversion of a civil partnership.

[(5A) Subsection (5B) applies where regulations under this section provide for a fee to be payable to a superintendent registrar or registrar.

(5B) The regulations may provide for such part of the fee as may be specified in or determined in accordance with the regulations to be payable by the superintendent registrar or registrar to the Registrar General in such circumstances as may be set out in the regulations.

(5C) The regulations may provide for the reduction, waiver or refund of part or all of a fee whether by conferring a discretion or otherwise.]

(6) Where a civil partnership is converted into a marriage under this section—
(a) the civil partnership ends on the conversion, and
(b) the resulting marriage is to be treated as having subsisted since the date the civil partnership was formed.

(7) In this section—

'England and Wales civil partnership' means a civil partnership which is formed by two people registering as civil partners of each other in England or Wales (see Part 2 of the Civil Partnership Act 2004);

'relevant armed forces personnel' means—

(a) a member of Her Majesty's forces;

(b) a civilian subject to service discipline (within the meaning of the Armed Forces Act 2006);

and for this purpose 'Her Majesty's forces' has the same meaning as in the Armed Forces Act 2006;

'relevant official' means—

(a) the Registrar General;

(b) a superintendent registrar;

(c) a registrar;

(d) a consular officer in the service of Her Majesty's government in the United Kingdom;

(e) a person authorised by the Secretary of State in respect of the solemnization of marriages or formation of civil partnerships in a country or territory in which Her Majesty's government in the United Kingdom has for the time being no consular representative.

10   Extra-territorial matters

(1) A marriage under—

(a) the law of any part of the United Kingdom (other than England and Wales), or

(b) the law of any country or territory outside the United Kingdom, is not prevented from being recognised under the law of England and Wales only because it is the marriage of a same sex couple.

(2) For the purposes of this section it is irrelevant whether the law of a particular part of the United Kingdom, or a particular country or territory outside the United Kingdom—

(a) already provides for marriage of same sex couples at the time when this section comes into force, or

(b) provides for marriage of same sex couples from a later time.

(3) *****

Effect of extension of marriage

11   Effect of extension of marriage

(1) In the law of England and Wales, marriage has the same effect in relation to same sex couples as it has in relation to opposite sex couples.

(2) The law of England and Wales (including all England and Wales legislation whenever passed or made) has effect in accordance with subsection (1).

(3)–(7) *****

*****

Succession to the Crown Act 2013

(2013, c. 20)

An Act to make succession to the Crown not depend on gender; to make provision about Royal Marriages; and for connected purposes.   [25th April 2013]

Territorial extent: United Kingdom

1   Succession to the Crown not to depend on gender

In determining the succession to the Crown, the gender of a person born after 28 October 2011 does not give that person, or that person's descendants, precedence over any other person (whenever born).

2   Removal of disqualification arising from marriage to a Roman Catholic

(1) A person is not disqualified from succeeding to the Crown or from possessing it as a result of marrying a person of the Roman Catholic faith.

(2) Subsection (1) applies in relation to marriages occurring before the time of the coming into force of this section where the person concerned is alive at that time (as well as in relation to marriages occurring after that time).

3   Consent of Sovereign required to certain Royal Marriages

(1) A person who (when the person marries) is one of the 6 persons next in the line of succession to the Crown must obtain the consent of Her Majesty before marrying.

(2) Where any such consent has been obtained, it must be—

(a) signified under the Great Seal of the United Kingdom,

(b) declared in Council, and

(c) recorded in the books of the Privy Council.

(3) The effect of a person's failure to comply with subsection (1) is that the person and the person's descendants from the marriage are disqualified from succeeding to the Crown.

(4)–(6) *****

*****

Care Act 2014

(2014, c. 23)

An Act to make provision to reform the law relating to care and support for adults and the law relating to support for carers; to make provision about safeguarding adults from abuse or neglect; to make provision about care standards; to establish and make provision about Health Education England; to establish and make provision about the Health Research Authority; to make provision about integrating care and support with health services; and for connected purposes.   [14th May 2014]

Territorial extent: United Kingdom but provisions for England reproduced here.

73   Human Rights Act 1998: provision of regulated care or support etc a public function

(1) This section applies where—

(a) in England, a registered care provider provides care and support to an adult or support to a carer, in the course of providing—

(i) personal care in a place where the adult receiving the personal care is living when the personal care is provided, or

(ii) residential accommodation together with nursing or personal care;

(b)–(d)* *****

In this section 'the care or support' means the care and support, support, advice, guidance, assistance or services provided as mentioned above, and 'the provider' means the person who provides the care or support.

(2) The provider is to be taken for the purposes of section 6(3)(b) of the Human Rights Act 1998 (acts of public authorities) to be exercising a function of a public nature in providing the care or support, if the requirements of subsection (3) are met.

(3) The requirements are that—

(a) the care or support is arranged by an authority listed in column 1 of the Table below, or paid for (directly or indirectly, and in whole or in part) by such an authority, and

(b) the authority arranges or pays for the care or support under a provision listed in the corresponding entry in column 2 of the Table.

TABLE	
Authority	*Provisions imposing duty or conferring power to meet needs*
Local authority in England	Sections 2, 18, 19, 20, 38 and 48 of this Act.

*   **Editor's Note:** Similar provisions for Wales, Scotland and Northern Ireland are included.

House of Lords Reform Act 2014

(2014, c. 24)

An Act to make provision for resignation from the House of Lords; and to make provision for the expulsion of Members of the House of Lords in specified circumstances.   [14th May 2014]

Territorial extent: United Kingdom

1 Resignation

(1) A member of the House of Lords who is a peer may retire or otherwise resign as a member of the House of Lords by giving notice in writing to the Clerk of the Parliaments.

(2) The notice must—

    (a) specify a date from which the resignation is to take effect, and

    (b) be signed by the peer and by a witness.

(3) At the beginning of that date the peer ceases to be a member of the House of Lords.

(4) Resignation may not be rescinded.

2 Non-attendance

(1) A member of the House of Lords who is a peer and does not attend the House of Lords during a Session ceases to be a member of the House at the beginning of the following Session.

(2) A peer 'does not attend the House of Lords during a Session' if, and only if, the Lord Speaker certifies that the peer—

    (a) at no time during the Session attended the House, having regard to attendance records kept by officials of the House, and

    (b) did not have leave of absence in respect of the Session, in accordance Standing with Standing Orders of the House.

(3) Subsection (1) does not apply to a peer in respect of attendance during a Session if—

    (a) the peer was disqualified from sitting or voting in the House, or suspended from its service, for the whole of the Session, or

    (b) the House resolves that subsection (1) should not apply to the peer by reason of special circumstances.

(4)–(6) *****

3 Conviction of serious offence

(1) A member of the House of Lords who is convicted of a serious offence ceases to be a member of the House of Lords.

(2) A person 'is convicted of a serious offence' if, and only if, the Lord Speaker certifies that the person, while a member of the House of Lords, has been—

    (a) convicted of a criminal offence, and

    (b) sentenced or ordered to be imprisoned or detained indefinitely or for more than one year.

(3) It is irrelevant for the purposes of subsection (2)—

    (a) whether the offence is committed at a time when the person is a member of the House of Lords;

    (b) whether any of the offence, conviction, sentence, order, imprisonment or detention occurs in the United Kingdom or elsewhere; (but see subsection (9)).

(4) The reference in subsection (2) to an offence is only to an offence committed on or after the day on which this section comes into force.

(5) The reference in subsection (2) to a person being sentenced or ordered to be imprisoned or detained indefinitely or for more than one year does not include such a sentence or order where the sentence or order is suspended.

(6) A certificate under subsection (2) takes effect when it is issued.

(7) If a person who has ceased to be a member of the House of Lords in accordance with this section is successful on appeal—

(a) the Lord Speaker must issue a further certificate to that effect, and

(b) on the issue of that certificate, the original certificate under subsection (2) shall be treated for the purposes of this Act as never having had effect.

(8) A person who has ceased to be a member of the House of Lords in accordance with this section 'is successful on appeal' if, and only if, the Lord Speaker certifies that—

(a) the conviction certified under subsection (2)(a) has been quashed, or

(b) the sentence or order certified under subsection (2)(b) has been—

(i) varied so that it is no longer a sentence or order that the person be imprisoned or detained indefinitely or for more than one year within the meaning of subsection (2)(b), or

(ii) replaced with another sentence or order that is not a sentence or order that the person be so imprisoned or detained.

(9) A certificate under subsection (2) in respect of a conviction outside the United Kingdom may be issued only if the House of Lords resolves that subsection (1) should apply; and where the House does so resolve the Lord Speaker must issue the certificate.

4 Effect of ceasing to be a member

(1) This section applies where a person ceases to be a member of the House of Lords in accordance with this Act.

(2) The person becomes disqualified from attending the proceedings of the House of Lords (including the proceedings of a Committee of the House).

(3) Accordingly, the person shall not be entitled to receive a writ to attend the House (whether under section 1 of the Life Peerages Act 1958, by virtue of the dignity conferred by virtue of appointment as a Lord of Appeal in Ordinary, by virtue of a hereditary peerage or as a Lord Spiritual) and may not attend the House in pursuance of a writ already received.

(4) If the person is a hereditary peer who is excepted from section 1 of the House of Lords Act 1999 by virtue of section 2 of that Act, the person ceases to be excepted from section 1 of that Act (and accordingly section 3 of that Act applies (removal of disqualification on voting in parliamentary elections or being an MP)).

(5) If the person is a peer other than a hereditary peer, the person is not, by virtue of that peerage, disqualified for—

(a) voting at elections to the House of Commons, or

(b) being, or being elected as, a member of that House.

(6) In relation to a peer who ceases to be a member of the House of Lords in accordance with this Act, any reference in section 1(3) or (4)(b) of the Representation of the People Act 1985 to a register of parliamentary electors is to be read as including—

(a) any register of local government electors in Great Britain, and

(b) any register of local electors in Northern Ireland,

which was required to be published on any date before the date on which the peer ceased to be a member.

(7) The Standing Orders of the House required by section 2(4) of the House of Lords Act 1999 (filling of vacancies) must make provision requiring the holding of a by-election to fill any vacancy which arises under this Act among the people excepted from section 1 of that Act in consequence of an election.

(8) Subject to section 3(7), a person who ceases to be a member of the House of Lords in accordance with this Act may not subsequently become a member of that House.

5 Certificate of Lord Speaker

(1) A certificate of the Lord Speaker under this Act shall be conclusive for all purposes.

(2) A certificate may be issued on the Lord Speaker's own initiative.

6, 7 *****

Counter-Terrorism and Security Act 2015

(2015, c. 6)

An Act to make provision in relation to terrorism; to make provision about retention of communications data, about information, authority to carry and security in relation to air, sea and rail transport and about reviews by the Special Immigration Appeals Commission against refusals to issue certificates of naturalisation; and for connected purposes.   [12th February 2015]

Territorial extent: United Kingdom (material reproduced here)

PART 1 TEMPORARY RESTRICTIONS ON TRAVEL

Chapter 1 Powers to Seize Travel Documents

1   Seizure of passports etc from persons suspected of involvement in terrorism

(1) Schedule 1 makes provision for the seizure and temporary retention of travel documents where a person is suspected of intending to leave Great Britain or the United Kingdom in connection with terrorism-related activity.

(2), (3) *****

Chapter 2 Temporary Exclusion from the United Kingdom

Imposition of temporary exclusion orders

2   Temporary exclusion orders

(1) A 'temporary exclusion order' is an order which requires an individual not to return to the United Kingdom unless—

(a) the return is in accordance with a permit to return issued by the Secretary of State before the individual began the return, or

(b) the return is the result of the individual's deportation to the United Kingdom.

(2) The Secretary of State may impose a temporary exclusion order on an individual if conditions A to E are met.

(3) Condition A is that the Secretary of State reasonably suspects that the individual is, or has been, involved in terrorism-related activity outside the United Kingdom.

(4) Condition B is that the Secretary of State reasonably considers that it is necessary, for purposes connected with protecting members of the public in the United Kingdom from a risk of terrorism, for a temporary exclusion order to be imposed on the individual.

(5) Condition C is that the Secretary of State reasonably considers that the individual is outside the United Kingdom.

(6) Condition D is that the individual has the right of abode in the United Kingdom.

(7) Condition E is that—

(a) the court gives the Secretary of State permission under section 3, or

(b) the Secretary of State reasonably considers that the urgency of the case requires a temporary exclusion order to be imposed without obtaining such permission.

(8) During the period that a temporary exclusion order is in force, the Secretary of State must keep under review whether condition B is met.

3   Temporary exclusion orders: prior permission of the court

(1) This section applies if the Secretary of State—

(a) makes the relevant decisions in relation to an individual, and

(b) makes an application to the court for permission to impose a temporary exclusion order on the individual.

(2) The function of the court on the application is to determine whether the relevant decisions of the Secretary of State are obviously flawed.

(3) The court may consider the application—

(a) in the absence of the individual,

(b) without the individual having been notified of the application, and

(c) without the individual having been given an opportunity (if the individual was aware of the application) of making any representations to the court.

(4) But that does not limit the matters about which rules of court may be made.

(5) In determining the application, the court must apply the principles applicable on an application for judicial review.

(6) In a case where the court determines that any of the relevant decisions of the Secretary of State is obviously flawed, the court may not give permission under this section.

(7) In any other case, the court must give permission under this section.

(8) Schedule 2 makes provision for references to the court etc where temporary exclusion orders are imposed in cases of urgency.

(9) Only the Secretary of State may appeal against a determination of the court under—

(a) this section, or

(b) Schedule 2;

and such an appeal may only be made on a question of law.

(10) In this section 'the relevant decisions' means the decisions that the following conditions are met—

(a) condition A;

(b) condition B;

(c) condition C;

(d) condition D.

4   Temporary exclusion orders: supplementary provision

(1) The Secretary of State must give notice of the imposition of a temporary exclusion order to the individual on whom it is imposed (the 'excluded individual').

(2) Notice of the imposition of a temporary exclusion order must include an explanation of the procedure for making an application under section 6 for a permit to return.

(3) A temporary exclusion order—

(a) comes into force when notice of its imposition is given; and

(b) is in force for the period of two years (unless revoked or otherwise brought to an end earlier).

(4) The Secretary of State may revoke a temporary exclusion order at any time.

(5) The Secretary of State must give notice of the revocation of a temporary exclusion order to the excluded individual.

(6) If a temporary exclusion order is revoked, it ceases to be in force when notice of its revocation is given.

(7) The validity of a temporary exclusion order is not affected by the excluded individual—

(a) returning to the United Kingdom, or

(b) departing from the United Kingdom.

(8) The imposition of a temporary exclusion order does not prevent a further temporary exclusion order from being imposed on the excluded individual (including in a case where an order ceases to be in force at the expiry of its two year duration).

(9) At the time when a temporary exclusion order comes into force, any British passport held by the excluded individual is invalidated.

(10) During the period when a temporary exclusion order is in force, the issue of a British passport to the excluded individual while he or she is outside the United Kingdom is not valid.

(11) In this section 'British passport' means a passport, or other document which enables or facilitates travel from one state to another (except a permit to return), that has been—

(a) issued by or for Her Majesty's Government in the United Kingdom, and

(b) issued in respect of a person's status as a British citizen.

Permit to return

5   Permit to return

(1) A 'permit to return' is a document giving an individual (who is subject to a temporary exclusion order) permission to return to the United Kingdom.

(2) The permission may be made subject to a requirement that the individual comply with conditions specified in the permit to return.

(3) The individual's failure to comply with a specified condition has the effect of invalidating the permit to return.

(4) A permit to return must state—

   (a) the time at which, or period of time during which, the individual is permitted to arrive on return to the United Kingdom;

   (b) the manner in which the individual is permitted to return to the United Kingdom; and

   (c) the place where the individual is permitted to arrive on return to the United Kingdom.

(5) Provision made under subsection (4)(a) or (c) may, in particular, be framed by reference to the arrival in the United Kingdom of a specific flight, sailing or other transport service.

(6) Provision made under subsection (4)(b) may, in particular, state—

   (a) a route,

   (b) a method of transport,

   (c) an airline, shipping line or other passenger carrier, or

   (d) a flight, sailing or other transport service,

which the individual is permitted to use to return to the United Kingdom.

(7) The Secretary of State may not issue a permit to return except in accordance with section 6 or 7.

(8) It is for the Secretary of State to decide the terms of a permit to return (but this is subject to section 6(3)).

6   Issue of permit to return: application by individual

(1) If an individual applies to the Secretary of State for a permit to return, the Secretary of State must issue a permit within a reasonable period after the application is made.

(2) But the Secretary of State may refuse to issue the permit if—

   (a) the Secretary of State requires the individual to attend an interview with a constable or immigration officer at a time and a place specified by the Secretary of State, and

   (b) the individual fails to attend the interview.

(3) Where a permit to return is issued under this section, the relevant return time must fall within a reasonable period after the application is made.

(4) An application is not valid unless it is made in accordance with the procedure for applications specified by the Secretary of State.

(5) In this section—

'application' means an application made by an individual to the Secretary of State for a permit to return to be issued;

'relevant return time' means—

   (a) the time at which the individual is permitted to arrive on return to the United Kingdom (in a case where the permit to return states such a time), or

   (b) the start of the period of time during which the individual is permitted to arrive on return to the United Kingdom (in a case where the permit to return states such a period).

7   Issue of permit to return: deportation or urgent situation

(1) The Secretary of State must issue a permit to return to an individual if the Secretary of State considers that the individual is to be deported to the United Kingdom.

(2) The Secretary of State may issue a permit to return to an individual if—

   (a) the Secretary of State considers that, because of the urgency of the situation, it is expedient to issue a permit to return even though no application has been made under section 6, and

(b) there is no duty to issue a permit to return under subsection (1).

(3) Subsection (1) or (2) applies whether or not any request has been made to issue the permit to return under that provision.

8   Permit to return: supplementary provision

(1) The Secretary of State may vary a permit to return.

(2) The Secretary of State may revoke a permit to return issued to an individual only if—

    (a) the permit to return has been issued under section 6 and the individual asks the Secretary of State to revoke it;

    (b) the permit to return has been issued under section 7(1) and the Secretary of State no longer considers that the individual is to be deported to the United Kingdom;

    (c) the permit to return has been issued under section 7(2) and the Secretary of State no longer considers that, because of the urgency of the situation, the issue of the permit to return is expedient;

    (d) the Secretary of State issues a subsequent permit to return to the individual; or

    (e) the Secretary of State considers that the permit to return has been obtained by misrepresentation.

(3) The making of an application for a permit to return to be issued under section 6 (whether or not resulting in a permit to return being issued) does not prevent a subsequent application from being made.

(4) The issuing of a permit to return (whether or not resulting in the individual's return to the United Kingdom) does not prevent a subsequent permit to return from being issued (whether or not the earlier permit is still in force).

Obligations after return to the United Kingdom

9   Obligations after return to the United Kingdom

(1) The Secretary of State may, by notice, impose any or all of the permitted obligations on an individual who—

    (a) is subject to a temporary exclusion order, and

    (b) has returned to the United Kingdom.

(2) The 'permitted obligations' are—

    (a) any obligation of a kind that may be imposed (on an individual subject to a TPIM notice) under these provisions of Schedule 1 to the Terrorism Prevention and Investigation Measures Act 2011—

        (i)   paragraph 10 (reporting to police station);

        (ii) paragraph 10A (attendance at appointments etc);

    (b) an obligation to notify the police, in such manner as a notice under this section may require, of—

        (i)   the individual's place (or places) of residence, and

        (ii) any change in the individual's place (or places) of residence.

(3) A notice under this section—

    (a) comes into force when given to the individual; and

    (b) is in force until the temporary exclusion order ends (unless the notice is revoked or otherwise brought to an end earlier).

(4) The Secretary of State may, by notice, vary or revoke any notice given under this section.

(5) The variation or revocation of a notice under this section takes effect when the notice of variation or revocation is given to the individual.

(6) The validity of a notice under this section is not affected by the individual—

    (a) departing from the United Kingdom, or

    (b) returning to the United Kingdom.

(7) The giving of any notice to an individual under this section does not prevent any further notice under this section from being given to that individual.

Offences and proceedings etc

10 Offences

(1) An individual subject to a temporary exclusion order is guilty of an offence if, without reasonable excuse, the individual returns to the United Kingdom in contravention of the restriction on return specified in the order.

(2) It is irrelevant for the purposes of subsection (1) whether or not the individual has a passport or other similar identity document.

(3) An individual subject to an obligation imposed under section 9 is guilty of an offence if, without reasonable excuse, the individual does not comply with the obligation.

(4) In a case where a relevant notice has not actually been given to an individual, the fact that the relevant notice is deemed to have been given to the individual under regulations under section 13 does not (of itself) prevent the individual from showing that lack of knowledge of the temporary exclusion order, or of the obligation imposed under section 9, was a reasonable excuse for the purposes of this section.

(5) An individual guilty of an offence under this section is liable—

    (a) on conviction on indictment, to imprisonment for a term not exceeding 5 years or to a fine, or to both;

    (b) on summary conviction in England and Wales, to imprisonment for a term not exceeding [the general limit in a magistrates' court] or to a fine, or to both;

    (c) on summary conviction in Northern Ireland, to imprisonment for a term not exceeding 6 months or to a fine not exceeding the statutory maximum, or to both;

    (d) on summary conviction in Scotland, to imprisonment for a term not exceeding 12 months or to a fine not exceeding the statutory maximum, or to both.

(6) Where an individual is convicted by or before a court of an offence under this section, it is not open to that court to make in respect of the offence—

    (a) an order under [section 80 of the Sentencing Code] (conditional discharge);

    (b) an order under section 227A of the Criminal Procedure (Scotland) Act 1995 (community pay-back orders); or

    (c) an order under Article 4(1)(b) of the Criminal Justice (Northern Ireland) Order 1996 (S.I. 1996/3160 (N.I. 24)) (conditional discharge in Northern Ireland).

(7) In this section—

'relevant notice' means—

    (a) notice of the imposition of a temporary exclusion order, or

    (b) notice under section 9 imposing an obligation;

'restriction on return' means the requirement specified in a temporary exclusion order in accordance with section 2(1).

(8) In section 2 of the UK Borders Act 2007 (detention at ports), in subsection (1A), for 'the individual is subject to a warrant for arrest' substitute 'the individual—

    (a) may be liable to be detained by a constable under section 14 of the Criminal Procedure (Scotland) Act 1995 in respect of an offence under section 10(1) of the Counter-Terrorism and Security Act 2015, or

    (b) is subject to a warrant for arrest.'

11 Review of decisions relating to temporary exclusion orders

(1) This section applies where an individual who is subject to a temporary exclusion order is in the United Kingdom.

(2) The individual may apply to the court to review any of the following decisions of the Secretary of State—

    (a) a decision that any of the following conditions was met in relation to the imposition of the temporary exclusion order—

        (i) condition A;

        (ii) condition B;

        (iii) condition C;

        (iv) condition D;

(b) a decision to impose the temporary exclusion order;

(c) a decision that condition B continues to be met;

(d) a decision to impose any of the permitted obligations on the individual by a notice under section 9.

(3) On a review under this section, the court must apply the principles applicable on an application for judicial review.

(4) On a review of a decision within subsection (2)(a) to (c), the court has the following powers (and only those powers)—

(a) power to quash the temporary exclusion order;

(b) power to give directions to the Secretary of State for, or in relation to, the revocation of the temporary exclusion order.

(5) If the court does not exercise either of its powers under subsection (4), the court must decide that the temporary exclusion order is to continue in force.

(6) On a review of a decision within subsection (2)(d), the court has the following powers (and only those powers)—

(a) power to quash the permitted obligation in question;

(b) if that is the only permitted obligation imposed by the notice under section 9, power to quash the notice;

(c) power to give directions to the Secretary of State for, or in relation to—

(i) the variation of the notice so far as it relates to that permitted obligation, or

(ii) if that is the only permitted obligation imposed by the notice, the revocation of the notice.

(7) If the court does not exercise any of its powers under subsection (6), the court must decide that the notice under section 9 is to continue in force.

(8) If the court exercises a power under subsection (6)(a) or (c)(i), the court must decide that the notice under section 9 is to continue in force subject to that exercise of that power.

(9) The power under this section to quash a temporary exclusion order, permitted obligation or notice under section 9 includes—

(a) in England and Wales or Northern Ireland, power to stay the quashing for a specified time, or pending an appeal or further appeal against the decision to quash; or

(b) in Scotland, power to determine that the quashing is of no effect for a specified time or pending such an appeal or further appeal.

(10) An appeal against a determination of the court on a review under this section may only be made on a question of law.

(11) For the purposes of this section, a failure by the Secretary of State to make a decision whether condition B continues to be met is to be treated as a decision that it continues to be met.

12–29   ***

30   Power to give directions: general

(1) Where the Secretary of State is satisfied that a specified authority has failed to discharge the duty imposed on it by section 26(1), the Secretary of State may give directions to the authority for the purpose of enforcing the performance of that duty.

[(2) A direction given under this section may be enforced—

(a) in England and Wales, on an application made on behalf of the Secretary of State, by a mandatory order,

(b) in Scotland, on an application made on behalf of the Secretary of State to the Court of Session, by an order of specific implement.]

(3) The Secretary of State must consult the Welsh Ministers before giving directions under subsection (1) so far as relating to the devolved Welsh functions of a [a devolved Welsh authority].

(4) The Secretary of State must consult the Scottish Ministers before giving directions under subsection (1) so far as relating to the devolved Scottish functions of a Scottish authority.

31   Freedom of expression in universities etc

(1) This section applies to a specified authority if it is the proprietor or governing body of—

(a) an institution that provides further education (within the meaning given by section 2(3) of the Education Act 1996), ...

(b) an institution that provides courses of a description mentioned in Schedule 6 to the Education Reform Act 1988 (higher education courses) [, or

(c) a post-16 education body within the meaning of the Further and Higher Education (Scotland) Act 2005].

(2) When carrying out the duty imposed by section 26(1), a specified authority to which this section applies—

(a) must have particular regard to the duty to ensure freedom of speech, if it is subject to that duty;

[(aa) must have particular regard to the need to ensure freedom of speech, if it is the proprietor of governing body of an institution mentioned in subsection (1)(c);]

(b) must have particular regard to the importance of academic freedom, if it is the proprietor or governing body of a qualifying institution.

(3) When issuing guidance under section 29 to specified authorities to which this section applies, the Secretary of State—

(a) must have particular regard to the duty to ensure freedom of speech, in the case of authorities that are subject to that duty;

[(aa) must have particular regard to the need to ensure freedom of speech, in the case of authorities that are proprietors or governing bodies of institutions mentioned in subsection (1)(c);]

(b) must have particular regard to the importance of academic freedom, in the case of authorities that are proprietors or governing bodies of qualifying institutions.

(4) When considering whether to give directions under section 30 to a specified authority to which this section applies, the Secretary of State—

(a) must have particular regard to the duty to ensure freedom of speech, in the case of an authority that is subject to that duty;

[(aa) must have particular regard to the need to ensure freedom of speech, in the case of authorities that are proprietors or governing bodies of institutions mentioned in subsection (1)(c);]

(b) must have particular regard to the importance of academic freedom, in the case of an authority that is the proprietor or governing body of a qualifying institution.

(5) In this section—

'the duty to ensure freedom of speech' means the duty imposed by section 43(1) of the Education (No. 2) Act 1986;

['the need to ensure freedom of speech' means the need to take such steps as are reasonably practicable to ensure that freedom of speech within the law is secured for members, students and employees of the institution in question and for visiting speakers;]

'academic freedom' means the freedom referred to in section 202(2)(a) of the Education Reform Act 1988;

'qualifying institution' has the meaning given by section 202(3) of that Act.

32 Monitoring of performance: further and higher education bodies

(1) In this section—

'monitoring authority' has the meaning given by subsection (4);

'relevant further education body' means the governing body or proprietor of an institution in England or Wales that—

(a) is subject to the duty imposed by section 26(1), and

(b) is subject to that duty because it is an institution at which more than 250 students are undertaking courses in preparation for examinations related to qualifications regulated by the Office of Qualifications and Examinations [, or to qualifications awarded by bodies in respect of the award of which they are recognised by Qualifications Wales under Part 3 of the Qualifications Wales Act 2015];

'relevant higher education body' means the governing body or proprietor of an institution in England or Wales that is subject to the duty imposed by section 26(1) because it is—

  (a) a qualifying institution within the meaning given by section 11 of the Higher Education Act 2004[, disregarding paragraphs (da) and (ea) of that section and the definition of 'institution' in section 21(1) of that Act], or

  (b) an institution at which more than 250 students are undertaking courses of a description mentioned in Schedule 6 to the Education Reform Act 1988 (higher education courses).

(2) A relevant further education body or relevant higher education body must give to the monitoring authority any information that the monitoring authority may require for the purposes of monitoring that body's performance in discharging the duty imposed by section 26(1).

(3) The information that the monitoring authority may require under subsection (2) includes information which specifies the steps that will be taken by the body in question to ensure that it discharges the duty imposed by section 26(1).

(4) The 'monitoring authority' for a relevant further education body or a relevant higher education body is—

  (a) the Secretary of State, or

  (b) a person to whom the Secretary of State delegates the function under subsection (2) in relation to that body.

The Secretary of State must consult the Welsh Ministers before delegating the function under subsection (2) in relation to institutions in Wales.

(5) A delegation under subsection (4)(b) must be made by giving notice in writing to the person to whom the delegation is made if—

  (a) that person is Her Majesty's Chief Inspector of Education, Children's Services and Skills or Her Majesty's Chief Inspector of Education and Training in Wales, and the function is delegated in relation to relevant further education bodies;

  (b) that person is the [Office for Students] or the Higher Education Funding Council for Wales, and the function is delegated in relation to relevant higher education bodies.

(6) Otherwise, a delegation under subsection (4)(b) must be made by regulations.

(7) The Secretary of State must publish any notice given under subsection (5).

(8) Regulations under subsection (6) are to be made by statutory instrument; and any such instrument is subject to annulment in pursuance of a resolution of either House of Parliament.

(9) In this section—

  (a) 'institution in England' means an institution whose activities are carried on, or principally carried on, in England, and includes the Open University;

  (b) 'institution in Wales' means an institution whose activities are carried on, or principally carried on, in Wales.

33   Power to give directions: section 32

(1) Where the Secretary of State is satisfied that a relevant further education body or a relevant higher education body has failed to comply with a requirement under section 32(2), the Secretary of State may give directions to the body for the purpose of enforcing compliance.

(2) A direction under this section may be enforced, on an application made on behalf of the Secretary of State, by a mandatory order.

(3) The Secretary of State must consult the Welsh Ministers before giving directions under subsection (1) in relation to institutions in Wales.

(4) In this section 'relevant further education body', 'relevant higher education body' and 'institution in Wales' have the same meaning as in section 32.

34   Enforcement

A failure in respect of a performance of a duty imposed by or under this Chapter does not confer a cause of action at private law.

*****

Criminal Justice and Courts Act 2015

(2015, c. 2)

An Act to make provision about how offenders are dealt with before and after conviction; to create offences involving ill-treatment or wilful neglect by a person providing health care or social care; to create an offence of the corrupt or other improper exercise of police powers and privileges; to make provision about offences committed by disqualified drivers; to create an offence of disclosing private sexual photographs or films with intent to cause distress; to amend the offence of meeting a child following sexual grooming; to amend the offence of possession of extreme pornographic images; to make provision about the proceedings and powers of courts and tribunals; to make provision about judicial review; and for connected purposes. [12th February 2015]

Territorial extent: England and Wales (material reproduced here)
*****

PART 4 JUDICIAL REVIEW IN THE HIGH COURT AND UPPER TRIBUNAL

84, 85 *****

86 Use of information about financial resources

(1) This section applies when the High Court, the Upper Tribunal or the Court of Appeal is determining by whom and to what extent costs of or incidental to judicial review proceedings are to be paid.

(2) The information to which the court or tribunal must have regard includes—

(a) information about the financing of the proceedings provided in accordance with section 31(3)(b) of the Senior Courts Act 1981 or section 16(3)(b) of the Tribunals, Courts and Enforcement Act 2007, and

(b) any supplement to that information provided in accordance with rules of court or Tribunal Procedure Rules.

(3) The court or tribunal must consider whether to order costs to be paid by a person, other than a party to the proceedings, who is identified in that information as someone who is providing financial support for the purposes of the proceedings or likely or able to do so.

(4) In this section 'judicial review proceedings' means—

(a) proceedings on an application for leave to apply for judicial review,

(b) proceedings on an application for judicial review,

(c) proceedings on an application for permission to apply for relief under section 15 of the Tribunals, Courts and Enforcement Act 2007 in a case arising under the law of England and Wales,

(d) proceedings on an application for such relief in such a case,

(e) any proceedings on an application for leave to appeal from a decision in proceedings described in paragraph (a), (b), (c) or (d), and

(f) proceedings on an appeal from such a decision.

87 Interveners and costs

(1) This section applies where—

(a) a person is granted permission to file evidence or make representations in judicial review proceedings, and

(b) at that time, the person is not a relevant party to the proceedings.

(2) That person is referred to in this section as an 'intervener'.

(3) A relevant party to the proceedings may not be ordered by the High Court or the Court of Appeal to pay the intervener's costs in connection with the proceedings.

(4) Subsection (3) does not prevent the court making an order if it considers that there are exceptional circumstances that make it appropriate to do so.

(5) On an application to the High Court or the Court of Appeal by a relevant party to the proceedings, if the court is satisfied that a condition described in subsection (6) is met in a stage of the

proceedings that the court deals with, the court must order the intervener to pay any costs specified in the application that the court considers have been incurred by the relevant party as a result of the intervener's involvement in that stage of the proceedings.

(6) Those conditions are that—

(a) the intervener has acted, in substance, as the sole or principal applicant, defendant, appellant or respondent;

(b) the intervener's evidence and representations, taken as a whole, have not been of significant assistance to the court;

(c) a significant part of the intervener's evidence and representations relates to matters that it is not necessary for the court to consider in order to resolve the issues that are the subject of the stage in the proceedings;

(d) the intervener has behaved unreasonably.

(7) Subsection 5 does not require the court to make an order if it considers that there are exceptional circumstances that make it inappropriate to do so.

(8) In determining whether there are exceptional circumstances that are relevant for the purposes of subsection (4) or (7), the court must have regard to criteria specified in rules of court.

(9) In this section, 'judicial review proceedings' means—

(a) proceedings on an application for leave to apply for judicial review,

(b) proceedings on an application for judicial review,

(c) any proceedings on an application for leave to appeal from a decision in proceedings described in paragraph (a) or (b), and

(d) proceedings on an appeal from such a decision,

and the proceedings described in paragraphs (a) to (d) are 'stages' of judicial review proceedings.

(10) For the purposes of this section, 'a relevant party' to judicial review proceedings means any of the following—

(a) a person who is or has been an applicant or defendant in the proceedings described in subsection 9(a), (b) or (c);

(b) a person who is or has been an appellant or respondent in the proceedings described in subsection 9(d);

(c) any other person who is or has been directly affected by the proceedings and on whom the application for judicial review, or for leave to apply for judicial review, has been served.

(11) If a person who is an intervener in judicial review proceedings becomes a relevant party to the proceedings, the person is to be treated for the purposes of subsections (3) and (5) as having been a relevant party, rather than an intervener, at all times when involved in the proceedings.

88 Capping of costs

(1) A costs capping order may not be made by the High Court or the Court of Appeal in connection with judicial review proceedings except in accordance with this section and sections 89 and 90.

(2) A 'costs capping order' is an order limiting or removing the liability of a party to judicial review proceedings to pay another party's costs in connection with any stage of the proceedings.

(3) The court may make a costs capping order only if leave to apply for judicial review has been granted.

(4) The court may make a costs capping order only on an application for such an order made by the applicant for judicial review in accordance with rules of court.

(5) Rules of court may, in particular, specify information that must be contained in the application, including—

(a) information about the source, nature and extent of financial resources available, or likely to be available, to the applicant to meet liabilities arising in connection with the application, and

(b) if the applicant is a body corporate that is unable to demonstrate that it is likely to have financial resources available to meet such liabilities, information about its members and about their ability to provide financial support for the purposes of the application.

(6) The court may make a costs capping order only if it is satisfied that—

(a) the proceedings are public interest proceedings,

(b) in the absence of the order, the applicant for judicial review would withdraw the application for judicial review or cease to participate in the proceedings, and

(c) it would be reasonable for the applicant for judicial review to do so.

(7) The proceedings are 'public interest proceedings' only if—

(a) an issue that is the subject of the proceedings is of general public importance,

(b) the public interest requires the issue to be resolved, and

(c) the proceedings are likely to provide an appropriate means of resolving it.

(8) The matters to which the court must have regard when determining whether proceedings are public interest proceedings include—

(a) the number of people likely to be directly affected if relief is granted to the applicant for judicial review,

(b) how significant the effect on those people is likely to be, and

(c) whether the proceedings involve consideration of a point of law of general public importance.

(9)–(11) *****

(12) In this section and sections 89 and 90—

'costs capping order' has the meaning given in subsection (2);

'the court' means the High Court or the Court of Appeal;

'judicial review proceedings' means—

(a) proceedings on an application for leave to apply for judicial review,

(b) proceedings on an application for judicial review,

(c) any proceedings on an application for leave to appeal from a decision in proceedings described in paragraph (a) or (b), and

(d) proceedings on an appeal from such a decision,

and the proceedings described in paragraphs (a) to (d) are 'stages' of judicial review proceedings.

(13) For the purposes of this section and section 89, in relation to judicial review proceedings—

(a) the applicant for judicial review is the person who is or was the applicant in the proceedings on the application for judicial review, and

(b) references to relief being granted to the applicant for judicial review include the upholding on appeal of a decision to grant such relief at an earlier stage of the proceedings.

89 Capping of costs: orders and their terms

(1) The matters to which the court must have regard when considering whether to make a costs capping order in connection with judicial review proceedings, and what the terms of such an order should be, include—

(a) the financial resources of the parties to the proceedings, including the financial resources of any person who provides, or may provide, financial support to the parties;

(b) the extent to which the applicant for the order is likely to benefit if relief is granted to the applicant for judicial review;

(c) the extent to which any person who has provided, or may provide, the applicant with financial support is likely to benefit if relief is granted to the applicant for judicial review;

(d) whether legal representatives for the applicant for the order are acting free of charge;

(e) whether the applicant for the order is an appropriate person to represent the interests of other persons or the public interest generally.

(2) A costs capping order that limits or removes the liability of the applicant for judicial review to pay the costs of another party to the proceedings if relief is not granted to the applicant for judicial review must also limit or remove the liability of the other party to pay the applicant's costs if it is.

(3) The Lord Chancellor may by regulations amend this section by adding to, omitting or amending the matters listed in subsection (1).

(4) Regulations under this section are to be made by statutory instrument.

(5) A statutory instrument containing regulations under this section may not be made unless a draft of the instrument has been laid before, and approved by a resolution of, each House of Parliament.

(6) In this section—

'free of charge' means otherwise than for or in expectation of fee, gain or reward;

'legal representative', in relation to a party to proceedings, means a person exercising a right of audience or conducting litigation on the party's behalf.

90   Capping of costs: environmental cases

(1) The Lord Chancellor may by regulations provide that sections 88 and 89 do not apply in relation to judicial review proceedings which, in the Lord Chancellor's opinion, have as their subject an issue relating entirely or partly to the environment.

(2) Regulations under this section—

(a) may make provision generally or only in relation to proceedings described in the regulations, and

(b) may include transitional, transitory or saving provision.

(3) Regulations under this section are to be made by statutory instrument.

(4) A statutory instrument containing regulations under this section is subject to annulment in pursuance of a resolution of either House of Parliament.

*****

European Union Referendum Act 2015

(2015, c. 36)

An Act to make provision for the holding of a referendum in the United Kingdom and Gibraltar on whether the United Kingdom should remain a member of the European Union.   [17th December 2015]

Territorial extent: United Kingdom and Gibraltar

The referendum

1   The referendum

(1) A referendum is to be held on whether the United Kingdom should remain a member of the European Union.

(2) The Secretary of State must, by regulations, appoint the day on which the referendum is to be held.

(3) The day appointed under subsection (2)—

(a) must be no later than 31 December 2017,

(b) must not be 5 May 2016, and

(c) must not be 4 May 2017.

(4) The question that is to appear on the ballot papers is—

'Should the United Kingdom remain a member of the European Union or leave the European Union?'

(5) The alternative answers to that question that are to appear on the ballot papers are—

'Remain a member of the European Union

Leave the European Union'.

(6) *******

2   Entitlement to vote in the referendum

(1) Those entitled to vote in the referendum are—

(a) the persons who, on the date of the referendum, would be entitled to vote as electors at a parliamentary election in any constituency,

(b) the persons who, on that date, are disqualified by reason of being peers from voting as electors at parliamentary elections but—

(i)   would be entitled to vote as electors at a local government election in any electoral area in Great Britain,

(ii) would be entitled to vote as electors at a local election in any district electoral area in Northern Ireland, or

(iii) would be entitled to vote as electors at a European Parliamentary election in any electoral region by virtue of section 3 of the Representation of the People Act 1985 (peers resident outside the United Kingdom), and

(c) the persons who, on the date of the referendum—

(i)   would be entitled to vote in Gibraltar as electors at a European Parliamentary election in the combined electoral region in which Gibraltar is comprised, and

(ii) fall within subsection (2).

(2) A person falls within this subsection if the person is either—

(a) a Commonwealth citizen, or

(b) a citizen of the Republic of Ireland.

(3) In subsection (1)(b)(i) 'local government election' includes a municipal election in the City of London (that is, an election to the office of mayor, alderman, common councilman or sheriff and also the election of any officer elected by the mayor, aldermen and liverymen in common hall).

3–5   *****

6   Duty to publish information on outcome of negotiations between member States

(1) The Secretary of State must publish a report which contains (alone or with other material)—

(a) a statement setting out what has been agreed by member States following negotiations relating to the United Kingdom's request for reforms to address concerns over its membership of the European Union, and

(b) the opinion of the Government of the United Kingdom on what has been agreed.

(2) The report must be published before the beginning of the final 10 week period.

(3) In this section 'the final 10 week period' means the period of 10 weeks ending with the date of the referendum.

(4) A copy of the report published under this section must be laid before Parliament by the Secretary of State.

7   Duty to publish information about membership of the European Union etc

(1) The Secretary of State must publish a report which contains (alone or with other material)—

(a) information about rights, and obligations, that arise under European Union law as a result of the United Kingdom's membership of the European Union, and

(b) examples of countries that do not have membership of the European Union but do have other arrangements with the European Union (describing, in the case of each country given as an example, those arrangements).

(2) The report must be published before the beginning of the final 10 week period.

(3) In this section 'the final 10 week period' means the period of 10 weeks ending with the date of the referendum.

(4) A copy of the report published under this section must be laid before Parliament by the Secretary of State.

*****

House of Lords (Expulsion and Suspension) Act 2015

(2015, c. 14)

An Act to make provision empowering the House of Lords to expel or suspend members.

[26th March 2015]

Territorial extent: United Kingdom

Expulsion and suspension of members of the House of Lords

1 Expulsion and suspension of members of the House of Lords

(1) Standing Orders of the House of Lords may make provision under which the House of Lords may by resolution—

(a) expel a member of the House of Lords, or

(b) suspend a member of the House of Lords for the period specified in the resolution.

(2) A person expelled by virtue of this section ceases to be a member.

(3) A person suspended by virtue of this section remains a member during the period of suspension, but during that period the person—

(a) is not entitled to receive writs of summons to attend the House of Lords, and

(b) despite any writ of summons previously issued to the person, is disqualified from sitting or voting in the House of Lords or a committee of the House of Lords.

(4) A resolution passed by virtue of subsection (1) must state that, in the opinion of the House of Lords, the conduct giving rise to the resolution—

(a) occurred after the coming into force of this Act, or

(b) occurred before the coming into force of this Act and was not public knowledge before that time.

2 *****

3 Effect of ceasing to be a member

A person expelled in accordance with section 1 is to be treated as if that person had ceased to be a member in accordance with the House of Lords Reform Act 2014, for the purposes of section 4(2) to (8) of that Act.

*****

Lords Spiritual (Women) Act 2015

(2015, c. 18)

An Act to make time-limited provision for vacancies among the Lords Spiritual to be filled by bishops who are women. [26th March 2015]

Territorial extent: United Kingdom

1 Vacancies among the Lords Spiritual

(1) This section applies where—

(a) a vacancy arises among the Lords Spiritual in the House of Lords in the 10 years beginning with the day on which this Act comes into force,

(b) at the time the vacancy arises there is at least one eligible bishop who is a woman, and

(c) the person who would otherwise be entitled to fill the vacancy under section 5 of the Bishoprics Act 1878 is a man.

(2) If at the time the vacancy arises there is only one eligible bishop who is a woman, the vacancy is to be filled by the issue of writs of summons to her.

(3) If at the time the vacancy arises there are two or more eligible bishops who are women, the vacancy is to be filled by the issue of writs of summons to the one whose election as a bishop of a diocese in England was confirmed first.

(4) In this section 'eligible bishop' means a bishop of a diocese in England who is not yet entitled in that capacity to the issue of writs of summons.

(5) The reference in subsection (1) to a vacancy does not include a vacancy arising by the avoidance of the see of Canterbury, York, London, Durham or Winchester.

*****

Modern Slavery Act 2015

(2015, c. 30)

An Act to make provision about slavery, servitude and forced or compulsory labour and about human trafficking, including provision for the protection of victims; to make provision for an Independent Anti-slavery Commissioner; and for connected purposes.   [26th March 2015]

Territorial extent: England and Wales (provisions reproduced here)

1   Slavery, servitude and forced or compulsory labour

(1) A person commits an offence if—

  (a) the person holds another person in slavery or servitude and the circumstances are such that the person knows or ought to know that the other person is held in slavery or servitude, or

  (b) the person requires another person to perform forced or compulsory labour and the circumstances are such that the person knows or ought to know that the other person is being required to perform forced or compulsory labour.

(2) In subsection (1) the references to holding a person in slavery or servitude or requiring a person to perform forced or compulsory labour are to be construed in accordance with Article 4 of the Human Rights Convention.

(3) In determining whether a person is being held in slavery or servitude or required to perform forced or compulsory labour, regard may be had to all the circumstances.

(4) For example, regard may be had—

  (a) to any of the person's personal circumstances (such as the person being a child, the person's family relationships, and any mental or physical illness) which may make the person more vulnerable than other persons;

  (b) to any work or services provided by the person, including work or services provided in circumstances which constitute exploitation within section 3(3) to (6).

(5) The consent of a person (whether an adult or a child) to any of the acts alleged to constitute holding the person in slavery or servitude, or requiring the person to perform forced or compulsory labour, does not preclude a determination that the person is being held in slavery or servitude, or required to perform forced or compulsory labour.

2   Human trafficking

(1) A person commits an offence if the person arranges or facilitates the travel of another person ('V') with a view to V being exploited.

(2) It is irrelevant whether V consents to the travel (whether V is an adult or a child).

(3) A person may in particular arrange or facilitate V's travel by recruiting V, transporting or transferring V, harbouring or receiving V, or transferring or exchanging control over V.

(4) A person arranges or facilitates V's travel with a view to V being exploited only if—

  (a) the person intends to exploit V (in any part of the world) during or after the travel, or

  (b) the person knows or ought to know that another person is likely to exploit V (in any part of the world) during or after the travel.

(5) 'Travel' means—

  (a) arriving in, or entering, any country,

  (b) departing from any country,

  (c) travelling within any country.

(6) A person who is a UK national commits an offence under this section regardless of—

  (a) where the arranging or facilitating takes place, or

  (b) where the travel takes place.

(7) A person who is not a UK national commits an offence under this section if—

  (a) any part of the arranging or facilitating takes place in the United Kingdom, or

  (b) the travel consists of arrival in or entry into, departure from, or travel within, the United Kingdom.

3   Meaning of exploitation

(1) For the purposes of section 2 a person is exploited only if one or more of the following subsections apply in relation to the person.

Slavery, servitude and forced or compulsory labour

(2) The person is the victim of behaviour—

   (a) which involves the commission of an offence under section 1, or

   (b) which would involve the commission of an offence under that section if it took place in England and Wales.

Sexual exploitation

(3) Something is done to or in respect of the person—

   (a) which involves the commission of an offence under—

      (i)   section 1(1)(a) of the Protection of Children Act 1978 (indecent photographs of children), or

      (ii) Part 1 of the Sexual Offences Act 2003 (sexual offences), as it has effect in England and Wales, or

   (b) which would involve the commission of such an offence if it were done in England and Wales.

Removal of organs etc

(4) The person is encouraged, required or expected to do anything—

   (a) which involves the commission, by him or her or another person, of an offence under section 32 or 33 of the Human Tissue Act 2004 (prohibition of commercial dealings in organs and restrictions on use of live donors) as it has effect in England and Wales, or

   (b) which would involve the commission of such an offence, by him or her or another person, if it were done in England and Wales.

Securing services etc by force, threats or deception

(5) The person is subjected to force, threats or deception designed to induce him or her—

   (a) to provide services of any kind,

   (b) to provide another person with benefits of any kind, or

   (c) to enable another person to acquire benefits of any kind.

Securing services etc from children and vulnerable persons

(6) Another person uses or attempts to use the person for a purpose within paragraph (a), (b) or (c) of subsection (5), having chosen him or her for that purpose on the grounds that—

   (a) he or she is a child, is mentally or physically ill or disabled, or has a family relationship with a particular person, and

   (b) an adult, or a person without the illness, disability, or family relationship, would be likely to refuse to be used for that purpose.

4   Committing offence with intent to commit offence under section 2

A person commits an offence under this section if the person commits any offence with the intention of committing an offence under section 2 (including an offence committed by aiding, abetting, counselling or procuring an offence under that section).

5   Penalties

(1) A person guilty of an offence under section 1 or 2 is liable—

   (a) on conviction on indictment, to imprisonment for life;

   (b) on summary conviction, to imprisonment for a term not exceeding [the general limit in a magistrates' court] or a fine or both.

(2) A person guilty of an offence under section 4 is liable (unless subsection (3) applies)—

   (a) on conviction on indictment, to imprisonment for a term not exceeding 10 years;

   (b) on summary conviction, to imprisonment for a term not exceeding [the general limit in a magistrates' court] or a fine or both.

(3) Where the offence under section 4 is committed by kidnapping or false imprisonment, a person guilty of that offence is liable, on conviction on indictment, to imprisonment for life.

(4) In relation to an offence committed before [2 May 2022], the references in subsections (1)(b) and (2)(b) to [the general limit in a magistrates' court] are to be read as references to 6 months.

*****

Recall of MPs Act 2015

(2015, c. 25)

An Act to make provision about the recall of members of the House of Commons; and for connected purposes.   [26th March 2015]

Territorial extent: United Kingdom

How an MP becomes subject to a recall petition process

1   How an MP becomes subject to a recall petition process

(1) An MP becomes subject to a recall petition process if—
   (a) the first, second or third recall condition has been met in relation to the MP, and
   (b) the Speaker gives notice of that fact under section 5.

(2) In this Act 'recall petition' means a petition calling—
   (a) for an MP to lose his or her seat in the House of Commons, and
   (b) for a by-election to be held to decide who should be the MP for the constituency in question.

(3) The first recall condition is that—
   (a) the MP has, after becoming an MP, been convicted in the United Kingdom of an offence and sentenced or ordered to be imprisoned or detained, and
   (b) the appeal period expires without the conviction, sentence or order having being overturned on appeal.

Sections 2 to 4 contain more about the first recall condition.

(4) The second recall condition is that, following on from a report from the Committee on Standards in relation to the MP, the House of Commons orders the suspension of the MP from the service of the House for a specified period of the requisite length.

(5) A specified period is 'of the requisite length' for the purposes of subsection (4) if—
   (a) where the period is expressed as a number of sitting days, the period specified is of at least 10 sitting days, or
   (b) in any other case, the period specified (however expressed) is a period of at least 14 days.

(6) For the purposes of subsection (4) it does not matter—
   (a) when the period of suspension starts, and
   (b) where that period is expressed as a number of sitting days, what provision (if any) is made by the House regarding what does, or does not, count as a sitting day for the purpose of calculating that period.

(7) The reference in subsection (4) to the Committee on Standards is to any committee of the House of Commons concerned with the standards of conduct of individual members of that House.

(8) Any question arising under subsection (7) is to be determined by the Speaker.

(9) The third recall condition is that—
   (a) the MP has, after becoming an MP, been convicted of an offence under section 10 of the Parliamentary Standards Act 2009 (offence of providing false or misleading information for allowances claims), and

(b) the appeal period expires without the conviction having been overturned on appeal.
Sections 2 to 4 contain more about the third recall condition.

(10) The provision made by or under this Act does not affect other ways in which an MP's seat may be vacated, whether—

(a) by the MP's disqualification—for example, under the Representation of the People Act 1981 (disqualification of certain offenders), or

(b) by the MP's death or otherwise.

(11) The loss by an MP of his or her seat under this Act as a result of a recall petition does not prevent him or her standing in the resulting by-election.

2 The first and third recall conditions: further provision

(1) In section 1(3) and (9) (the first and third recall conditions)—

(a) the reference to an offence includes an offence committed before the MP became an MP and an offence committed before the day on which section 1 comes into force, but

(b) the reference to an MP being convicted of an offence is only to an MP being convicted of an offence on or after the day on which section 1 comes into force.

(2) The reference in section 1(3) to an offence does not include an offence mentioned in section 1(9).

(3) The reference in section 1(3) to an MP being sentenced or ordered—

(a) includes the MP being sentenced or ordered where the sentence or order is suspended,

(b) does not include the MP being remanded in custody, and

(c) does not include the MP being authorised to be detained under mental health legislation if there is no sentence or order for imprisonment or detention other than under that legislation.

(4), (5) *****

3, 4 *****

5 Speaker's notice that first, second or third recall condition has been met

(1) As soon as reasonably practicable after becoming aware that the first, second or third recall condition has been met in relation to an MP, the Speaker must give notice of that fact to the petition officer for the MP's constituency.

(2) But subsection (1) does not apply if it would require the Speaker to give notice at a time—

(a) within the period of 6 months ending with the [last possible] polling day for the next parliamentary general election,

(b) when the MP is already subject to a recall petition process, or

(c) when the MP's seat has already been vacated (whether by the MP's disqualification or death, or otherwise).

[(2A)]–(7) *****

6–12 *****

13 Early termination of recall petition process

(1) This section applies where any of the following conditions is met at any time after the Speaker's notice is given but before notice of the outcome of the recall petition has been given under section 14(2)(b).

(2) The first condition is that [Parliament is dissolved.]

(3) The second condition is that the MP's seat is vacated (whether by the MP's disqualification or death, or otherwise).

(4) The third condition is that, in a case in which the first recall condition was met in relation to the MP, the conviction, sentence or order in question is overturned on appeal.

(5) The fourth condition is that, in a case in which the third recall condition was met in relation to the MP, the conviction in question is overturned on appeal.

(6) As soon as reasonably practicable after becoming aware that this section applies, the Speaker [(or, in a case where this section applies by virtue of the first condition, the person who was the Speaker immediately before Parliament was dissolved)] must notify the petition officer that the section applies, specifying which of the conditions above has been met.

(7)–(9) *****

14   Determination of whether recall petition successful

(1) This section applies unless the petition officer has received a notice under section 13(6) (early termination of recall petition process).

(2) As soon as reasonably practicable after the end of the signing period, the petition officer must—

(a)   determine whether the recall petition was successful,

(b)   notify the Speaker that the recall petition was successful or unsuccessful, as the case may be, and

(c)   having done that, give a public notice of the outcome of the recall petition in accordance with regulations under section 18.

(3)–(8) *****

15   Effect of successful petition

(1) If the petition officer notifies the Speaker under section 14(2)(b) that the recall petition was successful, the MP's seat becomes vacant on the giving of that notice.

(2) That does not apply if the seat has already been vacated (whether by the MP's disqualification or death, or otherwise).

(3) *****

*****

Investigatory Powers Act 2016

(2016, c. 25)

An Act to make provision about the interception of communications, equipment interference and the acquisition and retention of communications data, bulk personal datasets and other information; to make provision about the treatment of material held as a result of such interception, equipment interference or acquisition or retention; to establish the Investigatory Powers Commissioner and other Judicial Commissioners and make provision about them and other oversight arrangements; to make further provision about investigatory powers and national security; to amend sections 3 and 5 of the Intelligence Services Act 1994; and for connected purposes.   [29th November 2016]

Territorial extent: United Kingdom

PART 1   GENERAL PRIVACY PROTECTIONS

Overview and general privacy duties

1   Overview of Act

(1) This Act sets out the extent to which certain investigatory powers may be used to interfere with privacy.

(2) This Part imposes certain duties in relation to privacy and contains other protections for privacy.

(3) These other protections include offences and penalties in relation to—

(a)   the unlawful interception of communications, and

(b)   the unlawful obtaining of communications data.

(4) This Part also abolishes and restricts various general powers to obtain communications data and restricts the circumstances in which equipment interference, and certain requests about the interception of communications, can take place.

(5) Further protections for privacy—

  (a) can be found, in particular, in the regimes provided for by Parts 2 to 7 and in the oversight arrangements in Part 8, and

  (b) also exist—

    (i) by virtue of the Human Rights Act 1998,

    [(ii) in section 170 of the Data Protection Act 2018 (unlawful obtaining etc of personal data),]

    (iii) in section 48 of the Wireless Telegraphy Act 2006 (offence of interception or disclosure of messages),

    (iv) in sections 1 to 3A of the Computer Misuse Act 1990 (computer misuse offences),

    (v) in the common law offence of misconduct in public office, and

    (vi) elsewhere in the law.

(6) The regimes provided for by Parts 2 to 7 are as follows—

  (a) Part 2 and Chapter 1 of Part 6 set out circumstances (including under a warrant) in which the interception of communications is lawful and make further provision about the interception of communications and the treatment of material obtained in connection with it,

  (b) Part 3 and Chapter 2 of Part 6 set out circumstances in which the obtaining of communications data is lawful in pursuance of an authorisation or under a warrant and make further provision about the obtaining and treatment of such data,

  (c) Part 4 makes provision for the retention of certain communications data in pursuance of a notice,

  (d) Part 5 and Chapter 3 of Part 6 deal with equipment interference warrants, and

  (e) Part 7 deals with bulk personal dataset warrants.

(7) As to the rest of the Act—

  (a) Part 8 deals with oversight arrangements for regimes in this Act and elsewhere, and

  (b) Part 9 contains miscellaneous and general provisions including amendments to sections 3 and 5 of the Intelligence Services Act 1994 and provisions about national security and combined warrants and authorisations.

2 General duties in relation to privacy

(1) Subsection (2) applies where a public authority is deciding whether—

  (a) to issue, renew or cancel a warrant under Part 2, 5, 6 or 7,

  (b) to modify such a warrant,

  (c) to approve a decision to issue, renew or modify such a warrant,

  (d) to grant, approve or cancel an authorisation under Part 3,

  (e) to give a notice in pursuance of such an authorisation or under Part 4 or section 252, 253 or 257,

  (f) to vary or revoke such a notice,

  (g) to approve a decision to give or vary a notice under Part 4 or section 252, 253 or 257,

  (h) to approve the use of criteria under section 153, 194 or 222,

  (i) to give an authorisation under section 219(3)(b),

  (j) to approve a decision to give such an authorisation, or

  (k) to apply for or otherwise seek any issue, grant, giving, modification, variation or renewal of a kind falling within paragraph (a), (b), (d), (e), (f) or (i).

(2) The public authority must have regard to—

  (a) whether what is sought to be achieved by the warrant, authorisation or notice could reasonably be achieved by other less intrusive means,

(b) whether the level of protection to be applied in relation to any obtaining of information by virtue of the warrant, authorisation or notice is higher because of the particular sensitivity of that information,

(c) the public interest in the integrity and security of telecommunication systems and postal services, and

(d) any other aspects of the public interest in the protection of privacy.

(3) The duties under subsection (2)—

(a) apply so far as they are relevant in the particular context, and

(b) are subject to the need to have regard to other considerations that are also relevant in that context.

(4) The other considerations may, in particular, include—

(a) the interests of national security or of the economic well-being of the United Kingdom,

(b) the public interest in preventing or detecting serious crime,

(c) other considerations which are relevant to—

(i) whether the conduct authorised or required by the warrant, authorisation or notice is proportionate, or

(ii) whether it is necessary to act for a purpose provided for by this Act,

(d) the requirements of the Human Rights Act 1998, and

(e) other requirements of public law.

(5) For the purposes of subsection (2)(b), examples of sensitive information include—

(a) items subject to legal privilege,

(b) any information identifying or confirming a source of journalistic information, and

(c) relevant confidential information within the meaning given by paragraph 2(4) of Schedule 7 (certain information held in confidence and consisting of personal records, journalistic material or communications between Members of Parliament and their constituents).

(6) ...

3–86 *********

PART 4 RETENTION OF COMMUNICATIONS DATA

General

87 Powers to require retention of certain data

(1) The Secretary of State may, by notice (a 'retention notice') and subject as follows, require a telecommunications operator to retain relevant communications data if—

(a) the Secretary of State considers that the requirement is necessary and proportionate for one or more of the [following purposes—

(i) in the interests of national security,

(ii) for the applicable crime purpose (see subsection (10A)),

(iii) in the interests of the economic well-being of the United Kingdom so far as those interests are also relevant to the interests of national security,

(iv) in the interests of public safety,

(v) for the purpose of preventing death or injury or any damage to a person's physical or mental health, or of mitigating any injury or damage to a person's physical or mental health,

(vi) to assist investigations into alleged miscarriages of justice,] and

(b) the decision to give the notice has been approved by a Judicial Commissioner.

(2) A retention notice may—

(a) relate to a particular operator or any description of operators,

(b) require the retention of all data or any description of data,

(c) identify the period or periods for which data is to be retained,

(d) contain other requirements, or restrictions, in relation to the retention of data,

(e) make different provision for different purposes,

    (f) relate to data whether or not in existence at the time of the giving, or coming into force, of the notice.

(3) A retention notice must not require any data to be retained for more than 12 months beginning with—

    (a) in the case of communications data relating to a specific communication, the day of the communication concerned,

    (b) in the case of entity data which does not fall within paragraph (a) above but does fall within paragraph (a)(i) of the definition of 'communications data' in section 261(5), the day on which the entity concerned ceases to be associated with the telecommunications service concerned or (if earlier) the day on which the data is changed, and

    (c) in any other case, the day on which the data is first held by the operator concerned.

(4) A retention notice must not require an operator who controls or provides a telecommunication system ('the system operator') to retain data which—

    (a) relates to the use of a telecommunications service provided by another telecommunications operator in relation to that system,

    (b) is (or is capable of being) processed by the system operator as a result of being comprised in, included as part of, attached to or logically associated with a communication transmitted by means of the system as a result of the use mentioned in paragraph (a),

    (c) is not needed by the system operator for the functioning of the system in relation to that communication, and

    (d) is not retained or used by the system operator for any other lawful purpose,

and which it is reasonably practicable to separate from other data which is subject to the notice.

(5) A retention notice which relates to data already in existence when the notice comes into force imposes a requirement to retain the data for only so much of a period of retention as occurs on or after the coming into force of the notice.

(6) A retention notice comes into force—

    (a) when the notice is given to the operator (or description of operators) concerned, or

    (b) (if later) at the time or times specified in the notice.

(7) A retention notice is given to an operator (or description of operators) by giving, or publishing, it in such manner as the Secretary of State considers appropriate for bringing it to the attention of the operator (or description of operators) to whom it relates.

(8) A retention notice must specify—

    (a) the operator (or description of operators) to whom it relates,

    [(aa) each telecommunications service (or description of telecommunications service) to which it relates,]

    (b) the data which is to be retained,

    (c) the period or periods for which the data is to be retained,

    (d) any other requirements, or any restrictions, in relation to the retention of the data,

    (e) the information required by section 249(7) (the level or levels of contribution in respect of costs incurred as a result of the notice).

(9) The requirements or restrictions mentioned in subsection (8)(d) may, in particular, include—

    (a) a requirement to retain the data in such a way that it can be transmitted efficiently and effectively in response to requests,

    (b) requirements or restrictions in relation to the obtaining (whether by collection, generation or otherwise), generation or processing of—

        (i)   data for retention, or

        (ii) retained data.

(10) The fact that the data which would be retained under a retention notice relates to the activities in the British Islands of a trade union is not, of itself, sufficient to establish that the requirement to retain the data is necessary for one or more of the purposes falling within [sub-paragraphs (i) to (vi) of subsection (1)(a)].

[(10A) In this section, 'the applicable crime purpose' means—

    (a) to the extent that a retention notice relates to events data, the purpose of preventing or detecting serious crime;

(b) to the extent that a retention notice relates to entity data, the purpose of preventing or detecting crime or of preventing disorder.

(10B) In subsection (10A)(a), 'serious crime' means, in addition to crime which falls within paragraph (a) or (b) of the definition of 'serious crime' in section 263(1), crime where the offence, or one of the offences, which is or would be constituted by the conduct concerned is—

(a) an offence for which an individual who has reached the age of 18 (or, in relation to Scotland or Northern Ireland, 21) is capable of being sentenced to imprisonment for a term of 12 months or more (disregarding any enactment prohibiting or restricting the imprisonment of individuals who have no previous convictions), or

(b) an offence—

    (i) by a person who is not an individual, or

    (ii) which involves, as an integral part of it, the sending of a communication or a breach of a person's privacy.]

(11) In this Part 'relevant communications data' means communications data which may be used to identify, or assist in identifying, any of the following—

(a) the sender or recipient of a communication (whether or not a person),

(b) the time or duration of a communication,

(c) the type, method or pattern, or fact, of communication,

(d) the telecommunication system (or any part of it) from, to or through which, or by means of which, a communication is or may be transmitted, or

(e) the location of any such system,

and this expression therefore includes, in particular, internet connection records.

Safeguards

88 Matters to be taken into account before giving retention notices

(1) Before giving a retention notice, the Secretary of State must, among other matters, take into account—

(a) the likely benefits of the notice[, including in relation to one or more of the purposes mentioned in sub-paragraphs (i) to (vi) of section 87(1)(a) (purposes for which retention of communications data may be required)],

[(aa) the telecommunications services to which the retention notice relates,

(ab) the appropriateness of limiting the data to be retained by reference to—

    (i) location, or

    (ii) descriptions of persons to whom telecommunications services are provided,]

(b) the likely number of users (if known) of any telecommunications service to which the notice relates,

(c) the technical feasibility of complying with the notice,

(d) the likely cost of complying with the notice, and

(e) any other effect of the notice on the telecommunications operator (or description of operators) to whom it relates.

(2) Before giving such a notice, the Secretary of State must take reasonable steps to consult any operator to whom it relates.

89 Approval of retention notices by Judicial Commissioners

(1) In deciding whether to approve a decision to give a retention notice, a Judicial Commissioner must review the Secretary of State's conclusions as to whether the requirement to be imposed by the notice to retain relevant communications data is necessary and proportionate for one or more of the purposes falling within [sub paragraphs (i) to (vi) of section 87 (1) (a).]

(2) In doing so, the Judicial Commissioner must—

(a) apply the same principles as would be applied by a court on an application for judicial review, and

(b) consider the matters referred to in subsection (1) with a sufficient degree of care as to ensure that the Judicial Commissioner complies with the duties imposed by section 2 (general duties in relation to privacy).

(3) Where a Judicial Commissioner refuses to approve a decision to give a retention notice, the Judicial Commissioner must give the Secretary of State written reasons for the refusal.

(4) Where a Judicial Commissioner, other than the Investigatory Powers Commissioner, refuses to approve a decision to give a retention notice, the Secretary of State may ask the Investigatory Powers Commissioner to decide whether to approve the decision to give the notice.

90, 91 *****

92 Data integrity and security

(1) A telecommunications operator who retains relevant communications data by virtue of this Part must—

    (a) secure that the data is of the same integrity, and subject to at least the same security and protection, as the data on any system from which it is derived,

    (b) secure, by appropriate technical and organisational measures, that the data can be accessed only by specially authorised personnel, and

    (c) protect, by appropriate technical and organisational measures, the data against accidental or unlawful destruction, accidental loss or alteration, or unauthorised or unlawful retention, processing, access or disclosure.

(2) A telecommunications operator who retains relevant communications data by virtue of this Part must destroy the data if the retention of the data ceases to be authorised by virtue of this Part and is not otherwise authorised by law.

(3) The destruction of the data may take place at such monthly or shorter intervals as appear to the operator to be practicable.

93 Disclosure of retained data

A telecommunications operator must put in place adequate security systems (including technical and organisational measures) governing access to relevant communications data retained by virtue of this Part in order to protect against any unlawful disclosure.

Variation or revocation of notices

94 Variation or revocation of notices

(1) The Secretary of State may vary a retention notice.

(2) The Secretary of State must give, or publish, notice of the variation in such manner as the Secretary of State considers appropriate for bringing the variation to the attention of the telecommunications operator (or description of operators) to whom it relates.

(3) A variation comes into force—

    (a) when notice of it is given or published in accordance with subsection (2), or

    (b) (if later) at the time or times specified in the notice of variation.

(4) A retention notice may not be varied so as to require the retention of additional relevant communications data unless—

    (a) the Secretary of State considers that the requirement is necessary and proportionate for one or more of the purposes falling within [sub paragraphs (i) to (vi) of section 87 (1) (a)], and

    (b) subject to subsection (6), the decision to vary the notice has been approved by a Judicial Commissioner.

(5) The fact that additional relevant communications data which would be retained under a retention notice as varied relates to the activities in the British Islands of a trade union is not, of itself, sufficient to establish that the requirement to retain the data is necessary for one or more of the purposes falling within [sub paragraphs (i) to (vi) of section 87 (1) (a).]

(6) Subsection (4)(b) does not apply to a variation to which section 90(11) applies.

(7) Section 87(2) and (5) apply in relation to a retention notice as varied as they apply in relation to a retention notice, but as if the references to the notice coming into force included references to the variation coming into force.

(8) Sections 87(3), (4) and (8), 95 and 97, and subsections (1), (4), (13) and (16) of this section, apply in relation to a retention notice as varied as they apply in relation to a retention notice.

(9) Section 88 applies in relation to the making of a variation as it applies in relation to the giving of a retention notice (and, accordingly, the references to the notice in section 88(1)(a) to (e) are to be read as references to the variation).

(10) Section 89 applies in relation to a decision to vary to which subsection (4)(b) above applies as it applies in relation to a decision to give a retention notice (and, accordingly, the reference in subsection (1) of that section to the requirement to be imposed by the notice is to be read as a reference to the requirement to be imposed by the variation).

(11) Section 90 applies (but only so far as the variation is concerned) in relation to a retention notice as varied (other than one varied as mentioned in subsection (10)(a) of that section) as it applies in relation to a retention notice.

(12) Section 91 applies in relation to a decision under section 90(10) to vary or confirm a variation as it applies in relation to a decision to vary or confirm a retention notice (and, accordingly, the reference in subsection (1) of that section to the requirement to be imposed by the notice as varied or confirmed is to be read as a reference to the requirement to be imposed by the variation as varied or confirmed).

(13) The Secretary of State may revoke (whether wholly or in part) a retention notice.

(14) The Secretary of State must give or publish notice of the revocation in such manner as the Secretary of State considers appropriate for bringing the revocation to the attention of the operator (or description of operators) to whom it relates.

(15) A revocation comes into force—

(a) when notice of it is given or published in accordance with subsection (14), or

(b) (if later) at the time or times specified in the notice of revocation.

(16) The fact that a retention notice has been revoked in relation to a particular description of communications data and a particular operator (or description of operators) does not prevent the giving of another retention notice in relation to the same description of data and the same operator (or description of operators).

Enforcement

95   Enforcement of notices and certain other requirements and restrictions

(1) It is the duty of a telecommunications operator on whom a requirement or restriction is imposed by—

(a) a retention notice, or

(b) section 92 or 93,

to comply with the requirement or restriction.

(2) A telecommunications operator, or any person employed or engaged for the purposes of the business of a telecommunications operator, must not disclose the existence or contents of a retention notice to any other person.

(3) The Information Commissioner, or any member of staff of the Information Commissioner, must not disclose the existence or contents of a retention notice to any other person.

(4) Subsections (2) and (3) do not apply to a disclosure made with the permission of the Secretary of State.

(5) The duty under subsection (1) or (2) is enforceable by civil proceedings by the Secretary of State for an injunction, or for specific performance of a statutory duty under section 45 of the Court of Session Act 1988, or for any other appropriate relief.

Further and supplementary provision

96   *****

97   Extra-territorial application of Part 4

(1) A retention notice, and any requirement or restriction imposed by virtue of a retention notice or by section 92, 93 or 95(1) to (3), may relate to conduct outside the United Kingdom and persons outside the United Kingdom.

(2) But section 95(5), so far as relating to those requirements or restrictions, does not apply to a person outside the United Kingdom.

98   Part 4: interpretation

(1) In this Part—

'notice' means notice in writing,

'relevant communications data' has the meaning given by section 87(11),

'retention notice' has the meaning given by section 87(1).

(2) *****

99–226   ***

PART 8 OVERSIGHT ARRANGEMENTS

Chapter 1   Investigatory Powers Commissioner and other Judicial Commissioners

The Commissioners

227   Investigatory Powers Commissioner and other Judicial Commissioners

(1) The Prime Minister must appoint—

(a) the Investigatory Powers Commissioner, and

(b) such number of other Judicial Commissioners as the Prime Minister considers necessary for the carrying out of the functions of the Judicial Commissioners.

(2) A person is not to be appointed as the Investigatory Powers Commissioner or another Judicial Commissioner unless the person holds or has held a high judicial office (within the meaning of Part 3 of the Constitutional Reform Act 2005).

(3) A person is not to be appointed as the Investigatory Powers Commissioner unless recommended jointly by—

(a) the Lord Chancellor,

(b) the Lord Chief Justice of England and Wales,

(c) the Lord President of the Court of Session, and

(d) the Lord Chief Justice of Northern Ireland.

(4) A person is not to be appointed as a Judicial Commissioner under subsection (1)(b) unless recommended jointly by—

(a) the Lord Chancellor,

(b) the Lord Chief Justice of England and Wales,

(c) the Lord President of the Court of Session,

(d) the Lord Chief Justice of Northern Ireland, and

(e) the Investigatory Powers Commissioner.

(5) Before appointing any person under subsection (1), the Prime Minister must consult the Scottish Ministers.

(6) The Prime Minister must have regard to a memorandum of understanding agreed between the Prime Minister and the Scottish Ministers when exercising functions under subsection (1) or (5).

(7) The Investigatory Powers Commissioner is a Judicial Commissioner and the Investigatory Powers Commissioner and the other Judicial Commissioners are to be known, collectively, as the Judicial Commissioners.

(8) The Investigatory Powers Commissioner may, to such extent as the Investigatory Powers Commissioner may decide, delegate the exercise of functions of the Investigatory Powers Commissioner to any other Judicial Commissioner.

(9) Subsection (8) does not apply to the function of the Investigatory Powers Commissioner of making a recommendation under subsection (4)(e) or making an appointment under section 247(1).

[(9A) Subsection (8) applies to the functions of the Investigatory Powers Commissioner under section 60A or 65(3B) only where the Investigatory Powers Commissioner is unable to exercise the functions because of illness or absence or for any other reason.]

(10) The delegation under subsection (8) to any extent of functions by the Investigatory Powers Commissioner does not prevent the exercise of the functions to that extent by that Commissioner.

(11) Any function exercisable by a Judicial Commissioner or any description of Judicial Commissioners is exercisable by any of the Judicial Commissioners or (as the case may be) any of the Judicial Commissioners of that description.

(12) Subsection (11) does not apply to—

(a) any function conferred on the Investigatory Powers Commissioner by name (except so far as its exercise by any of the Judicial Commissioners or any description of Judicial Commissioners is permitted by a delegation under subsection (8)), or

(b) any function conferred on, or delegated under subsection (8) to, any other particular named Judicial Commissioner.

(13) References in any enactment—

(a) to a Judicial Commissioner are to be read as including the Investigatory Powers Commissioner, and

(b) to the Investigatory Powers Commissioner are to be read, so far as necessary for the purposes of subsection (8), as references to the Investigatory Powers Commissioner or any other Judicial Commissioner.

228 Terms and conditions of appointment

(1) Subject as follows, each Judicial Commissioner holds and vacates office in accordance with the Commissioner's terms and conditions of appointment.

(2) Each Judicial Commissioner is to be appointed for a term of three years.

(3) A person who ceases to be a Judicial Commissioner (otherwise than under subsection (5)) may be re-appointed under section 227(1).

(4) A Judicial Commissioner may not, subject to subsection (5), be removed from office before the end of the term for which the Commissioner is appointed unless a resolution approving the removal has been passed by each House of Parliament.

(5) A Judicial Commissioner may be removed from office by the Prime Minister if, after the appointment of the Commissioner—

(a) a bankruptcy order is made against the Commissioner or the Commissioner's estate is sequestrated or the Commissioner makes a composition or arrangement with, or grants a trust deed for, the Commissioner's creditors,

(b) any of the following orders is made against the Commissioner—

(i) a disqualification order under the Company Directors Disqualification Act 1986 or the Company Directors Disqualification (Northern Ireland) Order 2002,

(ii) an order under section 429(2)(b) of the Insolvency Act 1986 (failure to pay under county court administration order),

(iii) an order under section 429(2) of the Insolvency Act 1986 (disabilities on revocation of county court administration order),

(c) the Commissioner's disqualification undertaking is accepted under section 7 or 8 of the Company Directors Disqualification Act 1986 or under the Company Directors Disqualification (Northern Ireland) Order 2002, or

(d) the Commissioner is convicted in the United Kingdom, the Channel Islands or the Isle of Man of an offence and receives a sentence of imprisonment (whether suspended or not).

229 *****

230 Additional directed oversight functions

(1) So far as directed to do so by the Prime Minister and subject to subsection (2), the Investigatory Powers Commissioner must keep under review the carrying out of any aspect of the functions of—

(a) an intelligence service,

(b) a head of an intelligence service, or

(c) any part of Her Majesty's forces, or of the Ministry of Defence, so far as engaging in intelligence activities.

(2) Subsection (1) does not apply in relation to anything which is required to be kept under review by the Investigatory Powers Commissioner under section 229.

(3) The Prime Minister may give a direction under this section at the request of the Investigatory Powers Commissioner or the Intelligence and Security Committee of Parliament or otherwise.

(4) The Prime Minister must publish, in a manner which the Prime Minister considers appropriate, any direction under this section (and any revocation of such a direction) except so far as it appears to the Prime Minister that such publication would be contrary to the public interest or prejudicial to—

(a) national security,

(b) the prevention or detection of serious crime,

(c) the economic well-being of the United Kingdom, or

(d) the continued discharge of the functions of any public authority whose activities include activities that are subject to review by the Investigatory Powers Commissioner.

*****

European Union (Notification of Withdrawal) Act 2017

(2017, c. 9)

An Act to confer power on the Prime Minister to notify, under Article 50(2) of the Treaty on European Union, the United Kingdom's intention to withdraw from the EU. [16th March 2017]

Territorial extent: United Kingdom

1 Power to notify withdrawal from the EU

(1) The Prime Minister may notify, under Article 50(2) of the Treaty on European Union, the United Kingdom's intention to withdraw from the EU.

(2) This section has effect despite any provision made by or under the European Communities Act 1972 or any other enactment.

2 *****

European Union (Withdrawal) Act 2018

(2018, c. 16)

An Act to repeal the European Communities Act 1972 and make other provision in connection with the withdrawal of the United Kingdom from the EU. [26th June 2018]

Territorial extent: United Kingdom

Repeal of the ECA

1 Repeal of the European Communities Act 1972

The European Communities Act 1972 is repealed on exit day.

[1A Saving for ECA for implementation period]

[(1)–(4) …

(5) Subsections (1) to (4) are repealed on IP completion day.

(6) In this Act—

'the implementation period' means the transition or implementation period provided for by Part 4 of the withdrawal agreement and beginning with exit day and ending on IP completion day;

'IP completion day' (and related expressions) have the same meaning as in the European Union (Withdrawal Agreement) Act 2020 (see section 39(1) to (5) of that Act);

'withdrawal agreement' has the same meaning as in that Act (see section 39(1) and (6) of that Act).

(7) In this Act—

(a) references to the European Communities Act 1972 are to be read, so far as the context permits or requires, as being or (as the case may be) including references to that Act as it continues to have effect by virtue of subsections (2) to (4) above, and

(b) references to any Part of the withdrawal agreement or the EEA EFTA separation agreement include references to any other provisions of that agreement so far as applying to that Part.]

[1B   Saving for EU-derived domestic legislation for implementation period]

[(1)–(5) ...

(6) Subsections (1) to (5) are repealed on IP completion day.

(7) In this Act 'EU-derived domestic legislation' means any enactment so far as—

(a) made under section 2(2) of, or paragraph 1A of Schedule 2 to, the European Communities Act 1972,

(b) passed or made, or operating, for a purpose mentioned in section 2(2)(a) or (b) of that Act,

(c) relating to—

(i) anything which falls within paragraph (a) or (b), or

(ii) any rights, powers, liabilities, obligations, restrictions, remedies or procedures which are recognised and available in domestic law by virtue of section 2(1) of the European Communities Act 1972, or

(d) relating otherwise to the EU or the EEA,

but does not include any enactment contained in the European Communities Act 1972 or any enactment contained in this Act or the European Union (Withdrawal Agreement) Act 2020 or in regulations made under this Act or the Act of 2020.]

Retention of existing EU law [saved EU law at end of implementation period]

2   Saving for EU-derived domestic legislation

(1) EU-derived domestic legislation, as it has effect in domestic law immediately before [IP completion day], continues to have effect in domestic law on and after [IP completion day].

(2) ...

(3) This section is subject to section 5 and Schedule 1 (exceptions to savings and incorporation) [and section 5A (savings and incorporation: supplementary)].

3   Incorporation of direct EU legislation

(1) Direct EU legislation, so far as operative immediately before [IP completion day], forms part of domestic law on and after [IP completion day].

(2) In this Act 'direct EU legislation' means—

(a) any EU regulation, EU decision or EU tertiary legislation, as it has effect in EU law immediately before [IP completion day] and so far as—

(i) it is not an exempt EU instrument (for which see section 20(1) and Schedule 6), [and]

[(ai) it is applicable to and in the United Kingdom by virtue of Part 4 of the withdrawal agreement,

(bi) it neither has effect nor is to have effect by virtue of section 7A or 7B,]

(ii) ...

(iii) its effect is not reproduced in an enactment to which section 2(1) applies,

(b) any Annex to the EEA agreement, as it has effect in EU law immediately before [IP completion day] and so far as—

[(ai) it is applicable to and in the United Kingdom by virtue of Part 4 of the withdrawal agreement,

(bi) it neither has effect nor is to have effect by virtue of section 7A or 7B,]

(i) it refers to, or contains adaptations of, anything falling within paragraph (a), and

(ii) its effect is not reproduced in an enactment to which section 2(1) applies, or

(c) Protocol 1 to the EEA agreement (which contains horizontal adaptations that apply in relation to EU instruments referred to in the Annexes to that agreement), as it has effect in EU law immediately before [IP completion day and so far as—

    (i) it is applicable to and in the United Kingdom by virtue of Part 4 of the withdrawal agreement, and

    (ii) it neither has effect nor is to have effect by virtue of section 7A or 7B].

(3) For the purposes of this Act, any direct EU legislation is operative immediately before [IP completion day] if—

(a) in the case of anything which comes into force at a particular time and is stated to apply from a later time, it is in force and applies immediately before [IP completion day],

(b) in the case of a decision which specifies to whom it is addressed, it has been notified to that person before [IP completion day], and

(c) in any other case, it is in force immediately before [IP completion day].

(4) This section—

(a) brings into domestic law any direct EU legislation only in the form of the English language version of that legislation, and

(b) does not apply to any such legislation for which there is no such version,

but paragraph (a) does not affect the use of the other language versions of that legislation for the purposes of interpreting it.

(5) This section is subject to section 5 and Schedule 1 (exceptions to savings and incorporation) [and section 5A (savings and incorporation: supplementary)].

4   Saving for rights etc. under section 2(1) of the ECA

(1) Any rights, powers, liabilities, obligations, restrictions, remedies and procedures which, immediately before [IP completion day]—

(a) are recognised and available in domestic law by virtue of section 2(1) of the European Communities Act 1972, and

(b) are enforced, allowed and followed accordingly,

continue on and after [IP completion day] to be recognised and available in domestic law (and to be enforced, allowed and followed accordingly).

(2) Subsection (1) does not apply to any rights, powers, liabilities, obligations, restrictions, remedies or procedures so far as they—

(a) form part of domestic law by virtue of section 3, or

[(aa) are, or are to be, recognised and available in domestic law (and enforced, allowed and followed accordingly) by virtue of section 7A or 7B,] or

(b) arise under an EU directive (including as applied by the EEA agreement) and are not of a kind recognised by the European Court or any court or tribunal in the United Kingdom in a case decided before [IP completion day] (whether or not as an essential part of the decision in the case).

(3) This section is subject to section 5 and Schedule 1 (exceptions to savings and incorporation) [and section 5A (savings and incorporation: supplementary)].

5   Exceptions to savings and incorporation

(1) The principle of the supremacy of EU law does not apply to any enactment or rule of law passed or made on or after [IP completion day].

(2) Accordingly, the principle of the supremacy of EU law continues to apply on or after [IP completion day] so far as relevant to the interpretation, disapplication or quashing of any enactment or rule of law passed or made before [IP completion day].

(3) Subsection (1) does not prevent the principle of the supremacy of EU law from applying to a modification made on or after [IP completion day] of any enactment or rule of law passed or made before [IP completion day] if the application of the principle is consistent with the intention of the modification.

(4) The Charter of Fundamental Rights is not part of domestic law on or after [IP completion day].

(5) Subsection (4) does not affect the retention in domestic law on or after [IP completion day] in accordance with this Act of any fundamental rights or principles which exist irrespective of the Charter (and references to the Charter in any case law are, so far as necessary for this purpose, to be read as if they were references to any corresponding retained fundamental rights or principles).

(6) Schedule 1 (which makes further provision about exceptions to savings and incorporation) has effect.

[(7) Subsections (1) to (6) and Schedule 1 are subject to relevant separation agreement law (for which see section 7C).]

[5A   Savings and incorporation: supplementary]

[The fact that anything which continues to be, or forms part of, domestic law on or after IP completion day by virtue of section 2, 3 or 4 has an effect immediately before IP completion day which is time-limited by reference to the implementation period does not prevent it from having an indefinite effect on and after IP completion day by virtue of section 2, 3 or 4.]

6   Interpretation of retained EU law

(1) A court or tribunal—

    (a) is not bound by any principles laid down, or any decisions made, on or after [IP completion day] by the European Court, and

    (b) cannot refer any matter to the European Court on or after [IP completion day].

(2) Subject to this and subsections (3) to (6), a court or tribunal may have regard to anything done on or after [IP completion day] by the European Court, another EU entity or the EU so far as it is relevant to any matter before the court or tribunal.

(3) Any question as to the validity, meaning or effect of any retained EU law is to be decided, so far as that law is unmodified on or after [IP completion day] and so far as they are relevant to it—

    (a) in accordance with any retained case law and any retained general principles of EU law, and

    (b) having regard (among other things) to the limits, immediately before [IP completion day], of EU competences.

(4) But—

    (a)   the Supreme Court is not bound by any retained EU case law,

    (b)   the High Court of Justiciary is not bound by any retained EU case law when—

        (i)   sitting as a court of appeal otherwise than in relation to a compatibility issue (within the meaning given by section 288ZA(2) of the Criminal Procedure (Scotland) Act 1995) or a devolution issue (within the meaning given by paragraph 1 of Schedule 6 to the Scotland Act 1998), or

        (ii)   sitting on a reference under section 123(1) of the Criminal Procedure (Scotland) Act 1995,

    [(ba) a relevant court or relevant tribunal is not bound by any retained EU case law so far as is provided for by regulations under subsection (5A),] and

    (c)   no court or tribunal is bound by any retained domestic case law that it would not otherwise be bound by.

(5) In deciding whether to depart from any retained EU case law [by virtue of subsection (4)(a) or (b)], the Supreme Court or the High Court of Justiciary must apply the same test as it would apply in deciding whether to depart from its own case law.

[(5A) A Minister of the Crown may by regulations provide for—

    (a) a court or tribunal to be a relevant court or (as the case may be) a relevant tribunal for the purposes of this section,

(b) the extent to which, or circumstances in which, a relevant court or relevant tribunal is not to be bound by retained EU case law,

(c) the test which a relevant court or relevant tribunal must apply in deciding whether to depart from any retained EU case law, or

(d) considerations which are to be relevant to—

  (i) the Supreme Court or the High Court of Justiciary in applying the test mentioned in subsection (5), or

  (ii) a relevant court or relevant tribunal in applying any test provided for by virtue of paragraph (c) above.

(5B) Regulations under subsection (5A) may (among other things) provide for—

(a) the High Court of Justiciary to be a relevant court when sitting otherwise than as mentioned in subsection (4)(b)(i) and (ii),

(b) the extent to which, or circumstances in which, a relevant court or relevant tribunal not being bound by retained EU case law includes (or does not include) that court or tribunal not being bound by retained domestic case law which relates to retained EU case law,

(c) other matters arising in relation to retained domestic case law which relates to retained EU case law (including by making provision of a kind which could be made in relation to retained EU case law), or

(d) the test mentioned in paragraph (c) of subsection (5A) or the considerations mentioned in paragraph (d) of that subsection to be determined (whether with or without the consent of a Minister of the Crown) by a person mentioned in subsection (5C)(a) to (e) or by more than one of those persons acting jointly.

(5C) Before making regulations under subsection (5A), a Minister of the Crown must consult—

(a) the President of the Supreme Court,

(b) the Lord Chief Justice of England and Wales,

(c) the Lord President of the Court of Session,

(d) the Lord Chief Justice of Northern Ireland,

(e) the Senior President of Tribunals, and

(f) such other persons as the Minister of the Crown considers appropriate.

(5D) No regulations may be made under subsection (5A) after IP completion day.]

(6) Subsection (3) does not prevent the validity, meaning or effect of any retained EU law which has been modified on or after [IP completion day] from being decided as provided for in that subsection if doing so is consistent with the intention of the modifications.

[(6A) Subsections (1) to (6) are subject to relevant separation agreement law (for which see section 7C).]

(7) In this Act—

'retained case law' means—

(a) retained domestic case law, and

(b) retained EU case law;

'retained domestic case law' means any principles laid down by, and any decisions of, a court or tribunal in the United Kingdom, as they have effect immediately before [IP completion day] and so far as they—

(a) relate to anything to which section 2, 3 or 4 applies, and

(b) are not excluded by section 5 or Schedule 1,

(as those principles and decisions are modified by or under this Act or by other domestic law from time to time);

'retained EU case law' means any principles laid down by, and any decisions of, the European Court, as they have effect in EU law immediately before [IP completion day] and so far as they—

(a) relate to anything to which section 2, 3 or 4 applies, and

(b) are not excluded by section 5 or Schedule 1,

(as those principles and decisions are modified by or under this Act or by other domestic law from time to time);

'retained EU law' means anything which, on or after [IP completion day], continues to be, or forms part of, domestic law by virtue of section 2, 3 or 4 or subsection (3) or (6) above (as that body of law is added to or otherwise modified by or under this Act or by other domestic law from time to time);

'retained general principles of EU law' means the general principles of EU law, as they have effect in EU law immediately before [IP completion day] and so far as they—

(a) relate to anything to which section 2, 3 or 4 applies, and

(b) are not excluded by section 5 or Schedule 1,

(as those principles are modified by or under this Act or by other domestic law from time to time).

7 Status of retained EU law

(1) Anything which—

(a) was, immediately before exit day, primary legislation of a particular kind, subordinate legislation of a particular kind or another enactment of a particular kind, and

(b) continues to be domestic law on and after exit day by virtue of section [section 1A(2) or 1B(2)],

continues to be domestic law as an enactment of the same kind.

[(1A) Anything which—

(a) was, immediately before IP completion day, primary legislation of a particular kind, subordinate legislation of a particular kind or another enactment of a particular kind, and

(b) continues to be domestic law on and after IP completion day by virtue of section 2,

continues to be domestic law as an enactment of the same kind.]

(2) Retained direct principal EU legislation cannot be modified by any primary or subordinate legislation other than—

(a) an Act of Parliament,

(b) any other primary legislation (so far as it has the power to make such a modification), or

(c) any subordinate legislation so far as it is made under a power which permits such a modification by virtue of—

(i) paragraph 3, 5(3)(a) or (4)(a), 8(3), 10(3)(a) or (4)(a), 11(2)(a) or 12(3) of Schedule 8,

(ii) any other provision made by or under this Act,

(iii) any provision made by or under an Act of Parliament passed before, and in the same Session as, this Act, or

(iv) any provision made on or after the passing of this Act by or under primary legislation.

(3) Retained direct minor EU legislation cannot be modified by any primary or subordinate legislation other than—

(a) an Act of Parliament,

(b) any other primary legislation (so far as it has the power to make such a modification), or

(c) any subordinate legislation so far as it is made under a power which permits such a modification by virtue of—

(i) paragraph 3, 5(2) or (4)(a), 8(3), 10(2) or (4)(a) or 12(3) of Schedule 8,

(ii) any other provision made by or under this Act,

(iii) any provision made by or under an Act of Parliament passed before, and in the same Session as, this Act, or

(iv) any provision made on or after the passing of this Act by or under primary legislation.

(4) Anything which is retained EU law by virtue of section 4 cannot be modified by any primary or subordinate legislation other than—

(a) an Act of Parliament,

(b) any other primary legislation (so far as it has the power to make such a modification), or

(c) any subordinate legislation so far as it is made under a power which permits such a modification by virtue of—

(i) paragraph 3, 5(3)(b) or (4)(b), 8(3), 10(3)(b) or (4)(b), 11(2)(b) or 12(3) of Schedule 8,

(ii) any other provision made by or under this Act,

(iii) any provision made by or under an Act of Parliament passed before, and in the same Session as, this Act, or

(iv) any provision made on or after the passing of this Act by or under primary legislation.

(5) For other provisions about the status of retained EU law, see—

(a) section 5(1) to (3) [and (7)] (status of retained EU law in relation to other enactments or rules of law),

(b) section 6 (status of retained case law and retained general principles of EU law),

[(ba) section 7C (status of case law of European Court etc in relation to retained EU law which is relevant separation agreement law),]

(c) section 15(2) and Part 2 of Schedule 5 (status of retained EU law for the purposes of the rules of evidence),

(d) paragraphs 13 to 16 of Schedule 8 (affirmative and enhanced scrutiny procedure for, and information about, instruments which amend or revoke subordinate legislation under section 2(2) of the European Communities Act 1972 including subordinate legislation implementing EU directives),

(e) paragraphs 19 and 20 of that Schedule (status of certain retained direct EU legislation for the purposes of the Interpretation Act 1978), and

(f) paragraph 30 of that Schedule (status of retained direct EU legislation for the purposes of the Human Rights Act 1998).

(6) In this Act—

'retained direct minor EU legislation' means any retained direct EU legislation which is not retained direct principal EU legislation;

'retained direct principal EU legislation' means—

(a) any EU regulation so far as it—

(i) forms part of domestic law on and after exit day by virtue of section 3, and

(ii) was not EU tertiary legislation immediately before [IP completion day], or

(b) any Annex to the EEA agreement so far as it—

(i) forms part of domestic law on and after [IP completion day] by virtue of section 3, and

(ii) refers to, or contains adaptations of, any EU regulation so far as it falls within paragraph (a),

(as modified by or under this Act or by other domestic law from time to time).

[Further aspects of withdrawal]

[7A   General implementation of remainder of withdrawal agreement]

[(1) Subsection (2) applies to—

(a) all such rights, powers, liabilities, obligations and restrictions from time to time created or arising by or under the withdrawal agreement, and

(b)   all such remedies and procedures from time to time provided for by or under the withdrawal agreement,

as in accordance with the withdrawal agreement are without further enactment to be given legal effect or used in the United Kingdom.

(2) The rights, powers, liabilities, obligations, restrictions, remedies and procedures concerned are to be—

(a) recognised and available in domestic law, and

(b) enforced, allowed and followed accordingly.

(3) Every enactment (including an enactment contained in this Act) is to be read and has effect subject to subsection (2).

(4) This section does not apply in relation to Part 4 of the withdrawal agreement so far as section 2(1) of the European Communities Act 1972 applies in relation to that Part.

(5) See also (among other things)—

(a) Part 3 of the European Union (Withdrawal Agreement) Act 2020 (further provision about citizens' rights),

(b) section 20 of that Act (financial provision),

(c) section 7C of this Act (interpretation of law relating to withdrawal agreement etc),

(d) section 8B of this Act (power in connection with certain other separation issues),

(e) section 8C of this Act (power in connection with the Protocol on Ireland/Northern Ireland in withdrawal agreement), and

(f) Parts 1B and 1C of Schedule 2 to this Act (powers involving devolved authorities in connection with certain other separation issues and the Ireland/Northern Ireland Protocol).]

[7B   General implementation of EEA EFTA and Swiss agreements]

[(1) Subsection (2) applies to all such rights, powers, liabilities, obligations, restrictions, remedies and procedures as—

(a) would from time to time be created or arise, or (in the case of remedies or procedures) be provided for, by or under the EEA EFTA separation agreement or the Swiss citizens' rights agreement, and

(b) would, in accordance with Article 4(1) of the withdrawal agreement, be required to be given legal effect or used in the United Kingdom without further enactment,

if that Article were to apply in relation to the EEA EFTA separation agreement and the Swiss citizens' rights agreement, those agreements were part of EU law and the relevant EEA states and Switzerland were member States.

(2) The rights, powers, liabilities, obligations, restrictions, remedies and procedures concerned are to be—

(a) recognised and available in domestic law, and

(b) enforced, allowed and followed accordingly.

(3) Every enactment (other than section 7A but otherwise including an enactment contained in this Act) is to be read and has effect subject to subsection (2).

(4) See also (among other things)—

(a) Part 3 of the European Union (Withdrawal Agreement) Act 2020 (further provision about citizens' rights),

(b) section 7C of this Act (interpretation of law relating to the EEA EFTA separation agreement and the Swiss citizens' rights agreement etc),

(c) section 8B of this Act (power in connection with certain other separation issues), and

(d) Part 1B of Schedule 2 to this Act (powers involving devolved authorities in connection with certain other separation issues).

(5) In this section 'the relevant EEA states' means Norway, Iceland and Liechtenstein

(6) In this Act 'EEA EFTA separation agreement' and 'Swiss citizens' rights agreement' have the same meanings as in the European Union (Withdrawal Agreement) Act 2020 (see section 39(1) of that Act).]

[7C   Interpretation of relevant separation agreement law]

[(1) Any question as to the validity, meaning or effect of any relevant separation agreement law is to be decided, so far as they are applicable—

(a) in accordance with the withdrawal agreement, the EEA EFTA separation agreement and the Swiss citizens' rights agreement, and

(b) having regard (among other things) to the desirability of ensuring that, where one of those agreements makes provision which corresponds to provision made by another of those agreements, the effect of relevant separation agreement law in relation to the matters dealt with by the corresponding provision in each agreement is consistent.

(2) See (among other things)—

(a) Article 4 of the withdrawal agreement (methods and principles relating to the effect, the implementation and the application of the agreement),

    (b) Articles 158 and 160 of the withdrawal agreement (jurisdiction of the European Court in relation to Part 2 and certain provisions of Part 5 of the agreement),

    (c) Articles 12 and 13 of the Protocol on Ireland/Northern Ireland in the withdrawal agreement (implementation, application, supervision and enforcement of the Protocol and common provisions),

    (d) Article 4 of the EEA EFTA separation agreement (methods and principles relating to the effect, the implementation and the application of the agreement), and

    (e) Article 4 of the Swiss citizens' rights agreement (methods and principles relating to the effect, the implementation and the application of the agreement).

(3) In this Act 'relevant separation agreement law' means—

    (a) any of the following provisions or anything which is domestic law by virtue of any of them—

        (i) section 7A, 7B, 8B or 8C or Part 1B or 1C of Schedule 2 or this section, or

        (ii) Part 3, or section 20, of the European Union (Withdrawal Agreement) Act 2020 (citizens' rights and financial provision), or

    (b) anything not falling within paragraph (a) so far as it is domestic law for the purposes of, or otherwise within the scope of—

        (i) the withdrawal agreement (other than Part 4 of that agreement),

        (ii) the EEA EFTA separation agreement, or

        (iii) the Swiss citizens' rights agreement,

as that body of law is added to or otherwise modified by or under this Act or by other domestic law from time to time.]

Main powers in connection with withdrawal

8 Dealing with deficiencies arising from withdrawal

(1) A Minister of the Crown may by regulations make such provision as the Minister considers appropriate to prevent, remedy or mitigate—

    (a) any failure of retained EU law to operate effectively, or

    (b) any other deficiency in retained EU law,

arising from the withdrawal of the United Kingdom from the EU.

(2) Deficiencies in retained EU law are where the Minister considers that retained EU law—

    (a) contains anything which has no practical application in relation to the United Kingdom or any part of it or is otherwise redundant or substantially redundant,

    (b) confers functions on, or in relation to, EU entities which no longer have functions in that respect under EU law in relation to the United Kingdom or any part of it,

    (c) makes provision for, or in connection with, reciprocal arrangements between—

        (i) the United Kingdom or any part of it or a public authority in the United Kingdom, and

        (ii) the EU, an EU entity, a member State or a public authority in a member State,

    which no longer exist or are no longer appropriate,

    (d) makes provision for, or in connection with, other arrangements which—

        (i) involve the EU, an EU entity, a member State or a public authority in a member State, or

        (ii) are otherwise dependent upon the United Kingdom's membership of the EU [or Part 4 of the withdrawal agreement],

    and which no longer exist or are no longer appropriate,

    (e) makes provision for, or in connection with, any reciprocal or other arrangements not falling within paragraph (c) or (d) which no longer exist, or are no longer appropriate, as a result of the United Kingdom ceasing to be a party to any of the EU Treaties [or as a result of either the end of the implementation period or any other effect of the withdrawal agreement],

    [(ea) is not clear in its effect as a result of the operation of any provision of sections 2 to 6 or Schedule 1,]

(f) does not contain any functions or restrictions which—
  (i) were in an EU directive and in force immediately before [IP completion day] (including any power to make EU tertiary legislation), and
  (ii) it is appropriate to retain, or
(g) contains EU references which are no longer appropriate.

(3) There is also a deficiency in retained EU law where the Minister considers that there is—
(a) anything in retained EU law which is of a similar kind to any deficiency which falls within subsection (2), or
(b) a deficiency in retained EU law of a kind described, or provided for, in regulations made by a Minister of the Crown.

(4) But retained EU law is not deficient merely because it does not contain any modification of EU law which is adopted or notified, comes into force or only applies on or after [IP completion day].

(5) Regulations under subsection (1) may make any provision that could be made by an Act of Parliament.

(6) Regulations under subsection (1) may (among other things) provide for functions of EU entities or public authorities in member States (including making an instrument of a legislative character or providing funding) to be—
(a) exercisable instead by a public authority (whether or not established for the purpose) in the United Kingdom, or
(b) replaced, abolished or otherwise modified.

(7) But regulations under subsection (1) may not—
(a) impose or increase taxation or fees,
(b) make retrospective provision,
(c) create a relevant criminal offence,
(d) establish a public authority,
(e) …
(f) amend, repeal or revoke the Human Rights Act 1998 or any subordinate legislation made under it, or
(g) amend or repeal the Scotland Act 1998, the Government of Wales Act 2006 or the Northern Ireland Act 1998 (unless the regulations are made by virtue of paragraph 21(b) of Schedule 7 to this Act or are amending or repealing any provision of those Acts which modifies another enactment).

(8) No regulations may be made under this section after the end of the period of two years beginning with [IP completion day].

(9) The reference in subsection (1) to a failure or other deficiency arising from the withdrawal of the United Kingdom from the EU includes a reference to any failure or other deficiency arising m[—
(a) any aspect of that withdrawal, including (among other things)—
  (i) the end of the implementation period, or
  (ii) any other effect of the withdrawal agreement, or
(b) that withdrawal, or any such aspect of it, taken together] with the operation of any provision, or the interaction between any provisions, made by or under this Act [or the European Union (Withdrawal Agreement) Act 2020].

[8A   Supplementary power in connection with implementation period]

[(1) A Minister of the Crown may by regulations—
(a) provide for other modifications for the purposes of section 1B(3)(f)(i) (whether applying in all cases or particular cases or descriptions of case),
(b) provide for subsection (3) or (4) of section 1B not to apply to any extent in particular cases or descriptions of case,
(c) make different provision in particular cases or descriptions of case to that made by subsection (3) or (4) of that section,

(d) modify any enactment contained in this Act in consequence of any repeal made by section 1A(5) or 1B(6), or

(e) make such provision not falling within paragraph (a), (b), (c) or (d) as the Minister considers appropriate for any purpose of, or otherwise in connection with, Part 4 of the withdrawal agreement.

(2) The power to make regulations under subsection (1) may (among other things) be exercised by modifying any provision made by or under an enactment.

(3) In subsection (2) 'enactment' does not include primary legislation passed or made after IP completion day.

(4) No regulations may be made under subsection (1) after the end of the period of two years beginning with IP completion day.]

[8B Power in connection with certain other separation issues]

[(1) A Minister of the Crown may by regulations make such provision as the Minister considers appropriate—

(a) to implement Part 3 of the withdrawal agreement (separation provisions),

(b) to supplement the effect of section 7A in relation to that Part, or

(c) otherwise for the purposes of dealing with matters arising out of, or related to, that Part (including matters arising by virtue of section 7A and that Part).

(2) A Minister of the Crown may by regulations make such provision as the Minister considers appropriate—

(a) to implement Part 3 of the EEA EFTA separation agreement (separation provisions),

(b) to supplement the effect of section 7B in relation to that Part, or

(c) otherwise for the purposes of dealing with matters arising out of, or related to, that Part (including matters arising by virtue of section 7B and that Part).

(3) Regulations under this section may make any provision that could be made by an Act of Parliament.

(4) Regulations under this section may (among other things) restate, for the purposes of making the law clearer or more accessible, anything that forms part of domestic law by virtue of—

(a) section 7A above and Part 3 of the withdrawal agreement, or

(b) section 7B above and Part 3 of the EEA EFTA separation agreement.

(5) But regulations under this section may not—

(a) impose or increase taxation or fees,

(b) make retrospective provision,

(c) create a relevant criminal offence,

(d) establish a public authority,

(e) amend, repeal or revoke the Human Rights Act 1998 or any subordinate legislation made under it, or

(f) amend or repeal the Scotland Act 1998, the Government of Wales Act 2006 or the Northern Ireland Act 1998 (unless the regulations are made by virtue of paragraph 21(b) of Schedule 7 to this Act or are amending or repealing any provision of those Acts which modifies another enactment).

(6) In this section references to Part 3 of the withdrawal agreement or of the EEA EFTA separation agreement include references to any provision of EU law which is applied by, or referred to in, that Part (to the extent of the application or reference).]

[8C Power in connection with Ireland/Northern Ireland Protocol in withdrawal agreement]

[(1) A Minister of the Crown may by regulations make such provision as the Minister considers appropriate—

(a) to implement the Protocol on Ireland/Northern Ireland in the withdrawal agreement,

(b) to supplement the effect of section 7A in relation to the Protocol, or

(c) otherwise for the purposes of dealing with matters arising out of, or related to, the Protocol (including matters arising by virtue of section 7A and the Protocol).

(2) Regulations under subsection (1) may make any provision that could be made by an Act of Parliament (including modifying this Act).

(3) Regulations under subsection (1) may (among other things) make provision facilitating the access to the market within Great Britain of qualifying Northern Ireland goods.

(4) Such provision may (among other things) include provision about the recognition within Great Britain of technical regulations, assessments, registrations, certificates, approvals and authorisations issued by—

> (a) the authorities of a member State, or
>
> (b) bodies established in a member State,

in respect of qualifying Northern Ireland goods.

(5) Regulations under subsection (1) may (among other things) restate, for the purposes of making the law clearer or more accessible, anything that forms part of domestic law by virtue of section 7A and the Protocol.

[(5A) Regulations under subsection (1) may not amend, repeal or otherwise modify the operation of section 47 of the United Kingdom Internal Market Act 2020 ('the 2020 Act'), except by making—

> (a) provision of the sort that is contemplated by section 47(2) of the 2020 Act (permitted checks);
>
> (b) provision under subsection (6);
>
> (c) provision of the sort described in paragraph 21(b) of Schedule 7 (supplementary and transitional provision etc) in connection with—
>
>> (i)   provision within either of the preceding paragraphs;
>>
>> (ii) Articles 5 to 10 of the Northern Ireland Protocol ceasing to apply (and the resulting operation of section 55(1) of the 2020 Act).]

(6) A Minister of the Crown may by regulations define 'qualifying Northern Ireland goods' for the purposes of this Act.

(7) In this section any reference to the Protocol on Ireland/Northern Ireland includes a reference to—

> (a) any other provision of the withdrawal agreement so far as applying to the Protocol, and
>
> (b) any provision of EU law which is applied by, or referred to in, the Protocol (to the extent of the application or reference),

but does not include the second sentence of Article 11(1) of the Protocol (which provides that the United Kingdom and the Republic of Ireland may continue to make new arrangements that build on the provisions of the Belfast Agreement in other areas of North-South cooperation on the island of Ireland).]

9 ...

Devolution

10 [Protection for] North-South co-operation and ... prevention of new border arrangements

(1) In exercising any of the powers under this Act, a Minister of the Crown or devolved authority must—

> (a) act in a way that is compatible with the terms of the Northern Ireland Act 1998, and
>
> (b) have due regard to the joint report from the negotiators of the EU and the United Kingdom Government on progress during phase 1 of negotiations under Article 50 of the Treaty on European Union.

(2) Nothing in section 8 ... or 23(1) or (6) of this Act authorises regulations which—

> (a) diminish any form of North-South cooperation provided for by the Belfast Agreement ..., or
>
> (b) create or facilitate border arrangements between Northern Ireland and the Republic of Ireland after exit day which feature physical infrastructure, including border posts, or checks and controls, that did not exist before exit day and are not in accordance with an agreement between the United Kingdom and the EU.

[(3) A Minister of the Crown may not agree to the making of a recommendation by the Joint Committee under Article 11(2) of the Protocol on Ireland/Northern Ireland in the withdrawal agreement (recommendations as to North-South cooperation) to—

    (a) alter the arrangements for North-South co-operation as provided for by the Belfast Agreement,

    (b) establish a new implementation body, or

    (c) alter the functions of an existing implementation body.

    (4) In this section—

'the Belfast Agreement' has the meaning given by section 98 of the Northern Ireland Act 1998;

'implementation body' has the meaning given by section 55(3) of that Act.]

11   Powers involving devolved authorities corresponding to sections 8 [to 8C]

Schedule 2 (which confers powers to make regulations involving devolved authorities which correspond to the powers conferred by sections 8 [to 8C]) has effect.

12   *****

Parliamentary [oversight of withdrawal]

13   ...

[13A   Review of EU legislation during implementation period]

[(1) Subsection (2) applies where the European Scrutiny Select Committee of the House of Commons ('the ESC') publishes a report in respect of any EU legislation made, or which may be made, during the implementation period and the report—

    (a) states that, in the opinion of the ESC, the EU legislation raises a matter of vital national interest to the United Kingdom,

    (b) confirms that the ESC has taken such evidence as it considers appropriate as to the effect of the EU legislation and has consulted any Departmental Select Committee of the House of Commons which the ESC considers also has an interest in the EU legislation, and

    (c) sets out the wording of a motion to be moved in the House of Commons in accordance with subsection (2).

    (2) A Minister of the Crown must, within the period of 14 Commons sitting days beginning with the day on which the report is published, make arrangements for the motion mentioned in subsection (1)(c) to be debated and voted on by the House of Commons.

    (3) Subsection (4) applies where the EU Select Committee of the House of Lords ('the EUC') publishes a report in respect of any EU legislation made, or which may be made, during the implementation period and the report—

    (a) states that, in the opinion of the EUC, the EU legislation raises a matter of vital national interest to the United Kingdom,

    (b) confirms that the EUC has taken such evidence as it considers appropriate as to the effect of the EU legislation, and

    (c) sets out the wording of a motion to be moved in the House of Lords in accordance with subsection (4).

    (4) A Minister of the Crown must, within the period of 14 Lords sitting days beginning with the day on which the report is published, make arrangements for the motion mentioned in subsection (3)(c) to be debated and voted on by the House of Lords.

    (5) In this section—

'EU legislation' means—

    (a) any amendment to the Treaty on European Union, the Treaty on the Functioning of the European Union, the Euratom Treaty or the EEA agreement,

    (b) any EU directive, or

    (c) any EU regulation or EU decision which is not EU tertiary legislation;

'the European Scrutiny Select Committee of the House of Commons' means the Select Committee of the House of Commons known as the European Scrutiny Select Committee or any successor of that committee;

'the EU Select Committee of the House of Lords' means the Select Committee of the House of Lords known as the EU Select Committee or any successor of that committee.]

[13B]–15   *****

15A   Prohibition on extending implementation period

A Minister of the Crown may not agree in the Joint Committee to an extension of the implementation period.

15B   Ministerial co-chairs of the Joint Committee

The functions of the United Kingdom's co-chair of the Joint Committee, under Annex VIII of the withdrawal agreement (rules of procedure of the Joint Committee and specialised committees), are to be exercised personally by a Minister of the Crown (and, accordingly, only a Minister of the Crown may be designated as a replacement under Rule 1(3)).

15C   No use of written procedure in the Joint Committee

(1) The United Kingdom's co-chair of the Joint Committee may not consent to the Joint Committee using the written procedure provided for in Rule 9(1) of Annex VIII of the withdrawal agreement.

(2) In subsection (1) the reference to the United Kingdom's co-chair of the Joint Committee includes a reference to any designee of the co-chair designated under Rule 1(3) of Annex VIII of the withdrawal agreement.

16   ...

17   Family unity for those seeking asylum or other protection in Europe

[(1) A Minister of the Crown must, within the period of two months beginning with the day on which the European Union (Withdrawal Agreement) Act 2020 is passed, lay before Parliament a statement of policy in relation to any future arrangements between the United Kingdom and the EU about—

(a) unaccompanied children, who make an application for international protection to a member State, coming to the United Kingdom where it is in their best interests to join a relative who—

    (i)   is a lawful resident of the United Kingdom, or

    (ii) has made a protection claim which has not been decided, and

(b) unaccompanied children in the United Kingdom, who make a protection claim, going to a member State to join a relative there in equivalent circumstances.]

(2)–(4) *****

18, 19   ...

20–25, Schedule 1   *****

SCHEDULE 2 CORRESPONDING POWERS INVOLVING DEVOLVED AUTHORITIES

PART 1 DEALING WITH DEFICIENCIES ARISING FROM WITHDRAWAL

Power to deal with deficiencies

1.—(1) A devolved authority may by regulations make such provision as the devolved authority considers appropriate to prevent, remedy or mitigate—

(a) any failure of retained EU law to operate effectively, or

(b) any other deficiency in retained EU law,

arising from the withdrawal of the United Kingdom from the EU.

(2) A Minister of the Crown acting jointly with a devolved authority may by regulations make such provision as they consider appropriate to prevent, remedy or mitigate—

(a) any failure of retained EU law to operate effectively, or

(b) any other deficiency in retained EU law,

arising from the withdrawal of the United Kingdom from the EU.

(3) Section 8(2) to (9) apply for the purposes of this Part as they apply for the purposes of section 8 (including the references to the Minister in section 8(2) and (3) (but not the reference to a Minister of the Crown in section 8(3)(b)) being read as references to the devolved authority or (as the case may be) the Minister acting jointly with the devolved authority and the references to section 8(1) being read as references to sub-paragraph (1) or (2) above).

(4) Regulations under sub-paragraph (1) above are subject to paragraphs 2 to 7.

No power to make provision outside devolved competence

2.—(1) No provision may be made by a devolved authority acting alone in regulations under this Part unless the provision is within the devolved competence of the devolved authority.

(2) See paragraphs 8 to 11 for the meaning of 'devolved competence' for the purposes of this Part.

3....

Requirement for consultation in certain circumstances

4. No regulations may be made under this Part by a devolved authority acting alone so far as the regulations—

(a) are to come into force before [IP completion day], or

(b) remove (whether wholly or partly) reciprocal arrangements of the kind mentioned in section 8(2)(c) or (e),

unless the regulations are, to that extent, made after consulting with the Secretary of State.

Requirement for consent where it would otherwise be required

5.—(1) The consent of a Minister of the Crown is required before any provision is made by the Welsh Ministers acting alone in regulations under this Part so far as that provision, if contained in an Act of the National Assembly for Wales, would require the consent of a Minister of the Crown.

(2) The consent of the Secretary of State is required before any provision is made by a Northern Ireland department acting alone in regulations under this Part so far as that provision, if contained in an Act of the Northern Ireland Assembly, would require the consent of the Secretary of State.

(3) Sub-paragraph (1) or (2) does not apply if—

(a) the provision could be contained in subordinate legislation made otherwise than under this Act by the Welsh Ministers acting alone or (as the case may be) a Northern Ireland devolved authority acting alone, and

(b) no such consent would be required in that case.

(4) The consent of a Minister of the Crown is required before any provision is made by a devolved authority acting alone in regulations under this Part so far as that provision, if contained in—

(a) subordinate legislation made otherwise than under this Act by the devolved authority, or

(b) subordinate legislation not falling within paragraph (a) and made otherwise than under this Act by (in the case of Scotland) the First Minister or Lord Advocate acting alone or (in the case of Northern Ireland) a Northern Ireland devolved authority acting alone,

would require the consent of a Minister of the Crown.

(5) Sub-paragraph (4) does not apply if—

(a) the provision could be contained in—

(i) an Act of the Scottish Parliament, an Act of the National Assembly for Wales or (as the case may be) an Act of the Northern Ireland Assembly, or

    (ii) different subordinate legislation of the kind mentioned in sub-paragraph (4)(a) or (b) and of a devolved authority acting alone or (as the case may be) other person acting alone, and

(b) no such consent would be required in that case.

Requirement for joint exercise where it would otherwise be required

6.—(1) No regulations may be made under this Part by the Scottish Ministers, so far as they contain provision which relates to a matter in respect of which a power to make subordinate legislation otherwise than under this Act is exercisable by—

(a) the Scottish Ministers acting jointly with a Minister of the Crown, or

(b) the First Minister or Lord Advocate acting jointly with a Minister of the Crown,

unless the regulations are, to that extent, made jointly with the Minister of the Crown.

(2) No regulations may be made under this Part by the Welsh Ministers, so far as they contain provision which relates to a matter in respect of which a power to make subordinate legislation otherwise than under this Act is exercisable by the Welsh Ministers acting jointly with a Minister of the Crown, unless the regulations are, to that extent, made jointly with the Minister of the Crown.

(3) No regulations may be made under this Part by a Northern Ireland department, so far as they contain provision which relates to a matter in respect of which a power to make subordinate legislation otherwise than under this Act is exercisable by—

(a) a Northern Ireland department acting jointly with a Minister of the Crown, or

(b) another Northern Ireland devolved authority acting jointly with a Minister of the Crown,

unless the regulations are, to that extent, made jointly with the Minister of the Crown.

(4) Sub-paragraph (1), (2) or (3) does not apply if the provision could be contained in—

(a) an Act of the Scottish Parliament, an Act of the National Assembly for Wales or (as the case may be) an Act of the Northern Ireland Assembly without the need for the consent of a Minister of the Crown, or

(b) different subordinate legislation made otherwise than under this Act by—

    (i)   the Scottish Ministers, the First Minister or the Lord Advocate acting alone,

    (ii) the Welsh Ministers acting alone, or

    (iii) (as the case may be), a Northern Ireland devolved authority acting alone.

Requirement for consultation where it would otherwise be required

7.—(1) No regulations may be made under this Part by the Welsh Ministers acting alone, so far as they contain provision which, if contained in an Act of the National Assembly for Wales, would require consultation with a Minister of the Crown, unless the regulations are, to that extent, made after consulting with the Minister of the Crown.

(2) No regulations may be made under this Part by the Scottish Ministers acting alone, so far as they contain provision which relates to a matter in respect of which a power to make subordinate legislation otherwise than under this Act is exercisable by the Scottish Ministers, the First Minister or the Lord Advocate after consulting with a Minister of the Crown, unless the regulations are, to that extent, made after consulting with the Minister of the Crown.

(3) No regulations may be made under this Part by the Welsh Ministers acting alone, so far as they contain provision which relates to a matter in respect of which a power to make subordinate legislation otherwise than under this Act is exercisable by the Welsh Ministers after consulting with a Minister of the Crown, unless the regulations are, to that extent, made after consulting with the Minister of the Crown.

(4) No regulations may be made under this Part by a Northern Ireland department acting alone, so far as they contain provision which relates to a matter in respect of which a power to make subordinate legislation otherwise than under this Act is exercisable by a Northern Ireland department after consulting with a Minister of the Crown, unless the regulations are, to that extent, made after consulting with the Minister of the Crown.

(5) Sub-paragraph (2), (3) or (4) does not apply if—

(a) the provision could be contained in an Act of the Scottish Parliament, an Act of the National Assembly for Wales or (as the case may be) an Act of the Northern Ireland Assembly, and

(b) there would be no requirement for the consent of a Minister of the Crown, or for consultation with a Minister of the Crown, in that case.

(6) Sub-paragraph (2), (3) or (4) does not apply if—

(a) the provision could be contained in different subordinate legislation made otherwise than under this Act by—

   (i) the Scottish Ministers, the First Minister or the Lord Advocate acting alone,

   (ii) the Welsh Ministers acting alone, or

   (iii) (as the case may be), a Northern Ireland devolved authority acting alone, and

(b) there would be no requirement for the consent of a Minister of the Crown, or for consultation with a Minister of the Crown, in that case.

Meaning of devolved competence: Part 1

8.—(1) A provision is within the devolved competence of the Scottish Ministers for the purposes of this Part if—

(a) it would be within the legislative competence of the Scottish Parliament if it were contained in an Act of that Parliament . . ., or

(b) it meets the conditions in sub-paragraph (2).

(2) The conditions are—

(a) the provision—

   (i) amends or revokes subordinate legislation made before [IP completion day] by the Scottish Ministers, the First Minister or the Lord Advocate acting alone, or

   (ii) makes supplementary, incidental, consequential, transitional, transitory or saving provision in connection with any such amendment or revocation,

(b) the subject-matter of the provision does not go beyond the subject-matter of the subordinate legislation concerned,

(c) the provision only forms part of the law of Scotland,

(d) the provision does not confer or remove functions exercisable otherwise than in or as regards Scotland, and

(e) the provision does not modify any enactment so far as the enactment cannot, by virtue of paragraph 1, 4 or 5 of Schedule 4 to the Scotland Act 1998, be modified by an Act of the Scottish Parliament.

9.—(1) A provision is within the devolved competence of the Welsh Ministers for the purposes of this Part if—

(a) it would be within the legislative competence of the National Assembly for Wales if it were contained in an Act of the Assembly (. . . including any provision that could be made only with the consent of a Minister of the Crown), or

(b) it meets the conditions in sub-paragraph (2).

(2) The conditions are—

(a) the provision—

   (i) amends or revokes subordinate legislation made before [IP completion day] by the Welsh Ministers acting alone or the National Assembly for Wales constituted by the Government of Wales Act 1998, or

   (ii) makes supplementary, incidental, consequential, transitional, transitory or saving provision in connection with any such amendment or revocation,

(b) the subject-matter of the provision does not go beyond the subject-matter of the subordinate legislation concerned,

(c) the provision only forms part of the law of England and Wales,

(d) the provision does not confer or remove functions exercisable otherwise than in relation to Wales or the Welsh zone, and

(e) the provision does not modify any enactment so far as the enactment cannot, by virtue of paragraph 5, 6 or 7 of Schedule 7B to the Government of Wales Act 2006, be modified by an Act of the National Assembly for Wales.

10.—(1) A provision is within the devolved competence of a Northern Ireland department for the purposes of this Part if—

    (a) the provision, if it were contained in an Act of the Northern Ireland Assembly—

        (i) would be within the legislative competence of the Assembly . . ., and

        (ii) would not require the consent of the Secretary of State,

    (b) the provision—

        (i) amends or repeals Northern Ireland legislation, and

        (ii) would, if it were contained in an Act of the Northern Ireland Assembly, be within the legislative competence of the Assembly . . . and require the consent of the Secretary of State, or

    (c) the provision meets the conditions in sub-paragraph (2).

  (2) The conditions are—

    (a) the provision—

        (i) amends or revokes subordinate legislation made before [IP completion day] by a Northern Ireland devolved authority acting alone, or

        (ii) makes supplementary, incidental, consequential, transitional, transitory or saving provision in connection with any such amendment or revocation,

    (b) the subject-matter of the provision does not go beyond the subject-matter of the subordinate legislation concerned,

    (c) the provision only forms part of the law of Northern Ireland,

    (d) the provision does not confer or remove functions exercisable otherwise than in or as regards Northern Ireland,

    (e) the provision does not modify any enactment so far as the enactment cannot, by virtue of section 7 of the Northern Ireland Act 1998, be modified by an Act of the Northern Ireland Assembly, and

    (f) the provision does not deal with, or otherwise relate to, a matter to which paragraph 22 of Schedule 2, or paragraph 42 of Schedule 3, to the Northern Ireland Act 1998 applies.

11. References in paragraphs 8 to 10, in connection with the making of regulations under this Part, to the subject-matter of any provision or subordinate legislation are to be read as references to the subject-matter of the provision or subordinate legislation when the regulations concerned are made.

[PART 1A PROVISION IN CONNECTION WITH IMPLEMENTATION PERIOD]

[Supplementary power in connection with implementation period

11A.—(1) A devolved authority may by regulations—

    (a) provide for other modifications for the purposes of section 1B(3)(f)(i) (whether applying in all cases or particular cases or descriptions of case),

    (b) provide for subsection (3) or (4) of section 1B not to apply to any extent in particular cases or descriptions of case,

    (c) make different provision in particular cases or descriptions of case to that made by sub-section (3) or (4) of that section, or

    (d) make such provision not falling within paragraph (a), (b) or (c) as the devolved authority considers appropriate for any purpose of, or otherwise in connection with, Part 4 of the withdrawal agreement.

  (2) A Minister of the Crown acting jointly with a devolved authority may by regulations—

(a) provide for other modifications for the purposes of section 1B(3)(f)(i) (whether applying in all cases or particular cases or descriptions of case),

(b) provide for subsection (3) or (4) of section 1B not to apply to any extent in particular cases or descriptions of case,

(c) make different provision in particular cases or descriptions of case to that made by sub-section (3) or (4) of that section, or

(d) make such provision not falling within paragraph (a), (b) or (c) as they consider appropriate for any purpose of, or otherwise in connection with, Part 4 of the withdrawal agreement.

(3) The power to make regulations under this Part may (among other things) be exercised by modifying any provision made by or under an enactment.

(4) In sub-paragraph (3) 'enactment' does not include primary legislation passed or made after IP completion day.

(5) No regulations may be made under this Part after the end of the period of two years beginning with IP completion day.

(6) Regulations under sub-paragraph (1) are also subject to paragraphs 11B and 11C.

No power to make provision outside devolved competence

11B.—(1) No provision may be made by a devolved authority acting alone in regulations under this Part unless the provision is within the devolved competence of the devolved authority.

(2) See paragraphs 11D to 11F for the meaning of 'devolved competence' for the purposes of this Part.

Certain requirements for consent, joint exercise or consultation

11C. Paragraphs 5 to 7 apply for the purposes of this Part as they apply for the purposes of Part 1.

Meaning of devolved competence: Part 1A

11D. A provision is within the devolved competence of the Scottish Ministers for the purposes of this Part if—

(a) it would be within the legislative competence of the Scottish Parliament if it were contained in an Act of that Parliament (ignoring, in the case of regulations made under this Part before exit day, section 29(2)(d) of the Scotland Act 1998 so far as relating to EU law), or

(b) it is provision which could be made in other subordinate legislation by the Scottish Ministers, the First Minister or the Lord Advocate acting alone (ignoring, in the case of regulations made under this Part before exit day, section 57(2) of the Scotland Act 1998 so far as relating to EU law).

11E. A provision is within the devolved competence of the Welsh Ministers for the purposes of this Part if—

(a) it would be within the legislative competence of the National Assembly for Wales if it were contained in an Act of the Assembly (ignoring, in the case of regulations made under this Part before exit day, section 108A(2)(e) of the Government of Wales Act 2006 so far as relating to EU law but including any provision that could be made only with the consent of a Minister of the Crown), or

(b) it is provision which could be made in other subordinate legislation by the Welsh Ministers acting alone (ignoring, in the case of regulations made under this Part before exit day, section 80(8) of the Government of Wales Act 2006 so far as relating to EU law).

11F. A provision is within the devolved competence of a Northern Ireland department for the purposes of this Part if—

(a) the provision, if it were contained in an Act of the Northern Ireland Assembly—

      (i)   would be within the legislative competence of the Assembly (ignoring, in the case of regulations made under this Part before exit day, section 6(2)(d) of the Northern Ireland Act 1998 so far as relating to EU law), and

      (ii) would not require the consent of the Secretary of State,

  (b) the provision—

      (i)   amends or repeals Northern Ireland legislation, and

      (ii) would, if it were contained in an Act of the Northern Ireland Assembly, be within the legislative competence of the Assembly (ignoring, in the case of regulations made under this Part before exit day, section 6(2)(d) of the Northern Ireland Act 1998 so far as relating to EU law) and require the consent of the Secretary of State, or

  (c) the provision is provision which could be made in other subordinate legislation by any Northern Ireland devolved authority acting alone (ignoring, in the case of regulations made under this Part before exit day, section 24(1)(b) of the Northern Ireland Act 1998).]

[PART 1B PROVISION IN CONNECTION WITH CERTAIN OTHER SEPARATION ISSUES]

[Powers in connection with Part 3 of withdrawal agreement and EEA EFTA separation agreement

11G.—(1) A devolved authority may by regulations make such provision as the devolved authority considers appropriate—

  (a) to implement Part 3 of the withdrawal agreement (separation provisions),

  (b) to supplement the effect of section 7A in relation to that Part, or

  (c) otherwise for the purposes of dealing with matters arising out of, or related to, that Part (including matters arising by virtue of section 7A and that Part).

    (2) A Minister of the Crown acting jointly with a devolved authority may by regulations make such provision as they consider appropriate—

  (a) to implement Part 3 of the withdrawal agreement (separation provisions),

  (b) to supplement the effect of section 7A in relation to that Part, or

  (c) otherwise for the purposes of dealing with matters arising out of, or related to, that Part (including matters arising by virtue of section 7A and that Part).

    (3) A devolved authority may by regulations make such provision as the devolved authority considers appropriate—

  (a) to implement Part 3 of the EEA EFTA separation agreement (separation provisions),

  (b) to supplement the effect of section 7B in relation to that Part, or

  (c) otherwise for the purposes of dealing with matters arising out of, or related to, that Part (including matters arising by virtue of section 7B and that Part).

    (4) A Minister of the Crown acting jointly with a devolved authority may by regulations make such provision as they consider appropriate—

  (a) to implement Part 3 of the EEA EFTA separation agreement (separation provisions),

  (b) to supplement the effect of section 7B in relation to that Part, or

  (c) otherwise for the purposes of dealing with matters arising out of, or related to, that Part (including matters arising by virtue of section 7B and that Part).

    (5) Regulations under this Part may make any provision that could be made by an Act of Parliament.

    (6) Regulations under this Part may (among other things) restate, for the purposes of making the law clearer or more accessible, anything that forms part of domestic law by virtue of—

  (a) section 7A above and Part 3 of the withdrawal agreement, or

    (b) section 7B above and Part 3 of the EEA EFTA separation agreement.

  (7) But regulations under this Part may not—

    (a) impose or increase taxation or fees,

    (b) make retrospective provision,

    (c) create a relevant criminal offence,

    (d) establish a public authority,

    (e) amend, repeal or revoke the Human Rights Act 1998 or any subordinate legislation made under it, or

    (f) amend or repeal the Scotland Act 1998, the Government of Wales Act 2006 or the Northern Ireland Act 1998 (unless the regulations are made by virtue of paragraph 21(b) of Schedule 7 to this Act or are amending or repealing any provision of those Acts which modifies another enactment).

  (8) Regulations under sub-paragraph (1) or (3) are also subject to paragraphs 11H and 11I.

  (9) In this paragraph references to Part 3 of the withdrawal agreement or of the EEA EFTA separation agreement include references to any provision of EU law which is applied by, or referred to in, that Part (to the extent of the application or reference).

No power to make provision outside devolved competence

11H.—(1) No provision may be made by a devolved authority acting alone in regulations under this Part unless the provision is within the devolved competence of the devolved authority.

  (2) See paragraphs 11J to 11L for the meaning of 'devolved competence' for the purposes of this Part.

Certain requirements for consent, joint exercise or consultation

11I. Paragraphs 5 to 7 apply for the purposes of this Part as they apply for the purposes of Part 1.

Meaning of devolved competence: Part 1B

11J. A provision is within the devolved competence of the Scottish Ministers for the purposes of this Part if—

    (a) it would be within the legislative competence of the Scottish Parliament if it were contained in an Act of that Parliament . . ., or

    (b) it is provision which could be made in other subordinate legislation by the Scottish Ministers, the First Minister or the Lord Advocate acting alone. . . .

11K. A provision is within the devolved competence of the Welsh Ministers for the purposes of this Part if—

    (a) it would be within the legislative competence of the National Assembly for Wales if it were contained in an Act of the Assembly (. . . including any provision that could be made only with the consent of a Minister of the Crown), or

    (b) it is provision which could be made in other subordinate legislation by the Welsh Ministers acting alone. . . .

11L. A provision is within the devolved competence of a Northern Ireland department for the purposes of this Part if—

    (a) the provision, if it were contained in an Act of the Northern Ireland Assembly—

      (i)   would be within the legislative competence of the Assembly . . ., and

      (ii) would not require the consent of the Secretary of State,

    (b) the provision—

      (i)   amends or repeals Northern Ireland legislation, and

      (ii) would, if it were contained in an Act of the Northern Ireland Assembly, be within the legislative competence of the Assembly . . . and require the consent of the Secretary of State, or

    (c) the provision is provision which could be made in other subordinate legislation by any Northern Ireland devolved authority acting alone. . . .]

[PART 1C PROVISION IN CONNECTION WITH PROTOCOL ON IRELAND/NORTHERN IRELAND]

[Power in connection with protocol on Ireland/Northern Ireland]

11M.—(1) A devolved authority may by regulations make such provision as the devolved authority considers appropriate—

(a) to implement the Protocol on Ireland/Northern Ireland in the withdrawal agreement,

(b) to supplement the effect of section 7A in relation to the Protocol, or

(c) otherwise for the purposes of dealing with matters arising out of, or related to, the Protocol (including matters arising by virtue of section 7A and the Protocol).

(2) A Minister of the Crown acting jointly with a devolved authority may by regulations make such provision as they consider appropriate—

(a) to implement the Protocol on Ireland/Northern Ireland in the withdrawal agreement,

(b) to supplement the effect of section 7A in relation to the Protocol, or

(c) otherwise for the purposes of dealing with matters arising out of, or related to, the Protocol (including matters arising by virtue of section 7A and the Protocol).

(3) Regulations under this Part may make any provision that could be made by an Act of Parliament.

(4) Regulations under this Part may (among other things) make provision facilitating the access to the market within Great Britain of qualifying Northern Ireland goods.

(5) Such provision may (among other things) include provision about the recognition within Great Britain of technical regulations, assessments, registrations, certificates, approvals and authorisations issued by—

(a) the authorities of a member State, or

(b) bodies established in a member State,

in respect of qualifying Northern Ireland goods.

(6) Regulations under this Part may (among other things) restate, for the purposes of making the law clearer or more accessible, anything that forms part of domestic law by virtue of section 7A and the Protocol.

(7) Regulations under sub-paragraph (1) are also subject to paragraphs 11N and 11O.

(8) In this paragraph any reference to the Protocol on Ireland/Northern Ireland includes a reference to—

(a) any other provision of the withdrawal agreement so far as applying to the Protocol, and

(b) any provision of EU law which is applied by, or referred to in, the Protocol (to the extent of the application or reference),

but does not include the second sentence of Article 11(1) of the Protocol (which provides that the United Kingdom and the Republic of Ireland may continue to make new arrangements that build on the provisions of the Belfast Agreement in other areas of North-South cooperation on the island of Ireland).

No power to make provision outside devolved competence

11N.—(1) No provision may be made by a devolved authority acting alone in regulations under this Part unless the provision is within the devolved competence of the devolved authority.

(2) See paragraphs 11P to 11R for the meaning of 'devolved competence' for the purposes of this Part.

11O. Paragraphs 5 to 7 apply for the purposes of this Part as they apply for the purposes of Part 1.

Meaning of devolved competence: Part 1C

11P. A provision is within the devolved competence of the Scottish Ministers for the purposes of this Part if—

(a) it would be within the legislative competence of the Scottish Parliament if it were contained in an Act of that Parliament (ignoring section 29(2)(d) of the Scotland Act 1998 so far as relating to EU law), or

(b)   it is provision which could be made in other subordinate legislation by the Scottish Ministers, the First Minister or the Lord Advocate acting alone (ignoring section 57(2) of the Scotland Act 1998 so far as relating to EU law).

11Q.   A provision is within the devolved competence of the Welsh Ministers for the purposes of this Part if—

(a)   it would be within the legislative competence of the National Assembly for Wales if it were contained in an Act of the Assembly (ignoring section 108A(2)(e) of the Government of Wales Act 2006 so far as relating to EU law but including any provision that could be made only with the consent of a Minister of the Crown), or

(b)   it is provision which could be made in other subordinate legislation by the Welsh Ministers acting alone (ignoring section 80(8) of the Government of Wales Act 2006 so far as relating to EU law).

11R.   A provision is within the devolved competence of a Northern Ireland department for the purposes of this Part if—

(a)   the provision, if it were contained in an Act of the Northern Ireland Assembly—

(i)   would be within the legislative competence of the Assembly (ignoring section 6(2)(d) of the Northern Ireland Act 1998 so far as relating to EU law), and

(ii)   would not require the consent of the Secretary of State,

(b)   the provision—

(i)   amends or repeals Northern Ireland legislation, and

(ii)   would, if it were contained in an Act of the Northern Ireland Assembly, be within the legislative competence of the Assembly (ignoring section 6(2)(d) of the Northern Ireland Act 1998 so far as relating to EU law) and require the consent of the Secretary of State, or

(c)   the provision is provision which could be made in other subordinate legislation by any Northern Ireland devolved authority acting alone (ignoring section 24(1)(b) of the Northern Ireland Act 1998).]

*****

European Union (Future Relationship) Act 2020

(2020, c. 29)

An Act to make provision to implement, and make other provision in connection with, the Trade and Cooperation Agreement; to make further provision in connection with the United Kingdom's future relationship with the EU and its member States; to make related provision about passenger name record data, customs and privileges and immunities; and for connected purposes.   [31st December 2020]

Territorial extent: United Kingdom

1–28   *****

PART 3   GENERAL IMPLEMENTATION

General implementation of agreements

29   General implementation of agreements

(1)   Existing domestic law has effect on and after the relevant day with such modifications as are required for the purposes of implementing in that law the Trade and Cooperation Agreement or the Security of Classified Information Agreement so far as the agreement concerned is not otherwise so implemented and so far as such implementation is necessary for the purposes of complying with the international obligations of the United Kingdom under the agreement.

(2), (3)   *****

(4) In this section—

'domestic law' means the law of England and Wales, Scotland or Northern Ireland;

'existing domestic law' means—

    (a) an existing enactment, or

    (b) any other domestic law as it has effect on the relevant day;

'existing enactment' means an enactment passed or made before the relevant day;

'modifications' does not include any modifications of the kind which would result in a public bill in Parliament containing them being treated as a hybrid bill;

'relevant day', in relation to the Trade and Cooperation Agreement or the Security of Classified Information Agreement or any aspect of either agreement, means—

    (a) so far as the agreement or aspect concerned is provisionally applied before it comes into force, the time and day from which the provisional application applies, and

    (b) so far as the agreement or aspect concerned is not provisionally applied before it comes into force, the time and day when it comes into force;

and references to the purposes of (or having the effect of) implementing an agreement include references to the purposes of (or having the effect of) making provision consequential on any such implementation.

30 *****

Powers

31 Implementation power

(1) A relevant national authority may by regulations make such provision as the relevant national authority considers appropriate—

    (a) to implement the Trade and Cooperation Agreement, the Nuclear Cooperation Agreement, the Security of Classified Information Agreement or any relevant agreement, or

    (b) otherwise for the purposes of dealing with matters arising out of, or related to, the Trade and Cooperation Agreement, the Nuclear Cooperation Agreement, the Security of Classified Information Agreement or any relevant agreement.

(2) Regulations under this section may make any provision that could be made by an Act of Parliament (including modifying this Act).

(3) Regulations under this section may (among other things and whether with the same or a different effect) re-implement any aspect of—

    (a) the Trade and Cooperation Agreement,

    (b) the Nuclear Cooperation Agreement,

    (c) the Security of Classified Information Agreement, or

    (d) any relevant agreement,

which has already been implemented (whether by virtue of this Act or otherwise).

(4) But regulations under this section may not—

    (a) impose or increase taxation or fees,

    (b) make retrospective provision,

    (c) create a relevant criminal offence,

    (d) amend, repeal or revoke the Human Rights Act 1998 or any subordinate legislation made under it, or

    (e) amend or repeal the Scotland Act 1998, the Government of Wales Act 2006 or the Northern Ireland Act 1998 (unless the regulations are made by virtue of paragraph 27(b) of Schedule 5 to this Act or are amending or repealing any provision of those Acts which modifies another enactment).

(5) Subsection (4)(b) does not apply in relation to any regulations under this section which are for the purposes of replacing or otherwise modifying, or of otherwise making provision in connection with, the provision made by section 37(4) and (5).

(6) See also Part 2 of Schedule 5 (general restrictions on certain powers of devolved authorities: devolved competence etc).

(7) In this section 'relevant agreement' means—

(a) any future relationship agreement which is not the Trade and Cooperation Agreement, the Nuclear Cooperation Agreement or the Security of Classified Information Agreement, or

(b) any agreement which falls within [Article 361(4)] of the Trade and Cooperation Agreement (competition co-operation agreement) (including any agreement which so falls as modified or supplemented from time to time in accordance with any provision of it or of any future relationship agreement)

32   Powers relating to the start of agreements

(1) A relevant national authority may by regulations make such provision as the relevant national authority considers appropriate in connection with—

(a) the Trade and Cooperation Agreement, the Nuclear Cooperation Agreement or the Security of Classified Information Agreement (to any extent) coming into force, or becoming provisionally applied, later than IP completion day and after a period of time during which the agreement concerned was (to that extent) neither in force nor provisionally applied, or

(b) the ending, suspension or resumption of any provisional application of the Trade and Cooperation Agreement, the Nuclear Cooperation Agreement or the Security of Classified Information Agreement.

(2) Regulations under this section may make any provision that could be made by an Act of Parliament (including modifying this Act).

(3) Regulations under this section may not—

(a) create a relevant criminal offence,

(b) amend, repeal or revoke the Human Rights Act 1998 or any subordinate legislation made under it, or

(c) amend or repeal the Scotland Act 1998, the Government of Wales Act 2006 or the Northern Ireland Act 1998 (unless the regulations are made by virtue of paragraph 27(b) of Schedule 5 to this Act or are amending or repealing any provision of those Acts which modifies another enactment).

(4) See also Part 2 of Schedule 5 (general restrictions on certain powers of devolved authorities: devolved competence etc).

33   *****

Financial provision

34   *****

35   General financial provision

(1) There may be paid out of money provided by Parliament any expenditure incurred by a Minister of the Crown, government department or other public authority by virtue of any future relationship agreement.

(2) A Minister of the Crown, government department or devolved authority may incur expenditure, for the purpose of, or in connection with, preparing for anything about which provision may be made under a power to make subordinate legislation conferred or modified by or under this Act, before any such provision is made.

(3) There is to be paid out of money provided by Parliament—

(a) any expenditure incurred by a Minister of the Crown, government department or other public authority by virtue of this Act, and

(b) any increase attributable to this Act in the sums payable by virtue of any other Act out of money so provided.

(4) Subsection (3) is subject to any other provision made by or under this Act or any other enactment.

(5) In this section 'government department' means any department of the Government of the United Kingdom.

Parliamentary scrutiny

36 Requirements in Part 2 of CRAGA

Section 20 of the Constitutional Reform and Governance Act 2010 (treaties to be laid before Parliament before ratification) does not apply in relation to the Trade and Cooperation Agreement, the Nuclear Cooperation Agreement or the Security of Classified Information Agreement (but this does not affect whether that section applies in relation to any treaty which modifies or supplements the agreement concerned).

37 *****

38 Regulations

Schedule 5 contains provision about regulations under this Act (including provision about procedure).*

39 *****

European Union (Withdrawal Agreement) Act 2020

(2020, c. 1)

An Act to implement, and make other provision in connection with, the agreement between the United Kingdom and the EU under Article 50(2) of the Treaty on European Union which sets out the arrangements for the United Kingdom's withdrawal from the EU.   [23rd January 2020]

Territorial extent: United Kingdom

1–6 *****

PART 3 CITIZENS' RIGHTS

7–10 *****

11 Appeals etc. against citizens' rights immigration decisions

(1) A Minister of the Crown may by regulations make provision for, or in connection with, appeals against citizens' rights immigration decisions of a kind described in the regulations.

(2) For the purposes of this section, each of the following is a 'citizens' rights immigration decision'—

(a) a decision made in connection with entry clearance by virtue of relevant entry clearance immigration rules (see section 17);

(b) a decision made in connection with leave to enter or remain in the United Kingdom by virtue of residence scheme immigration rules (see section 17);

(c) a decision made in connection with entry clearance for the purposes of acquiring leave to enter or remain in relation to a healthcare right of entry;

(d) a decision made in connection with leave to enter or remain in the United Kingdom in relation to a healthcare right of entry;

(e) a decision made in connection with a right to enter or remain in the United Kingdom by virtue of regulations made under section 8 (frontier workers);

(f) a decision to make, or a refusal to revoke, a deportation order under section 5(1) of the Immigration Act 1971 in relation to a relevant person;

(g) any other decision made in connection with restricting the right of a relevant person to enter the United Kingdom.

(3) A Minister of the Crown may also by regulations make provision for, or in connection with, reviews (including judicial reviews) of decisions within subsection (2)(g).

(4) The power to make regulations under subsection (1) or (3) may (among other things) be exercised by modifying any provision made by or under an enactment.

(5)–(8) *****

12–14 *****

15 Independent Monitoring Authority for the Citizens' Rights Agreements

(1) A body corporate called the Independent Monitoring Authority for the Citizens' Rights Agreements is established.

(2) In this Part that body is referred to as 'the IMA'.

(3) *****

16–19 *****

PART 4   OTHER SUBJECT AREAS

20 Financial provision

(1) Any sum that is required to be paid to the EU or an EU entity to meet any obligation that the United Kingdom has by virtue of the withdrawal agreement is to be charged on and paid out of the Consolidated Fund or, if the Treasury so decides, the National Loans Fund.

(2) After 31 March 2021, subsection (1) does not apply in relation to any expenditure other than sums required to be paid in respect of the traditional own resources of the EU.

(3) Any money received by a Minister of the Crown or a government department by virtue of the withdrawal agreement is to be paid into the Consolidated Fund or, if the Treasury so decides, the National Loans Fund.

(4) A Minister of the Crown, government department or devolved authority may incur expenditure, for the purpose of, or in connection with, preparing for anything about which provision may be made under a power to make subordinate legislation conferred or modified by or under this Act, before any such provision is made.

(5) There is to be paid out of money provided by Parliament—

(a) any expenditure in relation to which subsection (1) does not apply which is incurred by a Minister of the Crown, government department or other public authority by virtue of this Act, and

(b) any increase attributable to this Act in the sums payable by virtue of any other Act out of money so provided.

(6), (7) *****

21–31 *****

32 Requirements in Part 2 of CRAGA

Section 20 of the Constitutional Reform and Governance Act 2010 (treaties to be laid before Parliament before ratification) does not apply in relation to the withdrawal agreement (but this does not affect whether that section applies in relation to any modification of the agreement).

33–37 *****

PART 5   GENERAL AND FINAL PROVISION

38 Parliamentary sovereignty

(1) It is recognised that the Parliament of the United Kingdom is sovereign.

(2) In particular, its sovereignty subsists notwithstanding—

(a) directly applicable or directly effective EU law continuing to be recognised and available in domestic law by virtue of section 1A or 1B of the European Union (Withdrawal) Act 2018 (savings of existing law for the implementation period),

(b) section 7A of that Act (other directly applicable or directly effective aspects of the withdrawal agreement),

(c) section 7B of that Act (deemed direct applicability or direct effect in relation to the EEA EFTA separation agreement and the Swiss citizens' rights agreement), and

(d) section 7C of that Act (interpretation of law relating to the withdrawal agreement (other than the implementation period), the EEA EFTA separation agreement and the Swiss citizens' rights agreement).

(3) Accordingly, nothing in this Act derogates from the sovereignty of the Parliament of the United Kingdom.

*****

Immigration and Social Security Co-ordination (EU Withdrawal) Act 2020

(2020, c. 20)

An Act to make provision to end rights to free movement of persons under retained EU law and to repeal other retained EU law relating to immigration; to confer power to modify retained direct EU legislation relating to social security co-ordination; and for connected purposes.   [11th November 2020]

Territorial extent: United Kingdom

PART 1 MEASURES RELATING TO ENDING FREE MOVEMENT

1   Repeal of the main retained EU law relating to free movement etc
Schedule 1 makes provision to—
(a) end rights to free movement of persons under retained EU law, including by repealing the main provisions of retained EU law relating to free movement, and
(b) end other EU-derived rights, and repeal other retained EU law, relating to immigration.

2*   *****

3   Protection claimants: legal routes from the EU and family reunion
(1) The Secretary of State must review, or arrange for a review of, the ways in which protection claimants who are in a member State are able to enter the United Kingdom lawfully.
(2) For the purposes of this section a 'protection claimant' is a person who—
(a) has made an application for international protection to a member State, or
(b) is not a national of a member State and is seeking to come to the United Kingdom from a member State for the purpose of making a protection claim.
(3) The review under subsection (1) must, in particular—
(a) consider the position of unaccompanied children in member States who are protection claimants and are seeking to come to the United Kingdom to join relatives there, and
(b) include a public consultation on that aspect of the review.
(4) The Secretary of State must, within the period of three months beginning with the day on which this Act is passed, lay before Parliament a statement providing further details about the review under subsection (1) and, in particular, about the aspect of the review described in subsection (3).
(5) After the review, the Secretary of State must—

---
* **Editor's Note:** Section 2 amended the Immigration Act 1971 in relation to Irish citizens. See Immigration Act 1971.

(a) prepare a report on the outcome of the review or arrange for such a report to be prepared, and

(b) publish the report and lay it before Parliament.

(6) *****

4, 5 *****

PART 2 SOCIAL SECURITY CO-ORDINATION

6   Power to modify retained direct EU legislation relating to social security co-ordination

(1) An appropriate authority may by regulations modify the retained direct EU legislation mentioned in subsection (2).

(2) The retained direct EU legislation is—

(a) Regulation (EC) No 883/2004 of the European Parliament and of the Council on the co-ordination of social security systems;

(b) Regulation (EC) No 987/2009 of the European Parliament and of the Council laying down the procedure for implementing Regulation (EC) No 883/2004;

(c) Regulation (EEC) No 1408/71 on the application of social security schemes to employed persons, to self-employed persons and to members of their families moving within the Community;

(d) Regulation (EEC) No 574/72 fixing the procedure for implementing Regulation (EEC) No 1408/71;

(e) Regulation (EC) No 859/2003 extending Regulation (EEC) No 1408/71 to nationals of non-EU Member Countries.

(3) The power to make regulations under subsection (1) includes power—

(a) to make different provision for different categories of person to whom they apply (and the categories may be defined by reference to a person's date of arrival in the United Kingdom, their immigration status, their nationality or otherwise);

(b) otherwise to make different provision for different purposes;

(c) to make supplementary, incidental, consequential, transitional, transitory or saving provision;

(d) to provide for a person to exercise a discretion in dealing with any matter.

(4) The power to make provision mentioned in subsection (3)(c) includes power to modify—

(a) any provision made by primary legislation passed before, or in the same Session as, this Act;

(b) any provision made under primary legislation before, or in the same Session as, this Act is passed;

(c) retained direct EU legislation which is not mentioned in subsection (2).

(5) EU-derived rights, powers, liabilities, obligations, restrictions, remedies and procedures cease to be recognised and available in domestic law so far as they are inconsistent with, or are otherwise capable of affecting the interpretation, application or operation of, provision made by regulations under this section.

(6) 'EU-derived rights, powers, liabilities, obligations, restrictions, remedies and procedures' means any rights, powers, liabilities, obligations, restrictions, remedies and procedures which continue to be recognised and available in domestic law by virtue of section 4 of the European Union (Withdrawal) Act 2018 (including as they are modified by domestic law from time to time).

(7) In this section, 'appropriate authority' means—

(a) the Secretary of State or the Treasury,

(b) a Northern Ireland department, or

(c) a Minister of the Crown acting jointly with a Northern Ireland department.

(8) Schedule 2 contains further provision about the power to make regulations under this section.

(9) Schedule 3 contains provision about the making of regulations under this section.

*****

United Kingdom Internal Market Act 2020

(2020, c. 27)

An Act to make provision in connection with the internal market for goods and services in the United Kingdom (including provision about the recognition of professional and other qualifications); to make provision in connection with provisions of the Northern Ireland Protocol relating to trade and state aid; to authorise the provision of financial assistance by Ministers of the Crown in connection with economic development, infrastructure, culture, sport and educational or training activities and exchanges; to make regulation of the provision of distortive or harmful subsidies a reserved or excepted matter; and for connected purposes. [17th December 2020]

Territorial extent: United Kingdom

PART 1 UK MARKET ACCESS: GOODS

Introductory

1 Purpose of Part 1

(1) This Part promotes the continued functioning of the internal market for goods in the United Kingdom by establishing the United Kingdom market access principles.

(2) The United Kingdom market access principles are—

(a) the mutual recognition principle for goods (see sections 2 to 4), and

(b) the non-discrimination principle for goods (see sections 5 to 9).

(3) Those principles have no direct legal effect except as provided by this Part.

Mutual recognition: goods

2 The mutual recognition principle for goods

(1) The mutual recognition principle for goods is the principle that goods which—

(a) have been produced in, or imported into, one part of the United Kingdom ('the originating part'), and

(b) can be sold there without contravening any relevant requirements that would apply to their sale,

should be able to be sold in any other part of the United Kingdom, free from any relevant requirements that would otherwise apply to the sale.

(2) Where goods are to be sold in a particular way in the other part of the United Kingdom, the condition in subsection (1)(b) has effect as if the reference to 'their sale' were a reference to their sale in that particular way.

So, for example, if goods are to be sold by auction, the condition is met if (and only if) they can be sold by auction in the originating part without contravening any applicable relevant requirements there.

(3) Where the principle applies in relation to a sale of goods in a part of the United Kingdom because the conditions in subsection (1)(a) and (b) are met, any relevant requirements there do not apply in relation to the sale.

3, 4 *******

Non-discrimination: goods

5   The non-discrimination principle for goods

(1) The non-discrimination principle for goods is the principle that the sale of goods in one part of the United Kingdom should not be affected by relevant requirements that directly or indirectly discriminate against goods that have a relevant connection with another part of the United Kingdom.

(2) For the purposes of the application of that principle in any given case—

  (a) the part of the United Kingdom where sale should not be affected is referred to as the 'destination part';

  (b) the goods that have a relevant connection with another part of the United Kingdom are referred to as the 'incoming goods';

  (c) that other part is referred to as the 'originating part'.

(3) *****

(4) Goods have a relevant connection with a part of the United Kingdom if they or any of their components—

  (a) are produced in that part,

  (b) are produced by a business based in that part, or

  (c) come from, or pass through, that part before reaching the destination part.

(5) *****

6   Relevant requirements for the purposes of the non-discrimination principle

(1), (2) *****

(3) A statutory provision is within the scope of the non-discrimination principle if it relates to any one or more of the following—

  (a) the circumstances or manner in which goods are sold (such as where, when, by whom, to whom, or the price or other terms on which they may be sold);

  (b) the transportation, storage, handling or display of goods;

  (c) the inspection, assessment, registration, certification, approval or authorisation of the goods or any similar dealing with them;

  (d) the conduct or regulation of businesses that engage in the sale of certain goods or types of goods.

(4)–(10) *****

7   The non-discrimination principle: direct discrimination

(1) A relevant requirement directly discriminates against incoming goods if, for the reason that the goods have the relevant connection with the originating part, the requirement applies to, or in relation to, the incoming goods in a way—

  (a) in which it does not or would not apply to local goods, and

  (b) that puts the incoming goods at a disadvantage compared to local goods.

(2) Goods are put at a disadvantage if it is made in any way more difficult, or less attractive, to sell or buy the goods or do anything in connection with their sale.

(3) 'Local goods', for the purposes of this section, are actual or hypothetical goods that—

  (a) lack the relevant connection of the incoming goods with the originating part, but

  (b) otherwise are materially the same as, and share the material circumstances of, the incoming goods.

(4) Goods ('the other goods') lack the relevant connection of the incoming goods with the originating part—

  (a) where the incoming goods have a relevant connection within section 5(4)(a), if the other goods, or (as the case may be) their components, were produced in the destination part;

(b) where the incoming goods have a relevant connection within section 5(4)(b), if the other goods, or (as the case may be) their components, were produced by a business based in the destination part;

(c) where the incoming goods have a relevant connection within section 5(4)(c), if the other goods, or (as the case may be) their components, came from the destination part and did not pass through anywhere outside that part.

8   The non-discrimination principle: indirect discrimination

(1) A relevant requirement indirectly discriminates against incoming goods if—

(a) it does not directly discriminate against the goods,

(b) it applies to, or in relation to, the incoming goods in a way that puts them at a disadvantage,

(c) it has an adverse market effect, and

(d) it cannot reasonably be considered a necessary means of achieving a legitimate aim.

(2) Goods are put at a disadvantage if it is made in any way more difficult, or less attractive, to sell or buy the goods or do anything in connection with their sale than if the requirement did not apply.

(3) A requirement has an adverse market effect if, because it—

(a) puts at a disadvantage the incoming goods (and any comparable goods that also have a relevant connection with the originating part and are also put at that disadvantage), but

(b) does not put at that disadvantage (at all or to the same extent) some or all comparable goods that have a relevant connection with the destination part and no other part of the United Kingdom,

it causes a significant adverse effect on competition in the market for such goods in the United Kingdom.

(4) 'Comparable goods' means like goods or interchangeable goods; and—

(a) 'like goods' are goods that are alike the incoming goods in all respects, or otherwise have characteristics closely resembling those of the incoming goods;

(b) 'interchangeable goods' are goods that, from the point of view of a purchaser of the goods, could reasonably be said to be interchangeable with the incoming goods.

(5) The application of subsection (3) is to be determined with regard both to the content of the requirement and to the way in which it operates, or is administered, in practice (as a whole or in particular classes of case).

(6) 'Legitimate aim' means one, or a combination, of the following aims—

(a) the protection of the life or health of humans, animals or plants;

(b) the protection of public safety or security.

(7) The Secretary of State may by regulations amend subsection (6) so as to add, vary or remove an aim.

(8) Regulations under subsection (7) are subject to affirmative resolution procedure.

(9) Before making regulations under subsection (7), the Secretary of State must seek the consent of the Scottish Ministers, the Welsh Ministers and the Department for the Economy in Northern Ireland.

(10) If consent to the making of the regulations is not given by any of those authorities within the period of one month beginning with the day on which it is sought from that authority, the Secretary of State may make the regulations without that consent.

(11) If regulations are made in reliance on subsection (10), the Secretary of State must publish a statement explaining why the Secretary of State decided to make the regulations without the consent of the authority or authorities concerned.

(12) The application of subsection (1)(d) is to be determined with regard, in particular, to—

(a) the effects of the requirement in all the circumstances, and

(b) the availability of alternative means of achieving the aim in question.

9, 10   *****

Supplementary

11   Modifications in connection with the Northern Ireland Protocol

(1) The United Kingdom market access principles for goods apply, in relation to the sale of goods in a part of the United Kingdom other than Northern Ireland, with the following modifications.

(For provision affecting the application of those principles in relation to the sale of goods in Northern Ireland, see, in particular, the Northern Ireland Protocol and sections 7A, 7C and 8C of the European Union (Withdrawal) Act 2018.)

(2) The mutual recognition principle for goods applies in relation to all qualifying Northern Ireland goods as if they were produced in, or imported into, Northern Ireland.

(3) That principle does not apply in relation to goods produced in, or imported into, Northern Ireland that are not qualifying Northern Ireland goods, unless subsection (4) applies.

(4) If goods falling within subsection (3) are moved in a way that would, but for the fact that Northern Ireland is a part of the United Kingdom, amount for the purposes of the mutual recognition principle for goods to the importation of the goods into England, Scotland or Wales, the goods are to be regarded for the purposes of that principle as having been so imported.

(5) Goods that are not qualifying Northern Ireland goods do not have a relevant connection with Northern Ireland for the purposes of the non-discrimination principle for goods (despite section 5(4)).

(6) Subsection (7) applies for the purposes of paragraph 1 of Schedule 1 in a case where Northern Ireland is the 'affected part' within the meaning of sub-paragraph (2) of that paragraph.

(7) In determining whether the condition in sub-paragraph (3) of that paragraph is met, a pest or disease is to be taken to be present in Northern Ireland if it is, or may be, present in qualifying Northern Ireland goods (including when the goods are in Great Britain).

(8) In this section 'qualifying Northern Ireland goods' has the same meaning as in section 47.

12   *******

13   Duty to review the use of Part 1 amendment powers

(1) In this section 'the Part 1 amendment powers' are the powers conferred by sections 6(5), 8(7) and 10(2) (powers to amend certain provisions of Part 1).

(2) The Secretary of State must, during the permitted period—
(a) carry out a review of any use that has been made of the Part 1 amendment powers,
(b) prepare a report of the review, and
(c) lay a copy of the report before Parliament.

(3) In carrying out the review the Secretary of State must—
(a) consult the Scottish Ministers, the Welsh Ministers and the Department for the Economy in Northern Ireland,
(b) consider any relevant reports made, or advice given, by the Competition and Markets Authority under Part 4, and
(c) assess the impact and effectiveness of any changes made under the Part 1 amendment powers.

(4) The permitted period is the period beginning with the third anniversary of the passing of this Act and ending with the fifth anniversary.

(5) *******

14–16   *******

PART 2   UK MARKET ACCESS: SERVICES

17   Services: overview

(1) This Part governs the regulation of service providers in the United Kingdom.

(2) It makes provision that limits the application and effect of authorisation requirements and regulatory requirements.

(3) An authorisation requirement is a legislative requirement that a service provider must have the permission of a regulator before carrying on a business of providing particular services.

(4) A regulatory requirement is a legislative requirement that would if not satisfied (whether at a particular point or on a continuing basis) prevent a service provider from carrying on a business of providing particular services.

(5) The following are neither authorisation requirements nor regulatory requirements for the purposes of this Part—

(a) relevant requirements as defined for the purposes of the mutual recognition principle for goods (see section 3);

(b) provision of the sort described in section 24(1) or 28(1) (professional qualifications and regulation) to the extent it has the effect described there;

(c) a requirement that—

(i) is in force, or otherwise has effect, on the day before the day on which this section comes into force and has not been substantively changed after that day, or

(ii) comes into force, or otherwise takes effect, on or after the day on which this section comes into force if it re-enacts or replicates (without substantive change) a legislative requirement in force or having effect immediately before that day;

(d) a requirement that applies to a service provider, but which also applies to persons who do not provide services (for example, a requirement imposing duties on employers);

(e) a requirement to notify, or register with, a regulator;

(f) a requirement to provide evidence of being authorised to provide services in a part of the United Kingdom other than the part in which the requirement applies.

(6) Subsection (5)(c) does not exclude (and, accordingly, references to authorisation requirements do include) an authorisation requirement that applies in a part of the United Kingdom if, after the relevant day, a corresponding authorisation requirement in another part of the United Kingdom is substantively changed.

(7) For the purposes of subsection (6)—

(a) an authorisation requirement corresponds to another authorisation requirement if it relates to the same, or substantially the same, services;

(b) the 'relevant day' is the day before the day on which this section comes into force.

(8) For the purposes of this section, an authorisation requirement is substantively changed if a legislative requirement that would, if not satisfied, prevent a service provider from satisfying the authorisation requirement is substantively changed.

(9) In this Part—

'service provider' means a person—

(a) that provides, or intends to provide, services in the course of the person's business, and

(b) that has a permanent establishment in the United Kingdom through which that business is wholly or partly carried on;

'permanent establishment'—

(a) in relation to a company, is to be read in accordance with Chapter 2 of Part 24 of the Corporation Tax Act 2010, and

(b) in relation to any other person, is to be read in accordance with that Chapter but as if references in that Chapter to a company were references to that person.

18   *****

19 Services: mutual recognition of authorisation requirements

(1) An authorisation requirement in relation to the provision of services in one part of the United Kingdom does not apply to a person who is authorised to provide those services in another part of the United Kingdom.

(2) A person is authorised to provide services in a part of the United Kingdom if they have the permission of a regulator that exercises regulatory functions in relation to the whole of that part to carry on a business of providing those services in that part.

(3) But, for the purposes of this section, a person is not to be treated as authorised to provide services in a part of the United Kingdom where the permission to provide those services only relates to their provision in relation to particular premises or to a particular place or piece of infrastructure.

(4) Subsection (1) does not apply to an authorisation requirement to the extent it can reasonably be justified as a response to a public health emergency.

20   Direct discrimination in the regulation of services

(1) A regulatory requirement that directly discriminates against a service provider is of no effect in relation to that service provider.

(2) A regulatory requirement directly discriminates against a service provider if—

(a) it has, or would have, the effect of treating the service provider less favourably than other service providers, and

(b) the reason for that less favourable treatment is the service provider's relevant connection, or lack of relevant connection, to a part of the United Kingdom.

(3) A regulatory requirement is not to be taken to directly discriminate against a service provider to the extent the requirement can reasonably be justified as a response to a public health emergency.

(4) For the purposes of this section, a service provider has a relevant connection to a part of the United Kingdom if the service provider—

(a) has a registered office, place of business or residence in that part,

(b) provides services from that part, or

(c) has members, partners, officers or staff with a registered office, place of business, or residence in that part.

21   Indirect discrimination in the regulation of services

(1) A regulatory requirement that indirectly discriminates against an incoming service provider is of no effect in relation to that incoming service provider.

(2) A regulatory requirement indirectly discriminates against an incoming service provider if—

(a) it does not directly discriminate against the incoming service provider (within the meaning of section 20),

(b) it puts the incoming service provider at a relevant disadvantage,

(c) it has an adverse market effect, and

(d) it cannot reasonably be considered a necessary means of achieving a legitimate aim.

(3) A regulatory requirement puts an incoming service provider at a relevant disadvantage if—

(a) it puts the incoming service provider at a disadvantage in relation to the provision of services in the part of the United Kingdom in which the requirement applies, and

(b) it does not put, or would not put, each local service provider at that disadvantage in relation to the provision of those services in that part (at all or to the same extent).

(4) A regulatory requirement puts a service provider at a disadvantage in relation to the provision of services in a part of the United Kingdom if it makes it in any way more difficult, or less attractive, for the service provider to provide the services in that part.

(5) A regulatory requirement has an adverse market effect if, by putting an incoming service provider (or incoming service providers) at a relevant disadvantage in relation to the provision of services, it has a significant adverse effect on competition in the market for those services in the United Kingdom.

(6)–(13) *****

22   Duty to review the use of Part 2 amendment powers

(1) In this section 'the Part 2 amendment powers' are the powers conferred by sections 18(2) and 21(8) (powers to amend certain provisions of Part 2).

(2) The Secretary of State must, during the permitted period—

(a) carry out a review of any use that has been made of the Part 2 amendment powers,

(b) prepare a report of the review, and

(c) lay a copy of the report before Parliament.

(3) In carrying out the review the Secretary of State must—

(a) consult the Scottish Ministers, the Welsh Ministers and the Department for the Economy in Northern Ireland,

(b) consider any relevant reports made, or advice given, by the Competition and Markets Authority under Part 4, and

(c) assess the impact and effectiveness of any changes made under the Part 2 amendment powers.

(4) The permitted period is the period beginning with the third anniversary of the passing of this Act and ending with the fifth anniversary.

(5) *****

23 *****

PART 3 UK MARKET ACCESS: PROFESSIONAL QUALIFICATIONS AND REGULATION

24   Access to professions on grounds of qualifications or experience

(1) Subsection (2) applies in relation to provision applying in a part of the United Kingdom ('the relevant part') that limits the ability to practise a profession in that part to individuals who have certain qualifications or experience.

(2) A qualified UK resident (see section 25) is to be treated for the purposes of the provision (and any related provision) as if the qualified UK resident had the qualifications or experience required to be able to practise the profession.

(3) Provision does not fall within subsection (1) by making the ability of an individual to continue to practise a particular profession, having started to do so on a fully qualified basis, subject to continuing requirements as to training, learning or other forms of experience.

(4) Subsections (1) and (2) are subject to sections 26 and 27.

25   Meaning of 'qualified' UK resident

(1) A UK resident is 'qualified' in relation to a profession for the purposes of section 24(2) if, in any part of the United Kingdom other than the relevant part ('the other part'), the resident is qualified (within the meaning of subsections (3) to (5)) to undertake the full range of corresponding activity.

(2) In this section—

(a) 'corresponding activity' means activity that is the same as, or substantially corresponds to, relevant professional activity;

(b) 'the full range' of corresponding activity is a range of corresponding activity that substantially corresponds to the full range of relevant professional activity;

(c) 'relevant professional activity' means activity that, in the relevant part, ordinarily comprises the practice of the profession in question.

(3) To the extent that—

(a) corresponding activity is ordinarily undertaken by practitioners of a particular profession in the other part, and

(b) provision applying in the other part limits the ability to practise that profession to individuals who have certain qualifications or experience,

a UK resident is qualified to undertake the corresponding activity if the resident has the qualifications or experience required to be able to practise the profession in the other part.

(4) To the extent that—

(a) the position is not as described in subsection (3)(a) and (b), and

(b) provision applying in the other part limits the ability to undertake corresponding activity to individuals who have certain qualifications or experience,

a UK resident is qualified to undertake the corresponding activity if the resident has the qualifications or experience required to do so in the other part.

(5) To the extent that the position is not as described in subsection (3)(a) and (b) or (4)(b), any UK resident is qualified to undertake corresponding activity in the other part.

(6) For the purposes of subsection (3)—

(a) it does not matter that corresponding activity may also be undertaken by individuals who are not practitioners of a profession;

(b) to the extent that corresponding activity is ordinarily undertaken by practitioners of more than one profession regulated as mentioned in subsection (3)(b), a UK resident is qualified in relation to that activity only if the resident has qualifications or experience required to be able to practise whichever of those professions most closely corresponds to the profession in the relevant part.

(7) For the purposes of subsections (3) and (4)—

(a) qualifications may be relied on only if they were obtained in the United Kingdom, and

(b) experience may be relied on only if it was obtained mainly in the United Kingdom

26–45   *****

PART 5 NORTHERN IRELAND PROTOCOL

Northern Ireland's place in the UK internal market and customs territory

46   Northern Ireland's place in the UK internal market and customs territory

(1) An appropriate authority must have special regard to the following matters when exercising any function for a relevant purpose—

(a) the need to maintain Northern Ireland's integral place in the United Kingdom's internal market;

(b) the need to respect Northern Ireland's place as part of the customs territory of the United Kingdom; and

(c) the need to facilitate the free flow of goods between Great Britain and Northern Ireland with the aim of—

(i) streamlining trade between Great Britain and Northern Ireland, and

(ii) maintaining and strengthening the integrity and smooth operation of the internal market in the United Kingdom.

(2) A function is exercised for 'a relevant purpose' if it is exercised for—

(a) the purpose of—

(i) implementing, or

(ii) otherwise dealing with matters arising out of, or related to,

the Northern Ireland Protocol,

(b) the purpose of enabling or facilitating a purpose described in paragraph (a) to be achieved, or

(c) a purpose relating to movement of goods within the United Kingdom (including movement that involves movement in a country or territory outside the United Kingdom).

(3) In this section 'appropriate authority' means—

(a) a Minister of the Crown;

(b) the Scottish Ministers;

(c) the Welsh Ministers;

(d) the First Minister and deputy First Minister in Northern Ireland acting jointly, a Northern Ireland Minister or a Northern Ireland department;

(e) any other person who exercises functions of a public nature.

Unfettered access

47   Unfettered access to UK internal market for Northern Ireland goods

(1) On or after IP completion day, an appropriate authority must not exercise any function in a way that would—

(a) result in an existing kind of NI-GB check, control or administrative process being used—

(i) for the first time, or

        (ii) for a new purpose or to a new extent; or

    (b) result in a new kind of NI-GB check, control or administrative process—

        (i)   being introduced, or

        (ii) being used.

(2) This section does not prevent the exercise of a function if the exercise—

    (a) is necessary for the administration of arrangements which have the purpose of facilitating access for qualifying Northern Ireland goods to the internal market in the United Kingdom,

    (b) is necessary to secure compliance with, or to give effect to, any international obligation or arrangement to which the United Kingdom is a party (whenever the United Kingdom becomes a party to it),

    (c) is necessary where goods have been declared for a voluntary customs procedure,

    (d) is necessary for the purposes of VAT or excise duty in consequence of the Northern Ireland Protocol,

    (e) is necessary for the purpose of dealing with a threat to biosecurity in Great Britain, or

    (f) is necessary for the purpose of dealing with a threat to food or feed safety in Great Britain.

(3) Subsection (2)(b) authorises (in particular) the exercise of a function in relation to a check, control or administrative process if the exercise is necessary to secure compliance with, or to give effect to, Article 6(1) of the Northern Ireland Protocol.

(4) For the purposes of this section the exercise of a function 'is necessary for the purposes of VAT or excise duty in consequence of the Northern Ireland Protocol' if—

    (a) the appropriate authority exercising the functions is the Treasury, the Commissioners for Her Majesty's Revenue and Customs, or the Director of Border Revenue,

    (b) the function is exercised for the purposes of VAT or excise duty (including for the purposes of preventing double taxation, partial or complete non-taxation, or evasion), and

    (c) the appropriate authority exercising the function considers that the exercise is necessary in consequence of the Northern Ireland Protocol.

(5) For the purposes of this section the exercise of a function 'is necessary for the purpose of dealing with a threat to biosecurity in Great Britain' if the exercise of the function consists of—

    (a) the making, or operation, of legislation which satisfies the conditions set out in paragraph 1 of Schedule 1, or

    (b) any other activity which satisfies the conditions set out in paragraph 1(2), (3), (4) and (6) of Schedule 1 (reading any reference in those conditions to 'legislation' as a reference to the activity in question).

(6) In determining for the purposes of subsection (5)(b) whether the condition in paragraph 1(3) of Schedule 1 is met, a pest or disease is to be taken to be present in Northern Ireland if it is, or may be, present in qualifying Northern Ireland goods (including when the goods are in Great Britain).

(7) For the purposes of this section the exercise of a function 'is necessary for the purpose of dealing with a threat to food or feed safety in Great Britain' if the exercise of the function consists of—

    (a) the making, or operation, of legislation which satisfies the conditions set out in paragraph 2 of Schedule 1, or

    (b) any other activity which satisfies the conditions set out in paragraph 2(2), (3), (4) and (6) of Schedule 1 (reading any reference in those conditions to 'legislation' as a reference to the activity in question).

(8) For the purposes of this section—

    (a) an 'NI-GB' check, control or administrative process is one applicable to the direct movement of qualifying Northern Ireland goods from Northern Ireland to Great Britain;

    (b) an 'existing kind' of NI-GB check, control or administrative process is one that—

        (i)   was in use or available for use immediately before IP completion day, or

        (ii) is the same as, or substantially similar to, one that was in use or available for use immediately before IP completion day (the 'predecessor');

(c) a 'new kind of' NI-GB check, control or administrative process is one that is not of an existing kind;

(d) where an NI-GB check, control or administrative process is of an existing kind because of paragraph (b)(ii), that check, control or administrative process and the predecessor are to be treated as a single function for the purpose of determining whether subsection (1)(a) prevents its exercise;

(e) the purpose for which, or extent to which, a function would be used is 'new' if the function has not been used for that purpose, or to that extent, before IP completion day.

(9) A Minister of the Crown may by regulations amend this section so that it applies to a type of movement instead of, or in addition to, a type of movement to which it already applies (whether that type of movement is direct movement or another type of movement provided for by regulations under this subsection).

(10) Regulations under subsection (9) are subject to affirmative resolution procedure.

(11) In this section—

'appropriate authority' means—

(a) a Minister of the Crown;

(b) the Scottish Ministers;

(c) the Welsh Ministers;

(d) the First Minister and deputy First Minister in Northern Ireland acting jointly, a Northern Ireland Minister or a Northern Ireland department;

(e) any other person who exercises functions of a public nature;

'declared for a voluntary customs procedure' means declared, in accordance with the Taxation (Cross-border Trade) Act 2018, for a special Customs procedure or temporary storage;

'direct movement' means movement that does not involve movement by land in a country or territory other than the United Kingdom;

'excise duty' means any excise duty under—

(a) the Alcoholic Liquor Duties Act 1979,

(b) the Hydrocarbon Oil Duties Act 1979, or

(c) the Tobacco Products Duty Act 1979;

'qualifying Northern Ireland goods'—

(a) has the same meaning that it has in the European Union (Withdrawal) Act 2018, including any meaning defined for the purposes of that Act from time to time by regulations made under the power conferred by section 8C(6) of that Act (and, if those regulations provide for different meanings to be defined for different purposes of that Act, regulations under section 8C(6) may make provision about the meaning or meanings that are to apply for the purposes of this section);

(b) is to be taken to have had, immediately before IP completion day, the same meaning that it has (under paragraph (a)) at the time when this section comes into force.

48, 49 ******

PART 6 FINANCIAL ASSISTANCE

50 Power to provide financial assistance for economic development etc

(1) A Minister of the Crown may, out of money provided by Parliament, provide financial assistance to any person for, or in connection with, any of the following purposes—

(a) promoting economic development in the United Kingdom or any area of the United Kingdom;

(b) providing infrastructure at places in the United Kingdom (including infrastructure in connection with any of the other purposes mentioned in this section);

(c) supporting cultural activities, projects and events that the Minister considers directly or indirectly benefit the United Kingdom or particular areas of the United Kingdom;

(d) supporting activities, projects and events relating to sport that the Minister considers directly or indirectly benefit the United Kingdom or particular areas of the United Kingdom;

(e) supporting international educational and training activities and exchanges;

(f) supporting educational and training activities and exchanges within the United Kingdom.

(2) In this section—

'infrastructure' includes—

(a) water, electricity, gas, telecommunications, sewerage or other services (for example, the provision of heat),

(b) railway facilities (including rolling stock), roads or other transport facilities,

(c) health, educational, cultural or sports facilities,

(d) court or prison facilities, and

(e) housing;

'promoting', in relation to economic development, includes taking any measure likely to contribute directly or indirectly to economic development (which might include, for example, measures relating to social inclusion);

'providing', in relation to infrastructure, includes acquiring, designing, constructing, converting, improving, operating and repairing infrastructure;

'sport' includes any physical recreation.

*****

Dissolution and Calling of Parliament Act 2022

(2022, c. 11)

An Act to make provision about the dissolution and calling of Parliament, including provision for the repeal of the Fixed-term Parliaments Act 2011; and for connected purposes.   [24th March 2022]

Territorial extent: United Kingdom

1   Repeal of the Fixed-term Parliaments Act 2011

The Fixed-term Parliaments Act 2011 is repealed.

2   Revival of prerogative powers to dissolve Parliament and to call a new Parliament

(1) The powers relating to the dissolution of Parliament and the calling of a new Parliament that were exercisable by virtue of Her Majesty's prerogative immediately before the commencement of the Fixed-term Parliaments Act 2011 are exercisable again, as if the Fixed-term Parliaments Act 2011 had never been enacted.

(2) For the purposes of subsection (1), the powers relating to the calling of a new Parliament include powers to order the issue of—

(a) writs of summons to attend the House of Lords, and

(b) writs for parliamentary elections (see rule 3 in Schedule 1 to the Representation of the People Act 1983).

3   Non-justiciability of revived prerogative powers

A court or tribunal may not question—

(a) the exercise or purported exercise of the powers referred to in section 2,

(b) any decision or purported decision relating to those powers, or

(c) the limits or extent of those powers.

4   Automatic dissolution of Parliament after five years

If it has not been dissolved earlier, a Parliament dissolves at the beginning of the day that is the fifth anniversary of the day on which it first met.

*****

Part II

EU Law and Brexit

Consolidated versions of the Treaty on European Union and the Treaty on the Functioning of the European Union*

CONSOLIDATED VERSION OF THE TREATY ON EUROPEAN UNION

Title I Common Provisions

Article 1

By this Treaty, the HIGH CONTRACTING PARTIES establish among themselves a EUROPEAN UNION, hereinafter called 'the Union' on which the Member States confer competences to attain objectives they have in common.

This Treaty marks a new stage in the process of creating an ever closer union among the peoples of Europe, in which decisions are taken as openly as possible and as closely as possible to the citizen.

The Union shall be founded on the present Treaty and on the Treaty on the Functioning of the European Union (hereinafter referred to as 'the Treaties'). Those two Treaties shall have the same legal value. The Union shall replace and succeed the European Community.

Article 2

The Union is founded on the values of respect for human dignity, freedom, democracy, equality, the rule of law and respect for human rights, including the rights of persons belonging to minorities. These values are common to the Member States in a society in which pluralism, non-discrimination, tolerance, justice, solidarity and equality between women and men prevail.

Article 3

1. The Union's aim is to promote peace, its values and the well-being of its peoples.

2. The Union shall offer its citizens an area of freedom, security and justice without internal frontiers, in which the free movement of persons is ensured in conjunction with appropriate measures with respect to external border controls, asylum, immigration and the prevention and combating of crime.

3. The Union shall establish an internal market. It shall work for the sustainable development of Europe based on balanced economic growth and price stability, a highly competitive social market economy, aiming at full employment and social progress, and a high level of protection and improvement of the quality of the environment. It shall promote scientific and technological advance.

* **Editor's Note:** This is the consolidated version of both the Treaty on European Union and the Treaty on the Functioning of the European Union as amended by the Treaty of Lisbon, signed on 13 December 2007 in Lisbon.

It shall combat social exclusion and discrimination, and shall promote social justice and protection, equality between women and men, solidarity between generations and protection of the rights of the child.

It shall promote economic, social and territorial cohesion, and solidarity among Member States.

It shall respect its rich cultural and linguistic diversity, and shall ensure that Europe's cultural heritage is safeguarded and enhanced.

4. The Union shall establish an economic and monetary union whose currency is the euro.

5. In its relations with the wider world, the Union shall uphold and promote its values and interests and contribute to the protection of its citizens. It shall contribute to peace, security, the sustainable development of the Earth, solidarity and mutual respect among peoples, free and fair trade, eradication of poverty and the protection of human rights, in particular the rights of the child, as well as to the strict observance and the development of international law, including respect for the principles of the United Nations Charter.

6. The Union shall pursue its objectives by appropriate means commensurate with the competences which are conferred upon it in the Treaties.

Article 4   *****

Article 5

1. The limits of Union competences are governed by the principle of conferral. The use of Union competences is governed by the principles of subsidiarity and proportionality.

2. Under the principle of conferral, the Union shall act only within the limits of the competences conferred upon it by the Member States in the Treaties to attain the objectives set out therein. Competences not conferred upon the Union in the Treaties remain with the Member States.

3. Under the principle of subsidiarity, in areas which do not fall within its exclusive competence, the Union shall act only if and in so far as the objectives of the proposed action cannot be sufficiently achieved by the Member States, either at central level or at regional and local level, but can rather, by reason of the scale or effects of the proposed action, be better achieved at Union level.

The institutions of the Union shall apply the principle of subsidiarity as laid down in the Protocol on the application of the principles of subsidiarity and proportionality. National Parliaments ensure compliance with the principle of subsidiarity in accordance with the procedure set out in that Protocol.

4. Under the principle of proportionality, the content and form of Union action shall not exceed what is necessary to achieve the objectives of the Treaties.

The institutions of the Union shall apply the principle of proportionality as laid down in the Protocol on the application of the principles of subsidiarity and proportionality.

Article 6

1. The Union recognises the rights, freedoms and principles set out in the Charter of Fundamental Rights of the European Union of 7 December 2000, as adapted at Strasbourg, on 12 December 2007, which shall have the same legal value as the Treaties.

The provisions of the Charter shall not extend in any way the competences of the Union as defined in the Treaties.

The rights, freedoms and principles in the Charter shall be interpreted in accordance with the general provisions in Title VII of the Charter governing its interpretation and application and with due regard to the explanations referred to in the Charter, that set out the sources of those provisions.

2. The Union shall accede to the European Convention for the Protection of Human Rights and Fundamental Freedoms. Such accession shall not affect the Union's competences as defined in the Treaties.

3. Fundamental rights, as guaranteed by the European Convention for the Protection of Human Rights and Fundamental Freedoms and as they result from the constitutional traditions common to the Member States, shall constitute general principles of the Union's law.

Articles 7–10   *****

Article 11

1. The institutions shall, by appropriate means, give citizens and representative associations the opportunity to make known and publicly exchange their views in all areas of Union action.

2. The institutions shall maintain an open, transparent and regular dialogue with representative associations and civil society.

3. The European Commission shall carry out broad consultations with parties concerned in order to ensure that the Union's actions are coherent and transparent.

4. Not less than one million citizens who are nationals of a significant number of Member States may take the initiative of inviting the European Commission, within the framework of its powers, to submit any appropriate proposal on matters where citizens consider that a legal act of the Union is required for the purpose of implementing the Treaties.

The procedures and conditions required for such a citizens' initiative shall be determined in accordance with the first paragraph of Article 24 of the Treaty on the Functioning of the European Union.

Article 12   *****

Title III Provisions on the Institutions

Article 13

1. The Union shall have an institutional framework which shall aim to promote its values, advance its objectives, serve its interests, those of its citizens and those of the Member States, and ensure the consistency, effectiveness and continuity of its policies and actions.

The Union's institutions shall be:
— the European Parliament,
— the European Council,
— the Council,
— the European Commission (hereinafter referred to as 'the Commission'),
— the Court of Justice of the European Union,
— the European Central Bank,
— the Court of Auditors.

2. Each institution shall act within the limits of the powers conferred on it in the Treaties, and in conformity with the procedures, conditions and objectives set out in them. The institutions shall practice mutual sincere cooperation.

3. The provisions relating to the European Central Bank and the Court of Auditors and detailed provisions on the other institutions are set out in the Treaty on the Functioning of the European Union.

4. The European Parliament, the Council and the Commission shall be assisted by an Economic and Social Committee and a Committee of the Regions acting in an advisory capacity.

Article 14

1. The European Parliament shall, jointly with the Council, exercise legislative and budgetary functions. It shall exercise functions of political control and consultation as laid down in the Treaties. It shall elect the President of the Commission.

2. The European Parliament shall be composed of representatives of the Union's citizens. They shall not exceed seven hundred and fifty in number, plus the President. Representation of citizens shall be degressively proportional, with a minimum threshold of six members per Member State. No Member State shall be allocated more than ninety-six seats.

The European Council shall adopt by unanimity, on the initiative of the European Parliament and with its consent, a decision establishing the composition of the European Parliament, respecting the principles referred to in the first subparagraph.

3. The members of the European Parliament shall be elected for a term of five years by direct universal suffrage in a free and secret ballot.

4. The European Parliament shall elect its President and its officers from among its members.

Article 15

1. The European Council shall provide the Union with the necessary impetus for its development and shall define the general political directions and priorities thereof. It shall not exercise legislative functions.

2. The European Council shall consist of the Heads of State or Government of the Member States, together with its President and the President of the Commission. The High Representative of the Union for Foreign Affairs and Security Policy shall take part in its work.

3. The European Council shall meet twice every six months, convened by its President. When the agenda so requires, the members of the European Council may decide each to be assisted by a minister and, in the case of the President of the Commission, by a member of the Commission. When the situation so requires, the President shall convene a special meeting of the European Council.

4. Except where the Treaties provide otherwise, decisions of the European Council shall be taken by consensus.

5. The European Council shall elect its President, by a qualified majority, for a term of two and a half years, renewable once. In the event of an impediment or serious misconduct, the European Council can end the President's term of office in accordance with the same procedure.

6. The President of the European Council:
   (a) shall chair it and drive forward its work;
   (b) shall ensure the preparation and continuity of the work of the European Council in cooperation with the President of the Commission, and on the basis of the work of the General Affairs Council;
   (c) shall endeavour to facilitate cohesion and consensus within the European Council;
   (d) shall present a report to the European Parliament after each of the meetings of the European Council.

The President of the European Council shall, at his level and in that capacity, ensure the external representation of the Union on issues concerning its common foreign and security policy, without prejudice to the powers of the High Representative of the Union for Foreign Affairs and Security Policy.

The President of the European Council shall not hold a national office.

Article 16

1. The Council shall, jointly with the European Parliament, exercise legislative and budgetary functions. It shall carry out policy-making and coordinating functions as laid down in the Treaties.

2. The Council shall consist of a representative of each Member State at ministerial level, who may commit the government of the Member State in question and cast its vote.

3. The Council shall act by a qualified majority except where the Treaties provide otherwise.

4. As from 1 November 2014, a qualified majority shall be defined as at least 55 % of the members of the Council, comprising at least fifteen of them and representing Member States comprising at least 65 % of the population of the Union.

A blocking minority must include at least four Council members, failing which the qualified majority shall be deemed attained.

The other arrangements governing the qualified majority are laid down in Article 238(2) of the Treaty on the Functioning of the European Union.

5. The transitional provisions relating to the definition of the qualified majority which shall be applicable until 31 October 2014 and those which shall be applicable from 1 November 2014 to 31 March 2017 are laid down in the Protocol on transitional provisions.

6. The Council shall meet in different configurations, the list of which shall be adopted in accordance with Article 236 of the Treaty on the Functioning of the European Union.

The General Affairs Council shall ensure consistency in the work of the different Council configurations. It shall prepare and ensure the follow-up to meetings of the European Council, in liaison with the President of the European Council and the Commission.

The Foreign Affairs Council shall elaborate the Union's external action on the basis of strategic guidelines laid down by the European Council and ensure that the Union's action is consistent.

7. A Committee of Permanent Representatives of the Governments of the Member States shall be responsible for preparing the work of the Council.

8. The Council shall meet in public when it deliberates and votes on a draft legislative act. To this end, each Council meeting shall be divided into two parts, dealing respectively with deliberations on Union legislative acts and non-legislative activities.

9. The Presidency of Council configurations, other than that of Foreign Affairs, shall be held by Member State representatives in the Council on the basis of equal rotation, in accordance with the conditions established in accordance with Article 236 of the Treaty on the Functioning of the European Union.

Article 17

1. The Commission shall promote the general interest of the Union and take appropriate initiatives to that end. It shall ensure the application of the Treaties, and of measures adopted by the institutions pursuant to them. It shall oversee the application of Union law under the control of the Court of Justice of the European Union. It shall execute the budget and manage programmes. It shall exercise coordinating, executive and management functions, as laid down in the Treaties. With the exception of the common foreign and security policy, and other cases provided for in the Treaties, it shall ensure the Union's external representation. It shall initiate the Union's annual and multiannual programming with a view to achieving interinstitutional agreements.

2. Union legislative acts may only be adopted on the basis of a Commission proposal, except where the Treaties provide otherwise. Other acts shall be adopted on the basis of a Commission proposal where the Treaties so provide.

3. The Commission's term of office shall be five years.

The members of the Commission shall be chosen on the ground of their general competence and European commitment from persons whose independence is beyond doubt.

In carrying out its responsibilities, the Commission shall be completely independent. Without prejudice to Article 18(2), the members of the Commission shall neither seek nor take instructions from any Government or other institution, body, office or entity. They shall refrain from any action incompatible with their duties or the performance of their tasks.

4. The Commission appointed between the date of entry into force of the Treaty of Lisbon and 31 October 2014, shall consist of one national of each Member State, including its President and the High Representative of the Union for Foreign Affairs and Security Policy who shall be one of its Vice-Presidents.

5. As from 1 November 2014, the Commission shall consist of a number of members, including its President and the High Representative of the Union for Foreign Affairs and Security Policy, corresponding to two thirds of the number of Member States, unless the European Council, acting unanimously, decides to alter this number.

The members of the Commission shall be chosen from among the nationals of the Member States on the basis of a system of strictly equal rotation between the Member States, reflecting the demographic and geographical range of all the Member States. This system shall be established unanimously by the European Council in accordance with Article 244 of the Treaty on the Functioning of the European Union.

6. The President of the Commission shall:
   (a) lay down guidelines within which the Commission is to work;
   (b) decide on the internal organisation of the Commission, ensuring that it acts consistently, efficiently and as a collegiate body;
   (c) appoint Vice-Presidents, other than the High Representative of the Union for Foreign Affairs and Security Policy, from among the members of the Commission.

A member of the Commission shall resign if the President so requests. The High Representative of the Union for Foreign Affairs and Security Policy shall resign, in accordance with the procedure set out in Article 18(1), if the President so requests.

7. Taking into account the elections to the European Parliament and after having held the appropriate consultations, the European Council, acting by a qualified majority, shall propose to the European Parliament a candidate for President of the Commission. This candidate shall be elected by

the European Parliament by a majority of its component members. If he does not obtain the required majority, the European Council, acting by a qualified majority, shall within one month propose a new candidate who shall be elected by the European Parliament following the same procedure.

The Council, by common accord with the President-elect, shall adopt the list of the other persons whom it proposes for appointment as members of the Commission. They shall be selected, on the basis of the suggestions made by Member States, in accordance with the criteria set out in paragraph 3, second subparagraph, and paragraph 5, second subparagraph.

The President, the High Representative of the Union for Foreign Affairs and Security Policy and the other members of the Commission shall be subject as a body to a vote of consent by the European Parliament. On the basis of this consent the Commission shall be appointed by the European Council, acting by a qualified majority.

8. The Commission, as a body, shall be responsible to the European Parliament. In accordance with Article 234 of the Treaty on the Functioning of the European Union, the European Parliament may vote on a motion of censure of the Commission. If such a motion is carried, the members of the Commission shall resign as a body and the High Representative of the Union for Foreign Affairs and Security Policy shall resign from the duties that he carries out in the Commission.

Article 18

1. The European Council, acting by a qualified majority, with the agreement of the President of the Commission, shall appoint the High Representative of the Union for Foreign Affairs and Security Policy. The European Council may end his term of office by the same procedure.

2. The High Representative shall conduct the Union's common foreign and security policy. He shall contribute by his proposals to the development of that policy, which he shall carry out as mandated by the Council. The same shall apply to the common security and defence policy.

3. The High Representative shall preside over the Foreign Affairs Council.

4. The High Representative shall be one of the Vice-Presidents of the Commission. He shall ensure the consistency of the Union's external action. He shall be responsible within the Commission for responsibilities incumbent on it in external relations and for coordinating other aspects of the Union's external action. In exercising these responsibilities within the Commission, and only for these responsibilities, the High Representative shall be bound by Commission procedures to the extent that this is consistent with paragraphs 2 and 3.

Article 19

1. The Court of Justice of the European Union shall include the Court of Justice, the General Court and specialised courts. It shall ensure that in the interpretation and application of the Treaties the law is observed.

Member States shall provide remedies sufficient to ensure effective legal protection in the fields covered by Union law.

2. The Court of Justice shall consist of one judge from each Member State. It shall be assisted by Advocates-General.

The General Court shall include at least one judge per Member State.

The Judges and the Advocates-General of the Court of Justice and the Judges of the General Court shall be chosen from persons whose independence is beyond doubt and who satisfy the conditions set out in Articles 253 and 254 of the Treaty on the Functioning of the European Union. They shall be appointed by common accord of the governments of the Member States for six years. Retiring Judges and Advocates-General may be reappointed.

3. The Court of Justice of the European Union shall, in accordance with the Treaties:
   (a) rule on actions brought by a Member State, an institution or a natural or legal person;
   (b) give preliminary rulings, at the request of courts or tribunals of the Member States, on the interpretation of Union law or the validity of acts adopted by the institutions;
   (c) rule in other cases provided for in the Treaties.
   *****

Article 27

1. The High Representative of the Union for Foreign Affairs and Security Policy, who shall chair the Foreign Affairs Council, shall contribute through his proposals towards the preparation of the

common foreign and security policy and shall ensure implementation of the decisions adopted by the European Council and the Council.

2. The High Representative shall represent the Union for matters relating to the common foreign and security policy. He shall conduct political dialogue with third parties on the Union's behalf and shall express the Union's position in international organisations and at international conferences.

3. In fulfilling his mandate, the High Representative shall be assisted by a European External Action Service. This service shall work in cooperation with the diplomatic services of the Member States and shall comprise officials from relevant departments of the General Secretariat of the Council and of the Commission as well as staff seconded from national diplomatic services of the Member States. The organisation and functioning of the European External Action Service shall be established by a decision of the Council. The Council shall act on a proposal from the High Representative after consulting the European Parliament and after obtaining the consent of the Commission.

*****

Article 47
The Union shall have legal personality.

Article 48
1. The Treaties may be amended in accordance with an ordinary revision procedure. They may also be amended in accordance with simplified revision procedures.

Ordinary revision procedure

2. The Government of any Member State, the European Parliament or the Commission may submit to the Council proposals for the amendment of the Treaties. These proposals may, inter alia, serve either to increase or to reduce the competences conferred on the Union in the Treaties. These proposals shall be submitted to the European Council by the Council and the national Parliaments shall be notified.

3. If the European Council, after consulting the European Parliament and the Commission, adopts by a simple majority a decision in favour of examining the proposed amendments, the President of the European Council shall convene a Convention composed of representatives of the national Parliaments, of the Heads of State or Government of the Member States, of the European Parliament and of the Commission. The European Central Bank shall also be consulted in the case of institutional changes in the monetary area. The Convention shall examine the proposals for amendments and shall adopt by consensus a recommendation to a conference of representatives of the governments of the Member States as provided for in paragraph 4.

The European Council may decide by a simple majority, after obtaining the consent of the European Parliament, not to convene a Convention should this not be justified by the extent of the proposed amendments. In the latter case, the European Council shall define the terms of reference for a conference of representatives of the governments of the Member States.

4. A conference of representatives of the governments of the Member States shall be convened by the President of the Council for the purpose of determining by common accord the amendments to be made to the Treaties.

The amendments shall enter into force after being ratified by all the Member States in accordance with their respective constitutional requirements.

5. If, two years after the signature of a treaty amending the Treaties, four fifths of the Member States have ratified it and one or more Member States have encountered difficulties in proceeding with ratification, the matter shall be referred to the European Council.

Simplified revision procedures

6. The Government of any Member State, the European Parliament or the Commission may submit to the European Council proposals for revising all or part of the provisions of Part Three of the Treaty on the Functioning of the European Union relating to the internal policies and action of the Union.

The European Council may adopt a decision amending all or part of the provisions of Part Three of the Treaty on the Functioning of the European Union. The European Council shall act by unanimity after consulting the European Parliament and the Commission, and the European Central Bank in the case of institutional changes in the monetary area. That decision shall not enter into force until it is approved by the Member States in accordance with their respective constitutional requirements.

The decision referred to in the second subparagraph shall not increase the competences conferred on the Union in the Treaties.

7. Where the Treaty on the Functioning of the European Union or Title V of this Treaty provides for the Council to act by unanimity in a given area or case, the European Council may adopt a decision authorising the Council to act by a qualified majority in that area or in that case. This subparagraph shall not apply to decisions with military implications or those in the area of defence.

Where the Treaty on the Functioning of the European Union provides for legislative acts to be adopted by the Council in accordance with a special legislative procedure, the European Council may adopt a decision allowing for the adoption of such acts in accordance with the ordinary legislative procedure.

Any initiative taken by the European Council on the basis of the first or the second subparagraph shall be notified to the national Parliaments. If a national Parliament makes known its opposition within six months of the date of such notification, the decision referred to in the first or the second subparagraph shall not be adopted. In the absence of opposition, the European Council may adopt the decision.

For the adoption of the decisions referred to in the first and second subparagraphs, the European Council shall act by unanimity after obtaining the consent of the European Parliament, which shall be given by a majority of its component members.

*****

CONSOLIDATED VERSION OF THE TREATY ON THE FUNCTIONING OF THE EUROPEAN UNION

PART ONE (PRINCIPLES)

Article 1

1. This Treaty organises the functioning of the Union and determines the areas of, delimitation of, and arrangements for exercising its competences.

2. This Treaty and the Treaty on European Union constitute the Treaties on which the Union is founded. These two Treaties, which have the same legal value, shall be referred to as 'the Treaties'.

Title I Categories and Areas of Union Competence

Article 2

1. When the Treaties confer on the Union exclusive competence in a specific area, only the Union may legislate and adopt legally binding acts, the Member States being able to do so themselves only if so empowered by the Union or for the implementation of Union acts.

2. When the Treaties confer on the Union a competence shared with the Member States in a specific area, the Union and the Member States may legislate and adopt legally binding acts in that area. The Member States shall exercise their competence to the extent that the Union has not exercised its competence. The Member States shall again exercise their competence to the extent that the Union has decided to cease exercising its competence.

3. The Member States shall coordinate their economic and employment policies within arrangements as determined by this Treaty, which the Union shall have competence to provide.

4. The Union shall have competence, in accordance with the provisions of the Treaty on European Union, to define and implement a common foreign and security policy, including the progressive framing of a common defence policy.

5. In certain areas and under the conditions laid down in the Treaties, the Union shall have competence to carry out actions to support, coordinate or supplement the actions of the Member States, without thereby superseding their competence in these areas.

Legally binding acts of the Union adopted on the basis of the provisions of the Treaties relating to these areas shall not entail harmonisation of Member States' laws or regulations.

6. The scope of and arrangements for exercising the Union's competences shall be determined by the provisions of the Treaties relating to each area.

Articles 3–6   ***

Title II Provisions Having General Application

Article 7
The Union shall ensure consistency between its policies and activities, taking all of its objectives into account and in accordance with the principle of conferral of powers.

Article 8
In all its activities, the Union shall aim to eliminate inequalities, and to promote equality, between men and women.

Article 9
In defining and implementing its policies and activities, the Union shall take into account requirements linked to the promotion of a high level of employment, the guarantee of adequate social protection, the fight against social exclusion, and a high level of education, training and protection of human health.

Article 10
In defining and implementing its policies and activities, the Union shall aim to combat discrimination based on sex, racial or ethnic origin, religion or belief, disability, age or sexual orientation.

Article 11
Environmental protection requirements must be integrated into the definition and implementation of the Union policies and activities, in particular with a view to promoting sustainable development.

Article 12
Consumer protection requirements shall be taken into account in defining and implementing other Union policies and activities.

Articles 13–16   ***

Article 17
1. The Union respects and does not prejudice the status under national law of churches and religious associations or communities in the Member States.

2. The Union equally respects the status under national law of philosophical and non-confessional organisations.

3. Recognising their identity and their specific contribution, the Union shall maintain an open, transparent and regular dialogue with these churches and organisations.

PART TWO (NON-DISCRIMINATION AND CITIZENSHIP OF THE UNION)

Article 18
Within the scope of application of the Treaties, and without prejudice to any special provisions contained therein, any discrimination on grounds of nationality shall be prohibited.

The European Parliament and the Council, acting in accordance with the ordinary legislative procedure, may adopt rules designed to prohibit such discrimination.

Article 19

1. Without prejudice to the other provisions of the Treaties and within the limits of the powers conferred by them upon the Union, the Council, acting unanimously in accordance with a special legislative procedure and after obtaining the consent of the European Parliament, may take appropriate action to combat discrimination based on sex, racial or ethnic origin, religion or belief, disability, age or sexual orientation.

2. By way of derogation from paragraph 1, the European Parliament and the Council, acting in accordance with the ordinary legislative procedure, may adopt the basic principles of Union incentive measures, excluding any harmonisation of the laws and regulations of the Member States, to support action taken by the Member States in order to contribute to the achievement of the objectives referred to in paragraph 1.

Article 20

1. Citizenship of the Union is hereby established. Every person holding the nationality of a Member State shall be a citizen of the Union. Citizenship of the Union shall be additional to and not replace national citizenship.

2. Citizens of the Union shall enjoy the rights and be subject to the duties provided for in the Treaties. They shall have, *inter alia*:

    (a) the right to move and reside freely within the territory of the Member States;

    (b) the right to vote and to stand as candidates in elections to the European Parliament and in municipal elections in their Member State of residence, under the same conditions as nationals of that State;

    (c) the right to enjoy, in the territory of a third country in which the Member State of which they are nationals is not represented, the protection of the diplomatic and consular authorities of any Member State on the same conditions as the nationals of that State;

    (d) the right to petition the European Parliament, to apply to the European Ombudsman, and to address the institutions and advisory bodies of the Union in any of the Treaty languages and to obtain a reply in the same language.

These rights shall be exercised in accordance with the conditions and limits defined by the Treaties and by the measures adopted thereunder.

Articles 21–25   *****

PART THREE (UNION POLICIES AND INTERNAL ACTIONS)

Title I The Internal Market

Article 26

1. The Union shall adopt measures with the aim of establishing or ensuring the functioning of the internal market, in accordance with the relevant provisions of the Treaties.

2. The internal market shall comprise an area without internal frontiers in which the free movement of goods, persons, services and capital is ensured in accordance with the provisions of the Treaties.

3. The Council, on a proposal from the Commission, shall determine the guidelines and conditions necessary to ensure balanced progress in all the sectors concerned.

Article 27   *****

Title II Free Movement of Goods

Article 28

1. The Union shall comprise a customs union which shall cover all trade in goods and which shall involve the prohibition between Member States of customs duties on imports and exports and

of all charges having equivalent effect, and the adoption of a common customs tariff in their relations with third countries.

2. The provisions of Article 30 and of Chapter 2 of this Title shall apply to products originating in Member States and to products coming from third countries which are in free circulation in Member States.

Articles 29–33 *****

Chapter 3 (Prohibition of Quantitative Restrictions between Member States)

Article 34

Quantitative restrictions on imports and all measures having equivalent effect shall be prohibited between Member States.

Article 35 *****

Article 36

The provisions of Articles 34 and 35 shall not preclude prohibitions or restrictions on imports, exports or goods in transit justified on grounds of public morality, public policy or public security; the protection of health and life of humans, animals or plants; the protection of national treasures possessing artistic, historic or archaeological value; or the protection of industrial and commercial property. Such prohibitions or restrictions shall not, however, constitute a means of arbitrary discrimination or a disguised restriction on trade between Member States.

Articles 37–44 *****

Title IV Free Movement of Persons, Services and Capital

Chapter 1 (Workers)

Article 45

1. Freedom of movement for workers shall be secured within the Union.

2. Such freedom of movement shall entail the abolition of any discrimination based on nationality between workers of the Member States as regards employment, remuneration and other conditions of work and employment.

3. It shall entail the right, subject to limitations justified on grounds of public policy, public security or public health:

    (a) to accept offers of employment actually made;

    (b) to move freely within the territory of Member States for this purpose;

    (c) to stay in a Member State for the purpose of employment in accordance with the provisions governing the employment of nationals of that State laid down by law, regulation or administrative action;

    (d) to remain in the territory of a Member State after having been employed in that State, subject to conditions which shall be embodied in regulations to be drawn up by the Commission.

4. The provisions of this Article shall not apply to employment in the public service.

Article 46, 47 *****

Article 48

The European Parliament and the Council shall, acting in accordance with the ordinary legislative procedure, adopt such measures in the field of social security as are necessary to provide freedom of movement for workers; to this end, they shall make arrangements to secure for employed and self-employed migrant workers and their dependants:

    (a) aggregation, for the purpose of acquiring and retaining the right to benefit and of calculating the amount of benefit, of all periods taken into account under the laws of the several countries;

    (b) payment of benefits to persons resident in the territories of Member States.

Where a member of the Council declares that a draft legislative act referred to in the first subparagraph would affect important aspects of its social security system, including its scope, cost or financial structure, or would affect the financial balance of that system, it may request that the matter be referred to the European Council. In that case, the ordinary legislative procedure shall be suspended. After discussion, the European Council shall, within four months of this suspension, either:

    (a) refer the draft back to the Council, which shall terminate the suspension of the ordinary legislative procedure; or

    (b) take no action or request the Commission to submit a new proposal; in that case, the act originally proposed shall be deemed not to have been adopted.

Chapter 2 (Right of Establishment)

Article 49

Within the framework of the provisions set out below, restrictions on the freedom of establishment of nationals of a Member State in the territory of another Member State shall be prohibited. Such prohibition shall also apply to restrictions on the setting-up of agencies, branches or subsidiaries by nationals of any Member State established in the territory of any Member State.

Freedom of establishment shall include the right to take up and pursue activities as self-employed persons and to set up and manage undertakings, in particular companies or firms within the meaning of the second paragraph of Article 54, under the conditions laid down for its own nationals by the law of the country where such establishment is effected, subject to the provisions of the Chapter relating to capital.

Articles 50–53 *****

Article 54

Companies or firms formed in accordance with the law of a Member State and having their registered office, central administration or principal place of business within the Union shall, for the purposes of this Chapter, be treated in the same way as natural persons who are nationals of Member States.

'Companies or firms' means companies or firms constituted under civil or commercial law, including cooperative societies, and other legal persons governed by public or private law, save for those which are non-profit-making.

Article 55 *****

Chapter 3 (Services)

Article 56

Within the framework of the provisions set out below, restrictions on freedom to provide services within the Union shall be prohibited in respect of nationals of Member States who are established in a Member State other than that of the person for whom the services are intended.

The European Parliament and the Council, acting in accordance with the ordinary legislative procedure, may extend the provisions of the Chapter to nationals of a third country who provide services and who are established within the Union.

Article 57

Services shall be considered to be 'services' within the meaning of the Treaties where they are normally provided for remuneration, in so far as they are not governed by the provisions relating to freedom of movement for goods, capital and persons.

'Services' shall in particular include:

(a) activities of an industrial character;

(b) activities of a commercial character;

(c) activities of craftsmen;

(d) activities of the professions.

Without prejudice to the provisions of the Chapter relating to the right of establishment, the person providing a service may, in order to do so, temporarily pursue his activity in the Member State where the service is provided, under the same conditions as are imposed by that State on its own nationals.
*****

Chapter 4 (Judicial Cooperation in Criminal Matters)

Article 82

1. Judicial cooperation in criminal matters in the Union shall be based on the principle of mutual recognition of judgments and judicial decisions and shall include the approximation of the laws and regulations of the Member States in the areas referred to in paragraph 2 and in Article 83.

The European Parliament and the Council, acting in accordance with the ordinary legislative procedure, shall adopt measures to:

(a) lay down rules and procedures for ensuring recognition throughout the Union of all forms of judgments and judicial decisions;

(b) prevent and settle conflicts of jurisdiction between Member States;

(c) support the training of the judiciary and judicial staff;

(d) facilitate cooperation between judicial or equivalent authorities of the Member States in relation to proceedings in criminal matters and the enforcement of decisions.

2. To the extent necessary to facilitate mutual recognition of judgments and judicial decisions and police and judicial cooperation in criminal matters having a cross-border dimension, the European Parliament and the Council may, by means of directives adopted in accordance with the ordinary legislative procedure, establish minimum rules. Such rules shall take into account the differences between the legal traditions and systems of the Member States.

They shall concern:

(a) mutual admissibility of evidence between Member States;

(b) the rights of individuals in criminal procedure;

(c) the rights of victims of crime;

(d) any other specific aspects of criminal procedure which the Council has identified in advance by a decision; for the adoption of such a decision, the Council shall act unanimously after obtaining the consent of the European Parliament.

Adoption of the minimum rules referred to in this paragraph shall not prevent Member States from maintaining or introducing a higher level of protection for individuals.

3. *****

Article 83

1. The European Parliament and the Council may, by means of directives adopted in accordance with the ordinary legislative procedure, establish minimum rules concerning the definition of criminal offences and sanctions in the areas of particularly serious crime with a cross-border dimension resulting from the nature or impact of such offences or from a special need to combat them on a common basis.

These areas of crime are the following: terrorism, trafficking in human beings and sexual exploitation of women and children, illicit drug trafficking, illicit arms trafficking, money laundering, corruption, counterfeiting of means of payment, computer crime and organised crime.

On the basis of developments in crime, the Council may adopt a decision identifying other areas of crime that meet the criteria specified in this paragraph. It shall act unanimously after obtaining the consent of the European Parliament.

2., 3. *****

Articles 84–86 *****

Chapter 5 (Police Cooperation)

Article 87

1. The Union shall establish police cooperation involving all the Member States' competent authorities, including police, customs and other specialised law enforcement services in relation to the prevention, detection and investigation of criminal offences.

2. For the purposes of paragraph 1, the European Parliament and the Council, acting in accordance with the ordinary legislative procedure, may establish measures concerning:

(a) the collection, storage, processing, analysis and exchange of relevant information;

(b) support for the training of staff, and cooperation on the exchange of staff, on equipment and on research into crime-detection;

(c) common investigative techniques in relation to the detection of serious forms of organised crime.

3. The Council, acting in accordance with a special legislative procedure, may establish measures concerning operational cooperation between the authorities referred to in this Article. The Council shall act unanimously after consulting the European Parliament.

In case of the absence of unanimity in the Council, a group of at least nine Member States may request that the draft measures be referred to the European Council. In that case, the procedure in the Council shall be suspended. After discussion, and in case of a consensus, the European Council shall, within four months of this suspension, refer the draft back to the Council for adoption.

Within the same timeframe, in case of disagreement, and if at least nine Member States wish to establish enhanced cooperation on the basis of the draft measures concerned, they shall notify the European Parliament, the Council and the Commission accordingly. In such a case, the authorisation to proceed with enhanced cooperation referred to in Article 20(2) of the Treaty on European Union and Article 329(1) of this Treaty shall be deemed to be granted and the provisions on enhanced cooperation shall apply.

The specific procedure provided for in the second and third subparagraphs shall not apply to acts which constitute a development of the Schengen *acquis*.

*****

Title VII Common Rules on Competition, Taxation and Approximation of Laws

Chapter 1 (Rules on Competition)

Section 1 Rules applying to undertakings

Article 101

1. The following shall be prohibited as incompatible with the internal market: all agreements between undertakings, decisions by associations of undertakings and concerted practices which may affect trade between Member States and which have as their object or effect the prevention, restriction or distortion of competition within the internal market, and in particular those which:

(a) directly or indirectly fix purchase or selling prices or any other trading conditions;

(b) limit or control production, markets, technical development, or investment;

(c) share markets or sources of supply;

(d) apply dissimilar conditions to equivalent transactions with other trading parties, thereby placing them at a competitive disadvantage;

(e) make the conclusion of contracts subject to acceptance by the other parties of supplementary obligations which, by their nature or according to commercial usage, have no connection with the subject of such contracts.

2. Any agreements or decisions prohibited pursuant to this Article shall be automatically void.

3. The provisions of paragraph 1 may, however, be declared inapplicable in the case of:

— any agreement or category of agreements between undertakings,

— any decision or category of decisions by associations of undertakings,

— any concerted practice or category of concerted practices,

which contributes to improving the production or distribution of goods or to promoting technical or economic progress, while allowing consumers a fair share of the resulting benefit, and which does not:

(a) impose on the undertakings concerned restrictions which are not indispensable to the attainment of these objectives;

(b) afford such undertakings the possibility of eliminating competition in respect of a substantial part of the products in question.

Articles 102–106 *****

Section 2 Aids granted by States

Article 107

1. Save as otherwise provided in the Treaties, any aid granted by a Member State or through State resources in any form whatsoever which distorts or threatens to distort competition by favouring certain undertakings or the production of certain goods shall, in so far as it affects trade between Member States, be incompatible with the internal market.

2. The following shall be compatible with the internal market:

(a) aid having a social character, granted to individual consumers, provided that such aid is granted without discrimination related to the origin of the products concerned;

(b) aid to make good the damage caused by natural disasters or exceptional occurrences;

(c) aid granted to the economy of certain areas of the Federal Republic of Germany affected by the division of Germany, in so far as such aid is required in order to compensate for the economic disadvantages caused by that division. Five years after the entry into force of the Treaty of Lisbon, the Council, acting on a proposal from the Commission, may adopt a decision repealing this point.

3. The following may be considered to be compatible with the internal market:

(a) aid to promote the economic development of areas where the standard of living is abnormally low or where there is serious underemployment, and of the regions referred to in Article 349, in view of their structural, economic and social situation;

(b) aid to promote the execution of an important project of common European interest or to remedy a serious disturbance in the economy of a Member State;

(c) aid to facilitate the development of certain economic activities or of certain economic areas, where such aid does not adversely affect trading conditions to an extent contrary to the common interest;

(d) aid to promote culture and heritage conservation where such aid does not affect trading conditions and competition in the Union to an extent that is contrary to the common interest;

(e) such other categories of aid as may be specified by decision of the Council on a proposal from the Commission.

Articles 108–113 *****

Chapter 3 (Approximation of Laws)

Article 114

1. Save where otherwise provided in the Treaties, the following provisions shall apply for the achievement of the objectives set out in Article 26. The European Parliament and the Council shall, acting in accordance with the ordinary legislative procedure and after consulting the Economic and Social Committee, adopt the measures for the approximation of the provisions laid down by law, regulation or administrative action in Member States which have as their object the establishment and functioning of the internal market.

2. Paragraph 1 shall not apply to fiscal provisions, to those relating to the free movement of persons nor to those relating to the rights and interests of employed persons.

3. The Commission, in its proposals envisaged in paragraph 1 concerning health, safety, environmental protection and consumer protection, will take as a base a high level of protection, taking account in particular of any new development based on scientific facts. Within their respective powers, the European Parliament and the Council will also seek to achieve this objective.

4. If, after the adoption of a harmonisation measure by the European Parliament and the Council, by the Council or by the Commission, a Member State deems it necessary to maintain national provisions on grounds of major needs referred to in Article 36, or relating to the protection of the environment or the working environment, it shall notify the Commission of these provisions as well as the grounds for maintaining them.

5.–10. *****

Articles 115–118 *****

Title VIII Economic and Monetary Policy

Article 119

1. For the purposes set out in Article 3 of the Treaty on European Union, the activities of the Member States and the Union shall include, as provided in the Treaties, the adoption of an economic policy which is based on the close coordination of Member States' economic policies, on the internal market and on the definition of common objectives, and conducted in accordance with the principle of an open market economy with free competition.

2. Concurrently with the foregoing, and as provided in the Treaties and in accordance with the procedures set out therein, these activities shall include a single currency, the euro, and the definition and conduct of a single monetary policy and exchange-rate policy the primary objective of both of which shall be to maintain price stability and, without prejudice to this objective, to support the general economic policies in the Union, in accordance with the principle of an open market economy with free competition.

3. These activities of the Member States and the Union shall entail compliance with the following guiding principles: stable prices, sound public finances and monetary conditions and a sustainable balance of payments.

Articles 120–150 *****

Title X Social Policy

Article 151

The Union and the Member States, having in mind fundamental social rights such as those set out in the European Social Charter signed at Turin on 18 October 1961 and in the 1989 Community Charter of the Fundamental Social Rights of Workers, shall have as their objectives the promotion of employment, improved living and working conditions, so as to make possible their harmonisation while the improvement is being maintained, proper social protection, dialogue between management and labour, the development of human resources with a view to lasting high employment and the combating of exclusion.

To this end the Union and the Member States shall implement measures which take account of the diverse forms of national practices, in particular in the field of contractual relations, and the need to maintain the competitiveness of the Union economy.

They believe that such a development will ensue not only from the functioning of the internal market, which will favour the harmonisation of social systems, but also from the procedures provided for in the Treaties and from the approximation of provisions laid down by law, regulation or administrative action.

Article 152   *****

Article 153

1. With a view to achieving the objectives of Article 151, the Union shall support and complement the activities of the Member States in the following fields:
    (a) improvement in particular of the working environment to protect workers' health and safety;
    (b) working conditions;
    (c) social security and social protection of workers;
    (d) protection of workers where their employment contract is terminated;
    (e) the information and consultation of workers;
    (f) representation and collective defence of the interests of workers and employers, including co-determination, subject to paragraph 5;
    (g) conditions of employment for third-country nationals legally residing in Union territory;
    (h) the integration of persons excluded from the labour market, without prejudice to Article 166;
    (i) equality between men and women with regard to labour market opportunities and treatment at work;
    (j) the combating of social exclusion;
    (k) the modernisation of social protection systems without prejudice to point (c).
2. To this end, the European Parliament and the Council:
    (a) may adopt measures designed to encourage cooperation between Member States through initiatives aimed at improving knowledge, developing exchanges of information and best practices, promoting innovative approaches and evaluating experiences, excluding any harmonisation of the laws and regulations of the Member States;
    (b) may adopt, in the fields referred to in paragraph 1(a) to (i), by means of directives, minimum requirements for gradual implementation, having regard to the conditions and technical rules obtaining in each of the Member States. Such directives shall avoid imposing administrative, financial and legal constraints in a way which would hold back the creation and development of small and medium-sized undertakings.

The European Parliament and the Council shall act in accordance with the ordinary legislative procedure after consulting the Economic and Social Committee and the Committee of the Regions.

In the fields referred to in paragraph 1(c), (d), (f) and (g), the Council shall act unanimously, in accordance with a special legislative procedure, after consulting the European Parliament and the said Committees.

The Council, acting unanimously on a proposal from the Commission, after consulting the European Parliament, may decide to render the ordinary legislative procedure applicable to paragraph 1(d), (f) and (g).

3. A Member State may entrust management and labour, at their joint request, with the implementation of directives adopted pursuant to paragraph 2, or, where appropriate, with the implementation of a Council decision adopted in accordance with Article 155.

In this case, it shall ensure that, no later than the date on which a directive or a decision must be transposed or implemented, management and labour have introduced the necessary measures by agreement, the Member State concerned being required to take any necessary measure enabling it at any time to be in a position to guarantee the results imposed by that directive or that decision.

4. The provisions adopted pursuant to this Article:
- shall not affect the right of Member States to define the fundamental principles of their social security systems and must not significantly affect the financial equilibrium thereof,
- shall not prevent any Member State from maintaining or introducing more stringent protective measures compatible with the Treaties.

5. The provisions of this Article shall not apply to pay, the right of association, the right to strike or the right to impose lock-outs.

Article 154

1. The Commission shall have the task of promoting the consultation of management and labour at Union level and shall take any relevant measure to facilitate their dialogue by ensuring balanced support for the parties.

2. To this end, before submitting proposals in the social policy field, the Commission shall consult management and labour on the possible direction of Union action.

3. If, after such consultation, the Commission considers Union action advisable, it shall consult management and labour on the content of the envisaged proposal. Management and labour shall forward to the Commission an opinion or, where appropriate, a recommendation.

4. On the occasion of the consultation referred to in paragraphs 2 and 3, management and labour may inform the Commission of their wish to initiate the process provided for in Article 155. The duration of this process shall not exceed nine months, unless the management and labour concerned and the Commission decide jointly to extend it.

Article 155

1. Should management and labour so desire, the dialogue between them at Union level may lead to contractual relations, including agreements.

2. Agreements concluded at Union level shall be implemented either in accordance with the procedures and practices specific to management and labour and the Member States or, in matters covered by Article 153, at the joint request of the signatory parties, by a Council decision on a proposal from the Commission. The European Parliament shall be informed.

The Council shall act unanimously where the agreement in question contains one or more provisions relating to one of the areas for which unanimity is required pursuant to Article 153(2).

Article 156

With a view to achieving the objectives of Article 151 and without prejudice to the other provisions of the Treaties, the Commission shall encourage cooperation between the Member States and facilitate the coordination of their action in all social policy fields under this Chapter, particularly in matters relating to:
- employment,
- labour law and working conditions,
- basic and advanced vocational training,
- social security,
- prevention of occupational accidents and diseases,
- occupational hygiene,
- the right of association and collective bargaining between employers and workers.

To this end, the Commission shall act in close contact with Member States by making studies, delivering opinions and arranging consultations both on problems arising at national level and on those of concern to international organisations, in particular initiatives aiming at the establishment of guidelines and indicators, the organisation of exchange of best practice, and the preparation of the necessary elements for periodic monitoring and evaluation. The European Parliament shall be kept fully informed.

Before delivering the opinions provided for in this Article, the Commission shall consult the Economic and Social Committee.

Article 157

1. Each Member State shall ensure that the principle of equal pay for male and female workers for equal work or work of equal value is applied.

2. For the purpose of this Article, 'pay' means the ordinary basic or minimum wage or salary and any other consideration, whether in cash or in kind, which the worker receives directly or indirectly, in respect of his employment, from his employer.

Equal pay without discrimination based on sex means:

(a) that pay for the same work at piece rates shall be calculated on the basis of the same unit of measurement;

(b) that pay for work at time rates shall be the same for the same job.

3. The European Parliament and the Council, acting in accordance with the ordinary legislative procedure, and after consulting the Economic and Social Committee, shall adopt measures to ensure the application of the principle of equal opportunities and equal treatment of men and women in matters of employment and occupation, including the principle of equal pay for equal work or work of equal value.

4. With a view to ensuring full equality in practice between men and women in working life, the principle of equal treatment shall not prevent any Member State from maintaining or adopting measures providing for specific advantages in order to make it easier for the underrepresented sex to pursue a vocational activity or to prevent or compensate for disadvantages in professional careers.

Articles 158–215   *****

Title V International Agreements

Article 216

1. The Union may conclude an agreement with one or more third countries or international organisations where the Treaties so provide or where the conclusion of an agreement is necessary in order to achieve, within the framework of the Union's policies, one of the objectives referred to in the Treaties, or is provided for in a legally binding Union act or is likely to affect common rules or alter their scope.

2. Agreements concluded by the Union are binding upon the institutions of the Union and on its Member States.

Article 217

The Union may conclude with one or more third countries or international organisations agreements establishing an association involving reciprocal rights and obligations, common action and special procedure.

Articles 218–222   *****

PART SIX (INSTITUTIONAL AND FINANCIAL PROVISIONS)

Title I Institutional Provisions

Chapter 1 (The Institutions)

Section 1 The European Parliament

Article 223

1. The European Parliament shall draw up a proposal to lay down the provisions necessary for the election of its Members by direct universal suffrage in accordance with a uniform procedure in all Member States or in accordance with principles common to all Member States.

The Council, acting unanimously in accordance with a special legislative procedure and after obtaining the consent of the European Parliament, which shall act by a majority of its component

Members, shall lay down the necessary provisions. These provisions shall enter into force following their approval by the Member States in accordance with their respective constitutional requirements.

2. The European Parliament, acting by means of regulations on its own initiative in accordance with a special legislative procedure after seeking an opinion from the Commission and with the approval of the Council, shall lay down the regulations and general conditions governing the performance of the duties of its Members. All rules or conditions relating to the taxation of Members or former Members shall require unanimity within the Council.

Article 224

The European Parliament and the Council, acting in accordance with the ordinary legislative procedure, by means of regulations, shall lay down the regulations governing political parties at European level referred to in Article 10(4) of the Treaty on European Union and in particular the rules regarding their funding.

Article 225

The European Parliament may, acting by a majority of its component Members, request the Commission to submit any appropriate proposal on matters on which it considers that a Union act is required for the purpose of implementing the Treaties. If the Commission does not submit a proposal, it shall inform the European Parliament of the reasons.

Article 226

In the course of its duties, the European Parliament may, at the request of a quarter of its component Members, set up a temporary Committee of Inquiry to investigate, without prejudice to the powers conferred by the Treaties on other institutions or bodies, alleged contraventions or maladministration in the implementation of Union law, except where the alleged facts are being examined before a court and while the case is still subject to legal proceedings.

The temporary Committee of Inquiry shall cease to exist on the submission of its report.

The detailed provisions governing the exercise of the right of inquiry shall be determined by the European Parliament, acting by means of regulations on its own initiative in accordance with a special legislative procedure, after obtaining the consent of the Council and the Commission.

Article 227

Any citizen of the Union, and any natural or legal person residing or having its registered office in a Member State, shall have the right to address, individually or in association with other citizens or persons, a petition to the European Parliament on a matter which comes within the Union's fields of activity and which affects him, her or it directly.

Article 228

1. A European Ombudsman, elected by the European Parliament, shall be empowered to receive complaints from any citizen of the Union or any natural or legal person residing or having its registered office in a Member State concerning instances of maladministration in the activities of the Union institutions, bodies, offices or agencies, with the exception of the Court of Justice of the European Union acting in its judicial role. He or she shall examine such complaints and report on them.

In accordance with his duties, the Ombudsman shall conduct inquiries for which he finds grounds, either on his own initiative or on the basis of complaints submitted to him direct or through a Member of the European Parliament, except where the alleged facts are or have been the subject of legal proceedings. Where the Ombudsman establishes an instance of maladministration, he shall refer the matter to the institution, body, office or agency concerned, which shall have a period of three months in which to inform him of its views. The Ombudsman shall then forward a report to the European Parliament and the institution, body, office or agency concerned. The person lodging the complaint shall be informed of the outcome of such inquiries.

The Ombudsman shall submit an annual report to the European Parliament on the outcome of his inquiries.

2. The Ombudsman shall be elected after each election of the European Parliament for the duration of its term of office. The Ombudsman shall be eligible for reappointment.

The Ombudsman may be dismissed by the Court of Justice at the request of the European Parliament if he no longer fulfils the conditions required for the performance of his duties or if he is guilty of serious misconduct.

3. The Ombudsman shall be completely independent in the performance of his duties. In the performance of those duties he shall neither seek nor take instructions from any Government, institution, body, office or entity. The Ombudsman may not, during his term of office, engage in any other occupation, whether gainful or not.

4. The European Parliament acting by means of regulations on its own initiative in accordance with a special legislative procedure shall, after seeking an opinion from the Commission and with the approval of the Council, lay down the regulations and general conditions governing the performance of the Ombudsman's duties.

Article 229

The European Parliament shall hold an annual session. It shall meet, without requiring to be convened, on the second Tuesday in March.

The European Parliament may meet in extraordinary part-session at the request of a majority of its component Members or at the request of the Council or of the Commission.

Article 230

The Commission may attend all the meetings and shall, at its request, be heard.

The Commission shall reply orally or in writing to questions put to it by the European Parliament or by its Members.

The European Council and the Council shall be heard by the European Parliament in accordance with the conditions laid down in the Rules of Procedure of the European Council and those of the Council.

Article 231

Save as otherwise provided in the Treaties, the European Parliament shall act by a majority of the votes cast.

The Rules of Procedure shall determine the quorum.

Article 232

The European Parliament shall adopt its Rules of Procedure, acting by a majority of its Members.

The proceedings of the European Parliament shall be published in the manner laid down in the Treaties and in its Rules of Procedure.

Article 233

The European Parliament shall discuss in open session the annual general report submitted to it by the Commission.

Article 234

If a motion of censure on the activities of the Commission is tabled before it, the European Parliament shall not vote thereon until at least three days after the motion has been tabled and only by open vote.

If the motion of censure is carried by a two-thirds majority of the votes cast, representing a majority of the component Members of the European Parliament, the members of the Commission shall resign as a body and the High Representative of the Union for Foreign Affairs and Security Policy shall resign from duties that he or she carries out in the Commission. They shall remain in office and continue to deal with current business until they are replaced in accordance with Article 17 of the Treaty on European Union. In this case, the term of office of the members of the Commission appointed to replace them shall expire on the date on which the term of office of the members of the Commission obliged to resign as a body would have expired.

Section 2 The European Council

Article 235

1. Where a vote is taken, any member of the European Council may also act on behalf of not more than one other member.

Article 16(4) of the Treaty on European Union and Article 238(2) of this Treaty shall apply to the European Council when it is acting by a qualified majority. Where the European Council decides by vote, its President and the President of the Commission shall not take part in the vote.

Abstentions by members present in person or represented shall not prevent the adoption by the European Council of acts which require unanimity.

2. The President of the European Parliament may be invited to be heard by the European Council.

3. The European Council shall act by a simple majority for procedural questions and for the adoption of its Rules of Procedure.

4. The European Council shall be assisted by the General Secretariat of the Council.

Article 236

The European Council shall adopt by a qualified majority:
  (a) a decision establishing the list of Council configurations, other than those of the General Affairs Council and of the Foreign Affairs Council, in accordance with Article 16(6) of the Treaty on European Union;
  (b) a decision on the Presidency of Council configurations, other than that of Foreign Affairs, in accordance with Article 16(9) of the Treaty on European Union.

Section 3 The Council

Article 237

The Council shall meet when convened by its President on his own initiative or at the request of one of its Members or of the Commission.

Article 238

1. Where it is required to act by a simple majority, the Council shall act by a majority of its component members.

2. By way of derogation from Article 16(4) of the Treaty on European Union, as from 1 November 2014 and subject to the provisions laid down in the Protocol on transitional provisions, where the Council does not act on a proposal from the Commission or from the High Representative of the Union for Foreign Affairs and Security Policy, the qualified majority shall be defined as at least 72 % of the members of the Council, representing Member States comprising at least 65 % of the population of the Union.

3. As from 1 November 2014 and subject to the provisions laid down in the Protocol on transitional provisions, in cases where, under the Treaties, not all the members of the Council participate in voting, a qualified majority shall be defined as follows:
  (a) A qualified majority shall be defined as at least 55 % of the members of the Council representing the participating Member States, comprising at least 65 % of the population of these States.
  A blocking minority must include at least the minimum number of Council members representing more than 35 % of the population of the participating Member States, plus one member, failing which the qualified majority shall be deemed attained;
  (b) By way of derogation from point (a), where the Council does not act on a proposal from the Commission or from the High Representative of the Union for Foreign Affairs and Security Policy, the qualified majority shall be defined as at least 72 % of the members of the Council representing the participating Member States, comprising at least 65 % of the population of these States.

4. Abstentions by Members present in person or represented shall not prevent the adoption by the Council of acts which require unanimity.

Articles 239–243 *****

Section 4 The Commission

Article 244

In accordance with Article 17(5) of the Treaty on European Union, the Members of the Commission shall be chosen on the basis of a system of rotation established unanimously by the European Council and on the basis of the following principles:

(a) Member States shall be treated on a strictly equal footing as regards determination of the sequence of, and the time spent by, their nationals as members of the Commission; consequently, the difference between the total number of terms of office held by nationals of any given pair of Member States may never be more than one;

(b) subject to point (a), each successive Commission shall be so composed as to reflect satisfactorily the demographic and geographical range of all the Member States.

Articles 245–250 *****

Section 5 The Court of Justice of the European Union

Article 251

The Court of Justice shall sit in chambers or in a Grand Chamber, in accordance with the rules laid down for that purpose in the Statute of the Court of Justice of the European Union.

When provided for in the Statute, the Court of Justice may also sit as a full Court.

Article 252

The Court of Justice shall be assisted by eight Advocates-General. Should the Court of Justice so request, the Council, acting unanimously, may increase the number of Advocates-General.

It shall be the duty of the Advocate-General, acting with complete impartiality and independence, to make, in open court, reasoned submissions on cases which, in accordance with the Statute of the Court of Justice of the European Union, require his involvement.

Article 253

The Judges and Advocates-General of the Court of Justice shall be chosen from persons whose independence is beyond doubt and who possess the qualifications required for appointment to the highest judicial offices in their respective countries or who are jurisconsults of recognised competence; they shall be appointed by common accord of the governments of the Member States for a term of six years, after consultation of the panel provided for in Article 255.

Every three years there shall be a partial replacement of the Judges and Advocates-General, in accordance with the conditions laid down in the Statute of the Court of Justice of the European Union.

The Judges shall elect the President of the Court of Justice from among their number for a term of three years. He may be re-elected.

Retiring Judges and Advocates-General may be reappointed.

The Court of Justice shall appoint its Registrar and lay down the rules governing his service.

The Court of Justice shall establish its Rules of Procedure. Those Rules shall require the approval of the Council.

Article 254

The number of Judges of the General Court shall be determined by the Statute of the Court of Justice of the European Union. The Statute may provide for the General Court to be assisted by Advocates-General.

The members of the General Court shall be chosen from persons whose independence is beyond doubt and who possess the ability required for appointment to high judicial office. They shall be appointed by common accord of the governments of the Member States for a term of six years, after consultation of the panel provided for in Article 255. The membership shall be partially renewed every three years.

Retiring members shall be eligible for reappointment.

The Judges shall elect the President of the General Court from among their number for a term of three years. He may be re-elected.

The General Court shall appoint its Registrar and lay down the rules governing his service.

The General Court shall establish its Rules of Procedure in agreement with the Court of Justice. Those Rules shall require the approval of the Council.

Unless the Statute of the Court of Justice of the European Union provides otherwise, the provisions of the Treaties relating to the Court of Justice shall apply to the General Court.

Article 255

A panel shall be set up in order to give an opinion on candidates' suitability to perform the duties of Judge and Advocate-General of the Court of Justice and the General Court before the governments of the Member States make the appointments referred to in Articles 253 and 254.

The panel shall comprise seven persons chosen from among former members of the Court of Justice and the General Court, members of national supreme courts and lawyers of recognised competence, one of whom shall be proposed by the European Parliament. The Council shall adopt a decision establishing the panel's operating rules and a decision appointing its members. It shall act on the initiative of the President of the Court of Justice.

Article 256

1. The General Court shall have jurisdiction to hear and determine at first instance actions or proceedings referred to in Articles 263, 265, 268, 270 and 272, with the exception of those assigned to a specialised court set up under Article 257 and those reserved in the Statute for the Court of Justice. The Statute may provide for the General Court to have jurisdiction for other classes of action or proceeding.

Decisions given by the General Court under this paragraph may be subject to a right of appeal to the Court of Justice on points of law only, under the conditions and within the limits laid down by the Statute.

2. The General Court shall have jurisdiction to hear and determine actions or proceedings brought against decisions of the specialised courts.

Decisions given by the General Court under this paragraph may exceptionally be subject to review by the Court of Justice, under the conditions and within the limits laid down by the Statute, where there is a serious risk of the unity or consistency of Union law being affected.

3. The General Court shall have jurisdiction to hear and determine questions referred for a preliminary ruling under Article 267, in specific areas laid down by the Statute.

Where the General Court considers that the case requires a decision of principle likely to affect the unity or consistency of Union law, it may refer the case to the Court of Justice for a ruling.

Decisions given by the General Court on questions referred for a preliminary ruling may exceptionally be subject to review by the Court of Justice, under the conditions and within the limits laid down by the Statute, where there is a serious risk of the unity or consistency of Union law being affected.

Article 257

The European Parliament and the Council, acting in accordance with the ordinary legislative procedure, may establish specialised courts attached to the General Court to hear and determine at first instance certain classes of action or proceeding brought in specific areas. The European Parliament and the Council shall act by means of regulations either on a proposal from the Commission after consultation of the Court of Justice or at the request of the Court of Justice after consultation of the Commission.

The regulation establishing a specialised court shall lay down the rules on the organisation of the court and the extent of the jurisdiction conferred upon it.

Decisions given by specialised courts may be subject to a right of appeal on points of law only or, when provided for in the regulation establishing the specialised court, a right of appeal also on matters of fact, before the General Court.

The members of the specialised courts shall be chosen from persons whose independence is beyond doubt and who possess the ability required for appointment to judicial office. They shall be appointed by the Council, acting unanimously.

The specialised courts shall establish their Rules of Procedure in agreement with the Court of Justice. Those Rules shall require the approval of the Council.

Unless the regulation establishing the specialised court provides otherwise, the provisions of the Treaties relating to the Court of Justice of the European Union and the provisions of the Statute of the Court of Justice of the European Union shall apply to the specialised courts. Title I of the Statute and Article 64 thereof shall in any case apply to the specialised courts.

Article 258

If the Commission considers that a Member State has failed to fulfil an obligation under the Treaties, it shall deliver a reasoned opinion on the matter after giving the State concerned the opportunity to submit its observations.

If the State concerned does not comply with the opinion within the period laid down by the Commission, the latter may bring the matter before the Court of Justice of the European Union.

Article 259

A Member State which considers that another Member State has failed to fulfil an obligation under the Treaties may bring the matter before the Court of Justice of the European Union.

Before a Member State brings an action against another Member State for an alleged infringement of an obligation under the Treaties, it shall bring the matter before the Commission.

The Commission shall deliver a reasoned opinion after each of the States concerned has been given the opportunity to submit its own case and its observations on the other party's case both orally and in writing.

If the Commission has not delivered an opinion within three months of the date on which the matter was brought before it, the absence of such opinion shall not prevent the matter from being brought before the Court.

Article 260

1. If the Court of Justice of the European Union finds that a Member State has failed to fulfil an obligation under the Treaties, the State shall be required to take the necessary measures to comply with the judgment of the Court.

2. If the Commission considers that the Member State concerned has not taken the necessary measures to comply with the judgment of the Court, it may bring the case before the Court after giving that State the opportunity to submit its observations. It shall specify the amount of the lump sum or penalty payment to be paid by the Member State concerned which it considers appropriate in the circumstances.

If the Court finds that the Member State concerned has not complied with its judgment it may impose a lump sum or penalty payment on it.

This procedure shall be without prejudice to Article 259.

3. When the Commission brings a case before the Court pursuant to Article 258 on the grounds that the Member State concerned has failed to fulfil its obligation to notify measures transposing a directive adopted under a legislative procedure, it may, when it deems appropriate, specify the amount of the lump sum or penalty payment to be paid by the Member State concerned which it considers appropriate in the circumstances.

If the Court finds that there is an infringement it may impose a lump sum or penalty payment on the Member State concerned not exceeding the amount specified by the Commission. The payment obligation shall take effect on the date set by the Court in its judgment.

Article 261

Regulations adopted jointly by the European Parliament and the Council, and by the Council, pursuant to the provisions of the Treaties, may give the Court of Justice of the European Union unlimited jurisdiction with regard to the penalties provided for in such regulations.

Article 262   *****

Article 263

The Court of Justice of the European Union shall review the legality of legislative acts, of acts of the Council, of the Commission and of the European Central Bank, other than recommendations and opinions, and of acts of the European Parliament and of the European Council intended to produce legal effects *vis-à-vis* third parties. It shall also review the legality of acts of bodies, offices or agencies of the Union intended to produce legal effects *vis-à-vis* third parties.

It shall for this purpose have jurisdiction in actions brought by a Member State, the European Parliament, the Council or the Commission on grounds of lack of competence, infringement of an essential procedural requirement, infringement of the Treaties or of any rule of law relating to their application, or misuse of powers.

The Court shall have jurisdiction under the same conditions in actions brought by the Court of Auditors, by the European Central Bank and by the Committee of the Regions for the purpose of protecting their prerogatives.

Any natural or legal person may, under the conditions laid down in the first and second paragraphs, institute proceedings against an act addressed to that person or which is of direct and individual concern to them, and against a regulatory act which is of direct concern to them and does not entail implementing measures.

Acts setting up bodies, offices and agencies of the Union may lay down specific conditions and arrangements concerning actions brought by natural or legal persons against acts of these bodies, offices or agencies intended to produce legal effects in relation to them.

The proceedings provided for in this Article shall be instituted within two months of the publication of the measure, or of its notification to the plaintiff, or, in the absence thereof, of the day on which it came to the knowledge of the latter, as the case may be.

Article 264

If the action is well founded, the Court of Justice of the European Union shall declare the act concerned to be void.

However, the Court shall, if it considers this necessary, state which of the effects of the act which it has declared void shall be considered as definitive.

Articles 265, 266   *****

Article 267

The Court of Justice of the European Union shall have jurisdiction to give preliminary rulings concerning:

       (a) the interpretation of the Treaties;

       (b) the validity and interpretation of acts of the institutions, bodies, offices or agencies of the Union;

Where such a question is raised before any court or tribunal of a Member State, that court or tribunal may, if it considers that a decision on the question is necessary to enable it to give judgment, request the Court to give a ruling thereon.

Where any such question is raised in a case pending before a court or tribunal of a Member State against whose decisions there is no judicial remedy under national law, that court or tribunal shall bring the matter before the Court.

If such a question is raised in a case pending before a court or tribunal of a Member State with regard to a person in custody, the Court of Justice of the European Union shall act with the minimum of delay.

Articles 268–274   *****

Article 275

The Court of Justice of the European Union shall not have jurisdiction with respect to the provisions relating to the common foreign and security policy nor with respect to acts adopted on the basis of those provisions.

However, the Court shall have jurisdiction to monitor compliance with Article 40 of the Treaty on European Union and to rule on proceedings, brought in accordance with the conditions laid down in the fourth paragraph of Article 263 of this Treaty, reviewing the legality of decisions providing for restrictive measures against natural or legal persons adopted by the Council on the basis of Chapter 2 of Title V of the Treaty on European Union.

Articles 276–287   *****

Chapter 2   (Legal Acts of the Union, Adoption Procedures and Other Provisions)

Section 1   The legal acts of the Union

Article 288

To exercise the Union's competences, the institutions shall adopt regulations, directives, decisions, recommendations and opinions.

A regulation shall have general application. It shall be binding in its entirety and directly applicable in all Member States.

A directive shall be binding, as to the result to be achieved, upon each Member State to which it is addressed, but shall leave to the national authorities the choice of form and methods.

A decision shall be binding in its entirety. A decision which specifies those to whom it is addressed shall be binding only on them.

Recommendations and opinions shall have no binding force.

Articles 289–293   *****

Article 294

1. Where reference is made in the Treaties to the ordinary legislative procedure for the adoption of an act, the following procedure shall apply.

2. The Commission shall submit a proposal to the European Parliament and the Council.

First reading

3. The European Parliament shall adopt its position at first reading and communicate it to the Council.

4. If the Council approves the European Parliament's position, the act concerned shall be adopted in the wording which corresponds to the position of the European Parliament.

5. If the Council does not approve the European Parliament's position, it shall adopt its position at first reading and communicate it to the European Parliament.

6. The Council shall inform the European Parliament fully of the reasons which led it to adopt its position at first reading. The Commission shall inform the European Parliament fully of its position.

Second reading

7. If, within three months of such communication, the European Parliament:
   (a) approves the Council's position at first reading or has not taken a decision, the act concerned shall be deemed to have been adopted in the wording which corresponds to the position of the Council;
   (b) rejects, by a majority of its component members, the Council's position at first reading, the proposed act shall be deemed not to have been adopted;
   (c) proposes, by a majority of its component members, amendments to the Council's position at first reading, the text thus amended shall be forwarded to the Council and to the Commission, which shall deliver an opinion on those amendments.

8. If, within three months of receiving the European Parliament's amendments, the Council, acting by a qualified majority:

(a) approves all those amendments, the act in question shall be deemed to have been adopted;

(b) does not approve all the amendments, the President of the Council, in agreement with the President of the European Parliament, shall within six weeks convene a meeting of the Conciliation Committee.

9. The Council shall act unanimously on the amendments on which the Commission has delivered a negative opinion.

Conciliation

10. The Conciliation Committee, which shall be composed of the members of the Council or their representatives and an equal number of members representing the European Parliament, shall have the task of reaching agreement on a joint text, by a qualified majority of the members of the Council or their representatives and by a majority of the members representing the European Parliament within six weeks of its being convened, on the basis of the positions of the European Parliament and the Council at second reading.

11. The Commission shall take part in the Conciliation Committee's proceedings and shall take all necessary initiatives with a view to reconciling the positions of the European Parliament and the Council.

12. If, within six weeks of its being convened, the Conciliation Committee does not approve the joint text, the proposed act shall be deemed not to have been adopted.

Third reading

13. If, within that period, the Conciliation Committee approves a joint text, the European Parliament, acting by a majority of the votes cast, and the Council, acting by a qualified majority, shall each have a period of six weeks from that approval in which to adopt the act in question in accordance with the joint text. If they fail to do so, the proposed act shall be deemed not to have been adopted.

14. The periods of three months and six weeks referred to in this Article shall be extended by a maximum of one month and two weeks respectively at the initiative of the European Parliament or the Council.

Special provisions

15. Where, in the cases provided for in the Treaties, a legislative act is submitted to the ordinary legislative procedure on the initiative of a group of Member States, on a recommendation by the European Central Bank, or at the request of the Court of Justice, paragraph 2, the second sentence of paragraph 6, and paragraph 9 shall not apply.

In such cases, the European Parliament and the Council shall communicate the proposed act to the Commission with their positions at first and second readings. The European Parliament or the Council may request the opinion of the Commission throughout the procedure, which the Commission may also deliver on its own initiative. It may also, if it deems it necessary, take part in the Conciliation Committee in accordance with paragraph 11.

Articles 295–334 *****

PART SEVEN (GENERAL AND FINAL PROVISIONS)

Articles 335–351 *****

Article 352

1. If action by the Union should prove necessary, within the framework of the policies defined in the Treaties, to attain one of the objectives set out in the Treaties, and the Treaties have not provided the necessary powers, the Council, acting unanimously on a proposal from the Commission and after obtaining the consent of the European Parliament, shall adopt the appropriate measures. Where the measures in question are adopted by the Council in accordance with a special legislative

procedure, it shall also act unanimously on a proposal from the Commission and after obtaining the consent of the European Parliament.

2. Using the procedure for monitoring the subsidiarity principle referred to in Article 5(3) of the Treaty on European Union, the Commission shall draw national Parliaments' attention to proposals based on this Article.

3. Measures based on this Article shall not entail harmonisation of Member States' laws or regulations in cases where the Treaties exclude such harmonisation.

4. This Article cannot serve as a basis for attaining objectives pertaining to the common foreign and security policy and any acts adopted pursuant to this Article shall respect the limits set out in Article 40, second paragraph, of the Treaty on European Union.

Article 353–355   *****

Article 356
This Treaty is concluded for an unlimited period.
*****

PROTOCOLS

PROTOCOL (NO 1) ON THE ROLE OF NATIONAL PARLIAMENTS IN THE EUROPEAN UNION

Article 1
Commission consultation documents (green and white papers and communications) shall be forwarded directly by the Commission to national Parliaments upon publication. The Commission shall also forward the annual legislative programme as well as any other instrument of legislative planning or policy to national Parliaments, at the same time as to the European Parliament and the Council.

Article 2
Draft legislative acts sent to the European Parliament and to the Council shall be forwarded to national Parliaments.

For the purposes of this Protocol, 'draft legislative acts' shall mean proposals from the Commission, initiatives from a group of Member States, initiatives from the European Parliament, requests from the Court of Justice, recommendations from the European Central Bank and requests from the European Investment Bank for the adoption of a legislative act.

Draft legislative acts originating from the Commission shall be forwarded to national Parliaments directly by the Commission, at the same time as to the European Parliament and the Council.

Draft legislative acts originating from the European Parliament shall be forwarded to national Parliaments directly by the European Parliament.

Draft legislative acts originating from a group of Member States, the Court of Justice, the European Central Bank or the European Investment Bank shall be forwarded to national Parliaments by the Council.

Article 3
National Parliaments may send to the Presidents of the European Parliament, the Council and the Commission a reasoned opinion on whether a draft legislative act complies with the principle of subsidiarity, in accordance with the procedure laid down in the Protocol on the application of the principles of subsidiarity and proportionality.

If the draft legislative act originates from a group of Member States, the President of the Council shall forward the reasoned opinion or opinions to the governments of those Member States.

If the draft legislative act originates from the Court of Justice, the European Central Bank or the European Investment Bank, the President of the Council shall forward the reasoned opinion or opinions to the institution or body concerned.

Article 4

An eight-week period shall elapse between a draft legislative act being made available to national Parliaments in the official languages of the Union and the date when it is placed on a provisional agenda for the Council for its adoption or for adoption of a position under a legislative procedure. Exceptions shall be possible in cases of urgency, the reasons for which shall be stated in the act or position of the Council. Save in urgent cases for which due reasons have been given, no agreement may be reached on a draft legislative act during those eight weeks. Save in urgent cases for which due reasons have been given, a ten-day period shall elapse between the placing of a draft legislative act on the provisional agenda for the Council and the adoption of a position.

Article 5

The agendas for and the outcome of meetings of the Council, including the minutes of meetings where the Council is deliberating on draft legislative acts, shall be forwarded directly to national Parliaments, at the same time as to Member States' governments.

Article 6

When the European Council intends to make use of the first or second subparagraphs of Article 48(7) of the Treaty on European Union, national Parliaments shall be informed of the initiative of the European Council at least six months before any decision is adopted.

Article 7

The Court of Auditors shall forward its annual report to national Parliaments, for information, at the same time as to the European Parliament and to the Council.

Article 8

Where the national Parliamentary system is not unicameral, Articles 1 to 7 shall apply to the component chambers.

9, 10 *****
*****

European Communities Act 1972*

(1972, c. 68)

An Act to make provision in connection with the enlargement of the European Communities to include the United Kingdom, together with (for certain purposes) the Channel Islands, the Isle of Man and Gibraltar.   *[17th October 1972]*

Territorial extent: United Kingdom

PART I GENERAL PROVISIONS

1 *Short title and interpretation*

(1) *This Act may be cited as the European Communities Act 1972.*

(2) *In this Act ...*

['the EU' *means the European Union, being the Union established by the Treaty on European Union signed at Maastricht on 7th February 1992 (as amended by any later Treaty);*]

---

* **Editor's Note:** Section 1 of the European Union (Withdrawal) Act 2018 states that: 'The European Communities Act 1972 is repealed on exit day.' Exit day was 31 January 2020. Though the effect of the 1972 Act was initially saved by s. 1A(2) European Union (Withdrawal Agreement) Act 2020 to allow for the implementation period, when this expired on 31 December 2020, the 1972 Act was repealed. This said, a few important sections of the European Communities Act 1972 are here included for their historic importance.

'*the Communities*' *means the European Economic Community, the European Coal and Steel Community and the European Atomic Energy Community;*

'*the Treaties*' *or* ['*the EU Treaties*'] *means, subject to subsection (3) below, the pre-accession treaties, that is to say, those described in Part I of Schedule 1 to this Act, taken with—*

***** *[list omitted]**

and any expression defined in Schedule 1 to this Act has the meaning there given to it.

(3) If Her Majesty by Order in Council declares that a treaty specified in the Order is to be regarded as one of [the EU Treaties] as herein defined, the Order shall be conclusive that it is to be so regarded; but a treaty entered into by the United Kingdom after the 22nd January 1972, other than a pre-accession treaty to which the United Kingdom accedes on terms settled on or before that date, shall not be so regarded unless it is so specified, nor be so specified unless a draft of the Order in Council has been approved by resolution of each House of Parliament.

*(4) For purposes of subsections (2) and (3) above, '*treaty*' includes any international agreement, and any protocol or annex to a treaty or international agreement.*

2   *General implementation of Treaties*

(1) All such rights, powers, liabilities, obligations and restrictions from time to time created or arising by or under the Treaties, and all such remedies and procedures from time to time provided for by or under the Treaties, as in accordance with the Treaties are without further enactment to be given legal effect or used in the United Kingdom shall be recognised and available in law, and be enforced, allowed and followed accordingly; and the expression ['enforceable EU right*'] and similar expressions shall be read as referring to one to which this subsection applies.*

(2) Subject to Schedule 2 to this Act, at any time after its passing Her Majesty may by Order in Council, and any designated Minister or department may by [order, rules, regulations or schemes], make provision—

     (a) for the purpose of implementing any [EU obligation] of the United Kingdom, or enabling any such obligation to be implemented, or of enabling any rights enjoyed or to be enjoyed by the United Kingdom under or by virtue of the Treaties to be exercised; or

     (b) for the purpose of dealing with matters arising out of or related to any such obligation or rights or the coming into force, or the operation from time to time, of subsection (1) above;

and in the exercise of any statutory power or duty, including any power to give directions or to legislate by means of orders, rules, regulations or other subordinate instrument, the person entrusted with the power or duty may have regard to the [objects of the EU] and to any such obligation or rights as aforesaid.

*In this subsection '*designated Minister or Department*' means such Minister of the Crown or government department as may from time to time be designated by Order in Council in relation to any matter or for any purpose, but subject to such restrictions or conditions (if any) as may be specified by the Order in Council.*

(3) There shall be charged on and issued out of the Consolidated Fund or, if so determined by the Treasury, the National Loans Fund the amounts required to meet any [EU obligation] to make payments to [the EU or a member State], or any [EU obligation] in respect of contributions to the capital or reserves of the European Investment Bank or in respect of loans to the Bank, or to redeem any notes or obligations issued or created in respect of any such [EU obligation]; and, except as otherwise provided by or under any enactment,—

     (a) any other expenses incurred under or by virtue of the Treaties or this Act by any Minister of the Crown or government department may be paid out of moneys provided by Parliament; and

---

* **Editor's Note:** The full list of Treaties in s. 1(2) includes those adopted and ratified by the United Kingdom since 1972 as well as the original treaties, so that major constitutional changes such as the incorporation of the Single European Act of 1986, the Maastricht Treaty 1992 and the Lisbon Treaty are achieved by amendments to the subsection.

    (b) *any sums received under or by virtue of the Treaties or this Act by any Minister of the Crown or government department, save for such sums as may be required for disbursements permitted by any other enactment, shall be paid into the Consolidated Fund or, if so determined by the Treasury, the National Loans Fund.*

    (4) The provision that may be made under subsection (2) above includes, subject to Schedule 2 to this Act, any such provision (of any such extent) as might be made by Act of Parliament, and any enactment passed or to be passed, other than one contained in this Part of this Act, shall be construed and have effect subject to the foregoing provisions of this section; but, except as may be provided by any Act passed after this Act, Schedule 2 shall have effect in connection with the powers conferred by this and the following sections of this Act to make Orders in Council [or orders, rules, regulations or schemes].

    (5), (6) *******

3 Decisions on, and proof of, Treaties and [EU instruments], etc

    (1) For the purposes of all legal proceedings any question as to the meaning or effect of any of the Treaties, or as to the validity, meaning or effect of any [EU instrument], shall be treated as a question of law (and, if not referred to the European Court, be for determination as such in accordance with the principles laid down by and any relevant decision of [the European Court]).

    (2) Judicial notice shall be taken of the Treaties, of the [Official Journal of the European Union] and of any decision of, or expression of opinion by [the European Court] on any such question as aforesaid; and the Official Journal shall be admissible as evidence of any instrument or other act thereby communicated of [the EU] or of any [EU institution].

    (3), (4), (5) *******

*****

Section 2   **SCHEDULE 2**

PROVISIONS AS TO SUBORDINATE LEGISLATION

    1.—*(1) The powers conferred by section 2(2) of this Act to make provision for the purposes mentioned in section 2(2)(a) and (b) shall not include power—*

    (a) *to make any provision imposing or increasing taxation; or*

    (b) *to make any provision taking effect from a date earlier than that of the making of the instrument containing the provision; or*

    (c) *to confer any power to legislate by means of orders, rules regulations or other subordinate instrument, other than rules of procedure for any court or tribunal; or*

    (d) *to create any new criminal offence punishable with imprisonment for more than two years or punishable on summary conviction with imprisonment for more than [the prescribed term] or with a fine of more than [level 5 on the standard scale] (if not calculated on a daily basis) or with a fine of more than [£100 a day].*

    (2) Sub-paragraph (1)(c) above shall not be taken to preclude the modification of a power to legislate conferred otherwise than under section 2(2), or the extension of any such power to purposes of the like nature as those for which it was conferred; and a power to give directions as to matters of administration is not to be regarded as a power to legislate within the meaning of sub-paragraph (1)(c).

    [1A.—*(1) Where—*

    (a) *subordinate legislation makes provision for a purpose mentioned in section 2(2) of this Act,*

    (b) *the legislation contains a reference to a [EU instrument] or any provision of a [EU instrument], and*

    (c) *it appears to the person making the legislation that it is necessary or expedient for the reference to be construed as a reference to that instrument or that provision as amended from time to time, the subordinate legislation may make express provision to that effect.*

(2) In this paragraph 'subordinate legislation' means any Order in Council, order, rules, regulations, scheme, warrant, byelaws or other instrument made after the coming into force of this paragraph under any Act, Act of the Scottish Parliament [, Measure or Act of the National Assembly for Wales] or Northern Ireland legislation passed or made before or after the coming into force of this paragraph.]

2.—(1) Subject to paragraph 3 below, where a provision contained in any section of this Act confers power to make [any order, rules, regulations or scheme] (otherwise than by modification or extension of an existing power), the power shall be exercisable by statutory instrument.

(2) Any statutory instrument containing an Order in Council or [any order, rules, regulations or scheme] made in the exercise of a power so conferred, if made without a draft having been approved by resolution of each House of Parliament, shall be subject to annulment in pursuance of a resolution of either House.

[2A.—(1) This paragraph applies where, pursuant to paragraph 2(2) above, a draft of a statutory instrument containing provision made in exercise of the power conferred by section 2(2) of this Act is laid before Parliament for approval by resolution of each House of Parliament and—

    (a) the instrument also contains provision made in exercise of a power conferred by any other enactment; and

    (b) apart from this paragraph, any of the conditions in sub-paragraph (2) below applies in relation to the instrument so far as containing that provision.

(2) The conditions referred to in sub-paragraph (1)(b) above are that—

    (a) the instrument, so far as containing the provision referred to in sub-paragraph (1)(a) above, is by virtue of any enactment subject to annulment in pursuance of a resolution of either House of Parliament;

    (b) the instrument so far as containing that provision is by virtue of any enactment required to be laid before Parliament after being made and to be approved by resolution of each House of Parliament in order to come into or remain in force;

    (c) in a case not falling within paragraph (a) or (b) above, the instrument so far as containing that provision is by virtue of any enactment required to be laid before Parliament after being made;

    (d) the instrument or a draft of the instrument so far as containing that provision is not by virtue of any enactment required at any time to be laid before Parliament.

(3) Where this paragraph applies in relation to the draft of a statutory instrument—

    (a) the instrument, so far as containing the provision referred to in sub-paragraph (1)(a) above, may not be made unless the draft is approved by a resolution of each House of Parliament;

    (b) in a case where the condition in sub-paragraph (2)(a) above is satisfied, the instrument so far as containing that provision is not subject to annulment in pursuance of a resolution of either House of Parliament;

    (c) in a case where the condition in sub-paragraph (2)(b) above is satisfied, the instrument is not required to be laid before Parliament after being made (and accordingly any require-ment that the instrument be approved by each House of Parliament in order for it to come into or remain in force does not apply); and

    (d) in a case where the condition in sub-paragraph (2)(c) above is satisfied, the instrument so far as containing that provision is not required to be laid before Parliament after being made.

(4) In this paragraph, references to an enactment are to an enactment passed or made before or after the coming into force of this paragraph.

2B.—(1) This paragraph applies where, pursuant to paragraph 2(2) above, a statutory instru-ment containing provision made in exercise of the power conferred by section 2(2) of this Act is laid before Parliament under section 5 of the Statutory Instruments Act 1946 (instruments subject to annul-ment) and—

    (a) the instrument also contains provision made in exercise of a power conferred by any other enactment; and

    (b) apart from this paragraph, either of the conditions in sub-paragraph (2) below applies in relation to the instrument so far as containing that provision.

(2) *The conditions referred to in sub-paragraph (1)(b) above are that—*

   (a) *the instrument so far as containing the provision referred to in sub-paragraph (1)(a) above is by virtue of any enactment required to be laid before Parliament after being made but—*

      (i) *is not subject to annulment in pursuance of a resolution of either House of Parliament; and*

      (ii) *is not by virtue of any enactment required to be approved by resolution of each House of Parliament in order to come into or remain in force;*

   (b) *the instrument or a draft of the instrument so far as containing that provision is not by virtue of any enactment required at any time to be laid before Parliament.*

(3) *Where this paragraph applies in relation to a statutory instrument, the instrument, so far as containing the provision referred to in sub-paragraph (1)(a) above, is subject to annulment in pursuance of a resolution of either House of Parliament.*

(4) *In this paragraph, references to an enactment are to an enactment passed or made before or after the coming into force of this paragraph.*

2C. *Paragraphs 2A and 2B above apply to a Scottish statutory instrument containing provision made in the exercise of the power conferred by section 2(2) of this Act (and a draft of any such instrument) as they apply to any other statutory instrument containing such provision (or, as the case may be, any draft of such an instrument), but subject to the following modifications—*

   (a) *references to Parliament and to each or either House of Parliament are to be read as references to the Scottish Parliament;*

   (b) *references to an enactment include an enactment comprised in, or in an instrument made under, an Act of the Scottish Parliament; and*

   (c) *the reference in paragraph 2B(1) to section 5 of the Statutory Instruments Act 1946 is to be read as a reference to [section 28 of the Interpretation and Legislative Reform (Scotland) Act 2010 (asp 10)].]*

*****

European Union Charter of Fundamental Rights (2000)*

Preamble

The peoples of Europe, in creating an ever closer union among them, are resolved to share a peaceful future based on common values.

Conscious of its spiritual and moral heritage, the Union is founded on the indivisible, universal values of human dignity, freedom, equality and solidarity; it is based on the principles of democracy and the rule of law. It places the individual at the heart of its activities, by establishing the citizenship of the Union and by creating an area of freedom, security and justice.

The Union contributes to the preservation and to the development of these common values while respecting the diversity of the cultures and traditions of the peoples of Europe as well as the national identities of the Member States and the organisation of their public authorities at national, regional and local levels; it seeks to promote balanced and sustainable development and ensures free movement of persons, goods, services and capital, and the freedom of establishment.

To this end, it is necessary to strengthen the protection of fundamental rights in the light of changes in society, social progress and scientific and technological developments by making those rights more visible in a Charter.

This Charter reaffirms, with due regard for the powers and tasks of the Community and the Union and the principle of subsidiarity, the rights as they result, in particular, from the constitutional traditions and international obligations common to the Member States, the European Convention for the Protection of Human Rights and Fundamental Freedoms, the Social Charters adopted by the Union and by the Council of Europe and the case law of the Court of Justice of the European Union and of the European Court of Human Rights. In this context the Charter will be interpreted by the courts of the Union and the Member States with due regard to the explanations prepared under the authority of the Praesidium of the Convention which drafted the Charter and updated under the responsibility of the Praesidium of the European Convention.

Enjoyment of these rights entails responsibilities and duties with regard to other persons, to the human community and to future generations.

The Union therefore recognises the rights, freedoms and principles set out hereafter.

Chapter I Dignity

Article 1   Human dignity
Human dignity is inviolable. It must be respected and protected.

Article 2   Right to life
1. Everyone has the right to life.
2. No one shall be condemned to the death penalty, or executed.

Article 3   Right to the integrity of the person
1. Everyone has the right to respect for his or her physical and mental integrity.
2. In the fields of medicine and biology, the following must be respected in particular:
   • the free and informed consent of the person concerned, according to the procedures laid down by law,
   • the prohibition of eugenic practices, in particular those aiming at the selection of persons,
   • the prohibition on making the human body and its parts as such a source of financial gain,
   • the prohibition of the reproductive cloning of human beings.

Article 4   Prohibition of torture and inhuman or degrading treatment or punishment
No one shall be subjected to torture or to inhuman or degrading treatment or punishment.

Article 5   Prohibition of slavery and forced labour
1. No one shall be held in slavery or servitude.
2. No one shall be required to perform forced or compulsory labour.
3. Trafficking in human beings is prohibited.

Chapter II Freedoms

Article 6   Right to liberty and security
Everyone has the right to liberty and security of person.

Article 7   Respect for private and family life
Everyone has the right to respect for his or her private and family life, home and communications.

Article 8   Protection of personal data
1. Everyone has the right to the protection of personal data concerning him or her.
2. Such data must be processed fairly for specified purposes and on the basis of the consent of the person concerned or some other legitimate basis laid down by law. Everyone has the right of access to data which has been collected concerning him or her, and the right to have it rectified.
3. Compliance with these rules shall be subject to control by an independent authority.

Article 9   Right to marry and right to found a family
The right to marry and the right to found a family shall be guaranteed in accordance with the national laws governing the exercise of these rights.

Article 10   Freedom of thought, conscience and religion

1. Everyone has the right to freedom of thought, conscience and religion. This right includes freedom to change religion or belief and freedom, either alone or in community with others and in public or in private, to manifest religion or belief, in worship, teaching, practice and observance.

2. The right to conscientious objection is recognised, in accordance with the national laws governing the exercise of this right.

Article 11   Freedom of expression and information

1. Everyone has the right to freedom of expression. This right shall include freedom to hold opinions and to receive and impart information and ideas without interference by public authority and regardless of frontiers.

2. The freedom and pluralism of the media shall be respected.

Article 12   Freedom of assembly and of association

1. Everyone has the right to freedom of peaceful assembly and to freedom of association at all levels, in particular in political, trade union and civic matters, which implies the right of everyone to form and to join trade unions for the protection of his or her interests.

2. Political parties at Union level contribute to expressing the political will of the citizens of the Union.

Article 13   Freedom of the arts and sciences

The arts and scientific research shall be free of constraint. Academic freedom shall be respected.

Article 14   Right to education

1. Everyone has the right to education and to have access to vocational and continuing training.

2. This right includes the possibility to receive free compulsory education.

3. The freedom to found educational establishments with due respect for democratic principles and the right of parents to ensure the education and teaching of their children in conformity with their religious, philosophical and pedagogical convictions shall be respected, in accordance with the national laws governing the exercise of such freedom and right.

Article 15   Freedom to choose an occupation and right to engage in work

1. Everyone has the right to engage in work and to pursue a freely chosen or accepted occupation.

2. Every citizen of the Union has the freedom to seek employment, to work, to exercise the right of establishment and to provide services in any Member State.

3. Nationals of third countries who are authorised to work in the territories of the Member States are entitled to working conditions equivalent to those of citizens of the Union.

Article 16   Freedom to conduct a business

The freedom to conduct a business in accordance with Community law and national laws and practices is recognised.

Article 17   Right to property

1. Everyone has the right to own, use, dispose of and bequeath his or her lawfully acquired possessions. No one may be deprived of his or her possessions, except in the public interest and in the cases and under the conditions provided for by law, subject to fair compensation being paid in good time for their loss. The use of property may be regulated by law insofar as is necessary for the general interest.

2. Intellectual property shall be protected.

Article 18   Right to asylum

The right to asylum shall be guaranteed with due respect for the rules of the Geneva Convention of 28 July 1951 and the Protocol of 31 January 1967 relating to the status of refugees and in accordance with the Treaty on European Union and the Treaty on the Functioning of the European Union (hereinafter referred to as 'the Treaties').

Article 19　Protection in the event of removal, expulsion or extradition

1. Collective expulsions are prohibited.

2. No one may be removed, expelled or extradited to a State where there is a serious risk that he or she would be subjected to the death penalty, torture or other inhuman or degrading treatment or punishment.

Chapter III　Equality

Article 20　Equality before the law

Everyone is equal before the law.

Article 21　Non-discrimination

1. Any discrimination based on any ground such as sex, race, colour, ethnic or social origin, genetic features, language, religion or belief, political or any other opinion, membership of a national minority, property, birth, disability, age or sexual orientation shall be prohibited.

2. Within the scope of application of the Treaty establishing the European Community and of the Treaty on European Union, and without prejudice to the special provisions of those Treaties, any discrimination on grounds of nationality shall be prohibited.

Article 22　Cultural, religious and linguistic diversity

The Union shall respect cultural, religious and linguistic diversity.

Article 23　Equality between men and women

Equality between men and women must be ensured in all areas, including employment, work and pay.

The principle of equality shall not prevent the maintenance or adoption of measures providing for specific advantages in favour of the under-represented sex.

Article 24　The rights of the child

1. Children shall have the right to such protection and care as is necessary for their well-being. They may express their views freely. Such views shall be taken into consideration on matters which concern them in accordance with their age and maturity.

2. In all actions relating to children, whether taken by public authorities or private institutions, the child's best interests must be a primary consideration.

3. Every child shall have the right to maintain on a regular basis a personal relationship and direct contact with both his or her parents, unless that is contrary to his or her interests.

Article 25　The rights of the elderly

The Union recognises and respects the rights of the elderly to lead a life of dignity and independence and to participate in social and cultural life.

Article 26　Integration of persons with disabilities

The Union recognises and respects the right of persons with disabilities to benefit from measures designed to ensure their independence, social and occupational integration and participation in the life of the community.

Chapter IV　Solidarity

Article 27　Workers' right to information and consultation within the undertaking

Workers or their representatives must, at the appropriate levels, be guaranteed information and consultation in good time in the cases and under the conditions provided for by Community law and national laws and practices.

Article 28 Right of collective bargaining and action

Workers and employers, or their respective organisations, have, in accordance with Community law and national laws and practices, the right to negotiate and conclude collective agreements at the appropriate levels and, in cases of conflicts of interest, to take collective action to defend their interests, including strike action.

Article 29 Right of access to placement services

Everyone has the right of access to a free placement service.

Article 30 Protection in the event of unjustified dismissal

Every worker has the right to protection against unjustified dismissal, in accordance with Community law and national laws and practices.

Article 31 Fair and just working conditions

1. Every worker has the right to working conditions which respect his or her health, safety and dignity.

2. Every worker has the right to limitation of maximum working hours, to daily and weekly rest periods and to an annual period of paid leave.

Article 32 Prohibition of child labour and protection of young people at work

The employment of children is prohibited. The minimum age of admission to employment may not be lower than the minimum school-leaving age, without prejudice to such rules as may be more favourable to young people and except for limited derogations.

Young people admitted to work must have working conditions appropriate to their age and be protected against economic exploitation and any work likely to harm their safety, health or physical, mental, moral or social development or to interfere with their education.

Article 33 Family and professional life

1. The family shall enjoy legal, economic and social protection.

2. To reconcile family and professional life, everyone shall have the right to protection from dismissal for a reason connected with maternity and the right to paid maternity leave and to parental leave following the birth or adoption of a child.

Article 34 Social security and social assistance

1. The Union recognises and respects the entitlement to social security benefits and social services providing protection in cases such as maternity, illness, industrial accidents, dependency or old age, and in the case of loss of employment, in accordance with the procedures laid down by Community law and national laws and practices.

2. Everyone residing and moving legally within the European Union is entitled to social security benefits and social advantages in accordance with Community law and national laws and practices.

3. In order to combat social exclusion and poverty, the Union recognises and respects the right to social and housing assistance so as to ensure a decent existence for all those who lack sufficient resources, in accordance with the procedures laid down by Community law and national laws and practices.

Article 35 Health care

Everyone has the right of access to preventive health care and the right to benefit from medical treatment under the conditions established by national laws and practices. A high level of human health protection shall be ensured in the definition and implementation of all Union policies and activities.

Article 36 Access to services of general economic interest

The Union recognises and respects access to services of general economic interest as provided for in national laws and practices, in accordance with the Treaties, in order to promote the social and territorial cohesion of the Union.

Article 37   Environmental protection

A high level of environmental protection and the improvement of the quality of the environment must be integrated into the polices of the Union and ensured in accordance with the principle of sustainable development.

Article 38   Consumer protection

Union policies shall ensure a high level of consumer protection.

Chapter V   Citizens' Rights

Article 39   Right to vote and to stand as a candidate at elections to the European Parliament

1. Every citizen of the Union has the right to vote and to stand as a candidate at elections to the European Parliament in the Member State in which he or she resides, under the same conditions as nationals of that State.

2. Members of the European Parliament shall be elected by direct universal suffrage in a free and secret ballot.

Article 40   Right to vote and to stand as a candidate at municipal elections

Every citizen of the Union has the right to vote and to stand as a candidate at municipal elections in the Member State in which he or she resides under the same conditions as nationals of that State.

Article 41   Right to good administration

1. Every person has the right to have his or her affairs handled impartially, fairly and within a reasonable time by the institutions and bodies of the Union.

2. This right includes:
   - the right of every person to be heard, before any individual measure which would affect him or her adversely is taken;
   - the right of every person to have access to his or her file, while respecting the legitimate interests of confidentiality and of professional and business secrecy;
   - the obligation of the administration to give reasons for its decisions.

3. Every person has the right to have the Union make good any damage caused by its institutions or by its servants in the performance of their duties, in accordance with the general principles common to the laws of the Member States.

4. Every person may write to the institutions of the Union in one of the languages of the Treaties and must have an answer in the same language.

Article 42   Right of access to documents

Any citizen of the Union, and any natural or legal person residing or having its registered office in a Member State, has a right of access to documents of the institutions, bodies, offices and agencies of the Union, whatever their medium.

Article 43   European Ombudsman

Any citizen of the Union and any natural or legal person residing or having its registered office in a Member State has the right to refer to the European Ombudsman cases of maladministration in the activities of the institutions, bodies, offices or agencies of the Union, with the exception of the Court of Justice of the European Union acting in its judicial role.

Article 44   Right to petition

Any citizen of the Union and any natural or legal person residing or having its registered office in a Member State has the right to petition the European Parliament.

Article 45   Freedom of movement and of residence

1. Every citizen of the Union has the right to move and reside freely within the territory of the Member States.

2. Freedom of movement and residence may be granted, in accordance with the Treaties, to nationals of third countries legally resident in the territory of a Member State.

Article 46   Diplomatic and consular protection

Every citizen of the Union shall, in the territory of a third country in which the Member State of which he or she is a national is not represented, be entitled to protection by the diplomatic or consular authorities of any Member State, on the same conditions as the nationals of that Member State.

Chapter VI Justice

Article 47   Right to an effective remedy and to a fair trial

Everyone whose rights and freedoms guaranteed by the law of the Union are violated has the right to an effective remedy before a tribunal in compliance with the conditions laid down in this Article. Everyone is entitled to a fair and public hearing within a reasonable time by an independent and impartial tribunal previously established by law. Everyone shall have the possibility of being advised, defended and represented.

Legal aid shall be made available to those who lack sufficient resources insofar as such aid is necessary to ensure effective access to justice.

Article 48   Presumption of innocence and right of defence

1. Everyone who has been charged shall be presumed innocent until proved guilty according to law.

2. Respect for the rights of the defence of anyone who has been charged shall be guaranteed.

Article 49   Principles of legality and proportionality of criminal offences and penalties

1. No one shall be held guilty of any criminal offence on account of any act or omission which did not constitute a criminal offence under national law or international law at the time when it was committed. Nor shall a heavier penalty be imposed than that which was applicable at the time the criminal offence was committed. If, subsequent to the commission of a criminal offence, the law provides for a lighter penalty, that penalty shall be applicable.

2. This Article shall not prejudice the trial and punishment of any person for any act or omission which, at the time when it was committed, was criminal according to the general principles recognised by the community of nations.

3. The severity of penalties must not be disproportionate to the criminal offence.

Article 50   Right not to be tried or punished twice in criminal proceedings for the same criminal offence

No one shall be liable to be tried or punished again in criminal proceedings for an offence for which he or she has already been finally acquitted or convicted within the Union in accordance with the Law.

Chapter VII General Provisions Governing the Interpretation and Application of the Charter

Article 51   Field of application

1. The provisions of this Charter are addressed to the institutions, bodies, offices and agencies of the Union with due regard for the principle of subsidiarity and to the Member States only when they are implementing Union law. They shall therefore respect the rights, observe the principles and promote the application thereof in accordance with their respective powers and respecting the limits of the powers of the Union as conferred on it in the Treaties.

2. The Charter does not extend the field of application of Union law beyond the powers of the Union or establish any new power or task for the Union, or modify powers and tasks as defined in the Treaties.

Article 52   Scope and interpretation of rights and principles

1. Any limitation on the exercise of the rights and freedoms recognised by this Charter must be provided for by law and respect the essence of those rights and freedoms. Subject to the principle of proportionality, limitations may be made only if they are necessary and genuinely meet objectives of general interest recognized by the Union or the need to protect the rights and freedoms of others.

2. Rights recognised by this Charter for which provision is made in the Treaties shall be exercised under the conditions and within the limits defined by those Treaties.

3. Insofar as this Charter contains rights which correspond to rights guaranteed by the Convention for the Protection of Human Rights and Fundamental Freedoms, the meaning and scope of those rights shall be the same as those laid down by the said Convention. This provision shall not prevent Union law providing more extensive protection.

4. In so far as this Charter recognises fundamental rights as they result from the constitutional traditions common to the Member States, those rights shall be interpreted in harmony with those traditions.

5. The provisions of this Charter which contain principles may be implemented by legislative and executive acts taken by institutions, bodies, offices and agencies of the Union, and by acts of Member States when they are implementing Union law, in the exercise of their respective powers. They shall be judicially cognisable only in the interpretation of such acts and in the ruling on their legality.

6. Full account shall be taken of national laws and practices as specified in the Charter.

7. The explanations drawn up as a way of providing guidance in the interpretation of this Charter shall be given due regard by the courts of the Union and of the Member States.

Article 53   Level of protection

Nothing in this Charter shall be interpreted as restricting or adversely affecting human rights and fundamental freedoms as recognised, in their respective fields of application, by Union law and international law and by international agreements to which the Union, or all the Member States are party, including the European Convention for the Protection of Human Rights and Fundamental Freedoms, and by the Member States' constitutions.

Article 54   Prohibition of abuse of rights

Nothing in this Charter shall be interpreted as implying any right to engage in any activity or to perform any act aimed at the destruction of any of the rights and freedoms recognised in this Charter or at their limitation to a greater extent than is provided for herein.

Agreement on the withdrawal of the United Kingdom of Great Britain and Northern Ireland from the European Union and the European Atomic Energy Community*

(12th November 2019)

Preamble

THE EUROPEAN UNION AND THE EUROPEAN ATOMIC ENERGY COMMUNITY

AND

THE UNITED KINGDOM OF GREAT BRITAIN AND NORTHERN IRELAND,

CONSIDERING that on 29 March 2017 the United Kingdom of Great Britain and Northern Ireland ('United Kingdom'), following the outcome of a referendum held in the United Kingdom and its sovereign decision to leave the European Union, notified its intention to withdraw from the European Union ('Union') and the European Atomic Energy Community ('Euratom') in accordance with Article 50 of the Treaty on European Union ('TEU'), which applies to Euratom by virtue of Article 106a of the Treaty establishing the European Atomic Energy Community ('Euratom Treaty'),

---

* **Editor's Note:** The Agreement runs to 185 Articles and includes numerous Protocols and Annexes. It is not possible to reproduce the entire Agreement here. Selected areas have been chosen for inclusion.

WISHING to set out the arrangements for the withdrawal of the United Kingdom from the Union and Euratom, taking account of the framework for their future relationship,

NOTING the guidelines of 29 April and 15 December 2017 and of 23 March 2018 provided by the European Council in the light of which the Union is to conclude the Agreement setting out the arrangements for the withdrawal of the United Kingdom from the Union and Euratom,

RECALLING that, pursuant to Article 50 TEU, in conjunction with Article 106a of the Euratom Treaty, and subject to the arrangements laid down in this Agreement, the law of the Union and of Euratom in its entirety ceases to apply to the United Kingdom from the date of entry into force of this Agreement,

STRESSING that the objective of this Agreement is to ensure an orderly withdrawal of the United Kingdom from the Union and Euratom,

RECOGNISING that it is necessary to provide reciprocal protection for Union citizens and for United Kingdom nationals, as well as their respective family members, where they have exercised free movement rights before a date set in this Agreement, and to ensure that their rights under this Agreement are enforceable and based on the principle of non-discrimination; recognising also that rights deriving from periods of social security insurance should be protected,

RESOLVED to ensure an orderly withdrawal through various separation provisions aiming to prevent disruption and to provide legal certainty to citizens and economic operators as well as to judicial and administrative authorities in the Union and in the United Kingdom, while not excluding the possibility of relevant separation provisions being superseded by the agreement(s) on the future relationship,

CONSIDERING that it is in the interest of both the Union and the United Kingdom to determine a transition or implementation period during which—notwithstanding all consequences of the United Kingdom's withdrawal from the Union as regards the United Kingdom's participation in the institutions, bodies, offices and agencies of the Union, in particular the end, on the date of entry into force of this Agreement, of the mandates of all members of institutions, bodies and agencies of the Union nominated, appointed or elected in relation to the United Kingdom's membership of the Union—Union law, including international agreements, should be applicable to and in the United Kingdom, and, as a general rule, with the same effect as regards the Member States, in order to avoid disruption in the period during which the agreement(s) on the future relationship will be negotiated,

RECOGNISING that, even if Union law will be applicable to and in the United Kingdom during the transition period, the specificities of the United Kingdom as a State having withdrawn from the Union mean that it will be important for the United Kingdom to be able to take steps to prepare and establish new international arrangements of its own, including in areas of Union exclusive competence, provided such agreements do not enter into force or apply during that period, unless so authorised by the Union,

RECALLING that the Union and the United Kingdom have agreed to honour the mutual commitments undertaken while the United Kingdom was a member of the Union through a single financial settlement,

CONSIDERING that in order to guarantee the correct interpretation and application of this Agreement and compliance with the obligations under this Agreement, it is essential to establish provisions ensuring overall governance, in particular binding dispute-settlement and enforcement rules that fully respect the autonomy of the respective legal orders of the Union and of the United Kingdom as well as the United Kingdom's status as a third country,

ACKNOWLEDGING that, for an orderly withdrawal of the United Kingdom from the Union, it is also necessary to establish, in separate protocols to this Agreement, durable arrangements addressing the very specific situations relating to Ireland/Northern Ireland and to the Sovereign Base Areas in Cyprus,

ACKNOWLEDGING further that, for an orderly withdrawal of the United Kingdom from the Union, it is also necessary to establish, in a separate protocol to this Agreement, the specific arrangements in respect of Gibraltar applicable in particular during the transition period,

UNDERLINING that this Agreement is founded on an overall balance of benefits, rights and obligations for the Union and the United Kingdom,

NOTING that in parallel with this Agreement, the Parties have made a Political Declaration setting out the framework for the future relationship between the European Union and the United Kingdom of Great Britain and Northern Ireland,

CONSIDERING that there is a need for both the United Kingdom and the Union to take all necessary steps to begin as soon as possible from the date of entry into force of this Agreement, the formal negotiations of one or several agreements governing their future relationship with a view to ensuring that, to the extent possible, those agreements apply from the end of the transition period,

HAVE AGREED AS FOLLOWS:

PART ONE   COMMON PROVISIONS

Article 1   Objective

This Agreement sets out the arrangements for the withdrawal of the United Kingdom of Great Britain and Northern Ireland ('United Kingdom') from the European Union ('Union') and from the European Atomic Energy Community ('Euratom').

Article 2   Definitions

For the purposes of this Agreement, the following definitions shall apply:

(a) 'Union law' means:

    (i) the Treaty on European Union ('TEU'), the Treaty on the Functioning of the European Union ('TFEU') and the Treaty establishing the European Atomic Energy Community ('Euratom Treaty'), as amended or supplemented, as well as the Treaties of Accession and the Charter of Fundamental Rights of the European Union, together referred to as 'the Treaties';

    (ii) the general principles of the Union's law;

    (iii) the acts adopted by the institutions, bodies, offices or agencies of the Union;

    (iv) the international agreements to which the Union is party and the international agreements concluded by the Member States acting on behalf of the Union;

    (v) the agreements between Member States entered into in their capacity as Member States of the Union;

    (vi) acts of the Representatives of the Governments of the Member States meeting within the European Council or the Council of the European Union ('Council');

    (vii) the declarations made in the context of intergovernmental conferences which adopted the Treaties;

(b) 'Member States' means the Kingdom of Belgium, the Republic of Bulgaria, the Czech Republic, the Kingdom of Denmark, the Federal Republic of Germany, the Republic of Estonia, Ireland, the Hellenic Republic, the Kingdom of Spain, the French Republic, the Republic of Croatia, the Italian Republic, the Republic of Cyprus, the Republic of Latvia, the Republic of Lithuania, the Grand Duchy of Luxembourg, Hungary, the Republic of Malta, the Kingdom of the Netherlands, the Republic of Austria, the Republic of Poland, the Portuguese Republic, Romania, the Republic of Slovenia, the Slovak Republic, the Republic of Finland and the Kingdom of Sweden;

(c) 'Union citizen' means any person holding the nationality of a Member State;

(d) 'United Kingdom national' means a national of the United Kingdom, as defined in the New Declaration by the Government of the United Kingdom of Great Britain and Northern Ireland of 31 December 1982 on the definition of the term 'nationals'[1] together

---

[1] OJ C 23, 28.1.1983, p. 1.

with DeclarationNo 63 annexed to the Final Act of the intergovernmental conference which adopted the Treaty of Lisbon[2];

(e) 'transition period' means the period provided in Article 126;

(f) 'day' means a calendar day, unless otherwise provided in this Agreement or in provisions of Union law made applicable by this Agreement.

Article 3   Territorial scope

1. Unless otherwise provided in this Agreement or in Union law made applicable by this Agreement, any reference in this Agreement to the United Kingdom or its territory shall be understood as referring to:

(a) the United Kingdom;

(b) Gibraltar, to the extent that Union law was applicable to it before the date of entry into force of this Agreement;

(c) the Channel Islands and the Isle of Man, to the extent that Union law was applicable to them before the date of entry into force of this Agreement;

(d) the Sovereign Base Areas of Akrotiri and Dhekelia in Cyprus, to the extent necessary to ensure the implementation of the arrangements set out in the Protocol on the Sovereign Base Areas of the United Kingdom of Great Britain and Northern Ireland in Cyprus annexed to the Act concerning the conditions of accession of the Czech Republic, the Republic of Estonia, the Republic of Cyprus, the Republic of Latvia, the Republic of Lithuania, the Republic of Hungary, the Republic of Malta, the Republic of Poland, the Republic of Slovenia and the Slovak Republic to the European Union;

(e) the overseas countries and territories listed in Annex II to the TFEU having special relations with the United Kingdom,[3] where the provisions of this Agreement relate to the special arrangements for the association of the overseas countries and territories with the Union.

2. Unless otherwise provided in this Agreement or in Union law made applicable by this Agreement, any reference in this Agreement to Member States, or their territory, shall be understood as covering the territories of the Member States to which the Treaties apply as provided in Article 355 TFEU.

Article 4   Methods and principles relating to the effect, the implementation and the application of this Agreement

1. The provisions of this Agreement and the provisions of Union law made applicable by this Agreement shall produce in respect of and in the United Kingdom the same legal effects as those which they produce within the Union and its Member States.

Accordingly, legal or natural persons shall in particular be able to rely directly on the provisions contained or referred to in this Agreement which meet the conditions for direct effect under Union law.

2. The United Kingdom shall ensure compliance with paragraph 1, including as regards the required powers of its judicial and administrative authorities to disapply inconsistent or incompatible domestic provisions, through domestic primary legislation.

3. The provisions of this Agreement referring to Union law or to concepts or provisions thereof shall be interpreted and applied in accordance with the methods and general principles of Union law.

4. The provisions of this Agreement referring to Union law or to concepts or provisions thereof shall in their implementation and application be interpreted in conformity with the relevant case

---

[2] OJ C 306, 17.12.2007, p. 270.

[3] Anguilla, Bermuda, British Antarctic Territory, British Indian Ocean Territory, British Virgin Islands, Cayman Islands, Falkland Islands, Montserrat, Pitcairn, Saint Helena, Ascension and Tristan da Cunha, South Georgia and the South Sandwich Islands, and Turks and Caicos Islands.

law of the Court of Justice of the European Union handed down before the end of the transition period.

5. In the interpretation and application of this Agreement, the United Kingdom's judicial and administrative authorities shall have due regard to relevant case law of the Court of Justice of the European Union handed down after the end of the transition period.

Article 5 Good faith

The Union and the United Kingdom shall, in full mutual respect and good faith, assist each other in carrying out tasks which flow from this Agreement.

They shall take all appropriate measures, whether general or particular, to ensure fulfilment of the obligations arising from this Agreement and shall refrain from any measures which could jeopardise the attainment of the objectives of this Agreement.

This Article is without prejudice to the application of Union law pursuant to this Agreement, in particular the principle of sincere cooperation.

Article 6 References to Union law

1. With the exception of Parts Four and Five, unless otherwise provided in this Agreement all references in this Agreement to Union law shall be understood as references to Union law, including as amended or replaced, as applicable on the last day of the transition period.

2. Where in this Agreement reference is made to Union acts or provisions thereof, such reference shall, where relevant, be understood to include a reference to Union law or provisions thereof that, although replaced or superseded by the act referred to, continue to apply in accordance with that act.

3. For the purposes of this Agreement, references to provisions of Union law made applicable by this Agreement shall be understood to include references to the relevant Union acts supplementing or implementing those provisions.

Article 7 References to the Union and to Member States

1. For the purposes of this Agreement, all references to Member States and competent authorities of Member States in provisions of Union law made applicable by this Agreement shall be understood as including the United Kingdom and its competent authorities, except as regards:

(a) the nomination, appointment or election of members of the institutions, bodies, offices and agencies of the Union, as well as the participation in the decision-making and the attendance in the meetings of the institutions;

(b) the participation in the decision-making and governance of the bodies, offices and agencies of the Union;

(c) the attendance in the meetings of the committees referred to in Article 3(2) of Regulation (EU) No 182/2011 of the European Parliament and of the Council,[4] of Commission expert groups or of other similar entities, or in the meetings of expert groups or similar entities of bodies, offices and agencies of the Union, unless otherwise provided in this Agreement.

2. Unless otherwise provided in this Agreement, any reference to the Union shall be understood as including Euratom.

Article 8 Access to networks, information systems and databases

Unless otherwise provided in this Agreement, at the end of the transition period the United Kingdom shall cease to be entitled to access any network, any information system and any database established on the basis of Union law. The United Kingdom shall take appropriate measures to ensure that it does not access a network, information system or database which it is no longer entitled to access.

---

[4] Regulation (EU) No 182/2011 of the European Parliament and of the Council of 16 February 2011 laying down the rules and general principles concerning mechanisms for control by Member States of the Commission's exercise of implementing powers (OJ L 55, 28.2.2011, p. 13).

PART TWO CITIZENS' RIGHTS

Title I General provisions

Articles 9 Definitions

(a), (b)   *****

(c) 'host State' means:

   (i)   in respect of Union citizens and their family members, the United Kingdom, if they exercised their right of residence there in accordance with Union law before the end of the transition period and continue to reside there thereafter;

   (ii) in respect of United Kingdom nationals and their family members, the Member State in which they exercised their right of residence in accordance with Union law before the end of the transition period and in which they continue to reside thereafter;

(d), (e)   *****

Articles 10–12 *****

Title II Rights and obligations

Chapter 1 Rights related to residence, residence documents

Article 13 Residence rights

1. Union citizens and United Kingdom nationals shall have the right to reside in the host State under the limitations and conditions as set out in Articles 21, 45 or 49 TFEU and in Article 6(1), points (a), (b) or (c) of Article 7(1), Article 7(3), Article 14, Article 16(1) or Article 17(1) of Directive 2004/38/EC.

2. Family members who are either Union citizens or United Kingdom nationals shall have the right to reside in the host State as set out in Article 21 TFEU and in Article 6(1), point (d) of Article 7(1), Article 12(1) or (3), Article 13(1), Article 14, Article 16(1) or Article 17(3) and (4) of Directive 2004/38/EC, subject to the limitations and conditions set out in those provisions.

3. Family members who are neither Union citizens nor United Kingdom nationals shall have the right to reside in the host State under Article 21 TFEU and as set out in Article 6(2), Article 7(2), Article 12(2) or (3), Article 13(2), Article 14, Article 16(2), Article 17(3) or (4) or Article 18 of Directive 2004/38/EC, subject to the limitations and conditions set out in those provisions.

4. The host State may not impose any limitations or conditions for obtaining, retaining or losing residence rights on the persons referred to in paragraphs 1, 2 and 3, other than those provided for in this Title. There shall be no discretion in applying the limitations and conditions provided for in this Title, other than in favour of the person concerned.

Article 14   Right of exit and of entry

1. Union citizens and United Kingdom nationals, their respective family members, and other persons, who reside in the territory of the host State in accordance with the conditions set out in this Title shall have the right to leave the host State and the right to enter it, as set out in Article 4(1) and the first subparagraph of Article 5(1) of Directive 2004/38/EC, with a valid passport or national identity card in the case of Union citizens and United Kingdom nationals, and with a valid passport in the case of their respective family members and other persons who are not Union citizens or United Kingdom nationals.

Five years after the end of the transition period, the host State may decide no longer to accept national identity cards for the purposes of entry to or exit from its territory if such cards do not include a chip that complies with the applicable International Civil Aviation Organisation standards related to biometric identification.

2. No exit visa, entry visa or equivalent formality shall be required of holders of a valid document issued in accordance with Article 18 or 26.

3. Where the host State requires family members who join the Union citizen or United Kingdom national after the end of the transition period to have an entry visa, the host State shall grant such persons every facility to obtain the necessary visas. Such visas shall be issued free of charge as soon as possible, and on the basis of an accelerated procedure.

Article 15   Right of permanent residence

1. Union citizens and United Kingdom nationals, and their respective family members, who have resided legally in the host State in accordance with Union law for a continuous period of 5 years or for the period specified in Article 17 of Directive 2004/38/EC, shall have the right to reside permanently in the host State under the conditions set out in Articles 16, 17 and 18 of Directive 2004/38/EC. Periods of legal residence or work in accordance with Union law before and after the end of the transition period shall be included in the calculation of the qualifying period necessary for acquisition of the right of permanent residence.

2. Continuity of residence for the purposes of acquisition of the right of permanent residence shall be determined in accordance with Article 16(3) and Article 21 of Directive 2004/38/EC.

3. Once acquired, the right of permanent residence shall be lost only through absence from the host State for a period exceeding 5 consecutive years.

Articles 16–21   *****

Article 22   Related rights

In accordance with Article 23 of Directive 2004/38/EC, irrespective of nationality, the family members of a Union citizen or United Kingdom national who have the right of residence or the right of permanent residence in the host State or the State of work shall be entitled to take up employment or self-employment there.

Article 23   *****

Chapter 2   Rights of workers and self-employed persons

Article 24   Rights of workers

1. Subject to the limitations set out in Article 45(3) and (4) TFEU, workers in the host State and frontier workers in the State or States of work shall enjoy the rights guaranteed by Article 45 TFEU and the rights granted by Regulation (EU) No 492/2011 of the European Parliament and of the Council.[5] These rights include:

(a) the right not to be discriminated against on grounds of nationality as regards employment, remuneration and other conditions of work and employment;

(b) the right to take up and pursue an activity in accordance with the rules applicable to the nationals of the host State or the State of work;

(c) the right to assistance afforded by the employment offices of the host State or the State of work as offered to own nationals;

(d) the right to equal treatment in respect of conditions of employment and work, in particular as regards remuneration, dismissal and in case of unemployment, reinstatement or re-employment;

(e) the right to social and tax advantages;

(f) collective rights;

(g) the rights and benefits accorded to national workers in matters of housing;

(h) the right for their children to be admitted to the general educational, apprenticeship and vocational training courses under the same conditions as the nationals of the host State or the State of work, if such children are residing in the territory where the worker works.

---

[5] Regulation (EU) No 492/2011 of the European Parliament and of the Council of 5 April 2011 on freedom of movement for workers within the Union (OJ L 141, 27.5.2011, p. 1).

2. Where a direct descendant of a worker who has ceased to reside in the host State is in education in that State, the primary carer for that descendant shall have the right to reside in that State until the descendant reaches the age of majority, and after the age of majority if that descendant continues to need the presence and care of the primary carer in order to pursue and complete his or her education.

3. Employed frontier workers shall enjoy the right to enter and exit the State of work in accordance with Article 14 of this Agreement and shall retain the rights they enjoyed as workers there, provided they are in one of the circumstances set out in points (a), (b), (c) and (d) of Article 7(3) of Directive 2004/38/EC, even where they do not move their residence to the State of work.

Article 25   Rights of self-employed persons

1. Subject to the limitations set out in Articles 51 and 52 TFEU, self-employed persons in the host State and self-employed frontier workers in the State or States of work shall enjoy the rights guaranteed by Articles 49 and 55 TFEU. These rights include:

    (a) the right to take up and pursue activities as self-employed persons and to set up and manage undertakings under the conditions laid down by the host State for its own nationals, as set out in Article 49 TFEU;

    (b) the rights as set out in points (c) to (h) of Article 24(1) of this Agreement.

2. Article 24(2) shall apply to direct descendants of self-employed workers.

3. Article 24(3) shall apply to self-employed frontier workers.

Articles 26–39   *****

PART THREE SEPARATION PROVISIONS

Title I Goods placed on the market

Article 40   Definitions

    (a) 'making available on the market' means any supply of a good for distribution, consumption or use on the market in the course of a commercial activity, whether in return for payment or free of charge;

    (b) 'placing on the market' means the first making available of a good on the market in the Union or the United Kingdom;

    (c) 'supply of a good for distribution, consumption or use' means that an existing and individually identifiable good, after the stage of manufacturing has taken place, is the subject matter of a written or verbal agreement between two or more legal or natural persons for the transfer of ownership, any other property right, or possession concerning the good in question, or is the subject matter of an offer to a legal or natural person or persons to conclude such an agreement;

    (d) 'putting into service' means the first use of a good within the Union or the United Kingdom by the end user for the purposes for which it was intended or, in the case of marine equipment, placing on board;

    (e) 'market surveillance' means the activities carried out and measures taken by market surveillance authorities to ensure that goods comply with the applicable requirements and do not endanger health, safety or any other aspect of public interest protection;

    (f) 'market surveillance authority' means an authority of a Member State or of the United Kingdom responsible for carrying out market surveillance on its territory;

    (g) 'conditions for the marketing of goods' means requirements concerning the characteristics of goods such as levels of quality, performance, safety or dimensions, including on the composition of such goods or on the terminology, symbols, testing and testing methods, packaging, marking, labelling, and conformity assessment procedures used in relation to such goods; the term also covers requirements concerning production methods and processes, where these have an effect on product characteristics;

(h) 'conformity assessment body' means a body that performs conformity assessment activities including calibration, testing, certification and inspection;

(i) 'notified body' means a conformity assessment body authorised to carry out third-party conformity assessment tasks under Union law harmonising the conditions for the marketing of goods;

(j) 'animal products' means products of animal origin, animal by-products and derived products, as referred to in points (29), (30) and (31) of Article 4 of Regulation (EU) 2016/429 of the European Parliament and of the Council,[6] respectively, feed of animal origin, and food and feed containing products of animal origin.

Article 41   Continued circulation of goods placed on the market

1. Any good that was lawfully placed on the market in the Union or the United Kingdom before the end of the transition period may:

(a) be further made available on the market of the Union or of the United Kingdom and circulate between these two markets until it reaches its end-user;

(b) where provided in the applicable provisions of Union law, be put into service in the Union or in the United Kingdom.

2. The requirements set out in Articles 34 and 35 TFEU and the relevant Union law governing the marketing of goods, including the conditions for the marketing of goods, applicable to the goods concerned shall apply in respect of the goods referred to in paragraph 1.

3. Paragraph 1 shall apply to all existing and individually identifiable goods within the meaning of Title II of Part Three of the TFEU, with the exception of the circulation between the Union market and the United Kingdom's market or vice-versa of:

(a) live animals and germinal products;

(b) animal products.

4. In respect of a movement of live animals or of germinal products between a Member State and the United Kingdom, or vice-versa, the provisions of Union law listed in Annex II shall apply, provided that the date of departure was before the end of the transition period.

5. This Article shall be without prejudice to the possibility for the United Kingdom, a Member State or the Union to take measures to prohibit or restrict the making available on its market of a good referred to in paragraph 1, or a category of such goods, where and to the extent permitted by Union law.

6. The provisions of this Title shall be without prejudice to any applicable rules on modalities of sale, intellectual property, customs procedures, tariffs and taxes.

Articles 42–69   *****

Title VII Data and information processed or obtained before the end of the transition period, or on the basis of this agreement

Article 70   *****

Article 71   Protection of personal data

1. Union law on the protection of personal data shall apply in the United Kingdom in respect of the processing of personal data of data subjects outside the United Kingdom, provided that the personal data:

(a) were processed under Union law in the United Kingdom before the end of the transition period; or

---

[6] Regulation (EU) 2016/429 of the European Parliament and of the Council of 9 March 2016 on transmissible animal diseases and amending and repealing certain acts in the area of animal health ('Animal Health Law') (OJ L 84, 31.3.2016, p. 1).

(b) are processed in the United Kingdom after the end of the transition period on the basis of this Agreement.

2. Paragraph 1 shall not apply to the extent the processing of the personal data referred to therein is subject to an adequate level of protection as established in applicable decisions under Article 45(3) of Regulation (EU) 2016/679 or Article 36(3) of Directive (EU) 2016/680.

3. To the extent that a decision referred to in paragraph 2 has ceased to be applicable, the United Kingdom shall ensure a level of protection of personal data essentially equivalent to that under Union law on the protection of personal data in respect of the processing of personal data of data subjects referred to in paragraph 1.

Article 72   Confidential treatment and restricted use of data and information in the United Kingdom

Without prejudice to Article 71, in addition to Union law on the protection of personal data, the provisions of Union law on confidential treatment, restriction of use, storage limitation and requirement to erase data and information shall apply in respect of data and information obtained by authorities or official bodies of or in the United Kingdom or by contracting entities, as defined in Article 4 of Directive 2014/25/EU of the European Parliament and of the Council,[7] that are of or in the United Kingdom:

(a) before the end of the transition period; or

(b) on the basis of this Agreement.

Article 73   Treatment of data and information obtained from the United Kingdom

The Union shall not treat data and information obtained from the United Kingdom before the end of the transition period, or obtained after the end of the transition period on the basis of this Agreement, differently from data and information obtained from a Member State, on the sole ground of the United Kingdom having withdrawn from the Union.

Article 74   Information security

1. The provisions of Union law on the protection of EU classified information and Euratom classified information shall apply in respect of classified information that was obtained by the United Kingdom either before the end of the transition period or on the basis of this Agreement or that was obtained from the United Kingdom by the Union or a Member State either before the end of the transition period or on the basis of this Agreement.

2. The obligations resulting from Union law regarding industrial security shall apply to the United Kingdom in cases where the tendering, contracting or grant award procedure for the classified contract, classified subcontract or classified grant agreement was launched before the end of the transition period.

3., 4. *****

Articles 75–78   *****

Title IX Euratom related issues

Article 79   *****

Article 80   End of Community responsibility for matters related to the United Kingdom

1. The United Kingdom shall have sole responsibility for ensuring that all ores, source materials and special fissile materials covered by the Euratom Treaty and present on the territory of the

---

[7] Directive 2014/25/EU of the European Parliament and of the Council of 26 February 2014 on procurement by entities operating in the water, energy, transport and postal services sectors and repealing Directive 2004/17/EC (OJ L 94, 28.3.2014, p. 243).

United Kingdom at the end of the transition period are handled in accordance with relevant and applicable international treaties and conventions, including but not limited to international treaties and conventions on nuclear safety, safeguards, non-proliferation and physical protection of nuclear materials, and international treaties and conventions on safety of spent fuel management and the safety of radioactive waste management.

2. The United Kingdom shall have sole responsibility for ensuring its compliance with international obligations arising as a consequence of its membership of the International Atomic Energy Agency or as a consequence of the Treaty on the Non-Proliferation of Nuclear Weapons or any other relevant international treaties or conventions to which the United Kingdom is a party.

Articles 81–85   *****

Title X Union judicial and administrative procedures

Chapter 1   Judicial procedures

Article 86   Pending cases before the Court of Justice of the European Union

1. The Court of Justice of the European Union shall continue to have jurisdiction in any proceedings brought by or against the United Kingdom before the end of the transition period. Such jurisdiction shall apply to all stages of proceedings, including appeal proceedings before the Court of Justice and proceedings before the General Court where the case is referred back to the General Court.

2. The Court of Justice of the European Union shall continue to have jurisdiction to give preliminary rulings on requests from courts and tribunals of the United Kingdom made before the end of the transition period.

3. For the purposes of this Chapter, proceedings shall be considered as having been brought before the Court of Justice of the European Union, and requests for preliminary rulings shall be considered as having been made, at the moment at which the document initiating the proceedings has been registered by the registry of the Court of Justice or the General Court, as the case may be.

Article 87   New cases before the Court of Justice

1. If the European Commission considers that the United Kingdom has failed to fulfil an obligation under the Treaties or under Part Four of this Agreement before the end of the transition period, the European Commission may, within 4 years after the end of the transition period, bring the matter before the Court of Justice of the European Union in accordance with the requirements laid down in Article 258 TFEU or the second subparagraph of Article 108(2) TFEU, as the case may be. The Court of Justice of the European Union shall have jurisdiction over such cases.

2. If the United Kingdom does not comply with a decision referred to in Article 95(1) of this Agreement, or fails to give legal effect in the United Kingdom's legal order to a decision, as referred to in that provision, that was addressed to a natural or legal person residing or established in the United Kingdom, the European Commission may, within 4 years from the date of the decision concerned, bring the matter to the Court of Justice of the European Union in accordance with the requirements laid down in Article 258 TFEU or the second subparagraph of Article 108(2) TFEU, as the case may be. The Court of Justice of the European Union shall have jurisdiction over such cases.

3. In deciding to bring matters under this Article, the European Commission shall apply the same principles in respect of the United Kingdom as in respect of any Member State.

Article 88   Procedural rules

The provisions of Union law governing the procedure before the Court of Justice of the European Union shall apply in respect of the proceedings and requests for preliminary rulings referred to in this Title.

Article 89 Binding force and enforceability of judgments and orders

1. Judgments and orders of the Court of Justice of the European Union handed down before the end of the transition period, as well as such judgments and orders handed down after the end of the transition period in proceedings referred to in Articles 86 and 87, shall have binding force in their entirety on and in the United Kingdom.

2. If, in a judgment referred to in paragraph 1, the Court of Justice of the European Union finds that the United Kingdom has failed to fulfil an obligation under the Treaties or this Agreement, the United Kingdom shall take the necessary measures to comply with that judgment.

3. Articles 280 and 299 TFEU shall apply in the United Kingdom in respect of the enforcement of the judgments and orders of the Court of Justice of the European Union referred to in paragraph 1 of this Article.

Article 90 Right to intervene and participate in the procedure

Until the judgments and orders of the Court of Justice of the European Union in all proceedings and requests for preliminary rulings referred to in Article 86 have become final, the United Kingdom may intervene in the same way as a Member State or, in the cases brought before the Court of Justice of the European Union in accordance with Article 267 TFEU, participate in the procedure before the Court of Justice of the European Union in the same way as a Member State. During that period, the Registrar of the Court of Justice of the European Union shall notify the United Kingdom, at the same time and in the same manner as the Member States, of any case referred to the Court of Justice of the European Union for a preliminary ruling by a court or tribunal of a Member State.

The United Kingdom may also intervene or participate in the procedure before the Court of Justice of the European Union in the same way as a Member State:

(a) in relation to cases which concern a failure to fulfil obligations under the Treaties, where the United Kingdom was subject to the same obligations before the end of the transition period, and where such cases are brought before the Court of Justice of the European Union in accordance with Articles 258 TFEU before the end of the period referred to in Article 87(1) or, as the case may be, until the moment, after the end of that period, at which the last judgment or order rendered by the Court of Justice of the European Union on the basis of Article 87(1) has become final;

(b) in relation to cases which concern acts or provisions of Union law which were applicable before the end of the transition period to and in the United Kingdom and which are brought before Court of Justice of the European Union in accordance with Article 267 TFEU before the end of the period referred to in Article 87(1) or, as the case may be, until the moment, after the end of that period, at which the last judgment or order rendered by the Court of Justice on the basis of Article 87(1) has become final; and

(c) in relation to the cases referred to in Article 95(3).

Article 91 Representation before the Court

1. Without prejudice to Article 88, where, before the end of the transition period, a lawyer authorised to practise before the courts or tribunals of the United Kingdom represented or assisted a party in proceedings before the Court of Justice of the European Union or in relation to requests for preliminary rulings made before the end of the transition period, that lawyer may continue to represent or assist that party in those proceedings or in relation to those requests. This right shall apply to all stages of proceedings, including appeal proceedings before the Court of Justice and proceedings before the General Court after a case has been referred back to it.

2. Without prejudice to Article 88, lawyers authorised to practise before the courts or tribunals of the United Kingdom may represent or assist a party before the Court of Justice of the European Union in the cases referred to in Article 87 and Article 95(3). Lawyers authorised to practise before the courts or tribunals of the United Kingdom may also represent or assist the United Kingdom in the proceedings covered by Article 90 in which the United Kingdom has decided to intervene or participate.

3. When representing or assisting a party before the Court of Justice of the European Union in the cases referred to in paragraphs 1 and 2, lawyers authorised to practise before the courts or tribunals of the United Kingdom shall in every respect be treated as lawyers authorised to practise before courts or tribunals of Member States representing or assisting a party before the Court of Justice of the European Union.

Chapter 2 Administrative procedures

Article 92   Ongoing administrative procedures

1. The institutions, bodies, offices and agencies of the Union shall continue to be competent for administrative procedures which were initiated before the end of the transition period concerning:

(a) compliance with Union law by the United Kingdom, or by natural or legal persons residing or established in the United Kingdom; or

(b) compliance with Union law relating to competition in the United Kingdom.

2., 3. *****

4. The Union shall provide the United Kingdom with a list of all individual ongoing administrative procedures that fall within the scope of paragraph 1 within 3 months after the end of the transition period. By way of derogation from the first sentence, in the case of individual ongoing administrative procedures of the European Banking Authority, the European Securities and Markets Authority, and the European Insurance and Occupational Pensions Authority, the Union shall provide the United Kingdom with a list of such ongoing administrative procedures within 1 month after the end of the transition period.

5. In an administrative procedure on State aid governed by Regulation (EU) 2015/1589, the European Commission shall be bound in relation to the United Kingdom by the applicable case law and best practices, as if the United Kingdom were still a Member State. In particular, the European Commission shall, within a reasonable period of time, adopt one of the following decisions:

(a) a decision finding that the measure does not constitute aid pursuant to Article 4(2) of Regulation (EU) 2015/1589;

(b) a decision not to raise objections pursuant to Article 4(3) of Regulation (EU) 2015/1589;

(c) a decision to initiate formal investigation proceedings pursuant to Article 4(4) of Regulation (EU) 2015/1589.

Article 93   *****

Article 94   Procedural rules

1. The provisions of Union law governing the different types of administrative procedures covered by this Chapter shall apply to the procedures referred to in Articles 92, 93 and 96.

2. When representing or assisting a party in relation to the administrative procedures referred to in Articles 92 and 93, the lawyers authorised to practise before the courts or tribunals of the United Kingdom shall in every respect be treated as lawyers authorised to practise before courts or tribunals of Member States who represent or assist a party in relation to such administrative procedures.

3. Article 128(5) shall apply to the extent necessary for any procedures referred to in Articles 92 and 93 after the end of the transition period.

Article 95   Binding force and enforceability of decisions

1. Decisions adopted by institutions, bodies, offices and agencies of the Union before the end of the transition period, or adopted in the procedures referred to in Articles 92 and 93 after the end of the transition period, and addressed to the United Kingdom or to natural and legal persons residing or established in the United Kingdom, shall be binding on and in the United Kingdom.

2. Unless otherwise agreed between the European Commission and the designated national competition authority of the United Kingdom, the European Commission shall continue to be competent to monitor and enforce commitments given or remedies imposed in, or in relation to, the United Kingdom in connection with any proceedings for the application of Articles 101 or 102 TFEU

conducted by the European Commission under Regulation (EC) No 1/2003 or proceedings conducted by the European Commission under Regulation (EC) No 139/2004 in connection with the control of concentrations between undertakings. If so agreed between the European Commission and the designated national competition authority of the United Kingdom, the European Commission shall transfer the monitoring and enforcement of such commitments or remedies in the United Kingdom to the designated national competition authority of the United Kingdom.

3. The legality of a decision referred to in paragraph 1 of this Article shall be reviewed exclusively by the Court of Justice of the European Union in accordance with Article 263 TFEU.

4. Article 299 TFEU shall apply in the United Kingdom in respect of the enforcement of decisions referred to in paragraph 1 of this Article that impose pecuniary obligations on natural and legal persons residing or established in the United Kingdom.

Articles 96–125 *****

PART FOUR TRANSITION

Article 126 Transition period
There shall be a transition or implementation period, which shall start on the date of entry into force of this Agreement and end on 31 December 2020.

Article 127 Scope of the transition
1. Unless otherwise provided in this Agreement, Union law shall be applicable to and in the United Kingdom during the transition period.
*****

Article 128 Institutional arrangements
1. Notwithstanding Article 127, during the transition period Article 7 shall apply.

2. For the purposes of the Treaties, during the transition period, the parliament of the United Kingdom shall not be considered to be a national parliament of a Member State, except as regards Article 1 of Protocol (No 1) on the role of national parliaments in the European Union and, in respect of proposals which are in the public domain, Article 2 of that Protocol.

3. During the transition period, provisions of the Treaties which grant institutional rights to Member States enabling them to submit proposals, initiatives or requests to the institutions shall be understood as not including the United Kingdom.[8]

4.–6. *****

7. During the transition period, where draft Union acts identify or refer directly to specific Member State authorities, procedures, or documents, the United Kingdom shall be consulted by the Union on such drafts, with a view to ensuring the proper implementation and application of those acts by and in the United Kingdom.

Article 129 Specific arrangements relating to the Union's external action
1. Without prejudice to Article 127(2), during the transition period, the United Kingdom shall be bound by the obligations stemming from the international agreements concluded by the Union, by Member States acting on its behalf, or by the Union and its Member States acting jointly, as referred to in point (a)(iv) of Article 2.[9]

2.–7. *****

Articles 130–132 *****

---

[8] This should in particular concern Articles 7, 30, 42(4), 48(2) to (6) and 49 TEU and Articles 25, 76(b), 82(3), 83(3), 86(1), 87(3), 135, 218(8), 223(1), 262, 311 and 341 TFEU.

[9] The Union will notify the other parties to these agreements that during the transition period the United Kingdom is to be treated as a Member State for the purposes of these agreements.

PART FIVE FINANCIAL PROVISIONS

Chapter 1 General provisions

Article 133   Currency to be used between the Union and the United Kingdom

Without prejudice to the applicable Union law concerning the Union's own resources, all amounts, liabilities, calculations, accounts and payments referred to in this Part shall be drawn up and implemented in euro.

Articles 134–139   *****

Articles 140   Outstanding commitments

1. Unless otherwise provided for in this Agreement, the United Kingdom shall be liable to the Union for the United Kingdom's share of the budgetary commitments of the Union budget and the budgets of the Union decentralised agencies outstanding on 31 December 2020 and for the United Kingdom's share of the commitments made in 2021 on the carryover of commitment appropriations from the budget for 2020.

   *****

2. *****

3. The Union shall, by 31 March of each year, starting in 2022, with regard to the commitments referred to in paragraph 1, communicate to the United Kingdom:

   (a) information on the amount of commitments outstanding on 31 December of the previous year and on the payments and decommitments made in the previous year, including an update of the list referred to in paragraph 2;

   (b) an estimate of the expected payments in the current year based on the level of payment appropriations in the budget;

   (c) an estimate of the expected contribution of the United Kingdom to the payments referred to in point (b); and

   (d) other information, such as a medium term payment forecast.

4. The annual amount payable shall be calculated as the United Kingdom's share of the estimate referred to in point (b) of paragraph 3 adjusted by the difference between the payments made by the United Kingdom in the previous year and the United Kingdom's share of the payments made by the Union in the previous year on the outstanding commitments referred to in paragraph 1, reduced by the amount of net financial corrections in relation to programmes and activities financed under the MFF 2014-2020 or previous financial perspectives and reduced by the proceeds of any infringement procedures concerning the failure of a Member State to make available own resources related to financial years until 2020, provided that those amounts have been received by the budget in the previous year and are definitive. The annual amount payable by the United Kingdom shall not be adjusted in the given year.

   In 2021, the annual amount payable by the United Kingdom shall be reduced by the United Kingdom's share in the financing of the budget for 2020 of the amount of payment appropriations carried over from 2020 to 2021 in accordance with Articles 12 and 13 of the Financial Regulation and by the United Kingdom's share of the total amount of traditional own resources made available to the Union in January and February 2021 in respect of which the Union's entitlements were established in accordance with Article 2 of Regulation (EU, Euratom) No 609/2014 in November and December 2020. The Union shall also reimburse to the United Kingdom the United Kingdom's share of the total amount of traditional own resources made available by the Member States after 31 December 2020 for goods released for free circulation in respect of ending or discharge of temporary storage or customs procedures referred to in Article 49(2) started before or on this date.

5. At the request of the United Kingdom, made at the earliest after 31 December 2028, the Union shall make an estimate of the remaining amounts to be paid by the United Kingdom under this Article, on the basis of a rule taking into account the amount of outstanding commitments at

the end of the year and an estimate of any decommitments on those outstanding commitments, any financial corrections and any proceeds from the infringement procedures after the end of the year. After the confirmation by the United Kingdom of the acceptance of the proposal to the Committee on the financial provisions referred to in point (f) of Article 165(1) and the Joint Committee, the United Kingdom shall pay the estimated amount, as adjusted in accordance with paragraph 4 of this Article, in relation to the payments made by the United Kingdom in the previous year. The payment of the amounts referred to in this paragraph shall extinguish the remaining obligations of the United Kingdom or the Union under this Article.

Articles 141–144   *****

Article 145   The European Coal and Steel Community
The Union shall be liable to the United Kingdom for its share of the net assets of the European Coal and Steel Community in liquidation on 31 December 2020.

The Union shall reimburse the United Kingdom for the relevant amount in five equal annual instalments on 30 June of each year, starting on 30 June 2021.

Article 146   Union investment in the EIF
The Union shall be liable to the United Kingdom for its share of the Union's investment in the paid-in capital of the EIF on 31 December 2020.

The Union shall reimburse the United Kingdom for the relevant amount in five equal annual instalments on 30 June of each year starting on 30 June 2021.

Articles 147–157   *****

PART SIX INSTITUTIONAL AND FINAL PROVISIONS

Title I Consistent interpretation and application

Article 158   References to the Court of Justice of the European Union concerning Part Two
1. Where, in a case which commenced at first instance within 8 years from the end of the transition period before a court or tribunal in the United Kingdom, a question is raised concerning the interpretation of Part Two of this Agreement, and where that court or tribunal considers that a decision on that question is necessary to enable it to give judgment in that case, that court or tribunal may request the Court of Justice of the European Union to give a preliminary ruling on that question.

However, where the subject matter of the case before the court or tribunal in the United Kingdom is a decision on an application made pursuant to Article 18(1) or (4) or pursuant to Article 19, a request for a preliminary ruling may be made only where the case commenced at first instance within a period of 8 years from the date from which Article 19 applies.

2. The Court of Justice of the European Union shall have jurisdiction to give preliminary rulings on requests pursuant to paragraph 1. The legal effects in the United Kingdom of such preliminary rulings shall be the same as the legal effects of preliminary rulings given pursuant to Article 267 TFEU in the Union and its Member States.

3. In the event that the Joint Committee adopts a decision under Article 132(1), the period of eight years referred to in the second subparagraph of paragraph 1 shall be automatically extended by the corresponding number of months by which the transition period is extended.

Articles 159, 160   *****

Article 161   Procedures before the Court of Justice of the European Union
1. Where a court or tribunal of a Member State refers a question concerning the interpretation of this Agreement to the Court of Justice of the European Union for a preliminary ruling, the

decision of the national court or tribunal containing that question shall be notified to the United Kingdom.

2. The provisions of Union law governing procedures brought before the Court of Justice of the European Union in accordance with Article 267 TFEU shall apply *mutatis mutandis* to requests for a ruling of the Court of Justice of the European Union made pursuant to Article 158 of this Agreement.

The provisions of Union law governing the procedure before the Court of Justice of the European Union shall apply in respect of the proceedings before the Court of Justice of the European Union and requests for preliminary rulings made in accordance with Article 160 of this Agreement.

3. In the cases brought before the Court of Justice of the European Union in accordance with paragraph 1 and Articles 158 and 160 of this Agreement and Article 12 of the Protocol on the Sovereign Base Areas:

    (a) the United Kingdom may participate in the proceedings before the Court of Justice of the European Union in the same way as a Member State;

    (b) lawyers authorised to practise before the courts or tribunals of the United Kingdom shall be entitled to represent or assist any parties to such proceedings before the Court of Justice of the European Union; in such cases those lawyers shall in every respect be treated as lawyers authorised to practise before courts of Member States representing or assisting a party before the Court of Justice of the European Union.

Article 162   Participation of the European Commission in cases pending in the United Kingdom

Where the consistent interpretation and application of this Agreement so requires, the European Commission may submit written observations to the courts and tribunals of the United Kingdom in pending cases where the interpretation of the Agreement is concerned. The European Commission may, with the permission of the court or tribunal in question, also make oral observations. The European Commission shall inform the United Kingdom of its intention to submit observations before formally making such submissions.

Article 163   *****

Title II Institutional provisions

Article 164   Joint Committee

1. A Joint Committee, comprising representatives of the Union and of the United Kingdom, is hereby established. The Joint Committee shall be co-chaired by the Union and the United Kingdom.

2. The Joint Committee shall meet at the request of the Union or the United Kingdom, and in any event shall meet at least once a year. The Joint Committee shall set its meeting schedule and its agenda by mutual consent. The work of the Joint Committee shall be governed by the rules of procedure set out in Annex VIII to this Agreement.

3. The Joint Committee shall be responsible for the implementation and application of this Agreement. The Union and the United Kingdom may each refer to the Joint Committee any issue relating to the implementation, application and interpretation of this Agreement.

4. The Joint Committee shall:

    (a) supervise and facilitate the implementation and application of this Agreement;

    (b) decide on the tasks of the specialised committees and supervise their work;

    (c) seek appropriate ways and methods of preventing problems that might arise in areas covered by this Agreement or of resolving disputes that may arise regarding the interpretation and application of this Agreement;

    (d) consider any matter of interest relating to an area covered by this Agreement;

    (e) adopt decisions and make recommendations as set out in Article 166; and

    (f) adopt amendments to this Agreement in the cases provided for in this Agreement.

5. The Joint Committee may:

(a) delegate responsibilities to specialised committees, except those responsibilities referred to in points (b), (e) and (f) of paragraph 4;

(b) establish specialised committees other than those established by Article 165, in order to assist the Joint Committee in the performance of its tasks;

(c) change the tasks assigned to specialised committees and dissolve any of those committees;

(d) except in relation to Parts One, Four and Six, until the end of the fourth year following the end of the transition period, adopt decisions amending this Agreement, provided that such amendments are necessary to correct errors, to address omissions or other deficiencies, or to address situations unforeseen when this Agreement was signed, and provided that such decisions may not amend the essential elements of this Agreement;

(e) adopt amendments to the rules of procedure set out in Annex VIII; and

(f) take such other actions in the exercise of its functions as decided by the Union and the United Kingdom.

6. The Joint Committee shall issue an annual report on the functioning of this Agreement.

Article 165   Specialised committees

1. The following specialised committees are hereby established:

(a) the Committee on citizens' rights;

(b) the Committee on the other separation provisions;

(c) the Committee on issues related to the implementation of the Protocol on Ireland/ Northern Ireland;

(d) the Committee on issues related to the implementation of the Protocol relating to the Sovereign Base Areas in Cyprus;

(e) the Committee on issues related to the implementation of the Protocol on Gibraltar; and

(f) the Committee on the financial provisions.

Those specialised committees shall comprise representatives of the Union and representatives of the United Kingdom.

2. The work of the specialised committees shall be governed by the rules of procedure set out in Annex VIII to this Agreement.

Unless otherwise provided in this Agreement, or unless the co-chairs decide otherwise, the specialised committees shall meet at least once a year. Additional meetings may be held at the request of the Union, the United Kingdom, or of the Joint Committee. They shall be co-chaired by representatives of the Union and of the United Kingdom. The specialised committees shall set their meeting schedule and agenda by mutual consent. The specialised committees may draw up draft decisions and recommendations and refer them for adoption by the Joint Committee.

3. The Union and the United Kingdom shall ensure that their respective representatives on the specialised committees have the appropriate expertise with respect to the issues under discussion.

4. The specialised committees shall inform the Joint Committee of their meeting schedules and agenda sufficiently in advance of their meetings, and shall report to the Joint Committee on the results and conclusions of each of their meetings. The creation or existence of a specialised committee shall not prevent the Union or the United Kingdom from bringing any matter directly to the Joint Committee.

Article 166   Decisions and recommendations

1. The Joint Committee shall, for the purposes of this Agreement, have the power to adopt decisions in respect of all matters for which this Agreement so provides and to make appropriate recommendations to the Union and the United Kingdom.

2. The decisions adopted by the Joint Committee shall be binding on the Union and the United Kingdom, and the Union and the United Kingdom shall implement those decisions. They shall have the same legal effect as this Agreement.

3. The Joint Committee shall adopt its decisions and make its recommendations by mutual consent.

Title III Dispute settlement

Articles 167, 168 *****

Article 169 Consultations and communications within the Joint Committee

1. The Union and the United Kingdom shall endeavour to resolve any dispute regarding the interpretation and application of the provisions of this Agreement by entering into consultations in the Joint Committee in good faith, with the aim of reaching a mutually agreed solution. A party wishing to commence consultations shall provide written notice to the Joint Committee.

2. Any communication or notification between the Union and the United Kingdom provided for in this Title shall be made within the Joint Committee.

Article 170 Initiation of the arbitration procedure

1. Without prejudice to Article 160, if no mutually agreed solution has been reached within 3 months after a written notice has been provided to the Joint Committee in accordance with Article 169(1), the Union or the United Kingdom may request the establishment of an arbitration panel. Such request shall be made in writing to the other party and to the International Bureau of the Permanent Court of Arbitration. The request shall identify the subject matter of the dispute to be brought before the arbitration panel and a summary of the legal arguments in support of the request.

2. *****

Articles 171–174 *****

Article 175 Compliance with the arbitration panel ruling

The arbitration panel ruling shall be binding on the Union and the United Kingdom. The Union and the United Kingdom shall take any measures necessary to comply in good faith with the arbitration panel ruling and shall endeavour to agree on the period of time to comply with the ruling in accordance with the procedure in Article 176.

Articles 176–181 *****

Title IV Final provisions

Article 182 Protocols and Annexes

The Protocol on Ireland/Northern Ireland, the Protocol relating to the Sovereign Base Areas in Cyprus, the Protocol on Gibraltar, and Annexes I to IX shall form an integral part of this Agreement.

Article 183 *****

Article 184 Negotiations on the future relationship

The Union and the United Kingdom shall use their best endeavours, in good faith and in full respect of their respective legal orders, to take the necessary steps to negotiate expeditiously the agreements governing their future relationship referred to in the Political Declaration of 17 October 2019 and to conduct the relevant procedures for the ratification or conclusion of those agreements, with a view to ensuring that those agreements apply, to the extent possible, as from the end of the transition period.

Article 185 *****

*****

Protocol on Ireland/Northern Ireland

The Union and the United Kingdom,

HAVING REGARD to the historic ties and enduring nature of the bilateral relationship between Ireland and the United Kingdom,

RECALLING that the United Kingdom's withdrawal from the Union presents a significant and unique challenge to the island of Ireland, and reaffirming that the achievements, benefits and commitments of the peace process will remain of paramount importance to peace, stability and reconciliation there,

RECOGNISING that it is necessary to address the unique circumstances on the island of Ireland through a unique solution in order to ensure the orderly withdrawal of the United Kingdom from the Union,

AFFIRMING that the Good Friday or Belfast Agreement of 10 April 1998 between the Government of the United Kingdom, the Government of Ireland and the other participants in the multi-party negotiations (the '1998 Agreement'), which is annexed to the British-Irish Agreement of the same date (the 'British-Irish Agreement'), including its subsequent implementation agreements and arrangements, should be protected in all its parts,

RECOGNISING that cooperation between Northern Ireland and Ireland is a central part of the 1998 Agreement and is essential for achieving reconciliation and the normalisation of relationships on the island of Ireland, and recalling the roles, functions and safeguards of the Northern Ireland Executive, the Northern Ireland Assembly and the North-South Ministerial Council (including cross-community provisions), as set out in the 1998 Agreement,

NOTING that Union law has provided a supporting framework for the provisions on Rights, Safeguards and Equality of Opportunity of the 1998 Agreement,

RECOGNISING that Irish citizens in Northern Ireland, by virtue of their Union citizenship, will continue to enjoy, exercise and have access to rights, opportunities and benefits, and that this Protocol should respect and be without prejudice to the rights, opportunities and identity that come with citizenship of the Union for the people of Northern Ireland who choose to assert their right to Irish citizenship, as defined in Annex 2 of the British-Irish Agreement 'Declaration on the Provisions of Paragraph (vi) of Article 1 in Relation to Citizenship',

EMPHASISING that in order to ensure democratic legitimacy, there should be a process to ensure democratic consent in Northern Ireland to the application of Union law under this Protocol,

RECALLING the commitment of the United Kingdom to protect North-South cooperation and its guarantee of avoiding a hard border, including any physical infrastructure or related checks and controls,

NOTING that nothing in this Protocol prevents the United Kingdom from ensuring unfettered market access for goods moving from Northern Ireland to the rest of the United Kingdom's internal market,

UNDERLINING the Union's and the United Kingdom's shared aim of avoiding controls at the ports and airports of Northern Ireland, to the extent possible in accordance with applicable legislation and taking into account their respective regulatory regimes as well as the implementation thereof,

RECALLING the commitments of the Union and the United Kingdom reflected in the Joint Report from the negotiators of the European Union and the United Kingdom Government on progress during phase 1 of negotiations under Article 50 TEU on the United Kingdom's orderly withdrawal from the European Union of 8 December 2017,

RECALLING that the Union and the United Kingdom have carried out a mapping exercise which shows that North-South cooperation relies to a significant extent on a common Union legal and policy framework,

NOTING that therefore the United Kingdom's withdrawal from the Union gives rise to substantial challenges to the maintenance and development of North-South cooperation,

RECALLING that the United Kingdom remains committed to protecting and supporting continued North-South and East-West cooperation across the full range of political, economic, security, societal and agricultural contexts and frameworks for cooperation, including the continued operation of the North-South implementation bodies,

ACKNOWLEDGING the need for this Protocol to be implemented so as to maintain the necessary conditions for continued North-South cooperation, including for possible new arrangements in accordance with the 1998 Agreement,

RECALLING the Union's and the United Kingdom's commitments to the North South PEACE and INTERREG funding programmes under the current multi-annual financial framework and to the maintaining of the current funding proportions for the future programme,

AFFIRMING the commitment of the United Kingdom to facilitate the efficient and timely transit through its territory of goods moving from Ireland to another Member State or to a third country, and vice versa,

DETERMINED that the application of this Protocol should impact as little as possible on the everyday life of communities in both Ireland and Northern Ireland,

UNDERLINING their firm commitment to no customs and regulatory checks or controls and related physical infrastructure at the border between Ireland and Northern Ireland,

RECALLING that Northern Ireland is part of the customs territory of the United Kingdom and will benefit from participation in the United Kingdom's independent trade policy,

HAVING REGARD to the importance of maintaining the integral place of Northern Ireland in the United Kingdom's internal market,

MINDFUL that the rights and obligations of Ireland under the rules of the Union's internal market and customs union must be fully respected,

HAVE AGREED UPON the following provisions, which shall be annexed to the Withdrawal Agreement:

Article 1   Objectives

1. This Protocol is without prejudice to the provisions of the 1998 Agreement in respect of the constitutional status of Northern Ireland and the principle of consent, which provides that any change in that status can only be made with the consent of a majority of its people.

2. This Protocol respects the essential State functions and territorial integrity of the United Kingdom.

3. This Protocol sets out arrangements necessary to address the unique circumstances on the island of Ireland, to maintain the necessary conditions for continued North-South cooperation, to avoid a hard border and to protect the 1998 Agreement in all its dimensions.

Article 2   Rights of individuals

1. The United Kingdom shall ensure that no diminution of rights, safeguards or equality of opportunity, as set out in that part of the 1998 Agreement entitled Rights, Safeguards and Equality of Opportunity results from its withdrawal from the Union, including in the area of protection against discrimination, as enshrined in the provisions of Union law listed in Annex 1 to this Protocol, and shall implement this paragraph through dedicated mechanisms.

2. The United Kingdom shall continue to facilitate the related work of the institutions and bodies set up pursuant to the 1998 Agreement, including the Northern Ireland Human Rights Commission, the Equality Commission for Northern Ireland and the Joint Committee of representatives of the Human Rights Commissions of Northern Ireland and Ireland, in upholding human rights and equality standards.

Article 3   Common Travel Area

1. The United Kingdom and Ireland may continue to make arrangements between themselves relating to the movement of persons between their territories (the 'Common Travel Area'), while fully respecting the rights of natural persons conferred by Union law.

2. The United Kingdom shall ensure that the Common Travel Area and the rights and privileges associated therewith can continue to apply without affecting the obligations of Ireland under Union

law, in particular with respect to free movement to, from and within Ireland for Union citizens and their family members, irrespective of their nationality.

Article 4   Customs territory of the United Kingdom

Northern Ireland is part of the customs territory of the United Kingdom.

Accordingly, nothing in this Protocol shall prevent the United Kingdom from including Northern Ireland in the territorial scope of any agreements it may conclude with third countries, provided that those agreements do not prejudice the application of this Protocol.

In particular, nothing in this Protocol shall prevent the United Kingdom from concluding agreements with a third country that grant goods produced in Northern Ireland preferential access to that country's market on the same terms as goods produced in other parts of the United Kingdom.

Nothing in this Protocol shall prevent the United Kingdom from including Northern Ireland in the territorial scope of its Schedules of Concessions annexed to the General Agreement on Tariffs and Trade 1994.

Article 5   Customs, movements of goods

1. No customs duties shall be payable for a good brought into Northern Ireland from another part of the United Kingdom by direct transport, notwithstanding paragraph 3, unless that good is at risk of subsequently being moved into the Union, whether by itself or forming part of another good following processing.

The customs duties in respect of a good being moved by direct transport to Northern Ireland other than from the Union or from another part of the United Kingdom shall be the duties applicable in the United Kingdom, notwithstanding paragraph 3, unless that good is at risk of subsequently being moved into the Union, whether by itself or forming part of another good following processing.

No duties shall be payable by, as relief shall be granted to, residents of the United Kingdom for personal property, as defined in point (c) of Article 2(1) of Council Regulation 1186/2009,[10] brought into Northern Ireland from another part of the United Kingdom.

2. For the purposes of the first and second subparagraphs of paragraph 1, a good brought into Northern Ireland from outside the Union shall be considered to be at risk of subsequently being moved into the Union unless it is established that that good:

    (a) will not be subject to commercial processing in Northern Ireland; and

    (b) fulfils the criteria established by the Joint Committee in accordance with the fourth subparagraph of this paragraph.

For the purposes of this paragraph, 'processing' means any alteration of goods, any transformation of goods in any way, or any subjecting of goods to operations other than for the purpose of preserving them in good condition or for adding or affixing marks, labels, seals or any other documentation to ensure compliance with any specific requirements.

Before the end of the transition period, the Joint Committee shall by decision establish the conditions under which processing is to be considered not to fall within point (a) of the first subparagraph, taking into account in particular the nature, scale and result of the processing.

Before the end of the transition period, the Joint Committee shall by decision establish the criteria for considering that a good brought into Northern Ireland from outside the Union is not at risk of subsequently being moved into the Union. The Joint Committee shall take into consideration, inter alia:

    (a) the final destination and use of the good;

    (b) the nature and value of the good;

    (c) the nature of the movement; and

    (d) the incentive for undeclared onward-movement into the Union, in particular incentives resulting from the duties payable pursuant to paragraph 1.

---

[10] Council Regulation (EC) No 1186/2009 of 16 November 2009 setting up a Community system of reliefs from customs duty (OJ L 324, 10.12.2009, p. 23).

The Joint Committee may amend at any time its decisions adopted pursuant to this paragraph.

In taking any decision pursuant to this paragraph, the Joint Committee shall have regard to the specific circumstances in Northern Ireland.

3. Legislation as defined in point (2) of Article 5 of Regulation (EU) No 952/2013 shall apply to and in the United Kingdom in respect of Northern Ireland (not including the territorial waters of the United Kingdom). However, the Joint Committee shall establish the conditions, including in quantitative terms, under which certain fishery and aquaculture products, as set out in Annex I to Regulation (EU) 1379/2013 of the European Parliament and of the Council,[11] brought into the customs territory of the Union defined in Article 4 of Regulation (EU) No 952/2013 by vessels flying the flag of the United Kingdom and having their port of registration in Northern Ireland are exempted from duties.

4. The provisions of Union law listed in Annex 2 to this Protocol shall also apply, under the conditions set out in that Annex, to and in the United Kingdom in respect of Northern Ireland.

5. Articles 30 and 110 TFEU shall apply to and in the United Kingdom in respect of Northern Ireland. Quantitative restrictions on exports and imports shall be prohibited between the Union and Northern Ireland.

6. Customs duties levied by the United Kingdom in accordance with paragraph 3 are not remitted to the Union.

Subject to Article 10, the United Kingdom may in particular:

(a) reimburse duties levied pursuant to the provisions of Union law made applicable by paragraph 3 in respect of goods brought into Northern Ireland;
(b) provide for circumstances in which a customs debt which has arisen is to be waived in respect of goods brought into Northern Ireland;
(c) provide for circumstances in which customs duties are to be reimbursed in respect of goods that can be shown not to have entered the Union; and
(d) compensate undertakings to offset the impact of the application of paragraph 3.

In taking decisions under Article 10, the European Commission shall take the circumstances in Northern Ireland into account as appropriate.

7. No duties shall be payable on consignments of negligible value, on consignments sent by one individual to another or on goods contained in travellers' personal baggage, under the conditions set out in the legislation referred to in paragraph 3.

Article 6   Protection of the UK internal market

1. Nothing in this Protocol shall prevent the United Kingdom from ensuring unfettered market access for goods moving from Northern Ireland to other parts of the United Kingdom's internal market. Provisions of Union law made applicable by this Protocol which prohibit or restrict the exportation of goods shall only be applied to trade between Northern Ireland and other parts of the United Kingdom to the extent strictly required by any international obligations of the Union. The United Kingdom shall ensure full protection under international requirements and commitments that are relevant to the prohibitions and restrictions on the exportation of goods from the Union to third countries as set out in Union law.

2. Having regard to Northern Ireland's integral place in the United Kingdom's internal market, the Union and the United Kingdom shall use their best endeavours to facilitate the trade between Northern Ireland and other parts of the United Kingdom, in accordance with applicable legislation and taking into account their respective regulatory regimes as well as the implementation thereof. The Joint Committee shall keep the application of this paragraph under constant review and shall adopt appropriate recommendations with a view to avoiding controls at the ports and airports of Northern Ireland to the extent possible.

---

[11] Regulation (EU) No 1379/2013 of the European Parliament and of the Council of 11 December 2013 on the common organisation of the markets in fishery and aquaculture products amending Council Regulations (EC) No 1184/2006 and (EC) No 1224/2009 and repealing Council Regulation (EC) No 104/2000 (OJ L 354, 28.12.2013, p. 1).

3. Nothing in this Protocol shall prevent a product originating from Northern Ireland from being presented as originating from the United Kingdom when placed on the market in Great Britain.

4. Nothing in this Protocol shall affect the law of the United Kingdom regulating the placing on the market in other parts of the United Kingdom of goods from Northern Ireland that comply with or benefit from technical regulations, assessments, registrations, certificates, approvals or authorisations governed by provisions of Union law referred to in Annex 2 to this Protocol.

Article 7   Technical regulations, assessments, registrations, certificates, approvals and authorisations

1. Without prejudice to the provisions of Union law referred to in Annex 2 to this Protocol, the lawfulness of placing goods on the market in Northern Ireland shall be governed by the law of the United Kingdom as well as, as regards goods imported from the Union, by Articles 34 and 36 TFEU.

2., 3. *****

Articles 8–13   *****

Article 14   Specialised Committee

The Committee on issues related to the implementation of the Protocol on Ireland/Northern Ireland established by Article 165 of the Withdrawal Agreement ('Specialised Committee') shall:

(a) facilitate the implementation and application of this Protocol;

(b) examine proposals concerning the implementation and application of this Protocol from the North-South Ministerial Council and North-South Implementation bodies set up under the 1998 Agreement;

(c) consider any matter of relevance to Article 2 of this Protocol brought to its attention by the Northern Ireland Human Rights Commission, the Equality Commission for Northern Ireland, and the Joint Committee of representatives of the Human Rights Commissions of Northern Ireland and Ireland;

(d) discuss any point raised by the Union or the United Kingdom that is of relevance to this Protocol and gives rise to a difficulty; and

(e) make recommendations to the Joint Committee as regards the functioning of this Protocol.

Article 15   Joint consultative working group

1. A joint consultative working group on the implementation of this Protocol ('working group') is hereby established. It shall serve as a forum for the exchange of information and mutual consultation.

2. The working group shall be composed of representatives of the Union and the United Kingdom and shall carry out its functions under the supervision of the Specialised Committee, to which it shall report. The working group shall have no power to take binding decisions other than the power to adopt its own rules of procedure referred to in paragraph 6.

3.–7. *****

Article 16   Safeguards

1. If the application of this Protocol leads to serious economic, societal or environmental difficulties that are liable to persist, or to diversion of trade, the Union or the United Kingdom may unilaterally take appropriate safeguard measures. Such safeguard measures shall be restricted with regard to their scope and duration to what is strictly necessary in order to remedy the situation. Priority shall be given to such measures as will least disturb the functioning of this Protocol.

2. If a safeguard measure taken by the Union or the United King-dom, as the case may be, in accordance with paragraph 1 creates an imbalance between the rights and obligations under this Protocol, the Union or the United Kingdom, as the case may be, may take such proportionate rebalancing measures as are strictly necessary to remedy the imbalance. Priority shall be given to such measures as will least disturb the functioning of this Protocol.

3. Safeguard and rebalancing measures taken in accordance with paragraphs 1 and 2 shall be governed by the procedures set out in Annex 7 to this Protocol.

Article 17   *****

Article 18   Democratic consent in Northern Ireland

1. Within 2 months before the end of both the initial period and any subsequent period, the United Kingdom shall provide the opportunity for democratic consent in Northern Ireland to the continued application of Articles 5 to 10.

2. For the purposes of paragraph 1, the United Kingdom shall seek democratic consent in Northern Ireland in a manner consistent with the 1998 Agreement. A decision expressing democratic consent shall be reached strictly in accordance with the unilateral declaration concerning the operation of the 'Democratic consent in Northern Ireland' provision of the Protocol on Ireland/ Northern Ireland made by the United Kingdom on 17 October 2019, including with respect to the roles of the Northern Ireland Executive and Assembly.

3. The United Kingdom shall notify the Union before the end of the relevant period referred to in paragraph 5 of the outcome of the process referred to in paragraph 1.

4. Where the process referred to in paragraph 1 has been undertaken and a decision has been reached in accordance with paragraph 2, and the United Kingdom notifies the Union that the outcome of the process referred to in paragraph 1 is not a decision that the Articles of this Protocol referred to in that paragraph should continue to apply in Northern Ireland, then those Articles and other provisions of this Protocol, to the extent that those provisions depend on those Articles for their application, shall cease to apply 2 years after the end of the relevant period referred to in paragraph 5. In such a case the Joint Committee shall address recommendations to the Union and to the United Kingdom on the necessary measures, taking into account the obligations of the parties to the 1998 Agreement. Before doing so, the Joint Committee may seek an opinion from institutions created by the 1998 Agreement.

5. For the purposes of this Article, the initial period is the period ending 4 years after the end of the transition period. Where the decision reached in a given period was on the basis of a majority of Members of the Northern Ireland Assembly, present and voting, the subsequent period is the 4 year period following that period, for as long as Articles 5 to 10 continue to apply. Where the decision reached in a given period had cross-community support, the subsequent period is the 8-year period following that period, for as long as Articles 5 to 10 continue to apply.

6. For the purposes of paragraph 5, cross-community support means:
    (a) a majority of those Members of the Legislative Assembly present and voting, including a majority of the unionist and nationalist designations present and voting; or
    (b) a weighted majority (60 %) of Members of the Legislative Assembly present and voting, including at least 40 % of each of the nationalist and unionist designations present and voting.

Article 19   Annexes

Annexes 1 to 7 shall form an integral part of this Protocol.[*]
******[**]

---

[*] **Editor's Note:** Annexes 1–7 set out the various provisions of Union law and procedures relevant to the foregoing Articles. They are not reproduced here.

[**] **Editor's Note:** The Agreement then goes on to set out further Protocols and Annexes pertaining to 'Sovereign base areas of the United Kingdom of Great Britain and Northern Ireland in Cyprus'; to 'Gibraltar'.

Other Constitutional Materials

The Constitution of the United States (1787)

We the People of the United States, in order to form a more perfect Union, establish Justice, ensure Domestic Tranquillity, provide for the common Defence, promote the general Welfare, and secure the Blessings of Liberty to ourselves and our Posterity, do ordain and establish this CONSTITUTION for the United States of America.

Articles I–VII *****

Amendments to the Constitution

Article I*
Congress shall make no law respecting an establishment of religion, or prohibiting the free exercise thereof; or abridging the freedom of speech or of the press; or the right of the people peaceably to assemble, and to petition the government for a redress of grievances.

Article II
A well-regulated militia being necessary to the security of a free state, the right of the people to keep and bear arms shall not be infringed.

Article III
No soldier shall, in time of peace, be quartered in any house without the consent of the owner, nor in time of war but in a manner to be prescribed by law.

Article IV
The right of the people to be secure in their persons, houses, papers, and effects, against unreasonable searches and seizures, shall not be violated, and no warrants shall issue but upon probable cause, supported by oath or affirmation, and particularly describing the place to be searched, and the persons or things to be seized.

Article V
No person shall be held to answer for a capital or other infamous crime unless on a presentment or indictment of a grand jury, except in cases arising in the land or naval forces, or in the militia, when in actual service, in time of war or public danger; nor shall any person be subject for the same offence to be twice put in jeopardy of life or limb; nor shall be compelled in any criminal case to be a witness against himself, nor be deprived of life, liberty, or property, without due process of law; nor shall private property be taken for public use without just compensation.

Article VI
In all criminal prosecutions, the accused shall enjoy the right to a speedy and public trial, by an impartial jury of the state and district wherein the crime shall have been committed, which district shall

* **Editor's Note:** The first ten amendments were adopted at the first session of Congress, and were declared to be in force, 15 December 1791.

have been previously ascertained by law, and to be informed of the nature and cause of the accusation; to be confronted with the witnesses against him; to have compulsory process for obtaining witnesses in his favor, and to have the assistance of counsel for his defence.

Article VII

In suits at common law, where the value in controversy shall exceed twenty dollars, the right of trial by jury shall be preserved, and no fact tried by a jury shall be otherwise re-examined in any court of the United States than according to the rules of the common law.

Article VIII

Excessive bail shall not be required, nor excessive fines imposed, nor cruel and unusual punishments inflicted.

Article IX

The enumeration in the constitution of certain rights shall not be construed to deny or disparage others retained by the people.

Article X

The powers not delegated to the United States by the constitution, nor prohibited by it to the states, are reserved to the states respectively, or to the people.

Articles XI–XIII   *****

Article XIV*

1. All persons born or naturalized in the United States, and subject to the jurisdiction thereof, are citizens of the United States and of the state wherein they reside. No state shall make or enforce any law which shall abridge the privileges or immunities of citizens of the United States; nor shall any state deprive any person of life, liberty, or property without due process of law; nor deny to any person within its jurisdiction the equal protection of the law.

2.–4. *****

5. The Congress shall have power to enforce, by appropriate legislation, the provisions of this article.

*****

United Nations Universal Declaration of Human Rights (December 1948)**

Preamble

Whereas recognition of the inherent dignity and of the equal and inalienable rights of all members of the human family is the foundation of freedom, justice and peace in the world,

Whereas disregard and contempt for human rights have resulted in barbarous acts which have outraged the conscience of mankind, and the advent of a world in which human beings shall enjoy freedom of speech and belief and freedom from fear and want has been proclaimed as the highest aspiration of the common people,

Whereas it is essential, if man is not to be compelled to have recourse, as a last resort, to rebellion against tyranny and oppression, that human rights should be protected by the rule of law,

Whereas it is essential to promote the development of friendly relations between nations,

Whereas the peoples of the United Nations have in the Charter reaffirmed their faith in fundamental human rights, in the dignity and worth of the human person and in the equal rights of men and women and have determined to promote social progress and better standards of life in larger freedom,

---

* **Editor's Note:** Declared in force, 28 July 1868.
** © 1948 United Nations. Reproduced with permission of the United Nations.

Whereas Member States have pledged themselves to achieve, in co-operation with the United Nations, the promotion of universal respect for and observance of human rights and fundamental freedoms,

Whereas a common understanding of these rights and freedoms is of the greatest importance for the full realization of this pledge,

Now, Therefore THE GENERAL ASSEMBLY proclaims THIS UNIVERSAL DECLARATION OF HUMAN RIGHTS as a common standard of achievement for all peoples and all nations, to the end that every individual and every organ of society, keeping this Declaration constantly in mind, shall strive by teaching and education to promote respect for these rights and freedoms and by progressive measures, national and international, to secure their universal and effective recognition and observance, both among the peoples of Member States themselves and among the peoples of territories under their jurisdiction.

Article 1
All human beings are born free and equal in dignity and rights. They are endowed with reason and conscience and should act towards one another in a spirit of brotherhood.

Article 2
Everyone is entitled to all the rights and freedoms set forth in this Declaration, without distinction of any kind, such as race, colour, sex, language, religion, political or other opinion, national or social origin, property, birth or other status. Furthermore, no distinction shall be made on the basis of the political, jurisdictional or international status of the country or territory to which a person belongs, whether it be independent, trust, non-self-governing or under any other limitation of sovereignty.

Article 3
Everyone has the right to life, liberty and security of person.

Article 4
No one shall be held in slavery or servitude; slavery and the slave trade shall be prohibited in all their forms.

Article 5
No one shall be subjected to torture or to cruel, inhuman or degrading treatment or punishment.

Article 6
Everyone has the right to recognition everywhere as a person before the law.

Article 7
All are equal before the law and are entitled without any discrimination to equal protection of the law. All are entitled to equal protection against any discrimination in violation of this Declaration and against any incitement to such discrimination.

Article 8
Everyone has the right to an effective remedy by the competent national tribunals for acts violating the fundamental rights granted him by the constitution or by law.

Article 9
No one shall be subjected to arbitrary arrest, detention or exile.

Article 10
Everyone is entitled in full equality to a fair and public hearing by an independent and impartial tribunal, in the determination of his rights and obligations and of any criminal charge against him.

Article 11
(1) Everyone charged with a penal offence has the right to be presumed innocent until proved guilty according to law in a public trial at which he has had all the guarantees necessary for his defence.

(2) No one shall be held guilty of any penal offence on account of any act or omission which did not constitute a penal offence, under national or international law, at the time when it was committed. Nor shall a heavier penalty be imposed than the one that was applicable at the time the penal offence was committed.

Article 12

No one shall be subjected to arbitrary interference with his privacy, family, home or correspondence, nor to attacks upon his honour and reputation. Everyone has the right to the protection of the law against such interference or attacks.

Article 13

(1) Everyone has the right to freedom of movement and residence within the borders of each state.

(2) Everyone has the right to leave any country, including his own, and to return to his country.

Article 14

(1) Everyone has the right to seek and to enjoy in other countries asylum from persecution.

(2) This right may not be invoked in the case of prosecutions genuinely arising from non-political crimes or from acts contrary to the purposes and principles of the United Nations.

Article 15

(1) Everyone has the right to a nationality.

(2) No one shall be arbitrarily deprived of his nationality nor denied the right to change his nationality.

Article 16

(1) Men and women of full age, without any limitation due to race, nationality or religion, have the right to marry and to found a family. They are entitled to equal rights as to marriage, during marriage and at its dissolution.

(2) Marriage shall be entered into only with the free and full consent of the intending spouses.

(3) The family is the natural and fundamental group unit of society and is entitled to protection by society and the State.

Article 17

(1) Everyone has the right to own property alone as well as in association with others.

(2) No one shall be arbitrarily deprived of his property.

Article 18

Everyone has the right to freedom of thought, conscience and religion; this right includes freedom to change his religion or belief, and freedom, either alone or in community with others and in public or private, to manifest his religion or belief in teaching, practice, worship and observance.

Article 19

Everyone has the right to freedom of opinion and expression; this right includes freedom to hold opinions without interference and to seek, receive and impart information and ideas through any media and regardless of frontiers.

Article 20

(1) Everyone has the right to freedom of peaceful assembly and association.

(2) No one may be compelled to belong to an association.

Article 21

(1) Everyone has the right to take part in the government of his country, directly or through freely chosen representatives.

(2) Everyone has the right of equal access to public service in his country.

(3) The will of the people shall be the basis of the authority of government; this will shall be expressed in periodic and genuine elections which shall be by universal and equal suffrage and shall be held by secret vote or by equivalent free voting procedures.

Article 22

Everyone, as a member of society, has the right to social security and is entitled to realization, through national effort and international co-operation and in accordance with the organization and resources of each State, of the economic, social and cultural rights indispensable for his dignity and the free development of his personality.

Article 23

(1) Everyone has the right to work, to free choice of employment, to just and favourable conditions of work and to protection against unemployment.

(2) Everyone, without any discrimination, has the right to equal pay for equal work.

(3) Everyone who works has the right to just and favourable remuneration ensuring for himself and his family an existence worthy of human dignity, and supplemented, if necessary, by other means of social protection.

(4) Everyone has the right to form and to join trade unions for the protection of his interests.

Article 24

Everyone has the right to rest and leisure, including reasonable limitation of working hours and periodic holidays with pay.

Article 25

(1) Everyone has the right to a standard of living adequate for the health and well-being of himself and of his family, including food, clothing, housing and medical care and necessary social services, and the right to security in the event of unemployment, sickness, disability, widowhood, old age or other lack of livelihood in circumstances beyond his control.

(2) Motherhood and childhood are entitled to special care and assistance. All children, whether born in or out of wedlock, shall enjoy the same social protection.

Article 26

(1) Everyone has the right to education. Education shall be free, at least in the elementary and fundamental stages. Elementary education shall be compulsory. Technical and professional education shall be made generally available and higher education shall be equally accessible to all on the basis of merit.

(2) Education shall be directed to the full development of the human personality and to the strengthening of respect for human rights and fundamental freedoms. It shall promote understanding, tolerance and friendship among all nations, racial or religious groups, and shall further the activities of the United Nations for the maintenance of peace.

(3) Parents have a prior right to choose the kind of education that shall be given to their children.

Article 27

(1) Everyone has the right freely to participate in the cultural life of the community, to enjoy the arts and to share in scientific advancement and its benefits.

(2) Everyone has the right to the protection of the moral and material interests resulting from any scientific, literary or artistic production of which he is the author.

Article 28

Everyone is entitled to a social and international order in which the rights and freedoms set forth in this Declaration can be fully realized.

Article 29

(1) Everyone has duties to the community in which alone the free and full development of his personality is possible.

(2) In the exercise of his rights and freedoms, everyone shall be subject only to such limitations as are determined by law solely for the purpose of securing due recognition and respect for the rights and freedoms of others and of meeting the just requirements of morality, public order and the general welfare in a democratic society.

(3) These rights and freedoms may in no case be exercised contrary to the purposes and principles of the United Nations.

Article 30

Nothing in this Declaration may be interpreted as implying for any State, group or person any right to engage in any activity or to perform any act aimed at the destruction of any of the rights and freedoms set forth herein.

European Convention for the Protection of Human Rights and Fundamental Freedoms (1950)*

[The European Convention on Human Rights]

The Governments signatory hereto, being Members of the Council of Europe.

Considering the Universal Declaration of Human Rights proclaimed by the General Assembly of the United Nations on 10 December 1948;

Considering that this Declaration aims at securing the universal and effective recognition and observance of the Rights therein declared;

Considering that the aim of the Council of Europe is the achievement of greater unity between its Members and that one of the methods by which the aim is to be pursued is the maintenance and further realization of Human Rights and Fundamental Freedoms;

Reaffirming their profound belief in those Fundamental Freedoms which are the foundation of justice and peace in the world and are best maintained on the one hand by an effective political democracy and on the other by a common understanding and observance of the Human Rights upon which they depend;

Being resolved, as the Governments of European countries which are like-minded and have a common heritage of political traditions, ideals, freedom and the rule of law to take the first steps for the collective enforcement of certain of the Rights stated in the Universal Declaration;

Have agreed as follows:

Article 1 Obligation to respect human rights

The High Contracting Parties shall secure to everyone within their jurisdiction the rights and freedoms defined in Section I of this Convention.

Section I Rights and Freedoms

Article 2 Right to life

1. Everyone's right to life shall be protected by law. No one shall be deprived of his life intentionally save in the execution of a sentence of a court following his conviction of a crime for which this penalty is provided by law.

2. Deprivation of life shall not be regarded as inflicted in contravention of this article when it results from the use of force which is no more than absolutely necessary:
    (a) in defence of any person from unlawful violence;
    (b) in order to effect a lawful arrest or to prevent the escape of a person lawfully detained;
    (c) in action lawfully taken for the purpose of quelling a riot or insurrection.

Article 3 Prohibition of torture

No one shall be subjected to torture or to inhuman or degrading treatment or punishment.

Article 4 Prohibition of slavery and forced labour

1. No one shall be held in slavery or servitude.
2. No one shall be required to perform forced or compulsory labour.
3. For the purpose of this article the term 'forced or compulsory labour' shall not include:
    (a) any work required to be done in the ordinary course of detention imposed according to the provisions of Article 5 of this Convention or during conditional release from such detention;

(b) any service of a military character or, in case of conscientious objectors in countries where they are recognized, service exacted instead of compulsory military service;

(c) any service exacted in case of an emergency or calamity threatening the life or well-being of the community;

(d) any work or service which forms part of normal civic obligations.

Article 5 Right to liberty and security

1. Everyone has the right to liberty and security of person. No one shall be deprived of his liberty save in the following cases and in accordance with a procedure prescribed by law:

(a) the lawful detention of a person after conviction by a competent court;

(b) the lawful arrest or detention of a person for non-compliance with the lawful order of a court or in order to secure the fulfilment of any obligation prescribed by law;

(c) the lawful arrest or detention of a person effected for the purpose of bringing him before the competent legal authority on reasonable suspicion of having committed an offence or when it is reasonably considered necessary to prevent his committing an offence or fleeing after having done so;

(d) the detention of a minor by lawful order for the purpose of educational supervision or his lawful detention for the purpose of bringing him before the competent legal authority;

(e) the lawful detention of persons for the prevention of the spreading of infectious diseases, of persons of unsound mind, alcoholics or drug addicts, or vagrants;

(f) the lawful arrest or detention of a person to prevent his effecting an unauthorized entry into the country or of a person against whom action is being taken with a view to deportation or extradition.

2. Everyone who is arrested shall be informed promptly, in a language which he understands, of the reasons for his arrest and of any charge against him.

3. Everyone arrested or detained in accordance with the provisions of paragraph 1(c) of this article shall be brought promptly before a judge or other officer authorized by law to exercise judicial power and shall be entitled to trial within a reasonable time or to release pending trial. Release may be conditioned by guarantees to appear for trial.

4. Everyone who is deprived of his liberty by arrest or detention shall be entitled to take proceedings by which the lawfulness of his detention shall be decided speedily by a court and his release ordered if the detention is not lawful.

5. Everyone who has been the victim of arrest or detention in contravention of the provisions of this article shall have an enforceable right to compensation.

Article 6 Right to a fair trial

1. In the determination of his civil rights and obligations or of any criminal charge against him, everyone is entitled to a fair and public hearing within a reasonable time by an independent and impartial tribunal established by law. Judgment shall be pronounced publicly but the press and public may be excluded from all or part of the trial in the interest of morals, public order or national security in a democratic society, where the interests of juveniles or the protection of the private life of the parties so require, or to the extent strictly necessary in the opinion of the court in special circumstances where publicity would prejudice the interests of justice.

2. Everyone charged with a criminal offence shall be presumed innocent until proved guilty according to law.

3. Everyone charged with a criminal offence has the following minimum rights:

(a) to be informed promptly, in a language which he understands and in detail, of the nature and cause of the accusation against him;

(b) to have adequate time and facilities for the preparation of his defence;

(c) to defend himself in person or through legal assistance of his own choosing or, if he has not sufficient means to pay for legal assistance, to be given it free when the interests of justice so require;

(d) to examine or have examined witnesses against him and to obtain the attendance and examination of witnesses on his behalf under the same conditions as witnesses against him;

(e) to have the free assistance of an interpreter if he cannot understand or speak the language used in court.

Article 7   No punishment without law

1. No one shall be held guilty of any criminal offence on account of any act or omission which did not constitute a criminal offence under national or international law at the time when it was committed. Nor shall a heavier penalty be imposed than the one that was applicable at the time the criminal offence was committed.

2. This article shall not prejudice the trial and punishment of any person for any act or omission which, at the time when it was committed, was criminal according to the general principles of law recognized by civilized nations.

Article 8   Right to respect for private and family life

1. Everyone has the right to respect for his private and family life, his home and his correspondence.

2. There shall be no interference by a public authority with the exercise of this right except such as is in accordance with the law and is necessary in a democratic society in the interests of national security, public safety or the economic well-being of the country, for the prevention of disorder or crime, for the protection of health or morals, or for the protection of the rights and freedoms of others.

Article 9   Freedom of thought, conscience and religion

1. Everyone has the right to freedom of thought, conscience and religion; this right includes freedom to change his religion or belief, and freedom, either alone or in community with others and in public or private, to manifest his religion or belief, in worship, teaching, practice and observance.

2. Freedom to manifest one's religion or beliefs shall be subject only to such limitations as are prescribed by law and are necessary in a democratic society in the interests of public safety, for the protection of public order, health or morals, or for the protection of the rights and freedoms of others.

Article 10   Freedom of expression

1. Everyone has the right to freedom of expression. This right shall include freedom to hold opinions and to receive and impart information and ideas without interference by public authority and regardless of frontiers. This article shall not prevent States from requiring the licensing of broadcasting, television or cinema enterprises.

2. The exercise of these freedoms, since it carries with it duties and responsibilities, may be subject to such formalities, conditions, restrictions or penalties as are prescribed by law and are necessary in a democratic society, in the interests of national security, territorial integrity or public safety, for the prevention of disorder or crime, for the protection of health or morals, for the protection of the reputation or rights of others, for preventing the disclosure of information received in confidence, or for maintaining the authority and impartiality of the judiciary.

Article 11   Freedom of assembly and association

1. Everyone has the right to freedom of peaceful assembly and to freedom of association with others, including the right to form and to join trade unions for the protection of his interests.

2. No restrictions shall be placed on the exercise of these rights other than such as are prescribed by law and are necessary in a democratic society in the interests of national security or public safety, for the prevention of disorder or crime, of the protection of health or morals or for the protection of the rights and freedoms of others. This article shall not prevent the imposition of lawful restrictions on the exercise of these rights by members of the armed forces, of the police or of the administration of the State.

Article 12   Right to marry

Men and women of marriageable age have the right to marry and to found a family, according to the national laws governing the exercise of this right.

Article 13   Right to an effective remedy

Everyone whose rights and freedoms as set forth in this Convention are violated shall have an effective remedy before a national authority notwithstanding that the violation has been committed by persons acting in an official capacity.

Article 14   Prohibition of discrimination

The enjoyment of the rights and freedoms set forth in this Convention shall be secured without discrimination on any ground such as sex, race, colour, language, religion, political or other opinion, national or social origin, association with a national minority, property, birth or other status.

Article 15   Derogation in time of emergency

1. In time of war or other public emergency threatening the life of the nation any High Contracting Party may take measures derogating from its obligations under this Convention to the extent strictly required by the exigencies of the situation, provided that such measures are not inconsistent with its other obligations under international law.

2. No derogation from Article 2, except in respect of deaths resulting from lawful acts of war, or from Articles 3, 4 (paragraph 1) and 7 shall be made under this provision.

3. Any High Contracting Party availing itself of this right of derogation shall keep the Secretary-General of the Council of Europe fully informed of the measures which it has taken and the reasons therefor. It shall also inform the Secretary-General of the Council of Europe when such measures have ceased to operate and the provisions of the Convention are again being fully executed.

Article 16   Restrictions on political activity of aliens

Nothing in Articles 10, 11, and 14 shall be regarded as preventing the High Contracting Parties from imposing restrictions on the political activity of aliens.

Article 17   Prohibition of abuse of rights

Nothing in this Convention may be interpreted as implying for any State, group or person any right to engage in any activity or perform any act aimed at the destruction of any of the rights and freedoms set forth herein or at their limitation to a greater extent than is provided for in the Convention.

Article 18   Limitation on use of restrictions on rights

The restrictions permitted under this Convention to the said rights and freedoms shall not be applied for any purpose other than those for which they have been prescribed.

Section II European Court of Human Rights

Article 19   Establishment of the Court

To ensure the observance of the engagements undertaken by the High Contracting Parties in the Convention and the protocols thereto, there shall be set up a European Court of Human Rights, hereinafter referred to as 'the Court'. It shall function on a permanent basis.

Article 20   Number of judges

The Court shall consist of a number of judges equal to that of the High Contracting Parties.

Article 21   Criteria for office

1. The judges shall be of high moral character and must either possess the qualifications required for appointment to high judicial office or be jurisconsults of recognised competence.

2. The judges shall sit on the Court in their individual capacity.

3. During their term of office the judges shall not engage in any activity which is incompatible with their independence, impartiality or with the demands of a full-time office; all questions arising from the application of this paragraph shall be decided by the Court.

Article 22   Election of judges

The judges shall be elected by the Parliamentary Assembly with respect to each High Contracting Party by a majority of votes cast from a list of three candidates nominated by the High Contracting Party.

Article 23   Terms of office and dismissal

1. The judges shall be elected for a period of nine years. They may not be re-elected.

2. The terms of office of judges shall expire when they reach the age of 70.

3. The judges shall hold office until replaced. They shall, however, continue to deal with such cases as they already have under consideration.

4. No judge may be dismissed from office unless the other judges decide by a majority of two-thirds that that judge has ceased to fulfil the required conditions.

Article 24   Registry and rapporteurs

1. The Court shall have a registry, the functions and organisation of which shall be laid down in the rules of the Court.

2. When sitting in a single-judge formation, the Court shall be assisted by rapporteurs who shall function under the authority of the President of the Court. They shall form part of the Court's registry.

Article 25   Plenary Court

The plenary Court shall

    (a) elect its President and one or two Vice-Presidents for a period of three years; they may be re-elected;

    (b) set up Chambers, constituted for a fixed period of time;

    (c) elect the Presidents of the Chambers of the Court; they may be re-elected;

    (d) adopt the rules of the Court;

    (e) elect the Registrar and one or more Deputy Registrars;

    (f) make any request under Article 26, paragraph 2.

Article 26   Single-judge formation, committees, Chambers and Grand Chamber

1. To consider cases brought before it, the Court shall sit in a single-judge formation, in committees of three judges, in Chambers of seven judges and in a Grand Chamber of seventeen judges. The Court's Chambers shall set up committees for a fixed period of time.

2. At the request of the plenary Court, the Committee of Ministers may, by a unanimous decision and for a fixed period, reduce to five the number of judges of the Chambers.

3. When sitting as a single judge, a judge shall not examine any application against the High Contracting Party in respect of which that judge has been elected.

4. There shall sit as an *ex officio* member of the Chamber and the Grand Chamber the judge elected in respect of the High Contracting Party concerned. If there is none or if that judge is unable to sit, a person chosen by the President of the Court from a list submitted in advance by that Party shall sit in the capacity of judge.

5. The Grand Chamber shall also include the President of the Court, the Vice-Presidents, the Presidents of the Chambers and other judges chosen in accordance with the rules of the Court. When a case is referred to the Grand Chamber under Article 43, no judge from the Chamber which rendered the judgment shall sit in the Grand Chamber, with the exception of the President of the Chamber and the judge who sat in respect of the High Contracting Party concerned.

Article 27   Competence of single judges

1. A single judge may declare inadmissible or strike out of the Court's list of cases an application submitted under Article 34, where such a decision can be taken without further examination.

2. The decision shall be final.

3. If the single judge does not declare an application inadmissible or strike it out, that judge shall forward it to a committee or to a Chamber for further examination.

Article 28   Competence of committees

1. In respect of an application submitted under Article 34, a committee may, by a unanimous vote,

    (a) declare it inadmissible or strike it out of its list of cases, where such decision can be taken without further examination; or

    (b) declare it admissible and render at the same time a judgment on the merits, if the underlying question in the case, concerning the interpretation or the application of the

Convention or the Protocols thereto, is already the subject of well-established case-law of the Court.

2. Decisions and judgments under paragraph 1 shall be final.

3. If the judge elected in respect of the High Contracting Party concerned is not a member of the committee, the committee may at any stage of the proceedings invite that judge to take the place of one of the members of the committee, having regard to all relevant factors, including whether that Party has contested the application of the procedure under paragraph 1.b.

Article 29 Decisions by Chambers on admissibility and merits

1. If no decision is taken under Article 27 or 28, or no judgment rendered under Article 28, a Chamber shall decide on the admissibility and merits of individual applications submitted under Article 34. The decision on admissibility may be taken separately.

2. A Chamber shall decide on the admissibility and merits of inter-State applications submitted under Article 33. The decision on admissibility shall be taken separately unless the Court, in exceptional cases, decides otherwise.

Article 30 Relinquishment of jurisdiction to the Grand Chamber

Where a case pending before a Chamber raises a serious question affecting the interpretation of the Convention or the protocols thereto, or where the resolution of a question before the Chamber might have a result inconsistent with a judgment previously delivered by the Court, the Chamber may, at any time before it has rendered its judgment, relinquish jurisdiction in favour of the Grand Chamber, unless one of the parties to the case objects.

Article 31 Powers of the Grand Chamber

The Grand Chamber shall:

(a) determine applications submitted either under Article 33 or Article 34 when a Chamber has relinquished jurisdiction under Article 30 or when the case has been referred to it under Article 43;

(b) decide on issues referred to the Court by the Committee of Ministers in accordance with Article 46, paragraph 4; and

(c) consider requests for advisory opinions submitted in Article 47.

Article 32 Jurisdiction of the Court

1. The jurisdiction of the Court shall extend to all matters concerning the interpretation and application of the Convention and the protocols thereto which are referred to it as provided in Articles 33, 34 and 47.

2. In the event of dispute as to whether the Court has jurisdiction, the Court shall decide.

Article 33 Inter-State cases

Any High Contracting Party may refer to the Court any alleged breach of the provisions of the Convention and the protocols thereto by another High Contracting Party.

Article 34 Individual applications

The Court may receive applications from any person, non-governmental organisation or group of individuals claiming to be the victim of a violation by one of the High Contracting Parties of the rights set forth in the Convention or the protocols thereto. The High Contracting Parties undertake not to hinder in any way the effective exercise of this right.

Article 35 Admissibility criteria

1. The Court may only deal with the matter after all domestic remedies have been exhausted, according to the generally recognised rules of international law, and within a period of six months from the date on which the final decision was taken.

2. The Court shall not deal with any individual application submitted under Article 34 that:

(a) is anonymous; or

(b) is substantially the same as a matter that has already been examined by the Court or has already been submitted to another procedure of international investigation or settlement and contains no relevant new information.

3. The Court shall declare inadmissible any individual application submitted under Article 34 if it considers that:

    (a) the application is incompatible with the provisions of the Convention or the Protocols thereto, manifestly ill-founded, or an abuse of the right of individual application; or

    (b) the applicant has not suffered a significant disadvantage, unless respect for human rights as defined in the Convention and the Protocols thereto requires an examination of the application on the merits and provided that no case may be rejected on this ground which has not been duly considered by a domestic tribunal.

4. The Court shall reject any application which it considers inadmissible under this Article. It may do so at any stage of the proceedings.

Article 36   Third party intervention

1. In all cases before a Chamber or the Grand Chamber, a High Contracting Party one of whose nationals is an applicant shall have the right to submit written comments and to take part in hearings.

2. The President of the Court may, in the interest of the proper administration of justice, invite any High Contracting Party which is not a party to the proceedings or any person concerned who is not the applicant to submit written comments or take part in hearings.

3. In all cases before a Chamber of the Grand Chamber, the Council of Europe Commissioner for Human Rights may submit written comments and take part in hearings.

Article 37   Striking out applications

1. The Court may at any stage of the proceedings decide to strike an application out of its list of cases where the circumstances lead to the conclusion that:

    (a) the applicant does not intend to pursue his application; or

    (b) the matter has been resolved; or

    (c) for any other reason established by the Court, it is no longer justified to continue the examination of the application.

However, the Court shall continue the examination of the application if respect for human rights as defined in the Convention and the protocols thereto so requires.

2. The Court may decide to restore an application to its list of cases if it considers that the circumstances justify such a course.

Article 38   Examination of the case

The Court shall examine the case together with the representatives of the parties and, if need be, undertake an investigation, for the effective conduct of which the High Contracting Parties concerned shall furnish all necessary facilities.

Article 39   Friendly settlements

1. At any stage of the proceedings, the Court may place itself at the disposal of the parties concerned with a view to securing a friendly settlement of the matter on the basis of respect for human rights as defined in the Convention and the Protocols thereto.

2. Proceedings conducted under paragraph 1 shall be confidential.

3. If a friendly settlement is effected, the Court shall strike the case out of its list by means of a decision which shall be confined to a brief statement of the facts and of the solution reached.

4. This decision shall be transmitted to the Committee of Ministers, which shall supervise the execution of the terms of the friendly settlement as set out in the decision.

Article 40   Public hearings and access to documents

1. Hearings shall be public unless the Court in exceptional circumstances decides otherwise.

2. Documents deposited with the Registrar shall be accessible to the public unless the President of the Court decides otherwise.

Article 41   Just satisfaction

If the Court finds that there has been a violation of the Convention or the protocols thereto, and if the internal law of the High Contracting Party concerned allows only partial reparation to be made, the Court shall, if necessary, afford just satisfaction to the injured party.

Article 42   Judgments of Chambers

Judgments of Chambers shall become final in accordance with the provisions of Article 44, paragraph 2.

Article 43   Referral to the Grand Chamber

1. Within a period of three months from the date of the judgment of the Chamber, any party to the case may, in exceptional cases, request that the case be referred to the Grand Chamber.

2. A panel of five judges of the Grand Chamber shall accept the request if the case raises a serious question affecting the interpretation or application of the Convention or the protocols thereto, or a serious issue of general importance.

3. If the panel accepts the request, the Grand Chamber shall decide the case by means of a judgment.

Article 44   Final judgments

1. The judgment of the Grand Chamber shall be final.

2. The judgment of a Chamber shall become final:
   (a)   when the parties declare that they will not request that the case be referred to the Grand Chamber; or
   (b)   three months after the date of the judgment, if reference of the case to the Grand Chamber has not been requested; or
   (c)   when the panel of the Grand Chamber rejects the request to refer under Article 43.

3. The final judgment shall be published.

Article 45   Reasons for judgments and decisions

1. Reasons shall be given for judgments as well as for decisions declaring applications admissible or inadmissible.

2. If a judgment does not represent, in whole or in part, the unanimous opinion of the judges, any judge shall be entitled to deliver a separate opinion.

Article 46   Binding force and execution of judgments

1. The High Contracting Parties undertake to abide by the final judgment of the Court in any case to which they are parties.

2. The final judgment of the Court shall be transmitted to the Committee of Ministers, which shall supervise its execution.

3. If the Committee of Ministers considers that the supervision of the execution of a final judgment is hindered by a problem of interpretation of the judgment, it may refer the matter to the Court for a ruling on the question of interpretation. A referral decision shall require a majority vote of two thirds of the representatives entitled to sit on the Committee.

4. If the Committee of Ministers considers that a High Contracting Party refuses to abide by a final judgment in a case to which it is a party, it may, after serving formal notice on that Party and by decision adopted by a majority vote of two thirds of the representatives entitled to sit on the Committee, refer to the Court the question whether that Party has failed to fulfil its obligation under paragraph 1.

5. If the Court finds a violation of paragraph 1, it shall refer the case to the Committee of Ministers for consideration of the measures to be taken. If the Court finds no violation of paragraph 1, it shall refer the case to the Committee of Ministers, which shall close its examination of the case.

Article 47   Advisory opinions

1. The Court may, at the request of the Committee of Ministers, give advisory opinions on legal questions concerning the interpretation of the Convention and the protocols thereto.

2. Such opinions shall not deal with any question relating to the content or scope of the rights or freedoms defined in Section I of the Convention and the protocols thereto, or with any other question which the Court or the Committee of Ministers might have to consider in consequence of any such proceedings as could be instituted in accordance with the Convention.

3. Decisions of the Committee of Ministers to request an advisory opinion of the Court shall require a majority vote of the representatives entitled to sit on the Committee.

Article 48   Advisory jurisdiction of the Court

The Court shall decide whether a request for an advisory opinion submitted by the Committee of Ministers is within its competence as defined in Article 47.

Article 49   Reasons for advisory opinions

1. Reasons shall be given for advisory opinions of the Court.

2. If the advisory opinion does not represent, in whole or in part, the unanimous opinion of the judges, any judge shall be entitled to deliver a separate opinion.

3. Advisory opinions of the Court shall be communicated to the Committee of Ministers.

Article 50   Expenditure on the Court

The expenditure on the Court shall be borne by the Council of Europe.

Article 51   Privileges and immunities of judges

The judges shall be entitled, during the exercise of their functions, to the privileges and immunities provided for in Article 40 of the Statute of the Council of Europe and in the agreements made thereunder.

Section III Miscellaneous Provisions

Article 52   *****

Article 53   Safeguard for existing human rights

Nothing in this Convention shall be construed as limiting or derogating from any of the human rights and fundamental freedoms which may be ensured under the laws of any High Contracting Party or under any other agreement to which it is a Party.

Articles 54–56   *****

Article 57   Reservations

1. Any State may, when signing this Convention or when depositing its instrument of ratification, make a reservation in respect of any particular provision of the Convention to the extent that any law then in force in its territory is not in conformity with the provision. Reservations of a general character shall not be permitted under this article.

2. Any reservation made under this article shall contain a brief statement of the law concerned.
*****

Protocols

Enforcement of certain Rights and Freedoms not included in Section I of the Convention

The Governments signatory hereto, being Members of the Council of Europe,

Being resolved to take steps to ensure the collective enforcement of certain rights and freedoms other than those already included in Section I of the Convention for the Protection of Human Rights and Fundamental Freedoms signed at Rome on 4th November 1950 (hereinafter referred to as 'the Convention'),

Have agreed as follows:

Article 1   Protection of property

Every natural or legal person is entitled to the peaceful enjoyment of his possessions. No one shall be deprived of his possessions except in the public interest and subject to the conditions provided for by law and by the general principles of international law.

The preceding provisions shall not, however, in any way impair the right of a State to enforce such laws as it deems necessary to control the use of property in accordance with the general interest or to secure the payment of taxes or other contributions or penalties.

Article 2   Right to education

No person shall be denied the right to education. In the exercise of any functions which it assumes in relation to education and to teaching, the State shall respect the right of parents to ensure such education and teaching in conformity with their own religious and philosophical convictions.

Article 3   Right to free elections

The High Contracting Parties undertake to hold free elections at reasonable intervals by secret ballot, under conditions which will ensure the free expression of the opinion of the people in the choice of the legislature.
*****

4.   *Protecting certain additional rights*

The Governments signatory hereto, being Members of the Council of Europe.*

Being resolved to take steps to ensure the collective enforcement of certain rights and freedoms other than those already included in Section I of the Convention for the Protection of Human Rights and Fundamental Freedoms signed at Rome on 4 November 1950 (hereinafter referred to as 'the Convention') and in Articles 1 to 3 of the First Protocol to the Convention, signed at Paris on 20 March 1952,

Have agreed as follows:

Article 1   Prohibition of imprisonment for debt

No one shall be deprived of his liberty merely on the ground of inability to fulfil a contractual obligation.

Article 2   Freedom of movement

1. Everyone lawfully within the territory of a State shall, within that territory, have the right to liberty of movement and freedom to choose his residence.

2. Everyone shall be free to leave any country, including his own.

3. No restrictions shall be placed on the exercise of these rights other than such as are in accordance with law and are necessary in a democratic society in the interests of national security or public safety, for the maintenance of 'ordre public', for the prevention of crime, for the protection of health or morals, or for the protection of the rights and freedoms of others.

4. The rights set forth in paragraph 1 may also be subject, in particular areas, to restrictions imposed in accordance with law and justified by the public interest in a democratic society.

Article 3   Prohibition of expulsion of nationals

1. No one shall be expelled, by means either of an individual or of a collective measure, from the territory of the State of which he is a national.

2. No one shall be deprived of the right to enter the territory of the State of which he is a national.

Article 4   Prohibition of collective expulsion of aliens

Collective expulsion of aliens is prohibited.
*****

13.   *The Death Penalty*

Article 1   Abolition of the death penalty

The death penalty shall be abolished. No one shall be condemned to such penalty or executed.
*****

---

* **Editor's Note:** This Protocol has not yet been ratified by the United Kingdom.

The Ministerial Code (2022)

1 Ministers of the crown

1.1 Ministers of the Crown are expected to maintain high standards of behaviour and to behave in a way that upholds the highest standards of propriety.

1.2 Ministers should be professional in all their dealings and treat all those with whom they come into contact with consideration and respect. Working relationships, including with civil servants, ministerial and parliamentary colleagues and parliamentary staff should be proper and appropriate. Harassing, bullying or other inappropriate or discriminating behaviour wherever it takes place is not consistent with the Ministerial Code and will not be tolerated.

1.3 The Ministerial Code should be read against the background of the overarching duty on Ministers to comply with the law and to protect the integrity of public life. They are expected to observe the Seven Principles of Public Life set out at Annex A, and the following principles of Ministerial conduct:

    a.   The principle of collective responsibility applies to all Government Ministers;

    b.   Ministers have a duty to Parliament to account, and be held to account, for the policies, decisions and actions of their departments and agencies;

    c.   It is of paramount importance that Ministers give accurate and truthful information to Parliament, correcting any inadvertent error at the earliest opportunity. Ministers who knowingly mislead Parliament will be expected to offer their resignation to the Prime Minister;

    d.   Ministers should be as open as possible with Parliament and the public, refusing to provide information only when disclosure would not be in the public interest, which should be decided in accordance with the relevant statutes and the Freedom of Information Act 2000;

    e.   Ministers should similarly require civil servants who give evidence before Parliamentary Committees on their behalf and under their direction to be as helpful as possible in providing accurate, truthful and full information in accordance with the duties and responsibilities of civil servants as set out in the Civil Service Code;

    f.   Ministers must ensure that no conflict arises, or appears to arise, between their public duties and their private interests;

    g.   Ministers should not accept any gift or hospitality which might, or might reasonably appear to, compromise their judgement or place them under an improper obligation; h. Ministers in the House of Commons must keep separate their roles as Minister and constituency Member;

    i.   Ministers must not use government resources for Party political purposes; and

    j.   Ministers must uphold the political impartiality of the Civil Service and not ask civil servants to act in any way which would conflict with the Civil Service Code as set out in the Constitutional Reform and Governance Act 2010.

1.4 It is not the role of the Cabinet Secretary or other officials to enforce the Code. The Prime Minister's Independent Adviser has a role, set out in Terms of Reference published by the Prime Minister, in advising the Prime Minister and Ministers about adherence to the Code. Ministers are expected to provide the Independent Adviser with all information reasonably necessary for the discharge of his role. Investigations into adherence to the Ministerial Code may occur:

    a.   If there is an allegation about a breach of the Code, and the Prime Minister, having consulted the Cabinet Secretary, feels that it warrants further investigation, he may ask the Cabinet Office to investigate the facts of the case and/or refer the matter to the Independent Adviser on Ministers' interests.

    b.   Where the Independent Adviser believes that an alleged breach of the Code warrants further investigation and that matter has not already been referred to him, he may initiate an investigation. Before doing so, the Independent Adviser will consult the Prime Minister who will normally give his consent. However, where there are public interest reasons for doing so, the Prime Minister may raise concerns about a proposed investigation such that the Independent Adviser does not proceed. In such an event, the Independent Adviser may still require that the reasons for an investigation not proceeding be made public unless this would undermine the grounds that have led to the investigation not proceeding.

1.5 The Code provides guidance to Ministers on how they should act and arrange their affairs in order to uphold these standards. It lists the principles which may apply in particular situations. It applies to all members of the Government and covers Parliamentary Private Secretaries in paragraphs 3.7–3.12.

1.6 Ministers are personally responsible for deciding how to act and conduct themselves in the light of the Code and for justifying their actions and conduct to Parliament and the public. However, Ministers only remain in office for so long as they retain the confidence of the Prime Minister. He is the ultimate judge of the standards of behaviour expected of a Minister and the appropriate consequences of a breach of those standards.

1.7 Where the Prime Minister determines that a breach of the expected standards has occurred, he may ask the Independent Adviser for confidential advice on the appropriate sanction. The final decision rests with the Prime Minister. Where the Prime Minister retains his confidence in the Minister, available sanctions include requiring some form of public apology, remedial action, or removal of ministerial salary for a period.

1.8 Ministers must also comply at all times with the requirements which Parliament itself has laid down in relation to the accountability and responsibility of Ministers. For Ministers in the Commons, these are set by the Resolution carried on 19 March 1997 (Official Report columns 1046–47), the terms of which are repeated at b. to e. above. For Ministers in the Lords, the Resolution can be found in the Official Report of 20 March 1997 column 1057. Ministers must also comply with the Codes of Conduct for their respective Houses and also any requirements placed on them by the Independent Parliamentary Standards Authority.

2 Ministers and the government

2.1 The principle of collective responsibility requires that Ministers should be able to express their views frankly in the expectation that they can argue freely in private while maintaining a united front when decisions have been reached. This in turn requires that the privacy of opinions expressed in Cabinet and Ministerial Committees, including in correspondence, should be maintained.

2.2 The business of the Cabinet and Ministerial Committees consists in the main of:

    a.   questions which significantly engage the collective responsibility of the Government because they raise major issues of policy or because they are of critical importance to the public;

    b.   questions on which there is an unresolved argument between departments

2.3 The internal process through which a decision has been made, or the level of Committee by which it was taken should not be disclosed. Neither should the individual views of Ministers or advice provided by civil servants as part of that internal process be disclosed. Decisions reached by the Cabinet or Ministerial Committees are binding on all members of the Government. They are, however, normally announced and explained as the decision of the Minister concerned. On occasion, it may be desirable to emphasise the importance of a decision by stating specifically that it is the decision of Her Majesty's Government. This, however, is the exception rather than the rule. Ministers also have an obligation to ensure decisions agreed in Cabinet and Cabinet Committees (and in write-rounds) are implemented. Ministers should take special care in discussing issues which are the responsibility of other Ministers, consulting ministerial colleagues as appropriate.

2.4 Matters wholly within the responsibility of a single Minister and which do not significantly engage collective responsibility need not be brought to the Cabinet or to a Ministerial Committee unless the Minister wishes to inform his colleagues or to have their advice. No definitive criteria can be given for issues which engage collective responsibility. The Cabinet Secretariats can advise where departments are unsure, however, the final decision rests with the Prime Minister. When there is a difference between departments, it should not be referred to the Cabinet until other means of resolving it have been exhausted. It is the responsibility of the initiating department to ensure that proposals have been discussed with other interested departments and the outcome of these discussions should be reflected in the memorandum or letter submitted to Cabinet or a Cabinet Committee.

2.5 Cabinet and Cabinet Committee meetings take precedence over all other Ministerial business apart from the Privy Council, although it is understood that Ministers may occasionally have to be absent for reasons of Parliamentary business and international commitments. A Minister may delegate attendance at Cabinet Committees to a junior Ministerial colleague (although there may be exceptions for particular meetings at the discretion of the Chair), but officials cannot attend Cabinet Committee meetings in place of a Minister. There are restrictions on officials attending Cabinet Committees. If exceptionally officials or advisers need to attend, they should inform the secretariat. The Ministerial chair of the Committee must agree attendance of officials and advisers in advance.

2.6 Before publishing a policy statement (white paper) or a consultation paper (green paper), departments should consider whether it raises issues which require full collective ministerial consideration through the appropriate Cabinet Committee. The expectation is that most such papers will need collective agreement prior to publication. Any Command Paper containing a major statement of Government policy should be circulated to the Cabinet before publication. This rule applies to Papers containing major statements even when no issue requiring collective consideration is required.

2.7 Ministers relinquishing office should hand back to their department any Cabinet documents and/or other departmental papers in their possession.

2.8 On a change of Government, the Cabinet Secretary on behalf of the outgoing Prime Minister, issues special instructions about the disposal of Cabinet papers of the outgoing Administration.

2.9 By convention and at the Government's discretion, former Ministers are allowed reasonable access to the papers of the period when they were in office. With the exception of former Prime Ministers, access is limited to former Ministers personally. Subject to compliance with the 'Radcliffe' Rules (paragraph 8.10), former Ministers may have access in the Cabinet Office to copies of Cabinet or Cabinet Committee papers which were issued to them when in office, and access in the relevant department to other official papers which they are known to have handled at the time. The requirements of paragraph 2.13 below also apply.

2.10–2.14 *****

3 Ministers and appointments

3.1 Civil service appointments must be made in accordance with the requirements of the Constitutional Reform and Governance Act 2010. Ministerial involvement in such appointments is set out in the Civil Service Commission's Recruitment Principles. Public appointments should be made in accordance with the requirements of the law and, where appropriate, the Governance Code issued by the Cabinet Office. Ministers have a duty to ensure that influence over civil service and public appointments is not abused for partisan purposes.

3.2 With the exception of the Prime Minister, Cabinet Ministers may each appoint up to two special advisers. The Prime Minister may also authorise the appointment of special advisers for Ministers who regularly attend Cabinet. All appointments, including exceptions to this rule, require the prior written approval of the Prime Minister, and no commitments to make such appointments should be entered into in the absence of such approval. All special advisers will be appointed under terms and conditions set out in the Model Contract for Special Advisers and the Code of Conduct for Special Advisers.

3.3 All special advisers must uphold their responsibility to the Government as a whole, not just to their appointing Minister. The responsibility for the management and conduct of special advisers, including discipline, rests with the Minister who made the appointment. Individual Ministers will be accountable to the Prime Minister, Parliament and the public for their actions and decisions in respect of their special advisers. It is, of course, also open to the Prime Minister to terminate employment by withdrawing his consent to an individual appointment.

3.4, 3.5 *****

3.6 Cabinet Ministers and Ministers of State may appoint Parliamentary Private Secretaries. All appointments require the prior written approval of the Prime Minister. The Chief Whip should also be consulted and no commitments to make such appointments should be entered into until such approval is received.

3.7 Parliamentary Private Secretaries are not members of the Government. However, they must ensure that no conflict arises, or appears to arise, between their role as a Parliamentary Private Secretary, and their private interests.

3.8 Official information given to them should generally be limited to what is necessary for the discharge of their Parliamentary and political duties. This need not preclude them from being brought into departmental discussions where appropriate, but any such access should be approved by the relevant appointing Minister. They should not have access to information classified at secret or above. Any proposal to visit a secure government establishment requires the approval of the Head of the establishment.

3.9 Parliamentary Private Secretaries are expected to support the Government in divisions in the House. No Parliamentary Private Secretary who votes against the Government can retain his or her position.

3.10 Parliamentary Private Secretaries should not make statements in the House nor put Questions on matters affecting the department with which they are connected. They are not precluded from serving on Select Committees, but they should withdraw from any involvement with inquiries into their appointing Minister's department, and they should avoid associating themselves with recommendations critical of or embarrassing to the Government. They should also exercise discretion in any statements outside the House.

3.11, 3.12 *****

4   Ministers and their departments

4.1 The Prime Minister is responsible for the overall organisation of the executive and the allocation of functions between Ministers in charge of departments.

4.2 The Prime Minister's approval must be sought where changes are proposed that affect this allocation and the responsibilities for the discharge of ministerial functions. This applies whether the functions in question are derived from statute or from the exercise of the Royal Prerogative, or are general administrative responsibilities.

4.3 The Prime Minister's written approval must be sought where it is proposed to transfer functions: a. between Ministers in charge of departments; and b. between junior Ministers within a department unless the changes are de minimis.

4.4 In addition, the Prime Minister's written approval should be sought for proposals to allocate new functions to a particular Minister where the function does not fall wholly within the field of responsibilities of one Minister, or where there is disagreement about who should be responsible.

4.5 Unresolved disputes concerning the allocation of functions should be referred to the Cabinet Secretary before a submission is made to the Prime Minister.

4.6 The Minister in charge of a department is solely accountable to Parliament for the exercise of the powers on which the administration of that department depends. The Minister's authority may, however, be delegated to a Minister of State, a Parliamentary Secretary, or to an official. It is desirable that Ministers in charge should devolve to their junior Ministers responsibility for a defined range of departmental work, particularly in connection with Parliament.

4.7 A Minister's proposal for the assignment of duties to junior Ministers, together with any proposed 'courtesy titles' descriptive of their duties should be agreed in writing with the Prime Minister, copied to the Cabinet Secretary.

4.8 Ministers of State and Parliamentary Secretaries will be authorised to supervise the day-to-day administration of a defined range of subjects. This arrangement does not relieve the Permanent Secretary of general responsibility for the organisation and discipline of the department or of the duty to advise on matters of policy. Any conflict of view between junior Ministers and the Permanent Secretary should be resolved by reference to the Minister in charge of the department. If the dispute cannot be resolved it should be referred to the Prime Minister and the Cabinet Secretary.

4.9 Departments should ensure appropriate arrangements are made for Ministerial cover when Ministers are absent from London.

4.10 The Prime Minister's prior approval should be sought for the arrangements for superintending the work of a department when the Minister in charge will be absent. Special care must be taken over the exercise of statutory powers. Ministers should seek legal advice in cases of doubt.

4.11 Ministers who wish to take maternity leave (of up to 6 months), or other extended absence from Government, must seek the permission of the Prime Minister. Where the Prime Minister agrees to such a request, the Minister must not exercise their functions as a Minister during their period of absence unless this is agreed by the Permanent Secretary and the Minister who is temporarily covering the Ministerial responsibilities.

4.12 The Prime Minister must be consulted in good time about any proposal to set up:
   a. Royal Commissions: these can only be set up with the sanction of the Cabinet and after The Queen's approval has been sought by the Prime Minister;
   b. Public inquiries under the Inquiries Act 2005.

4.13 The Lord Chancellor and Secretary of State for Justice should also be consulted where there is a proposal to appoint a judge to the above.

5 Ministers and civil servants

5.1 Ministers must uphold the political impartiality of the Civil Service, and not ask civil servants to act in any way which would conflict with the Civil Service Code and the requirements of the Constitutional Reform and Governance Act 2010. Ministers should be professional in their working relationships with the Civil Service and treat all those with whom they come into contact with consideration and respect.

5.2–5.7 *****

6 Ministers' constituency and party interests

6.1 Ministers are provided with facilities at Government expense to enable them to carry out their official duties. These facilities should not generally be used for Party or constituency activities.

6.2 Government property should not generally be used for constituency work or party political activities. A particular exception is recognised in the case of official residences. Where Ministers host Party or personal events in these residences it should be at their own or Party expense with no cost falling to the public purse.

6.3 *****

6.4 Where Ministers have to take decisions within their departments which might have an impact on their own constituencies, they must take particular care to avoid any possible conflict of interest. Within departments, the Minister should advise their Permanent Secretary and, in the case of junior Ministers, their Secretary of State and Permanent Secretary of the interest and responsibilities should be arranged to avoid any conflict of interest.

6.5 Ministers are free to make their views about constituency matters known to the responsible Minister by correspondence, leading deputations or by personal interview provided they make clear that they are acting as their constituents' representative and not as a Minister.

6.6–6.8 *****

6.9 Ministers in the Commons who are asked by members of the public to submit cases to the Parliamentary Commissioner for Administration should act no differently from other MPs in deciding whether to refer complaints to the Commissioner on the merits of the individual case.

6.10 Where a complaint from a constituent is against the Minister's own department the Minister should ask a neighbouring MP to take up the constituent's case on his or her behalf.

7 Ministers' private interests

7.1 Ministers must ensure that no conflict arises, or could reasonably be perceived to arise, between their public duties and their private interests, financial or otherwise.

7.2 It is the personal responsibility of each Minister to decide whether and what action is needed to avoid a conflict or the perception of a conflict, taking account of advice received from their Permanent Secretary and the Independent Adviser on Ministers' interests.

7.3 On appointment to each new office, Ministers must provide their Permanent Secretary with a full list in writing of all interests which might be thought to give rise to a conflict. The list should also cover interests of the Minister's spouse or partner and close family which might be thought to give rise to a conflict.

7.4–7.6 *****

7.7 Ministers must scrupulously avoid any danger of an actual or perceived conflict of interest between their Ministerial position and their private financial interests. They should be guided by the general principle that they should either dispose of the interest giving rise to the conflict or take alternative steps to prevent it. In reaching their decision they should be guided by the advice given to them by their

Permanent Secretary and the independent adviser on Ministers' interests. Ministers' decisions should not be influenced by the hope or expectation of future employment with a particular firm or organisation.

7.8, 7.9 *****

7.10 Where a Minister is allocated an official residence, they must ensure that all personal tax liabilities, including council tax, are properly discharged, and that they personally pay such liabilities. Ministers who occupy an official residence will not be able to claim accommodation expenses from the Independent Parliamentary Standards Authority.

7.11 When they take up office, Ministers should give up any other public appointment they may hold. Where exceptionally it is proposed that such an appointment should be retained, the Minister should seek the advice of their Permanent Secretary and the Independent Adviser on Ministers' interests.

7.12 Ministers should take care to ensure that they do not become associated with non-public organisations whose objectives may in any degree conflict with Government policy and thus give rise to a conflict of interest.

7.13 Ministers should not therefore normally accept invitations to act as patrons of, or otherwise offer support to, pressure groups, or organisations dependent in whole or in part on Government funding. There is normally less objection to a Minister associating him or herself with a charity, subject to the points above, but Ministers should take care to ensure that in participating in any fundraising activity, they do not place, or appear to place, themselves under an obligation as Ministers to those to whom appeals are directed and for this reason they should not approach individuals or companies personally for this purpose. In all such cases, the Minister should consult their Permanent Secretary and where appropriate the independent adviser on Ministers' interests.

7.14 In order to avoid any conflict of interest, Ministers on taking up office should give up membership or chairmanship of a Select Committee or All Party Parliamentary Group. This is to avoid any risk of criticism that a Minister is seeking to influence the Parliamentary process. It is also to avoid being drawn into a situation whereby their membership of a Committee could result in the belief that ministerial support is being given to a particular policy or funding proposal.

7.15 There is, of course, no objection to a Minister holding trade union membership but care must be taken to avoid any actual or perceived conflict of interest. Accordingly, Ministers should arrange their affairs so as to avoid any suggestion that a union of which they are a member has any undue influence; they should take no active part in the conduct of union affairs, should give up any office they may hold in a union and should receive no remuneration from a union. A nominal payment purely for the purpose of protecting a Minister's future pension rights is acceptable.

7.16–7.18 *****

7.19 The rules governing the acceptance of foreign awards set by the Committee on the Grant of Honours, Decorations and Medals apply. Ministers should not normally, whilst holding office, accept decorations from foreign countries. Where such an award is offered directly to a Minister and it would be difficult or embarrassing to decline, they can receive the award but should inform the Foreign and Commonwealth Office (FCO) as soon as possible. Generally, permission to wear will not be granted but the minister will be able to retain the award as a keepsake. Where the FCO considers the case for restricted permission to wear might merit a national interest case exception, the FCO will consult the Prime Minister who will make the final decision.

7.20 It is a well-established and recognised rule that no Minister should accept gifts, hospitality or services from anyone which would, or might appear to, place him or her under an obligation. The same principle applies if gifts etc are offered to a member of their family.

7.21 This is primarily a matter which must be left to the good sense of Ministers. But any Minister in doubt or difficulty over this should seek the advice of their Permanent Secretary.

7.22 Gifts given to Ministers in their Ministerial capacity become the property of the Government and do not need to be declared in the Register of Members' or Peers' Interests. Gifts of small value, currently this is set at £140, may be retained by the recipient. Gifts of a higher value should be handed over to the department for disposal unless the recipient wishes to purchase the gift abated by £140. There is usually no customs duty or import VAT payable on the importation of official gifts received overseas. HMRC can advise on any cases of doubt. If a Minister wishes to retain a gift he or she will be liable for any tax it may attract. Departments will publish, on a quarterly basis, details of gifts received and given by Ministers valued at more than £140.

7.23 Gifts given to Ministers as constituency MPs or members of a political Party fall within the rules relating to the Registers of Members' and Lords' Interests.

7.24 Departments will publish, quarterly, details of hospitality received by Ministers in a Ministerial capacity. Hospitality accepted as an MP or Peer should be declared in the Register of Members' or Lords' Interests respectively.

7.25 On leaving office, Ministers will be prohibited from lobbying Government for two years. They must also seek advice from the independent Advisory Committee on Business Appointments (ACoBA) about any appointments or employment they wish to take up within two years of leaving office. Former Ministers must ensure that no new appointments are announced, or taken up, before the Committee has been able to provide its advice. To ensure that Ministers are fully aware of their future obligations in respect of outside appointments after leaving office, the Business Appointment Rules are attached at Annex B. Former Ministers must abide by the advice of the Committee which will be published by the Committee when a role is announced or taken up.

8   Ministers and the presentation of policy

8.1 Official facilities paid for out of public funds should be used for Government publicity and advertising but may not be used for the dissemination of material which is essentially party political. The conventions governing the work of the Government Communication Service are set out in the Government Communication Service's Propriety Guidance—Guidance on Government Communications.

8.2 In order to ensure the effective coordination of Cabinet business, the policy content and timing of all major announcements, speeches, press releases and new policy initiatives should be cleared in draft with the No 10 Press and Private Offices at least 24 hours in advance. All major interviews and media appearances, both print and broadcast, should also be agreed with the No 10 Press Office.

8.3 In all cases other than those described in paragraph 6.6, the principle of collective responsibility applies (see also paragraph 2.1). Ministers should ensure that their statements are consistent with collective Government policy. Ministers should take special care in referring to subjects which are the responsibility of other Ministers (see also paragraph 2.3).

8.4 Ministers must only use official machinery, including social media, for distributing texts of speeches relating to Government business. Speeches made in a party political context should not be distributed via official machinery.

8.5 Ministers invited to broadcast on radio, television and/or webcasts in a political or private capacity should consider if such a broadcast would have a bearing on another department's responsibilities, in which case they should clear the matter with the ministerial colleague concerned before agreeing to the invitation.

8.6 Ministers may contribute to a book, journal or newspaper, including a local newspaper in their constituency, provided that publication will not be at variance with their obligations to Parliament and their duty to observe the principle of collective Ministerial responsibility. No payment should be accepted for such articles.

8.7 Any Minister wishing to practice regular journalism must have the prior approval of the No 10 Press Office.

8.8 Ministers should not accept payment for speeches or media articles of an official nature or which directly draw on their responsibilities or experience as Ministers or with a view to donating the fee to charity. If the organisation in question insists on making a donation to a charity then it should be a charity of the organisation's choice. This is to avoid any criticism that a Minister is using his or her official position to influence or take the credit for donations to charity.

8.9 Ministers may not, while in office, write and publish a book on their ministerial experience. Nor, while serving as a Minister, may they enter into any agreement to publish their memoirs on leaving their ministerial position.

8.10 Former Ministers intending to publish their memoirs are required to submit the draft manuscript in good time before publication to the Cabinet Secretary and to conform to the principles set out in the Radcliffe report of 1976 (Cmnd 6386).

8.11–8.16 *****

9 Ministers and parliament

9.1 When Parliament is in session, the most important announcements of Government policy should be made in the first instance, in Parliament.

9.2–9.7 *****

10 Travel by ministers

10.1 Ministers must ensure that they always make efficient and cost-effective travel arrangements. Official transport should not normally be used for travel arrangements arising from Party or private business, except where this is justified on security grounds.

10.2–10.9 *****

10.10 Ministers intending to make an official visit within the United Kingdom must inform in advance, and in good time, the MPs whose constituencies are to be included within the itinerary.

10.11 Similar courtesies should be extended when UK Ministers are visiting the constituencies of members of the Scottish Parliament, the National Assembly for Wales and the Northern Ireland Assembly.

10.12 Ministers who are planning official visits to Scotland, Wales and Northern Ireland should inform the Secretary of State concerned.

10.13 Ministers are permitted to use an official car for official business and for home to office journeys within a reasonable distance of London on the understanding that they are using the time to work. Where practicable, Ministers are encouraged to use public transport.

10.14 *****

10.15 Where a visit is a mix of political and official engagements, it is important that the department and the Party each meet a proper proportion of the actual cost.

10.16–10.18 *****

Annex A
The Seven Principles of Public Life

Selflessness

Holders of public office should act solely in terms of the public interest.

Integrity

Holders of public office must avoid placing themselves under any obligation to people or organisations that might try inappropriately to influence their work. They should not act or take decisions in order to gain financial or other material benefits for themselves, their family, or their friends. They must declare and resolve any interests and relationships.

Objectivity

Holders of public office must act and take decisions impartially, fairly and on merit, using the best evidence and without discrimination or bias.

Accountability

Holders of public office are accountable for their decisions and actions and must submit themselves to whatever scrutiny necessary to ensure this.

Openness

Holders of public office should act and take decisions in an open and transparent manner. Information should not be withheld from the public unless there are clear and lawful reasons for doing so.

Honesty

Holders of public office should be truthful.

Leadership

Holders of public office should exhibit these principles in their own behaviour. They should actively promote and robustly support the principles and be willing to challenge poor behaviour wherever it occurs.

*****

Part IV

PACE Codes*

Code A Code of Practice for the exercise by: Police Officers of Statutory Powers of stop and search

Police Officers and Police Staff of requirements to record public encounters

General
This code of practice must be readily available at all police stations for consultation by police officers, police staff, detained persons and members of the public. The notes for guidance included are not provisions of this code, but are guidance to police officers and others about its application and interpretation. Provisions in the annexes to the code are provisions of this code.
*****

1 Principles governing stop and search
1.1 Powers to stop and search must be used fairly, responsibly, with respect for people being searched and without unlawful discrimination. Under the Equality Act 2010, section 149, when police officers are carrying out their functions, they also have a duty to have due regard to the need to eliminate unlawful discrimination, harassment and victimisation, to advance equality of opportunity between people who share a relevant protected characteristic and people who do not share it, and to take steps to foster good relations between those persons. The Children Act 2004, section 11, also requires chief police officers and other specified persons and bodies to ensure that in the discharge of their functions they have regard to the need to safeguard and promote the welfare of all persons under the age of 18.

1.2 The intrusion on the liberty of the person stopped or searched must be brief and detention for the purposes of a search must take place at or near the location of the stop.

1.3 If these fundamental principles are not observed the use of powers to stop and search may be drawn into question. Failure to use the powers in the proper manner reduces their effectiveness. Stop and search can play an important role in the detection and prevention of crime, and using the powers fairly makes them more effective.

* **Editor's Note**: For the legal status of the Codes and other issues relating to them, see ss. 66 and 67 of the Police and Criminal Evidence Act 1984 (*supra*). The Codes have been revised regularly in accordance with s. 67(7) of the Act. The most recent revised versions of the Codes are reproduced here: Code A—search of persons and vehicles came into effect on 17 January 2023; Code C—detention, treatment and questioning of persons by police officers came into effect on 21 August 2019; and Code G—statutory powers of arrest—is included as issued on 12 November 2012. The Codes apply only to England and Wales. A Welsh language edition of the Codes is available.

1.4 The primary purpose of stop and search powers is to enable officers to allay or confirm suspicions about individuals without exercising their power of arrest. Officers may be required to justify the use or authorisation of such powers, in relation both to individual searches and the overall pattern of their activity in this regard, to their supervisory officers or in court. Any misuse of the powers is likely to be harmful to policing and lead to mistrust of the police. Officers must also be able to explain their actions to the member of the public searched. The misuse of these powers can lead to disciplinary action.

1.5 An officer must not search a person, even with his or her consent, where no power to search is applicable. Even where a person is prepared to submit to a search voluntarily, the person must not be searched unless the necessary legal power exists, and the search must be in accordance with the relevant power and the provisions of this Code. The only exception, where an officer does not require a specific power, applies to searches of persons entering sports grounds or other premises carried out with their consent given as a condition of entry.

1.6 Evidence obtained from a search to which this Code applies may be open to challenge if the provisions of this Code are not observed.

2   Types of stop and search powers

2.1 This code applies, subject to paragraph 1.03, to powers of stop and search as follows:

(a) powers which require reasonable grounds for suspicion, before they may be exercised; that articles unlawfully obtained or possessed are being carried such as section 1 of PACE for stolen and prohibited articles and section 23 of the Misuse of Drugs Act 1971 for controlled goods;

(b) authorised under section 60 of the Criminal Justice and Public Order Act 1994, based upon a reasonable belief that incidents involving serious violence may take place or that people are carrying dangerous instruments or offensive weapons within any locality in the police area or that it is expedient to use the powers to find such instruments or weapons that have been used in incidents of serious violence;

(c) [Not Used]

(d) the powers in Schedule 5 to the Terrorism Prevention and Investigation Measures (TPIM) Act 2011 to search an individual who has not been arrested, conferred by:
    (i) paragraph 6(2)(a) at the time of serving a TPIM notice;
    (ii) paragraph 8(2)(a) under a search warrant for compliance purposes; and
    (iii) paragraph 10 for public safety purposes.

(e) powers to search a person who has not been arrested in the exercise of a power to search premises.

(a) Stop and search powers requiring reasonable grounds for suspicion—explanation

2.2 Reasonable grounds for suspicion is the legal test which a police officer must satisfy before they can stop and detain individuals or vehicles to search them under powers such as section 1 of PACE (to find stolen or prohibited articles) and section 23 of the Misuse of Drugs Act 1971 (to find controlled drugs). This test must be applied to the particular circumstances in each case and is in two parts:

(i) Firstly, the officer must have formed a genuine suspicion in their own mind that they will find the object for which the search power being exercised allows them to search (see Annex A, second column, for examples); and

(ii) Secondly, the suspicion that the object will be found must be reasonable. This means that there must be an objective basis for that suspicion based on facts, information and/or intelligence which are relevant to the likelihood that the object in question will be found, so that a reasonable person would be entitled to reach the same conclusion based on the same facts and information and/or intelligence.

Officers must therefore be able to explain the basis for their suspicion by reference to intelligence or information about, or some specific behaviour by, the person concerned.

2.2A The exercise of these stop and search powers depends on the likelihood that the person searched is in possession of an item for which they may be searched; it does not depend on the person concerned being suspected of committing an offence in relation to the object of the search.

A police officer who has reasonable grounds to suspect that a person is in innocent possession of a stolen or prohibited article, controlled drug or other item for which the officer is empowered to search, may stop and search the person even though there would be no power of arrest. This would apply when a child under the age of criminal responsibility (10 years) is suspected of carrying any such item, even if they knew they had it.

Personal factors can never support reasonable grounds for suspicion

2.2B Reasonable suspicion can never be supported on the basis of personal factors. This means that unless the police have information or intelligence which provides a description of a person suspected of carrying an article for which there is a power to stop and search, the following cannot be used, alone or in combination with each other, or in combination with any other factor, as the reason for stopping and searching any individual, including any vehicle which they are driving or are being carried in:

    (a) A person's physical appearance with regard, for example, to any of the 'relevant protected characteristics' set out in the Equality Act 2010, section 149, which are age, disability, gender reassignment, pregnancy and maternity, race, religion or belief, sex and sexual orientation (see paragraph 1.1 and Note 1A), or the fact that the person is known to have a previous conviction; and

    (b) Generalisations or stereotypical images that certain groups or categories of people are more likely to be involved in criminal activity.

2.3 [Not Used]

2.4 Reasonable grounds for suspicion should normally be linked to accurate and current intelligence or information, relating to articles for which there is a power to stop and search, being carried by individuals or being in vehicles in any locality. This would include reports from members of the public or other officers describing:

- a person who has been seen carrying such an article or a vehicle in which such an article has been seen.
- crimes committed in relation to which such an article would constitute relevant evidence, for example, property stolen in a theft or burglary, an offensive weapon or bladed or sharply pointed article used to assault or threaten someone or an article used to cause criminal damage to property.

2.4A Searches based on accurate and current intelligence or information are more likely to be effective. Targeting searches in a particular area at specified crime problems not only increases their effectiveness but also minimises inconvenience to law-abiding members of the public. It also helps in justifying the use of searches both to those who are searched and to the public. This does not, however, prevent stop and search powers being exercised in other locations where such powers may be exercised and reasonable suspicion exists.

2.5 [Not Used]

2.6 Where there is reliable information or intelligence that members of a group or gang habitually carry knives unlawfully or weapons or controlled drugs, and wear a distinctive item of clothing or other means of identification in order to identify themselves as members of that group or gang, that distinctive item of clothing or other means of identification may provide reasonable grounds to stop and search any person believed to be a member of that group or gang.

2.6A A similar approach would apply to particular organised protest groups where there is reliable information or intelligence:

    (a) that the group in question arranges meetings and marches to which one or more members bring articles intended to be used to cause criminal damage and/or injury to others in support of the group's aims;

    (b) that at one or more previous meetings or marches arranged by that group, such articles have been used and resulted in damage and/or injury; and

    (c) that on the subsequent occasion in question, one or more members of the group have brought with them such articles with similar intentions.

These circumstances may provide reasonable grounds to stop and search any members of the group to find such articles (see *Note 9A*). See also *paragraphs 2.12 to 2.18*, 'Searches authorised under section 60 of the Criminal Justice and Public Order Act 1994', when serious violence is anticipated at meetings and marches.

Reasonable grounds for suspicion based on behaviour, time and location

2.6B Reasonable suspicion may also exist without specific information or intelligence and on the basis of the behaviour of a person. For example, if an officer encounters someone on the street at night who is obviously trying to hide something, the officer may (depending on the other surrounding circumstances) base such suspicion on the fact that this kind of behaviour is often linked to stolen or prohibited articles being carried. An officer who forms the opinion that a person is acting suspiciously or that they appear to be nervous must be able to explain, with reference to specific aspects of the person's behaviour or conduct which they have observed, why they formed that opinion. A hunch or instinct which cannot be explained or justified to an objective observer can never amount to reasonable grounds.

2.7 [Not Used]

2.8 [Not Used]

2.8A All police officers must recognise that searches are more likely to be effective, legitimate and secure public confidence when their reasonable grounds for suspicion are based on a range of objective factors. The overall use of these powers is more likely to be effective when up-to-date and accurate intelligence or information is communicated to officers and they are well-informed about local crime patterns. Local senior officers have a duty to ensure that those under their command who exercise stop and search powers have access to such information, and the officers exercising the powers have a duty to acquaint themselves with that information (see *paragraphs 5.1 to 5.6*).

2.9 An officer who has reasonable grounds for suspicion may detain the person concerned in order to carry out a search. Before carrying out a search the officer may ask questions about the person's behaviour or presence in circumstances which gave rise to the suspicion. As a result of questioning the detained person, the reasonable grounds for suspicion necessary to detain that person may be confirmed or, because of a satisfactory explanation, be dispelled. Questioning may also reveal reasonable grounds to suspect the possession of a different kind of unlawful article from that originally suspected. Reasonable grounds for suspicion however cannot be provided retrospectively by such questioning during a person's detention or by refusal to answer any questions asked.

2.10 If, as a result of questioning before a search, or other circumstances which come to the attention of the officer, there cease to be reasonable grounds for suspecting that an article of a kind for which there is a power to stop and search is being carried, no search may take place. In the absence of any other lawful power to detain, the person is free to leave at will and must be so informed.

2.11 There is no power to stop or detain a person in order to find grounds for a search. Police officers have many encounters with members of the public which do not involve detaining people against their will and do not require any statutory power for an officer to speak to a person. However, if reasonable grounds for suspicion emerge during such an encounter, the officer may detain the person to search them, even though no grounds existed when the encounter began. As soon as detention begins, and before searching, the officer must inform the person that they are being detained for the purpose of a search and take action in accordance with paragraphs 3.8 to 3.11.

2.12–2.26 *****

(e) Powers to search in the exercise of a power to search premises

2.27 The following powers to search premises also authorise the search of a person, not under arrest, who is found on the premises during the course of the search:

(a) section 139B of the Criminal Justice Act 1988 under which a constable may enter school premises and search the premises and any person on those premises for any bladed or pointed article or offensive weapon;

(b) under a warrant issued under section 23(3) of the Misuse of Drugs Act 1971 to search premises for drugs or documents but only if the warrant specifically authorises the search of persons found on the premises; and

(c)   under a search warrant or order issued under paragraph 1, 3 or 11 of Schedule 5 to the Terrorism Act 2000 to search premises and any person found there for material likely to be of substantial value to a terrorist investigation.

2.28 Before the power under section 139 B of the Criminal Justice Act 1988 may be exercised, the constable must have reasonable grounds to suspect that an offence under section 139A or 139AA of the Criminal Justice Act 1988 (having a bladed or pointed article or offensive weapon on school premises) has been or is being committed. A warrant to search premises and persons found therein may be issued under section 23(3) of the Misuse of Drugs Act 1971 if there are reasonable grounds to suspect that controlled drugs or certain documents are in the possession of a person on the premises.

2.29 The powers in paragraph 2.27 do not require prior specific grounds to suspect that the person to be searched is in possession of an item for which there is an existing power to search. However, it is still necessary to ensure that the selection and treatment of those searched under these powers is based upon objective factors connected with the search of the premises, and not upon personal prejudice.

3   Conduct of searches

3.1 All stops and searches must be carried out with courtesy, consideration and respect for the person concerned. This has a significant impact on public confidence in the police. Every reasonable effort must be made to minimise the embarrassment that a person being searched may experience.

3.2 The co-operation of the person to be searched must be sought in every case, even if the person initially objects to the search. A forcible search may be made only if it has been established that the person is unwilling to co-operate or resists. Reasonable force may be used as a last resort if necessary to conduct a search or to detain a person or vehicle for the purposes of a search.

3.3 The length of time for which a person or vehicle may be detained must be reasonable and kept to a minimum. Where the exercise of the power requires reasonable suspicion, the thoroughness and extent of a search must depend on what is suspected of being carried, and by whom. If the suspicion relates to a particular article which is seen to be slipped into a person's pocket, then, in the absence of other grounds for suspicion or an opportunity for the article to be moved elsewhere, the search must be confined to that pocket. In the case of a small article which can readily be concealed, such as a drug, and which might be concealed anywhere on the person, a more extensive search may be necessary. In the case of searches mentioned in paragraph 2.1(b) and (d), which do not require reasonable grounds for suspicion, officers may make any reasonable search to look for items for which they are empowered to search.

3.4 The search must be carried out at or near the place where the person or vehicle was first detained.

3.5 There is no power to require a person to remove any clothing in public other than an outer coat, jacket or gloves except under section 60AA of the Criminal Justice and Public Order Act 1994 (which empowers a constable to require a person to remove any item worn to conceal identity). A search in public of a person's clothing which has not been removed must be restricted to superficial examination of outer garments. This does not, however, prevent an officer from placing his or her hand inside the pockets of the outer clothing, or feeling round the inside of collars, socks and shoes if this is reasonably necessary in the circumstances to look for the object of the search or to remove and examine any item reasonably suspected to be the object of the search.

For the same reasons, subject to the restrictions on the removal of headgear, a person's hair may also be searched in public (see paragraphs 3.1 and 3.3).

3.6 Where on reasonable grounds it is considered necessary to conduct a more thorough search (e.g. by requiring a person to take off a T-shirt), this must be done out of public view, for example, in a police van unless paragraph 3.7 applies, or police station if there is one nearby. Any search involving the removal of more than an outer coat, jacket, gloves, headgear or footwear, or any other item concealing identity, may only be made by an officer of the same sex as the person searched and may not be made in the presence of anyone of the opposite sex unless the person being searched specifically requests it.

3.7 Searches involving exposure of intimate parts of the body must not be conducted as a routine extension of a less thorough search, simply because nothing is found in the course of the initial search. Searches involving exposure of intimate parts of the body may be carried out only at a nearby police station or other nearby location which is out of public view (but not a police vehicle). These searches must be conducted in accordance with paragraph 11 of Annex A to Code C except that an intimate search mentioned in paragraph 11(f) of Annex A to Code C may not be authorised or carried out under any stop and search powers. The other provisions of Code C do not apply to the conduct and recording of searches of persons detained at police stations in the exercise of stop and search powers.

Steps to be taken prior to a search

3.8 Before any search of a detained person or attended vehicle takes place the officer must take reasonable steps, if not in uniform (see paragraph 3.9), to show their warrant card to the person to be searched or in charge of the vehicle to be searched and whether or not in uniform, to give that person the following information:

- (a) that they are being detained for the purposes of a search;
- (b) the officer's name (except in the case of enquiries linked to the investigation of terrorism, or otherwise where the officer reasonably believes that giving their name might put them in danger, in which case a warrant or other identification number shall be given) and the name of the police station to which the officer is attached;
- (c) the legal search power which is being exercised; and
- (d) a clear explanation of:
  - (i) the object of the search in terms of the article or articles for which there is a power to search; and
  - (ii) in the case of:
    - the power under section 60 of the Criminal Justice and Public Order Act 1994 (see *paragraph 2.1(b)*), the nature of the power, the authorisation and the fact that it has been given;
    - the powers in Schedule 5 to the Terrorism Prevention and Investigation Measures Act 2011 (see *paragraph 2.1(e)* and *2.18A*):
      - the fact that a TPIM notice is in force or, (in the case of paragraph 6(2)(a)) that a TPIM notice is being served;
      - the nature of the power being exercised.
      For a search under paragraph 8 of Schedule 5, the warrant must be produced and the person provided with a copy of it.
    - all other powers requiring reasonable suspicion (see *paragraph 2.1(a)*), the grounds for that suspicion. This means explaining the basis for the suspicion by reference to information and/or intelligence about, or some specific behaviour by, the person concerned
- (e) that they are entitled to a copy of the record of the search if one is made (see section 4 below) if they ask within 3 months from the date of the search and:
  - (i) if they are not arrested and taken to a police station as a result of the search and it is practicable to make the record on the spot, that immediately after the search is completed they will be given, if they request, either:
    - a copy of the record, or
    - a receipt which explains how they can obtain a copy of the full record or access to an electronic copy of the record, or
  - (ii) if they are arrested and taken to a police station as a result of the search, that the record will be made at the station as part of their custody record and they will be given, if they request, a copy of their custody record which includes a record of the search as soon as practicable whilst they are at the station.

3.9 Stops and searches under the powers mentioned in paragraphs 2.1(b) may be undertaken only by a constable in uniform.

3.10 The person should also be given information about police powers to stop and search and the individual's rights in these circumstances.

3.11 If the person to be searched, or in charge of a vehicle to be searched, does not appear to understand what is being said, or there is any doubt about the person's ability to understand English, the officer must take reasonable steps to bring information regarding the person's rights and any relevant provisions of this Code to his or her attention. If the person is deaf or cannot understand English and is accompanied by someone, then the officer must try to establish whether that person can interpret or otherwise help the officer to give the required information.

4 Recording requirements

(a) Searches which do not result in an arrest

4.1 When an officer carries out a search in the exercise of any power to which this Code applies and the search does not result in the person searched or person in charge of the vehicle searched being arrested and taken to a police station, a record must be made of it, electronically or on paper, unless there are exceptional circumstances which make this wholly impracticable (e.g. in situations involving public disorder or when the recording officer's presence is urgently required elsewhere). If a record is to be made, the officer carrying out the search must make the record on the spot unless this is not practicable, in which case, the officer must make the record as soon as practicable after the search is completed.

4.2 If the record is made at the time, the person who has been searched or who is in charge of the vehicle that has been searched must be asked if they want a copy and if they do, they must be given immediately, either:
- a copy of the record, or
- a receipt which explains how they can obtain a copy of the full record or access to an electronic copy of the record.

4.2A An officer is not required to provide a copy of the full record or a receipt at the time if they are called to an incident of higher priority.

(b) Searches which result in an arrest

4.2B If a search in the exercise of any power to which this Code applies results in a person being arrested and taken to a police station, the officer carrying out the search is responsible for ensuring that a record of the search is made as part of their custody record. The custody officer must then ensure that the person is asked if they want a copy of the record and if they do, that they are given a copy as soon as practicable.

(c) Record of search

4.3 The record of a search must always include the following information:
- (a) A note of the self defined ethnicity, and if different, the ethnicity as perceived by the officer making the search, of the person searched or of the person in charge of the vehicle searched (as the case may be);
- (b) The date, time and place the person or vehicle was searched;
- (c) The object of the search in terms of the article or articles for which there is a power to search;
- (d) In the case of:
  - the power under section 60 of the Criminal Justice and Public Order Act 1994 (see *paragraph 2.1(b)*), the nature of the power, the authorisation and the fact that it has been given;
  - the powers in Schedule 5 to the Terrorism Prevention and Investigation Measures Act 2011 (see paragraph 2.1(e) and 2.18A):
    - the fact that a TPIM notice is in force or, (in the case of paragraph 6(2)(a)) that a TPIM notice is being served;
    - the nature of the power, and

— for a search under paragraph 8, the date the search warrant was issued, the fact that the warrant was produced and a copy of it provided and the warrant must also be endorsed by the constable executing it to state whether anything was found and whether anything was seized, and

• all other powers requiring reasonable suspicion (see *paragraph 2.1(a)*), the grounds for that suspicion.

(e) subject to paragraph 3.8(b), the identity of the officer carrying out the search.

4.3A For the purposes of completing the search record, there is no requirement to record the name, address and date of birth of the person searched or the person in charge of a vehicle which is searched. The person is under no obligation to provide this information and they should not be asked to provide it for the purpose of completing the record.

4.4 Nothing in paragraph 4.3 requires the names of police officers to be shown on the search record or any other record required to be made under this code in the case of enquiries linked to the investigation of terrorism or otherwise where an officer reasonably believes that recording names might endanger the officers. In such cases the record must show the officers' warrant or other identification number and duty station.

4.5 A record is required for each person and each vehicle searched. However, if a person is in a vehicle and both are searched, and the object and grounds of the search are the same, only one record need be completed. If more than one person in a vehicle is searched, separate records for each search of a person must be made. If only a vehicle is searched, the self-defined ethnic background of the person in charge of the vehicle must be recorded, unless the vehicle is unattended.

4.6 The record of the grounds for making a search must, briefly but informatively, explain the reason for suspecting the person concerned, by reference to information and/or intelligence about or some specific behaviour by the person concerned.

4.7 Where officers detain an individual with a view to performing a search, but the need to search is eliminated as a result of questioning the person detained, a search should not be carried out and a record is not required.

4.8 After searching an unattended vehicle, or anything in or on it, an officer must leave a notice in it (or on it, if things on it have been searched without opening it) recording the fact that it has been searched.

4.9 The notice must include the name of the police station to which the officer concerned is attached and state where a copy of the record of the search may be obtained and how (if applicable) an electronic copy may be accessed and where any application for compensation should be directed.

4.10 The vehicle must if practicable be left secure.

4.10A–4.20 *****

5   Monitoring and supervising the use of stop and search powers

5.1 Any misuse of stop and search powers is likely to be harmful to policing and lead to mistrust of the police by the local community and by the public in general. Supervising officers must monitor the use of stop and search powers and should consider in particular whether there is any evidence that they are being exercised on the basis of stereotyped images or inappropriate generalisations. Supervising officers should satisfy themselves that the practice of officers under their supervision in stopping, searching and recording is fully in accordance with this Code. Supervisors must also examine whether the records reveal any trends or patterns which give cause for concern, and if so take appropriate action to address this.

5.2 Senior officers with area or force-wide responsibilities must also monitor the broader use of stop and search powers and, where necessary, take action at the relevant level.

5.3 Supervision and monitoring must be supported by the compilation of comprehensive statistical records of stops and searches at force, area and local level. Any apparently disproportionate use of the powers by particular officers or groups of officers or in relation to specific sections of the community should be identified and investigated.

5.4 In order to promote public confidence in the use of the powers, forces in consultation with police and crime commissioners must make arrangements for the records to be scrutinised by representatives of the community, and to explain the use of the powers at a local level.

Suspected misuse of powers by individual officers

5.5 Police supervisors must monitor the use of stop and search powers by individual officers to ensure that they are being applied appropriately and lawfully. Monitoring takes many forms, such as direct supervision of the exercise of the powers, examining stop and search records (particularly examining the officer's documented reasonable grounds for suspicion) and asking the officer to account for the way in which they conducted and recorded particular searches or through complaints about a stop and search that an officer has carried out.

5.6 Where a supervisor identifies issues with the way that an officer has used a stop and search power, the facts of the case will determine whether the standards of professional behaviour as set out in the Code of Ethics (see http://www.college.police.uk/en/20972.htm) have been breached and which formal action is pursued. Improper use might be a result of poor performance or a conduct matter, which will require the supervisor to take appropriate action such as performance or misconduct procedures. It is imperative that supervisors take both timely and appropriate action to deal with all such cases that come to their notice.

Notes for guidance

Officers exercising stop and search powers

1 This code does not affect the ability of an officer to speak to or question a person in the ordinary course of the officer's duties without detaining the person or exercising any element of compulsion. It is not the purpose of the code to prohibit such encounters between the police and the community with the co-operation of the person concerned and neither does it affect the principle that all citizens have a duty to help police officers to prevent crime and discover offenders. This is a civic rather than a legal duty; but when a police officer is trying to discover whether, or by whom, an offence has been committed he or she may question any person from whom useful information might be obtained, subject to the restrictions imposed by Code C. A person's unwillingness to reply does not alter this entitlement, but in the absence of a power to arrest, or to detain in order to search, the person is free to leave at will and cannot be compelled to remain with the officer.

1A In paragraphs 1.1 and 2.2B(a), 'relevant protected characteristic' includes: age, disability, gender reassignment, pregnancy and maternity, race, religion or belief, sex and sexual orientation.

1B Innocent possession means that the person does [not] have the guilty knowledge that they are carrying an unlawful item which is required before an arrest on suspicion that the person has committed an offence in respect of the item sought (if arrest is necessary—see PACE Code G) and/or a criminal prosecution) can be considered. It is not uncommon for children under the age of criminal responsibility to be used by older children and adults to carry stolen property, drugs and weapons and, in some cases, firearms, for the criminal benefit of others, either:

- *in the hope that police may not suspect they are being used for carrying the items; or*
- *knowing that if they are suspected of being couriers and are stopped and searched, they cannot be arrested or prosecuted for any criminal offence.*

Stop and search powers therefore allow the police to intervene effectively to break up criminal gangs and groups that use young children to further their criminal activities.

1BA Whenever a child under 10 is suspected of carrying unlawful items for someone else, or is found in circumstances which suggest that their welfare and safety may be at risk, the facts should be reported and actioned in accordance with established force safeguarding procedures. This will be in addition to treating them as a potentially vulnerable or intimidated witness in respect of their status as a witness to the serious criminal offence(s) committed by those using them as couriers. Safeguarding considerations will also apply to other persons aged under 18 who are stopped and searched under any of the powers to which this Code applies. See paragraph 1.1 with regard to the requirement under the Children Act 2004, section 11, for chief police officers and other specified persons and bodies, to ensure that in the discharge of their functions, they have regard to the need to safeguard and promote the welfare of all persons under the age of 18.

2 In some circumstances preparatory questioning may be unnecessary, but in general a brief conversation or exchange will be desirable not only as a means of avoiding unsuccessful searches, but to explain the grounds for the stop/search, to gain cooperation and reduce any tension there might be surrounding the stop/search.

3 Where a person is lawfully detained for the purpose of a search, but no search in the event takes place, the detention will not thereby have been rendered unlawful.

4 Many people customarily cover their heads or faces for religious reasons – for example, Muslim women, Sikh men, Sikh or Hindu women, or Rastafarian men or women. A police officer cannot order the removal of a head or face covering except where there is reason to believe that the item is being worn by the individual wholly or mainly for the purpose of disguising identity, not simply because it disguises identity. Where there may be religious sensitivities about ordering the removal of such an item, the officer should permit the item to be removed out of public view. Where practicable, the item should be removed in the presence of an officer of the same sex as the person and out of sight of anyone of the opposite sex.

5 A search of a person in public should be completed as soon as possible.

6 A person may be detained under a stop and search power at a place other than where the person was first detained, only if that place, be it a police station or elsewhere, is nearby. Such a place should be located within a reasonable travelling distance using whatever mode of travel (on foot or by car) is appropriate. This applies to all searches under stop and search powers, whether or not they involve the removal of clothing or exposure of intimate parts of the body (see paragraphs 3.6 and 3.7) or take place in or out of public view. It means, for example, that a search under the stop and search power in section 23 of the Misuse of Drugs Act 1971 which involves the compulsory removal of more than a person's outer coat, jacket or gloves cannot be carried out unless a place which is both nearby the place they were first detained and out of public view, is available. If a search involves exposure of intimate parts of the body and a police station is not nearby, particular care must be taken to ensure that the location is suitable in that it enables the search to be conducted in accordance with the requirements of paragraph 11 of Annex A to Code C.

7 A search in the street itself should be regarded as being in public for the purposes of paragraphs 3.6 and 3.7 above, even though it may be empty at the time a search begins. Although there is no power to require a person to do so, there is nothing to prevent an officer from asking a person voluntarily to remove more than an outer coat, jacket or gloves in public.

8 [Not Used]

9 Other means of identification might include jewellery, insignias, tattoos or other features which are known to identify members of the particular gang or group.

9A–23 *****

24–25 [Not Used]

Annexes A–C and F   *****

Code C Code of Practice for the detention, treatment and questioning of persons by Police Officers

1   General

1.0 The powers and procedures in this Code must be used fairly, responsibly, with respect for the people to whom they apply and without unlawful discrimination. Under the Equality Act 2010, section 149 (Public sector Equality Duty), police forces must, in carrying out their functions, have due regard to the need to eliminate unlawful discrimination, harassment, victimisation and any other conduct which is prohibited by that Act, to advance equality of opportunity between people who share a relevant protected characteristic and people who do not share it, and to foster good relations between those persons. The Equality Act also makes it unlawful for police officers to discriminate against, harass or victimise any person on the grounds of the 'protected character-istics' of age, disability, gender reassignment, race, religion or belief, sex and sexual orientation, marriage and civil partnership, pregnancy and maternity, when using their powers.

1.1 All persons in custody must be dealt with expeditiously, and released as soon as the need for detention no longer applies.

1.1A A custody officer must perform the functions in this Code as soon as practicable. A custody officer will not be in breach of this Code if delay is justifiable and reasonable steps are taken to prevent unnecessary delay. The custody record shall show when a delay has occurred and the reason.

1.2 This Code of Practice must be readily available at all police stations for consultation by:

- police officers;
- police staff;
- detained persons;
- members of the public.

1.3 The provisions of this Code:

- include the *Annexes*
- do not include the *Notes for Guidance which* form guidance to police officers and others about its application and interpretation.

1.4 If at any time an officer has any reason to suspect that a person of any age may be vulnerable (see *paragraph 1.13(d)*), in the absence of clear evidence to dispel that suspicion, that person shall be treated as such for the purposes of this Code and to establish whether any such reason may exist in relation to a person suspected of committing an offence (see *paragraph 10.1* and *Note 10A*), the custody officer in the case of a detained person, or the officer investigating the offence in the case of a person who has not been arrested or detained, shall take, or cause to be taken, (see *paragraph 3.5* and *Note 3F*) the following action:

(a) reasonable enquiries shall be made to ascertain what information is available that is relevant to any of the factors described in *paragraph 1.13(d) as* indicating that the person may be vulnerable might apply;

(b) a record shall be made describing whether any of those factors appear to apply and provide any reason to suspect that the person may be vulnerable or (as the case may be) may not be vulnerable; and

(c) the record mentioned in sub-paragraph (b) shall be made available to be taken into account by police officers, police staff and any others who, in accordance with the provisions of this or any other Code, are required or entitled to communicate with the person in question. This would include any solicitor, appropriate adult and health care professional and is particularly relevant to communication by telephone or by means of a live link (see *paragraphs 12.9A* (interviews), *13.12* (interpretation), and *15.3C, 15.11A, 15.11B, 15.11C* and *15.11D* (reviews and extension of detention)).

See *Notes 1G, 1GA, 1GB* and *1GC*.

1.5 Anyone who appears to be under 18, shall, in the absence of clear evidence that they are older and subject to *paragraph 1.5A*, be treated as a juvenile for the purposes of this Code and any other Code.

1.5A [Not Used]

1.6 If a person appears to be blind, seriously visually impaired, deaf, unable to read or speak or has difficulty orally because of a speech impediment, they shall be treated as such for the purposes of this Code in the absence of clear evidence to the contrary.

1.7 'The appropriate adult' means, in the case of a:

(a) juvenile:

(i) the parent, guardian or, if the juvenile is in the care of a local authority or voluntary organisation, a person representing that authority or organisation (see *Note 1B*);

(ii) a social worker of a local authority (see *Note 1C*);

(iii) failing these, some other responsible adult aged 18 or over who is not:
- a police officer;
- employed by the police;
- under the direction or control of the chief officer of a police force; or

       – a person who provides services under contractual arrangements (but without being employed by the chief officer of a police force), to assist that force in relation to the discharge of its chief officer's functions,

    whether or not they are on duty at the time.

    See *Note 1F.*

  (b) person who is vulnerable (see *paragraph 1.4* and *Note 1D.*

    (i) a relative, guardian or other person responsible for their care or custody;

    (ii) someone experienced in dealing with vulnerable persons but who is not:

        – a police officer;

        – employed by the police;

        – under the direction or control of the chief officer of a police force; or

        – a person who provides services under contractual arrangements (but without being employed by the chief officer of a police force), to assist that force in relation to the discharge of its chief officer's functions, whether or not they are on duty at the time;

    (iii) failing these, some other responsible adult aged 18 or over other than a person described in the bullet points in *sub-paragraph (b)(ii)* above.

1.7A The role of the appropriate adult is to safeguard the rights, entitlements and welfare of juveniles and vulnerable persons (see *paragraphs 1.4* and *1.5*) to whom the provisions of this and any other Code of Practice apply. For this reason, the appropriate adult is expected, amongst other things, to:

- support, advise and assist them when, in accordance with this Code or any other Code of Practice, they are given or asked to provide information or participate in any procedure;
- observe whether the police are acting properly and fairly to respect their rights and entitlements, and inform an officer of the rank of inspector or above if they consider that they are not;
- assist them to communicate with the police whilst respecting their right to say nothing unless they want to as set out in the terms of the caution (see *paragraphs 10.5* and *10.6*);
- help them to understand their rights and ensure that those rights are protected and respected (see *paragraphs 3.15, 3.17, 6.5A* and *11.17*).

1.8 If this Code requires a person be given certain information, they do not have to be given it if at the time they are incapable of understanding what is said, are violent or may become violent or in urgent need of medical attention, but they must be given it as soon as practicable.

1.9–1.17 *****

Notes for guidance

1A Although certain sections of this Code apply specifically to people in custody at police stations, a person who attends a police station or other location voluntarily to assist with an investigation should be treated with no less consideration, e.g. offered or allowed refreshments at appropriate times, and enjoy an absolute right to obtain legal advice or communicate with anyone outside the police station or other location (see paragraphs 3.21 and 3.22.
*****

2 Custody records

2.1A When a person:

- is brought to a police station under arrest;
- is arrested at the police station having attended there voluntarily; or
- attends a police station to answer bail

they must be brought before the custody officer as soon as practicable after their arrival at the station or if applicable, following their arrest after attending the police station voluntarily. This applies to designated and non-designated police stations. A person is deemed to be 'at a police station' for these purposes if they are within the boundary of any building or enclosed yard which forms part of that police station.

2.1 A separate custody record must be opened as soon as practicable for each person brought to a police station under arrest or arrested at the station having gone there voluntarily or attending a police station in answer to street bail. All information recorded under this Code must be recorded as soon as practicable in the custody record unless otherwise specified. Any audio or video recording made in the custody area is not part of the custody record.

2.2 If any action requires the authority of an officer of a specified rank, subject to *paragraph 2.6A*, their name and rank must be noted in the custody record.

2.3 The custody officer is responsible for the custody record's accuracy and completeness and for making sure the record or copy of the record accompanies a detainee if they are transferred to another police station. The record shall show the:

- time and reason for transfer;
- time a person is released from detention.

2.3A If a person is arrested and taken to a police station as a result of a search in the exercise of any stop and search power to which PACE Code A (Stop and search) or the 'search powers code' issued under TACT applies, the officer carrying out the search is responsible for ensuring that the record of that stop and search, is made as part of the person's custody record. The custody officer must then ensure that the person is asked if they want a copy of the search record and if they do, that they are given a copy as soon as practicable. The person's entitlement to a copy of the search record which is made as part of their custody record is in addition to, and does not affect, their entitlement to a copy of their custody record or any other provisions of section 2 (Custody records) of this Code.

2.4 The detainee's solicitor and appropriate adult must be permitted to inspect the whole of the detainee's custody record as soon as practicable after their arrival at the station and at any other time on request, whilst the person is detained. This includes the following specific records relating to the reasons for the detainee's arrest and detention and the offence concerned, to which paragraph 3.1(b) refers:

(a) The information about the circumstances and reasons for the detainee's arrest as recorded in the custody record in accordance with paragraph 4.3 of Code G. This applies to any further offences for which the detainee is arrested whilst in custody;

(b) The record of the grounds for each authorisation to keep the person in custody. The authorisations to which this applies are the same as those described at items (i)(a) to (d) in the table in paragraph 2 of Annex M of this Code.

Access to the records in sub-paragraphs (a) and (b) is in addition to the requirements in paragraphs 3.4(b), 11.1A, 15.0, 15.7A(c) and 16.7A to make certain documents and materials available and to provide information about the offence and the reasons for arrest and detention.

Access to the custody record for the purposes of this paragraph must be arranged and agreed with the custody officer and may not unreasonably interfere with the custody officer's duties. A record shall be made when access is allowed and whether it includes the records described in sub-paragraphs (a) and (b) above.

2.4A When a detainee leaves police detention or is taken before a court they, their legal representative or appropriate adult shall be given, on request, a copy of the custody record as soon as practicable. This entitlement lasts for 12 months after release.

2.5 The detainee, appropriate adult or legal representative shall be permitted to inspect the original custody record after the detainee has left police detention provided they give reasonable notice of their request. Any such inspection shall be noted in the custody record.

2.6–2.7 *****

3   Initial action

(a) Detained persons—normal procedure

3.1 When a person is brought to a police station under arrest or arrested at the station having gone there voluntarily, the custody officer must make sure the person is told clearly about

(a) the following continuing rights which may be exercised at any stage during the period in custody:

(i) the right to consult privately with a solicitor and that free independent legal advice is available as in *section 6*;

    (ii) the right to have someone informed of their arrest as in *section 5*;

    (iii) the right to consult the Codes of Practice; and

    (iv) if applicable, their right to interpretation and translation (see paragraph 3.12) and their right to communicate with their High Commission, Embassy or Consulate (see paragraph 3.12A).

  (b) their right to be informed about the offence and (as the case may be) any further offences for which they are arrested whilst in custody and why they have been arrested and detained in accordance with paragraphs 2.4, 3.4(a) and 11.1A of this Code and paragraph 3.3 of Code G.

3.2 The detainee must also be given a written notice, which contains information:

  (a) to allow them to exercise their rights by setting out:

    (i)   their rights under paragraph 3.1, paragraph 3.12 and 3.12A;

    (ii)   the arrangements for obtaining legal advice, see section 6;

    (iii) their right to a copy of the custody record as in paragraph 2.4A;

    (iv) their right to remain silent as set out in the caution in the terms prescribed in section 10;

    (v)   their right to have access to materials and documents which are essential to effectively challenging the lawfulness of their arrest and detention for any offence and (as the case may be) any further offences for which they are arrested whilst in custody, in accordance with paragraphs 3.4(b), 15.0, 15.7A(c) and 16.7A of this Code;

    (vi) the maximum period for which they may be kept in police detention without being charged, when detention must be reviewed and when release is required.

    (vii) their right to medical assistance in accordance with section 9 of this Code

    (viii) their right, if they are prosecuted, to have access to the evidence in the case before their trial in accordance with the Criminal Procedure and Investigations Act 1996, the Attorney General's Guidelines on Disclosure, the common law and the Criminal Procedure Rules; and

  (b) briefly setting out their other entitlements while in custody, by:

    (i)   mentioning:

        – the provisions relating to the conduct of interviews;

        – the circumstances in which an appropriate adult should be available to assist the detainee and their statutory rights to make representations whenever the need for their detention is reviewed.

    (ii)   listing the entitlements in this Code, concerning

        – reasonable standards of physical comfort;

        – adequate food and drink;

        – access to toilets and washing facilities, clothing, medical attention, and exercise when practicable;

        – personal needs relating to health, hygiene and welfare concerning the provision of menstrual and any other health, hygiene and welfare products needed by the detainee in question and speaking about these in private to a member of the custody staff (see *paragraphs 9.3A* and *9.3B*).

3.2A The detainee must be given an opportunity to read the notice and shall be asked to sign the custody record to acknowledge receipt of the notice. Any refusal to sign must be recorded on the custody record.

3.3 [Not Used]

3.3A An 'easy read' illustrated version should also be provided if available.

3.4 (a) The custody officer shall:

     • record the offence(s) that the detainee has been arrested for and the reason(s) for the arrest on the custody record. See *paragraph 10.3 and Code C paragraphs 2.2 and 4.3*;

     • note on the custody record any comment the detainee makes in relation to the arresting officer's account but shall not invite comment. If the arresting officer is not physically present when the detainee is brought to a police station, the arresting officer's account must be made available to the custody officer remotely or by a third party on the arresting officer's behalf. If the custody officer authorises a person's detention, subject to paragraph 1.8, that officer must record the grounds for detention in the detainee's presence and at the same time, inform them of the grounds. The detainee must be informed of the grounds for their detention before they are questioned about any offence;

- note any comment the detainee makes in respect of the decision to detain them but shall not invite comment;
- not put specific questions to the detainee regarding their involvement in any offence, nor in respect of any comments they may make in response to the arresting officer's account or the decision to place them in detention. Such an exchange is likely to constitute an interview as in *paragraph 11.1A* and require the associated safeguards in *section 11*.
  Note: This sub-paragraph also applies to any further offences and grounds for detention which come to light whilst the person is detained. See *paragraph 11.13* in respect of unsolicited comments.

(b) Documents and materials which are essential to effectively challenging the lawfulness of the detainee's arrest and detention must be made available to the detainee or their solicitor. Documents and materials will be 'essential' for this purpose if they are capable of undermining the reasons and grounds which make the detainee's arrest and detention necessary. The decision about whether particular documents or materials must be made available for the purpose of this requirement therefore rests with the custody officer who determines whether detention is necessary, in consultation with the investigating officer who has the knowledge of the documents and materials in a particular case necessary to inform that decision. A note should be made in the detainee's custody record of the fact that documents or materials have been made available under this sub-paragraph and when. The investigating officer should make a separate note of what is made available and how it is made available in a particular case. This sub-paragraph also applies (with modifications) for the purposes of sections 15 (Reviews and extensions of detention) and 16 (Charging detained persons).

3.5 The custody officer or other custody staff as directed by the custody officer shall:

(a) ask the detainee, whether at this time, they:
   (i)   would like legal advice, see *paragraph 6.5*;
   (ii) want someone informed of their detention, see *section 5*;
(b) ask the detainee to sign the custody record to confirm their decisions in respect of (a);
(c) determine whether the detainee:
   (i)   is, or might be, in need of medical treatment or attention, see *section 9*;
   (ii) is a juvenile and/or vulnerable and therefore requires an appropriate adult (see *paragraphs 1.4, 1.5,* and *3.15*);
   (iia) wishes to speak in private with a member of the custody staff who may be of the same sex about any matter concerning their personal needs relating to health, hygiene and welfare (see *paragraph 9.3A*);
   (iii) requires:
     - help to check documentation (see *paragraph 3.20*);
     - an interpreter (see *paragraph 3.12* and *Note 13B*).
(ca) if the detainee is a female aged 18 or over, ask if they require or are likely to require any menstrual products whilst they are in custody (see *paragraph 9.3B*). For girls under 18, see *paragraph 3.20A*;
(d) record the decision and actions taken as applicable in respect of (c) and (ca).

Where any duties under this paragraph have been carried out by custody staff at the direction of the custody officer, the outcomes shall, as soon as practicable, be reported to the custody officer who retains overall responsibility for the detainee's care and treatment and ensuring that it complies with this Code.

3.6–3.10 *****

3.11 If video cameras are installed in the custody area, notices shall be prominently displayed showing cameras are in use. Any request to have video cameras switched off shall be refused.

3.12–3.20C *****

(d) Persons attending a police station or elsewhere voluntarily

3.21 Anybody attending a police station or other location (see *paragraph 3.22*) voluntarily to assist police with the investigation of an offence may leave at will unless arrested. The person may only be prevented from leaving at will if their arrest on suspicion of committing the offence is necessary in accordance with Code G.

Action if arrest becomes necessary

(a) If during a person's voluntary attendance at a police station or other location it is decided for any reason that their arrest is necessary, they must:
- be informed at once that they are under arrest and of the grounds and reasons as required by Code G, and
- be brought before the custody officer at the police station where they are arrested or (as the case may be) at the police station to which they are taken after being arrested elsewhere. The custody officer is then responsible for making sure that a custody record is opened and that they are notified of their rights in the same way as other detainees as required by this Code.

Information to be given when arranging a voluntary interview

(b) If the suspect's arrest is not necessary but they are cautioned as required in *section 10*, the person who, after describing the nature and circumstances of the suspected offence, gives the caution must at the same time, inform them that they are not under arrest and that they are not obliged to remain at the station or other location (see *paragraph 3.22* and *Note 3I*). The rights, entitlements and safeguards that apply to the conduct and recording of interviews with suspects are not diminished simply because the interview is arranged on a voluntary basis. For the purpose of arranging a voluntary interview (see *Code G Note 2F*), the duty of the interviewer reflects that of the custody officer with regard to detained suspects. As a result:

(i) the requirement in *paragraph 3.5(c)(ii)* to determine whether a detained suspect requires an appropriate adult, help to check documentation or an interpreter shall apply equally to a suspect who has not been arrested; and

(ii) the suspect must not be asked to give their informed consent to be interviewed until after they have been informed of the rights, entitlements and safeguards that apply to voluntary interviews. These are set out in *paragraph 3.21A* and the interviewer is responsible for ensuring that the suspect is so informed and for explaining these rights, entitlements and safeguards.

3.21A The interviewer must inform the suspect that the purpose of the voluntary interview is to question them to obtain evidence about their involvement or suspected involvement in the offence(s) described when they were cautioned and told that they were not under arrest. The interviewer shall then inform the suspect that the following matters will apply if they agree to the voluntary interview proceeding:

(a) Their right to information about the offence(s) in question by providing sufficient information to enable them to understand the nature of any such offence(s) and why they are suspected of committing it. This is in order to allow for the effective exercise of the rights of the defence as required by *paragraph 11.1A*. It applies whether or not they ask for legal advice and includes any further offences that come to light and are pointed out during the voluntary interview and for which they are cautioned.

(b) Their right to free (see *Note 3J*) legal advice by:

(i) explaining that they may obtain free and independent legal advice if they want it, and that this includes the right to speak with a solicitor on the telephone and to have the solicitor present during the interview;

(ii) asking if they want legal advice and recording their reply; and

(iii) if the person requests advice, securing its provision before the interview by contacting the Defence Solicitor Call Centre and explaining that the time and place of the interview will be arranged to enable them to obtain advice and that the interview will be delayed until they have received the advice unless, in accordance with *paragraph 6.6(c)* (Nominated solicitor not available and duty solicitor declined) or *paragraph 6.6(d)* (Change of mind), an officer of the rank of inspector or above agrees to the interview proceeding; or

(iv) if the person declines to exercise the right, asking them why and recording any reasons given (see *Note 6K*).

Note: When explaining the right to legal advice and the arrangements, the interviewer must take care not to indicate, except to answer a direct question, that the time taken to arrange and complete the voluntary interview might be reduced if:

- the suspect does not ask for legal advice or does not want a solicitor present when they are interviewed; or
- the suspect asks for legal advice or (as the case may be) asks for a solicitor to be present when they are interviewed, but changes their mind and agrees to be interviewed without waiting for a solicitor.

(c) Their right, if in accordance with *paragraph 3.5(c)(ii)* the interviewer determines:

(i) that they are a juvenile or are vulnerable; or

(ii) that they need help to check documentation (see *paragraph 3.20*), to have the appropriate adult present or (as the case may be) to have the necessary help to check documentation; and that the interview will be delayed until the presence of the appropriate adult or the necessary help, is secured.

(d) If they are a juvenile or vulnerable and do not want legal advice, their appropriate adult has the right to ask for a solicitor to attend if this would be in their best interests and the appropriate adult must be so informed. In this case, action to secure the provision of advice if so requested by their appropriate adult will be taken without delay in the same way as if requested by the person (see *subparagraph (b)(iii)*). However, they cannot be forced to see the solicitor if they are adamant that they do not wish to do so (see *paragraphs 3.19* and *6.5A*).

(e) Their right to an interpreter, if in accordance with, *paragraphs 3.5(c)(ii)* and *3.12*, the interviewer determines that they require an interpreter and that if they require an interpreter, making the necessary arrangements in accordance with *paragraph 13.1ZA* and that the interview will be delayed to make the arrangements.

(f) That interview will be arranged for a time and location (see *paragraph 3.22* and *Note 3I*) that enables:

(i) the suspect's rights described above to be fully respected; and

(ii) the whole of the interview to be recorded using an authorised recording device in accordance with Code E (Code of Practice on Audio recording of interviews with suspects) or (as the case may be) Code F (Code of Practice on visual recording with sound of interviews with suspects); and

(g) That their agreement to take part in the interview also signifies their agreement for that interview to be audio-recorded or (as the case may be) visually recorded with sound.

3.21B The provision by the interviewer of factual information described in *paragraph 3.21A* and, if asked by the suspect, further such information, does not constitute an interview for the purpose of this Code and when that information is provided:

(a) the interviewer must remind the suspect about the caution as required in *section 10* but must not invite comment about the offence or put specific questions to the suspect regarding their involvement in any offence, nor in respect of any comments they may make when given the information. Such an exchange is itself likely to constitute an interview as in *paragraph 11.1A* and require the associated interview safeguards in *section 11*.

(b) Any comment the suspect makes when the information is given which might be relevant to the offence, must be recorded and dealt with in accordance with *paragraph 11.13*.

(c) The suspect must be given a notice summarising the matters described in *paragraph 3.21A* and which includes the arrangements for obtaining legal advice. If a specific notice is not available, the notice given to detained suspects with references to detention-specific requirements and information redacted, may be used.

(d) For juvenile and vulnerable suspects (see *paragraphs 1.4* and *1.5*):

(i) the information must be provided or (as the case may be) provided again, together with the notice, in the presence of the appropriate adult;

(ii) if cautioned in the absence of the appropriate adult, the caution must be repeated in the appropriate adult's presence (see *paragraph 10.12*);

(iii) the suspect must be informed of the decision that an appropriate is required and the reason (see *paragraph 3.5(c)(ii)*);

(iv) the suspect and the appropriate adult shall be advised:

- that the duties of the appropriate adult include giving advice and assistance in accordance with *paragraphs 1.7A* and *11.17*; and
- that they can consult privately at any time.

(v) their informed agreement to be interviewed voluntarily must be sought and given in the presence of the appropriate adult and for a juvenile, the agreement of a parent or guardian of the juvenile is also required.

3.22 If the other location mentioned in *paragraph 3.21* is any place or premises for which the interviewer requires the informed consent of the suspect and/or occupier (if different) to remain, for example, the suspect's home (see *Note 3I*), then the references that the person is 'not obliged to remain' and that they 'may leave at will' mean that the suspect and/or occupier (if different) may also withdraw their consent and require the interviewer to leave.

Commencement of voluntary interview—general

3.22A Before asking the suspect any questions about their involvement in the offence they are suspected of committing, the interviewing officer must ask them to confirm that they agree to the interview proceeding. This confirmation shall be recorded in the interview record made in accordance with section 11 of this Code (written record) or Code E or Code F.

Documentation

3.22B Action taken under *paragraphs 3.21A* to *3.21B* shall be recorded. The record shall include the date time and place the action was taken, who was present and anything said to or by the suspect and to or by those present.

3.23–3.24 [Not Used] *****

3.25, 3.26 *****

4   Detainee's property

(a) Action

4.1 The custody officer is responsible for:

(a) ascertaining what property a detainee:

(i) has with them when they come to the police station, whether on:

- arrest or re-detention on answering to bail;
- commitment to prison custody on the order or sentence of a court;
- lodgement at the police station with a view to their production in court from prison custody;
- transfer from detention at another station or hospital;
- detention under the Mental Health Act 1983, section 135 or 136;
- remand into police custody on the authority of a court.

(ii) might have acquired for an unlawful or harmful purpose while in custody;

(b) the safekeeping of any property taken from a detainee which remains at the police station.

The custody officer may search the detainee or authorise their being searched to the extent they consider necessary, provided a search of intimate parts of the body or involving the removal of more than outer clothing is only made as in *Annex A*. A search may only be carried out by an officer of the same sex as the detainee.

4.2–4.5 *****

5   Right not to be held incommunicado

(a) Action

5.1 Subject to *paragraph 5.7B*, any person arrested and held in custody at a police station or other premises may, on request, have one person known to them or likely to take an interest in their welfare informed at public expense of their whereabouts as soon as practicable. If the person cannot be contacted the detainee may choose up to two alternatives. If they cannot be contacted, the person in charge of detention or the investigation has discretion to allow further attempts until the information has been conveyed.

5.2 The exercise of the above right in respect of each person nominated may be delayed only in accordance with *Annex B*.

5.3 The above right may be exercised each time a detainee is taken to another police station.

5.4 If the detainee agrees, they may at custody officer's discretion, receive visits from friends, family or others likely to take an interest in their welfare, or in whose welfare the detainee has an interest.

5.5 If a friend, relative or person with an interest in the detainee's welfare enquires about their whereabouts, this information shall be given if the suspect agrees and *Annex B* does not apply.

5.6 The detainee shall be given writing materials, on request, and allowed to telephone one person for a reasonable time. Either or both these privileges may be denied or delayed if an officer of inspector rank or above considers sending a letter or making a telephone call may result in any of the consequences in:

> (a) *Annex B paragraphs 1* and *2* and the person is detained in connection with an indictable offence;
>
> (b) [Not Used]

Nothing in this paragraph permits the restriction or denial of the rights in *paragraphs 5.1* and *6.1*.

5.7 Before any letter or message is sent, or telephone call made, the detainee shall be informed that what they say in any letter, call or message (other than in a communication to a solicitor) may be read or listened to and may be given in evidence. A telephone call may be terminated if it is being abused. The costs can be at public expense at the custody officer's discretion.

5.7A Any delay or denial of the rights in this section should be proportionate and should last no longer than necessary.

5.7B, 5.8 *****

6   Right to legal advice

(a) Action

6.1 Unless *Annex B* applies, all detainees must be informed that they may at any time consult and communicate privately with a solicitor, whether in person, in writing or by telephone, and that free independent legal advice is available.

6.2 [Not Used]

6.3 A poster advertising the right to legal advice must be prominently displayed in the charging area of every police station.

6.4 No police officer should, at any time, do or say anything with the intention of dissuading any person who is entitled to legal advice in accordance with this Code, whether or not they have been arrested and are detained, from obtaining legal advice.

6.5 The exercise of the right of access to legal advice may be delayed only as in *Annex B*. Whenever legal advice is requested, and unless *Annex B* applies, the custody officer must act without delay to secure the provision of such advice. If the detainee has the right to speak to a solicitor in person but declines to exercise the right the officer should point out that the right includes the right to speak with a solicitor on the telephone. If the detainee continues to waive this right, or a detainee whose right to free legal advice is limited to telephone advice from the Criminal Defence Service (CDS) Direct declines to exercise that right, the officer should ask them why and any reasons should be recorded on the custody record or the interview record as appropriate. Reminders of the right to legal advice must be given as in *paragraphs 3.5, 11.2, 15.4, 16.4, 16.5, 2B of Annex A, 3 of Annex K* and *5 of Annex M* of this Code and *Code D, paragraphs 3.17(ii)* and *6.3*. Once it is clear a detainee does not want to speak to a solicitor in person or by telephone they should cease to be asked their reasons.

6.5A In the case of a person who is a juvenile or is vulnerable, an appropriate adult should consider whether legal advice from a solicitor is required. If such a detained person wants to exercise the right to legal advice, the appropriate action should be taken and should not be delayed until the appropriate adult arrives. If the person indicates that they do not want legal advice, the appropriate adult has the right to ask for a solicitor to attend if this would be in the best interests of the person and must be so informed. In this case, action to secure the provision of advice if so requested by the appropriate adult shall be taken without delay in the same way as when requested by the person. However, the person cannot be forced to see the solicitor if they are adamant that they do not wish to do so.

6.6 A detainee who wants legal advice may not be interviewed or continue to be interviewed until they have received such advice unless:

(a) *Annex B* applies, when the restriction on drawing adverse inferences from silence in *Annex C* will apply because the detainee is not allowed an opportunity to consult a solicitor; or

(b) an officer of superintendent rank or above has reasonable grounds for believing that:

    (i) the consequent delay might:

- lead to interference with, or harm to, evidence connected with an offence;
- lead to interference with, or physical harm to, other people;
- lead to serious loss of, or damage to, property;
- lead to alerting other people suspected of having committed an offence but not yet arrested for it;
- hinder the recovery of property obtained in consequence of the commission of an offence.

    (ii) when a solicitor, including a duty solicitor, has been contacted and has agreed to attend, awaiting their arrival would cause unreasonable delay to the process of investigation.

Note: In these cases the restriction on drawing adverse inferences from silence in *Annex C* will apply because the detainee is not allowed an opportunity to consult a solicitor.

(c) the solicitor the detainee has nominated or selected from a list:

    (i) cannot be contacted;

    (ii) has previously indicated they do not wish to be contacted; or

    (iii) having been contacted, has declined to attend; and

- the detainee has been advised of the Duty Solicitor Scheme but has declined to ask for the duty solicitor;
- in these circumstances the interview may be started or continued without further delay provided an officer of inspector rank or above has agreed to the interview proceeding.

Note: The restriction on drawing adverse inferences from silence in *Annex C* will not apply because the detainee is allowed an opportunity to consult the duty solicitor;

(d) the detainee changes their mind about wanting legal advice or (as the case may be) about wanting a solicitor present at the interview and states that they no longer wish to speak to a solicitor. In these circumstances, the interview may be started or continued without delay provided that:

    (i) an officer of inspector rank or above:

- speaks to the detainee to enquire about the reasons for their change of mind, and
- makes, or directs the making of, reasonable efforts to ascertain the solicitor's expected time of arrival and to inform the solicitor that the suspect has stated that they wish to change their mind and the reason (if given);

    (ii) the detainee's reason for their change of mind (if given) and the outcome of the action in (i) are recorded in the custody record;

    (iii) the detainee, after being informed of the outcome of the action in (i) above, confirms in writing that they want the interview to proceed without speaking or further speaking to a solicitor or (as the case may be) without a solicitor being present and do not wish to wait for a solicitor by signing an entry to this effect in the custody record;

    (iv) an officer of inspector rank or above is satisfied that it is proper for the interview to proceed in these circumstances and:

- gives authority in writing for the interview to proceed and if the authority is not recorded in the custody record, the officer must ensure that the custody record shows the date and time of the authority and where it is recorded, and
- takes or directs the taking of, reasonable steps to inform the solicitor that the authority has been given and the time when the interview is expected to commence, and records or causes to be recorded, the outcome of this action in the custody record.

    (v) When the interview starts and the interviewer reminds the suspect of their right to legal advice (see *paragraph 11.2*, Code E *paragraph 4.5* and Code F *paragraph 4.5*), the interviewer shall then ensure that the following is recorded in the written interview record or the interview record made in accordance with Code E or F:

- confirmation that the detainee has changed their mind about wanting legal advice or (as the case may be) about wanting a solicitor present and the reasons for it if given;
- the fact that authority for the interview to proceed has been given and, subject to *paragraph 2.6A*, the name of the authorising officer;
- that if the solicitor arrives at the station before the interview is completed, the detainee will be so informed without delay and *a break will be taken* to allow them to speak to the solicitor if they wish, unless *paragraph 6.6(a)* applies, and
- that at any time during the interview, the detainee may again ask for legal advice and that if they do, a break will be taken to allow them to speak to the solicitor, unless *paragraph 6.6(a), (b), or (c)* applies.

Note: In these circumstances, the restriction on drawing adverse inferences from silence in *Annex C* will not apply because the detainee is allowed an opportunity to consult a solicitor if they wish.

6.7 If *paragraph 6.6(a)* applies, where the reason for authorising the delay ceases to apply, there may be no further delay in permitting the exercise of the right in the absence of a further authorisation unless *paragraph 6.6(b), (c) or (d)* applies. If *paragraph 6.6(b)(i)* applies, once sufficient information has been obtained to avert the risk, questioning must cease until the detainee has received legal advice unless *paragraph 6.6(a), (b)(ii), (c) or (d)* applies.

6.8 A detainee who has been permitted to consult a solicitor shall be entitled on request to have the solicitor present when they are interviewed unless one of the exceptions in *paragraph 6.6* applies.

6.9 The solicitor may only be required to leave the interview if their conduct is such that the interviewer is unable properly to put questions to the suspect.

6.10 If the interviewer considers a solicitor is acting in such a way, they will stop the interview and consult an officer not below superintendent rank, if one is readily available, and otherwise an officer not below inspector rank not connected with the investigation. After speaking to the solicitor, the officer consulted will decide if the interview should continue in the presence of that solicitor. If they decide it should not, the suspect will be given the opportunity to consult another solicitor before the interview continues and that solicitor given an opportunity to be present at the interview.

6.11 The removal of a solicitor from an interview is a serious step and, if it occurs, the officer of superintendent rank or above who took the decision will consider if the incident should be reported to the Solicitors Regulation Authority. If the decision to remove the solicitor has been taken by an officer below superintendent rank, the facts must be reported to an officer of superintendent rank or above who will similarly consider whether a report to the Solicitors Regulation Authority would be appropriate. When the solicitor concerned is a duty solicitor, the report should be both to the Solicitors Regulation Authority and to the Legal Aid Agency.

6.12–6.17 *****

Notes for guidance

6ZA No police officer or police staff shall indicate to any suspect, except to answer a direct question, that the period for which they are liable to be detained, or if not detained, the time taken to complete the interview, might be reduced:

- *if they do not ask for legal advice or do not want a solicitor present when they are interviewed; or*
- *if they have asked for legal advice or (as the case may be) asked for a solicitor to be present when they are interviewed but change their mind and agree to be interviewed without waiting for a solicitor.*

6A In considering if paragraph 6.6(b) applies, the officer should, if practicable, ask the solicitor for an estimate of how long it will take to come to the station and relate this to the time detention is permitted, the time of day (i.e. whether the rest period under paragraph 12.2 is imminent) and the requirements of other investigations. If the solicitor is on their way or is to set off immediately, it will not normally be appropriate to begin an interview before they arrive. If it appears necessary to begin an interview before the solicitor's arrival, they should be given an indication of how long the police would be able to wait before 6.6(b) applies so there is an opportunity to make arrangements for someone else to provide legal advice.

*6B *****

6B1–6C [Not Used]

6D The solicitor's only role in the police station is to protect and advance the legal rights of their client. On occasions this may require the solicitor to give advice which has the effect of the client avoiding giving evidence which strengthens a prosecution case. The solicitor may intervene in order to seek clarification, challenge an improper question to their client or the manner in which it is put, advise their client not to reply to particular questions, or if they wish to give their client further legal advice. Paragraph 6.9 only applies if the solicitor's approach or conduct prevents or unreasonably obstructs proper questions being put to the suspect or the suspect's response being recorded. Examples of unacceptable conduct include answering questions on a suspect's behalf or providing written replies for the suspect to quote.

6E An officer who takes the decision to exclude a solicitor must be in a position to satisfy the court the decision was properly made. In order to do this they may need to witness what is happening.

6F If an officer of at least inspector rank considers a particular solicitor or firm of solicitors is persistently sending probationary representatives who are unsuited to provide legal advice, they should inform an officer of at least superintendent rank, who may wish to take the matter up with the Solicitors Regulation Authority.

6G Subject to the constraints of Annex B, a solicitor may advise more than one client in an investigation if they wish. Any question of a conflict of interest is for the solicitor under their professional code of conduct. If, however, waiting for a solicitor to give advice to one client may lead to unreasonable delay to the interview with another, the provisions of paragraph 6.6(b) may apply.

6H In addition to a poster in English, a poster or posters containing translations into Welsh, the main minority ethnic languages and the principal European languages should be displayed wherever they are likely to be helpful and it is practicable to do so.

6I [Not Used]

6J Whenever a detainee exercises their right to legal advice by consulting or communicating with a solicitor, they must be allowed to do so in private. This right to consult or communicate in private is fundamental. If the requirement for privacy is compromised because what is said or written by the detainee or solicitor for the purpose of giving and receiving legal advice is overheard, listened to, or read by others without the informed consent of the detainee, the right will effectively have been denied. When a detainee speaks to a solicitor on the telephone, they should be allowed to do so in private unless this is impractical because of the design and layout of the custody area or the location of telephones. However, the normal expectation should be that facilities will be available, unless they are being used, at all police stations to enable detainees to speak in private to a solicitor either face to face or over the telephone.

6K A detainee is not obliged to give reasons for declining legal advice and should not be pressed to do so.

7   Citizens of independent Commonwealth countries or foreign nationals

(a) Action

7.1 A detainee who is a citizen of an independent Commonwealth country or a national of a foreign country, including the Republic of Ireland, has the right, upon request, to communicate at any time with the appropriate High Commission, Embassy or Consulate. That detainee must be informed as soon as practicable of this right and asked if they want to have their High Commission, Embassy or Consulate told of their whereabouts and the grounds for their detention. Such a request should be acted upon as soon as practicable.

7.2 *******

7.3 Consular officers may, if the detainee agrees, visit one of their nationals in police detention to talk to them and, if required, to arrange for legal advice. Such visits shall take place out of the hearing of a police officer.

7.4 Notwithstanding the provisions of consular conventions, if the detainee claims that they are a refugee or have applied or intend to apply for asylum, the custody officer must ensure that UK Visas and Immigration (UKVI) (formerly the UK Border Agency) is informed as soon as practicable of the claim. UKVI will then determine whether compliance with relevant international obligations requires notification of the arrest to be sent and will inform the custody officer as to what action police need to take.

7.5 *******

8   Conditions of detention

(a) Action

8.1 So far as it is practicable, not more than one detainee should be detained in each cell.

8.2 Cells in use must be adequately heated, cleaned and ventilated. They must be adequately lit, subject to such dimming as is compatible with safety and security to allow people detained overnight to sleep. No additional restraints shall be used within a locked cell unless absolutely necessary and then only restraint equipment, approved for use in that force by the Chief Officer, which is reasonable and necessary in the circumstances having regard to the detainee's demeanour and with a view to ensuring their safety and the safety of others. If a detainee is deaf or a vulnerable person, particular care must be taken when deciding whether to use any form of approved restraints.

8.3 Blankets, mattresses, pillows and other bedding supplied shall be of a reasonable standard and in a clean and sanitary condition.

8.4 Access to toilet and washing facilities must be provided. This must take account of the dignity of the detainee.

8.5 If it is necessary to remove a detainee's clothes for the purposes of investigation, for hygiene, health reasons or cleaning, removal shall be conducted with proper regard to the dignity, sensitivity and vulnerability of the detainee and replacement clothing of a reasonable standard of comfort and cleanliness shall be provided. A detainee may not be interviewed unless adequate clothing has been offered.

8.6 At least two light meals and one main meal should be offered in any 24 hour period. Drinks should be provided at meal times and upon reasonable request between meals. Whenever necessary, advice shall be sought from the appropriate health care professional, on medical and dietary matters. As far as practicable, meals provided shall offer a varied diet and meet any specific dietary needs or religious beliefs the detainee may have. The detainee may, at the custody officer's discretion, have meals supplied by their family or friends at their expense.

8.7 Brief outdoor exercise shall be offered daily if practicable.

8.8 A juvenile shall not be placed in a police cell unless no other secure accommodation is available and the custody officer considers it is not practicable to supervise them if they are not placed in a cell or that a cell provides more comfortable accommodation than other secure accommodation in the station. A juvenile may not be placed in a cell with a detained adult.

8.9–8.11 *****

9 Care and treatment of detained persons

(a) General

9.1 Nothing in this section prevents the police from calling an appropriate healthcare professional to examine a detainee for the purposes of obtaining evidence relating to any offence in which the detainee is suspected of being involved.

9.2 If a complaint is made by, or on behalf of, a detainee about their treatment since their arrest, or it comes to notice that a detainee may have been treated improperly, a report must be made as soon as practicable to an officer of inspector rank or above not connected with the investigation. If the matter concerns a possible assault or the possibility of the unnecessary or unreasonable use of force, an appropriate health care professional must also be called as soon as practicable.

9.3–9.4 *****

(b) Clinical treatment and attention

9.5 The custody officer must make sure a detainee receives appropriate clinical attention as soon as reasonably practicable if the person:

    (a) appears to be suffering from physical illness; or

    (b) is injured; or

    (c) appears to be suffering from a mental disorder; or

    (d) appears to need clinical attention.

9.5A This applies even if the detainee makes no request for clinical attention and whether or not they have already received clinical attention elsewhere. If the need for attention appears urgent, e.g. when indicated as in *Annex H*, the nearest available health care professional or an ambulance must be called immediately.

9.5B–9.17 *****

10 Cautions

(a) When a caution must be given

10.1 A person whom there are grounds to suspect of an offence, see *Note 10A*, must be cautioned before any questions about an offence, or further questions if the answers provide the grounds for suspicion, are put to them if either the suspect's answers or silence, (i.e. failure or refusal to answer or answer satisfactorily) may be given in evidence to a court in a prosecution. A person need not be cautioned if questions are for other necessary purposes, e.g.:

    (a) solely to establish their identity or ownership of any vehicle;

    (b) to obtain information in accordance with any relevant statutory requirement, see *paragraph 10.9*;

    (c) in furtherance of the proper and effective conduct of a search, e.g. to determine the need to search in the exercise of powers of stop and search or to seek cooperation while carrying out a search; or

    (d) to seek verification of a written record as in *paragraph 11.13*;

    (e) [Not Used]

10.2 Whenever a person not under arrest is initially cautioned, or reminded that they are under caution, that person must at the same time be told they are not under arrest and must be informed of the provisions of *paragraphs 3.21* to *3.21B* which explain that they need to agree to be interviewed, how they may obtain legal advice according to whether they are at a police station or elsewhere and the other rights and entitlements that apply to a voluntary interview. See *Note 10C*.

10.3 A person who is arrested, or further arrested, must be informed at the time if practicable, or if not, as soon as it becomes practicable thereafter, that they are under arrest and the grounds and reasons for their arrest, see *paragraph 3.4, Note 10B* and *Code G, paragraphs 2.2* and *4.3*.

10.4 As required by *Code G, section 3*, a person who is arrested, or further arrested, must also be cautioned unless:

    (a) it is impracticable to do so by reason of their condition or behaviour at the time;

    (b) they have already been cautioned immediately prior to arrest as in *paragraph 10.1*.

(b) Terms of the cautions

10.5 The caution which must be given on:

(a) arrest; or

(b) all other occasions before a person is charged or informed they may be prosecuted, see *section 16*,

should, unless the restriction on drawing adverse inferences from silence applies, see *Annex C*, be in the following terms:

'You do not have to say anything. But it may harm your defence if you do not mention when questioned something which you later rely on in Court. Anything you do say may be given in evidence.'

[Where the use of the Welsh Language is appropriate, a constable may provide the caution directly in Welsh in the following terms:

'Does dim rhaid i chi ddweud dim byd. Ond gall niweidio eich amddiffyniad os na fyddwch chi'n sôn, wrth gael eich holi, am rywbeth y byddwch chi'n dibynnu arno nes ymlaen yn y Llys. Gall unrhyw beth yr ydych yn ei ddweud gael ei roi fel tystiolaeth.']

10.6 *Annex C, paragraph 2* sets out the alternative terms of the caution to be used when the restriction on drawing adverse inferences from silence applies.

10.7 Minor deviations from the words of any caution given in accordance with this Code do not constitute a breach of this Code, provided the sense of the relevant caution is preserved.

10.8 After any break in questioning under caution, the person being questioned must be made aware they remain under caution. If there is any doubt the relevant caution should be given again in full when the interview resumes.

10.9 When, despite being cautioned, a person fails to co-operate or to answer particular questions which may affect their immediate treatment, the person should be informed of any relevant consequences and that those consequences are not affected by the caution. Examples are when a person's refusal to provide:

- their name and address when charged may make them liable to detention;
- particulars and information in accordance with a statutory requirement, e.g. under the Road Traffic Act 1988, may amount to an offence or may make the person liable to a further arrest.

10.10, 10.11 *****

(d) Juveniles and vulnerable persons

10.11A The information required in *paragraph 10.11* must not be given to a suspect who is a juvenile or a vulnerable person unless the appropriate adult is present.

10.12 If a juvenile or a vulnerable person is cautioned in the absence of the appropriate adult, the caution must be repeated in the appropriate adult's presence.

10.12A [Not Used].

(e) Documentation

10.13 A record shall be made when a caution is given under this section, either in the interviewer's pocket book or in the interview record.

Notes for guidance

10A There must be some reasonable, objective grounds for the suspicion, based on known facts or information which are relevant to the likelihood the offence has been committed and the person to be questioned committed it.

10B An arrested person must be given sufficient information to enable them to understand that they have been deprived of their liberty and the reason they have been arrested, e.g. when a person is arrested on suspicion of committing an offence they must be informed of the suspected offence's nature, when and where it was committed. The suspect must also be informed of the reason or reasons why the arrest is considered necessary. Vague or technical language should be avoided.

10C The restriction on drawing inferences from silence, see Annex C, paragraph 1, does not apply to a person who has not been detained and who therefore cannot be prevented from seeking legal advice if they want, see paragraph 3.21.

10D If it appears a person does not understand the caution, the person giving it should explain it in their own words.

10E It may be necessary to show to the court that nothing occurred during an interview break or between interviews which influenced the suspect's recorded evidence. After a break in an interview or at the beginning of a subsequent interview, the interviewing officer should summarise the reason for the break and confirm this with the suspect.

*****

11   Interviews—general

(a) Action

11.1A An interview is the questioning of a person regarding their involvement or suspected involvement in a criminal offence or offences which, under paragraph 10.1, must be carried out under caution. Before a person is interviewed, they and, if they are represented, their solicitor must be given sufficient information to enable them to understand the nature of any such offence, and why they are suspected of committing it (see paragraphs 3.4(a) and 10.3), in order to allow for the effective exercise of the rights of the defence. However, whilst the information must always be sufficient for the person to understand the nature of any offence (see Note 11ZA), this does not require the disclosure of details at a time which might prejudice the criminal investigation. The decision about what needs to be disclosed for the purpose of this requirement therefore rests with the investigating officer who has sufficient knowledge of the case to make that decision. The officer who discloses the information shall make a record of the information disclosed and when it was disclosed. This record may be made in the interview record, in the officer's pocket book or other form provided for this purpose. Procedures under the Road Traffic Act 1988, section 7 or the Transport and Works Act 1992, section 31 do not constitute interviewing for the purpose of this Code.

11.1 Following a decision to arrest a suspect, they must not be interviewed about the relevant offence except at a police station or other authorised place of detention, unless the consequent delay would be likely to:

    (a) lead to:
- interference with, or harm to, evidence connected with an offence;
- interference with, or physical harm to, other people; or
- serious loss of, or damage to, property;

    (b) lead to alerting other people suspected of committing an offence but not yet arrested for it; or

    (c) hinder the recovery of property obtained in consequence of the commission of an offence.

Interviewing in any of these circumstances shall cease once the relevant risk has been averted or the necessary questions have been put in order to attempt to avert that risk.

11.2 Immediately prior to the commencement or re-commencement of any interview at a police station or other authorised place of detention, the interviewer should remind the suspect of their entitlement to free legal advice and that the interview can be delayed for legal advice to be obtained, unless one of the exceptions in *paragraph 6.6* applies. It is the interviewer's responsibility to make sure all reminders are recorded in the interview record.

11.3 [Not Used]

11.4 At the beginning of an interview the interviewer, after cautioning the suspect, *see section 10*, shall put to them any significant statement or silence which occurred in the presence and hearing of a police officer or other police staff before the start of the interview and which have not been put to the suspect in the course of a previous interview. See *Note 11A*. The interviewer shall ask the suspect whether they confirm or deny that earlier statement or silence and if they want to add anything.

11.4A A significant statement is one which appears capable of being used in evidence against the suspect, in particular a direct admission of guilt. A significant silence is a failure or refusal to answer a question or answer satisfactorily when under caution, which might, allowing for the restriction on drawing adverse inferences from silence, see *Annex C*, give rise to an inference under the Criminal Justice and Public Order Act 1994, Part III.

11.5 No interviewer may try to obtain answers or elicit a statement by the use of oppression. Except as in *paragraph 10.9*, no interviewer shall indicate, except to answer a direct question, what action will be taken by the police if the person being questioned answers questions, makes a statement or refuses to do either. If the person asks directly what action will be taken if they answer questions, make a statement or refuse to do either, the interviewer may inform them what action the police propose to take provided that action is itself proper and warranted.

11.6 The interview or further interview of a person about an offence with which that person has not been charged or for which they have not been informed they may be prosecuted, must cease when:

    (a) the officer in charge of the investigation is satisfied all the questions they consider relevant to obtaining accurate and reliable information about the offence have been put to the suspect, this includes allowing the suspect an opportunity to give an innocent explanation and asking questions to test if the explanation is accurate and reliable, e.g. to clear up ambiguities or clarify what the suspect said;

    (b) the officer in charge of the investigation has taken account of any other available evidence; and

    (c) the officer in charge of the investigation, or in the case of a detained suspect, the custody officer, see *paragraph 16.1*, reasonably believes there is sufficient evidence to provide a realistic prospect of conviction for that offence.

This paragraph does not prevent officers in revenue cases or acting under the confiscation provisions of the Criminal Justice Act 1988 or the Drug Trafficking Act 1994 from inviting suspects to complete a formal question and answer record after the interview is concluded.

(b) Interview records

11.7 (a) An accurate record must be made of each interview, whether or not the interview takes place at a police station

    (b) The record must state the place of interview, the time it begins and ends, any interview breaks and, subject to *paragraph 2.6A*, the names of all those present; and must be made on the forms provided for this purpose or in the interviewer's pocket book or in accordance with the Codes of Practice E or F;

    (c) Any written record must be made and completed during the interview, unless this would not be practicable or would interfere with the conduct of the interview, and must constitute either a verbatim record of what has been said or, failing this, an account of the interview which adequately and accurately summarises it.

11.8–11.14 *****

(c) Juveniles and vulnerable persons

11.15 A juvenile or vulnerable person must not be interviewed regarding their involvement or suspected involvement in a criminal offence or offences, or asked to provide or sign a written statement under caution or record of interview, in the absence of the appropriate adult unless *paragraphs 11.1, 11.18 to 11.20 apply*.

11.16 Juveniles may only be interviewed at their place of education in exceptional circumstances and only when the principal or their nominee agrees. Every effort should be made to notify the parent(s) or other person responsible for the juvenile's welfare and the appropriate adult, if this is a different person, that the police want to interview the juvenile and reasonable time should be allowed to enable the appropriate adult to be present at the interview. If awaiting the appropriate adult would cause unreasonable delay, and unless the juvenile is suspected of an offence against the educational establishment, the principle or their nominee can act as the appropriate adult for the purposes of the interview.

11.17 If an appropriate adult is present at an interview, they shall be informed:

- they are not expected to act simply as an observer; and
- the purpose of their presence is to:
  - advise the person being interviewed;
  - observe whether the interview is being conducted properly and fairly; and
  - facilitate communication with the person being interviewed.

11.17A The appropriate adult may be required to leave the interview if their conduct is such that the interviewer is unable properly to put questions to the suspect. This will include situations where the appropriate adult's approach or conduct prevents or unreasonably obstructs proper questions being put to the suspect or the suspect's responses being recorded (see *Note 11F*). If the interviewer considers an appropriate adult is acting in such a way, they will stop the interview and consult an officer not below superintendent rank, if one is readily available, and otherwise an officer not below inspector rank not connected with the investigation. After speaking to the appropriate adult, the officer consulted must remind the adult that their role under *paragraph 11.17* does not allow them to obstruct proper questioning and give the adult an opportunity to respond. The officer consulted will then decide if the interview should continue without the attendance of that appropriate adult. If they decide it should, another appropriate adult must be obtained before the interview continues, unless the provisions of *paragraph 11.18* below apply.

(d) Vulnerable suspects—urgent interviews at police stations

11.18 *****

11.19 These interviews may not continue once sufficient information has been obtained to avert the consequences in *paragraph 11.1(a) to (c)*.

11.20 A record shall be made of the grounds for any decision to interview a person under *paragraph 11.18*.

(e) Conduct and recording of Interviews at police stations—use of live link

11.21 When a suspect in police detention is interviewed using a live link by a police officer who is not at the police station where the detainee is held, the provisions of this section that govern the conduct and making a written record of that interview, shall be subject to *paragraph 12.9B* of this Code.

(f) Witnesses

11.22 The provisions of this Code and Codes E and F which govern the conduct and recording of interviews do not apply to interviews with, or taking statements from, witnesses.

Notes for guidance

11ZA The requirement in paragraph 11.1A for a suspect to be given sufficient information about the offence applies prior to the interview and whether or not they are legally represented. What is sufficient will depend on the circumstances of the case, but it should normally include, as a minimum, a description of the facts relating to the suspected offence that are known to the officer, including the time and place in question. This aims to avoid suspects being confused or unclear about what they are supposed to have done and to help an innocent suspect to clear the matter up more quickly.

11A Paragraph 11.4 does not prevent the interviewer from putting significant statements and silences to a suspect again at a later stage or a further interview.

11B The Criminal Procedure and Investigations Act 1996 Code of Practice, paragraph 3.5 states 'In conducting an investigation, the investigator should pursue all reasonable lines of enquiry, whether these point towards or away from the suspect. What is reasonable will depend on the particular circumstances.' Interviewers should keep this in mind when deciding what questions to ask in an interview.

11C Although juveniles or vulnerable persons are often capable of providing reliable evidence, they may, without knowing or wishing to do so, be particularly prone in certain circumstances to providing information that may be unreliable, misleading or self-incriminating. Special care should always be taken when questioning such a person, and the appropriate adult should be involved if there is any doubt about a person's age, mental state or capacity. Because of the risk of unreliable evidence it is also important to obtain corroboration of any facts admitted whenever possible. Because of the risks, which the presence of the appropriate adult is intended to minimise, officers of superintendent rank or above should exercise their discretion under paragraph 11.18(a) to authorise the commencement of an interview in the appropriate adult's absence only in exceptional cases, if it is necessary to avert one or more of the specified risks in paragraph 11.1.

11D Juveniles should not be arrested at their place of education unless this is unavoidable. When a juvenile is arrested at their place of education, the principal or their nominee must be informed.

11E Significant statements described in paragraph 11.4 will always be relevant to the offence and must be recorded. When a suspect agrees to read records of interviews and other comments and sign them as correct, they should be asked to endorse the record with, e.g. 'I agree that this is a correct record of what was said' and add their signature. If the suspect does not agree with the record, the interviewer should record the details of any disagreement and ask the suspect to read these details and sign them to the effect that they accurately reflect their disagreement. Any refusal to sign should be recorded.

11F The appropriate adult may intervene if they consider it is necessary to help the suspect understand any question asked and to help the suspect to answer any question. Paragraph 11.17A only applies if the appropriate adult's approach or conduct prevents or unreasonably obstructs proper questions being put to the suspect or the suspect's response being recorded. Examples of unacceptable conduct include answering questions on a suspect's behalf or providing written replies for the suspect to quote. An officer who takes the decision to exclude an appropriate adult must be in a position to satisfy the court the decision was properly made. In order to do this they may need to witness what is happening and give the suspect's solicitor (if they have one) who witnessed what happened, an opportunity to comment.

12   Interviews in police stations

(a) Action
When interviewer and suspect are present at the same police station

12.1 If a police officer wants to interview or conduct enquiries which require the presence of a detainee, the custody officer is responsible for deciding whether to deliver the detainee into the officer's custody. An investigating officer who is given custody of a detainee takes over responsibility for the detainee's care and safe custody for the purposes of this Code until they return the detainee to the custody officer when they must report the manner in which they complied with the Code whilst having custody of the detainee.

12.2 Except as below, in any period of 24 hours a detainee must be allowed a continuous period of at least 8 hours for rest, free from questioning, travel or any interruption in connection with the investigation concerned. This period should normally be at night or other appropriate time which takes account of when the detainee last slept or rested. If a detainee is arrested at a police station after going there voluntarily, the period of 24 hours runs from the time of their arrest and not the time of arrival at the police station. The period may not be interrupted or delayed, except:

    (a) when there are reasonable grounds for believing not delaying or interrupting the period would:
        (i) involve a risk of harm to people or serious loss of, or damage to, property;
        (ii) delay unnecessarily the person's release from custody; or
        (iii) otherwise prejudice the outcome of the investigation;
    (b) at the request of the detainee, their appropriate adult or legal representative;
    (c) when a delay or interruption is necessary in order to:
        (i) comply with the legal obligations and duties arising under *section 15*; or
        (ii) to take action required under *section 9* or in accordance with medical advice.

If the period is interrupted in accordance with *(a)*, a fresh period must be allowed. Interruptions under *(b)* and *(c)*, do not require a fresh period to be allowed.

12.3 *****

12.4 As far as practicable interviews shall take place in interview rooms which are adequately heated, lit and ventilated.

12.5 A suspect whose detention without charge has been authorised under PACE, because the detention is necessary for an interview to obtain evidence of the offence for which they have been arrested, may choose not to answer questions but police do not require the suspect's consent or agreement to interview them for this purpose. If a suspect takes steps to prevent themselves being questioned or further questioned, e.g. by refusing to leave their cell to go to a suitable interview room or by trying to leave the interview room, they shall be advised their consent or agreement to interview is not required. The suspect shall be cautioned as in *section 10*, and informed if they fail or refuse to co-operate, the interview may take place in the cell and that their failure or refusal to co-operate may be given in evidence. The suspect shall then be invited to co-operate and go into the interview room. If they refuse and the custody officer considers, on reasonable grounds, that the interview should not be delayed, the custody officer has discretion to direct that the interview be conducted in a cell.

12.6 People being questioned or making statements shall not be required to stand.

12.7 Before the interview commences each interviewer shall, subject to *paragraph 2.6A*, identify themselves and any other persons present to the interviewee.

12.8 Breaks from interviewing should be made at recognised meal times or at other times that take account of when an interviewee last had a meal. Short refreshment breaks shall be provided at approximately two hour intervals, subject to the interviewer's discretion to delay a break if there are reasonable grounds for believing it would:

    (i)   involve a:
- risk of harm to people;
- serious loss of, or damage to, property;

    (ii) unnecessarily delay the detainee's release; or

    (iii) otherwise prejudice the outcome of the investigation.

12.9 If during the interview a complaint is made by or on behalf of the interviewee concerning the provisions of any of the Codes, or it comes to the interviewer's notice that the interviewee may have been treated improperly, the interviewer should:

    (i)   record the matter in the interview record; and

    (ii) inform the custody officer, who is then responsible for dealing with it as in *section 9*.

Interviewer not present at the same station as the detainee—use of live link

12.9A Amendments to PACE, section 39, allow a person in police detention to be interviewed using a live link (see *paragraph 1.13(e)(i)*) by a police officer who is not at the police station where the detainee is held. Subject to *sub-paragraphs (a)* to *(f)* below, the custody officer is responsible for deciding on a case by case basis whether a detainee is fit to be interviewed (see *paragraph 12.3*) and should be delivered into the physical custody of an officer who is not involved in the investigation, for the purpose of enabling another officer who is investigating the offence for which the person is detained and who is not at the police station where the person is detained, to interview the detainee by means of a live link (see *Note 12ZA*).

    (a) The custody officer must be satisfied that the live link to be used provides for accurate and secure communication with the suspect. The provisions of *paragraph 13.13* shall apply to communications between the interviewing officer, the suspect and anyone else whose presence at the interview or, (as the case may be) whose access to any communications between the suspect and the interviewer, has been authorised by the custody officer or the interviewing officer.

    (b) Each decision must take account of the age, gender and vulnerability of the suspect, the nature and circumstances of the offence and the investigation and the impact on the suspect of carrying out the interview by means of a live link. For this reason, the custody officer must consider whether the ability of the particular suspect, to communicate confidently and effectively for the purpose of the interview is likely to be adversely affected or otherwise undermined or limited if the interviewing officer is not physically present and a live-link is used (see *Note 12ZB*). Although a suspect for whom an appropriate adult is required may be more likely to be adversely affected as described, it is important to note that a person who does not require an appropriate adult may also be adversely impacted if interviewed by means of a live link.

    (c) If the custody officer is satisfied that interviewing the detainee by means of a live link would not adversely affect or otherwise undermine or limit the suspect's ability to communicate confidently and effectively for the purpose of the interview, the officer must so inform the suspect, their solicitor and (if applicable) the appropriate adult. At the same time, the operation of the live-link must be explained and demonstrated to them (see *Note 12ZC*), they must be advised of the chief officer's obligations concerning the security of live-link communications under *paragraph 13.13* and they must be asked if they wish to make representations that the live-link should not be used or if they require more information about the operation of the arrangements. They must also be told that at any time live-link is in use, they may make representations to the custody officer or the interviewer that its operation should cease and that the physical presence of the interviewer should be arranged.

When the authority of an inspector is required

(d) If:

    (i)   representations are made that a live-link should not be used to carry out the interview, or that at any time it is in use, its operation should cease and the physical presence of the interviewer arranged; and

    (ii) the custody officer in consultation with the interviewer is unable to allay the concerns raised;

then live-link may not be used, or (as the case may be) continue to be used, unless authorised in writing by an officer of the rank of inspector or above in accordance with *sub-paragraph (e)*.

(e) Authority may be given if the officer is satisfied that interviewing the detainee by means of a live link is necessary and justified. In making this decision, the officer must have regard to:

    (i)   the circumstances of the suspect;

    (ii) the nature and seriousness of the offence;

    (iii) the requirements of the investigation, including its likely impact on both the suspect and any victim(s);

    (iv) the representations made by the suspect, their solicitor and (if applicable) the appropriate adult that a live-link should not be used (*see sub-paragraph (b)*);

    (v) the impact on the investigation of making arrangements for the physical presence of the interviewer (see *Note 12ZD*); and

    (vi) the risk if the interviewer is not physically present, evidence obtained using link interpretation might be excluded in subsequent criminal proceedings; and

    (vii) the likely impact on the suspect and the investigation of any consequential delay to arrange for the interviewer to be physically present with the suspect.

(f) The officer given custody of the detainee and the interviewer take over responsibility for the detainee's care, treatment and safe custody for the purposes of this Code until the detainee is returned to the custody officer. On that return, both must report the manner in which they complied with the Code during period in question.

12.9B When a suspect detained at a police station is interviewed using a live link in accordance with *paragraph 12.9A*, the officer given custody of the detainee at the police station and the interviewer who is not present at the police station, take over responsibility for ensuring compliance with the provisions of *sections 11* and *12* of this Code, or Code E (Audio recording) or Code F (Audio visual recording) that govern the conduct and recording of that interview. In these circumstances:

(a) the interviewer who is not at the police station where the detainee is held must direct the officer having physical custody of the suspect at the police station, to take the action required by those provisions and which the interviewer would be required to take if they were present at the police station.

(b) the officer having physical custody of the suspect at the police station must take the action required by those provisions and which would otherwise be required to be taken by the interviewer if they were present at the police station. This applies whether or not the officer has been so directed by the interviewer but in such a case, the officer must inform the interviewer of the action taken.

(c) during the course of the interview, the officers in (a) and (b) may consult each other as necessary to clarify any action to be taken and to avoid any misunderstanding. Such consultations must, if in the hearing of the suspect and any other person present with the suspect (for example, a solicitor, appropriate adult or interpreter) be recorded in the interview record.

12.10–12.14 *****

13–15 *****

16   Charging detained persons

(a) Action

16.1 When the officer in charge of the investigation reasonably believes there is sufficient evidence to provide a realistic prospect of conviction for the offence (see *paragraph 11.6*), they shall without delay, and subject to the following qualification, inform the custody officer who will be responsible for considering whether the detainee should be charged. When a person is detained in respect of more than one offence it is permissible to delay informing the custody officer until the above conditions are satisfied in respect of all the offences, but see *paragraph 11.6*. If the detainee is a juvenile or a vulnerable person, any resulting action shall be taken in the presence of the appropriate adult if they are present at the time.

16.1A Where guidance issued by the Director of Public Prosecutions under PACE, section 37A is in force the custody officer must comply with that Guidance in deciding how to act in dealing with the detainee.

16.1B Where in compliance with the DPP's Guidance the custody officer decides that the case should be immediately referred to the CPS to make the charging decision, consultation should take place with a Crown Prosecutor as soon as is reasonably practicable. Where the Crown Prosecutor is unable to make the charging decision on the information available at that time, the detainee may be released without charge and on bail (with conditions if necessary) under section 37(7)(a). In such circumstances, the detainee should be informed that they are being released to enable the Director of Public Prosecutions to make a decision under section 37B.

16.2 When a detainee is charged with or informed they may be prosecuted for an offence, they shall, unless the restriction on drawing adverse inferences from silence applies, see *Annex C*, be cautioned as follows:

'You do not have to say anything. But it may harm your defence if you do not mention now something which you later rely on in court. Anything you do say may be given in evidence.'

[Where the use of the Welsh Language is appropriate, a constable may provide the caution directly in Welsh in the following terms:

'Does dim rhaid i chi ddweud dim byd. Ond gall niweidio eich amddiffyniad os na fyddwch chi'n sôn, wrth gael eich holi, am rywbeth y byddwch chi'n dibynnu arno nes ymlaen yn y Llys. Gall unrhyw beth yr ydych yn ei ddweud gael ei roi fel tystiolaeth.']

Annex C, paragraph 2 sets out the alternative terms of the caution to be used when the restriction on drawing adverse inferences from silence applies.

16.3 When a detainee is charged they shall be given a written notice showing particulars of the offence and, subject to *paragraph 2.6A*, the officer's name and the case reference number. As far as possible the particulars of the charge shall be stated in simple terms, but they shall also show the precise offence in law with which the detainee is charged. The notice shall begin:

'You are charged with the offence(s) shown below.' Followed by the caution.

If the detainee is a juvenile, mentally disordered or otherwise mentally vulnerable, the notice should be given to the appropriate adult.

16.4 If, after a detainee has been charged with or informed they may be prosecuted for an offence, an officer wants to tell them about any written statement or interview with another person relating to such an offence, the detainee shall either be handed a true copy of the written statement or the content of the interview record brought to their attention. Nothing shall be done to invite any reply or comment except to:

    (a) caution the detainee, *'You do not have to say anything, but anything you do say may be given in evidence.'* [Where the use of the Welsh Language is appropriate, caution the detainee in the following terms: 'Does dim rhaid i chi ddweud dim byd, ond gall unrhyw beth yr ydych yn ei ddweud gael ei roi fel tystiolaeth.']; and

    (b) remind the detainee about their right to legal advice.

16.4A If the detainee:
- cannot read, the document may be read to them;
- is a juvenile, mentally disordered or otherwise mentally vulnerable, the appropriate adult shall also be given a copy, or the interview record shall be brought to their attention.

16.5 A detainee may not be interviewed about an offence after they have been charged with, or informed they may be prosecuted for it, unless the interview is necessary:
- to prevent or minimise harm or loss to some other person, or the public;
- to clear up an ambiguity in a previous answer or statement;
- in the interests of justice for the detainee to have put to them, and have an opportunity to comment on, information concerning the offence which has come to light since they were charged or informed they might be prosecuted.

Before any such interview, the interviewer shall:
   (a) caution the detainee, *'You do not have to say anything, but anything you do say may be given in evidence.'* [Where the use of the Welsh Language is appropriate, the interviewer shall caution the detainee, 'Does dim rhaid i chi ddweud dim byd, ond gall unrhyw beth yr ydych yn ei ddweud gael ei roi fel tystiolaeth.'];
   (b) remind the detainee about their right to legal advice.

16.6–16.10 *****

17   *****

Annex A   *****

Annex B Delay in notification of arrest and whereabouts or allowing access to legal advice

A   Persons detained under PACE

1. The exercise of the rights in *Section 5* or *Section 6*, or both, may be delayed if the person is in police detention, as in PACE, section 118(2), in connection with an indictable offence, has not yet been charged with an offence and an officer of superintendent rank or above, or inspector rank or above only for the rights in *Section 5*, has reasonable grounds for believing their exercise will:
   (i)   lead to:
      - interference with, or harm to, evidence connected with an indictable offence; or
      - interference with, or physical harm to, other people; or
   (ii) lead to alerting other people suspected of having committed an indictable offence but not yet arrested for it; or
   (iii) hinder the recovery of property obtained in consequence of the commission of such an offence.
2. These rights may also be delayed if the officer has reasonable grounds to believe that:
   (i)   the person detained for an indictable offence has benefited from their criminal conduct (decided in accordance with Part 2 of the Proceeds of Crime Act 2002); and
   (ii) the recovery of the value of the property constituting that benefit will be hindered by the exercise of either right.
3. Authority to delay a detainee's right to consult privately with a solicitor may be given only if the authorising officer has reasonable grounds to believe the solicitor the detainee wants to consult will, inadvertently or otherwise, pass on a message from the detainee or act in some other way which will have any of the consequences specified under *paragraph 1* or *2*. In these circumstances the detainee must be allowed to choose another solicitor.
4. If the detainee wishes to see a solicitor, access to that solicitor may not be delayed on the grounds they might advise the detainee not to answer questions or the solicitor was initially asked to attend the police station by someone else. In the latter case the detainee must be told the solicitor has

come to the police station at another person's request, and must be asked to sign the custody record to signify whether they want to see the solicitor.

5. The fact the grounds for delaying notification of arrest may be satisfied does not automatically mean the grounds for delaying access to legal advice will also be satisfied.

6. These rights may be delayed only for as long as grounds exist and in no case beyond 36 hours after the relevant time as in PACE, section 41. If the grounds cease to apply within this time, the detainee must, as soon as practicable, be asked if they want to exercise either right, the custody record must be noted accordingly, and action taken in accordance with the relevant section of the Code.

7. A detained person must be permitted to consult a solicitor for a reasonable time before any court hearing.

*****

<h1 style="text-align:center">Annexes C–L *****</h1>

Code G Code of Practice for the Statutory Power of Arrest by Police Officers

1 Introduction

1.1 This Code of Practice deals with the statutory power of police to arrest a person who is involved, or suspected of being involved, in a criminal offence. The power of arrest must be used fairly, responsibly, with respect for people suspected of committing offences and without unlawful discrimination. The Equality Act 2010 makes it unlawful for police officers to discriminate against, harass or victimise any person on the grounds of the 'protected characteristics' of age, disability, gender reassignment, race, religion or belief, sex and sexual orientation, marriage and civil partnership, pregnancy and maternity when using their powers. When police forces are carrying out their functions they also have a duty to have regard to the need to eliminate unlawful discrimination, harassment and victimisation and to take steps to foster good relations.

1.2 The exercise of the power of arrest represents an obvious and significant interference with the Right to Liberty and Security under Article 5 of the European Convention on Human Rights set out in Part I of Schedule 1 to the Human Rights Act 1998.

1.3 The use of the power must be fully justified and officers exercising the power should consider if the necessary objectives can be met by other, less intrusive means. Absence of justification for exercising the powers of arrest may lead to challenges should the case proceed to court. It could also lead to civil claims against police for unlawful arrest and false imprisonment. When the power of arrest is exercised it is essential that it is exercised in a non-discriminatory and proportionate manner which is compatible with the Right to Liberty under Article 5.

1.4 Section 24 of the Police and Criminal Evidence Act 1984 (as substituted by section 110 of the Serious Organised Crime and Police Act 2005) provides the statutory power for a constable to arrest without warrant for all offences. If the provisions of the Act and this Code are not observed, both the arrest and the conduct of any subsequent investigation may be open to question.

1.5 This code of practice must be readily available at all police stations for consultation by police officers and police staff, detained persons and members of the public.

1.6 *****

2 Elements of arrest under section 24 PACE

2.1 A lawful arrest requires two elements:

A person's involvement or suspected involvement or attempted involvement in the commission of a criminal offence;

AND

Reasonable grounds for *believing* that the person's arrest is necessary.
- both elements must be satisfied, and
- it can never be necessary to arrest a person unless there are reasonable grounds to suspect them of committing an offence.

2.2 The arrested person must be informed that they have been arrested, even if this fact is obvious, and of the relevant circumstances of the arrest in relation to both the above elements. The custody officer must be informed of these matters on arrival at the police station. See *paragraphs 2.9, 3.3* and *Note 3* and *Code C paragraph 3.4*.

(a) Involvement in the commission of an offence

2.3 A constable may arrest without warrant in relation to any offence anyone:
- who is about to commit an offence <u>or</u> is in the act of committing an offence;
- whom the officer has reasonable grounds for suspecting is about to commit an offence <u>or</u> to be committing an offence;
- whom the officer has reasonable grounds to suspect of being guilty of an offence which he or she has reasonable grounds for suspecting has been committed;
- anyone who is guilty of an offence which has been committed or anyone whom the officer has reasonable grounds for suspecting to be guilty of that offence.

2.3A There must be some reasonable, objective grounds for the suspicion, based on known facts and information which are relevant to the likelihood the offence has been committed and the person liable to arrest committed it.

(b) Necessity criteria

2.4 The power of arrest is <u>only</u> exercisable if the constable has reasonable grounds for *believing* that it is necessary to arrest the person. The statutory criteria for what may constitute necessity are set out in paragraph 2.9 and it remains an operational decision at the discretion of the constable to decide:
- which one or more of the necessity criteria (if any) which applies to the individual; and
- if any of the criteria do apply, whether to arrest, grant street bail after arrest, report for summons or for charging by post, issue a penalty notice or take any other action that is open to the officer.

2.5 In applying the criteria, the arresting officer has to be satisfied that at least one of the reasons supporting the need for arrest is satisfied.

2.6 Extending the power of arrest to all offences provides a constable with the ability to use that power to deal with any situation. However applying the necessity criteria requires the constable to examine and justify the reason or reasons why a person needs to be arrested or (as the case may be) further arrested, for an offence for the custody officer to decide whether to authorise their detention for that offence.

2.7 The criteria in paragraph 2.9 below which are set out in section 24 of PACE as substituted by section 110 of the Serious Organised Crime and Police Act 2005 <u>are</u> exhaustive. However, the circumstances that may satisfy those criteria remain a matter for the operational discretion of individual officers. Some examples are given to illustrate what those circumstances might be and what officers might consider when deciding whether arrest is necessary.

2.8 In considering the individual circumstances, the constable must take into account the situation of the victim, the nature of the offence, the circumstances of the suspect and the needs of the investigative process.

2.9 When it is practicable to tell a person why their arrest is necessary (as required by paragraphs 2.2, 3.3 and *Note 3*), the constable should outline the facts, information and other circumstances which provide the grounds for believing that their arrest is necessary and which the officer considers satisfy one or more of the statutory criteria in sub-paragraphs (a) to (f), namely:
- (a) to enable the name of the person in question to be ascertained (in the case where the constable does not know, and cannot readily ascertain, the person's name, or has

reasonable grounds for doubting whether a name given by the person as his name is his real name):

An officer might decide that a person's name cannot be readily ascertained if they fail or refuse to give it when asked, particularly after being warned that failure or refusal is likely to make their arrest necessary (see *Note 2D*). Grounds to doubt a name given may arise if the person appears reluctant or hesitant when asked to give their name or to verify the name they have given.

Where mobile fingerprinting is available and the suspect's name cannot be ascertained or is doubted, the officer should consider using the power under section 61(6A) of PACE (see *Code D paragraph 4.3(e)*) to take and check the fingerprints of a suspect as this may avoid the need to arrest solely to enable their name to be ascertained.

(b) correspondingly as regards the person's address:

An officer might decide that a person's address cannot be readily ascertained if they fail or refuse to give it when asked, particularly after being warned that such a failure or refusal is likely to make their arrest necessary. See *Note 2D*. Grounds to doubt an address given may arise if the person appears reluctant or hesitant when asked to give their address or is unable to provide verifiable details of the locality they claim to live in. When considering reporting to consider summons or charging by post as alternatives to arrest, an address would be satisfactory if the person will be at it for a sufficiently long period for it to be possible to serve them with the summons or requisition and charge; or, that some other person at that address specified by the person will accept service on their behalf. When considering issuing a penalty notice, the address should be one where the person will be in the event of enforcement action if the person does not pay the penalty or is convicted and fined after a court hearing.

(c) to prevent the person in question:

(i) causing physical injury to himself or any other person;
This might apply where the suspect has already used or threatened violence against others and it is thought likely that they may assault others if they are not arrested.

(ii) suffering physical injury;
This might apply where the suspect's behaviour and actions are believed likely to provoke, or have provoked, others to want to assault the suspect unless the suspect is arrested for their own protection.

(iii) causing loss or damage to property;
This might apply where the suspect is a known persistent offender with a history of serial offending against property (theft and criminal damage) and it is thought likely that they may continue offending if they are not arrested.

(iv) committing an offence against public decency (only applies where members of the public going about their normal business cannot reasonably be expected to avoid the person in question);
This might apply when an offence against public decency is being committed in a place to which the public have access and is likely to be repeated in that or some other public place at a time when the public are likely to encounter the suspect.

(v) causing an unlawful obstruction of the highway;
This might apply to any offence where its commission causes an unlawful obstruction which it is believed may continue or be repeated if the person is not arrested, particularly if the person has been warned that they are causing an obstruction.

(d) to protect a child or other vulnerable person from the person in question.
This might apply when the health (physical or mental) or welfare of a child or vulnerable person is likely to be harmed or is at risk of being harmed, if the person is not arrested in cases where it is not practicable and appropriate to make alternative arrangements to prevent the suspect from having any harmful or potentially harmful contact with the child or vulnerable person.

(e) to allow the prompt and effective investigation of the offence or of the conduct of the person in question.

This may arise when it is thought likely that unless the person is arrested and then either taken in custody to the police station or granted 'street bail' to attend the station later, see *Note 2J*, further action considered necessary to properly investigate their involvement in the offence would be frustrated, unreasonably delayed or otherwise hindered and therefore be impracticable. Examples of such actions include:

(i) *interviewing the suspect* on occasions when the person's voluntary attendance is not considered to be a practicable alternative to arrest, because for example:

- it is thought unlikely that the person would attend the police station voluntarily to be interviewed.
- it is necessary to interview the suspect about the outcome of other investigative action for which their arrest is necessary, see (ii) to (v) below.
- arrest would enable the special warning to be given in accordance with Code C paragraphs 10.10 and 10.11 when the suspect is found:
  - in possession of incriminating objects, or at a place where such objects are found;
  - at or near the scene of the crime at or about the time it was committed.
- the person has made false statements and/or presented false evidence;
- it is thought likely that the person:
  - may steal or destroy evidence;
  - may collude or make contact with, co-suspects or conspirators;
  - may intimidate or threaten or make contact with, witnesses.

(ii) when considering arrest in connection with the investigation of an *indictable offence*, there is a need:

- to enter and search without a search warrant any premises occupied or controlled by the arrested person or where the person was when arrested or immediately before arrest;
- to prevent the arrested person from having contact with others;
- to detain the arrested person for more than 24 hours before charge.

(iii) when considering arrest in connection with any *recordable offence* and it is necessary to secure or preserve evidence of that offence by taking fingerprints, footwear impressions or samples from the suspect for evidential comparison or matching with other material relating to that offence, for example, from the crime scene.

(iv) when considering arrest in connection with any offence and it is necessary to search, examine or photograph the person to obtain evidence.

(v) when considering arrest in connection with an offence to which the statutory Class A drug testing requirements in Code C section 17 apply, to enable testing when it is thought that drug misuse might have caused or contributed to the offence.

(f) to prevent any prosecution for the offence from being hindered by the disappearance of the person in question. This may arise when it is thought that:

- if the person is not arrested they are unlikely to attend court if they are prosecuted;
- the address given is not a satisfactory address for service of a summons or a written charge and requisition to appear at court because the person will not be at it for a sufficiently long period for the summons or charge and requisition to be served and no other person at that specified address will accept service on their behalf.

3   Information to be given on arrest

(a) Cautions—when a caution must be given*
3.1–3.7 *****

---

* **Editor's Note:** Code G at this point replicates the material taken from Code C, paras 10.3 to 10.7 (*supra*).

4 Records of arrest

(a) General

4.1 The arresting officer is required to record in his pocket book or by other methods used for recording information:

- the nature and circumstances of the offence leading to the arrest;
- the reason or reasons why arrest was necessary;
- the giving of the caution; and
- anything said by the person at the time of arrest.

4.2 Such a record should be made at the time of the arrest unless impracticable to do. If not made at that time, the record should then be completed as soon as possible thereafter.

4.3 On arrival at the police station or after being first arrested at the police station, the arrested person must be brought before the custody officer as soon as is practicable and a custody record must be opened in accordance with section 2 of Code C. The information given by the arresting officer on the circumstances and reason or reasons for arrest shall be recorded as part of the custody record. Alternatively, a copy of the record made by the officer in accordance with *paragraph 4.1* above shall be attached as part of the custody record. See *paragraph 2.2* and *Code C paragraphs 3.4 and 10.3.*

4.4 The custody record will serve as a record of the arrest. Copies of the custody record will be provided in accordance with paragraphs 2.4 and 2.4A of Code C and access for inspection of the original record in accordance with paragraph 2.5 of Code C.

(b) Interviews and arrests

4.5 Records of interview, significant statements or silences will be treated in the same way as set out in sections 10 and 11 of Code C and in Code E and F (audio and visual recording of interviews).

Notes for guidance

1 For the purposes of this Code, 'offence' means any statutory or common law offence for which a person may be tried by a magistrates' court or the Crown court and punished if convicted. Statutory offences include assault, rape, criminal damage, theft, robbery, burglary, fraud, possession of controlled drugs and offences under road traffic, liquor licensing, gambling and immigration legislation and local government byelaws. Common law offences include murder, manslaughter, kidnapping, false imprisonment, perverting the course of justice and escape from lawful custody.

1A, 1B *****

2 Facts and information relevant to a person's suspected involvement in an offence should not be confined to those which tend to indicate the person has committed or attempted to commit the offence. Before making a decision to arrest, a constable should take account of any facts and information that are available, including claims of innocence made by the person, that might dispel the suspicion.

2A–2J *****

3 An arrested person must be given sufficient information to enable them to understand they have been deprived of their liberty and the reason they have been arrested, as soon as practicable after the arrest, e.g. when a person is arrested on suspicion of committing an offence they must be informed of the nature of the suspected offence and when and where it was committed. The suspect must also be informed of the reason or reasons why arrest is considered necessary. Vague or technical language should be avoided. When explaining why one or more of the arrest criteria apply, it is not necessary to disclose any specific details that might undermine or otherwise adversely affect any investigative processes. An example might be the conduct of a formal interview when prior disclosure of such details might give the suspect an opportunity to fabricate an innocent explanation or to otherwise conceal lies from the interviewer.

4 Nothing in this Code requires a caution to be given or repeated when informing a person not under arrest they may be prosecuted for an offence. However, a court will not be able to draw any inferences under the Criminal Justice and Public Order Act 1994, section 34, if the person was not cautioned.

5 If it appears a person does not understand the caution, the people giving it should explain it in their own words.

6 Certain powers available as the result of an arrest – for example, entry and search of premises, detention without charge beyond 24 hours, holding a person incommunicado and delaying access to legal advice – only apply in respect of indictable offences and are subject to the specific requirements on authorisation as set out in PACE and the relevant Code of Practice.

Please see the prelims for the following tables of contents